D1318982

SOCIAL PSYCHOLOGY

Studying Human Interaction

SOCIAL PSYCHOLOGY

Studying Human Interaction

Charles Emerson Kimble

University of Dayton

 Wm. C. Brown Publishers

Book Team

Editor *Michael Lange*
Production Editor *Michelle M. Kiefer*
Art Editor *Barbara J. Grantham*
Photo Editor *Carol M. Smith*
Permissions Editor *Mavis M. Oeth*
Visuals Processor *Jodi Wagner*

 Wm. C. Brown Publishers

President *G. Franklin Lewis*
Vice President, Publisher *George Wm. Bergquist*
Vice President, Publisher *Thomas E. Doran*
Vice President, Operations and Production *Beverly Kolz*
National Sales Manager *Virginia S. Moffat*
Advertising Manager *Ann M. Knepper*
Marketing Manager *Kathy Law Laube*
Production Editorial Manager *Colleen A. Yonda*
Production Editorial Manager *Julie A. Kennedy*
Publishing Services Manager *Karen J. Slaght*
Manager of Visuals and Design *Faye M. Schilling*

Cover illustration: © Steve Johnson.

Cover and interior design by Mary K. Sailer.

The credits section for this book begins on page 599, and is considered an extension of the copyright page.

Copyright © 1990 by Wm. C. Brown Publishers. All rights reserved

Library of Congress Catalog Card Number: 89–61204

ISBN 0–697–03093–8

No part of this publication may be reproduced, stored in a retrieval system, or transmitted, in any form or by any means, electronic, mechanical, photocopying, recording, or otherwise, without the prior written permission of the publisher.

Printed in the United States of America by Wm. C. Brown Publishers, 2460 Kerper Boulevard, Dubuque, IA 52001

10 9 8 7 6 5 4 3 2 1

Dedicated with love to all my
family, near and far; especially
Marty and the kids, Emily, Lauren,
Daniel, and Andrew.

BRIEF CONTENTS

CONTENTS

Preface

PART 1

Society and the Individual

Interpersonal Perceptions and Judgments

PART 3

Social Influence and Group Dynamics

PART 4

Social Relations

PART 5

Environmental Influences

PREFACE

Social psychology has been a consuming interest of mine since I was introduced to the field by Elliot Aronson (and then Robert Wicklund, Robert Helmreich, Judson Mills, and Jerald Jellison) two decades ago. Before that, I had been interested in what makes people tick in social situations; but I did not know how to study the topic systematically to gain more understanding. Since that introduction, gaining more knowledge about this fascinating subject has been the focus of my professional career. In this book, I hope to communicate that interest and knowledge about social psychology to readers.

Most social psychology students are not psychology majors. With this in mind, we have tried to produce a book which will appeal to a wide range of students, but will at the same time cover the basic areas and approaches of social psychology. To this end, we have concluded each chapter with an applications section to show ways in which the principles and findings of the chapter have been or could be applied to increase understanding of ourselves, others, and events in our everyday lives. We prefer this combining of basic and applied social psychology to the practice of presenting applied social psychology in separate chapters with little relationship to basic social psychology.

Another feature of the book is the presentation of Research Trailblazers boxes in six chapters. These capsules are intended to highlight research programs on selected topics and to describe those research approaches in greater detail. There are also summaries of social psychological theories in five chapters. They cover sociobiology, attribution, cognitive dissonance, social impact, and equity theories. You will discover that these are not the only theories covered. Likewise, the research programs highlighted are not the only studies described in considerable detail. In fact, we hope that professors will find that the coverage is thorough enough that they can entrust topics they do not emphasize to the book's treatment of those topics.

In each chapter, we have printed key terms in bold type with definitions of those terms in the same sentence or nearby in the text and in the glossary at the back of the book. In addition to this student aid, we presented specific results of many studies in figures and tables to give a more concrete illustration of the research. There are also figures used to represent schematically the relationships between various sets of variables in the text.

After the introductory chapter, the book is divided into five parts. Part 1, Society and the Individual, contains chapter 2, Personal Development, which describes how individuals develop differently due to the social contexts they experience. Chapter 3, The Self, presents concepts about the self and how they are related to social behavior. Part 2, Interpersonal Perceptions and Judgments, focuses on the evaluations of people and events that we make in the chapters concerning Impressions, Social Cognition, and Attitudes. Part 3, Social Influence and Group Dynamics, covers persuasion, obedience, conformity, compliance, group processes, and communication. Part 4, Social Relations, presents first positive, then negative, interpersonal attitudes and behaviors in the chapters on attraction, altruism and helping, aggression, and prejudice and discrimination. Part 5, Environmental Influences, contains coverage of the physical environment and social behavior in chapter 15 and stress in chapter 16. Individual professors may, of course, choose to arrange these chapters in some other order or emphasize some and not others.

For instructors, we have a *Resource Manual and Test Item File* to accompany this textbook. It includes ideas for additional lecture material, class discussion, classroom demonstrations, out-of-class projects and films related to the textbook to enrich the course. The test item file includes many different types of objective items to make test construction easier. The test item file is also available on diskette upon adoption. The *Student Study Guide* has interesting exercises to help students review the test material. Both of these aids were written by Joanna L. Newman of Antioch College with the assistance of James Rotton, Edward Hirt, Frank Kardes, and myself.

Acknowledgments

Many people contributed to the production of this book, and I want to acknowledge their efforts. First, my coauthors deserve much credit. Edward Hirt and Frank Kardes, former students of mine who earned their doctorates from Indiana University's strong social psychology program, wrote chapter 5, Social Cognition, The Study of Social Judgments. I appreciate their lending their expertise and writing skill to this project. They are currently faculty members at the University of Wisconsin and the University of Cincinnati, respectively. James Rotton, a former departmental colleague, wrote chapter 15, The Physical Environment and Social Behavior, and chapter 16, Stress. Jim, a Purdue University Ph.D. who is now Professor of Psychology at Florida International University, is a much-published social psychologist, environmental psychologist, and statistician. His interest and expertise in these areas is evident in his chapters.

Joanna Newman, a University of Kansas Ph.D. now teaching at Antioch College, was the primary author of the *Resource Manual and Test Item File* and the *Student Study Guide*. Joanna is a superior teacher and an excellent social psychologist. Her creative approach to teaching is reflected in the resource material she has written. Joanna, Jim, Ed, and Frank are not only respected professionals, but valued friends. Their friendship, cooperativeness, and productivity have made our collaboration on this book a pleasant experience.

I would be remiss if I did not acknowledge the support of many of my colleagues at the University of Dayton. All of my departmental colleagues have been friendly and supportive over the years. Eliot Butter, Frank DaPolito, Don Polzella, Ron Katsuyama, and Sam Bower have readily directed me to resources in their areas of expertise. Kelly Williams of the Biology Department has been a source of encouragement, support, and sociobiological information over the years. Kenneth Kuntz, department chairperson, and others in university administration have been very supportive in meeting equipment and computer needs and in enabling me to take leaves at the University of Texas at El Paso and the University of Kansas in recent years. Barbara Deschapelles, Robert McAdams, and Jim Baccus of the Office of Computing Activities have been helpful in organizing bibliographic files and handling computer snags. Several students—Kevin Miller, Leah Lawrence, in particular; and Sheri Farrell, Deborah Connelie, Nanthapol Charoenpakdi, Gary Sturgeon, and Amy Robbins—helped in compiling the bibliography, and Brenda Hartman-Bowers helped index the book.

I am very grateful to Dan Batson, Jack Brehm, and Howard Baumgartel for offering me a visiting position at the University of Kansas in 1985–1986. There I wrote several chapters of this book, taught, and enjoyed the opportunity to interact with Lawrence Wrightsman, Paul Gump, Sharon Brehm, Howard Rosenfeld, C. R. Snyder, the three gentlemen listed above, and others. In addition, I had the opportunity to meet Fritz and Grace Heider and to help host a colloquium series honoring Fritz Heider on his 90th birthday. That was a special privilege because the five distinguished speakers whom I got to know through that series; Robert Abelson, Alice Eagly, Edward E. Jones, Steven J. Sherman, and Abraham Tesser; are such prominent contributors to social psychology.

I appreciate the efforts, suggestions, and recommendations of the following reviewers who read and commented on all or parts of this manuscript:

John R. Braun *University of Bridgeport*	Eugene Indenbaum *SUNY-Farmingdale*
Peter Chroman *College of San Mateo*	David E. Johnson *John Brown University*
Clive M. Davis *Syracuse University*	Martin F. Kaplan *Northern Illinois University*
David K. Dodd *Eastern Illinois University*	Art Skibbe *Appalachian State University*
Tracy B. Henley *The University of Tennessee— Knoxville*	James M. Thomas *University of Nebraska at Omaha*
	Fred W. Whitford *Montana State University*

Their suggestions and guidance improved the final product substantially.

Last but not least, I want to thank the people at Wm. C. Brown Publishers who helped me put this book together. I want to thank Michael D. Lange, Psychology Editor, for his encouragement and direction. I am grateful to Michelle M. Kiefer, Production Editor, and the production staff for their many efforts to bring this project to fruition.

Charles E. Kimble
University of Dayton

CHAPTER 1

Introduction to Social Psychology

Studying Human Interactions

Social psychologists study the causes, consequences, and patterns of human interaction. They are not alone in their interest in interpersonal events. Most people have a profound interest in how they relate to each other. Looking at such popular magazines as *People, Cosmopolitan, Psychology Today, Redbook,* or *Ms.* should convince you of that interest.

Social interactions form the core of human existence. Birthdays, weddings, anniversaries, reunions, and funerals are milestones of life marked by interactions of differing strengths among people. Religious ceremonies, sports events, artistic performances, and political rallies feature the actions of some central individuals before audiences. Most of us eat, drink, and make merry with other people. Everything from conversations to sexual encounters requires the participation of at least two people.

Love and hate are decidedly social emotions. Anxiety and joy are usually associated with interactions with others. Disturbances in one's close relationships are a major reason why people seek the help of a counselor, clergy, clinical psychologist, or psychiatrist. Behavior, aggressive and otherwise, that infringes on the rights and comfort of others often leads to involuntary commitment to mental institutions or imprisonment. At the same time, experiences shared with others are usually more pleasant than events experienced alone. There should be little wonder that people show interest in the nature of human transactions.

What Social Psychologists Study

Social psychology is the study of human interactions. Describing, explaining, and examining the effects of social interactions on the thoughts, attitudes, and behaviors of people are central interests of social psychologists. While the focus is on social interactions among humans, social psychologists often represent elements of interactions symbolically in their investigations. Also, some researchers focus on the antecedents or products of interactions rather than the interactions per se. Consequently, many studies which do not deal with real interactions are included within the domain of social psychology.

In their approach to understanding human interactions, social psychologists emphasize the impact of the situation, as perceived and interpreted by the individual, on behavior. Roger Barker (1968) has stressed the influence of the psychological environment on behavior. He says that behavior settings, which are the social/physical situations in which human behaviors occur (Wicker, 1979), affect people's behaviors more than their personality traits do. For instance, Barker would contend that your behavior in a history class is more like other students' behavior in that class than it is like your own behavior somewhere else. The same is true for your behavior at a basketball game, a rock concert, or an aerobics class. You act the same way others do in the situation. Working from a social cognition perspective, Schank and Abelson (1977) have pointed out that we all seem to have common scripts that we enact when particular situational cues appear. As you will learn in reading this book, the situational context of behavior does have a strong influence on the behavior.

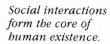

Social interactions form the core of human existence.

Situations and settings have a strong influence on behavior.

Social
Psychological
Findings

Now we will attempt to give you a flavor of the many aspects of life social psychologists study. The range of interests of social psychologists is quite broad, and their interests overlap with those of other disciplines. The major categories of sociopsychological interests are reflected in the chapters of this book. Some of the major findings and explanatory concepts will be presented briefly now to give you an overview.

What would your reaction be if you saw a stranger yelling at another person in a public place?

You would probably conclude that the stranger was a hostile, aggressive person. Social psychologists have shown that most people believe a person's behavior is determined more by the person's characteristics than by the situation in which he or she acts. This effect has been called the fundamental attribution error (Ross, 1977) and the observer's attribution bias (Jones & Nisbett, 1971). This phenomenon is called the observer's bias because it occurs only when we are trying to evaluate someone else's behavior. It does not occur when we are trying to judge the causes of our own behavior. It raises the possibility of misjudgment occurring in therapist-client, teacher-student, manager-employee, and judge-offender interactions. The impact of such a misjudgment can be seen in the Rosenhan (1973) study in which pseudopatients were incorrectly diagnosed after very little observation as having a mental disorder (usually schizophrenia) and hospitalized. The therapists apparently jumped to the conclusion that personality traits of the pseudopatients caused them to act the way they did and the behavior and the traits were judged abnormal because the setting was a mental health admissions interview. Their subsequent behavior was judged abnormal and unlikely to change because it was caused by the personality traits. Such a bias nearly always works to the disadvantage of the lower-status person being evaluated (i.e., the client, student, employee, and offender in the interactions cited above).

If your teacher believed you were going to do very well in this course, would his or her expectations affect your performance?

Another important and consistent finding is that our expectations and beliefs about a person often have a profound effect on how that person behaves. This phenomenon is called the self-fulfilling prophecy. We subtly, and sometimes blatantly, communicate our expectations about how a person will perform and recognition of these expectations make that person act differently. The classic demonstration of the self-fulfilling prophecy occurred when teachers were led to expect certain students, designated as "intellectual bloomers," to show marked academic improvement during the school year. These students, who were really no different from other students, did score significantly higher on intelligence tests administered at the end of the year than the control students (Rosenthal & Jacobson, 1968). Other investigators (Snyder, Tanke, & Berscheid, 1977; Eden, 1984) have shown that the self-fulfilling prophecy also operates in social and other nonacademic situations.

The boss tells you to hurt another person. Would you do it?

One of the most chronicled findings of social psychology is the ability of an authority figure to make almost anyone act in an immoral, irresponsible, harmful manner in certain situations (Milgram, 1974). In the most basic obedience study conducted by Milgram, 62.5 percent of his male subjects shocked a middle-aged man up to the 450-volt level, and 100 percent (all of them!) shocked him up to the 300-volt level. This is certainly a strong enough shock to do terrible damage if the victim had been connected into the circuit as he was believed to have been (the victim was not really being shocked). We will discuss the situational factors involved in eliciting such obedience and the implications of these and related findings in chapter 8, Social Influence: Obedience, Conformity, and Compliance.

If you were asked—not required—to debate in favor of the death penalty and did so even though you were opposed to capital punishment, would it change your attitude?

A consistent finding in the area of attitude change research has been that you can change a person's attitude by subtly compelling that person to act in a way that is consistent with the new attitude you want him or her to adopt (Bem, 1967; Festinger & Carlsmith, 1959). The implication of the many studies is that how a person behaves affects his or her subsequent attitudes, given that the individual was not blatantly forced to behave that way. There is still disagreement about whether cognitive dissonance or self-perception causes public behavior to affect attitudes, but the effect is consistent and strong.

Joan has consistently and repeatedly been rewarded for getting good grades. Lately, she is not as interested in schoolwork as she once was. Why?

A somewhat paradoxical effect that has been well substantiated is that giving a person a reward for doing some activity can undermine that person's intrinsic motivation to do that activity later (Deci, 1975; Lepper, Greene, & Nisbett, 1973). The individual's perspective on why he or she did the activity is altered by receiving the extrinsic reward. Again, there is theoretical conflict about why rewards have this effect. Lepper et al. (1973) take the self-perception position that the external reward makes the individual see her- or himself as less internally motivated. Deci (1975, 1980) takes the competence motivation position that some rewards communicate to the individual that his or her activity is being controlled by the reward-giver while not giving the person any information about how competently he or she is performing. The individual's desire for mastery and independence makes him or her lose interest in the rewarded task. Regardless of the explanation, this motivation-undermining effect indicates that we must take care in administering positive reinforcements or we may obtain undesired outcomes.

The first secret ballot indicated that all jurors weakly and tentatively supported acquittal. After discussion, they vigorously endorsed the decision to acquit. Why?

Group polarization refers to the fact that individuals adopt a more extreme position in the same direction after engaging in group discussion than the position they held before (Kogan & Wallach, 1964; Myers, 1978). Group discussion polarizes the positions of participants, but it does not increase conflict in the group because everyone gravitates toward the same extreme. As a result, groups that interact make riskier or more cautious decisions than individuals do. Why this effect occurs will be discussed in chapter 9, Group Processes.

You notice that you do not work as hard on a group class project as you do on an individual art project. It sounds like a case of social loafing.

Social loafing refers to the fact that individuals who believe they are involved in a group effort exert less effort than those who are acting alone (Latané, Williams, & Harkins, 1979). Such social loafing occurs on many kinds of tasks (e.g., tugs-of-war, clapping, cheering, joint manual tasks, and group signal-detection tasks) and in Eastern and Western cultures (Latané, 1983). This effect suggests that monitoring individual performance and limiting the number of people working on the same task are necessary to make activities most productive.

Your new roommate likes different music than you do. Her political attitudes are much different from yours. Will you like her?

You probably won't like her. In the area of interpersonal attraction, the most consistent finding is that people who hold similar attitudes like each other more than people who have dissimilar attitudes (Byrne, 1961, 1972). While this set of results is consistent with the old adage, "Birds of a feather flock together," other interpersonal truisms, such as "Opposites attract" and "Absence makes the heart grow fonder," have generally been proven false. Also, similarity of personality usually does not enhance attraction between the two parties. There are several theories about why attitude similarity leads to attraction which will be discussed in chapter 11, Interpersonal Attraction: Friends and Lovers.

These eight sets of findings are only a brief sample of effects social psychologists have uncovered in recent years. They are among the most stable and replicable findings in the field. To apply even these findings to new situations, it is important to know why they occurred. Social psychological theories are useful for uncovering these mysteries.

Large group activities can inhibit individual effort and encourage social loafing.

Theories are conceptual frameworks that help us understand facts and predict new relationships between events, thoughts, and behavior. To say that something is "just a theory, not a fact" is to misunderstand the nature of a theory. Theories never will be facts when they grow up. Theories are sets of ideas used to understand known facts and to chart the course for discovering new facts. The eight sets of findings previously described are some of the known facts of social psychology. If a theory does not account for known facts in its domain and the hypotheses (predictions) derived from it are disproved by new data, the theory should be discarded or revamped.

Most of the theories in social psychology are fairly narrow in scope and account for only a few phenomena. Some of the broadest and most established theories will be presented in later chapters where the facts they attempt to explain are discussed. Capsule commentaries will be presented on the following prominent theories: sociobiology, attribution, cognitive dissonance, social impact, and equity. You will see that all these theories have different central topics to which they are applied. They are not attempts to explain the same facts. Most social psychological theories have separate domains of application, but you will notice later in this book that there are areas of overlap where competing explanations are offered by different theories.

Social Psychological Theories

Table 1.1   A Chronology of Important Events in the History of Social Psychology to 1970

1897—Norman Triplett published the first social psychological experiment in which he investigated the effects of the presence of other performers on individual performance.

1908—Edward Ross, a sociologist, and William McDougall, a psychologist, wrote the first two books in the field entitled *Social Psychology.*

1913—Max Ringelmann, a French agricultural engineer, published an article on how individual effort decreases when one works in a cooperative group rather than alone. Because the research was conducted in the 1880s, it could be considered the first social psychological experiment, antedating Triplett (Kravitz & Martin, 1986).

1922—*Journal of Abnormal Psychology* became the *Journal of Abnormal and Social Psychology.*

1924—Floyd Allport published the first empirically-based social psychology textbook in which he focused on how the presence of others affects individual performance.

1934—Richard LaPiere published an article on the marked differences between the positive behaviors and the negative attitudes expressed toward Chinese customers by lodging and eating establishments.

—*Mind, Self and Society from the Standpoint of a Social Behaviorist* by George Herbert Mead was published from the class notes of Mead's students.

1935—Muzafer Sherif reported his work on the formation of group norms in ambiguous situations.

1938—B. F. Skinner published the book, *The Behavior of Organisms.*

1939—John Dollard and his associates at Yale published the book, *Frustration and Aggression.*

1943—Theodore Newcomb described his work on political attitude change among Bennington College students in the book, *Personality and Social Change.*

1947—Kenneth and Mamie Clark presented their study on how growing up in American society affected young black children.

1949—Samuel Stouffer and associates published their extensive study of the attitudes and adjustment of the American soldier.

1951—Solomon Asch demonstrated how different patterns of group opinion affect conformity even in unambiguous situations.

A Short History of Social Psychology

It is hard to know where to begin a history of social psychology. Freud's psychoanalytic approach starting before the twentieth century certainly influenced some social psychological thinking, as did William James' (1890) theorizing about the self. Behaviorism from John B. Watson (1913) to E. L. Thorndike (1933) to B. F. Skinner (1938) has affected early and current thinking about social behavior. The French sociological thinkers of the nineteenth century, Tarde, Durkheim, and LeBon, gave us early perspectives on group and crowd behavior and the collective mind. The first social psychology textbooks were written early in the twentieth century. As table 1.1 indicates, there were many significant events in the history of social psychology which occurred before, or early in, the twentieth century.

1953—Carl Hovland, Irving Janis, and Harold Kelley published *Communication and Persuasion.*

1954—Gordon Allport, brother of Floyd Allport, published *The Nature of Prejudice.*

—Several social scientists presented a "friend of the court" brief to the Supreme Court in the Brown v. Topeka Board of Education school desegregation case.

1957—Leon Festinger published the book, *A Theory of Cognitive Dissonance.*

1958—Fritz Heider described his view of common sense psychology in the book, *The Psychology of Interpersonal Relations.*

1963—Stanley Milgram gave his first account of how many people will obey authority figures and hurt other people on command.

1965—Roger Brown published *Social Psychology.*

—E. E. Jones and Keith Davis presented their attribution theory about how people infer others' dispositions from observing characteristics of their behavior.

—The *Journal of Personality and Social Psychology* split from the *Journal of Abnormal and Social Psychology.*

—Robert Zajonc reviewed how the presence of other people affects individual performance in the article, "Social Facilitation."

1966—Konrad Lorenz, the ethologist, presented an instinctive view of aggression in the book, *On Aggression.*

—Elaine Walster and her associates examined the effect of physical attractiveness on initial interpersonal attraction.

1967—Harold Kelley described how we attribute the causes of behavior to persons, stimuli, and/or circumstances in his attribution theory.

—E. E. Jones and Harold Gerard's *Foundations of Social Psychology* gave us a comprehensive view of experimental social psychology.

1969—Irving Piliavin, Judith Rodin, and Jane Piliavin presented their research on helping of a fallen passenger on the New York City subway.

1970—Bibb Latané and John Darley's book, *The Unresponsive Bystander: Why Doesn't He Help?*, described their program of research on helping in emergencies and inspired much more research on that topic.

Modern social psychology began during an era of oppression. Hitler's rise in the 1930s led many Europeans to flee to America. One of those European refugees was Kurt Lewin. Lewin brought both a theoretical and a practical orientation to American social psychology. His field theory approach, which posited that behavior is determined by the combination of characteristics of the person and the environment that he or she is currently experiencing, had a social and interpersonal emphasis that earlier theories didn't. Lewin not only brought a new theoretical perspective to social psychology, but he also insisted on testing ideas experimentally. Lewin's attention and enthusiasm also extended to social problems and applying social psychology to solving them. He even investigated ways of persuading homemakers to use unusual but edible organ meats (tongue, brain, kidneys) to conserve resources in supporting the war effort.

Kurt Lewin.

During his American academic career (1933–1947) at Cornell, Stanford, Iowa, Harvard, and MIT; Lewin influenced many people and the development of social psychology. He established the Research Center for Group Dynamics at MIT in 1944, and the center is still thriving at the University of Michigan. Many of today's most influential social psychologists were Lewin's students. Leon Festinger, the originator of cognitive dissonance theory; Stanley Schachter, writer of theories about emotion and affiliation; Harold Kelley, a leading theorist on attribution; Roger Barker, the originator of ecological psychology; Dorwin Cartwright, a prominent group dynamics researcher; and Morton Deutsch, a leading researcher on conflict and justice, are just a few of those students. Festinger (1980), Barker (1979), and Cartwright (1979) have written accounts of how Kurt Lewin invigorated the field of social psychology. Among the students of Lewin's students (the third generation) are some of the most prominent women social psychologists of today: Elaine Hatfield (formerly Walster) and Ellen Berscheid, leaders in equity theory and interpersonal attraction research; and Jane Piliavin, a leading researcher on helping and altruism. Many of the most prominent social psychologists today can trace their academic lineage directly to Lewin.

Another immigrant from pre-World War II Europe was Fritz Heider. In 1947, he migrated with Roger Barker to Kansas, where he and his wife, Grace, lived until his death in 1988. In 1958, Heider wrote a book, *The Psychology of Interpersonal Relations,* which introduced both balance theory and attribution theory to social psychology. Both theories, which you will learn about later in this book, have thriving research traditions.

An immigrant from Turkey between the two world wars, Muzafer Sherif influenced the course of social psychology over several decades until his death in 1988. In 1935, he showed how individuals are affected by group norms. In the 1950s and 1960s, he made major contributions with his social judgment theory and his field experiments on the development and reduction of prejudice.

Else Frenkel-Brunswik and Egon Brunswik, psychologists at the University of Vienna, also fled to America as Hitler rose to power. Egon Brunswik's lens model of perception has been applied in many areas of psychology. Else Frenkel-Brunswik made a substantial contribution to personality and social psychology when she coauthored the book, *The Authoritarian Personality,* with T. W. Adorno, D. J. Levinson, and R. N. Sanford in 1950. In this book, they described a rigid, dogmatic type of personality. Such authoritarian people were prone to display anti-Semitism and other types of ethnic prejudice according to the research of Frenkel-Brunswik and many others. The work on authoritarianism was a major impetus to the research on prejudice by social psychologists.

By 1950, social psychology was beginning to branch out. It was no longer possible to say that the hotbed of the discipline was at a few schools or in a particular region. The Yale attitude change group under Carl Hovland was becoming influential. The Research Center for Group Dynamics moved from MIT to Michigan in 1948, making the University of Michigan another focal point for social psychology. Festinger moved his brand of social psychology to Minnesota and subsequently to Stanford, creating strong programs in both universities.

Edward E. Jones, now famous for his work in attribution, interpersonal attraction, and self-presentation, went to Duke in 1952 with his new Harvard Ph.D. and created a social psychological tradition in the South. Today there are strong social psychology programs in colleges and universities all over the United States and Canada.

Methods in Social Psychology

In order to understand social psychology and most other disciplines, it is important to know how data are collected and what are considered meaningful results. It should be obvious by now that social psychology has adopted an empirical approach to understanding life's events. An empirical approach requires the investigator to translate his or her ideas or "conceptual variables" into observable events to make them testable. Some theories we encounter in everyday life do not appear testable. Some of Freud's ideas about unconscious processes have been criticized for being untestable. Prognosticators such as Jeanne Dixon usually phrase their predictions so loosely—"Something significant will happen to a member of the Kennedy family this year"—that they can be interpreted as true after the fact. The scientific, empirical approach requires a researcher to be more specific in identifying what he or she is studying than that. It requires such researchers to specify operational definitions for their independent and dependent variables beforehand. An **operational definition** is a statement of what concrete measures or techniques will be used to determine levels of variables. Operational definitions are described in the method sections of empirical psychological articles. For instance, intelligence may be operationally defined as the individuals' scores on the Wechsler Adult Intelligence Scale, a prominent and reliable measure of intelligence.

Social psychology has adopted an empirical approach that requires clearly measurable hypotheses rather than vague predictions.

   What are independent variables and dependent variables? Independent and dependent variables are determined by the investigator's hypotheses. An **independent variable** is the hypothesized cause for variation in another event or condition, a **dependent variable.** So an **hypothesis** specifies a cause-effect relationship between an independent variable and a dependent variable. The same variable could be an independent variable in one study and a dependent variable in another study, depending on the investigator's hypothesis. Working from the adage, "Birds of a feather flock together," an investigator may test the hypothesis that attitude similarity causes attraction. In such a study, attitude similarity would be the independent variable and attraction would be the dependent variable. On the other hand, an investigator could harbor the idea that birds that flock together become of the same feather or that liking someone causes a person to agree with that person. If a study were conducted to test this idea, attraction would be the independent variable and attitude similarity would be the dependent variable. To know the independent variables and dependent variables in a study, you must know the investigator's hypothesis. It should be a fruitful exercise for you to look up an article cited in this textbook and determine what the hypotheses, independent variables, dependent variables, and operational definitions are in the study.

Basic Dimensions
of Investigations

Studies in social psychology can be categorized on four basic methodological dimensions. These dimensions are (1) **experiments** versus **correlational studies,** (2) laboratory versus field settings, (3) self-report versus observational dependent variables, and (4) behavioral versus behavioral estimate dependent variables. Let us consider the four basic dimensions now.

Experiments versus
Correlational
Studies

There are two ways experimental independent variables are different from correlational independent variables. Investigators manipulate or systematically vary levels of *experimental* independent variables, and they randomly assign subjects to the different experimental conditions. In contrast, investigators measure *correlational* independent variables as they naturally occur, and subjects place themselves in different correlational conditions by how they respond to particular items or by their personal attributes (e.g., sex, race). Some investigators examine experimental and correlational independent variables in the same study. For example, an investigator could examine sex differences in behavior in two or more randomly assigned social situations. In such a study, sex would be a correlational variable and the social situation would be an experimental variable. Studies in which an independent variable is manipulated but subjects are not randomly assigned to conditions are called quasi-experimental studies (cf. Cook & Campbell, 1979). Such studies can be very useful in evaluating social, educational, or governmental programs where the evaluator does not have complete control over events (Oskamp, 1984).

Advantages of Experiments   There are many advantages to using experimental independent variables to evaluate cause and effect relationships. By virtue of manipulating the independent variable, it is possible to know what was introduced and when it was experienced. In a correlational study, the independent variable can be measured before the dependent variable, but the investigator does not know that the independent variable was experienced first. By being able to control the time sequence of events, an experimenter knows that the independent variable occurred first. For one event to cause another, it must occur first. Experimental variables allow one to know that this condition for inferring a cause-effect relationship is met.

Correlational and experimental variables are equally good at establishing covariation of the independent and dependent variables, another condition necessary for inferring causality. Covariation simply means that two variables vary together. That covariation can take the form of a positive correlation wherein high values of one variable go with high values of the other and low values coincide with other low values. For example, Adorno, Frenkel-Brunswik, Levinson, and Sanford (1950) found that people who were high in authoritarianism, a rigid, dogmatic type of personality, scored higher in ethnic prejudice than people low in authoritarianism. Covariation can also take the form of a negative correlation in which high values on one variable coincide with low values of the other and vice versa. For example, Belmont and Marolla (1973) found that the more brothers and sisters a person had, the lower his or her intelligence score. This somewhat disconcerting finding to those of us from large families will be discussed fully in chapter 2.

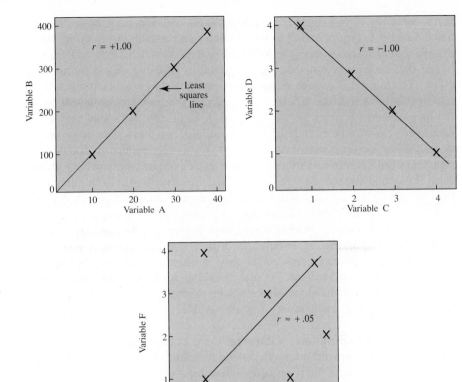

Figure 1.1
*Scattergram examples
of two perfect
correlations and a
correlation
approaching zero. The
x's represent one
individual's scores on
the two variables.*

The Correlation Coefficient   Statistically, correlations can range from −1.00 to +1.00. Both of these correlations indicate a perfect relationship between the two variables as graphed in figure 1.1. Such correlations seldom occur in psychology unless you are talking about two people rating quite objective events or stimuli. The important point to remember is that the positive or negative sign has nothing to do with the strength of the relationship. It is only related to the direction of the correlation. The degree to which the correlation departs from zero indicates the strength of the correlation. So, +.90 and −.90 are equally strong correlations. The more the values in the scattergram depart from the least squares line, the lower the correlation.

Random Assignment   Perhaps the most significant way that experimental variables are different from correlational variables is in the random assignment of subjects to conditions. Random assignment to conditions means that the investigator determines which condition a subject will participate in beforehand by referring to a table with numbers in a random sequence or by obtaining randomly ordered numbers from a computer. If 4 were the first number to appear, then the first subject would be assigned to Experimental Condition 4, as the investigator had defined it before referring to the random number table. In this way, one is assured that characteristics of the subjects didn't affect which condition they were in and that each subject had an equal probability of being picked for any condition. Assuming that enough subjects participate in the experiment, random assignment assures that the different experimental groups were equivalent before the independent variables were introduced. Kirk (1968) has stated that extraneous variables can be eliminated from a study in two ways. The two ways are to hold those factors constant or to cause them to vary randomly. Random assignment of subjects to conditions enables one to eliminate troublesome variables using the second method. So experimental variables assure you that nothing other than the manipulated independent variable caused the results to occur, enabling you to make a more certain cause-effect judgment.

The real beauty of random assignment is that you do not have to know whether the contaminating variable is introversion-extraversion, self-esteem, sexual orientation, sex, race, or social class in order to eliminate its effects on your results. On the other hand, in order to hold such a factor constant, you have to know what it is. So most social psychologists insist on conducting true experiments (with random assignment) if at all possible.

Disadvantages of Experiments   Others believe that staunch experimentalists are like the man in the proverb who was looking for a lost object under a light. After others helped him look for it for a few minutes, someone asked him if he had dropped it in the area. His reply was, "No, but the light's better here." Critics of experimentalists argue that they are examining wrong or less interesting variables simply because the methods are better suited to studying them. It is certainly true that if an investigator will not use correlational variables, he or she severely limits what can be studied. Sex, race, all personality variables, and all ability variables such as intelligence are unalterable personal characteristics that cannot be manipulated. Other factors, such as growing up in an affluent or impoverished home or being reared with strict or permissive parenting, also cannot be manipulated for ethical reasons. Can you imagine researchers telling parents that their infant daughter will have to live in a poor home because she was randomly assigned to the impoverished living condition. Many aspects of clinical medicine, for instance, are also based on correlational research by necessity because you can't tinker with live humans. Other psychologists, including ecological psychologists, have argued that behavior outside its natural, unmanipulated setting is not worth studying. Tunnell (1977) contended that we should strive to study the most natural settings, stimuli, and responses possible. Because of the interest in personality factors and other correlational variables mentioned, many social psychologists incorporate correlational variables into their experiments.

Social psychology studies can be conducted in a laboratory or a field setting. Most studies are conducted in a laboratory of one kind or another. However many helping studies are conducted in the field. For instance, Piliavin, Rodin, and Piliavin (1969) used the New York City subways as their field setting. Compliance and persuasion studies also often employ field settings. For example, Freedman and Fraser (1966) used subjects' own homes as their field settings. Dutton and Aron (1974) actually conducted part of their study on arousal and interpersonal attraction on an unstable bridge high above a deep gorge near Vancouver, British Columbia. Pennebaker, Dyer, Caulkins, Litowitz, Ackreman, Anderson, and McGraw (1979) even used honky-tonks, haunts, and hangouts near the University of Virginia campus for their settings. Is nothing sacred? We will see later that all studies in ecological psychology (e.g., Barker & Gump, 1964) and ethology (e.g., Cunningham, 1979) are conducted in field settings because of their insistence on studying behavior in natural habitats.

Some advantages of using field settings are that you are likely to see natural, uncontrived behavior in those settings. Results may be more generalizable to other everyday settings and people because they have been obtained in normal settings and with many different types of people. Some methodologists argue that you cannot use random assignment in the field to conduct a true experiment. That is not true; you can, but many investigators don't, choosing to do quasi experiments instead. The real problem is that you may get peculiar, unrepresentative subjects in some field settings, for instance, on Vancouver bridges. However, some college sophomores at particular universities in laboratory studies may not be representative of other people either, and the issue is seldom raised there.

How are laboratory settings different from field settings? Perhaps not in the ways you might think. Laboratories can be typical scientific laboratories, but they can also be classrooms, cubicles, nooks, and crannies. Basically, they are anywhere a subject has been asked to come to participate in a study. Field settings, on the other hand, are anywhere people are conducting their normal activities, unaware that they are being studied. The key difference between a laboratory and a field study is the subjects' agreement to participate and their awareness of the nature of the study. Not all deception studies are field studies. In most deception studies, the subject knows that he or she has chosen to participate in a psychological study. However, a study would be a field study if the data of interest is collected before or after the subject believes the study is being conducted at a laboratory site.

The major advantage of conducting a laboratory study is greater control over the environment. By controlling the events that occur in the setting, the investigator can hold possible troublesome variables constant by seeing that they never occur or they occur the same way every time. Another advantage is an ethical one. The researcher can disabuse the subject of any deceptions or misperceptions after the data is collected because the subject knows that he or she is being studied. In a field study, subjects are seldom debriefed because they never know they are being studied.

Laboratory versus Field Settings

The physical effects of drinking camel's milk would have to be investigated correlationally rather than experimentally for ethical reasons.

CHARLIE, by Rodrigues. © 1987 by Tribune Media Services. Reprinted by permission.

Social psychologists often conduct studies in field settings, such as on the Capilano bridge in Vancouver, to observe natural behavior and reactions.

Imagine the problems debriefing male subjects who were observed with a periscope as they urinated in a restroom (cf. Middlemist, Knowles, & Matter, 1976). Though conducting the study stirred ethical controversy (Koocher, 1977), it is probably better that subjects never knew they were being observed. Field researchers must be careful they do not harm their subjects or put them in situations they would not ordinarily experience, because field researchers usually don't have the opportunity to undo the harm they have done by debriefing.

One other point—these methodological dimensions are independent of each other. That is, researchers can conduct laboratory experiments, field experiments, laboratory correlational studies, or field correlational studies. Just because a study is done in a laboratory doesn't make it an experiment. Only manipulation of independent variables and random assignment of subjects to conditions make a study an experiment. It might be enlightening to examine studies in this discipline or others to see what kinds of studies they are.

Self-Report versus Observational Dependent Variables

Most of us have little difficulty agreeing on physical events. The sun always sets in the west; many people get married every year; a few people can run a mile in less than four minutes; and most people watch television more than an hour a day. All of the events are observed or recorded happenings. There are also many social behaviors that can be observed. Social psychologists can take advantage of these observable events and behaviors in building an objective discipline. The job for psychologists is tougher when they have to depend on individuals' self-reports about their attitudes or feelings. A person may express a particular attitude for many reasons other than the legitimate reason. Subjects may disguise their actual feelings or attitudes. If a social psychologist uses effective questionnaire or interview items in an appropriate setting, he or she can eliminate many of the extraneous reasons and obtain dependable measures.

It seems obvious that observational measures are used with events or behaviors which are happening or have been recorded so they can be observed later. Typically, two or more trained observers judge whether or how long particular behaviors occurred. On the other hand, self-report measures are used with variables that are not directly observable such as attitudes, moods, personality traits, or any past events not recorded on tape or film. Self-report measures are responses by subjects indicating their position typically marked on a scale associated with a statement or question. A typical self-report measure would be a 7-point Likert scale (named for its originator, Rensis Likert) used by the subject to indicate extent of agreement/disagreement with an attitude statement, such as the following:

Baseball players who use cocaine should be banned
from baseball for life.

1	2	3	4	5	6	7
Disagree strongly						Agree strongly

Observational dependent variables are best for many studies because the bottom line for those studies is "How does the independent variable affect behavior?" Observational techniques allow you to assess the occurrence or extent of behavior. Observational measures are less subject to distorted recall than self-reports because the behaviors are visible and/or audible to observers who are motivated to be objective. One problem with observations is that at least two observers should see each event to ensure that the observations are reliable. Another problem, especially with naturalistic observations, is that much time may pass before the behaviors of interest occur. A researcher must be astute in picking settings to maximize the number of observations in a period of time. Time sampling, whereby an observer may watch, for instance, for five minutes beginning every half-hour, may be used to maximize efficiency. It is analogous to time-lapse photography. Radloff and Helmreich (1968) used time sampling to observe men living in an undersea compartment for a month via video cameras in the compartment. In laboratory experiments (Kimble, Forte, & Yoshikawa, 1981; Kimble & Olszewski, 1980), researchers used videotaped observations to see how eye contact is used in expressing different emotions. So these techniques can be used in experiments and correlational studies, in the laboratory, and in the field.

New technologies such as video recording have helped social psychologists conquer problems of distorted recall and long-term observation.

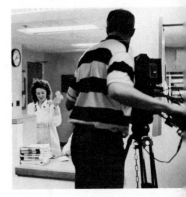

Self-reports enable psychologists to study otherwise unobservable events. These events can be unobservable because they happened in the past or because they are private events occurring within a person's body with no outward signs. Other types of events could be unobservable both because they happened in the past and because the individual does not wish to report them, as in the case of sexual practices. Only by assurance of confidentiality, anonymity, and upholding high ethical standards can sex researchers like Kinsey and his associates in the forties gain self-reports of such behaviors. Self-reports are obviously valuable in the study of attitudes, attributions, and personality characteristics. They are also valuable in assessing the effects of earlier events, such as childhood experiences, on current psychological outcomes. Some observational techniques, such as the galvanic skin response of lie detector tests, have been used to gain access to thoughts and feelings. However, their validity is uncertain unless parallel self-report information is obtained.

Self-reports can afford access to unobservable events very efficiently. There is no time lost in waiting for something to happen as in observational studies. Information about events occurring over a long period of time can be obtained in minutes by asking the subject. Also, if the reports are recorded in a standard form like the Likert item shown previously, they can be scored quickly by one person without ambiguity. In contrast, observations of highly variable behavior can be quite difficult to categorize. Self-report measures are quite common in studies of attributions and attitudes. One attitude study concerning cognitive dissonance (Knox & Inkster, 1968) even involved self-report measures of confidence of bettors as they went to or came from the $2 window at a racetrack.

Surveys and Archival Data   Surveys and polls are self-report measures commonly used by political groups, newspapers and television, political scientists, sociologists, and social psychologists. The purpose of such surveys is usually to find out what proportion of a particular large group (U.S. voters, for example) responds in a particular way (e.g., for Jesse Jackson for president). They are designed to discover how different people feel about an issue, not to answer questions about cause-effect relationships. Representative sampling is very important in these surveys in order to assure that your sample responds the way the entire large group would. Bias can creep into a survey in various ways. The Literary Digest poll in 1936 indicated that Alf Landon would win the presidency, but the incumbent Franklin D. Roosevelt actually won by a landslide. The problem was not the size of their sample, which was much larger than those used today. The problem was that the phone and car owners who responded (only 20 to 25 percent responded) were not representative of Depression era voters. Phone-in polls conducted by newspapers or television are biased because they get responses from only the most interested and partisan individuals, who are not representative of all the people potentially involved. QUBE television, which obtains responses from viewers via a response box in their homes, have some of the sampling problems Literary Digest had. Differences in time zones can even affect survey responses because viewerships are different at different times. The major TV networks have become acquainted with time zone effects with the controversy over releasing election results before polls are closed in western areas of the country.

Archival research is typically done on self-report data. The U.S. Census Bureau, the FBI, and the University of Michigan Survey Research Center are prominent sources for archival data. Rotton, Barry, and Kimble (1985) recently used the Census Bureau's City-County Databook to assess the relationships between climate and crime. While data collected in the census every decade are self-report data, other archives such as the burglary rate reported by the FBI are recorded observations. Such archival research can be valuable in assessing the impact of laws (Campbell, 1970).

Behavior versus Behavioral Estimates

In social psychology, we either put people into situations where they have to act or react and record their responses or we ask them to estimate how they or others would respond in hypothetical situations. In the first type of study, we are using behaviors as our dependent variables. In the second type of study, we are using behavioral estimates as dependent variables. In an attitude study, the self-reported attitudes would be regarded as behaviors, not as estimates of behavior. The feature distinguishing these two types of studies is personal involvement. The situation has more impact in behavioral studies. In fact, some studies that claim to study behavior have so little impact on and involve test subjects so little that they are really only obtaining behavioral estimates. Studies by Byrne and his associates (cf. Byrne, 1971) are examples. In these studies, subjects read attitude responses and indicate how much they "would" like the person who made them. "Would" is the important term here. It indicates that subjects are only estimating their response. Since they never see or hear the person, estimates of their attraction is all they could give.

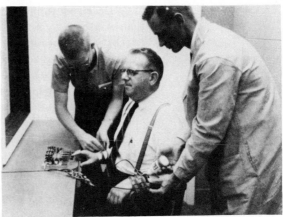

Experimental realism is another term for the impact that behavioral studies have. This impact evokes emotional as well as cognitive responses. If there are emotional components to the responses you are studying, it is important to create realistic situations with impact or to observe behavior in powerful, naturally occurring situations. If you are studying dispassionate, cognitive processes, estimates of behavior are probably better measures.

The Use of Deceptions   Deception is often used to create the situations that evoke behavior in social psychological studies. However, deception is not always necessary to create an involving situation. Many group interaction studies create interest, involvement and natural behavior without deception.

Milgram's (1974) studies on obedience demonstrated some of the advantages of using deception to create situations with greater impact. Using deception, Milgram created a compelling situation in which over 60 percent of the subjects obeyed the experimenter's command to shock a victim at a very dangerous level (450 volts). Milgram also wrote a description of this experimental situation and procedures and took it and a picture of the shock apparatus to Harvard Medical School. There he asked 40 psychiatrists to estimate how many people in such a situation would shock a victim up to 450 volts. Their average estimate was that far less than 1 percent of the subjects would administer such shock!

Which results best represented human nature? If we believe that the subjects thought the victim was really being shocked, we must trust the behavioral study more than the behavioral estimate. The reactions of filmed subjects, Milgram's descriptions in the literature, and an account by one of my professors in graduate school make me believe that the subjects thought they were actually shocking the victim. My graduate professor told us that when he was in graduate school at Yale, he took his car to a garage for repairs. As he was chatting with the mechanic, he said that he was studying psychology at Yale. Whereupon the mechanic lowered his car to the floor and told him to get out. The mechanic was still suffering nightmares from having been one of Milgram's subjects two years earlier!

Stanley Milgram's studies on obedience, in which subjects were ordered to shock a man demonstrated the advantages of deception as a research technique.

(Copyright 1965 by Stanley Milgram. From the film Obedience, *distributed by the New York University Film Library)*

Deceiving subjects by telling them you are interested in something other than what you are really studying has at least two other advantages in addition to experimental realism or impact. It reduces hypothesis guessing by the subjects by minimizing the demand characteristics of the situation. **Demand characteristics** are simply cues in the situation that may enable subjects to infer the connection between independent variables and dependent variables (the hypothesis) that the investigator is examining. By telling them that he or she is interested in other factors, the investigator diverts subjects' attention away from the real hypothesis. There are other means of reducing demand characteristics, such as embedding the critical dependent measure among meaningless filler items. It is important to reduce hypothesis guessing because subjects may not give a natural response if they know that response is being scrutinized. An investigator may get the desired results, but for the wrong reason (because the subjects want to act appropriately) in such studies.

The third advantage of using deception is that investigators can avoid getting socially desirable responses from subjects. Especially in a psychology study, a subject may be motivated to "fake good" or to appear well adjusted. Such motivation leads subjects to respond in unnatural ways, invalidating the results of the study. In a deception study, a subject may not know which items to fake and he or she may be so involved in the study that he or she is not motivated to act artificially. It should be obvious that social psychologists use deception for legitimate reasons. (See table 1.2.)

Ethics in Social Psychological Studies

Subjects' reactions in the Milgram obedience studies highlight the importance of ethical considerations in social psychology. Two guiding principles for social psychologists are to minimize physical and psychological harm to subjects and to assure that they leave the subject as well or better than they were before participating in the study. Milgram could not restore his subjects to their original mental state. Even though he told them that their victim was not really being shocked and thoroughly debriefed them after the session, the subjects learned something unpleasant about themselves that they could not discard when the experimental session was over, namely, they knew that they would harm someone badly if they were ordered to do so. Because of the continuing psychological harm to the subjects, Milgram was forced to discontinue his studies of obedience in the 1960s. Fortunately for him and social psychology, Milgram found other fruitful research areas to study until his death in 1984.

Recent ethical guidelines from the American Psychological Association emphasize minimizing harm to subjects, minimizing the use of deception, obtaining consent to participate from subjects after informing them of the nature of the experience, providing full disclosure of purposes and procedures of the study immediately after subjects' participation, and protecting the privacy of subjects. Individual psychology departments urge investigators to make participation an educational experience for students by describing the research fully

Table 1.2 Advantages and Disadvantages of Different Methods in Social Psychology

	Experiments	Correlational studies
Advantage	Can make cause-effect inferences	Can assess topics that can't be studied experimentally for practical or ethical reasons
Disadvantage	Can't use to assess some topics	Can't make cause-effect inferences

	Field setting	Laboratory setting
Advantage	More natural behavior	Better control
Disadvantage	Usually unable to debrief, disabuse subjects	Artificiality of situation and subjects' responses

	Self-reports	Observations
Advantage	Provide access to unobservable moods, attitudes, thoughts	Enable direct measurement of behaviors
Disadvantage	Susceptible to lying, distortions of memory	Time-consuming; multiple observers needed

	Behavioral studies	Behavior estimate studies
Advantage	Involving, high impact, experimental realism	Useful in cognitive, unemotional studies
Disadvantage	Sometimes requires the use of deception	Uninvolved subjects may not be able to accurately estimate how they would behave

Social psychologists are not the only ones who use deception. However, deception can only be justified by the value of the information obtained and the fact that no lasting physical or psychological harm is done.

THE FAR SIDE, by Gary Larson. © 1987 by Universal Press Syndicate. Reprinted by permission. All Rights Reserved.

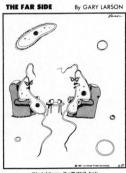

THE FAR SIDE   By GARY LARSON

"He told you *that*? Well, he's pulling your flagellum, Nancy."

after subjects participate. Deception is still widely used in studies where the benefits of its use are judged to outweigh the costs. When deception is used, obtaining prior informed consent is a problem. Obviously, subjects can't be fully informed beforehand in those cases. However, they should be informed of any unpleasant experiences they might encounter in the study such as receiving electrical shock or being asked personal questions. All other ethical standards, including full debriefing immediately after the session and assurance of anonymity and confidentiality of responses, should be readily met in social psychological studies. Researchers should answer all questions and reduce any uneasiness subjects may have about the experience. It is important that we maintain and deserve the trust of the public in conducting this research. Participants should leave a study thinking it has been a pleasant, rewarding experience.

Applications of Knowledge about Methods

The student of social psychology must apply his or her knowledge of methods to understand the significance of findings in social psychology and other fields. That knowledge enables students to judge the merits of a particular study, to compare it to their own experiences, and to decide whether it has any use in their personal lives or work. Understanding of methods means a person does not have to depend on authorities to tell him or her what life is or how the world works. Instead, that person can look at what has been found and see how the results were obtained to make his or her decisions.

Such a consumer of social psychology should appreciate that systematic data collection is important. Single cases may be dramatic, fascinating, and useful in illustrating a point; but they cannot be considered dependable data. They can be an impetus for conducting systematic research, but we should be reluctant to draw conclusions from them. The sudden death of Jim Fixx, the man who wrote the book on running, may have led many people to conclude that strenuous exercise is dangerous for your health. For people like Jim Fixx, who had a history of heart trouble in his family, who had been overweight, who had smoked for years, and whose everyday diet was high in fats and carbohydrates, running is dangerous. However, for many other people, strenuous exercise is invigorating and life-lengthening. Overgeneralization from the single case is the problem with drawing such conclusions.

Another point that a student of social psychology should consider in evaluating results is that they are true for most people most of the time if the study has been properly conducted. That means that you would probably act the same way in a similar situation. It is always easy for us to say, "yes, that's how those other people act." Unless the results only occur for the other sex or for another type of personality (e.g., highly self-conscious people), the results are applicable to us all. So we should gain some self-understanding from considering the theories and findings in this book.

Many social psychologists use their knowledge of methods and design as consultants for public and private agencies or companies. Social psychologists may consult with research firms, which often use sophisticated experimental studies. Mental health agencies, local government programs, or marketing firms are more likely to want help doing survey types of studies such as needs assessments (studies designed to determine the needs of a particular community or set of consumers). Social psychologists may be more likely to use quasi-experimental or correlational methods to do program evaluations for mental health, criminal justice, or other social service agencies.

Many of the public agencies and private concerns where these research and evaluation studies are conducted should be encouraged to use more rigorous, systematic methods. Donald Campbell (Campbell & Stanley, 1966; Cook & Campbell, 1979) has been a leader in pointing out how better methods can be used in applied settings. Legislative bodies should be encouraged to enact evaluation components in more of the programs they pass in order to see if they are attaining the desired outcomes.

Summary

Social psychology was presented as the study of the causes, consequences, and patterns of human interaction. Several prominent sociopsychological findings were also described. Facets of the observer attribution bias, the self-fulfilling prophecy, obedience to authority, the effect of behavior on attitudes, the motivation-undermining effects of rewards, the group polarization effect, social loafing, and the effect of attitude similarity on attraction were briefly discussed. Theories are conceptual frameworks to aid in understanding facts and uncovering new relationships. A brief history of social psychology emphasizing the influence of immigrants to America between the two world wars, such as Kurt Lewin, Else Frenkel-Brunswik, Fritz Heider, and Muzafer Sherif was presented.

The major dimensions of methods in social psychology were outlined. Manipulation of independent variables with random assignment of subjects is preferred over correlational variables unless it is impossible or impractical to manipulate the factors. Laboratory studies offer more precision and control, but field studies usually yield more natural responses. Systematic observation of behavior is usually the preferred means of assessing dependent variables, but many elements of psychology are unobservable. Self-report measures are necessary to assess these attitudes, attributions, and traits. Behavioral dependent measures are preferred over estimates of behavior unless one is dealing with cognitive processes such as attribution. Deception can sometimes be used to create situations with impact, but special care must be taken to ensure that subjects are treated ethically in those studies.

It is very important that consumers and practitioners of social psychology understand that results can only be meaningful and useful if appropriate, systematic methods were used to obtain them.

Society and the Individual

CHAPTER 2

Personal Development

I. Early Experience and development
  A. Attachment and later relationships
  B. Learning to behave
    1. Operant conditioning
    2. Classical conditioning
    3. Observational learning
II. Individual aspects of development
  A. Physical appearance and development
  B. Sex roles and development
    1. Psychological sex differences
    2. Fear of success in women
    3. Femininity, masculinity, and androgyny

III. Family aspects of development
  A. Family constellation and intelligence
  B. Family constellation and social behavior
  C. Childrearing practices and self-esteem
IV. Urban-rural environments and development
  A. Undermanning in small towns
  B. Urban villages and city life
  C. Critical mass and city life
  D. Overload and city life
V. Other influences on development
VI. Applications of Personal Development Information
Summary

". . . as the twig is bent, the tree's inclined"

—*Moral Essays*, Epistle I, To Lord Cobham, Alexander Pope.

". . . the difference between a lady and a flower girl is not how she behaves, but how she's treated."

—*Pygmalion*, George Bernard Shaw

Individual differences in how we act, feel, and think in social situations as adults arise partly from our past social experiences. It seems appropriate to start this account of personal development at the beginning: childhood. **Socialization** is a term used to describe how adults teach a society's rules to children to make those children fit into the society better. Children who live in different circumstances are treated differently or socialized differently. In a way, the self, which will be covered in the next chapter, is the product of all our socialization experiences. This chapter will deal with how these differences in treatment affect personal development.

One reason we are interested in personal development is because this study should help each of us to understand better our place in society. We should be able to understand why we act, think, and feel the way we do. Further, if we learn that certain characteristics or other background factors have consistent effects on how people develop, we should appreciate the differences between people more. Knowing the origins of these differences should facilitate communication and cooperation between people of different backgrounds.

Early Experience and Development

Socialization affects our understanding of ourselves and our place in society. It begins in early childhood.

Your behavior today is determined by your understanding of the current situation, your genetic physical and mental makeup, your past environments, and how you experienced those environments through your mental and physical faculties. Clearly, our past experiences affect our present patterns of thinking and behaving, and our earliest experiences should have great impact on the development that follows.

Sigmund Freud emphasized the importance of early experience for later development and the interplay of individual sensitivities and environmental events with his **psychosexual stages** of development. He observed that very young infants were particularly responsive to feeding practices and schedules (the **oral stage**), slightly older infants were sensitive to toilet training practices by which society made the child curb her or his natural impulses (the **anal stage**), and 5 and 6-year-olds were attuned to genital stimulation (the **phallic stage**). Overindulgence or deprivation during any of the oral, anal, or phallic stages can lead to fixation of psychic energy at that stage and impaired development later. Also, problems in resolving the Oedipus (boys' desire for their mothers) or Electra (girls' desire for their fathers) complex at the end of the phallic stage can lead to fixations and problem behaviors later. Even though there is still debate over the validity of some of his positions, Freud's theories have been very beneficial in directing attention to the early years of development.

Harlow's (1958) studies with infant monkeys who had been isolated from their mothers showed that infants need the touching, holding, and caressing provided by their mothers for normal development. Harlow's studies even showed that baby monkeys will stay with terrycloth mothers who provide contact comfort over wire mothers who contain the food source. Stories about overburdened orphanages and children reared in isolation from adult physical attention seem to lend credence to the generalizability of Harlow's findings to humans. In the 1940s (Spitz, 1945), there were reports that well-nourished babies in orphanages grew listless and died from lack of physical attention. However, those reports have been discredited by indications that there were physical problems as well as psychological ones. An eminent developmental psychologist, Jerome Kagan (1984) has stated, after conducting research on the topic for years, that early childhood isolation and deprivation must be very extreme for it to alter normal maturation. Such a statement makes one doubt that the contact experiences of bottle-fed and breast-fed babies, for instance, would be different enough to have any psychological impact.

A recent investigation (Hazan & Shaver, 1987) examined how infants' relationship with their mother (or primary caregiver) affects their approach to adult love relationships. When an infant is separated from its mother during the second year (1–2), attachment theory (Bowlby, 1973) states that the child first protests by crying and seeking her, then the child displays despair with passivity and sad expressions, and finally shows detachment with active disregard or avoidance of mother upon her return. Bowlby suggested that the nature of attachment in this first relationship laid the groundwork for reactions to later relationships.

Attachment and Later Relationships

How the child has been treated during its first year affects the security of the **attachment** relationship with the mother (Ainsworth, Blehar, Waters, & Wall, 1978). Ainsworth and her associates theorized that if the mother were sensitive and responsive to the infant's needs, the child would respond *securely* upon separation and return of the mother by going to her first and then quickly returning to exploring and playing. If the mother were unresponsive when she was needed and intrusive when she wasn't (generally out of synch with the infant's needs), the child would respond *anxiously/ambivalently* by clinging to the mother some of the time and acting angrily toward her at others. If the mother had consistently rebuffed the infant's attempts to establish physical contact, the child would act *avoidantly* by staying away and not looking at the mother upon her return. Ainsworth's laboratory observations have shown that these three patterns of response do occur. In a review of these studies with American infants, Campos, Barrett, Lamb, Goldsmith, and Stenberg (1983) found that 62 percent of infants were secure, 23 percent were avoidant, and 15 percent were anxious/ambivalent.

In their studies, Hazan and Shaver found interesting indications that this earliest relationship does affect one's approach to loving others later in life. In a newspaper questionnaire sample and in a college student sample (see table 2.1), they found that 56 percent of respondents described their feelings in close relationships in secure ways, 25 percent (newspaper, 23 percent college) used

Table 2.1 Adult Attachment Types and Their Frequencies (Newspaper Sample)

Question

Which of the following best describes your feelings?

Answers and percentages

Secure ($N = 319$, 56 percent): I find it relatively easy to get close to others and am comfortable depending on them and having them depend on me. I don't often worry about being abandoned or about someone getting too close to me.

Avoidant ($N = 145$, 25 percent): I am somewhat uncomfortable being close to others; I find it difficult to trust them completely, difficult to allow myself to depend on them. I am nervous when anyone gets too close, and often, love partners want me to be more intimate than I feel comfortable being.

Anxious/Ambivalent ($N = 110$, 19 percent): I find that others are reluctant to get as close as I would like. I often worry that my partner doesn't really love me or won't want to stay with me. I want to merge completely with another person, and this desire sometimes scare people away.

Note. Twenty-one subjects failed to answer this question, and 25 checked more than one answer alternative.

From C. Hazen and P. Shaver, "Romantic Love Conceptualized as an Attachment Process," in the *Journal of Personality and Social Psychology* [52: 511–524, (1987)]. Copyright 1987 by the American Psychological Association (Washington, D.C.). Reprinted by permission.

avoidant terms, and 19 percent (newspaper, 20 percent college) used anxious/ambivalent terms. These percentages for the three types of reactions to relationships were practically identical and quite similar to the percentages of the types of behavioral reactions among infants. From these results and other correlational data, Hazan and Shaver suggest that the nature of our first relationship shapes our reactions to later close relationships.

Learning to Behave

Operant Conditioning

Parents and other caretakers can have a substantial impact on how children act. It is assumed that children acquire behaviors through operant conditioning, classical conditioning, and observational learning. **Operant conditioning,** as described by B. F. Skinner (1938), occurs when a child does something and that act is followed by reinforcement, punishment, or no action. If a particular response such as saying "Mama" is followed by reinforcement, it will be repeated. If a response such as throwing food is followed by punishment, it will be less likely to be repeated. If a response such as hitting is ignored consistently (i.e., it is followed by no action), it will also be less likely to occur again. Table 2.2 shows which kinds of events are likely to be reinforcing and which are likely to be punishing if they follow a child's response.

So, presenting a positive stimulus is normally reinforcing, and presenting a negative stimulus is ordinarily punishing. Removing a pleasant stimulus is usually punishing and removing an unpleasant stimulus is usually reinforcing. There is often confusion between punishment and negative reinforcement. Remember, punishment decreases the likelihood of response in the future; reinforcement increases it. One example of how termination of an aversive stimulus is reinforcing is when a baby stops crying when her father changes her wet diaper. She is negatively reinforcing his behavior and he is likely to change her diaper when she cries later. This example also illustrates that reinforcement does not have to be

Table 2.2 Reinforcing and Punishing Events		
	Appetitive (+) Stimulus	Aversive (−) Stimulus
Start or increase	Positive reinforcement (getting food or praise)	Punishment (getting spanked)
Stop or reduce	Punishment (toys, TV privileges taken)	Negative reinforcement (restraints removed)

planned to work and that children influence the behavior of parents as well as vice versa. Skinner and other behavior modification advocates usually prefer to extinguish a behavior by ignoring it rather than using punishment. Sometimes inappropriate behaviors are learned because a parent or teacher unknowingly reinforces a child by treating the child in what he or she thinks is a negative way and the child perceives it as positive. A child may acquire many aggressive habits this way.

Classical conditioning can lead to strong emotional responses to stimuli or events that were originally neutral. The idea from Pavlovian classical conditioning is that if neutral events are paired consistently with positive or negative unconditioned stimuli (UCS) that elicit pleasurable or fearful unconditioned responses, those neutral events will eventually elicit the emotional response. Some young children may become fearful of doctors, nurses, and doctors' offices because they are consistently paired with getting shots. Part of the child's bonding to his or her mother may grow out of her consistently being paired with pleasurable unconditioned stimuli such as food and affection. Other children develop inordinate attachments to blankets or other objects that probably grow out of similar complex classical conditioning.

Classical Conditioning

    Dog obedience training is an example of a combination of classical and operant conditioning. A verbal command such as "heel," which is certainly a neutral stimulus to most dogs, can eventually elicit the desired behavior if it is paired with (followed by) pulling on a choke collar (UCS) enough times. That is an example of classical conditioning. Praising other desired acts by the dog is an example of operant conditioning by positive reinforcement.

Observational learning (cf. Bandura, 1977b) is another way that children learn to behave. This learning can occur whenever the child sees someone else perform in a way that he or she is capable of repeating. In observational learning, another person models the behavior and the child imitates it, especially if the other person (model) was rewarded for doing the behavior. The newly-acquired behavior is not always performed immediately after seeing the model perform, and it may not be performed exactly as the model performed it. Nonetheless, the child can retain a mental representation of the act and perform it later at an appropriate time. Our oldest daughter demonstrated observational learning in her language

Observational Learning

Children acquire language through observational learning.
News America Syndicate

patterns when she was one and a half years old, much to our amusement and dismay. We had just driven 1,000 miles in two days to visit relatives. It had been an arduous ordeal and apparently my language had occasionally been more colorful than desired. As we went through a parking lot on the second day, our car hit a pothole and jarred us badly. From the back seat, we heard a soft "g _____ it." We tried to keep our laughter to a minimum so as not to reinforce the behavior. The next morning as we were having breakfast, I juggled and nearly dropped a syrup container. Again Emily uttered a quiet, "g _____ it." She had obviously learned the appropriate times to say it, but did not show the emotional expression that such an expletive requires! Probably, many parents have observed such examples of observational learning.

Observational learning or imitation is probably the most common way that individuals acquire behavior. Two important questions about observational learning follow: What behaviors are most likely to be learned? What models are likely to be imitated? Behavior that is salient, attention-getting, seen repeatedly, and simple enough for the child to retain and reproduce is likely to be learned (Bandura, 1977b). Behaviors seen and heard on television are as likely to have these characteristics and be imitated as are behaviors observed live. That is why there is much interest and concern about what children see on television. Parents who are interested in how their children are going to act and think in the future should attend to what the children see on TV today. Actions are also more likely to be imitated than words (Rushton, 1979).

Parents, siblings, teachers, neighborhood kids, and schoolmates are the ones who interact most with young children and are likely to be imitated most due to the frequent contact. Parents, same-sex peers (cf. Bandura, Ross, & Ross, 1963), slightly older children, teachers, and TV or entertainment heroes are likely to be imitated because they are liked or admired. Young people who imitate appearance or mannerisms of Cyndy Lauper, Tina Turner, Michael Jackson, Mr. T.,

Brian Bosworth, or Boy George are ample evidence of the influence of entertainment figures. However, parents who interact with their children often in nurturant, affectionate ways are the models who are most likely to be imitated, at least by young children. The relative positivity and frequency of the interactions between parent (or other model) and child determines identification and imitation in most cases (Bandura, 1977b).

Individual Aspects of Development

Many characteristics of the individual affect how he or she is treated and such differential treatment affects the course of development. Certainly whether an infant is a smiling, active, and responsive baby instead of a fussy, irritable, colicky one affects how parents treat the infant. Such temperamental differences are often biologically determined (Buss & Plomin, 1975) and are not under the control of the baby, but they can affect the treatment the baby receives. Extreme cases, such as biologically determined early infantile autism (cf. Rimland, 1964) in which a baby is unresponsive from birth, distress parents and often leave them feeling guilty about their treatment of the child. Reports of child abuse of incessantly crying babies are extreme examples of babies' temperaments affecting the parents' response.

Physical Appearance and Development

The child's physical appearance is another individual characteristic that influences how he or she is treated early in life. Karen Dion (1972) found that undergraduate women rated physically attractive 7-year-old boys and girls who had intentionally hurt a dog or another child at school as less likely than unattractive children to commit a similar misdeed in the future. The college women also inferred that the unattractive children had more chronic antisocial dispositions than attractive children. Dion, Berscheid, and Walster (1972), in their study on the "what is beautiful is good" or physical attractiveness stereotype, found that college students rated photographed attractive college-age men and women as having more of many positive characteristics, such as being genuine, sensitive, outgoing, poised, and sophisticated, than unattractive men and women. They also estimated that these attractive people would have more occupational and marital success and happiness than unattractive people. It should be pointed out that on several variables attractive people were rated no more likely to be successful or happy than average appearance people. They were only rated more positively than the unattractive people on these dimensions. These studies suggest that attractive people are perceived more positively and are treated better than unattractive people and that this differential treatment begins at a young age.

Hobfoll and Penner (1978) conducted a study which indicated that such differential treatment over the years has impact on the individual's self-concept. They videotaped standardized interviews with men and women who were rated attractive or unattractive by independent judges. Then they had clinical psychology graduate students rate the positivity of their self-concepts from the videotapes or from the sound track alone without seeing their pictures. The most important result was that these students rated the attractive men and women as

Young children look up to and imitate older brothers and sisters.

having more positive self-concepts than the unattractive men and women regardless of whether or not they saw their pictures. It appears that years of being treated as attractive people made the attractive subjects project positive self-concepts in what they said and how they said it more than less attractive subjects projected.

Life histories of people disfigured by diseases, such as neurofibromatosis (Elephant Man's disease) or the bone disease experienced by Rocky Dennis, the California boy portrayed in the movie *Mask,* suggest that they are often treated poorly by others. They have considerable difficulty establishing heterosexual relationships. Most people are not so adversely affected by the physical attractiveness stereotype.

Sex Roles and Development

Gender is another characteristic that affects how a child is treated. Boys are traditionally covered with a blue blanket and girls with a pink blanket in the newborn nursery. There is a considerable amount of research indicating that adults treat infant boys and infant girls differently (e.g., Seavey, Katz, & Zalk, 1975), but parents interact with girls and boys less than a year old in similar ways (Field, 1978; Lamb, 1977). However, by the age of two, the kinds of toys girls and boys receive and the kinds of play they are encouraged to participate in have become radically different. With few exceptions, girls receive Cabbage Patch dolls and toy dishes, and boys receive balls and vehicles that turn into robots. Childrens' clothing, at least for special occasions, become more sex-specific as they grow older. By the time children are 3 years old, each girl has identified herself as a female and each boy has identified himself as a male (Kohlberg, 1969). Once they have cognitively labeled their sex, boys and girls tend to gravitate toward and develop interest in sex-typed activities. Most people in their environment reinforce the child's imitation of same-sex children and adults and reinforce what they consider to be sex-appropriate play (Bandura & Walters, 1963).

Childhood is just the beginning for differential treatment according to a person's sex. When the individual reaches adolescence, the difference in treatment between sexes becomes even greater. Bem and Bem (1970) have stated that gender-based treatment is so uniform and pervasive that our attitudes toward gender have become a "nonconscious ideology." That is, our ideas about how males and females should think and act have become so ingrained by this treatment that we seldom reflect thoughtfully on how we behave. We just act nonconsciously. So, women become nurses, teachers, secretaries, and homemakers; and men become doctors, engineers, executives, and breadwinners "naturally."

Perhaps with women's awareness groups and various other societal changes, these gender-based tendencies are weaker than they were in 1970. However, the failure of the Equal Rights Amendment, the current political climate, and accounts of how "enlightened, aware" people in the past have displayed gender bias make one doubt that substantial changes have occurred. Bem and Bem gave an account of how "equality-minded" radical men at Columbia University in 1968 told the radical women who had just helped them gain control of the administration building to cook them some food while the men talked strategy. Another example of the pervasiveness of the nonconscious ideology of sexism was the shocked response of a nonsexist fellow academician when she heard that the son of another faculty member had been playing with a doll. It turned out to be a GI Joe doll. Some expectations are hard to change even when more men and women are working side by side. For example, my sister-in-law was quite offended when her division leader did not ask her to go to an afternoon baseball game when he had asked all the men in her division in 1984. Parenthetically, those afternoon games used to be called "Businessmen's Specials"; now they are "Business Day Specials."

These differences in treatment contribute to the mental and behavioral sex differences documented by Maccoby and Jacklin (1974). Alice Eagly (1987) has presented compelling arguments that *social roles* or shared expectations about appropriate traits and behaviors form the basis for psychological sex differences. In particular, **gender roles,** social roles applied to persons based on their gender, contribute to sex differences by setting standards for males and females and by giving people gender-related skills and beliefs. The female gender role ascribes the *communal* qualities of selflessness, concern for others, and interpersonal sensitivity to girls and women (Bakan, 1966). Eagly further stated that the male gender role ascribes the *agentic* qualities of self-assertion, task-mindedness, and dominance to boys and men. These socially acquired qualities, skills, and beliefs, which develop from how females and males were treated, contribute to mental and behavioral differences between the sexes.

> *Psychological Sex Differences*

> *Acceptance of social roles may affect choice of sex-typed occupations, such as doctor or nurse.*

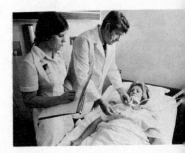

  This interpretation does not imply that psychological sex differences are wholly social and not biological in origin. One behavioral difference, the greater aggressiveness of males, seems to be due to hormonal, biological differences *and* the different treatments males and females receive. Patterns of aggressive behavior have been clearly related to the addition and reduction of testosterone, a male hormone, to the blood in rats (see chapter 13). One could also argue that the greater size and strength of males contributes indirectly to their learning to be aggressive because such behavior is more likely to produce rewards for them. The encouragement and reinforcement of aggression in males by other people in their environments must also contribute to this sex difference (cf. Bandura & Walters, 1963). Other psychological sex differences are predominantly caused by differences in treatment of males and females. These differences include greater conformity by women (Crutchfield, 1955; Eagly, 1987), greater dominance by men (Henley, 1977), and greater emotional expressiveness (Hall, 1984) and empathy by women (Hoffman, 1977; Maccoby & Jacklin, 1974).

  Studies of conformity and dominance have yielded inconsistent results. Conformity research is a good example. A meta-analysis, a method for quantitatively assessing research studies on a particular topic, by Cooper (1979) indicated that women conformed more than men in face-to-face group pressure type studies, but not in studies where written or stated summaries of group norms were the only form of pressure. A review by Eagly (1978) found similar results. One group norm study using fictitious group norms that was particularly instructive was conducted by Sistrunk and McDavid (1971). They gave men and women

Figure 2.1
*Average percentage
conformity by males
and females on
masculine, feminine,
and neutral items.*
*(From the study of Sistrunk &
McDavid, 1971.)*

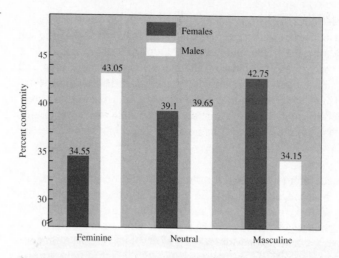

statements of fact and of opinion on topics of feminine, masculine, or neutral interest and asked them to indicate their agreement or disagreement with the statements. The experimenters gave the subjects fictitious majority answers of 200 students which were wrong for statements of fact and randomly varied for statements of opinion. Overall, there were no sex differences in conformity, but closer examination revealed that women conformed more on masculine-interest items, men conformed with the majority more on feminine-interest items, and there were no differences in conformity to neutral items. Presumably, men were unsure of their positions on feminine topics and women were unsure on masculine topics; therefore, they conformed to majority opinion in those instances. (See figure 2.1.) Eagly, Wood, and Fishbaugh (1981) found that men conformed less than women did when they believed their opinions would be seen by other members of the group, but there were no sex differences when their opinions were private. It was assumed that the males' nonconformity when their opinions were to be seen was due to their desire to live up to the masculine norm of independence. Both studies suggested that the contexts in which the response was given was important in determining whether men and women differ in conformity.

Research on dominance in conversations also suggests that sex difference findings are dependent on the contexts in which the conversations occur. Interrupting another person is a dominant behavior that men do more in mixed-sex dyadic conversations (Zimmerman & West, 1975). However, Dabbs and Ruback (1984), Duncan and Fiske (1977), and LaFrance and Carmen (1980) did not find sex differences in interruptions. Kimble, Yoshikawa, and Zehr (1981) found that men were more dominant in conversation than only some women. Those differences only occurred in mixed-sex groups, and they only occurred in structured rather than free discussions. So, these dominance differences were quite limited and qualified. Further, Kimble and Musgrove (1988) found that men dominated conversations in some ways and women dominated in others. Men talked louder and longer than women in arguments between a man and a woman, but women's visual behavior was more dominant in those same mixed-sex dyads.

Matina Horner (1970, 1972) has presented evidence that being treated as a female can create conflict in girls and women and hinder achievement. She said that others' expectations and womens' internalized expectations created conflict between being feminine and achieving success. Successful women, she said, feel anxious, guilty, unfeminine, and selfish (Horner, 1970). She used a projective technique, asking subjects to tell a story about a particular event or state of affairs, to see if women display fear of success more than men do. For instance, women were asked to respond to such statements as "After first-term finals, Anne finds herself at the top of her medical school class," while men were asked to respond to a similar statement concerning "John." Women's responses showed more fear of success or motive to avoid success in the forms of fear of social rejection (e.g., Anne is upset because she is ahead of her boyfriend in the class), concerns about normality or femininity (e.g., Anne feels guilty, unhappy, has a nervous breakdown), or denial (e.g., it was luck that Anne came out on top of her med school class). The last example is interesting because Deaux and Emswiller (1974) found that successful performance by women was often attributed to luck. In a separate study, Horner (1970) showed that women who displayed this fear of success did not perform well in competitive situations.

However, many investigators (e.g., Condry & Dyer, 1976; Gelbort & Winer, 1985; Tresemer, 1976) have raised questions about the fear of success methodology and have concluded that it is not clear that females show more fear of success than males. However, the concerns about competing with men and marital and maternal fulfillment seem to be alive as recently as 1978. Frieze, Parsons, Johnson, Ruble, and Zellman (1978) stated that single professional women reported that many men were threatened by a woman who was more successful than they were. So, many men were not potential marriage partners. Consequently, the most successful women were likely to remain single, while the most successful men were usually married. Regardless of whether women and girls develop an internalized fear of success, it appears that there are men's ploys and other factors that motivate females to "act dumb" or "take a back seat to males." Morgan and Mausner (1973) found that girls, regardless of their fear of success, purposely performed poorer so they would not beat boys. Lippa and Beavais (1983) found that women estimated their performance lower than males and chose lower difficulty levels (even when they chose feminine topics) on a computer quiz game.

The treatment a boy or girl receives by people in the individual's environment and the individual's biological and physical makeup affect the extent to which he or she develops masculine and/or feminine psychological characteristics. It should be emphasized that we are discussing psychological characteristics (i.e., ways of behaving, attitudes, and personality traits) that are typically associated with males or females, not physical characteristics, effeminate or masculine mannerisms, or sexual preferences. Some masculine characteristics are dominant, self-confident, aggressive, and ambitious (Bem, 1974). Some feminine characteristics are cheerful, compassionate, warmth, and understanding (Bem, 1974). Males tend to score high in **masculinity,** and females tend to score high in **femininity.** In a large scale validation sample of college students, Spence and Helmreich

Fear of Success in Women

Being competitive with males and being feminine are sometimes in conflict.
North America Syndicate

GRIN & BEAR IT   BY WAGNER

"Nobody will think you're less feminine if you strike him out."

Femininity, Masculinity, and Androgyny

(1978) found that 66 percent of the men were above the median in masculinity and 59 percent of the women scored above the median in femininity. So, there does appear to be some justification for calling these psychological traits masculine or feminine. It was not until the 1970s that investigators began to think of masculinity and femininity as separate dimensions, instead of the opposite ends of the same spectrum (cf. Constantinople, 1973). Sandra Bem's Sex Role Inventory (Bem, 1974) and Spence, Helmreich, and Stapp's (1975) Personal Attributes Questionnaire (PAQ) were the first instruments used to describe people as psychologically masculine, feminine, androgynous, and undifferentiated according to the following scheme:

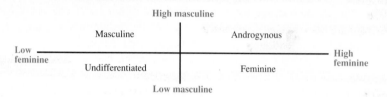

By dividing masculinity scores of the entire sample of subjects at the median and dividing femininity scores the same way, this four-category classification was obtained. **Androgynous** individuals are males and females who describe themselves as having many masculine and many feminine characteristics. In light of the fact that androgynous individuals are simultaneously aggressive and warm or ambitious and compassionate, it is accurate to say that they are more active, vivacious, and complex than other types of people. Undifferentiated individuals could be called inactive or less complex people since they characterize themselves as neither aggressive nor warm nor ambitious nor compassionate.

Bem (1975, 1979; Bem & Lenney, 1976) has consistently argued that androgynous people should be most well adjusted because they are more flexible, adaptable to different situations, and are not restricted to a sex-appropriate behavioral repertoire. Ickes and Barnes (1978) demonstrated convincingly that they acted in more socially adept ways and were liked better by opposite-sex persons in initial interactions. They surreptitiously videotaped couples as they waited on a couch for five minutes after just meeting. Ickes and Barnes had classified these men and women as masculine, feminine, or androgynous by earlier testing. It should be noted that they did not select any undifferentiated men or women, masculine women, or feminine men for observation. Only the masculine males and feminine females did not get along well or like each other much; the other three types of dyads, which all contained at least one androgynous person, interacted smoothly and liked each other. In a somewhat related vein, Coleman and Ganong (1985) found that androgynous persons reported that they acted in more loving ways toward their opposite-sex lovers than did masculine men, feminine women, or undifferentiated persons.

However, there are several studies in recent years which suggest that androgyny (high masculinity, high femininity) is not a superior type of personality to masculine or feminine ones. Antill (1983) found that the most satisfied married couples were those in which both the husband and the wife were feminine, not androgynous, masculine, or undifferentiated. Jones, Chernovetz, and Hansson (1978) found that, contrary to Bem's position, better flexibility and adjustment for both males and females was associated with masculinity, not androgyny. Lubinski, Tellegen, and Butcher (1981) also found that masculinity was most strongly associated with mental well-being. Zeldow, Clark, and Daugherty (1985) found that masculinity was associated with adjustment among medical students. They found that masculine men and women were more self-confident, emotionally stable, outgoing, and less depressed than those low in masculinity. Lubinski, Tellegen, and Butcher (1981, 1983) argued that androgyny was considered by Bem to be more than the simple combination of masculinity and femininity. They found no evidence that androgyny (conceived as the statistical interaction of masculinity and femininity) was related to personal well-being. Janet Spence (1983), a pioneer in this research and recent APA president, contended that Lubinski et al. should not have expected to find that androgyny was more than the sum of masculinity and femininity because no one else had. Spence also argued that the scale called masculinity on her PAQ and Bem's Sex Role Inventory should be regarded as a personality measure of dominance, and that femininity really was a measure of warmth. Unfortunately, boys are often only trained to be dominant, and girls are often only trained to be warm. Perhaps it would be best if both males and females had both types of responses in their repertoire.

Family Aspects of Development

A person's family environment affects how he or she acts, thinks, and feels. The ways a person is treated by and interacts with other members of his or her family may be affected by family size, the person's ordinal birth position (e.g., second-born child), age differences (spacing) among children in the family, sex of children, and presence of none, one, or both parents in the household.

Family Constellation and Intelligence

Belmont and Marolla (1973) related family sizes and birth positions of 386,114 nineteen-year-old men who took the Dutch Military examinations to their intelligence scores on a brief intelligence test. Figure 2.2 presents the results of this study. With the exception of only children, firstborns in small families were more intelligent than firstborns in large families. The same is true of second-borns, third-borns, etc. In general, children in small families were more intelligent than those in large families. There was a linear relationship between birth position and intelligence with firstborns being more intelligent than second-borns, second-borns than third-borns, etc.

Zajonc and his associates (Zajonc & Markus, 1975; Zajonc, Markus, & Markus, 1979) proposed a **confluence model** to explain how the combination of family constellation factors were related to intelligence. The confluence model suggested that the family intellectual environment in which the child was raised affects intelligence. The average family mental age for a firstborn child would be

$$\frac{(20 + 20)}{2} = 20,$$

where 20 is the maximum mental age used to represent the parents' mental age.

Figure 2.2
*Birth order, family
size, and intelligence.
Scores on an
intelligence test are
lower for later borns
and for large families.
The lowest scores are
achieved by last-borns
in a family size (FS) of
nine.*

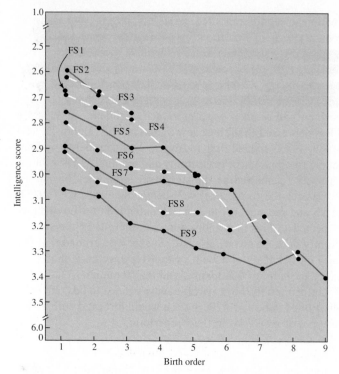

The average family mental age for a second-born child born two years later would
be

$$\frac{(20 + 20 + 2)}{3} = 14.$$

The family mental age for a third-born child born two years later would be

$$\frac{(20 + 20 + 4 + 2)}{4} = 11.5.$$

The decreasing family mental age with each subsequent child indicates that the
family environment for the younger children is less intellectually stimulating because of the older, still immature children present. The spacing between children
make a difference in that the family mental age for a second-born child with an
8-year-old sibling is 16, as opposed to 14 if the firstborn was only two. In general,
the model implied that the more adults and the fewer young children there were
in a family, the more time and energy the parents had to make the environment
a stimulating one for the children present. The model did not recognize that children may learn a great deal from their older brothers and sisters.

How would fathers who are absent much of the day affect the mental age
of the family environment? Children with only one parent in the household would
be expected to be especially disadvantaged according to the confluence model

with a family mental age of 11 [(20 + 2)/2] instead of 14 in our second-born example. The predicted effects of one-adult households on children's intelligence should be readily testable since the July 10, 1985 *Newsweek* indicated that by 1990, half of the households will be single-parent ones. This confluence model may actually reflect the amount of time parents have to interact with each subsequent child more than that there are more immature minds in the younger child's environment. Marjoribanks and Walberg's (1975) reanalysis of the Dutch data indicated that birth order accounted for very little of the differences in the intelligence scores, so the impact of these confluence factors may be minimal.

In fact, Ernst and Angst (1983) did an exhaustive review of family factors and intelligence and concluded that the relationship between birth order and intelligence was almost zero. Even Zajonc and Bargh (1980) concluded from a study of SAT scores that family factors, such as birth order and size, didn't account for much of the variability in intelligence. Ernst and Angst criticized Zajonc's confluence model for ignoring genetic and social factors. They concluded that social class and biological differences between parents of large and small families accounted for the family size and birth order relationships with intelligence better than Zajonc's ideas about stimulating and unstimulating family environments. Ernst and Angst (1983) also concluded from their review of many studies that the advantage of earlier born children in intelligence was extremely slight. The intelligence advantage of children in smaller families over those in larger ones was a little greater than the birth order advantage.

Family Constellation and Social Behavior

The different family environments of the firstborn child and later-born children also affect their social behavior. Because firstborn children initially interact only with adults in the family, they tend to become more adult-oriented than the more peer-oriented, later-born children (Markus, 1981). Firstborns achieve more educationally (Adams, 1972) and have higher self-esteem (Coopersmith, 1967; Schwab & Lundgren, 1978) than later-borns perhaps because they receive more care, attention, and direction from their parents than later-born children (Jacobs & Moss, 1976; Sears, Maccoby, & Levin, 1957). However, firstborn children display more anxiety (Howarth, 1980; Schachter, 1959) and fearfulness (Collard, 1968) than later-born children perhaps because more demands are made of them by their parents (Sears et al., 1957).

Miller and Maruyama (1976) reported that later-borns were rated as more socially skilled by their teachers and were more popular with their peers than firstborns in a large multiracial sample of California schoolchildren. They believed that later-born children were forced to become more socially skilled because of their low-power position in the family. For instance, you can imagine that the youngest child in a family where mother brings home one less soft drink than there are kids to drink them develops social skills in a hurry. Other possible reasons for this social skills difference are (1) later-borns learn to interact with other children because their older siblings bring friends to the home; (2) the older children model social behaviors they can imitate; and/or (3) the fewer parental demands give them more opportunities to develop their social skills. (See figure 2.3.)

Figure 2.3
*Average number of
times chosen as play
partner by classmates
for oldest, middle, and
youngest children in
their families.*
(From Miller & Maruyama, 1976.)

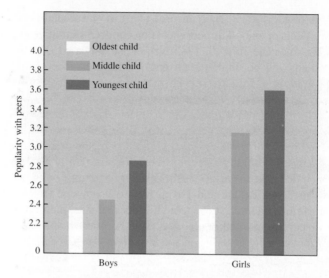

Ickes and Turner (1983), using only men and women who had at least one opposite-sex sibling and who were either the oldest or youngest child in their families as subjects, examined birth-order differences in social skills. They videotaped just-introduced, mixed-sex dyads consisting of (1) a firstborn woman and a firstborn man, (2) a firstborn woman and a last-born man, (3) a last-born woman and a firstborn man, or (4) a last-born woman and a last-born man. Using a hidden camera technique (Ickes, 1982) for studying initial interactions, they recorded the verbal and nonverbal behaviors of these dyads at their first meeting. Last-born men talked more and asked more questions than firstborn men. Women paired with last-born men smiled more, gave more verbal agreement and support (e.g., "right," "I see"), and liked their partners more than women with firstborn men. Last-born women initiated conversation more than firstborn women and were rated more likeable by their partners. Overall, last-borns of both sexes displayed better social skills than firstborns did. These studies on social behavior and the studies on intelligence indicate that perspectives and experiences of firstborn and later-born children in the same families are often quite different from each other. So, to expect people from the same home to act alike is often a mistake.

Childrearing Practices and Self-Esteem

One difference between firstborn children and later-born children lies in how their parents raise them (Sears et al., 1957). Firstborns are given more attention and care and more demands are made of them. Rothbart (1971) found that mothers put more pressure on firstborn children to achieve and were more anxious for them to perform well than later-borns' mothers did. Hilton (1967) found that mothers of firstborns were affectionate when their young child succeeded on a task and withheld affection when they didn't perform well more than mothers of later-born children did. A common scenario is a mother hovering over the first-born at the slightest whimper, while the fourth or fifth child may have to cry a half-hour to get the same attention. Doesn't everyone expect their firstborn to be at least a U.S. Senator? By the fourth or fifth, the same parents just hope the child can pass kindergarten.

Do you think these different expectations and childrearing practices affect the child? I do. In the last section, we noted that firstborn children were generally higher in self-esteem, achieved more educationally, were more anxious, less popular, and less socially skilled than later-born children. These psychological differences seem to be partly the product of firstborns being reared with conditional regard and later-borns being reared with unconditional regard or approval (cf. Kimble & Helmreich, 1972). Regard is *conditional* when the child has to perform up to certain standards to receive the regard or approval. Regard is *unconditional* when the child receives approval regardless of how the child performs. Of course, all children in some families may be reared predominantly with unconditional approval. To the extent that is true, all of those children should display the psychological characteristics of later-borns. In other words, it is the treatment the child receives, rather than his or her ordinal position in the family, that is important psychologically.

Kimble and Helmreich (1972) proposed that the quality and quantity of approval one receives from parents as a child influences the individual's later self-esteem. Conditional versus unconditional approval is the qualitative aspect of parents' treatment of children. If parents give approval only when the child performs acceptably according to parental standards, the approval, praise, or affection is called **conditional approval.** That is, the parents are using approval as a reinforcer for desired behavior. Under such conditions, the child would be expected to become sensitive or anxious about successful performance. If the parents give the same approval regardless of how the child behaves or performs, the approval is **unconditional approval** or regard. Rogers (1959) noted that unconditional positive regard was important in developing positive self-regard or self-esteem. Parenthetically, Fromm (1963) called unconditional approval "motherly love" and conditional approval "fatherly love." Unconditional approval lets the child know he or she is valued as a person, not for how she or he performs. If a person were reared with predominantly unconditional approval, he or she would be expected to develop a very secure sense of self-worth and would be invulnerable to the appraisals of others. These people whose parents have made few performance demands for their approval would be expected to display moderate self-esteem as adults. On the other hand, those who have received conditional approval as children would display either high or low self-esteem depending on how much approval they received early in life. If they could not and did not perform up to parental standards and received little approval, they would display low self-esteem as adults. If they could and did perform up to parental standards and received much approval, they would display high self-esteem as adults. However, these high self-esteem people may be insecure and susceptible to the appraisals of others. There was a stellar athlete of the 1960s who reported very conditional approval being given by his mother and who manifested high self-esteem in his autobiography. His mother was warm to him only when he gave the best piano recital, got top grades or excelled in athletics. He wrote about behavior problems that occurred regularly following or during interpersonal and athletic failures in adult life. He seemed to be very susceptible to the evaluations of others. Unfortunately, anecdotal evidence is about all we have on the developmental aspects of this theory of self-esteem. This theory implies that a mixture of unconditional and conditional approval (with reasonable standards tailored to the individual) in childrearing would produce adults who are productive and achievement-oriented *and* happy and secure in their feelings about themselves.

Urban-Rural Environments and Development

Are there differences between growing up in a city and growing up in a small town or in the country? Do any differences that exist affect the ways an individual comes to think, feel, and behave? There are theoretical positions which indicate that meaningful differences between urban and rural life are few (e.g., Gans, 1962), but others (e.g., Glass & Singer, 1972; Milgram, 1970) emphasize the detrimental features of city life. Ecological psychologists (Barker, 1968; Barker & Gump, 1964; Wicker, 1968) have pointed out some consistent differences between urban and rural life that lead to more positive outcomes for small town dwellers.

Undermanning in Small Towns

Let us consider the ecological psychologists' position first. Roger Barker (1968) has suggested that behavior is affected more by the behavior setting in which it occurs than by the personalities of the individuals involved. For instance, your behavior in your social psychology class is more like other students' behavior in the class than it is like your behavior in another type of behavior setting, such as a basketball game. So, the situation is affecting your behavior more than your personality is. A **behavior setting** (cf. Barker, 1968; Wicker, 1979) is an event occurring at a particular time and place involving people and objects in the environment with an agenda, functions, and roles to be executed. At first, people can usually choose to be in a particular behavior setting, but once entered, the behavior setting has a distinct influence of its own. Behavior settings can be undermanned (having too few people to execute the program of events smoothly), optimally manned (having the exact number of people needed to execute the program smoothly) or overmanned (having more people than needed).

Children and adults in small towns and villages are consistently involved in more undermanned behavior settings than people are in cities. This difference has psychological impact on the development of the individuals. Barker and Gump (1964) examined participation in extracurricular behavior settings in Kansas high schools with student bodies ranging from 35 to 2,287. Typical behavior settings were club meetings, class plays, student government meetings, football games, school dances, and fund-raising projects. They found that average students in small high schools participated in more settings, in more kinds of settings, had

One of many recent American Presidents with small town backgrounds.

more responsible and central positions, and had responsible positions in more diverse settings than students in large high schools (Gump & Friesen, 1964). Baird (1969) found that students in small colleges also reported more achievements than students in large colleges.

The best illustration of more extensive and diverse participation by students in small schools occurred at a football game in my hometown. Two six-man football teams, Nueces Canyon and Center Point, came to the big city, Uvalde (population 10–12,000), to play their regional championship game. Yes, they still play six-man football in places where they love their football and don't have enough players to field an eleven-man team. Just before halftime, I went below the stands and got in a soft drink line. Soon a Nueces Canyon player trotted by and went into the dressing room nearby. I got my drink and stood around, talking with friends. In a few minutes, the same kid came trotting by in a band uniform with a horn in his hand, heading for the halftime show. Now that's what I call diversified participation!

Gump and Friesen (1964) found that students in small schools reaped psychological benefits from their participation. They found that these students reported greater satisfaction from developing competence, being challenged, being involved in important activities, feeling responsible, and being valued than students in large schools did. Wicker (1968) corroborated these gains from participation and suggested that these benefits occurred more in small schools because the undermanned settings placed students in responsible jobs more often. Even though Baird (1969) found that participation in high school did not lead to greater college achievements, Wicker (1979) suggests that such diverse participation may have residual benefits. For instance, he says that participation in some activities may give you a lifelong appreciation for performances in that domain even though you may never excel yourself. Participating, feeling competent, and being recognized seemed so beneficial to Barker, Gump, and their students that they suggest cities should consider building smaller schools for their children.

Apparently, it is better to be a big fish in a small pond than a small fish in a big pond. It may seem coincidental to you, but if you look at the birthplace and childhood homes of recent presidents and presidential aspirants, you will note that they must have participated in many undermanned settings in their formative years. Dixon, Illinois (Ronald Reagan); Plains, Georgia (Jimmy Carter); Ceylon, Minnesota (Walter Mondale); Greenville, South Carolina (Jesse Jackson); Ottawa, Kansas (Gary Hart); Makando, Illinois (Paul Simon); Whittier, California (Richard Nixon); Mitchell, South Dakota (George McGovern); Stonewall, Texas (Lyndon Johnson); Abilene, Kansas (Dwight Eisenhower); and Independence, Missouri (Harry Truman) are a few examples. John F. Kennedy and George Bush are two striking exceptions to this residential rule in recent years. It seems likely that family wealth afforded them private schools small enough to allow them to participate in responsible positions in their formative years. It is important to remember that it is the degree of undermanning in specific behavior settings that makes the difference, not the size of the city or town (Wicker, 1968).

Urban Villages and City Life

Some theoreticians indicate that the size of the city or town makes very little difference to the person's everyday existence. Gans (1962) contends that a city is a group of **"urban villages"** or small communities. It is probably true that most people interact only with a few people at school or work, a few people who live near them, and, in some cases, relatives. However, many people in cities must make superficial contact with many people in their work life or in moving around the city. It is in these contacts that much of the interpersonal stress and conflict of the cities reside. Much of chapter 12 deals with whether people will help in emergency situations *among strangers*. There is little question that people will help friends and relatives in emergencies. Such interpersonal contacts with strangers are much more common in cities. As we will see later, everyday superficial contacts are often unpleasant because of the density and heterogeneity of cities. Also, the work of the ecological psychologists in Kansas implies that heavily populated behavior settings (such as at large high schools) in cities require a person to leave his or her urban village group and compete for recognition and participation opportunities. A positive feature of this competition is reflected in the song, "New York, New York": ". . . if I can make it there, I can make it anywhere. . . ." This competition also contributes to making city life more stressful than rural life for all except the most talented.

Critical Mass and City Life

Fischer (1984) argues that one of the major advantages of city life is that cities provide "critical masses" of people with common interests and values. **Critical mass** refers to a number of people adequate to sustain an activity. Many different subcultures can develop in cities where there are enough people with similar interests to create events that are important to the group. In small towns and villages, there may be only one or two people interested in ballet, opera, model airplaning, skydiving, jazz, or soccer. What Barker and his associates have not emphasized about undermanned behavior settings is that if there are an extremely low number of people available to participate, the event or behavior setting will never occur. Specialty schools focusing on music, drama, science, or technology within urban school districts and many occupational opportunities can flourish only when you have the critical masses provided by cities (see Freedman, 1975). Can you think of other opportunities afforded only by cities? This is another way in which individuals growing up in urban and rural areas will develop different skills and interests. This particular difference in urban and rural life obviously favors the urbanite.

Stanley Milgram (1970) emphasized that city residents experience "stimulus overload" in his article on the experience of living in cities. In his view, there are too many objects, people, and events bombarding the city dweller's senses for him or her to process everything. The urban inhabitant learns to adapt to this sensory overload by warding off some inputs, ignoring others, and giving others only superficial consideration. These actions taken to reduce inputs make human interactions in cities unpleasant, and they must take a psychological toll on the people who are involved in such interactions for years. Some examples of these actions follow:

Overload and City Life

1. Being brusque or curt with people to limit time used in interactions
2. Attending only to those people and events that are important to you and ignoring people of, for instance, other ethnic groups
3. Assuming an unfriendly demeanor and expression to ward off distracting interactions
4. Using physical barriers, signs, and unlisted telephone numbers to reduce unwanted inputs
5. Not being willing to use time to help others

All of these actions contribute to making city life unsavory. Those who are rich enough live in secluded, exclusive suburbs, are chauffeured to work, and work in quiet, isolated places to avoid these aspects of city life. Some recent studies have found that interactions with strangers in suburbs are friendlier than in cities but are still not as open and friendly as those in small towns (Newman and McCauley, 1977; Toepler, Diago, & Kimble, 1989). (See figure 2.4.) All of the factors described in this section make people who grow up in cities think, act, and feel differently than those who grow up in rural areas.

Other Influences on Development

There are many other social factors that affect how we behave, think, and feel as adults. The *culture* in which we grow up certainly affects our development. People from different countries and even people from different American subcultures display differences in time-mindedness or punctuality (Levine, 1985; Levine, West, & Reis, 1980), with Japan and the U.S. being among the most time-conscious and Brazil and Indonesia among the least. People from different cultures also display differences in nonverbal behavior (Jourard, 1966; Hall, 1966).

Figure 2.4
*Percentages of people
making eye contact
with and talking with
a stranger in a city,
suburb, and small
town.*
*(From Newman & McCauley,
1977.)*

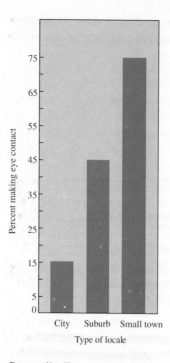

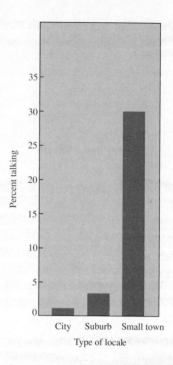

Generally, European-Americans, northern Europeans, and Japanese—people from "noncontact cultures"—are more inhibited and reserved than people from "contact cultures"—southern Europeans, Arabs, and Latin Americans. In America, blacks show more visual dominance (LaFrance & Mayo, 1976) and greater improvisational skills (Jones & Hochner, 1973) than whites. Hispanic-Americans value being "simpatico," agreeable, and pleasant in interactions more than Anglo-Americans do (Triandis, Marin, Lisansky, & Betancourt, 1984). Living in poverty affects the lifestyles of many subcultures (Lewis, 1966), and the effects of poverty are sometimes mistakenly seen as cultural characteristics. Characteristics of people reared in poverty include (1) a strong present-time orientation ("live for the moment"), (2) an inability to defer gratification, and (3) a sense of fatalism and resignation (Lewis, 1966; Mischel, 1981).

The roles we assume during our lives affect our attitudes and actions. **Roles** are positions or statuses most people believe should be enacted or fulfilled in particular ways. The gender roles we experience (Eagly, 1987) are a prominent type of role. Others' expectations about our roles provide subtle prescriptions about how we should behave. If we act publicly in these roles for a long enough time, our attitudes, even attitudes about ourselves, will be affected (Bem, 1967; Festinger & Carlsmith, 1959). If a president takes positions that encourage wars in foreign lands, his attitudes will become more warlike than they were originally. If a district attorney argues for the death penalty in many cases, she will come to support capital punishment more than she did before. Buss and Briggs (1984) even argue that there is sometimes behavioral spillover from roles to times and

Zimbardo's prison simulation study provided a graphic illustration of how roles can affect attitudes and polarize behavior.

situations when we aren't in those roles like the football player busting up furniture in the dormitory or the professor pontificating to his or her spouse on some esoteric topic.

Zimbardo's (cf. Haney, Banks, & Zimbardo, 1973) Stanford prison simulation study provides a graphic illustration of how assuming a role can affect one's conduct and attitudes. Zimbardo and his associates recruited college-age males to be prisoners and guards in their mock prison. They purposely chose only the most well-adjusted recruits so they could examine the effects of adopting prison roles on behavior without hearing the criticism that they got antisocial behavior because they had unsavory, maladjusted characters in their study. The opportunity to select people with stable personalities and to randomly assign them to the prisoner or guard roles were the major advantages of conducting this study over simply observing in a real prison.

They then attempted to make the prisoner role real to the recruits by making public arrests at their homes, fingerprinting them, booking them, disrobing and delousing them, and diminishing their personal identity by putting them in identical gowns, covering their hair with stockingcaps, and identifying them only by a prison number. The guard role was enhanced by putting those subjects in identical khaki uniforms, giving them reflecting sunglasses so others couldn't see their eyes, giving them billy clubs, and telling them that they should be addressed only as Mr. Correctional Officer. Beyond a few minimal instructions, they were on their own to enact the roles. Both prisoners and guards readily embellished the roles. Guards became cruel and demanding and prisoners became defiant. After six days, Zimbardo and his associates had to abort the study because of the toll it was taking, most noticeably on the prisoners. Two prisoners had to be released, one because of a rash that developed on his body and the other because of hysterical behavior. Zimbardo also expressed fears that even he was becoming too absorbed in the prison superintendent role. The study could be criticized for lack of rigorous control of events. It could also be argued that subjects simply enacted the roles as they had seen it done in movies or on television. However, it was a dramatic demonstration of how roles polarized behavior of the two groups and how roles can have strong psychological impact. Certainly the occupational, gender, and family roles of a lifetime shape our everyday behaviors and thoughts.

Applications of Personal Development Information

Citizens in general and parents in particular should be able to apply knowledge about how children learn to behave. Parents, teachers, and other child care workers should know and apply such knowledge in order to effect desired behavior. They should be aware of what they are reinforcing, what they are punishing, and what they are exposing children to that can be observed and imitated.

We should also be attuned to our tendency to sometimes act differently toward individuals because of their appearance, sex, or cultural group, and we should use this sensitivity to avoid bias that will have negative impact on these individuals. Parents and educators should be aware of the impact of family situations on children's development and guard against childrearing practices, such as exclusive conditional approval, that have negative consequences for children's self-esteem. Educational administrators should apply the knowledge that schools affording students the most opportunities to participate (i.e., small schools) are the most beneficial to both average and talented students.

Summary

Our early experiences affect how we act, feel, and think as adults. We learn to behave in particular ways through operant conditioning, classical conditioning, and observational learning. If a behavior is followed by reinforcement, it is likely to be repeated. If the behavior is followed by punishment or no event, it is unlikely to be repeated. Pairing a neutral stimulus with an unconditioned stimulus can make the neutral stimulus evoke strong emotional reactions. Children are most likely to imitate those people who treat them positively and who act in their presence often.

How the person is treated by others affects his or her development. Attractive young children are perceived to have more positive characteristics than unattractive children. Attractive people project more positive self-concepts apparently because of their positive interpersonal experiences. Boys and girls are treated differently. Women tend to be more emotionally expressive and less aggressive than men partly because of their different earlier experiences. Women are often put at a disadvantage because of sexism and internal conflict between being competitive and successful and being feminine. Androgynous people are those who have both masculine and feminine psychological characteristics. Androgynous individuals act in more socially adept ways in initial interactions and are more loving toward opposite-sex lovers than masculine men or feminine women are. One's position in the family affects how that person is treated and how he or she will behave. The facts that older children in the family and that children in smaller families are more intelligent have been explained through the idea that they experience more stimulating family environments. Younger children in the family are more socially skilled than their older brothers and sisters. Childrearing practices emphasizing conditional approval make children have unstable self-esteem.

The environment and culture in which a person grows up affect his or her adult thoughts and behaviors. Children growing up in rural areas are involved in more undermanned behavior settings and have more diverse participation opportunities. Urban children live in more stressful environments, especially when they have to leave their "urban villages." However, they have greater opportunities to develop special interests and skills because of the critical masses in the city. People from different cultures and subcultures develop differently. Certainly our occupational and family roles also affect our cognitive, emotional, and behavioral patterns.

The Self

What is the self? The **self** is (1) a set of thoughts and feelings a person has about oneself and (2) a characteristic way of responding to one's environment. Self has at least two major components: an evaluative part that weighs and assesses one's mental and physical state, and an active part that exhibits a particular style in responding to environmental events. There are many social psychologists who believe we develop a coherent sense of self which affects how we act and react in social situations (Berkowitz, 1988; Schlenker, 1985). In this chapter, we will consider the many facets of the self.

The Self as Actor

The product of the different shaping and socializing influences in the person's environment is the self. The *self* is a metaphor for (1) how a person acts, thinks, and feels toward his or her environment (the active part mentioned earlier); and (2) how one thinks and feels about oneself (the evaluative part). The concept of self implies that there is cohesiveness and continuity to the way an individual acts toward the environment and how one evaluates oneself. The first aspect of the self is the self as actor; the second aspect is the self as object of the person's own scrutiny.

Self-Identity

Self-identity is the description of features of the person that are important to the person. The study of self-identity requires the subject to reflect upon and evaluate her- or himself. When the subject does that, he or she is engaging the self as object. However, the descriptions the person supplies describe the self as actor. Therefore, self-identity is included in this self as actor section.

Self-identity has usually been assessed with the "Who am I?" form (Gordon, 1968; Zurcher, 1977), which requires respondents to complete the statement, "I am _____ " 20 times. The descriptive phrases typically used are physical descriptions (e.g., six feet tall), social statuses or roles (e.g., Jewish, father, Republican), or descriptions of personal traits or styles (e.g., trustworthy, loyal, friendly, courteous, kind). Sometimes personal tastes or interests are mentioned (e.g., jazz fan, Utah Jazz fan). It should be clear that people identify themselves by more than their physical and mental abilities. It also seems apparent that subjects often engage in self-presentation (i.e., present their most positive features) when they complete the "Who am I?" form.

An important feature of self-identity is its complexity. **Self-complexity** (Linville, 1985, 1987) is a measure of how much a person conceives of him- or herself as having few or many independent or unrelated aspects. That is, does the person see him- or herself as having few or many different roles, traits, or interests? If they were allowed to complete the "I am" statement as many times as they wanted, then the number of unrelated descriptions individuals generated should indicate their self-complexity. Linville argues that it is healthier to be more complex because a blow to one aspect of the self, such as failure on a test, would not have as much spillover effect if the self has many different compartments. Linville demonstrated that complex people were less prone to depression, perceived stress, and physical illness after experiencing stressful events than less complex people were. The implication is that we should develop ourselves in many different ways. That way, if our eggs are in separate baskets, we will not be as devastated if one basket drops.

Baumeister (1986) contends that for an aspect of a person to be a component of self-identity, the feature must *differentiate* the person from some other people through its distinctiveness and/or it must contribute to the *continuity* or unity of the self through its stable or long-standing nature. Some components of self-identity are acquired at birth without choice (sex, ethnic group); others are attained at one time and don't change (motherhood, college graduate). Other parts of our identity are more stressful because they demand choices of the individual (religious, political, other affiliations); still others are probably the most problematical for self-identity because they have upwardly-changing criteria and redefinition for good identity (salary, status in chosen field) (Baumeister, 1986).

William James wrote the following definition of self:

> A man's Self is the sum total of all that he can call his, not only his body and his psychic powers, but his clothes and his house, his wife and his children, his ancestors and friends, his reputation and works, his land and horses, and yacht and bank account. All these things give him the same emotions. If they wax and prosper, he feels triumphant; if they dwindle and die away, he feels cast down. (Schlenker, 1980, p. 48)

So, all of the things that a person has an attachment to and are important to him or her could be considered part of his or her self-identity.

Three studies by Cialdini, Borden, Thorne, Walker, Freeman, and Sloan (1976) indicated that a person's favorite college football team should be added to James' list. Cialdini and associates studied the fickleness of fans and their self-presentational behavior. They believed that students would try to associate themselves more closely to their team after it won than after it lost. To test this, they recorded the percentage of students attending introductory psychology classes at seven universities who wore school identified apparel and the percentage who wore apparel of another school on Mondays during football season. They found that these students wore their school insignias on Mondays after wins more than on Mondays after losses, but the tendency was not present at Arizona State, Michigan, and Southern California. It should be noted that all the schools sampled were football powers at the time. In two telephone studies, they found that students used the pronoun "we" when describing team victories more than they did in describing losses. However, most subjects used the same pronoun, "we" or "they," to describe the team in victories *and* losses. Again, the effect was not strong. (See figure 3.1.)

These results provide some indication that people attempt to associate themselves with positive images (winning teams). However, it is those fans who wore the insignias or said "we" after victories *and losses* that have incorporated the school's football team into their self-identities. There are probably plenty of them, and there are also probably many others who have incorporated them but

All things that a person has an attachment to can be considered part of his or her self-identity.

Figure 3.1
*Index (range from .00
to 1.00) of those
wearing school
apparel at seven
universities after
football wins and
losses/ties.*
(From Cialdini et al., 1976.)

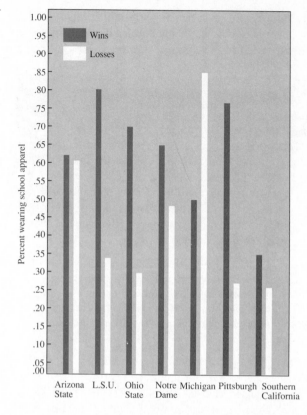

don't engage in self-presentation by wearing the school colors. It would be interesting to know the distinguishing backgrounds, characteristics, and motivations of such staunch fans of sports teams or performers, musical performers, or entertainment figures. Cialdini and his associates have described the tendency to identify with a winning sports team, entertainer, or famous person with whom we are only remotely associated as "basking in reflected glory." A recent study (Snyder, Lassegard & Ford, 1986) has shown that we not only bask in reflected glory, but that we dissociate ourselves from losers or "cut off reflected failure."

Is There a Real Self?

Many self-presentational approaches to explaining attitudes and behavior (Goffman, 1959; Schlenker, Forsyth, Leary, & Miller, 1980; Snyder, 1981; Tedeschi, 1981; Tedeschi, Schlenker, & Bonoma, 1971) imply that there is no real or true self. In their view, a person has no real attitudes. He or she only expresses positions to suit a particular audience or project a desired image. The person is a chameleon with no stable attitudinal, cognitive, or behavioral tendencies.

There have been and are dissenters, however. William James (1890) wrote of the pure ego as the self as knower or I. This self as knower does not judge or evaluate itself and is not aware of itself. Instead, it acts and reacts to circumstances in its environment. This knowing, acting self occurs when one's attention is focused on the environment (Duval & Wicklund, 1972). This nonevaluative aspect of the self is simply a person's way of behaving, thinking, and feeling. Baumeister (1982) agreed that "a 'true,' 'real,' or 'private' self is constructed not by self-presentation but through one's choices and performances" (Baumeister, 1982, p. 4). Buss and Briggs (1984) saw one's personal needs, impulses, and dispositional tendencies as influencing the individual's behavior apart from external self-presentation considerations. They referred to these needs, impulses, and tendencies as elements of individuality, but they also could be referred to as part of a core self as actor. Hogan, Jones, and Cheek (1985) have stated that a person's self-concept determines the roles he or she is willing to play (in a self-presentational sense) rather than being determined by the roles. They also saw this self-concept as growing out of interplay among the person's biological temperament, early family experiences, peer interactions, and culture. These factors influence the self-concept (or characteristic ways of acting, thinking, and feeling toward the environment) as was indicated by the previous chapter on socialization influences.

Self-presentation or impression management is behavior that people do to make themselves appear impressive. Buss and Briggs (1984) suggested that we often resort to pretense to make ourselves appear (1) to have positive social traits (e.g., warmth, sincerity); (2) to have some social abilities, such as sophistication or manners; (3) to be motivated, hardworking, and enthusiastic; (4) to be intelligent or to have some other specific ability (e.g., athletic, musical); (5) to be of high status or famous; or (6) to be moral (e.g., honest, loyal, benevolent). You can probably imagine specific traits or abilities most of us might try to project to particular audiences.

Which audiences do we act for? Do we act for real audiences present now, imagined future audiences, imagined past audiences or reference groups, or ourselves? Greenwald and Breckler (1985) and Schlenker (1980, 1985) said that we may act for all of these audiences. Greenwald and Breckler (1985) have emphasized that individuals do act for an inner audience (themselves). They stated that the presented self is a true, privately accepted self in the case of the inner audience. Greenwald and Breckler argued that most normal people see themselves as effective in attaining desired goals and avoiding undesired ones, and they genuinely believe this picture of themselves as good and capable. Individuals' belief in their own effectiveness is supported by findings that we readily accept credit for successes and deny our responsibility for failures or bad deeds (cf. Bradley [Weary], 1978; Harvey, Harris, & Barnes, 1975; Zuckerman, 1979).

The fact that people really believe in their good selves is supported by the finding that people make positive self-attributions when there is no audience other than themselves (Weary, Harvey, Schwieger, Olson, Perloff, & Pritchard, 1982). Other supporting evidence for this belief in the good self was provided when subjects made self-enhancing attributions even under conditions where dishonest responding was eliminated or minimized (Reiss, Rosenfeld, Melburg, & Tedeschi, 1981) and evidence that favorable, self-referent judgments were processed more

Self-Presentation

Which audiences do we act for? Present audiences, past audiences, or ourselves?

rapidly than unfavorable ones (Breckler & Greenwald, 1981). So, it appears that we believe that we are good, capable people and that many aspects of ourselves are presented in a positive way for no audience other than ourselves.

Baumeister (1982) has contended that we engage in self-presentational behavior to please the audience or to make our public image equivalent to our ideals of ourselves. Both of these ideas involve the public self. Therefore, Baumeister and most other researchers in this field view self-presentational behavior as behavior done under public scrutiny and nonself-presentational behavior as any behavior done under private circumstances. Baumeister has reviewed many studies comparing behavior done under public and private conditions and has concluded that attempting to present oneself in most favorable ways affects conforming and nonconforming behavior, altruistic behavior, attitude expressions, aggressive behavior, and many other facets of social life.

Buss and Briggs (1984) have discussed self-presentation as *pretense* or the portrayal of someone different from oneself. The opposite of this pretense is expressiveness, the uninhibited, unvarnished, candid expression of one's personal feelings and personality traits—what we might call one's true self. The dimension ranges from acting as if you are someone different as actors do; to a salesman, politician, teacher, or first date pretending to be more knowledgeable, bright, interested, or caring than he or she naturally is; to an honest, unexaggerated expression of one's self. Impression management or pretense is most likely to be used when there are economic rewards for doing so, when there is an audience, and when viewers do not know you well.

Some people are better at and more inclined to engage in pretense than others. People who adjust their behavior for each situation and audience have been called high **self-monitors** (Snyder, 1974). High self-monitors are sensitive to other people's cues as to the appropriateness of certain behaviors in the situation. They can control their behavior to present themselves in a positive way (Snyder, 1974). One implication of this behavioral style is that high self-monitors are inconsistent in their behavior from situation to situation. One might say that the behavior of low self-monitors is determined by their true selves (i.e., their attitudes and dispositions) and that the behavior of high self-monitors is determined by the social situation.

There have been a substantial number of empirical studies examining how self-monitors behave. Snyder and Monson (1975) found that high self-monitors acted in a conforming way when cues in the group situation called for conformity, and they acted in an autonomous way when the social cues indicated they should. On the other hand, the behavior of low self-monitors was the same (slightly autonomous) regardless of the group autonomy or conformity cues. Lippa (1976) found that high self-monitors could act in introverted, reserved ways or extraverted, gregarious ways depending on what the situation demanded. Low self-monitors did not follow situational demands as closely. Lippa (1978) found that high self-monitors acted in expressive, extraverted ways when they were given no acting instructions. Surprisingly, the measured extraversion of subjects was not related to their expressive behavior. Ickes and Barnes (1977) attempted to find out how high and low self-monitors behaved when there were no consistent cues for how they should behave. They put male dyads and female dyads of differing levels of self-monitoring characteristics in a waiting room and surreptitiously videotaped their interactions. High self-monitors apparently decided that the situation called for them to converse smoothly and pleasantly. They initiated conversation most often, felt they needed to talk more, and felt more self-conscious in the situation. They also were guided by their partner's behavior. High self-monitor/low self-monitor dyads experienced the most difficulty talking to each other as they had more periods of silence than any other dyads. However, the verbal and visual behaviors of high self-monitors were not consistently different from that of low self-monitors. Perhaps this lack of differences occurred because there were no consistent cues for the high self-monitors to read and react to.

Mark Snyder and Jeffry Simpson (1984) examined the relationships between an individual's self-monitoring and the individual's dating relationships. In four studies, they found that, relative to low self-monitors, high self-monitors displayed the following characteristics:

1. High self-monitors preferred to do casual activities with other-sex friends who were good at those activities rather than with their current dating partners.
2. High self-monitors were interested in changing their current dating partners.

Figure 3.2
Self-monitors, dating, and commitment.
(From Snyder & Simpson, 1984.)

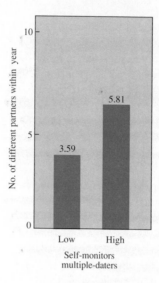

No. of different partners within year

Low   High

Self-monitors
multiple-daters

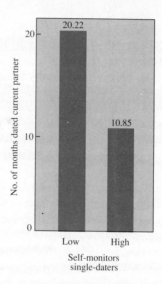

No. of months dated current partner

Low   High

Self-monitors
single-daters

3. High self-monitors dated more different people during the preceding year and, of those going with one person, high self-monitors had dated their current partners for a shorter time.
4. High self-monitors reported less positive change in intimacy as they dated a partner longer.

Overall, high self-monitors were less committed to the other person in the dating relationships than were low self-monitors. These results seem consistent with Buss and Briggs' (1984) idea that pretense is less likely to be used in interactions with someone who knows us well. Since high self-monitors are given to pretense, it makes sense that they would prefer not to have close relationships. (See figure 3.2.)

The Self as Object

Social Comparison and Self-Evaluation

How do we evaluate ourselves? First, we are motivated to evaluate ourselves positively (Bradley [Weary], 1978; Baumgardner & Brownlee, 1987; Greenwald & Breckler, 1985; Zuckerman, 1979). Festinger (1954) indicated in his social comparison theory that we are motivated to evaluate ourselves. Unless we are talking about variables that are easily measured, we generally evaluate ourselves by comparing ourselves to others. Festinger contended that we generally compare ourselves to similar others. Several years later, Goethals and Darley (1977) specified that similar others should mean other people who have similar characteristics other than the characteristic that you are trying to evaluate. So, if you are a 60-year-old, 5 ft. 9 in., 205 lb business executive who works 55 hours a week interested in evaluating your tennis-playing ability, you do not evaluate yourself by playing your 25-year-old, 6 ft. 3 in., 180 lb, nonworking son-in-law. Instead, you play someone who has similar physical characteristics and work schedule to find out how good you are. At the same time, you don't pick just anyone with whom you always have deuce games and split sets to evaluate yourself. You want to pick someone who has similar characteristics other than tennis-playing ability.

KUDZU

Sometimes social comparison is painful
KUDZU, by Marlette. © 1987 by permission of Doug Marlette and Creators Syndicate, Inc.

Self-Attribution

Once you have picked a sample of people who are like you, you are likely to use an attribution system like H. H. Kelley's (1967, 1972) to evaluate yourself. **Attribution** refers to the process by which we infer causes of events and behavior. Attribution theories can be used to determine whether some trait of yours caused an event to occur or some element in your environment caused it to occur. You may make internal, self-attributions or external attributions (Bem, 1965, 1967; Kelley, 1967). Kelley has contended that we usually look to *persons, stimuli,* or *circumstances* for the causes of events. A person is most likely to make a self-attribution if he or she performs better (or worse) than most people. This is similar to the social comparison theory that we evaluate our abilities or opinions by seeing how we stand relative to other similar people on those abilities or opinions. If we do the same thing consistently over time and circumstances (e.g., regardless of whether or not we are paid to do so), then we are also likely to make strong self-attributions (cf. Orvis, Cunningham, & Kelley, 1975; Harvey & Smith, 1977). Bem (1967) implied that if we campaigned door-to-door for a candidate for many weeks without pay, we and everyone else who knew the circumstances would know that we were strongly intrinsically motivated to help the candidate win. A person would be less likely to make a strong self-attribution if he or she was paid well to do the same campaigning. If a person reacted to or performed the same way for different stimuli (e.g., psychology tests), then he or she would also make strong self-attributions.

In summary, the following type of behavior indicates a confident self-attribution should be made:

1. Low consensus (it was different than other people's)
2. Low distinctiveness (it was the same toward many stimuli)
3. High consistency (it was the same under many conditions)

So if

Harold laughed at Steve Martin;
No one else laughed at Steve Martin [low consensus];
Harold laughed at Bill Cosby, George Burns, Joan Rivers, all comedians [low distinctiveness]; and
Harold always laughed at Steve Martin [high consistency];

then Harold would surmise that his laughter was caused by his peculiar appreciation of humor (a person attribution to himself).

Another feature of self-evaluation can be appreciated by considering yourself as a stimulus. For instance, you should conclude that you are a very likeable person if many people acted positively toward you [high consensus], they act more positively toward you than toward anyone else [high distinctiveness], and they always act positively toward you [high consistency]. So, high consensus, high distinctiveness, and high consistency of a behavior suggest that it was caused by a stimulus—in this case (Hansen, 1980; McArthur, 1972; Orvis, et al., 1975). We may gauge ourselves by examining other people's reactions to us in this manner (cf. Kimble, Arnold, & Hirt, 1985). This self-attribution procedure is an elaboration of the sociologist Cooley's (1902) notion of the "looking glass self." Charles Cooley believed that we infer who and how we are by examining others' reactions to us. Like a mirror, others' reactions reflect how we are. This self-attribution model may indicate what we look for in their reactions.

Self-Esteem

As self-attributions are how we think about ourselves, **self-esteem** is how we feel about ourselves. Generally, if a person is good at activities that others (parents, peers, siblings, etc.) have taught her or him to value, that person has high self-esteem. Greenwald and Breckler (1985) regard self-esteem as the expectation of success at personally important tasks. To Demo (1985), self-esteem consists of feeling good, liking yourself, being liked and treated well, feeling you are a success, and feeling capable of and comfortable with leading and influencing others. There are many effective measurement instruments of self-esteem. Demo (1985) found that the Coopersmith Self-Esteem Inventory (1967) and the Rosenberg Self-Esteem Scale (1965) were good self-report measures for teenagers.

Bandura's ideas about self-efficacy appear important to self-esteem in light of the definitions above. **Self-efficacy** is a person's belief that he or she can master situations and control events (cf. Bandura, 1977a). Self-efficacy has been shown to have a strong influence on performance (Bandura, 1982). Self-efficacy is the confidence element in the popular wisdom that "confidence breeds success and success breeds confidence." Bandura (1982) said self-efficacy is influenced by the following four factors:

1. Past accomplishments. "Success breeds confidence"
2. Vicarious experiences. Seeing others succeed or being told that similar others have succeeded
3. Verbal persuasion. Being told that you can succeed—within realistic limits
4. Reading one's own physiological state. Noting that you are not tense, aroused, or agitated in a demanding situation

Bandura and his associates (Bandura & Adams, 1977; Bandura, Adams, & Beyer, 1977; Bandura, Adams, Hardy, & Howells, 1980) found that all four of these factors contributed to less fearful performances by snake-phobics. Also, Bandura and Schunk (1981) showed that giving elementary school children proximal

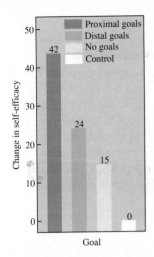
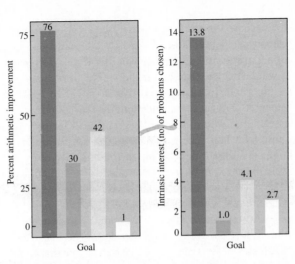

Figure 3.3
*Change in self-efficacy,
arithmetic
improvement and
intrinsic interest in
arithmetic after self
directed learning with
proximal, distal, and
no goals.*
(From Bandura & Schunk, 1981.)

goals—goals that were attainable in a single work session—improved their performance, made them feel more efficacious, and increased their intrinsic interest in mathematics problems more than giving them distal, remote goals or no goals at all. (See figure 3.3.) Frequent feedback indicating successful performance was important in many ways. One positive feature of achieving success on one task is that it may generalize to other tasks and make a person feel more efficacious in those areas as well. Since general self-efficacy is a major component of high self-esteem (Greenwald & Breckler, 1985), these results suggest some ways to improve individuals' self-esteem.

Two investigators (Snyder and Fromkin, 1980) have contended that self-esteem is related to uniqueness. They proposed that people value individuality. In fact, they cited a study by Ganster, McCuddy, and Fromkin (1977) showing that a person's self-esteem decreased when he or she was shown that the majority of people (80 percent) agreed with them on many attitudes. Also, McGuire, McGuire, Child, and Fujioka (1978) found that children mention their distinctive characteristics rather than their common characteristics when asked to describe themselves.

While we value being different when different means best; we do not value different when it means worst. Of course, we usually use the biased term, unique, when we are talking about very good conduct and another pejorative term, deviant, to describe very bad conduct. So, the words used to describe the behavior can affect how we evaluate it. Snyder and Fromkin also suggest that moderate similarity on attitude positions (which are not good, bad, best, or worst) is preferred to being unique. On such subjective issues, we apparently don't want to be like everyone else, but we don't want to be The Lone Ranger either—especially without Tonto! So when unique means best, we want to be unique. However, when there is no standard for goodness (no best or worst), we want to be like at least some other people.

Self-Esteem and
Need for Approval

As discussed in the last chapter, we (Kimble & Helmreich, 1972) believe that a person's self-esteem is affected by the quality and quantity of approval received from parents and others early in life. If a person received *unconditional* approval, it was expected that he or she would have a stable sense of self that would be invulnerable to current positive or negative feedback from others. It was also expected that these unconditionally-reared individuals would have moderate self-esteem and would not have a great need for social approval. On the other hand, those who had received *conditional* approval earlier and currently had low or high self-esteem depending on the quantity of approval they had earned earlier were expected to have greater need for social approval. Low and high self-esteem individuals were expected to work harder for social approval in a social situation than moderate self-esteem individuals.

To test these ideas, we divided our potential subjects into low, moderate, and high self-esteem groups based on their responses on a self-esteem inventory taken earlier in large groups. When they came to the lab individually, one of two experimental social situations was created for each subject. In the no contact condition, the subject completed a short attitude survey, and received "another subject's" attitude survey. This survey disagreed with his or her own on 75 percent of the items. The subject was asked to estimate his or her liking for the other subject based on that person's attitudes. The subject was told that the fictitious other subject would never see the subject's evaluation nor the subject, and the subject would be dismissed first to ensure that they would not meet. In the contact condition, everything was the same except before they evaluated the other subject, the experimenter told them that he would come back to pick up their evaluation, show it to the other subject, and then take them down to meet the other subject. In this contact condition, the subject could put his or her best foot forward and work for the other subject's approval by evaluating him or her more favorably. The results are presented in figure 3.4.

As you can see, the moderate self-esteem subjects acted as we expected by responding almost the same in the two experimental conditions. Also, the high self-esteem subjects acted as expected by responding more favorably when the other subject was going to see the evaluation than when he or she was not. That is, they worked hard for social approval. The low self-esteem subjects did the unexpected by evaluating the other subject less favorably in the contact condition than in the anonymous no contact condition.

How did we explain the behavior of the low self-esteem subjects? Our best explanation was that they were not willing to work for approval based on flattering the other subject. Low self-esteem subjects apparently desired approval of their unvarnished selves, rather than of their ingratiating behavior. This conduct is like the unsure lover who makes his or her partner prove his or her love by reacting positively when the unsure one treats the partner shabbily. Unfortunately, most people don't react approvingly of the person who puts his or her worst foot forward. Consequently, low self-esteem people are unlikely to win friends this way and their self-esteem will probably dip lower. This study does show that a person's self-esteem affects one's social behavior. Do you have other explanations for these results?

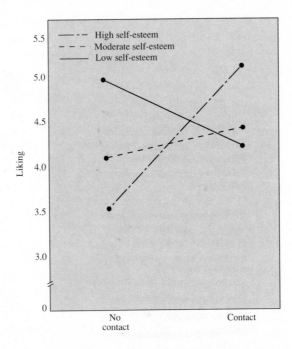

Figure 3.4
*Mean personal liking
scores for the self-
esteem groups at the
two levels of
postevaluation
contact.*
(From Kimble & Helmreich, 1972.)

We indicated earlier that most people have self-serving biases by which they take credit for success and avoid blame for failure (cf. Greenwald & Breckler, 1985). What happens when most of us are placed in a situation where we anticipate that we may fail? Do we try harder? Recent research (Berglas & Jones, 1978; Jones & Berglas, 1978) indicates that we do not. Instead, we engage in self-handicapping strategies in certain situations. Jones and Berglas (1978) suggested that many people will put themselves at a disadvantage before a difficult situation to avoid the inference that they did not have enough ability to succeed.

Picture this situation. The whole country expects you to break the long-standing world record in the long jump at the 1984 Olympics. You have already jumped closer to that record than any other jumper. With two jumps remaining, you have just jumped further than any other active jumper has jumped, but you are still almost a foot short of the world record. What do you do on your last two jumps? You pass; you do not jump! Later, you say you felt some tightness in a leg, and you didn't want to hurt it for a later running event. In this way, you can say to the world and to yourself, "I have the ability; I would have done it if it had not been for extenuating circumstances." Carl Lewis' self-handicapping strategy, if it really was one, had enabled him to avoid an inability explanation for his "failure" (just four Olympic gold medals!).

Another situation. You were in the top 5 percent of your class in your small high school. However, you are uncertain about how well you will perform at a major university. The first round of tests is coming up. Do you study long and hard? No, you go to bed without touching a book the night before an algebra exam and a biology exam. . . . The standardized departmental biology final is

Self-Handicapping

*Self-handicapping
could be one
explanation why Carl
Lewis passed on an
opportunity to break
the world long jump
record at the 1984
Summer Olympics.*

Research Trailblazers

Jones and Berglas (1978) first suggested that a person may put oneself at a disadvantage in order to escape the conclusion that they failed because of lack of ability. Berglas and Jones (1978) demonstrated that such self-handicapping is especially likely if a person has been successful in the past, but is doubtful that he or she can continue to succeed. Recently, putting oneself at a disadvantage before a threatening event occurs has been called **behavioral self-handicapping** (Leary & Shepperd, 1986).

C. R. Snyder and his associates (DeGree & Snyder, 1985; Smith, Snyder, & Handelsman, 1982; Smith, Snyder, & Perkins, 1983; Snyder, Smith, Augelli, & Ingram, 1985) at the University of Kansas have been studying a different kind of self-protective strategy, self-reported handicapping. **Self-reported handicaps** are claims that problem conditions or states of mind exist and are

hindering one's performance (Leary & Shepperd, 1986). In these studies, subjects only reported themselves to be at a disadvantage rather than placing themselves at a disadvantage. It is a different thing to tell your friends that you didn't study before a big exam when you actually did (self-reported handicap) than to not study (behavioral self-handicapping).

Snyder's research program has examined the use of self-reported test anxiety, hypochondriasis, shyness, and traumatic life history as self-handicapping strategies. They noted that Alfred Adler had preceded Jones and Berglas in suggesting that people sometimes use symptoms strategically to protect their sense of self. Also, Braginsky and Braginsky (1967) demonstrated that mental patients strategically displayed symptoms when it worked to their advantage.

the next morning. Do you burn the midnight oil? No, you go out with friends that night. Why do you behave in such a foolish way? You act that way so you can avoid having inability as an explanation for your failure. If you failed, you could say, "If I had just studied, I could have done it." If you succeeded, you could say, "I must really be smart if I did that well without studying." Perhaps you have known some new, academically insecure college students who used such a self-handicapping strategy. Fortunately, once the uncertainty about failure is removed, the individual is not motivated to self-handicap. So, when you feel self-efficacious, you can perform to the best of your ability.

These four studies used the same basic procedures to study self-reported handicapping. All subjects took Part I of an intelligence test or a social intelligence test. Before Part II of the test or a related task, subjects were told that test anxiety, physical health, shyness, or stressful background would have no impact on test performance (no self-handicapping condition), or they were told nothing about how the factor affected performance (self-handicapping condition). Then, subjects completed the appropriate dependent measures before Part II of the self-threatening test. The results of Smith et al. (1982) indicated that test-anxious women did report greater state anxiety in the self-handicapping condition. In all the studies, certain subjects reported more of the problem condition in the self-handicapping condition than in the no self-handicapping condition.

These studies demonstrated conclusively that these four types of self-reported disadvantages were used as self-handicaps. These studies examined self-handicapping as a self-presentational, public strategy designed to convince others that the individual had plenty of ability, which was encumbered by the handicapping conditions. They did not address whether people would privately use self-handicapping tactics to convince only themselves. The studies by Snyder and associates did not uncover whether people actually behaved to put themselves at a disadvantage. However, other studies (Berglas & Jones, 1978; Harris & Snyder, 1986; Kimble, Funk, & DaPolito, in press) have shown that behavioral self-handicapping occurs. There are several facets of self-handicapping to be studied yet.

Jones and Berglas (1978) suggested that low effort and excessive alcohol use are two prominent means of self-handicapping. Berglas and Jones (1978) demonstrated experimentally that subjects choose a performance-debilitating drug over a performance-enhancing one when they are fearful that they cannot maintain their level of performance on an intellectual task. Kolditz and Arkin (1982) found that individuals are more likely to engage in self-handicapping when their behavior is public than when it is private. They contended that self-handicapping is done more to affect others' attributions about the actor's ability than it is to affect self-attributions. What do you think?

Self-Awareness and Self-Consciousness

So far we have discussed the self as actor and the self as object. Now, we will examine when and how often a person thinks about himself or herself; that is, the extent to which he or she regards the self as object. **Self-awareness** refers to a state of consciousness wherein the individual's attention is focused on the self. Duval and Wicklund's (1972) self-awareness theory and Carver's (1979) model of self-attentive processes proposed that a person's attention fluctuates between being focused on the environment and being focused on the self. Originally, Duval and Wicklund defined self-focused attention as objective self-awareness and environment-focused attention as subjective self-awareness. Now, self-focused attention is simply referred to as self-awareness. A person can change from self-aware to not self-aware and back in a moment.

The presence of a camera, a mirror, or an audience increases a person's sense of self-awareness.

Many studies have demonstrated that situational factors can affect the proportion of attention focused on the self, and that self-focus affects attributions, affective states, and behavior (Carver & Scheier, 1978; Diener, 1979; Gibbons & Wicklund, 1982; Kimble, Hirt, & Arnold, 1985; Scheier, 1976; Scheier & Carver, 1977). Placing a person in front of a mirror or an audience increases self-focused attention. For instance, Diener (1979) found that placing a person alone before a larger audience made the subject more self-aware and made that person act more inhibitedly than if the person were not alone before a smaller audience. This study suggests one instance in which uniqueness had a negative impact on individuals' behaviors. Buss (1980) referred to mirror-induced self-focus as private self-awareness because it made subjects introspect on and evaluate their private selves. He referred to audience-induced self-focus as public self-awareness because it makes subjects think about how they present themselves to others. Generally, greater self-awareness makes people act in more evaluative, thoughtful, rational, and moral ways.

Self-consciousness refers to individual differences in the extent to which people direct their attention toward or away from the self. A self-conscious person is someone who is in a self-aware state much of the time. Fenigstein, Scheier, and Buss (1975) have developed the Self-Consciousness Scale to measure this personality trait. The scale has three subscales: private self-consciousness, public self-consciousness, and social anxiety. Private self-consciousness measures how introspective a person is (e.g., "I'm always trying to figure myself out."). Public self-consciousness measures the extent of focus on oneself in social situations (e.g., "I usually worry about the way I look."). Social anxiety assesses the extent of distracting emotionality during social interactions (e.g., "It takes me time to overcome shyness in new situations."). Several studies have shown that this personality trait produces attributional and affective reactions similar to those induced by manipulated self-focused attention (Buss & Scheier, 1976; Carver & Scheier, 1978; Fenigstein, 1979; Kimble & Zehr, 1982). It should be noted that very high self-consciousness is usually detrimental to performance.

Some interesting applications of social psychology by educators and psychotherapists have grown from self-attribution or self-perception theories (Bem, 1965, 1967, 1972). The first application to be discussed is how intrinsic interest or motivation can be affected by self-attribution. Lepper, Greene, and Nisbett (1973) studied the idea that giving a person rewards for doing tasks, such as schoolwork, can undermine that person's intrinsic motivation in doing the tasks. They gave preschool children either no reward, a reward they told the kids about beforehand, or a reward they did not tell the kids about beforehand to draw with multicolored pens in individual sessions. Later, they unobtrusively observed each child during a free play period in which the child could use the pens or four other items. The amount of free time the child spent using the pens was considered an indication of the child's **intrinsic motivation** to do the task. They found that the children who had received expected rewards in the earlier session had less intrinsic motivation than the kids who had not been given a reward. Lepper et al. suggested that they had turned play into work by rewarding the children. In attribution terms, they had changed a self-attribution of interest into an external attribution. Now, the children saw the drawing as something they only did if they were rewarded. Deci (1975) and his associates have demonstrated that rewards undermine intrinsic motivation in college students also. However, he offers a somewhat different explanation for the effect. Parents and teachers should be careful in offering rewards to children, especially for activities in which they are already interested.

The other application area stemming from self-attribution theory has been called **misattribution therapy** (Valins & Nisbett, 1972). The basic idea is that it is desirable to attribute problem thoughts and behaviors to external rather than internal causes. You might note that external attribution was undesirable in the intrinsic motivation research just discussed. As noted earlier (cf. Greenwald & Breckler, 1985), most people make self-serving or self-protecting attributions. However, depressed individuals do not show this beneficial bias (Alloy & Abramson, 1979; Lewinsohn, Mischel, Chaplin, & Barton, 1980).

Valins and Nisbett (1972) contend that if a person sees a problem as deriving from a characteristic of him- or herself (that is, he or she makes a self-attribution), that person would be likely to become more worried and distressed than if the individual attributed the problem to transient, situational factors. If depressives and others who are likely to make negative self-attributions could be convinced that the problem were situationally or externally induced, their state of mind would be improved. In effect, they said that the self-serving bias of ducking responsibility for negative events was beneficial in some circumstances.

Storms and Nisbett (1970) studied the effects of giving subjects an external attribution for insomnia. Subjects with sleeping problems were given a pill to take before bedtime. The pill was actually a placebo, but half of the subjects were told that it would arouse or agitate them physiologically, and the other half were told that it would have a calming or tranquilizing effect physiologically. Upon

Applications of Research on the Self

Intrinsic Motivation

Misattribution Therapy

awaking in the morning, each subject recorded how long it had taken him or her to get to sleep the night before for a few weeks. The "aroused" subjects reported going to sleep faster than the "tranquilized" subjects. How did that happen? Apparently, being able to attribute their usual agitated state to a pill put those subjects at ease and allowed them to sleep. The other subjects, being agitated even though they should have been calmed by the pill, made an even stronger self-attribution for the insomnia and had difficulty sleeping. So, being able to attribute a problem thought and behavior pattern to an external cause was beneficial to these insomniacs.

Brodt and Zimbardo (1981) attempted to affect the behavior of shy women by giving them an external, situational explanation for their uneasiness in an interaction with a man. They told shy and not-shy women that they were studying the effects of noise bombardment on physiological responses. They told the not-shy women and half of the shy women that noise bombardment caused heart pounding and increased pulse and that it had a carry-over effect for a few minutes. The other shy women were told that noise bombardment caused dry mouth and tremors. The shy women had previously reported heart pounding and faster pulse to be associated with their shyness. Therefore, the "heart-pounding, increased-pulse" subjects were expected to misattribute their symptoms to noise bombardment. Subjects were connected to electrical recording apparatus in a room with another subject (a male confederate) and heard a tone of varying frequency for three minutes. During a five-minute break, the man interacted with the woman using a rehearsed script as the investigators taped her talking. The shy women in the misattribution condition and the not-shy women talked more and changed the topic more than the other shy women did. Again, the opportunity to attribute symptoms to external causes had a positive impact on behavior.

However, it is important to remember that a therapist should only provide external, situational causes for problem aspects of clients' conduct. From the intrinsic motivation discussion previously, it should be clear that external causes for desirable ideas and behaviors is detrimental. It is also true that misattribution therapy would be inappropriate for psychopaths and alcoholics who tend to have plenty of external explanations for their behavior. However, an external attribution would probably prove helpful for shy people; people put in new, demanding situations; people experiencing sexual disfunction; neurotics; and phobics.

Self-Focus and Self-Evaluation

Another treatment for debilitating self-consciousness, such as shyness, is implied by the Diener (1979) study described in the section on self-awareness. Self-consciousness and/or social anxiety was augmented by placing the person in a unique position as the center of attention. When others shared the spotlight, self-consciousness was diminished. Those results were reminiscent of Zimbardo's (1977) account of his brother's experiences in grade school. The young boy was very shy because he wore braces on his legs. He would not go to school. Finally, his mother and his teacher agreed to a plan whereby he could wear a sack on his head at school. The sack/mask had a face painted on it, and the other children had been admonished not to remove it. He was able to participate and still escape the attention of others in this way. After over a year, his shyness had diminished enough that he discarded the mask for a special event at school and never wore it again. Being able to act without being the center of attention was helpful in this case and probably would be in others.

We sometimes experience anguish when we reconsider how we have failed or failed to measure up to our expectations. Many of us try to escape self-evaluation or self-consciousness. Use of alcohol and other drugs to alter our states of consciousness seem to be motivated by a desire to avoid or escape self-evaluation.

Several recent studies have looked at the connection between alcohol use and self-evaluation (cf. Hull & Young, 1983; Hull, Young, & Jouriles, 1986). Recall that privately self-conscious people are people who frequently introspect and evaluate how they are doing relative to their self-standards. Self-consciousness describes the personal trait of frequent self-focused attention; self-awareness describes the state of being self-focused as induced by environmental factors. Private self-awareness is the situational counterpart of the trait of self-consciousness. The important thing to remember in this context is that one must be self-focused in order to self-evaluate.

In the Hull and Young (1983) experiment, privately self-conscious subjects who had received failure feedback on an IQ test drank more wine in a subsequent wine-tasting task than did low self-conscious subjects who also failed. Thus, people who were self-evaluative and failed appeared to drink alcohol to escape self-awareness and self-evaluation. In another set of studies, Hull and his associates (Hull, Levenson, Young, & Sher, 1983) showed that drinking alcohol made subjects give less self-focused statements in a speech than those drinking tonic water. So, failure motivated self-conscious people to drink, and drinking alcohol does make people become less self-focused. Two field studies (Hull et al., 1986) examining the incidence of relapse after an alcohol detoxification program and the extent of alcohol use among high school students showed that experiencing failure in recent self-relevant life events and poor academic performance, respectively, was associated with greater alcohol consumption for privately self-conscious subjects more than others. So, one of the major motivations for alcohol consumption appears to be escaping recurrent thoughts about self-relevant failure experiences.

It is sometimes beneficial and desirable to minimize self-evaluation, especially if it is negative. Self-awareness theory suggests that ways to reduce self-focus are to focus on other people or events in our environments. For example, a recent study indicated that the greater pessimism of depressed people can be reduced by making them focus their attention away from themselves (Pyszczynski, Holt, & Greenberg, 1987). Also, if we act on our environment (that is, do something), we will have less opportunity to concentrate on self-evaluation. Many forms of entertainment may serve to reduce our self-awareness. Watching television, listening to music, or watching sports or artistic performances may be activities that are done partly to divert our consciousness from ourselves. Attending to others and events and keeping busy can be healthy ways to cope with life's stresses.

Sometimes alcohol is used to escape self-evaluation and gain happiness.

CHARLIE, by Rodrigues. © 1986 by Tribune Media Services, Inc. Reprinted by permission.

"Listen, everybody-Happy Hour ends in five minutes and it didn't go well at all. The proprietor, Mr. Mulcahy, just gave me special permission to go an extra hour—so let's do it right this time!"

Self-Discrepancy Theory

Recently, Tory Higgins (Higgins, 1987, 1989) has proposed Self-Discrepancy Theory that relates one's self-cognitions to different kinds of emotional vulner-abilities. In particular, Higgins begins by distinguishing between three distinct aspects of one's self: the actual self, the ideal self, and the ought self. The *actual self* is your representation of the attributes you (or someone else) believe you actually possess. The *ideal self* is your representation of the attributes that you (or someone else) would ideally like you to possess (i.e., hopes, aspirations, wishes for you). The *ought self* is your representation of the attributes that you (or someone else) believe you should or ought to possess (i.e., sense of your duty, obligation, or responsibilities). Furthermore, for each of these aspects of the self, Higgins distinguishes between two particular standpoints (or perspectives) on the self: (1) your personal standpoint; and (2) the standpoint of some significant *other* (e.g., mother, father, spouse, close friend).

Thus, an individual has six basic types of self-representations: actual/own, actual/other, ideal/own, ideal/other, ought/own, and ought/other. Higgins con-siders the actual/own (the attributes you believe you possess) and actual/other (e.g., the attributes your significant other(s) believes you possess) self-states as constituting a person's *self-concept*. The remaining four self-states are self-directive standards or *self-guides* we are motivated to meet. The basic assump-tion of Higgins' self-discrepancy theory is that we are motivated to reach a con-dition where our self-concept matches our relevant self-guides. To the extent that we perceive a discrepancy between our self-concept and our self-guides (i.e., we do not match up to our standards), we experience discomfort associated with specific emotional/motivational problems. The nature of these problems depends on the type of discrepancy that is most prominent.

For instance, discrepancies between the actual/own self and the ideal/own self (in which the person does not live up to his or her own ideals for him- or herself) result in the person being vulnerable to feelings of disappointment and dissatisfaction. Discrepancies between the actual/own and ideal/other selves (not living up to someone else's ideals for you) result in the person being vulnerable to feelings of shame and embarrassment. Discrepancies between the actual/own and ought/own selves (not fulfilling one's sense of duty) result in vulnerability to feelings of guilt, self-contempt, and uneasiness. Finally, discrepancies between the actual/own and ought/other selves (not matching the duties and obligations that someone else expects of you) result in feelings of fear, resentment, and feeling threatened (in anticipation of impending danger or harm from others).

This taxonomy specifies the types of emotions people experiencing certain kinds of self-discrepancies will experience. In general, discrepancies between one's self-concept and one's ideals result in dejection-related emotions (e.g., disap-pointment, embarrassment), whereas discrepancies between one's self-concept and one's sense of duty result in agitation-related emotions (e.g., fear, guilt, uneasiness). Discrepancies between these different aspects of self are computed by comparing the number of matches between attributes to the number of mis-matches between attributes (Higgins, Klein, & Strauman, 1985; Strauman & Higgins, in press).

Obviously, not all people have each of (or any of) these self-discrepancies. However, by using such a procedure, Higgins and his colleagues were able to identify people who did illustrate such discrepancies and could then test the predictions of their model. Namely, they wanted to see whether certain discrepancies were associated with specific emotions and feelings. The research indicated strong support for the model. Moreover, the intensity of the specified emotional discomfort experienced by the individual was significantly related to the magnitude of the discrepancy (Higgins, Bond, Klein, & Strauman, 1986).

Higgins' research has also shown that to the extent you make these discrepancies salient and accessible to these vulnerable individuals, you will see corresponding emotional responses. But there are some individuals for whom these self-discrepancies may be a pervasive part of the way they think about the world. Other research (e.g., Bargh & Thein, 1985; Higgins, King, & Mavin, 1982) has shown that these chronically accessible self-discrepancies strongly (and consistently) influence the way people interpret and remember social events. Thus, it may be important for clinicians to identify these people, for it is these individuals who might be most prone to certain disorders (e.g., dejected depression, agitated depression, anxiety).

Summary

The self has two parts: how we feel, think, and act toward the environment and how we think and feel about ourselves. How we act, think, and feel is affected by our past experiences and by our current audiences. We sometimes engage in self-presentation to affect others' images of us. Self-monitors are people who are especially good at pretense.

We are motivated to evaluate ourselves positively. We make self-attributions by comparing our conduct with that of similar other people and by weighing others' reactions to us. Our self-esteem is affected by how self-efficacious we perceive ourselves to be at activities others have taught us to value. We sometimes put ourselves at a disadvantage, so we and others do not conclude that our failures are caused by our inability to perform. Our consciousness is divided into self-focused attention and environment-focused attention. People who often focus on themselves are referred to as self-conscious. Situation-induced self-awareness and trait self-consciousness have similar effects on our behaviors and judgments.

Two applications of self-information grow out of self-perception or self-attribution theories. Intrinsic motivation is diminished by external attributions for the behavior; play is turned into work. Problem conditions, such as anxiety, shyness, or insomnia, may be improved by finding external attributions for the conditions. Also, people sometimes avoid self-evaluation by drinking alcohol, but there are more healthy ways to deal with negative experiences and thoughts. Self-discrepancy theory has shown that how we think about ourselves and how we think others perceive us affects our emotional reactions and mental health.

Interpersonal Perceptions and Judgments

Impressions

On a *Cheers* TV show, Norm Peterson, a burly bar regular, introduces himself and, while drinking beer from a can, sits down in the impeccable living room he has just decorated. An image-conscious yuppie couple is interested in hiring him as the interior decorator for their home. It is clear after a few minutes of conversation that unpretentious Norm is not making a good impression on them. After a whispered chat with his psychiatrist friend, Norm puts on airs, "I programmed myself to dream about your home last night," and gets the job. Later at the bar, the couple agrees to letting Norm also design their mountain residence; but only if he tells anyone who sees him there that he is the plumber.

It was love at first sight. We hit it off instantly.

Former President Reagan seems to be such a warm, positive, friendly man.

The television episode and quotations suggest that the way to win a job, a mate, a presidency is to make a good impression on people. The initial image you project to others is undoubtedly important. However, you must be able to sustain that impression or that job, marital partner, or presidency will be lost. The ability to communicate positive impressions is important early and later in a relationship.

The impression one creates is only partially under that person's control. The person whom one is trying to impress brings previous experience with others to the interaction; a whole system of attitudes, beliefs, cognitions, and perspectives developed from previous experience; and sometimes even information about the individual to the interaction. The actor has little control over those elements of the situation. In addition, the actor has little control over his or her appearance and mannerisms, especially nonverbal ones. All of these factors affect the impressions one person projects and the other person forms.

The two-way nature of impression formation should be emphasized. There must be an *actor* and a *perceiver* for **impression formation** to occur. Typically, the two or more people in an interaction will alternate between projecting information about themselves and forming impressions about others. All parties are motivated to make the interaction go smoothly and to help each other maintain "face" or self-respect (Goffman, 1959). This motivation and the unspoken rules of conversation make most interactions orderly, courteous, and comfortable.

In this chapter, we will discuss how the perceiver forms impressions and how those impressions affect later interactions. We will also discuss how the actor can manage impressions or present him- or herself as Norm Peterson did in the prologue. Self-presentation or impression management was introduced earlier in chapter 3. This chapter and chapter 10, in particular, focus on *patterns* of human interactions. You, the reader, should recognize some of these patterns of behavior in your everyday life. Greater understanding and recognition of these facts of life may help you have more positive and honest interactions with others.

The perceiver brings some preconceived ideas to every interaction. Among these ideas are *schemas, implicit personality theories,* and *stereotypes.* These three concepts are related to each other. They are so related that the *physical attractiveness stereotype,* the expectation that good-looking people possess other positive characteristics, could be considered an example of all three concepts. Expecting that "what is beautiful is good" is a **stereotype** in that it is a set of beliefs about members of a group (Hamilton, 1981), "good-looking people." **Implicit personality theories** describe an individual's ideas about what personality traits "go together," or are likely to appear in the same person (Schneider, 1973; Wegner & Vallacher, 1977). The physical attractiveness stereotype seems to be a common implicit personality theory because many people believe attractive people have marital competence, occupational competence, and certain personality traits (Dion et al., 1972). The yuppie couple in the opening example apparently held the implicit personality theory that a burly, beer-guzzling slob like Norm could not possibly have the sensitivity for color and design an interior decorator needs.

    Schema is a more basic term for these and other types of *knowledge structures* about elements in our environments (Hastie, 1981). Implicit personality theories and stereotypes are types of schemas. Other schemas are **gender schemas,** which describe a person's beliefs and expectations about male and female persons. Knowing that a person is female will imply to some people that she is interested in fashion, design, family, and domestic occupations because of her female gender schema (e.g., Sistrunk & McDavid, 1971). Such schemas are ways of thinking derived from past experiences, and they affect how perceivers form impressions of others. Schemas, stereotypes, and implicit personality theories assume great importance in impression formation because they exist before interacting with the individual and form the framework with which subsequent information about the individual is evaluated.

    Perceivers must also combine the information they have about an actor to form an impression. For example, in the television episode, the young couple knew that Norm had decorated the living room and was highly recommended by sophisticated friends. However, they also had preconceived ideas about how an interior decorator should look and act, and they observed Norm's appearance and behavior. How was all of that information combined?

    Information integration theory (Anderson, 1962, 1965, 1968; Kaplan & Anderson, 1973) indicates some ways a perceiver may process information about another person. This theory suggests that each bit of information about a person is given a positive, negative, or neutral evaluation (*value*) and its relevance or importance to the judgment at hand is weighed (*weight,* which is always positive). The value times the weight of each bit of information is summed with the $V \times W$ of other information to reach an overall judgment about the person. New information is simply added to the earlier sum to form a new impression. In this way, many types of information (descriptions, appearance, behaviors) are combined to form the overall impression, which can range from very positive to very

Social Perception

Components of Impression Formation

Perceivers' Preconceptions

Information integration theory suggests that each piece of information about someone is weighed by a receiver in order to reach an overall judgment. How do we put the pieces together?

negative. In our TV episode example, the beautiful living room and friends' recommendations of Norm as an interior decorator surely had created a positive first impression. However, when his appearance and behavior in contrast to their conception of a decorator was added, the overall impression became negative. Norm was able to change the impression to positive again by acting more refined and sophisticated.

Features of Actors

What are the major features of the actor that affect the perceiver's impression of that actor? The features can be grouped into five major categories. They are (1) the actor's appearance, (2) the actor's speech style, (3) the content of the actor's speech, (4) the actor's nonverbal mannerisms, and (5) information about the actor obtained from other sources. The first four factors of appearance and behavior usually have great impact on impression formation. As Heider (1958) indicated, they can "engulf the field" or overwhelm consideration of other information. Let us examine these factors in detail.

Physical attractiveness is often a prerequisite for performing in the visual media.

ZIGGY, by Tom Wilson. © 1987 by Universal Press Syndicate. Reprinted by permission.

Appearance   The first individual feature people attend to in interactions is the actor's appearance. In chapter 2, we discussed the influence of a person's appearance on that individual's personal development. In the previous paragraphs, we also mentioned the "what is beautiful is good" stereotype (Dion, et al., 1972). The existence of that stereotype means that if the actor is attractive to the perceiver, he or she will make a good first impression. Because of the attractiveness stereotype, the actor's behaviors will be interpreted to indicate that the actor is friendly, intelligent, etc. A word of caution here. A few studies (e.g., Sigall & Aronson, 1969; Sigall & Ostrove, 1975) have indicated that if a beautiful person acts negatively toward the perceiver or appears to be exploiting his or her good looks to his or her personal advantage, the perceiver will not have a positive impression of the actor.

Sociobiology and Appearance   What is a beautiful appearance? Many psychological studies on appearance have used facial appearance in snapshots alone. You might say that facial appearance is only a small part of the total picture. A few studies have examined preferences for different types of body forms (e.g., Wiggins, Wiggins, & Conger, 1968). Most people think the most attractive body types are those that accentuate the physical characteristics of the individual's sex. If people represented in the visual media are any indication, muscular men and women with accentuated breasts and hips are the preferred body types. Such body preferences are consistent with sociobiologists' emphasis on the importance of reproductive success in affecting social attitudes and behaviors. Likewise, sociobiologists might say that trimness is an attractive body feature because trimness implies fitness, health, and longevity, all important traits of prospective mates. Such fitness might also inspire jealousy in rivals of the same sex. In a sociobiological sense, bodily attractiveness is more relevant than facial attractiveness. Such attractive people might be expected to make good first impressions on heterosexual members of the other sex. However, they might make bad first impressions on same-sex persons.

Sociobiological Theory

Sociobiological theory was developed by a biologist, Edward O. Wilson (1975, 1978). He and others contend that much social behavior is determined by *evolutionary* considerations. Social behaviors are said to evolve because individuals who engage in particular social behaviors, such as headbutting in bighorn sheep, are more successful in producing offspring so that more members of future generations exhibit the behaviors (Barash, 1979). A primary motivation of individuals, according to sociobiologists, is to act in ways that will ensure the survival of their genes in future generations. So, it is not simply survival of the individual that motivates, but survival of others who are similar—who share the same genes. The more similar the other individuals, the harder a particular individual would work for their survival, given that those individuals still have reproductive potential. **Inclusive fitness** is an index of how successful an individual is in perpetuating his or her genes in future generations because it includes his or her reproductive success and the reproductive success of close and distant kin (Barash, 1979; Freedman, 1979; Wilson, 1975). It is the inclusion of the kinship group as well as the individual in genetic immortality evaluations that makes sociobiology more social than traditional evolutionary biology.

Genetic survival is thought to affect many social behaviors. An individual should be more altruistic and self-sacrificing toward his or her reproductively capable identical twin than to one's own children, more altruistic toward one's children than to one's siblings, more altruistic toward one's siblings than to one's cousins, more altruistic toward one's cousins than to one's fellow ethnic group member, and more altruistic toward one's fellow ethnic group member than toward a stranger who is physically dissimilar to him- or herself (Rushton, 1988).

Where does this genetic equation leave parents, spouses, and in-laws? Presumably, one would not sacrifice much for his or her parents when they are no longer reproductively active unless they could contribute to the care and survivability of the third generation (their grandchildren). Spouses should be treasured during their reproductive years because they enable the individual to pass on half of his or her genes to the next generation. Daughters- and sons-in-law would be admired to the extent that they are similar enough genetically that grandparents can see themselves in the grandchildren. It seems apparent that humans do not

(*Continued*)

follow these genetic dictates completely. They sometimes act positively toward genetically (reproductively) insignificant people. We will learn later that help given because it is likely to be reciprocated by the recipient is consistent with sociobiological tenets because it could contribute to the individual's survival. In this way, altruism could extend beyond the kinship group to those who live nearby and interact frequently.

Sociobiology also suggests that we will be competitive with and aggressive toward others who threaten our survival and our reproductive survival in our kin. Competition for desirable mates is an obvious social behavior implied by sociobiological theory. Indeed, fights and killings are too common between rivals for the same mate among humans. However, sociobiology also implies that aggression toward family members should be minimal, while evidence suggests that it is very common. It is hard to see how sociobiology could account for events such as the Easter

slayings by a 40+-year-old Hamilton, Ohio bachelor of his mother, his sister-in-law, his only brother, and his brother's eight children. In a few minutes, he completely destroyed his genetic future. Obviously, factors other than sociobiological ones are needed to account for some human aggression.

Sociobiology also addresses sex roles, including mating strategies, childrearing, and division of labor between the sexes. For instance, the optimal mating strategy for males to ensure genetic immortality is to mate with as many females as possible as many times as possible. Sociobiologists argue that such reproduction considerations put the male in the role of initiator or aggressor in sexually motivated encounters. The female, in addition to presenting herself as a desirable mate, must be selective in seeking a male who will be a good and constant provider for the children because she has to invest much time in pregnancy and childrearing. Barash (1979) even contends that a 70-year-old

A recent study on tactics of mate attraction from a sociobiological perspective verified some of these ideas about appearance and impression formation (D. Buss, 1988). College students were asked to report the frequency with which their closest same-sex friend had done certain acts in order to attract members of the other sex. Newlyweds were asked to self-report the frequency of actions done to win their new spouses. Students also rated the perceived effectiveness of these acts in winning favor with the other sex. Men reported that they displayed strength and athleticism, lifted weights, and flexed muscles often to make themselves attractive. Women reported that they wore makeup and stylish clothes, man marrying a 25-year-old woman is more prevalent and sensible than the other kind of May-December marriage because the older man can still reproduce and probably has many resources to provide. The typical age differences in married couples with the man being older can be explained in the same way.

While the central desire for inclusive fitness is helpful in explaining some social behavior, much more is needed to account for the complexities of much social behavior. After all, with the advent of new birth control techniques, most sexual behavior is nonreproductive. Since reproductive success for oneself and one's kin is humans' main goal according to sociobiology, such a state of affairs (no pun intended) should produce behavior patterns that sociobiologists might have trouble explaining. One problem sociobiologists have is methodological. They cannot use the standard scientific procedure of setting up certain conditions and then observing their outcomes to test the theory. All of their

Table 4.A A Summary of Sociobiology Theory

Motivation of the Individual
To maximize the survival of one's genes

Core Concept
Inclusive fitness = Reproductive success of individual and relatives

Focus of Theory
Biological influences on aggression, altruism, and sex role behavior

Assumption about Rationality/Awareness of People
Unaware, nonconscious actors because animals and humans act similarly

explanations are after-the-fact. The nature of the theory makes it virtually impossible to disconfirm. For instance, the fact that females do most of the child care in the world can probably be accounted for by sociobiological concepts, but that doesn't mean sociobiological factors make them care for the children.

dieted to improve their figures, and did many appearance-related acts. Men and women both reported that they usually kept themselves and their hair, in particular, well-groomed. For men, some actions rated effective were to diet, exercise, and keep fit. For women, actions rated effective were practically identical except that they did not include dieting. Many interpersonal acts, such as displaying a good sense of humor (the most effective for both sexes), were also important in making oneself attractive. However, the point was that appearance factors suggested by sociobiology were important in making good impressions.

*Genetic survival into
future generations
seems to be important
to many of us.*
News America Syndicate

Appearance and Control   Certainly a person has control over some features of his or her appearance. The current interest in jogging, aerobics, health clubs, and spas reflects, in part, many people's belief that they can achieve a trimmer, better appearance through these endeavors. Weight Watchers, Diet Workshop, and other diet programs are also indicators of many peoples' desire to look better. Another way that a person can control his or her appearance is through clothing. Molloy's (1975, 1977) books on dressing for success in corporate America indicate ways that individuals can create better impressions through their dress.

An aspect of appearance related to impression formation over which the actor has no control has been described by Crano and Messé (1982). A person's appearance may possess **cue similarity** for a particular perceiver. That is, his or her facial or bodily appearance may be similar to the appearance of someone the perceiver has known. If the perceiver liked the similar-looking past acquaintance, he or she will form a positive initial impression of the actor. If the perceiver disliked the past acquaintance, then his or her initial reaction to the actor is likely to be negative. A recent study (Lewicki, 1985) has shown that, indeed, if a person we have just met looks like another we know, we assume that the new person has similar personal qualities to the person we know. Obviously, the actor has no control over whom the perceiver has known in the past. Nevertheless, cue similarity may have considerable influence on reactions to a person's appearance.

Speech Style   Speech style refers to many different linguistic and paralinguistic characteristics of speech. The way a person speaks can have substantial influence on the impression we form of that person. Some paralinguistic features we will discuss are the rate, loudness, pitch, and variability or inflections of speech. They can affect our perceptions of how animated people are or how involved they are in what they are saying. Also, the presence or absence of unfilled (silent) and filled (uhs, ahs) pauses in speech affect impressions of the speaker, as we will see later.

Ethnic and regional accents are also likely to affect impression formation. Often, listeners are intrigued by unrecognized accents and will try to discover their origin. A contrived accent does not inspire the most positive impression of the speaker. However, it is often difficult to know if a particular accent is contrived or simply picked up through exposure. A high school friend may sound much different after a tour of duty in the Navy. Whether an unfamiliar, uncontrived accent causes you to form a good or bad impression of the speaker probably

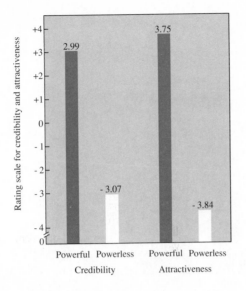
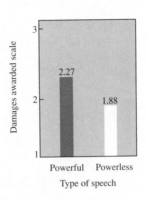

Figure 4.1
*Credibility and
attractiveness of
courtroom witness
using powerful or
powerless speech and
damages awarded
when witness's
testimony supported
greater damages.*

depends on whether you have a positive or a negative image of that ethnic group or region. Perhaps the cue similarity of the voice acts in the same way as cue similarity of appearance. That is, if a person talks like someone you have liked, then you will form a positive impression of the new person.

Speech style has been considered in another way. Speech styles can be powerful or powerless (Erickson, Lind, Johnson, & O'Barr, 1978). **Powerful speech** is straightforward and succinct. **Powerless speech** employs many qualifying words. Powerless speakers use many intensifiers (e.g., so, very, surely), hedges (e.g., kinda, I guess), hesitation forms (e.g., uh, well, you know), and questioning intonations in declarative statements. To test the differences in reactions to these speech styles, Erickson and her associates presented subjects with an audiotaped or printed segment of a male or a female witness's testimony in an automobile injury case. The witness's speech style was either powerful or powerless. The powerful speech style led to greater attraction to the witness and to greater acceptance of the witness's position. Erickson's findings are presented in figure 4.1. So, powerful speech leads to formation of a more positive impression than does powerless speech.

Indirect, Polite Speech   Sometimes a powerful speech style is considered blunt or too direct. In those situations, indirect speech is regarded as more polite (Brown, 1987; Brown & Levinson, 1978; Holtgraves, 1986; Searle, 1975). **Direct speech** involves utterances in which the sentence meaning is consistent with what the speaker wants to accomplish (e.g., "Get me a glass of lemonade."). **In indirect speech,** the speaker's intent is not obviously presented in the words of the sentence (e.g., "Could you get me a glass of lemonade?" or "It sure is hot in here."). Another form of indirect speech is to say nothing about the topic at hand if one's honest reply is likely to be offensive or threatening (e.g., "Did you notice my new blouse?" "It seems like clothes are getting too expensive these days."). Certainly,

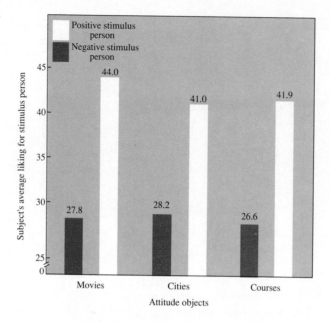

Figure 4.2
Liking ratings for persons who expressed positive or negative attitudes about movies, cities, and courses.

this indirect reply is more polite than "It looks terrible on you," but the transparency of the indirect comment may make the blouse-wearer dislike the second speaker anyway (Holtgraves, 1986). Generally, politeness is an endearing quality unless it embodies a thinly-veiled insult.

Content of Speech So far, we have been talking about how words are said. Now, we will consider the effects of what is said on impression formation. Some aspects of conversation content are the amount of personal information a person divulges (**self-disclosure**), the *responsiveness* of the second speaker to what the previous speaker said, the range of topics discussed, the amount of humorous or joking content, the self-centeredness of conversation topics, the *positivity* of conversational comments, and the amount of talking. Some of these elements of speech content relevant to impression formation have been studied, but other areas have barely been examined.

     Some research has been done on self-disclosure and impression formation or initial attraction. Generally speaking, a person who discloses more intimate information about him- or herself is liked better than someone who discloses little (Jourard & Friedman, 1970; Worthy, Gary, & Kahn, 1969). However, someone who discloses too much early in a relationship is likely to make a negative impression (Cozby, 1972). A person who is responsive to what another person has just said makes a better impression than someone who responds inappropriately (goes off on a tangent) or is unresponsive (Davis & Perkowitz, 1979). Also, those who talk more in group discussions are liked better than those who talk less (Ruback, Dabbs, & Hopper, 1984). The research of Folkes and Sears (1977) indicated that people who talk about positive feelings create more favorable impressions. (See figure 4.2.)

Almost no research has been done on the effect of displaying a sense of humor on impression formation. Yet, many public speakers use jokes and humorous stories to establish rapport with their audience. Some presidents, most notably John Kennedy and Ronald Reagan, have used their sense of humor effectively to create a favorable impression with American voters. One recent study (D. Buss, 1988) indicated that displaying a sense of humor is the most commonly used and the most effective tactic for attracting a mate for women and men. Another study (O'Quin & Aronoff, 1981) showed that a humorous comment did lead subjects to make more generous concessions in a bargaining situation. The effects of kinds and amounts of humorous comments on impression formation seem to be a ripe area for study.

Likewise, the effects of type and range of topics discussed and the effects of self-centered conversation have not been systematically studied. Discussion of a wider range of topics should produce more favorable impressions because such conversation would lead perceivers to see the speaker as multifaceted and interesting. We do discuss a wider range of topics with our closer friends (Altman & Taylor, 1973), suggesting that conversational breadth and favorable impressions go together. Self-centered talk in the form of using many first person pronouns or exclusively discussing topics of interest to you probably would not create a positive impression.

Nonverbal Mannerisms   Aspects of a person's nonverbal behavior in an initial encounter can have a profound effect on impression formation. If the nonverbal behavior were particularly uncommon, such as very little direct eye contact with the perceiver or very little smiling at the perceiver, attribution theory (Jones & Davis, 1965; Kelley, 1967) indicates that behavior would have greater impact on the impression formed. Perceivers may look for nonverbal signs of emotion (Ekman & Friesen, 1969). **Emotional leakage** occurs when a person's nonverbal actions betray an emotional state the person may wish to hide. Touching oneself frequently with one's hand(s) (such touches are called *self-adaptors*), excessive movement and rapid blinking are sometimes taken as indications that the actor is anxious (LeCompte, 1981). For example, President Nixon's eyelids would practically flutter when he talked about some personally sensitive issues on television. Most of us believe a person has little control over his or her nonverbal behavior, but there are some studies that indicate we can control our facial expressions during deception (Zuckerman, DePaulo, & Rosenthal, 1981).

Perceivers can form impressions of actors from their nonverbal behaviors as well. For instance, a perceiver might judge how dominant or high status an individual is by observing that person's body postures and visual behaviors. Mehrabian (1969) has shown that a person who adopts a more relaxed posture (with more backward lean, less direct orientation toward the perceiver, and asymmetrical placement of limbs) feels more dominant in that situation than does a person who adopts an attentive, erect, symmetrical posture. Exline, Ellyson, and Long (1975) have presented evidence that both high-status people and trait-dominant people tend to maintain more eye contact while speaking and less eye contact while listening than less dominant people. They call such visual behavior the **visual dominance pattern.** Whether displaying high or low dominance makes a good or a bad impression may depend on the actor's status relative to the perceiver. For example, a chief executive officer acting dominantly may be perceived positively, while a subordinate acting the same way would not.

We also make inferences about a person's honesty from his or her visual behavior. Hemsley and Doob (1978) found that subjects perceived witnesses who averted their eyes from their questioner in a courtroom setting as less credible than witnesses who maintained eye contact with their questioner. We will see later that perceivers do make judgments about whether or not an actor likes them from the actor's visual behavior.

Information from Other Sources   If a perceiver receives information about an actor before he or she interacts with the actor, the perceiver's impression may be affected. It often happens that we get information about people we are going to meet from friends and acquaintances, or we may make preliminary judgments about people from knowing their occupation or status or by observing their job or home setting. This preliminary expectation or set can change the way a perceiver interprets subsequent behavior or, if it is communicated to the actor by the perceiver's behavior, it can change the actor's subsequent behavior. The first effect may be called a **labeling effect,** and the second would be called a **self-fulfilling prophecy effect.**

A scene from "One Flew Over the Cuckoo's Nest." Social labeling can have a strong influence on the way people are perceived, even over long periods of time when their actions no longer fit the label.

The effect on impression formation of labeling or categorizing an individual before you meet him or her was clearly demonstrated in an early social psychological study (Kelley, 1950). Students in the same classroom were given a written description of a visiting lecturer as "warm" or "cold" before he gave a lecture to the class. Those who received the "warm" description formed a more favorable impression of the speaker than those students who received the "cold" description even though both sets of subjects heard the same talk.

Rosenhan's (1973) study on the experiences of normal "pseudopatients" in East and West Coast mental institutions (see p. 4) provides a striking example of this labeling effect. Perhaps it is not shocking that all eight pseudopatients were admitted as patients in all twelve mental hospitals they visited since they did describe some unusual symptoms during the admitting interview. What is surprising and distressing is that none of them were detected as sane by any of the staffs during their hospital stays. (Nearly one third of the other patients *did* say, without being asked, that the pseudopatients were sane.) The pseudopatients were judged psychotic by all hospitals (schizophrenic by all except one), and they were all released about one to two months later as "in remission." Schizophrenia in remission means that the person is still mentally disturbed, but he or she is not showing any symptoms right now!

These judgments occurred even though the pseudopatients acted normally from the moment they left the admitting room. Since the person was in a mental institution after being judged insane, doctors and nurses inferred that such ordinary behaviors as writing and waiting for the cafeteria to open were symptoms of their mental disorder.

It is possible that the failure to detect normalcy was not so much a matter of misinterpretation of observed behavior because of the label, but mere inattention by the staff. However, the failure to observe patients probably also grows from the label. On a children's unit at a state mental hospital where I worked one summer, the only patients who received much attention were those who were aggressing against other children. Psychiatrists spent approximately 10 minutes a week on the unit in the nurse's station checking charts to see if medication should be changed. They never saw patients except in the halls as they passed through. That experience is why I don't find it incredible that a blind woman spent 60 years in a southeast Ohio mental institution undetected as mentally competent until a student volunteer from Ohio University in the 1970s encountered her and managed to gain her release.

Kenneth Donaldson, a Florida mental patient for 15 years before he was ordered released by the U.S. Supreme Court in the late 1970s, stated that he was involuntarily committed to a mental institution without being seen by a judge or mental health personnel. That may have occurred partly because he had been labeled *paranoid schizophrenic* nearly 20 years earlier in New York. He also reported in his book, *Insanity Inside Out* (Donaldson, 1976), that he was seen by mental health professionals in individual sessions for about one hour a year. He learned from hospital records, which he obtained through the Freedom of Information Act, that those mental health professionals interpreted nearly everything he said in those interviews in ways that were consistent with the label, *paranoid schizophrenic*.

These studies and cases illustrate the dramatic effect of having information that causes labeling or categorizing of people. Of course, the common labels or categories we apply to others we know don't have such profound effects because we have revised our impressions of them with much added information (Kaplan & Anderson, 1973). However, the first impressions we form of individuals may persist and affect our later perceptions of them just as these labels do.

Jones and Nisbett (1972), in discussing the observer attribution bias, have pointed out several reasons why first impressions are likely to persist as we continue to interact with the person. One reason we continue to believe a certain impression of a person is because we fail to appreciate that the situations in which we commonly interact limit the behavior we see. Coparticipants do not realize that to observe the other participant both must be present and that both individuals are usually present in only a few types of settings. Another, related reason is that we usually see that person in only one role and we are not aware of how much that role limits the person's behavior. For instance, the student may never see his professor in her role as mother. If he did, he might see some very different behaviors and change his impression of her. Also, when the perceiver and the actor interact, it takes a very astute perceiver to realize that his or her own behavior limits the actor's behavior. For instance, you may think that a friend is a sports nut, but you may fail to realize that over half the time you are the one who initiates the topic of football, basketball, etc. In conversations with other

The Importance of First Impressions

people, he or she may be freer to talk about other topics. So settings, roles, and the perceiver's behaviors may limit the behaviors displayed and first impressions persist. In fact, a recent study has shown that active perceivers, who focus on regulating their behavior in conversations, are usually unable to take into account the constraints on actors' behaviors and adjust their impressions of them (Gilbert, Krull, & Pelham, 1988).

A fourth reason we may not get disconfirming evidence of an impression is that we typically compare notes about a person with other people who are similar to ourselves and who see that person in the same roles and settings that we do. A fifth reason impressions usually persist is that we are inclined to interpret behavior that is inconsistent with our impression as consistent. Jones and Nisbett (1972) note that a kind behavior by someone we have labeled as hostile will be seen as manipulative or insincere rather than benevolent. In this way, observers of Kenneth Donaldson saw the angry demands of a man who was being unjustly held as symptoms of his paranoia.

The Self-Fulfilling Prophecy and Its Effects

The other influence that a perceiver's impressions may have is to affect directly the behavior of the actor. This effect has been called the **self-fulfilling prophecy** or the *Pygmalion effect* (Merton, 1948; Jones, 1977; Jussim, 1986; Rosenthal, 1973; Rosenthal & Jacobson, 1968). In Greek mythology, Pygmalion sculpted a statue of a woman, Galatea. Galatea was brought to life by Pygmalion's desire for her to be alive. The self-fulfilling prophecy apparently has less profound effects than that in real life, but many studies have shown that the expectations of one person can affect the performance or behavior of another person.

One study (Rosenthal & Jacobson, 1968) examined the effects of teachers' expectations on students' performances using students from several grades and ability levels. Early in the school year, they presented teachers results from a test designed to identify "late bloomers." They told the teachers which students in their classes were likely to "bloom" academically that year. In fact, they had picked names of 20 percent of the students and designated them as bloomers randomly. The investigators did not return until the end of the school year. From a second intelligence test given to the students, Rosenthal and Jacobson discovered that the "bloomers" had improved their IQ scores significantly more than control or "nonbloomer" students had, especially in the lower grades. (See figure 4.3.)

Communication of Expectations

Since the only difference between the groups was the expectation of their teachers about their performance, those expectations had to be the cause of their improvement. However, the linkage between A's expectation and B's performance did not occur by magic. Rosenthal (1973) has contended that one person's expectations are translated into another person's behavior through *climate, feedback, input,* and *output.* By interpersonal climate, he means the warmth or supportiveness of the expectant person toward his or her target. In school settings that means the teacher would be friendlier and more encouraging toward the bloomers than toward the control students in the class. Feedback means that the teachers would

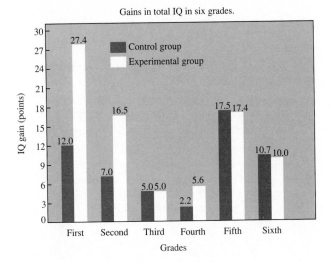

Gains in total IQ in six grades.

Figure 4.3
*The self-fulfilling
prophecy benefiting the
"bloomers"
(experimental group)
was strongest in the
first two grades.*

give clearer and more direct information to the bloomers about the correctness of their performance than to the nonbloomers. Input means the teachers would give more information and more demanding work projects to the bloomers than to their classmates. Output means that teachers would give more opportunities to respond to the bloomers than to the other students.

However, these four factors simply describe the way the expectant person acts differently because he or she has that expectation. Darley and Fazio (1980) have contended that self-fulfilling prophecy effects occur because the target person (the bloomer student in the Rosenthal and Jacobson study) also comes to believe that he or she can perform that well. In fact, Baumeister, Hamilton, and Tice (1985) found that other people's expectations that the target person could perform well actually had a negative effect on performance unless the target person became convinced that he or she could perform that well. Thinking that you can perform well is a big part of actually performing well, as Bandura's (1977a) ideas about self-efficacy have suggested.

Research suggests that in the self-fulfilling prophecy, the expectations of the perceiver affect the target person.

The **Galatea effect** affects the actor's self-expectations rather than the perceiver's expectations about the actor's performance as does the Pygmalion effect. The Galatea effect was examined when Eden and Ravid (1982) decided to deal with Galatea, the target person, directly instead of concerning themselves with Pygmalion. They manipulated the self-expectancies of military leadership trainees directly instead of manipulating their instructors' expectations. Having an authority figure tell randomly chosen trainees that they had the potential to succeed produced performance greater than controls and equal to Pygmalion condition subjects. They called this improved performance due to positive self-expectations the Galatea effect.

Wilson and Linville (1982) demonstrated a similar effect with struggling freshman students at Duke University. They found that persuading some of these students that the grades of college students like themselves generally improved during their college careers, resulted in a lower dropout rate and higher GPA in

The Galatea Effect

Figure 4.4
GPA change and dropout rates of struggling freshman students who were told that grades usually improved after the first year and students who weren't told that information.

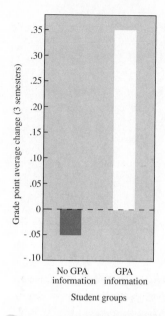

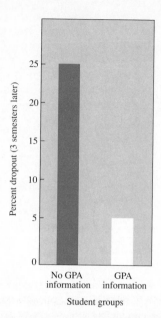

the next year for those students than for a comparison group of their peers. It is most important, and perhaps most expedient, to affect the expectations of the target person. Figure 4.4 displays the Galatea effect.

The Influence of the Self-Fulfilling Prophecy

However, the self-fulfilling prophecy is a very important interpersonal phenomenon. Rosenthal and Rubin (1978) reviewed over 300 studies on the effects of one person's expectations on another person's performance. Feldman and his associates (Feldman & Prohaska, 1979; Feldman & Theiss, 1982) have shown that the expectations of students affect the performance of teachers. Livingston (1969) pointed out how managers' expectations could affect workers' performance. King (1971) demonstrated the Pygmalion effect in industry, affecting the performance of welding and mechanic trainees by manipulating the expectations of their instructors. Eden (1984) reviewed the phenomenon in various organizational and military training situations. As we will see in chapter 14, many different kinds of expectations, including prejudices and stereotypes, can have self-fulfilling effects with negative outcomes.

The Self-Fulfilling Prophecy in a Social Interaction

One study (Snyder, Tanke, & Berscheid, 1977) demonstrated the self-fulfilling prophecy using a particular social stereotype, namely, the physical attractiveness stereotype. They put male and female students in separate cubicles connected by an intercom. They first photographed the man and presented a photograph of his "interaction partner" to him. Actually, the picture was not of the woman in the nearby cubicle. It was the photograph of either an unattractive woman or an attractive woman according to earlier ratings of photographs. So, there was no relationship between the appearance of his interaction partner and the picture, but the man was given the expectation that his partner was beautiful or homely by this manipulation. After receiving the picture but before talking to her, the man was asked to rate her on a number of personal characteristics. Then, the man and the woman engaged in a 10-minute unstructured interaction over the intercom as their voices were recorded. Later, judges rated the man's comments and the woman's comments separately on several qualities.

Men rated their partners as more sociable, poised, humorous, and socially adept if they were shown a picture of a beautiful woman. So, the men did form the predicted expectations. Were those expectations fulfilled in the behavior of their female partners? If so, how did the males influence the females? Judges rated the women's comments as more sociable, poised, sexually warm, and outgoing if their partners had been shown the picture of the beautiful woman. Their conversational actions constituted behavioral confirmation of the men's expectations. How did the men communicate their expectations? Judges rated the men who interacted with women whom they believed beautiful as more sociable, interesting, outgoing, socially adept, humorous, confident, and animated than those men who thought their partner was less attractive. Believing that they were talking to an attractive woman led these men to act in more charming ways and their women partners reciprocated that kind of behavior. We can assume that men and women bring out the best in attractive partners in face-to-face interactions every day because they believe the attractiveness stereotype.

Applications of Impression Formation Principles

We have already discussed the importance of creating favorable first impressions in finding and keeping jobs and in cementing personal relationships. We have also mentioned how appearance, speech style, nonverbal mannerisms, and other factors can influence impressions. These are elements of impression formation that all of us can observe in our lives. We should also be sensitive to the biases that the impressions we form can have on the outcomes and behavior of other people.

Impression Formation in the Courtroom

The impressions that are formed in courts of law have great impact on the outcomes of cases. Jurors form impressions about judges, attorneys, witnesses, and defendants in making their decisions. In jury selection, attorneys form impressions about prospective jurors and try to get a jury that will be sympathetic to their clients' position. Social psychologists have most commonly been used in trials to help attorneys select jurors who are likely to be receptive to the attorneys' side of the case (Weyant, 1986). These psychological consultants have usually worked for the defense in highly politicized cases, such as the criminal conspiracy case against antiwar activist, Father Phillip Berrigan (Schulman, Shaver, Colman, Emrick, & Christie, 1973). There are three legal ways to select the most favorable jurors:

1. Ask for a change of venue because of publicity or evidence that most local potential jurors have prejudged the case
2. Make a composition challenge stating that the jury panel from which jurors are selected is not representative of the court district
3. Ask that particular panel members not be allowed to serve on the jury during voire dire (Kairys, Schulman, & Harring, 1975)

Impression formation plays a key part in decision-making processes in the courtroom.

Voire dire is the interview procedure by which jury members are selected. An attorney can ask that a prospective juror be excluded without giving cause or because of apparent partiality against the attorney's client. However, only a few panel members may be excluded preemptively or without cause, so establishing partiality is important.

Consulting psychologists typically conduct a phone survey of registered voters in the district and perhaps in another district in order to make the case for a change of venue or a composition challenge (McConahay, Mullin, & Frederick, 1977). If respondents in the local district have prejudged the case more than respondents in another district, the lawyer can often persuade the judge to give a change of venue. If the representative phone sample of voters in the district is different from the jury panel racially or in some other demographic way, then a composition challenge can be made so another jury panel can be chosen.

The phone survey results can be helpful in voire dire also. Because jury panel members know that they may be struck from the jury if they display partiality, some panelists may respond dishonestly. Since the consultants know the demographics (i.e., race, sex, religion, and socioeconomic status) and attitudes of the telephone respondents toward the case and the demographic characteristics of the prospective juror, they can estimate what his or her honest responses would probably be. If respondents who were similar to the panelist in sex, race, age, and occupational status had certain attitudes toward the trial, the consultants would predict that the panelist probably thought the same way. The panelist might be selected or excluded based on that analysis.

In addition to the survey, consultants can help lawyers select receptive jurors by having the lawyers pose certain questions to the panelist during voire dire and observing the panelist's conduct. The panelist's nonverbal behavior may indicate that he or she is lying or has a negative attitude toward the defendant (Bonora, Linder, Christie, & Schulman, 1983). A lot of postural movements, touching oneself with hands frequently, or speaking in a higher pitch may indicate that the panelist is lying. Avoidance of looking at the defendant may indicate a negative attitude toward him or her. How deferential the prospective juror is toward the authority, the judge, may indicate whether or not the juror is biased toward the prosecution.

Lawyers should also be aware that their clients (e.g., defendants), witnesses, and the lawyers themselves need to impress the jurors and/or judge positively. An actor in the courtroom will certainly create more favorable impressions if he or she is responsive to questions asked (Davis & Perkowitz, 1979). There are also studies indicating that witnesses are most credible when they look at their questioners (Hemsley & Doob, 1978) and when they use a powerful speech style (Erickson et al., 1978). Lawyers should not only advise their witnesses to act in these ways, but they should adopt these behaviors themselves.

Summary

The impressions others form of us affect our work, relationships, and general well-being. The stereotypes, schemas, and implicit personality theories perceivers bring to the interaction and the way they integrate information about actors affect the impressions formed. Several characteristics and behaviors of actors affect the impressions perceivers form about them. A trim, attractive appearance usually leads perceivers to form a good general impression of the individual because of the physical attractiveness stereotype. What one says, how one says it, and how much one says affect the impression that is formed of that person. Nonverbal behaviors can leak anxiety or deceptiveness and affect impressions formed. Prior information from others can initiate labeling and self-fulfilling prophecy effects. The labeling effect is exemplified by the pseudopatients' experiences in mental institutions. The bloomers' improvement and women's responses to their partners' belief that they were beautiful and, therefore, sociable, etc. illustrate the impact that one person's expectations can have on another person's behavior. The application of impression formation principles to the courtroom was highlighted.

Social Cognition

The Study of Social Judgments
by Edward Hirt and Frank Kardes

Several years ago a grudge match was held between two rival college football teams. The game was very physical, fights erupted, players from both teams were injured. Following the game, two social psychologists showed films of the game to fans of each team (Hastorf & Cantril, 1954). Although the fans saw the same films, their perceptions of the game differed markedly. In each case, the fans saw more infractions committed by the opposing team than by the team they favored. Moreover, they perceived the actions of the opposing team as hostile and aggressive, while the retaliations of the favored team were perceived to be justified. Certainly, we have all experienced incidents similar to this. People often interpret the same events very differently. How is it that such divergent perceptions arise from the same events? What psychological mechanisms could account for this lack of objectivity?

A new pediatric clinic was established in a town in the Southwest. Soon a distressing pattern developed at the clinic. Well babies would stop breathing while they were being given routine inoculations. Each one was put on rescue equipment and was raced by ambulance to a large city hospital miles away. One of the seven or eight infants did not survive.

How could this mystery be unraveled? The covariation principle of Kelley's attribution theory, which will be discussed in this chapter, was used. That is, what people, events, drugs, etc. were associated with the babies being stricken? First, only babies treated at that clinic by the new pediatrician and the new nurse were stricken. So, the doctor and the nurse were under suspicion. Investigation uncovered that the doctor was fresh out of medical school and had no such incidents in her background. However, the nurse had worked on a hospital nursery shift that had become known as the "death shift" because so many babies had died during that work period. In fact, several babies had died in her arms in the hospital. The nurse was always giving the children shots when they stopped breathing in the clinic. So, the nurse was associated with several deadly incidents, with which the doctor and others were not. How was she making the children stop breathing? Ultimately, a partly empty vial of a drug which could stop children's breathing was found in the treatment room, and the mystery was solved. So the person, the situation, and the drug that covaried with these deadly incidents were uncovered; and the cause of the children's illnesses was clear. You will learn in this chapter that we use other attribution principles to judge people's dispositions, traits, and motives.

Amoebas may not, but people do think about social events.

THE FAR SIDE, by Gary Larson. 1988 CALENDAR. © 1988 by Universal Press Syndicate. Reprinted by permission. All Rights Reserved.

THE FAR SIDE   By GARY LARSON

"Stimulus, response! Stimulus, response! Don't you ever *think?*"

The field of social cognition focuses on how people think about social events. People are constantly making judgments about the traits, abilities, and feelings of themselves and others. We ask ourselves, "Do I like this person?" "Is he a nice guy?" Further, in order to better understand the world around us, we often try to explain why various events occur. If we knew why a particular person behaves as he or she does, we could predict his or her behavior with a relatively high degree of accuracy. In short, **social cognition** is the study of social judgment. A *judgment* refers to the assignment of an object to a cognitive category (Wyer & Carlston, 1979). For example, we often judge the degree to which we like or dislike an object, the size of an object, or the height of an object. We make judgments about the possible causes of social events, and we make judgments about the likelihood with which various social events occur. This chapter focuses on these judgments.

We will focus on three major classes of social judgment: trait judgments, causal judgments, and likelihood judgments. Within each of these classes, research has shown that people are not perfect social information processors. Consistent biases and errors emerge in social judgment. A clearer understanding of these biases and errors may enable cognitive social psychologists to understand the process by which people make judgments. This knowledge may lead to the development of training procedures that will improve the reliability and validity of human judgment.

Trait Judgments

Social stimuli are often ambiguous. The actions of others are frequently open to multiple interpretations. One factor that influences how people interpret ambiguous information is the accessibility of various constructs or concepts in memory. **Accessibility** refers to the ease with which a construct, such as hostility or friendliness, can be retrieved from memory (Bruner, 1957). The more accessible a particular construct is, the more likely it is that that construct will affect how ambiguous information will be interpreted. One way to increase the accessibility of a construct is through a process known as priming. **Priming** refers to techniques that unobtrusively expose people to judgment-relevant information. This process is illustrated by the following example.

Priming

Consider the results of an important experiment conducted by Higgins, Rholes, and Jones (1977). These researchers asked subjects to view some slides and told them to name the color of the background of each slide as quickly as possible. However, to make the task more difficult for subjects, they also asked subjects, after naming the background color, to name the "memory" word that they heard just prior to the presentation of the slide. Some of these "memory" words were trait adjectives (e.g., reckless, adventurous). Although subjects were not paying much attention to these memory words, it was hypothesized that asking subjects to remember these trait adjectives would "prime" these constructs (i.e., make these constructs highly accessible in memory for a short period of time). Half of the subjects received only favorable trait adjectives (e.g., adventurous, self-confident) and the remaining subjects received only unfavorable trait adjectives (e.g., reckless, conceited).

At the conclusion of the first experiment, subjects were asked to participate in a second seemingly unrelated experiment in which they read a description of a person named Donald. Donald's actions were ambiguous with respect to the trait adjectives that subjects received in Experiment 1. Subjects' task was to form an overall impression of Donald. As predicted, more favorable overall impressions of Donald were formed when subjects received favorable as opposed to unfavorable trait adjectives in the first experiment. This effect occurred even though subjects believed the two experiments were unrelated. Thus, without their knowledge, subjects' impressions of this person were influenced by the priming words they had received minutes earlier. The priming had subtly affected the way in which they viewed Donald.

Figure 5.1
Effects of priming on judgment as a function of the timing of three important events.
(From Srull & Wyer, 1980.)

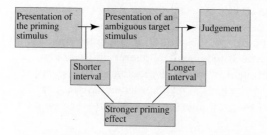

Moreover, because the way in which we perceive and interpret events has a strong impact on our behavior, priming effects can result in changes in later behavior. Herr (1986) found that subjects primed with hostile words not only judged Donald more hostile but also played a game with Donald more aggressively and competitively than subjects primed with nonhostile words. Advertisers as well often try to prime us into making positive evaluations of their products because these positive evaluations will produce higher sales.

However, priming effects do not always occur. There are some limitations. First, Higgins et al. found that priming effects did not occur in conditions in which subjects were exposed to trait adjectives that were *irrelevant* to the ambiguous behaviors described in the second study. That is, priming someone with hostile words should not affect judgments of intelligence. Thus, ambiguous behaviors are interpreted in terms of *relevant* constructs that happen to be accessible from memory when the ambiguous information is first encountered.

Secondly, subsequent research has shown that priming effects depend on the timing of three important events: (1) the presentation of the priming stimuli, (2) exposure to ambiguous information pertaining to the target stimulus, and (3) judgment formation (Srull & Wyer, 1979, 1980). Figure 5.1 illustrates the relationships among these three events. As the time between the presentation of the priming stimuli and the time of presentation of the ambiguous target information increases, priming effects decrease. This finding suggests that the priming procedures only increase the accessibility of a construct for a brief time. However, as the time between the presentation of the ambiguous information and the time of judgment increases, priming effects increase. This finding suggests that priming effects are not a result of accessible constructs at the time of judgment. They are a result of constructs that happen to be accessible when information about the target stimulus is first encoded or stored in memory.

Stereotyping

People are exposed to large amounts of information every day. When we observe the actions of others, we are exposed to a wide variety of behavioral information—including what the person says, how the person dresses, how smoothly and confidently the person acts, and so on. However, we do not encode or store all of this information in memory; instead, we seem to focus on only a subset of all of the available information. So, how do we decide which information to focus on?

Social cognition research has shown that people use *schemas* to encode incoming information. A *schema* is a knowledge structure in memory that organizes all of our knowledge about a particular domain (e.g., football, soap operas, fashion styles, chess). People who have a schema for a particular domain (e.g., chess) have stored in memory all of the commonalities of the game (the ways the different pieces can move, the positions on the board that a given piece can occupy) and are then able to focus on and encode only the important aspects of any moves or games they see (and can sift out the unimportant or irrelevant information). On the other hand, people who lack the schema cannot discriminate the important from the unimportant ("Was the black knight on a red or black square?") and cannot efficiently encode the incoming information.

Some schemas are unique to individuals (e.g., schemas for Egyptian hieroglyphics), while others are shared. One type of shared schema of particular interest is a stereotype. A *stereotype* is a schema that tells us what traits, features, and behaviors are typical for a given group of people (e.g., all straight A students are nerdy, wear glasses, and never date). Knowing what characteristics are typical of a given group enables us to make inferences about what traits, features, and behaviors are likely to be exhibited by any member of the stereotyped group. Hence, stereotypes are used to guide our *expectations* about other people. They are potentially useful because they reduce the flow of incoming information and make our complex social environments more manageable, but they are also potentially dangerous because, as we shall see, they are often based on biased information processing.

How are stereotypic beliefs formed? David Hamilton and his colleagues have conducted a series of experiments on the role of illusory correlation in stereotype formation (Hamilton & Gifford, 1976; Hamilton & Rose, 1980; Troiler & Hamilton, 1986). **Illusory correlation** refers to our tendency to overestimate the degree of association between two variables or events. For example, after reading a list of word pairs (lion—car), people overestimate the frequency of occurrence of word pairs that are high in associative strength (bread—butter) or distinctive because they are atypical (Chapman, 1967). Hamilton reasoned that minority groups are distinctive because they are, by definition, atypical. If a member of a minority group performs an atypical behavior, observers may overestimate the degree of association between the atypical group and the atypical behavior. To test this hypothesis, Hamilton and Gifford (1976) presented to subjects 29 sentences of the form: "John, a member of Group A, visited a sick friend in the hospital." Most of the sentences pertained to Group A (making Group A the majority group), and Group B was the minority group. The abstract labels A and B were employed to ensure that prior knowledge about the groups did not influence subjects' judgments. In addition, most of the behaviors described in these sentences were desirable, and some undesirable (atypical) behaviors were included. Although half of the behaviors associated with Group A were undesirable and half of the behaviors associated with Group B were desirable, subjects overestimated the extent to which the minority group performed undesirable, atypical behaviors. In a second study, atypical desirable behaviors were presented, and again, subjects overestimated the degree of co-occurrence between the minority group and atypical desirable behaviors.

What behaviors do you associate with each person?

Distinctiveness of either groups or behaviors is only one factor that affects correlational judgment. Another factor is the degree to which people expect two events to co-occur. Because stereotypic beliefs affect expectations about members of a particular group or category, we expect stereotyped groups to behave in stereotype-consistent ways (we expect all overweight people to be jolly). Moreover, because people tend to overestimate the degree to which their expectations are confirmed by the available evidence (Jennings, Amabile, & Ross, 1982; Rothbart, Evans, & Fulero, 1979; Trolier & Hamilton, 1986), we believe that our stereotypes are true and accurately reflect the world around us. In this way, stereotypes are self-perpetuating.

In a study on the consequences of stereotyping, half of the subjects were told that the target person was a librarian and half were told that the target person was a waitress (Cohen, 1981). Next, subjects watched a videotape in which the target person displayed many librarian features (e.g., she wore glasses, she owned many bookshelves) and many waitress features (she drank beer, she owned a bowling ball). Although all subjects watched the same videotape, subjects who thought the target person was a librarian subsequently recalled more librarian features, and subjects who thought the target person was a waitress recalled more waitress features. Thus, information that is consistent with our stereotypes is more memorable than information that is inconsistent or irrelevant (Cantor & Mischel, 1977; Cohen, 1981; Hamilton & Rose, 1980; Rothbart, Evans, & Fulero, 1979). This is one factor that makes stereotypes persist over time, even in the face of contradictory information.

A second factor that contributes to the persistence of stereotypes is that our own expectations and behaviors can elicit stereotype-consistent behavior from others. Imagine you were introduced to a person named Paul, who you had heard is a real jerk. When you meet him, you would probably be very cautious and defensive as he talks to you. After all, you don't want this jerk prying into your private life! He in turn would be likely to reciprocate your defensiveness or rudely end the conversation. Your expectations about this person have now been fulfilled and you are convinced that he really is a jerk. The problem is that we fail to realize that it is our own expectations and subsequent behavior that elicit the behavior of the other person. If we would have behaved otherwise, perhaps this person would have behaved quite differently. This sequence of events describes the phenomenon of *self-fulfilling prophecy* (Darley & Fazio, 1980; Jones, 1986).

Considered together, the studies suggest that although stereotypes seem to be emotional constructs (i.e., motivated distortions of reality), they are influenced by several cognitive mechanisms that operate outside of conscious awareness. Individuals are often unaware of the processes involved in forming and maintaining stereotypes, and they are often unaware that their behavior toward others is strongly influenced by their stereotypes.

Why do intelligent people seem industrious, skillful, determined, and imaginative? Why do cold people seem unpopular, humorless, pessimistic, and unhappy? One explanation for these perceptions is that people have notions about which traits "go together" or are correlated with one another. These notions are referred to as *implicit personality theories* (Bruner & Tagiuri, 1954; Rosenberg, Nelson, & Vivekanathan, 1968).

Person Memory

Sometimes, however, we encounter information that is incongruent with our initial impressions. Do we treat unexpected events differently from events that are consistent with our initial impressions? Do we focus our attention on unexpected events or do we ignore them? Are incongruent events more or less memorable than events that are congruent with our initial impressions?

Hastie and Kumar (1979) conducted a study designed to address these questions. Subjects were exposed to a list of sentences describing the behaviors of a target person. Most of the sentences described behaviors that were congruent with a given personality trait. For example, learning that the target person "won the chess tournament" would be consistent with the trait "intelligent." Subjects also studied some sentences that were incongruent with intelligence, such as he "made the same mistake three times." In addition, some irrelevant behaviors were included in the list, such as he "took the elevator to the third floor." After studying this information, subjects were unexpectedly asked to recall as much information as possible. The results indicated that subjects recalled a greater proportion of incongruent than congruent items and that the probability of recall was lowest for irrelevant items.

These results make some intuitive sense. When we attempt to form an impression of another person, we try to integrate all of the available information into a coherent, overall impression. Congruent information is easy to integrate because it fits so well with other information we have about the target person. Integrating incongruent information is difficult, however, and requires a great deal of effort on the part of the social perceiver. For instance, if we hear that a friendly person punches his neighbor in the nose, we are surprised by the (incongruent) event and have a hard time justifying or explaining it. The extensive and effortful processing of incongruent information makes that information more memorable, resulting in higher recall for the incongruent information than the congruent information.

One interesting implication of this explanation is that people will integrate incongruent information with congruent information only when attempting to form a coherent impression of another person. If they are not interested in the other person (e.g., they will never see this person again) or if other distracting tasks are preventing them from integrating information, they will not expend the necessary effort to integrate the incongruent information, and the memory advantage of incongruent information should decrease.

Previous research has dramatically demonstrated the importance of information integration in person memory (Hamilton, Katz, & Leirer, 1980; Wyer & Gordon, 1982). In one study, some subjects were instructed to form an impression of a target person, and some were told simply to memorize a list of sentences describing the behaviors of the target person (Hamilton et al., 1980). Later, subjects who received the impression instructions recalled significantly more information than subjects who were explicitly told to memorize the information! This is because subjects with the goal of forming an impression organize and relate the items of information in memory with one another. As a result, associations are formed between the items of information in memory. If items in memory are associated, then the recall of one item (she helped a neighbor) will cue the recall of other associated items (she gave money to a local charity). The more extensively we think about and relate information about a target person, the more associations among items there will be.

On the other hand, in simple rote memory tasks, people treat each item of information independently from the other items and a rich associative network will not be formed. Given that rich associative networks provide many different routes for accessing information, more information will subsequently be recalled when people integrate information than when they simply memorize information. Moreover, if the integration explanation is correct, instructing subjects to memorize information results in no advantage for incongruent information. Srull, Lichtenstein, and Rothbart (1985) tested this prediction and found that in the memory condition, probability of recall did not differ as a function of congruency. Thus, strong support was found for the integration explanation of the incongruency effect. (See figure 5.2.)

At this point, the reader may have noted an inconsistency between the findings reported in the stereotyping literature and the findings reported in the person memory literature. The stereotyping studies indicate that schema-consistent information is more memorable than schema-inconsistent information, whereas the person memory studies show the opposite effect. How can this be? One way to reconcile these findings is to examine a critical difference between the stereotyping and the person memory studies. In the stereotyping studies, subjects received information pertaining to a *group* of individuals, whereas in the person memory studies, subjects were exposed to information about a *single* target person. A group often (but not always) consists of a collection of unrelated individuals and there is no need to integrate information to form an impression of the group as a whole. We expect group members to differ somewhat from one another, and it is not surprising to learn that one member is different from the others. Inconsistent information is much more informative when forming an impression of a single individual, however, because we expect individuals to exhibit consistency between their traits and behaviors. Thus, congruent information should be more

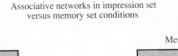

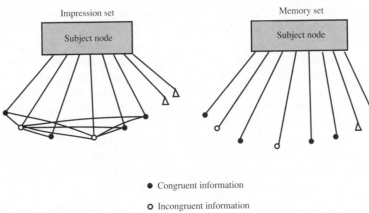

- ● Congruent information
- ○ Incongruent information
- △ Irrelevant information

Figure 5.2
More interconnections between incongruent and congruent information are formed in impression set than in memory set conditions. The rich associative network formed in impression set conditions facilitates recall.
(Figures adapted from Srull, Lichtenstein, & Rothbart, 1985, 319.)

memorable when subjects gather behavioral information about a group of individuals, whereas incongruent information should be more memorable when subjects integrate information pertaining to a single individual. Srull, Lichtenstein, and Rothbart (1985) found exactly this pattern of results.

Causal Judgments

In addition to our desire to make judgments about the enduring personality traits of others, we also show an overwhelming desire to understand the causes of social events. Whenever we read in the newspaper or see on television that some famous person has committed suicide or that an airline crash has occurred, we search for explanations as to *why* that event occurred. Everyday behaviors also elicit such causal thinking. When a clerk or waitress is rude to us, we typically ask those around us, "What's bothering him/her? Is it something I did?"

Attribution Theories

Attribution is the process by which most people decide why particular events occurred or why certain people acted the way they did. The three most prominent attribution theories have been Heider's (1958), Jones and Davis' (1965), and Kelley's (1967). Daryl Bem's (1965) self-perception theory should also be included among the prominent attribution theories. It will be discussed again in greater detail in later chapters.

Heider's Naive Psychology of Action

The field of attribution takes as its basis the writings and observations of Fritz Heider (1958). It was Heider who first conceptualized the process by which a person attempts to understand the cause of some action. Heider emphasized the importance of deciding whether an event or behavior was caused by internal or external factors. *Internal causes* refer to causes that reside within the person, such as the person's personality traits or dispositions (e.g., "she's just a nasty

*Was the drug incident
involving Dwight
Gooden due to an
internal cause or an
external situation
factor cause?*

*Correspondent
Inference Theory*

person"). *External causes* refer to causes residing in the situation or environment in which the behavior was performed (e.g., "She was having a bad day."). Heider also examined how people make finer judgments about internal causes. For instance, he described how people assess two different internal causes of performance level, motivation and ability.

We often use this distinction between internal and external causes in our everyday judgments. Did the student perform well because she is very skillful (internal) or because it was an easy task (external)? Did the client say that his family hates him because he is paranoid (internal) or because his family treats him badly (external)? Did Lieutenant Calley kill innocent men, women, children, and babies at My Lai because he was a hateful, murderous person (internal) or because he was under orders to do so (external)? Did she work so hard because she loved her job (internal) or because she was paid well (external)? Did he tell her how lovely she looked because he adores her (internal) or because that is what you're supposed to tell your date on prom night (external)? You can see how such decisions have many implications for how people feel and behave.

Heider's distinction of these different classes of attributions served as the basis for all of the later attribution theories. However, Heider himself never explicitly tested his notions in actual experiments and told us very little about the process by which people decide whether an event or behavior is due to an internal or external cause. Thus, subsequent attribution theories were proposed to explain the *process* by which people make causal attributions.

The next attribution theory was proposed by Jones and Davis (1965) and is called *correspondent inference theory*. These authors were particularly interested in how we infer the cause of a *single* instance of behavior (e.g., "Why did this waitress act rudely to me?"). According to this theory, the central concept of attribution is **correspondence,** which refers to the degree to which one can see a direct relationship between a behavior and a certain disposition (trait, attitude). If there are several plausible reasons why someone may have performed an action, correspondence is low and we cannot make a confident attribution about the cause of that person's behavior. However, if there is only a single plausible reason for performing an action, correspondence is high and one can confidently attribute the action to that cause. For Jones and Davis, one attempts to make a specific internal attribution for any action (and an external attribution is a default option made only when an internal cause cannot be found). Therefore, the Jones and Davis approach is designed to show how people distinguish between different internal causes of behavior.

As we mentioned before, social behavior is often ambiguous and the causes of behavior are not always apparent. Thus, it is often a difficult process to infer the true cause of a behavior. However, this theory suggests three factors that are particularly informative in determining the causes of behavior.

The **social desirability** of the behavior is the first factor to consider. Actions that are high in social desirability (i.e., behaviors that are ordinary and encouraged by society) are not particularly informative. They do not tell us much about the actor's personality. For instance, it is customary for tennis players at the end of a match to shake hands at the net before leaving the court. Suppose we observe that a tennis player (Ivan Lendl) shakes the hand of his opponent after a match. What can we infer about Ivan's level of sportsmanship? Not very much, since all the other players do this as well. However, suppose we observe a player (John McEnroe) refusing to shake hands with his opponent following a match. This behavior is very informative, and we would most likely infer that John McEnroe has poor sportsmanship. It is behavior that is *low* in social desirability—behavior that is atypical and inconsistent with role requirements (cf. Jones, Davis, & Gergen, 1961)—that provides a basis for making a dispositional inference about an actor.

A second factor to consider is the actor's degree of *choice* in performing the behavior. Actions that are freely chosen are informative because they reflect the actor's underlying preferences and dispositions (e.g., "I did it because I wanted to."). However, very often our actions are in direct response to external or situational concerns—situations in which we have little or no choice (e.g., "I had to do it.") Under such no choice conditions, we can infer nothing about the actor's underlying dispositions.

In an experiment designed to demonstrate this effect, Jones and Harris (1967) gave some subjects free choice in what type of essay (pro-Castro or anti-Castro) they wanted to write, while other subjects were simply assigned to a position. Observers (who were aware of the subject's condition, that is, whether the person had free choice or no choice) read the essay and were asked to estimate the writer's true position on the issue. As predicted, observers inferred that the attitudes of subjects in the free choice condition corresponded more closely to the position advocated in their essays than did the attitudes of the no choice subjects.

The third factor requires that we look at the actor's behavior in the context of other potential behaviors. We examine the actor's chosen behavior and ask the question, "Is there some effect or outcome that could only be obtained by performing the chosen behavior?" In order to answer this question, we must first outline the behavioral alternatives available to the actor and consider all of the effects associated with each behavioral choice. For instance, we could perform such an analysis on a student's choice of spring break vacation. In this example (see table 5.1), we will use three options: (1) going home, (2) going to the beach (Florida), and (3) going to the mountains (Colorado). Underneath each option, we have listed all of the effects associated with that choice. Imagine that this person chose to go to Florida. We now look for any effect(s) that are exclusive or unique to the chosen option (what we call **noncommon effects**). As we can see, all of the options involve getting away from school, so this effect does not help us explain why one would choose to go to Florida as opposed to any of the other options. Likewise, the expense of the trip does not tell us why a person would choose Florida over Colorado. The only effect exclusively gained by choosing the Florida option is the chance to get a suntan. Therefore, we would infer that the reason the person chose to go to Florida for spring break was to get a tan. A similar analysis could be performed to explain why one would choose Colorado or home as well.

Table 5.1   The Spring Break Vacation Dilemma: Effects Associated with Spring Break Vacation Options

Home	Florida	Colorado
Getting away from school	Getting away from school	Getting away from school
Inexpensive	Expensive	Expensive
Spend time with family	Get a suntan	Go skiing

Jones and Davis' theory serves a very important function in the field of attribution by specifying the factors that aid us in making dispositional inferences about another's behavior. The notion of looking for correspondence between a behavior and a particular disposition enables us to identify the specific dispositional cause associated with performing a particular behavior. In this way, we are able to examine more carefully the internal causes of behavior. However, this theory is not without some limitations. For instance, the scope of correspondent inference theory is limited to attributions made about a *single behavioral episode* rather than an entire sequence of behaviors. Also, the person making the attribution is a *passive observer* of the event (who tries to subjectively determine the cause of that event). Clearly, this situation does not encompass all of the possible situations in which we make attributions. In many cases, we are very active observers of the events around us, and we (like amateur sleuths or detectives) seek information from a variety of sources (for example, further observations of the actor's behavior, what other people know about the actor, etc.) that might be helpful in identifying the cause of behavior. Given these limitations, an alternative theory of attribution was proposed that dealt specifically with situations under which observers have the opportunity to collect multiple pieces of information about the actor in making an attribution.

Kelley's Attribution Theory

The attribution theory proposed by Harold Kelley (1967, 1971) deals specifically with situations in which observers have access to multiple pieces of information about the actor. Suppose, for instance, that you see your new next door neighbor John kick his dog after work. In Kelley's theory, our goal is to understand *why* this behavior occurred. Was it due to an internal or external cause? In order for an observer to adequately answer the question "why," Kelley argues that the observer needs to consider information concerning three dimensions of behavior.

First, one would need to know whether John acts this way in other situations. Has he kicked his dog on other occasions? Here, we are concerned with the *consistency* dimension of behavior across situations and over time. *In order to make an internal or external attribution in Kelley's theory, there must be high consistency.* In the event of low consistency (i.e., if John only kicked his dog this one time), we are unable to attribute this behavior to a stable internal cause (for example, "John is just a mean person") or a stable external cause (for example, "This dog provokes everyone to be nasty"). Instead, we would attribute this behavior to the specific circumstances (perhaps, John had had a terrible day at work or the dog had just dug up his prizewinning rose garden). It is important to note that an attribution to circumstances (a *circumstance* attribution) is both *unstable* (in the sense that it doesn't imply what might happen in a different situation) and *external* (i.e., something inherent to the situation rather than the person). In fact, one might consider a circumstance attribution to be the default attribution made only in situations in which observers cannot make a stable internal or external attribution.

The second dimension that we need to consider is the distinctiveness dimension. *Distinctiveness* refers to questions about how John responds to other dogs. Does he kick all dogs or is this behavior distinctive to this particular dog? If distinctiveness is high, it suggests that the cause of the behavior lies in this particular dog, and we make the attribution that something about this dog caused John to behave that way. Thus, high distinctiveness leads to stable external attributions to the target of the behavior (what is called a *stimulus* or *entity* attribution).

The third dimension discussed in Kelley's theory is the *consensus* dimension. Consensus refers to questions about how other people respond to this same dog. Does everybody kick this dog or is this behavior peculiar to John? If consensus is low (John and only John behaves this way), we would make the attribution that the cause of this behavior is something about John himself. Hence, we would make a stable internal attribution (what is called a *person* attribution) about John given low consensus.

Thus, according to Kelley's theory, there are three classes of attribution that people make—person attributions, stimulus attributions, or circumstance attributions—depending upon the patterns of information they receive. The patterns that lead to each of these attributions (see McArthur, 1972) are illustrated in table 5.2. The critical process that underlies which attribution is made for a behavior is the search for covariation. Kelley's **covariation principle** states that observers act as "naive scientists" trying to determine along which dimension(s)—consensus, distinctiveness, consistency—behavior is varying. If behavior is constant (invariant) across a particular dimension (for example, "John and everyone else kicks the dog"), then that dimension is eliminated from consideration as a possible causal agent. However, when behavior varies along a particular dimension (for example, "John kicks the dog but no one else does"), then we can confidently make a causal attribution to that dimension. Notice that in contrast to Jones and Davis' emphasis on the search for correspondence, Kelley's attribution theory emphasizes the search for covariation.

A person attribution would be made when one person acts differently than other people do (low consensus), in response to many different stimuli (low distinctiveness), under several different circumstances (high consistency). That is, if the behavior occurs only when one particular person is present, we infer that the person caused the behavior. A stimulus attribution would be made when information indicated that the act was common (high consensus), highly distinctive, and highly consistent. A circumstance attribution would be made when information indicated that the act was high in consensus, low in distinctiveness, and low in consistency. The fourth type of attribution shown, person by stimulus,

Table 5.2   Examples of Patterns of Attribution

Behavior: John kicked his dog.

Pattern 1

No one else kicks that dog.	Low consensus*	
John has kicked other dogs.	Low distinctiveness ---------------->	Person attribution
John has often kicked his dog.	High consistency	

Pattern 2

Everyone else kicks that dog.	High consensus	
John doesn't kick other dogs.	High distinctiveness* ------------->	Stimulus attribution
John has often kicked his dog.	High consistency	

Pattern 3

Everyone else kicks that dog.	High consensus	
John has kicked other dogs.	Low distinctiveness ---------------->	Circumstance attribution
John has seldom kicked his dog.	Low consistency*	

Pattern 4

No one else kicks that dog.	Low consensus*	
John doesn't kick other dogs.	High distinctiveness* ------------->	Person by stimulus attribution
John has often kicked his dog.	High consistency	

*Denotes covariation of dimension with behavior

The augmentation principle. This man must be an avid runner to be running in adverse conditions.

indicates that the combination of a particular person (John) and a particular stimulus (his dog) are needed for the behavior to occur. Such attributions are commonly made when the information pattern shown in table 5.2 is presented (Hewstone & Jaspars, 1987; Kimble, 1985; Kimble & Kardes, 1987).

The patterns of information illustrated in table 5.2 represent the ideal patterns of responses to these dimensions. However, in everyday life, situations that correspond to these ideal patterns are rare. What would happen in situations in which there appear to be several plausible causes of a behavior? In our discussion of correspondent inference theory, we said that situations in which there was poor correspondence between the behavior and a single disposition would lead to less confident attributions. Kelley further elaborated upon this idea in his presentation of the attributional principle of **discounting.** According to this principle, we tend to discount or downplay the importance of any particular cause of a behavior depending on the number of other potential causes for that behavior. For example, imagine that a clerk compliments you on your appearance. Then, this person tries to persuade you to buy an outfit that would further enhance your appearance. Normally, when someone pays us an unsolicited compliment, we would attribute very positive qualities to that person (he or she is very nice). However, in this situation, we would be likely to discount this cause of the clerk's behavior because another potential cause of that behavior (that is, the clerk was just trying to make a sale) is also present. Thus, as was the case in correspondent inference theory, our ability to confidently attribute the cause of some behavior to a particular cause is diminished by the presence of other potential causes of that behavior.

Table 5.3 A Summary of Attribution Theories

Motivation of individual
To understand the events and actions in one's environment

Core concepts
Actions are caused by internal factors, external factors, or both; correspondence; covariation

Focus of theories
Cognitive understanding of one's world and how causal conclusions affect reactions and behavior

Assumptions about rationality/awareness of people
Rational model with recognition of biases

Kelley also presented a second attributional principle, the **augmentation** principle, which refers to situations where there are inhibiting forces working against the occurrence of a particular behavior. Imagine a situation in which a student gets sick the week before a big test and cannot really study adequately for it. The student goes in to take the test feeling awful and unprepared, but the student ends up still getting an "A" on the test. What would be your attribution about this event? You would probably believe that this person must be really smart if he or she could still perform well under such adverse conditions. This situation demonstrates the principle of augmentation. You attribute even greater causal impact to a particular facilitating cause when there are inhibiting forces present, since this facilitating cause must be especially powerful to overcome the effects of these inhibiting factors. It should be noted that using a self-handicap (see chapter 3) enables one to *discount* lack of ability as the cause for failure and *augment* ability as the cause for success. (See table 5.3.)

A basic assumption of all the attribution theories is that humans are rational and logical information processors. In searching for the causes of behavior, we act as "intuitive scientists" (cf. Ross, 1977) observing certain factors and dimensions that allow us to make confident causal inferences. However, more recent research has identified several consistent errors and biases that creep into the attributional process. The study of these biases has caused many to question the inherent rationality of man as an information processor and decision maker. As we discuss these characteristic attributional biases, we will consider the implications that these errors have for understanding the process by which human beings make causal judgments.

Biases in the Attributional Process

The process of making causal attributions to internal versus external causes is one way of determining the relative importance of dispositional and situational forces in affecting a particular behavior. However, one critical observation made by Fritz Heider was that "behavior . . . has such salient properties [that] it tends to engulf the total field" (Heider, 1958, p. 54). In this statement, Heider notes that in many situations, we tend to focus too much on the behavior itself (and

The Fundamental Attribution Error

Table 5.4	Attributions of Attitudes to the Speech Writer	
	Essay	
Choice Condition	*Pro-Castro*	*Anti-Castro*
Choice	59.62	17.38
No Choice	44.10	22.87

Note: Higher numbers indicate more favorable attitudes toward Castro. The possible range of scores was from 10 (extremely anti-Castro) to 70 (extremely pro-Castro). The subjects' attitude toward Castro = 32.23. (From Jones & Harris, 1967.)

the dispositions that behavior implies) and not enough on the situation or context in which that behavior was performed. As a result, we tend to overemphasize dispositional causes and underestimate the situational forces affecting behavior. We also too often make dispositional attributions for behavior in situations where strong situational pressures exist. The pervasiveness of this phenomenon led Ross (1977) to characterize this bias as the **fundamental attribution error.**

A provocative demonstration of this error was obtained in an experiment mentioned earlier (Jones and Harris, 1967). In that experiment, subjects wrote essays that were either pro-Castro or anti-Castro under conditions of free choice or no choice. The results indicated that subjects made more correspondent inferences about the true attitudes of the essay writer when the writer had free choice as opposed to no choice. Although this result was obtained, it only tells part of the story that characterized this experiment. The data from this experiment is presented in table 5.4. As you can see, although more extreme attributions of the essay writer were made in the free choice condition, attributions of the no choice subjects were also strongly affected by their essay condition. Certainly, if these people were given no choice in which essay to write, their behavior in no way reflects their true underlying attitudes concerning this issue. Thus, attribution theory would expect that subjects would not be able to infer anything about these subjects' underlying dispositions from their behavior (and would most likely rate them at the midpoint of the scale). Yet, subjects' attributions of the true attitudes of these no choice essay writers indicated that subjects thought these writers truly believed the position they were told to argue. Thus, the behavior (the essay itself) determined the attributions subjects made, without considering that these writers had no choice in which type of essay they wrote.

Another interesting demonstration of the fundamental attribution error is presented in a clever study by Ross, Amabile, and Steinmetz (1977). In this study, subjects participated in a general knowledge quiz game, in which one person was assigned the role of quizmaster or questioner and the other the role of contestant or answerer. The questioner first composed a set of challenging general knowledge questions and then posed them to the contestant. Both participants then rated the questioner's and contestant's level of general knowledge. The performance of the contestants to the quizmasters' questions was generally poor (about 40 percent). However, subjects' attributions of the level of general knowledge indicated that both quizmasters and contestants rated the general knowledge of the quizmaster as high and the general knowledge of the contestant as low. Do you see any problem with these attributions? After all, the quizmasters effectively stumped the contestants fairly regularly with their questions, so they must be smarter, right? Wrong! It is critical in this situation to compare the roles of the participants. The quizmasters were in a very advantageous position. They could ask any question they pleased from their stores of general knowledge. However, the contestants had to answer whatever question the quizmasters asked. The contestants are at a clear disadvantage in that the quizmasters can ask about anything from opera to boxing to Biblical patriarchs. Thus, the differences in performance are probably more due to participants' social roles than to any real differences in knowledgeability. Yet, subjects' attributions reflected this fundamental tendency to assign dispositional causes to behavior. People who perform well do so because they are smart, people who perform poorly, regardless of the circumstances, are stupid.

One of the interesting aspects of the Ross et al. study was that both the quizmasters and the contestants made similar attributions about the cause of behaviors in this situation. To this point, we have focused only on the attributions made by observers of another person's behavior. Clearly, an important issue is the process by which we make attributions of *our own behavior*. What happens to the attribution process when self is involved? According to Bem's (1972) self-perception theory, the process in which actors make attributions about their own behavior is the same as the process by which observers make attributions of actors. According to Bem, there are many situations in which we behave a certain way and don't know why (situations where our attitudes are weak, ambiguous, or non-existent). In these situations, we act as observers of our own behavior and attempt to infer the causes of our behavior. Thus, according to Bem, the process of self-attribution is the same as that of observers.

The Actor/Observer Bias

However, research designed to compare the attributions made by actors and observers in the same situation (cf. Jones & Nisbett, 1971) finds differences between the attributions made by actors and observers. In particular, actors tend to attribute their behavior more to situational causes than observers do. We see instances of this actor-observer bias everyday. If we see someone in the cafeteria slip and drop their tray, we immediately perceive this person as a total klutz. However, if the same event happened to you, you make a far different attribution about the cause of that event—perhaps the floor was very slippery or something was on the bottom of your shoe. Thus, it seems clear that we are not as likely to make the fundamental attributional error when we are in the role of the actor as when we are in the role of observer.

Why might we see this discrepancy in the attributions made by actors and observers? One explanation would be that actors in many situations are interested in protecting their self-esteem. Therefore, they give themselves the benefit of the doubt in attributional situations (and make situational attributions for

These observers probably think the actor behaves that way because of her personality (an internal cause). The actor probably thinks she acts that way because of the situation she is in (an external cause).

events) but are not so lenient with others. While such an explanation makes intuitive sense in explaining the actor-observer bias for negative events, it has difficulty explaining why the same trend occurs for positive events. Why would an actor want to make situational explanations for his or her success?

A second explanation is the important source of this effect. This explanation states that the attributions we make in a situation are a function of our focus of attention. Consider the perspective that each person (the actor as opposed to the observer) has in an interaction situation. The actor is looking out at the other people and the situation. Thus, his or her focus of attention is on the environment. On the other hand, the observer is generally focusing on the person who is behaving in the situation. Thus, the observer's focus of attention is on the actor of the behavior. The divergent attributions that actors and observers make in a situation, then, may strictly be a function of their differing perspectives during the interaction situation.

Although this is an interesting explanation, how might we go about testing this notion? One way that one might test this explanation is to force actors to view the situation from the observers' perspective and vice versa. This manipulation was performed in an experiment by Storms (1973), who showed subjects videotapes of an earlier conversation. Some subjects saw a videotape taken from their same perspective (actors and observers saw what they originally had seen), while others were shown a videotape from a new perspective (actors were shown what the observers had seen, and observers were shown what the actors had seen). The results indicated that by shifting people to a new visual perspective, the actor-observer bias could be reversed. Thus, in the new perspective condition, actors made more disposition attributions than observers.

This research has several important implications. The general notion of focus of attention mediating attribution suggests that we will make dispositional attributions to whomever is our focus of attention in any situation (cf. Taylor & Fiske, 1975). However, in most group situations, it is often the person who is the most salient and distinctive (the most novel, the most provocatively dressed, the

	Stable	Unstable
Internal	Ability	Effort
External	Task difficulty	Luck

Figure 5.3
Two by two matrix from Weiner's model.

minority group member) who commands our attention. Research (McArthur & Post, 1977; Taylor & Fiske, 1978; Wolman & Frank, 1975) has shown that any manipulation that makes a particular member of the group salient (e.g., placing him or her at the head of the table, shining a spotlight on that person, minority status) leads to more dispositional attributions about that person and his or her influence on the group.

However, this research also suggests a method to avoid this actor-observer bias: shifting perspectives. In common vernacular, we use the term **empathy** to refer to the ability to take the perspective of another person and "see things from another person's eyes." The more we can empathize with another person, the less likely we will fall prey to the actor-observer bias and (if we are in the role of observers) make unwarranted dispositional attributions about other people. Experiments that have instructed subjects to empathize with different participants in an interaction situation (e.g., Gould & Sigall, 1977) have demonstrated that empathic observers tend to make more situational attributions.

Self-serving Biases in Attribution

The implication of the actor-observer bias is that actors always make situational attributions about their own behavior. Imagine yourself in an achievement situation in which you perform very well. Would you still attribute your success to situational causes? The attributions people make in achievement situations have been the focus of the research of Weiner and his colleagues (e.g., Weiner, Frieze, Kukla, Reed, Rest, and Rosenbaum, 1972). Weiner has borrowed from the earlier writings of Fritz Heider to suggest that attributions made in achievement situations vary along two critical dimensions: locus (internal/external) and stability (stable/unstable). The four corresponding attributions that people can make in achievement situations are ability (an internal stable attribution), effort (internal unstable), task difficulty (external stable), and luck (external unstable). Figure 5.3 illustrates these four possible classes of achievement attributions.

Weiner found that the way we make these types of attributions is to gather information relevant to these two dimensions (Frieze & Weiner, 1971). Thus, if we are trying to decide if a classmate's performance on a test should be attributed to an internal or external cause, we would want to ask for consensus information. How did other people do on the test? If others also did well, we would infer an external cause. If consensus were low, we would attribute the behavior to an internal cause. Attributions concerning the stability dimension require that we gather information concerning this person's (and others') past performance on such tasks. If present performance is consistent with past performance, we make a stable attribution. If present performance is not in line with past performance, we make an unstable attribution.

The Weiner model predicts that the same attributional process should occur for both success and failure. However, from our own everyday experiences, we know that our responses to success and failure are different. When we find that we did well on a test, we give ourselves credit for a fine performance (e.g., "I deserved it because I really knew the material well" or "I studied really hard for this one."). We make internal attributions (to ability or to effort) for our successes. Yet when we fail, to what do we attribute our failure? Do we attribute it to lack of ability or lack of effort? In most circumstances, we attribute our failure to external causes—either the test was too hard (task difficulty) or any number of excuses (bad luck, lack of sleep, illness, or not studying the right things) lead to our failure. This tendency to take credit for success but to externalize failure has been observed in many studies (cf. Miller and Ross, 1975) and has been labeled the **self-serving bias** (or egocentric bias).

Why would we want to engage in this self-serving bias? Certainly, the most apparent explanation for this bias is that it allows us to protect and enhance our self-esteem. We can enhance our self-esteem by taking credit for our successes and protect our self-esteem by externalizing our failures. In this way, we can maintain a positive self-image and a positive view of our abilities. Interestingly, it has been shown that this self-serving bias (although a distortion) is characteristic of mental health. Depressed individuals do not engage in this same self-serving bias (Peterson & Seligman, 1984). The term *depressive realism* (cf. Alloy & Abramson, 1979) was coined to express that depressed people do not show the same biases as normal individuals do. The implication then is that these biases are characteristic of mental health because they allow us to focus on our positive qualities and successes without dwelling on and becoming disillusioned by our failures and shortcomings. In this way, we maintain both a positive self-image and an optimistic view of the future.

Despite these positive benefits of self-serving bias, there are several situations in which it leads to problems. Imagine yourself in a group situation where the group receives a common outcome (for example, a group project). Suppose the group effort is successful and you receive some prize money. How should you split up the prize? Given what we know about the self-serving bias, each member of the group will want to take personal credit for the group's success and will believe that he or she was the deciding factor in the group's success. As a result, each person will feel like he or she is not receiving his or her fair share. This scenario is even more likely in the case of group failure. The self-serving bias tells us that people refuse to take the blame for failure ("It's not my fault"). Thus, if everyone in the group externalizes the failure, no one accepts the blame for failure. Inevitably, either of these situations can lead to interpersonal conflict and dissatisfaction.

Egocentric judgment seems to be operating here.

CATHY, by Cathy Guisewite. © 1987 by Universal Press Syndicate. Reprinted by permission. All Rights Reserved.

An interesting demonstration of this phenomenon was presented by Ross and Sicoly (1979). In one study, individual members of married couples were asked to estimate the extent of their responsibility for a list of twenty family activities (for example, housecleaning, grocery shopping, child care, etc.). The responses of both spouses for each responsibility were summed and compared. Consistently, these summed estimates totaled greater than 100 percent, indicating that each party overestimated his or her own contribution to that responsibility. For example, the husband might have said that he was responsible for the child care 50 percent of the time, while the wife estimated she was responsible for the child care 75 percent of the time (for a total of 125 percent). Thus, our own self-serving bias leads us to overestimate or overattribute our inputs to a group activity, a distortion that could cause problems for domestic tranquility.

Another egocentric bias that has been identified is the **false consensus effect.** We tend to believe that other people share our beliefs, values, and preferences. The initial demonstration of this effect was a study conducted by Ross, Greene, and House (1977). In this study, Ross et al. asked subjects whether they would be willing to walk around campus wearing a large sign which read "Eat at Joe's." As you might expect, some agreed (60 percent) and some refused (40 percent). After making their choice, subjects estimated what proportion of their peers would choose to wear the sign. The results indicated that those who agreed to wear the sign believed that many of their peers (62 percent) would do the same. However, those who refused to wear the sign believed that the majority of their peers (67 percent) would not wear the sign. Each group believed that their peers would act the same way as they did. As a consequence, people basically define behavior

The false consensus bias. These teenagers probably think that most of their peers smoke.

that is not like theirs as deviant and nonnormative, resulting in a greater willingness to draw correspondent (i.e., dispositional) inferences about people who don't act as they do (or would).

This false consensus bias has been observed in many contexts. For instance, adolescents who smoke believe that a greater proportion of their peers also smoke as compared to the estimates made by nonsmoker adolescents (Sherman, Presson, Chassin, Corty, & Olshavsky, 1983). On a more mundane level, people who prefer raw carrots to cooked carrots believe that the greater proportion of Americans also share the same preference (Sherman, Chassin, Presson, & Agostinelli, 1984). It seems a general tendency for people to want to believe that others would feel and act the same way as they do. However, this is a distortion of reality. Not everyone shares our thoughts, actions, and feelings. So, how do we get away with it? One interesting fact is that we tend to associate with people who share our beliefs and preferences. Even more, we tend to selectively expose ourselves only to people who we know will express views we sympathize with. For example, how many staunch Republicans attend Democratic rallies just to hear what the opposition is saying? Because we tend to affiliate with similar others, perhaps our estimates of the proportion of others who share our beliefs are a reflection of our tendency to selectively expose ourselves to similar others. Thus, there may be a grain of truth to the false consensus effect and many of these other seemingly motivational biases.

The Role of Expectations in Attributional Information Search

One of the fundamental notions of Kelley's attribution theory was that we act as "naive scientists" searching for information that will allow us to determine the dimension(s) along which behavior covaries. However, the studies that supported Kelley's theory (e.g., McArthur, 1972; Orvis, Cunningham, & Kelley, 1975) merely presented subjects with information concerning each of the dimensions of Kelley's model and measured the attributions that subjects made. Subjects did not have to seek out this information on their own; rather, it was given to them. Thus, an important issue that needed to be experimentally addressed was the information search process people use to make attributions. Do we really seek out information about all the dimensions along which behavior might vary before making an attribution?

This issue was studied experimentally by Hansen (1980). Hansen argued that perceiver's information search is guided by a principle of cognitive economy (we only do as much cognitive work as we have to). He also argued that for many behaviors, we form naive hypotheses about the most likely cause of that behavior. For example, Hansen gave some people the following behavioral description: "Twelve people work on twelve different puzzles. Some of the people fail to complete the puzzle, and some succeed in completing the puzzle." Other subjects were given a similar description, only the behavior was not puzzle solving, but was laughing at a movie. Hansen measured both subjects' intuitive hypotheses about the cause of these behavioral differences and their preferences for different sources of information. He found that subjects given the puzzle-solving description intuitively believed that differences among people accounted for the differences in ability to solve the puzzles. Subjects given the movie description intuitively believed that differences among the movies (stimulus) accounted for the observed behavioral differences (in laughing). Given these differing hypotheses, he found that subjects' preferences in information search were also affected. Subjects disposed toward person attributions of puzzle solving preferred distinctiveness information (how did these people do on other puzzles?); subjects disposed toward stimulus attributions of laughing preferred consensus information (did other people laugh at this movie?). Thus, Hansen's work indicated that people's information search during the attribution process is typically incomplete and guided by the individual's expectations. As a result, we do not take into account all of the relevant information necessary to make a confident attribution and increase the likelihood of making errors in attribution.

The results of Hansen's research are not particularly surprising. If we performed an exhaustive causal analysis for every behavior we encountered, we would be unable to function in our everyday lives. However, many researchers would argue that we don't even attempt to make any form of attribution for most behaviors we encounter. For instance, imagine we hear that a plane safely landed today. Do we automatically try to find a causal explanation for this plane's safe arrival? Certainly not. However, if we hear that a plane has crashed today, we are eager to learn why that event occurred. Thus, an important issue to consider is the question of when we engage in attributional thinking.

The "When" Question

Recently, Hastie (1984) has reviewed the literature on the types of situations that elicit attributional thinking. He identified four conditions that tend to produce causal (i.e., attributional) reasoning. First, whenever we are explicitly asked the question "Why," we must engage in some form of attributional processing to answer the question. Second, *unexpected events* tend to elicit causal thinking. Our plane example illustrates this point well. When something expected occurs (a safe arrival), we feel no need to explain or understand it. After all, that is what should have happened! However, unexpected events, such as plane crashes, need to be explained. We devote a great deal of time and effort to identifying the cause of such an event. Certainly, in the newspapers, much attention is given to the explanation and conjecture over the causes of unexpected events. Consider how much attention sports writers give to explaining losing streaks by successful teams (see Lau and Russell, 1980).

Most of us would want to know what caused this crash. An uneventful plane flight would not elicit any causal thinking.

A third situation that elicits attributional processing is *outcome dependency*. Outcome dependency is a situation in which you are dependent upon another person for desired outcomes. Outcome dependency is often manipulated by the anticipation of future interaction with another person (see Berscheid, Graziano, Monson, & Dermer, 1976). Obviously, when you interact with a person, you pay close attention to their behavior and try to figure out why they said something or behaved a certain way. When the behavior has direct implications for you, you are motivated to understand the cause(s) of that behavior.

The final situation that leads to attributional thinking is *task failure*. Several studies (Diener & Dweck, 1978; Wong & Weiner, 1981) have demonstrated that when subjects fail at a task, they are more likely to use attributional reasoning to explain the failure than when they succeed. However, failure may simply be another example of an unexpected event (since in most situations, we all expect to succeed). Thus, we might actually be able to assume task failure under the general topic of unexpected events.

Thus, it seems we engage in attributional thinking in only a few of our everyday situations. However, this finding does not in any way downplay its importance to our lives. In situations that are important to us, we use these principles to understand the causes of behavior. However, in most situations, we do not have the motivation and/or the time and energy to perform an exhaustive attributional analysis. What do we do in most situations, then? The next section of this chapter is devoted to the study of **cognitive heuristics,** which are rules of thumb we use to simplify the process of making everyday judgments.

Judgments of Likelihood/ Probability: Cognitive Heuristics

Bigger packages can give us the illusion that we are getting more for our money through a size-quantity heuristic.

It became clear that normative models of judgment (like attribution theory) did not represent the way we make most decisions. As a result, researchers in both social and cognitive psychology began to view humans not as intuitive scientists but as "cognitive misers" (cf. Fiske & Taylor, 1984) whose goal is to simplify the process of making judgments and decisions. As humans, we are limited capacity information processors. Given the tremendous amount of information we are exposed to every day, it is critical that we are very selective in attending to and processing only important matters. However, what do we do about the relatively unimportant or trivial matters that we must deal with every day?

Research in social cognition has found that we tend to rely on simple mental shortcuts or **heuristics** to make a number of judgments and decisions. An example is the price-quality heuristic that what is expensive must therefore be of high quality. The benefit of all heuristics is that they make it easy to make a quick decision. Namely, you should buy the most expensive product, and you will get the best product. After all, you get what you pay for! In most cases, such a strategy is quite reasonable because higher quality products are more expensive. However, there are some instances in which that may not be the case, and blind reliance on the heuristic could lead you to make a poor decision (i.e., wasting your money on an expensive but poor quality product). Hence, in some circumstances, the benefits of the heuristic are outweighed by the costs of the heuristic.

An intriguing example of our blind reliance on heuristics is found in a study by Langer, Blank, and Chanowitz (1978). A researcher asked people waiting in line to use the library copying machine a small request: "May I use the Xerox machine?" However, the form of the request was varied. For some subjects, the person made the request as follows: "Excuse me, I have five pages. May I use the Xerox machine because I'm in a rush?" In this condition, 94 percent of those asked complied with the request. For a second group of subjects, the request took the form, "Excuse me, I have five pages. May I use the Xerox machine?" To no surprise, the compliance rate to this request was only 60 percent, since the person made no effort to justify the request. A third condition was included, which Langer et al. labeled the "placebic reason" condition. Subjects were asked, "Excuse me, I have five pages. May I use the Xerox machine because I have to make some copies?" In this situation, the requester has given no true justification for being allowed to skip in line—why else would the person be in the Xerox line unless they had to "make some copies?" Yet in this condition, the compliance rate was a full 93 percent (as high as in the legitimate reason condition). The authors argued that it appears people's compliance to a request relies not on the legitimacy of the reason provided, but on the *mere fact that a reason* (legitimate or not) *was provided.* It was as if the word *because* signaled to people that it was ok to comply with the request—they gave a reason, so I'll let them go ahead!

Situations like the Langer et al. study are illustrative of the degree to which heuristics can dominate our decision making. Yet, it was not until the seminal work of Daniel Kahneman and Amos Tversky that the study of cognitive heuristics and their effects on judgment achieved prominence. These researchers have identified several pervasive judgmental heuristics and have noted situations in which an overreliance on these heuristics leads to errors of judgment. Our discussion of these heuristics will likewise focus on the errors or biases in judgment associated with each heuristic. It is important to keep in mind throughout this discussion that the goal of this research is not to show how people often fail to make good decisions in many situations, but to identify situations in which people make errors so we can *better understand the processes by which people make judgments* and can ultimately teach people to become better decision makers.

The first heuristic we will discuss is the availability heuristic. According to Tversky and Kahneman (1973), the **availability heuristic** refers to *situations in which people assess the frequency of a class or the probability of an event by the ease with which instances or occurrences (of that event) can be brought to mind.* For example, if you were to use the availability heuristic to judge how likely it is that the Los Angeles Lakers will win an upcoming game against the Sacramento Kings, you would think of the results of past games between these two teams (mostly victories by the Lakers). You would conclude on the basis of this brief search of memory that a Laker victory is very likely. In this way, use of the availability heuristic affords us the opportunity to make quick and accurate judgments and decisions.

The Availability Heuristic

However, there are some problems associated with using the availability heuristic as a basis for judgment. An example will serve to illustrate the nature of these problems:

> In the English language, which is more common—words that begin with the letter *k* or words that have *k* as the third letter?

Tversky and Kahneman (1973) posed this question to their subjects and found that most people believe that *k* is more commonly the first letter. Yet there are more than twice as many English words with *k* as the third letter as there are with *k* as the first letter. Thus, most people make an erroneous judgment to this problem. Why? Tversky and Kahneman argue that this error results from the use of the availability heuristic. For most people, it is easier to think of words starting with *k,* such as king, kangaroo, koala, and kayak, than it is to think of words having *k* in the third position. After all, that is the way the dictionary is set up! As a result, people judge that *k* occurs more frequently as the first letter of a word. Although, with a little more effort one can easily realize that there are many words in which *k* is the third letter, such as make, take, bike, hike, and coke. In this instance, then, the use of the availability heuristic leads one to make an error in judgment.

What determines whether or not availability is a good criterion for judgment? To adequately answer this question, it is important to consider exactly what the heuristic is saying. The availability heuristic states that something that is highly accessible (easily brought to mind) is therefore judged to be very frequent (or highly likely to occur). This logic is incorrect. Although it is true that things that are more frequent are typically more accessible in memory, it is not always the case that high accessibility implies high frequency. Events that are very salient, distinctive, or vivid—events that may not be (and often are not) very frequent—are also easily brought to mind and are highly accessible. Thus, overreliance on the availability heuristic leads us to erroneously judge the frequency of salient, distinctive, or vivid events as very high, even though they may be quite rare (Nisbett & Ross, 1980).

The implications of these errors in judgment associated with the use of the availability heuristic extend far beyond judgments about the frequency of words. (See table 5.5.) Some researchers have observed that people's estimates of the likelihood of various causes of death were best predicted not by their actual frequency, but by the amount of media attention given to those causes (Lichtenstein, Slovic, Fischhoff, Layman, & Combs, 1978). Subjects judged the frequency of death due to accidents, for instance, as more likely than death by stroke, even though strokes cause 85 percent more deaths per year than accidents. This error is quite understandable when one thinks of the disproportionate amount of media coverage reporting fatal accidents (television and newspaper accounts of automobile fatalities, plane crashes, train derailments, etc.) than to reporting deaths due to strokes. In this way, when one thinks about various causes of death, those causes of death that receive the most media attention will be most accessible in memory and (due to the operation of the availability heuristic) are judged as very likely. These results raise some important issues concerning the power of television and other media to affect our perceptions of the world (and our subsequent judgments based upon those perceptions).

Many of the phenomena we have discussed earlier in this chapter can be understood in terms of the availability heuristic. Priming procedures, for instance, make certain structures in memory more accessible and affect subsequent judgments. Many of the self-serving biases that we discussed earlier have been interpreted in terms of the availability heuristic. The false consensus effect, for instance, can be understood as the result of our tendency to make estimates of likelihood on the basis of the most accessible information. When asked to estimate the percentage of others that believe in abortion, we typically search through our memory and sample the opinions on abortion of all those people we can remember. Obviously, the opinions of those people who we know the best will come to mind most easily (are highly accessible) and will strongly influence our estimate. However, it is important to remember a point that we made earlier—that

Table 5.5 Bias in Judged Frequency of Death	
Most overestimated	**Most underestimated**
All accidents	Smallpox vaccination
Motor vehicle accidents	Diabetes
Pregnancy, childbirth, and abortion	Stomach cancer
Tornadoes	Lightning
Flood	Stroke
Botulism	Tuberculosis
All cancer	Asthma
Fire and flames	Emphysema
Venomous bite or sting	
Homicide	

Overestimated causes of death are dramatic, sensational, and get much newspaper coverage; underestimated causes are unsensational, claim one victim at a time, and are commonly nonfatal conditions. The overestimated causes are simply more available to the rater.

Source: Slovic, Fischhoff, & Lichtenstein (1979).

From Paul Slovic, Baruch Fischoff, and Sarah Lichtenstein, "Facts versus Fears: Understanding Perceived Risk" in *Judgment Under Uncertainty: Heuristics and Biases,* edited by D. Kahneman, P. Slovic, and A. Tversky (New York: Cambridge University Press, 1982) and *Societal Risk Assessment: How Safe is Safe Enough?,* edited by R. Schwing and W. A. Albers (1980) Copyright 1980 by Plenum Press.

most of our friends share our beliefs and opinions. Thus, this process results in most people estimating that the majority of others share their attitudes, beliefs, and opinions. Such an explanation argues that the false consensus effect is not a motivated bias designed to enhance one's self-esteem, but merely the result of relying on the availability heuristic in making these estimates.

A similar argument has been made for the egocentric bias (cf. Ross & Sicoly, 1979). The reason why we may overestimate our contributions to a marriage or team effort may be because our contributions are more accessible to us. We often don't notice all the times someone else does things for us; thus, their contributions are not as accessible.

Perhaps the most relevant illustration of availability biases is in the context of hypothesis-testing. An abundance of evidence has shown that people tend to adopt a confirmatory bias in hypothesis-testing (see Snyder & Swann, 1978; Mynatt, Doherty, & Tweney, 1978). It seems that when we have an hypothesis about what a person is like, we tend to look only for information that might confirm that hypothesis. Snyder and Swann (1978) gave subjects the hypothesis that a person was either an introvert or an extravert and then asked subjects to choose questions they would ask the person to test the validity of their hypothesis. Their findings illustrated that people try to confirm their initial hypothesis. Subjects who had the hypothesis that the person was an introvert chose such questions as "What makes you uncomfortable at parties?" Such a question assumes that the person is uncomfortable at parties; thus, almost any way one answers it, one will appear to be an introvert. Likewise, subjects with the extravert hypothesis chose such questions as "What would you do to liven up a party?" Again, any answer to this question would make one appear to have extraverted qualities. It is no surprise that Snyder and Swann found that subjects, after they had asked their questions, found confirmation for their initial hypothesis.

Hypothesis-Testing

In an interview, the interviewer tests his or her hypotheses about the other person.

There are many dangers associated with such a confirmatory bias. First, it does not allow for the possibility of hypothesis disconfirmation. An effective strategy to test hypotheses which never seems to be used is to seek out disconfirming information (see Sherman & Corty, 1984). In order to find whether a person is an introvert, for instance, why not ask whether the person ever goes to wild parties or ever enjoys talking to people that he or she doesn't know? Answers to these types of questions permits individuals to express either confirming or disconfirming responses (i.e., they could say that they do enjoy talking to new people and going to wild parties, evidence that would disconfirm the hypothesis that the person is an introvert). It can also more appropriately test the validity of their hypotheses.

Even more problematic is the fact that many times when people are presented with hypothesis-disconfirming information, they fail to use it (see Einhorn & Hogarth, 1978). As a result, people tend to hold onto false hypotheses, resulting in phenomena of illusory correlation and stereotype maintenance. In addition, it provides us with a false belief that our hypotheses are always correct, further solidifying the bias. Thus, the availability heuristic is used as a basis for judging the quality of our own judgments and decisions, allowing us to confirm our belief that we are good, effective decision makers.

The Representativeness Heuristic

Consider the following description:

> Jack is a 45-year-old man. He is married and has four children. He is generally conservative, careful, and ambitious. He shows no interest in political and social issues and spends most of his free time on his many hobbies which include home carpentry, sailing, and mathematical puzzles.

Given this description, what would you say is more likely to be Jack's occupation, lawyer or engineer? Kahneman and Tversky (1972) gave this problem to their subjects and found that an overwhelming majority of them thought that Jack must be an engineer. Yet, on what basis had subjects drawn this conclusion? Kahneman and Tversky argue that subjects match this description of Jack to their stereotype of the typical lawyer or the typical engineer. Since this description of Jack matches more closely our ideas of the typical engineer (e.g., conservative, mathematical), we judge that Jack is most likely an engineer.

Such a judgment reflects the operation of a second heuristic principle, namely the representativeness heuristic. According to Kahneman and Tversky (1972), the **representativeness heuristic** states that *an object is judged as probable and is categorized by the extent to which it represents the essential features of the typical member of that category.* Thus, the representativeness heuristic argues that we make judgments on the basis of overall similarity between an instance (our man Jack) and the prototype of the category (our stereotype of the typical engineer). If the match is good between the instance and the category prototype, then we categorize the object as a member of that category.

As with all of the heuristics we will discuss, this rule of thumb is a reasonable one in most instances. However, the heuristic does lead to some characteristic errors in judgment. One of the most notable errors of judgment associated with the use of the representativeness heuristic has been the fact that people tend to overrely on descriptive information and ignore relevant statistical information when making judgments. This error was dramatically demonstrated by Kahneman and Tversky (1972) using the Jack description mentioned previously. For one group of subjects, the description of Jack was prefaced with the following information:

A panel of psychologists have interviewed and administered personality tests of 30 engineers and 70 lawyers, all successful in their respective fields. On the basis of this information, thumbnail descriptions of the 30 engineers and 70 lawyers have been written. You will find one of these descriptions below, chosen at random from the 100 available descriptions. Please indicate the probability that the person described is an engineer, on a scale of 0 to 100%.

Another group of subjects received the same description, with one modification: The sample population was composed of 70 engineers and 30 lawyers. All subjects were then shown the description of Jack. Obviously, the likelihood that Jack is an engineer when the sample population (or what we refer to as the *base rate*) is 70 percent engineers is much greater than when the base rate is 30 percent engineers. Yet, Kahneman and Tversky found that the estimates subjects made were virtually identical in the two conditions (Jack is likely to be an engineer). Subjects ignored the base rate information and based their estimates entirely on the descriptive information about Jack. This result has been replicated with different problems, descriptions, and base rates, indicating a pervasive bias (known as the **base rate fallacy**) resulting from the use of the representativeness heuristic.

The base rate fallacy is reflected in many everyday decisions. Nisbett and Ross (1980) talk about a situation in which a student is deciding what course he or she should take. One source of information relevant to that decision is the course evaluation book, which lists the mean responses of students who took that particular course. This information is analogous to the base rate information in the previous problem. For this example, imagine that the course evaluation is favorable for the course you are considering. Another source of information is descriptive information from a student (or students) who took the course. Suppose you talk to a friend or acquaintance who took that course and ask them what they thought about the course, and they give you a bad review. They said the course was dull, stupid, and boring. Would you take the course? Subjects presented with this and similar situations tended to value the descriptive information (one person's opinion) more strongly than the base rate information (the consensus opinion of the class), again illustrating an insensitivity to base rates.

Suppose you flipped a coin six times. Which would be the most likely sequence of outcomes? (H = heads; T = tails)

    (a) HTHTHT
    (b) HTTHHT
    (c) HHHHHH
    (d) All of the above sequences are equally likely.

In fact, the correct answer to this problem is (d). However, most people would choose either (a) or (b) as the correct answer. Why? If you ask most people, they would say that (a) or (b) are more representative of a random sequence. When given a problem like the one shown, one way to judge the likelihood of the various random sequences is to match them to our intuitive notions about random events (like coin tosses). We all know that on the average we should see about 50 percent heads and 50 percent tails. However, this information does not imply that on any six throws of the coin we will necessarily see 3 heads and 3 tails. There will be considerable variability between the outcomes we will observe on any six throws. In fact, if you threw a coin 1,000 times, you would see many sequences or "runs" of heads (such as option (c) above) or tails. Similarly, if you charted the performance of a star baseball hitter over the course of the season, you would see many streaks of 0 for 15 as well as streaks of 12 for 15. However, the problem associated with the use of the representativeness heuristic is that it leads us to expect every random sequence will look "random." Thus, we tend to expect things to even out in the short run as well as in the long run. Kahneman and Tversky have labeled this effect *"belief in the law of small numbers"* (Tversky & Kahneman, 1971) and have identified several biases associated with this effect.

The Gambler's Fallacy   As a result of this misperception of randomness, one effect that we see is the so-called gambler's fallacy. The **gambler's fallacy** refers to the fact that gamblers will persist in their belief that their luck will turn around, that they are "due." As a result, you see that gamblers will maintain their behavior and continue to play despite losing incredible amounts of money because they believe their luck will change. While it is true that a streak of bad luck will not last forever and that *in the long run* the odds will even out for the gambler, the fallacy involved here deals with the fact that we think that things will even out *in the short run*. Any of you who are card players know that some nights you are hot and are getting good cards, and other nights you can't buy a good hand. Such streaks may last days, weeks, even months. Yet, the gambler's fallacy tells us we should just play one more hand; we're just getting warmed up; and the tides are turning in our favor.

    Announcers often exemplify this fallacy in their play-by-play of games. A hitter with a .330 average who is 0 for 3 in the game is "due" for a hit. A hitter with 25 home runs who hasn't hit one in a month is "due" for a home run. The fact is that each event is independent; thus, a coin doesn't think to itself, "Gee, I've come up heads six times in a row now; I'd better come up tails this time to even things out." Each coin toss has a .5 probability of coming up heads, whether

The gambler's fallacy. Expecting their luck to turn keeps these gamblers playing.

a given toss has been preceded by 10 heads in a row or 10 tails in a row. Yet the representativeness heuristic leads us to believe that streaks don't occur very often and cannot last, resulting in the gambler's fallacy.

Regression Effects   A second interesting effect associated with this misperception of randomness is an insensitivity to regression effects. *Regression to the mean* is a phenomenon that states that if someone obtains an extreme score at Time 1, their score at Time 2 will most likely be less extreme and closer to their mean level of performance. Thus, someone who has a 150 average in bowling that scores a 250 in a game will most likely not do as well the next time. Likewise, this same bowler who scores a 75 will most likely score higher the next time.

You may say that this effect seems contradictory to the gambler's fallacy. However, both of these effects can be satisfied simultaneously. The gambler's fallacy would predict that following an extreme score, one would see an extreme score in the opposite direction to bring the overall average back to normal. All that regression predicts is that an extreme score will be followed by a less extreme score. Thus, a 150 bowler who gets a 75 might get a second poor score the next game, but not one so extreme (a 100 game).

An interesting problem associated with insensitivity to regression occurs when we consider the way in which we allocate rewards and punishments (cf. Kahneman & Tversky, 1973; Schaffner, 1985). We typically allocate rewards after very good performances and allocate punishments after very poor performances. However, due to regression effects, we know that very good performances are most likely followed by poorer performances and very poor performances are followed by better performances. Thus, by regression effects alone, it will appear that rewards don't work and that punishment is effective.

Regression to the means dictated that Orel Hershiser could not repeat his Cy Young year of 1988.

Consider a scenario with a child who does exceptionally well on a test in school. You are so pleased that you reward the child. The next time, the child doesn't perform as well (due to regression to the mean). You think to yourself that it was a mistake to reward the child, that he or she didn't work as hard or became lazy. Likewise, you might punish a child after a very poor performance. The next time, the child would perform better (due to regression). Here, you would believe that the punishment was effective, it got the child working harder and taking school more seriously. Thus, an insensitivity to regression can have some dangerous consequences to the attributions we make about our own and others' performance.

The Anchoring and Adjustment Heuristic

A third heuristic that has been identified by Kahneman and Tversky is the **anchoring and adjustment heuristic.** Basically, this heuristic states that *people make estimates by beginning with a starting value (or anchor point) and adjusting this value until a final judgment is made.* In most sequential judgment tasks, this strategy is quite reasonable and will lead to accurate judgments. However, the error associated with this heuristic is that people typically rely too heavily on their initial anchor point and do not adjust sufficiently for subsequently received or considered information.

An initial demonstration of the operation of this heuristic is found in the following example. Subjects in this experiment were asked to judge the percentage of African countries in the United Nations. A number between 0 and 100 was determined by spinning a wheel. Subjects' task was to indicate first whether that number was higher or lower than the actual percentage, and to estimate the correct percentage by moving upward or downward from the given number. Their results indicated that subjects did not adjust sufficiently from the initial anchor point. Subjects who randomly received the number 10 as a starting point made an average final estimate of 25 percent. Subjects receiving the number 65 as a starting point made an average final estimate of 45 percent. Moreover, payoffs for accuracy did not reduce the anchoring effect. Thus, even with a randomly assigned initial anchor, subjects illustrated an overreliance on this anchor in making judgments.

This effect has many important implications. One of the most robust findings in the literature on impression formation is a primacy effect (see chapter 4), such that people form strong initial impressions of others that hold up despite subsequent information to the contrary. A second application of the anchoring and adjustment heuristic lies in the way we deal with conjunctive events. *Conjunctive events* refer to compound events that are composed of two or more unitary events (for example, Linda is a bank teller *and* is active in the feminist movement). One of the basic laws of probability is that the probability of a conjunctive event must be smaller than the probability of either of the unitary events. In fact, in computing the probability of a conjunctive event, we multiply the probabilities of each of the component events:

$$p \text{ (event A } \textbf{and} \text{ event B)} = p \text{ (event A)} \times p \text{ (event B)}$$

However, what we see is that people are very poor at judging the probability of compound events. An illustration of our problem in judging conjunctive events is found in many popular football pools. In many pools, participants choose the winners of five games from a list of games. If the person chooses all five games correctly, he or she wins the pool. Obviously, the best strategy is to choose games in which there are clear mismatches (with the highest probability of success). In these pools, there are games that appear to be mismatches, leading people to believe that their chances of winning the pool are good. However, even if someone could choose five games in which the probability of success was .7, the likelihood of *all five of those events occurring simultaneously* is .7 $\times$ .7 $\times$ .7 $\times$ .7 $\times$ .7 = .168. Because we tend to anchor on the high probability (.7) of each component event, we tend to overestimate the likelihood of conjunctive events. We do not adjust sufficiently for the fact that the probabilities are multiplied and diminish rapidly in value.

A similar bias exists in our estimation of the probability of disjunctive events. *Disjunctive events* refer to compound events that are satisfied if any one of the component events is satisfied (for example, Linda is a bank teller *or* is active in the feminist movement). In this case, we compute the probability of a disjunctive event by adding the probabilities of each of the component events:

$$p \text{ (event A \textbf{or} event B)} = p \text{ (event A)} + p \text{ (event B)}$$

Due to the anchoring and adjustment heuristic, people typically underestimate the probability of disjunctive events. One important implication of such an error is a false sense of security regarding the safety of nuclear power. While the probability of any one event going wrong is minuscule (perhaps 1 in 10,000), there are so many different ways that things could go wrong that these probabilities summate into a no longer negligible probability. Yet, people anchor on the probability of any component event and underestimate the likelihood of a nuclear mishap.

The Simulation Heuristic

The final heuristic that we will consider is the simulation heuristic (Kahneman & Tversky, 1982). The **simulation heuristic** states that the manner in which we judge the probability or likelihood of an event is like the process of running a simulation model. That is, we judge the likelihood of an event or outcome *by the ease or difficulty with which we can mentally construct scenarios that would produce that event (or result in that outcome)*. An event or outcome that is easy to imagine is judged to be highly likely; an event that is difficult to imagine is judged of low probability.

On first consideration, the simulation heuristic seems similar to the availability heuristic (see Sherman & Corty, 1984). Many people would argue that they are really one heuristic. However, there is an important distinction between them. Availability refers to the ease with which specific instances (already stored in memory) can be recalled. Simulation involves the active construction of scenarios for an event. Because recall and construction are distinct methods of bringing things to mind, they involve different processes and deserve to be treated independently.

Many phenomena are associated with the simulation heuristic. One of the most intriguing is Kahneman and Tversky's (1982) work on counterfactualizing. **Counterfactualizing** refers to the process of imagining how things could have been otherwise, how a different or alternative outcome might have occurred. Consider the following example:

> Mr. Crane and Mr. Tees were scheduled to leave the airport at the same time on different flights. They traveled from town in the same limousine, were caught in a traffic jam, and arrived at the airport 30 minutes after the scheduled departure time of their flights.
> Mr. Crane is told that his flight left on time.
> Mr. Tees is told that his flight was delayed, and just left five minutes ago.
> Who is more upset?

To no surprise, 96 percent of those sampled argued that Mr. Tees would be more upset. Why? The outcomes for both men were the same—both men missed their flights. The interesting point is that Mr. Tees could imagine or simulate many more ways he could have made his plane (and made up five minutes) than Mr. Crane could (in making up thirty minutes). The ease with which we can counterfactualize negative outcomes makes it especially difficult to cope with them effectively. Imagine the guilt experienced by a parent with a child who dies of an undiagnosed illness. It would be very easy to imagine how things could have been otherwise, and how this situation might have been prevented.

A related effect is the **hindsight bias** (Fischhoff & Beyth, 1975). Very often, when we know the outcome of an event, we believe that we "knew it all along." That is, when we judge the probability that we would have correctly predicted an outcome (knowing the true outcome), we tend to overestimate the probability that we would have predicted the correct outcome and find it hard to imagine how we could have predicted anything else. Anyone who has played the game of Trivial Pursuit knows that the other team always seems to get the easy questions, while your team seems to get an inordinate number of difficult questions. This observation exemplifies the simulation heuristic. In foresight, things are much more uncertain and there are several plausible alternative outcomes, making the prediction task a difficult one.

Our insensitivity to the hindsight bias results in a harsh response to people who have bad things happen to them. Armed with the right answer, we think people who miss those "easy" Trivial Pursuit questions are so stupid. Moreover, a consistent finding with regard to our response to victims of tragic circumstances is that we derogate victims and see them as deserving the negative events that befall them. By looking at others' decisions in hindsight, we believe that everything is predictable, that people should have known it ahead of time. According to the hindsight bias, bad outcomes result from bad decisions, and good outcomes result from good decisions. Thus, if something bad befalls someone (for example, she is the victim of abuse like Hedda Nussbaum or a governor like Michael Dukakis sets up a parole system which releases an inmate who then rapes again), we say that they should have known and should not have made that decision. The truth that sometimes good decisions don't work out is never realized due to our reliance on the simulation heuristic in the hindsight bias.

The hindsight bias. In Trivial Pursuit, the other team's questions seem easy because we see the answer and assume that we "knew it all along."

Another example of the operation of the simulation heuristic is illustrated in the **perseverance effect** (Ross, Lepper, & Hubbard, 1975), which is our tendency to stick to a belief which has been disconfirmed. In the landmark study of this effect, subjects performed the unusual task of distinguishing real from fictitious suicide notes. Subjects were then given false feedback concerning their performance. Afterward, subjects were told that the feedback was in fact bogus and in no way reflected their true level of performance. Then, subjects received the dependent measures, in which they were asked to predict their true level of performance at this task. The results indicated that subjects persevered in their belief in the accuracy of the feedback. Subjects who were falsely told that they had succeeded thought that they would do quite well, and subjects who were told that they failed persevered in their belief that they would do poorly. This effect has been found to be remarkably robust (Jennings, Lepper, & Ross, 1980; Lepper, Ross, & Lau, 1979), even in situations in which subjects clearly articulate their belief that the original feedback was false.

We sometimes belittle victims because, with the benefit of hindsight, we know they chose a bad course of action.

The effect seems to result from our simulations in response to the false feedback. Subjects construct an evidentiary base that justifies the feedback (for example, "I am a socially sensitive person who people come to with their problems, thus it makes sense that I would do well at this task"). When the debriefing discredits the original feedback, subjects still have stored in their memory these cognitions which suggest that they might succeed (or fail) at such a task. Thus, when asked to predict their true level of performance, subjects persevere in their beliefs because they already have the evidentiary basis to support and justify such a prediction. What subjects don't realize is that it would be easy for them to simulate how their performance at the task might have been otherwise, but we just don't seem to consider those alternative scenarios.

This observation brings up an important point regarding the use of the simulation heuristic. A common finding in the literature is that subjects who are asked to hypothetically imagine or explain a certain outcome (a win by a particular football team, or success at a task) tend to inflate their estimates of the likelihood of that future outcome (Ross, Lepper, Strack, & Steinmetz, 1977; Sherman, Skov, Hervitz, & Stock, 1981; Sherman, Zehner, Johnson, & Hirt, 1983). Thus, it seems that once a person creates one plausible scenario for an event, they stop the process. They fail to consider or construct alternative scenarios for the event (cf. Shaklee & Fischhoff, 1982). This use of a satisficing (rather than an optimizing) strategy produces these biases associated with the simulation heuristic and affects not only our likelihood judgments and predictions for future events but also our reconstructions of past events.

Reconstructing
the Past: Fact
or Fabrication?

In much of psychology, we rely on people's self-reports of their past feelings, attitudes, and behaviors. However, the question has been raised concerning just how accurate these memories of the past really are. Research in social cognition has shown that people's memory for information is often distorted by the particular schema used to encode and/or retrieve the information. For instance, in an experiment by Snyder and Uranowitz (1978), subjects read a story about a woman named Betty K. Before they were asked to recall the story information, subjects were told that Betty K was currently living either a heterosexual or lesbian lifestyle. Subjects' recall for the story was greatly affected by this information; that is, subjects found it difficult not to misrecall facts in Betty K's life to make them consistent with her current lifestyle. For example, when told that Betty K was a lesbian, subjects misrecalled that Betty K didn't date much and had trouble relating with her father and other male figures in her life.

As one can see from this example, it seems our present state of knowledge affects our recall of the past. Recently, Ross and Conway (1985) have argued that the primary method by which people attempt to recall past events, such as past behavior and past attitudes, involves two major steps. First, the person notes his or her present state (i.e., one's present attitude or behavior). Secondly, the person attempts to decide whether the past was different from the present. If a person holds an intuitive theory of stability (attitudes are stable over time), that person would infer their past attitude to be the same as their present attitude. Alternatively, a person holding an intuitive theory of change (wisdom increases but strength decreases over the lifespan) would say they were strong but foolish in the past (and are weak and wise now).

Ross and Conway (1985) have cited evidence from a number of studies that support this model of reconstruction. For instance, a number of studies (Bem & McConnell, 1970; Goethals & Reckman, 1973) have found that following attitude change, people incorrectly infer their past attitudes to be the same as their present attitudes. This reflects an intuitive theory that attitudes are stable over time. Thus, in recalling my past attitude toward capital punishment, I bring to mind my present attitude and can directly infer that I felt that same way in the past. In addition, Ross and his colleagues (Ross, McFarland, & Fletcher, 1981) have shown that recall of past behaviors can be similarly distorted. In this research, Ross et al. changed subjects' attitudes toward toothbrushing and found that subjects' recall of the frequency with which they had brushed their teeth over the past few weeks was significantly affected by their present (and newly changed) attitude. Those persuaded that toothbrushing was bad (e.g., scrapes the enamel off your teeth) recalled having brushed less frequently than those persuaded that toothbrushing was healthy.

Similarly, support for the model has been shown when people presumably hold intuitive theories of change. Conway and Ross (1984) found that subjects who had enrolled in a study skills improvement course actually did not improve relative to a control group. However, their recall of their past level of performance differed significantly. Subjects who had taken the study skills course recalled their past performance as much worse than it was so that it appeared they had improved. The present could not be changed, but subjects' recall of the past supported their intuitive theory of improvement.

As one can see, this process of reconstruction is totally theory-driven and does not involve any actual retrieval of past information. Instead, the past is inferred directly from the present. As a result, these results suggest we should only observe theory-consistent recall of the past. However, our question still needs to be answered. When will our recall of the past be accurate? According to this model, only in those cases in which our theory matches reality will our recall of the past be accurate.

Although many researchers would agree that such a "retrieval" process may occur, this process cannot explain all of the results we have. In a recent review, Alba and Hasher (1983) cited a number of studies in which people's recall of past information (for example, the details of past stories, conversations, TV shows) was quite accurate. Thus, some researchers (Hirt, 1987) have argued that Ross and Conway's theory-driven model of reconstruction is only one of many strategies one could use in retrieving past information.

In many situations, we do try to retrieve information from our memory (engaging in what we call data-driven processing). However, even if we engage in data-driven processing, it is often difficult not to allow our intuitive theories to guide our retrieval (as often occurs in hypothesis testing). Hirt (1987) has shown that even when people try to reaccess information from the past, their intuitive theories of stability or change influence and bias their recall.

How then might people avoid the biasing effects of intuitive theories? Hirt (1987) found that the best strategy for improving accuracy was to give people both accuracy incentives plus an alternative retrieval strategy. For instance, by giving people context reinstatement instructions (for example, try to put yourself back in the context in which you first received the information) as an alternative strategy, subjects were better able to ignore their intuitive theory and accurately retrieve the past information. However, for the alternative retrieval strategy to be effective, subjects have to be sufficiently motivated (via incentives) to use it.

This research has raised the issue of the interplay between cognitive and motivational factors in the recall of information. Under some conditions, we may not be motivated to be accurate—either because it is of little importance to us or because we would prefer to distort reality for our self-enhancement, such as believing that I used to be a good athlete or used to be very attractive. In such cases, a theory-driven mode of reconstructing the past may best serve these motives. It is quick, expends little effort, and can lead to the "recall" of the past that we want. Under other conditions, we may want or need to be accurate and have at our disposal other strategies that involve more data-driven, effortful processing. To the extent that we can ignore our theories in retrieval, such strategies may lead to accurate retrieval of the past. Thus, it seems clear that we have a number of retrieval strategies available to us.

Evaluating the Use of Heuristics

Given all this evidence which shows that the use of heuristics leads to characteristic biases and errors in judgment, it is important to ask why they persist. How is it that we can make it through life if we are such poor decision makers? One thing that we must keep in mind in answering this question is that these heuristics are generally good rules of thumb. Things that come to mind quite easily are usually more frequent, and most members of a category are similar to the prototypic member of that category. Moreover, when we consider the benefits of using heuristics as a basis for judgment (i.e., the speed and simplicity with which we can make decisions), the benefits may far outweigh the costs (any errors or biases in judgment). From a pragmatic point of view, we are information processors with a limited capacity. Given the volume of information that we must deal with each day, it is crucial that we utilize simplifying rules (like heuristics) to simplify our decision making with minimal costs.

A more dangerous problem with the use (and overuse) of heuristics is that very often we are not confronted with our errors in judgment. In many situations, (for example, a person perception situation), we might make an error in judging whether a person is nice or not. As a result, we do not pursue our relationship with this person any further. In this case, we will never know whether we made an error or not—we cannot see what might have been. Thus, for many errors in judgment, we never see the error.

Moreover, Sherman (1980) has demonstrated that subjects' errors in judgment can be self-erasing. In his study, some subjects were telephoned and asked to collect money for the American Cancer Society. Other subjects were asked merely to predict whether they would be willing to collect money for the charity. Forty-eight percent of the subjects *predicted* that they would be willing to perform this service, but only four percent of the subjects directly asked to collect the money actually complied. Hence, people tend to overestimate how much they would be willing to engage in socially desirable behavior.

However, in a second part of the study, subjects who had made predictions about their behavior were recontacted and asked to collect money for the American Cancer Society. The results indicated that 93 percent of those subjects who predicted that they would collect money actually volunteered to do so. Hence, even though subjects' original predictions were biased in a socially desirable direction, they subsequently behaved in a manner that confirmed their erroneous predictions. In this way, errors of prediction can be "self-erasing."

The volume of information we face each day leads us to use simplifying heuristics.

However, this is not to say that we never see mistakes and errors that we make. Despite the fact that we rarely (if ever) look for such information, inevitably we will sometimes learn of our mistakes. Interestingly, in such situations, we find that people still maintain the belief that they are good decision makers. In one study, Lord, Ross, and Lepper (1979) gave subjects who were initially pro (or anti) capital punishment a mixed set of evidence to evaluate. One would expect people to moderate their position in lieu of both positive and negative evidence. Instead, subjects' attitudes became more polarized in favor of their original position. Subjects took at face value the evidence favoring their position and criticized the evidence to the contrary. As a result of this process of *biased assimilation,* people can maintain their strong beliefs despite considerable contradictory evidence.

Hence, there seem to be many converging reasons why heuristics persist. By and large, they are accurate. Errors in judgment are rarely brought to our attention because the same heuristic principles that are used as a basis for judgment are used for judging the quality of our judgments. Even when errors in judgment are noted, processes of selective retrieval and biased assimilation can maintain (and even bolster) our belief in the quality of our judgments.

Research in social cognition has shown us how we try to understand ourselves, others, and the world around us. How we think about people and events affects our feelings, attitudes, and behaviors. In chapter 3, we discussed how we use attribution principles in evaluating ourselves. We use attributions to evaluate our performances and to understand how others are reacting to us. We sometimes use self-handicaps to avoid making undesirable self-attributions. If we attribute our engaging in activities to external causes (rewards), that attribution will undermine our intrinsic motivation for those activities. Misattribution therapy and self-discrepancy theory point to ways that social cognitions are related to mental health and how they may be changed.

Applications of Social Cognition Research

In chapter 4, we saw that the ways that people process information affect the impressions they form of others. Our schemas and expectations affect our impressions of others. The impressions we form influence how we behave toward others and can even affect their behavior through the self-fulfilling prophecy. In this chapter and chapter 4, we showed that jurors have to form impressions of others and make causal inferences about their behavior in making decisions. All of these previously discussed ideas are examples of how social cognition principles are applied.

The field of social cognition has begun to emphasize the applicability of its findings to contemporary issues within social psychology, such as stereotyping, as well as other areas within psychology, such as health behavior. Priming research suggests that our attitudes are affected by salient, vivid, repeated presentations. The judgments we make—whether rational or biased—affect our attitudes, motives, and behavior. Therefore, we need to know how we and others think to comprehend and cope with everyday events.

Summary

Social cognition involves the study of the psychological mechanisms that underlie human judgment and decision making. In this chapter, we focus on (1) social judgments, how we evaluate other people; (2) causal judgments, how we infer the causes of events and behaviors; and (3) probability judgments, how we estimate the likelihood of events and use them in making decisions.

Social judgments are constantly being made and they affect whether we like or dislike others. Preconceptions and stereotypes that are stored in memory guide our perceptions of others. Priming, systematically exposing people to judgment-relevant information, affects the ideas we have in memory and, consequently, our judgments of others. Stereotypes, schemas about characteristics of groups of people, are formed through illusory correlation between distinctive events and people, and affect our expectations about members of groups. Stereotype-consistent information receives much attention, whereas stereotype-inconsistent information is ignored. Consequently, stereotypes tend to persist in memory even when contradictory evidence is available.

Attribution theories specify how most people decide why particular events occurred or why certain people acted the way they did. In making causal judgments, the common focus is on individuals' deciding whether an event or behavior was caused by internal or external factors. Heider (1958) and Jones and Davis (1965) have examined how people make finer judgments about internal causes and Kelley (1967) has elaborated on the finer details of external causation. Jones and Davis examined how people infer specific dispositions and intentions from particular acts by comparing a person's chosen course of action with other options not exercised and with how other people would have behaved. Kelley has divided possible external causes into specific stimuli and more general circumstances in his model.

Several biases are associated with the attribution process. The fundamental attribution error refers to our tendency to overestimate dispositional causes and underestimate situational causes of behavior. Observers of behaviors display this bias by inferring that an actor's behavior had an internal cause (a personality trait, for instance). On the other hand, actors are likely to infer that their own behavior had a situational or external cause. These phenomena are known as the actor-observer bias. Self-serving biases, which usually involve the individual taking credit for success and ducking the blame for failure, have also been noted and studied. Moreover, it was noted that we are likely to make causal judgments only when (1) we are asked to, (2) unexpected events occur, (3) our outcomes are dependent on the person we are trying to understand, or (4) when we have failed.

Because we are bombarded with much information and we have limited capacity to handle it, we resort to cognitive shortcuts or heuristics. These judgmental strategies or heuristics enable us to make accurate judgments and decisions most of the time, but sometimes they lead to fallacious thinking. We may overestimate the probability of an event because of the ease with which it can be brought to mind (availability bias) or because this event seems typical of a class of events (representativeness bias). The gambler's fallacy, inaccurate perceptions of randomness, and nonregressive thinking are examples of the representativeness bias. The anchoring and adjustment bias occurs when a person relies too heavily on an initial judgment and does not adjust adequately for information received later. The simulation heuristic suggests that we often judge the likelihood of an event or outcome by mentally constructing scenarios by which the event or outcome could occur. If we can easily construct such scenarios, we overestimate the probability of the event or outcome. Hindsight bias, the perseverance effect, and inaccurate recollections of the past are products of the simulation heuristic.

The judgments a person makes have many implications. They can affect one's sense of self, intrinsic motivation, and mental well-being. Attributions made about others affect who you like and dislike, who you help, and who you aggress against. Thus, the study of principles of social cognition has important implications for understanding everyday events.

Attitudes

We all have attitudes. **Attitudes** are how we feel about the particular things, people, groups, events, and issues in our world. They are *evaluative judgments*—positive, negative, or neutral—about objects of thought (McGuire, 1985). Some of our attitudes are intensely felt; others may have very little meaning to us. Some people feel strongly about abortion, AIDS, capital punishment, communism, freedom of speech, nuclear war, and drug use. Other people couldn't care less about those objects of thought, but they may feel strongly about other topics. Strong *conviction* is issue specific; that is, if a person has intense attitudes about one topic, that person probably feels less fanatical about other topics (Abelson, 1988). In most cases, we feel strongly about matters that affect us and people like us most directly (Sivacek & Crano, 1982).

The Organization of Attitudes

What Constitutes an Attitude?

Some social psychologists believe that attitudes are constructed from beliefs and values (e.g., Jones & Gerard, 1967). For instance, attitudes are viewed as the conclusion of logical syllogisms which have a belief and a value as premises. What are beliefs? **Beliefs** are nonevaluative thoughts about characteristics of "objects" in our world. Beliefs are what we perceive as the facts of our world. **Values** are our evaluations of the goodness or badness of objects of thought. In Jones and Gerard's system, attitudes are the results of the logical combination of these cognitive and evaluative elements. The following syllogism demonstrates the system:

Belief	Easy access to guns produces more injuries and deaths.
Value	Producing injuries and deaths is bad.
Attitude	Easy access to guns is bad.

The conclusion of this logical syllogism, easy access to guns is bad, may serve as the value in the construction of an attitude toward gun control laws. Try to construct the syllogism.

On the other hand, a syllogism can be constructed which has the opposite attitudinal conclusion, such as the following:

Belief	Easy access to guns enables one to protect one's family.
Value	Being able to protect one's family is good.
Attitude	Easy access to guns is good.

The beliefs and values in these opposing syllogisms are indisputably true. The critical difference lies in which belief is emphasized because it has more impact or importance. In other words, is protecting one's family or limiting injuries and deaths by firearms more important? Many experiential and situational factors affect which action a particular person thinks is more important. Persuasive arguments designed to change the perceived importance of one of the two beliefs should be effective ways to change attitudes about easy access to guns.

Of course, we seldom analyze our attitudes in such detail. However, by examining the structure of attitudes, we can see how intricately organized attitudes can be. If there are several syllogisms that lead to the same attitudinal conclusion, then that attitude will be hard to refute. As mentioned earlier, the

Many of us have strong attitudes about issues.

conclusion of one syllogism may serve as a premise of another syllogism. Such linkages among attitudes suggest that a great deal of consistency will exist within a person's attitude network.

The intricacy of attitude organization that exists should also affect how a person will respond to new information (see Zajonc, 1960). That is, if a person has a well-developed, coherent network of attitudes in a particular domain; one would expect that he or she would be unlikely to alter the attitude network to fit the new information. Instead, this person would be likely to assimilate the information into the existing network. If there is no well-developed network, then the individual is likely to accommodate the existing ideas to the new information. That is, new information will have more impact if little evaluative information has preceded it. Information integration theory (see Kaplan & Anderson, 1973), presented earlier in chapter 4, also suggests that the earliest information on an issue has more impact than information processed after many judgments have been made.

The Functions of Attitudes

The organization of attitudes may also be affected by the function which particular attitudes serve (Katz, 1960, 1968). Katz contended that we may hold attitudes for four reasons:

1. To maximize rewards and minimize costs from our environments (*adjustment function*)
2. To protect oneself from internal conflicts and external threats to the self (*ego-defensive function*)
3. To indicate the kind of person he or she is (*value-expressive function*)
4. To establish meaning and order in one's world (*knowledge function*)

The function a particular attitude serves may determine its place in the attitude network (Herek, 1986; Shavitt & Brock, 1986). For instance, attitudes having an ego-defensive function and attitudes having a value-expressive function may be organized into a *self-schema* (see chapter 5). Attitudes serving an adjustment function and requiring knowledge of the rewarding or punishing nature of people in one's environment may have a separate network. Attitudes having a knowledge function may also have a separate organization. One would expect that attitudes in these three separate networks or organizations would show consistency within a network, but not necessarily between networks.

The Measurement of Attitudes

Social psychologists have been struggling with measuring attitudes from the beginning of this century. It ought to be easy, right? Just introduce an issue or topic and ask the subjects how positive or negative they are about the issue. How one structures the question or item can affect the responses. For instance, how general or specific the topic question is affects responses.

Because attitudes are unseen, or covert, judgments about objects, most investigators use self-report measures to determine what respondents are thinking. The most common self-report measures are Likert items, which call for the person

Figure 6.1
Examples of Likert items.

A Likert Attitude Item

I favor U.S. military intervention in Central America.

1	2	3	4	5
Disagree strongly		Neutral		Agree strongly

An Attraction Scale

I like my experimental participation partner.

1	2	3	4	5	6	7	8	9
Dislike very much	Dislike	Dislike somewhat	Dislike slightly	Neither like nor dislike	Like slightly	Like somewhat	Like	Like very much

---

Bipolar Scales in a Semantic Differential Format

The Bush Administration

Good	1 2 3 4 5 6 7 8	Bad
Unpleasant	1 2 3 4 5 6 7 8	Pleasant
Strong	1 2 3 4 5 6 7 8	Weak
Negative	1 2 3 4 5 6 7 8	Positive

A Unipolar Attitude Scale

Strict censorship of videotapes for young children is appropriate.

Not at all	1	2	3	4	5	6	Very appropriate

---

to agree or disagree with statements, and the semantic differential procedure, which requires that respondents evaluate the attitude object on a number of bipolar adjectives (see figure 6.1). Such closed-ended items are preferred over open-ended questions for ease of quantification and reliability of scoring. Usually, investigators use multiple items and even different types of measures about the same topic. High correlations between measures give assurance that the same conceptual variable is being measured and that the measures are valid.

Sometimes a single dimension scale is not enough. Recently, Abelson (1988) tried to assess the conviction with which certain attitudes on particular topics are held. To understand the strength of emotion behind some attitudes, he asked about the strength, importance to self, concern, amount of thought, amount of attitude

Table 6.1	Conviction Questions: A Longer List

Variable	Question
Courage	Have other people ever reacted negatively to your views?
Loyalty	Would friends (family) be disappointed if you changed views?
Longevity	How long have you held your views?
Strengthening	Have your views gotten stronger?
Instrumentality	Name some possible consequences if your views were enacted.
Instrumentality	Likelihood and value of those consequences.
Direct experience	Are your views based on the issue directly affecting you?
Moral values	Are views based on your moral sense of the way things should be?
Social comparison	Are views based on responses of people you care about?
Crystallization	Do views express the "real you"?
Steadfastness	Can you imagine yourself ever changing your mind?
Affects	Do you feel angry when you think about X? Fearful? Hopeful? Sympathetic?
Knowledge	Compared to most people, how much do you know about X?
Social support	Do most people agree with you about X?
Bandwagon	Is public support for your side increasing?
Uniqueness	Are your views ahead of the crowd?
Certainty	How correct do you think your views are?
Centrality	Name other issues that could come up when you discuss X.

From R. P. Abelson, "Conviction," in *The American Psychologist* [43:267–275 88)]. Copyright 1988 by the American Psychological Association (Washington, D.C.). Reprinted by permission.

expression to others, and willingness to work associated with specific issues. There are even more dimensions to attitudes, as can be seen in Abelson's extended list (see table 6.1).

What if the issue is a sensitive one so that subjects might be inclined to hide their true attitudes? Then more subtle approaches such as the bogus pipeline must be used. The **bogus pipeline** (Jones & Sigall, 1971) is a technique by which experimenters make subjects believe that they have a "pipeline" into their most secret attitudes so that subjects might as well respond honestly. Usually, subjects are connected to sophisticated looking equipment and asked to think about innocuous attitude objects. The equipment meter accurately indicates their attitudes one by one. Unbeknownst to the subjects, an assistant is setting the meter readings from subjects' attitude responses collected earlier. When the subject is convinced of the validity of the machine readings, more sensitive issues, such as attitudes about race (Sigall & Page, 1971) and women's rights (Faranda, Kaminski, & Giza, 1979), can be raised. (See figure 6.2.) Invariably, subjects' answers are more honest and more negative on paper-and-pencil items when they have been introduced to the bogus pipeline first and they thought they would be connected to the machine again.

Figure 6.2
*Whites characterized
Blacks as possessing
negative traits (stupid,
dirty, lazy) more and
positive traits
(intelligent, sensitive)
less under bogus
pipeline conditions
than under standard
conditions. The bogus
pipeline apparently
made subjects respond
with more honest
attitudes.*
(From Sigall & Page, 1971, Journal
of Personality and Social
Psychology.)

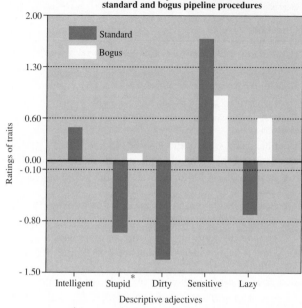

Whites' description of blacks under
standard and bogus pipeline procedures

*The bogus pipeline for intelligence was 0.00

**Behavioral
Measures**

So far, we have discussed only self-report questionnaire methods for measuring attitudes. There are a few other approaches. There are behavioral measures which are used to assess underlying attitudes. Typical *behavioral* measures of attitudes are how much time persons spend working on an activity (Deci, 1975; Lepper et al., 1973) when they are free to do other things and how many envelopes they stuff for a particular cause. There are many overt behaviors, verbal and non-verbal, that could potentially be used. Even a presidential candidate's nonverbal behavior has been observed to determine his attitude toward a potential running mate. Often, in the interest of saving time and trouble, psychologists use behavioroid measures instead (Carlsmith, Ellsworth & Aronson, 1976). A **behavioroid measure** is a report or agreement that a person will do certain behaviors or a certain number of behaviors (but the person is never actually required to do them). Subjects have been asked to allow a large sign to be erected in their yards (Freedman & Fraser, 1966), to chaperone a group of children to the zoo (Cialdini et al., 1975), and to make phone calls for an experimenter (Aronson & Cope, 1968) in order to assess their attitudes.

It is probably best to use physiological techniques as secondary or supplemental attitude measures to self-report or other behavioral measures. Lie detector measures, such as the galvanic skin response (GSR), are poor indicators of true attitudes unless a baseline (normal responding) has been established by asking other questions and unless the interview situation has been carefully controlled and structured. An approach similar to the GSR in attempting to assess covert attitudes from uncontrollable *physiological responses* is measuring pupil size. If a person's pupils become more dilated when shown a particular attitude object, that person presumably has a positive attitude or attraction toward that object (Atwood & Howell, 1971). However, there are many other factors, such as light level, where the person is looking, and physical condition of the subject, that can affect pupil dilation and make it an unstable indicator of attitudes. As with most physiological measures, pupil dilation is a better indication of attitude intensity than of the positive or negative nature of the attitude (Janisse & Peavler, 1974).

Attitudes and Behavior

Why should we study attitudes? Investigators have studied attitudes in order to be able *to predict behavior*. Ultimately, the way people act toward or against us has the greatest impact on our lives. Since attitudes are relatively enduring tendencies and remain consistent over several decades in a study of political attitudes (Newcomb, Koenig, Flacks, & Warwick, 1967), they should provide a good indication of how individuals will act. However, much research indicates that we cannot always predict how a person will behave from knowledge of the individual's attitudes (Wicker, 1969).

Attitude-Behavior Consistency

One study has shown that attitudes are sometimes overwhelmingly inconsistent with behavior (LaPiere, 1934). In the early thirties, LaPiere, an American sociologist, and a Chinese couple went on an extended trip together. They visited 251 eating and lodging establishments on the trip, and 250 of them served the three of them uneventfully. After the trip, LaPiere wrote a letter to each of these establishments to inquire if they accepted Chinese people into their places of business. Over 90 percent of those who replied were unwilling to accommodate Chinese people. These expressions of attitudes in the letters were diametrically opposite to the way the people had behaved when LaPiere and his associates had visited. Why?

Would La Piere's traveling companions have been accepted here? Probably, just as they were accepted almost 60 years ago.

In recent years, social psychologists have pinpointed many of the factors that affect attitude-behavior consistency. Some of these factors are evident in the LaPiere study. One methodological factor that was present in that study, which contributed to inconsistency and has not been emphasized in recent studies, is that one person may have expressed the attitude and another person actually behaved in the interaction with the Chinese couple. Of course, we would not expect perfect consistency between the attitudes of one person and the behavior of someone else, even if one person worked for the other.

Situational Factors

The situation in which the behavior must be enacted affects *attitude-behavior consistency*. There are many forces in particular situations that can overwhelm the influence of a single attitude on behavior. Ecological psychologists have presented evidence that the interaction situation may dictate our behaviors more than our personalities do (Barker, 1968), and the same may be true for attitudes. Schuman and Johnson (1976), in their review of the literature on attitude-behavior consistency to that time, contend that some behaviors are so dependent on particular situational contexts that attitudes are made useless in predicting

*Sometimes our
behaviors are
inconsistent with our
attitudes. Situational
factors can do that.*

FOR BETTER OR FOR WORSE, by
Lynn. © Universal Press Syndicate.
Reprinted by permission. All Rights
Reserved.

For Better or For Worse®    by Lynn Johnston

them. If the action had to be taken in a context where much of the audience would find the behavior offensive, it is likely that the behavior would be stifled. Those innkeepers and restauranteurs in the LaPiere study probably judged that refusing service would have created an unnecessary, undesirable disturbance in their establishment, especially with LaPiere being part of the audience. Ajzen and Fishbein (1980), in their **theory of reasoned action,** contended that if a person perceived that others believed he or she should not do a particular act, such *social norms* serve as powerful inhibitors of the action.

Noting the situational contexts for both the behavior and the expression of attitudes, Campbell (1963) has cast LaPiere's attitude-behavior inconsistency in a different light. He suggests that there is nothing inconsistent in a person expressing a rejecting attitude in a letter and behaving in an accepting way face-to-face. Such a person would have the same underlying attitude toward Chinese people. The difference lies in the expression of the attitude demanded in the two situations. In ordering the expression of controversial attitudes from easy to hard, stating beliefs should be easiest, followed by verbally expressing liking or disliking, and publicly behaving would be the hardest. This is essentially Campbell's position, and it implies that only people with especially strong anti-Chinese attitudes would behave in rejecting ways. However, people with milder anti-Chinese attitudes would express disliking for the Chinese indirectly in a letter.

This position suggests that nearly all the lodging and dining establishment managers were moderately biased against Chinese people. More generally, it suggests that (1) *behaviors* are the strongest forms of expression of attitudes, (2) expressions of *affective judgment* (as used on most attitude surveys) are intermediate forms, and (3) expressions of *beliefs* are the weakest forms of attitude expression. Behavioral results should not be consistent with the other forms of attitude expression unless the underlying attitude was strongly held, the attitude being assessed was uncontroversial, or the behavior was privately performed or had no meaningful audience.

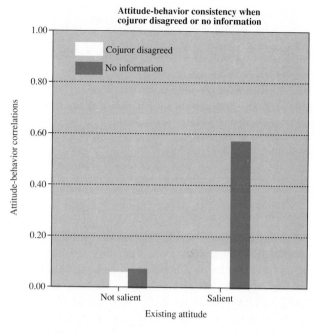

Attitude-behavior consistency when cojuror disagreed or no information

☐ Cojuror disagreed

■ No information

Attitude-behavior correlations

Existing attitude

Not salient   Salient

Figure 6.3
Subjects acted consistently with their attitudes toward affirmative action only when they had just been asked to think about their attitudes (Salient condition) before acting and there was no indication that their partner disagreed on affirmative action (No information). High positive correlations indicate attitude-behavior consistency.
(From Snyder & Swann, 1976, Journal of Personality and Social Psychology, 34, 1039.)

Attitudes will have no implications about behavior if you behave mindlessly. For instance, if the attitude is not made salient so that it is at the forefront of your awareness when you act, then it will not affect your behavior. A study of attitudes toward affirmative action showed that if subjects were told to think about their position on affirmative action before judging a sex discrimination case, consistency between their attitudes and their judgments was high. If they were not told to consider their position, attitudes and judgments were inconsistent (Snyder & Swann, 1976). (See figure 6.3.) In the LaPiere study, subjects were only asked to think about their attitudes weeks or months *after* they had behaved. What if those business managers had received the letter of inquiry about service to Chinese a day or two *before* LaPiere and his companions had arrived? Their actions would probably have been more consistent with their attitudes.

In everyday life, whether we will remember our attitudes spontaneously when we have to act depends on the strength of association between the target object and our evaluation (attitude) (Fazio, Powell, & Herr, 1983; Fazio, Sanbonmatsu, Powell, & Kardes, 1986). What determines the strength of *object-evaluation association?* If we have been asked to express the same attitude several times, we can access our attitude from memory readily (Powell & Fazio, 1984). Also, other everyday experiences affect the strength of our attitudes. One such factor is *direct experience* with the attitude object (Regan & Fazio, 1977; Fazio & Zanna, 1981). If you have thought about a situation or condition repeatedly or if you have had meaningful direct experience with the condition, the consistency between your attitude and your action should be high. It seems likely that LaPiere's subjects had not had frequent or involving direct experience with Chinese people in the situation presented to them.

Recalling the Attitude and Behavior

Table 6.2 Correlations between Attitude Measures and Behaviors	
Birth control behavior	*r*
Attitude toward birth control	.083
Attitude toward birth control pills	.323
Attitude toward using birth control pills	.525
Attitude toward using birth control pills during two years	.572
Birth or attempted conception behavior	*r*
Attitude toward children	−.007
Attitude toward having children	.187
Attitude toward having a child in the two-year period	.535

Note. Higher positive correlations indicate greater attitude-behavior consistency.

Correspondence between Attitudes and Behavior

Often, attitudes tell nothing about behavior because the attitude questions asked are not specific enough. Does a person's attitude toward birth control in general tell us whether he or she will practice birth control? It probably will not. Does a person's infatuation with Ferrari sports cars tell us whether that person will buy one? Information about one's income and life situation (married? children?) probably would tell you more. Does a person's distaste for divorce in general tell you whether he or she will file for one? A lot of other factors probably come into play.

One study examined the consistency between birth-giving and birth control attitudes and conception and birth control behavior (Davidson & Jaccard, 1979). One criterion behavior was use of birth control pills among married women during a two-year period. Another was birth or attempted conception during the two-year period. Using several attitude measures, they obtained the results shown in table 6.2.

It is apparent that the more specifically worded the attitude measure, the more consistent it was with behavior. Another feature of this effect is the correspondence of the target object evoked by the attitude statement with the target object toward which one must behave (Lord, Lepper, & Mackie, 1984). That is, if the Chinese person imagined (well-mannered, well-dressed?) when subjects received the letter was like the Chinese people who accompanied LaPiere to the subjects' businesses; then high attitude-behavior consistency would have been expected.

A Theory of Reasoned Action

Ajzen and Fishbein (1980; Fishbein & Ajzen, 1975), in presenting their theory of reasoned action, take the notion of attitude specificity a step further. They argue that attitudes about such global concepts as birth control are virtually useless in predicting behavior. Some attitudes, such as favoring or opposing war with Iran, are quite remote from the individual's everyday behavior. Only if that attitude was very important in deciding which presidential candidate to vote for could it be related to behavior. What one needs to know instead is a person's

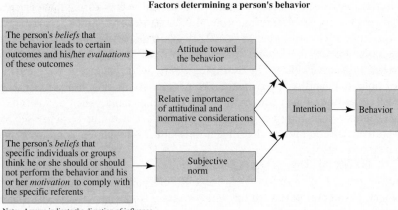

Factors determining a person's behavior

Note: Arrows indicate the direction of influence.

Figure 6.4
*A Theory of Reasoned
Action.*

*Icek Atzen/Martin Fishbein,
Understanding Attitudes and
Predicting Social Behavior,
© 1980, p. 8. Reprinted by
permission of Prentice Hall, Inc.,
Englewood Cliffs, New Jersey.*

attitude toward doing a particular behavior, such as using birth control or buying a dishwasher. Only if one uses attitudes about performing particular behaviors can an investigator obtain consistency between attitudes and behavior.

By using the *attitude toward the behavior* and the *subjective norm* depicted in figure 6.4, Ajzen and Fishbein have been quite successful in predicting behavior. By carefully measuring the belief and value elements of the attitude toward particular behaviors and the subjective norm, they have been able to predict such important behaviors as adhering to healthful diet and exercise regimens, women's occupational choices, buying decisions, voting, and taking alcoholism treatment. The *subjective norm* is essentially the subject's assessment of what important other people would like him or her to do in this particular case. In most cases, the person's beliefs about the consequences of the behavior and his or her evaluation of those outcomes which determined the person's attitude were more important factors in predicting the behavior than were the normative factors.

The more intense your mood when you have to act, the less likely it is that your behavior will be consistent with your attitude. *Moods* are positive or negative transitory emotional states. Moods are often caused or changed by everyday events. Receiving acclaim or approval, winning a contest, performing well on a test, or even recalling a favorable event can trigger a positive mood. Similarly, recent unpleasant events may put a person in a foul mood. Positive moods and negative moods increase helping (Berkowitz, 1987; Cialdini, Shaller, Beaman, Houlihan, Arps, & Fultz, 1987). Other studies have shown that if you are put in an irritable mood, you are likely to behave aggressively (Rotton, Frey, Barry, Milligan, & Fitzpatrick, 1979). These results suggest that intense moods may overwhelm the influence of attitudes on behavior, which would reduce attitude-behavior consistency.

Mood and Attitude-Behavior Consistency

The Formation of Attitudes

How are attitudes formed? The most obvious answer is through experience with the attitude objects. Learning principles, presented in chapter 2, summarize how experience affects attitudes. When an attitude object is experienced with a pleasant sensation, we develop a positive attitude toward that object according to *classical conditioning* principles. For example, a baby who repeatedly feels warm, comfortable, dry, and well-fed in the presence of its mother is likely to develop a positive attitude toward its mother. On the other hand, when an attitude object is experienced in conjunction with an unpleasant stimulus-response sequence, a negative attitude toward that object develops. Many phobias and aversions may develop in this way.

Operant conditioning principles indicate that if we are reinforced after acting toward some object, then we will develop positive attitudes toward that object. If something rewarding comes directly from the activity with the object, then one should also develop positive attitudes toward the object. So, if a child enjoys playing soccer or drawing pictures and the child's parents praise the child's efforts in those areas, then he or she should develop a positive attitude toward those endeavors because of the intrinsic enjoyment and the extrinsic rewards from parents. An exception to this principle is that excessive external rewards for already enjoyable activities may reduce positive attitudes toward the activities (Lepper, Greene, & Nisbett, 1973). On the other hand, if punishments follow action toward an object, then negative attitudes will develop. If the soccer player only gets tired and injured while playing and the child's parents criticize his or her play, negative attitudes toward playing soccer will develop.

Observational learning principles indicate ways indirect experiences can affect development of attitudes. For example, if you observe someone else acting toward an object and enjoying it, you are likely to form a positive attitude toward the object. Bandura's work on children's aggression suggests that when the children saw a model act aggressively toward toys, they formed positive attitudes toward acting aggressively. However, if we see someone avoiding acting with an object or being forced to act with the object, we are likely to form negative attitudes toward the object. For instance, if you saw someone being chased or bitten by a pitbull dog, you would probably develop an aversion to such dogs. The incidents observed do not have to be experienced by someone in your presence; instead, they may be portrayed in a story or in a mass media presentation. In addition, after a person develops facility with language, attitudes are adopted from hearing someone else express an affinity or aversion to some attitude object. The extent to which the observer identifies with the model affects whether the observer will adopt the same attitude (Bandura, 1977b).

These learning paradigms, especially those of classical and operant conditioning, indicate that a person's physical sensations are the root of attitude formation. The concepts of unconditioned stimulus and unconditioned response suggest that some stimuli always and without prior experience lead to a positive or negative physical sensation in the individual. These sensations are the basis for classical conditioning. Goosebumps upon hearing the national anthem would never occur without these primary sensations. In addition, the notion of primary reinforcers, such as food, in operant conditioning indicate that there is a biological basis for attitude formation. However, secondary reinforcers usually affect the behavior of adults and most children more than primary reinforcers.

The concept, "object of thought," (McGuire, 1985) indicates that the individual must be capable of perceiving and cognitively defining an object before he or she can frame an attitude about it. An object of thought is not always a physical object. It may be an activity, an idea, an issue, or a category of people. Young children may require experience with some of these "objects" before they can form an attitude. There may also be a fundamental difference in attitudes toward tangible objects or activities and toward abstract and remote ideas. Children cannot form attitudes about abstract ideas until they are cognitively mature (Kohlberg, 1966; Piaget, 1952). It is also likely that we develop stronger emotional reactions to tangible people and things than we do to abstract objects of thought. This suggests that we are unlikely to form intense attitudes toward abstract issues unless they are given tangible representations.

Though I have emphasized early experience, we do develop attitudes after childhood. Zajonc's work on mere exposure to attitude objects (see Moreland & Zajonc, 1979) and Fazio's use of multiple pairings of objects with evaluative adjectives to strengthen attitudes (see Fazio et al., 1986) indicate that simple cognitive consideration of objects develops attitudes toward those objects. Repeated experiences with and thinking about attitude objects certainly affects our attitudes.

Dramatic events or presentations can lead to the formation or change of attitudes. The effects of religious crusades and Nazi ceremonies (Merkl, 1980) with their impressive presentations on religious converts and German youth, respectively, illustrate how dramatic presentations can affect attitudes. The fact that the Little Rock school crisis in 1957 and the assassination of Martin Luther King, Jr. and associated events made the attitudes of white, middle-class west Texans more favorable toward school desegregation showed how events can shape attitudes (Riley & Pettigrew, 1976). (See figure 6.5.)

Multiple experiences with dramatic presentations should produce strong attitudes. This principle may be seen in how national anthem ceremonies foster nationalistic attitudes. Renditions of national anthems tend to be stirring, dramatic presentations. They are also experienced frequently. An acquaintance in graduate school suggested that such presentations serve to classically condition nationalistic fervor. He suggested that in order to counteract the development of nationalism, schools should have flag-raising, national anthem ceremonies daily but that they should use a different country's flag and anthem each day. This fanciful suggestion indicates an awareness of the importance of emotional involvement through dramatic presentations in the formation of attitudes.

The formation of attitudes can be affected by one's life experiences and by the time in the life cycle when they occur. Growing up in different cultures and subcultures—urban and rural, black and white, rich and poor, American and Soviet—can affect our adult attitudes, as suggested in chapter 2. *When* we experience life conditions can also be important. Sociologists have suggested that

Figure 6.5
(a) The 1957 Little Rock Central High School desegregation turmoil made middle-class Texas whites more favorable toward desegregation and lower-class Texas whites less favorable toward school desegregation. b) The Little Rock incidents made West Texans more favorable toward desegregation and East Texans less favorable. Overall, this dramatic incident made those who were originally negative more so and those who were positive more positive.

(From Riley & Pettigrew, 1976, Journal of Personality and Social Psychology.)

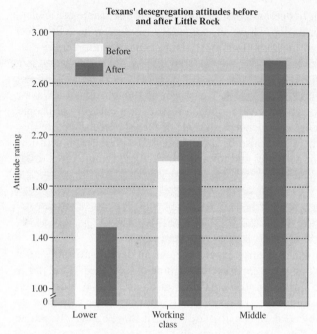

Texans' desegregation attitudes before and after Little Rock

(a)

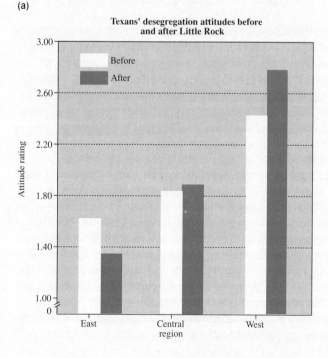

Texans' desegregation attitudes before and after Little Rock

Impressive displays and ceremonies can affect our attitudes.

people born at about the same time grow up sharing an historical period that shapes their attitudes (Kertzer, 1983; Ortega y Gasset, 1933). Further, Keniston (1968, 1971) has suggested that a person's political attitudes are often shaped by the political environment in the country when the individual is in his or her youth stage of development between the end of adolescence and before adulthood (ages 18–26). During that transition time, we are more attentive and receptive to the broader issues of the day. Consequently, events and public figures during that era of one's life can have a profound impact on the individual's attitudes. According to this view, the 20-year-olds of the mid-1950s, mid-1960s, and mid-1980s would be expected to have political attitude differences beyond their age and current life-status differences.

Cognitive Consistency

The idea that attitudes are organized leads us to expect that an individual's attitudes would be consistent with each other. We would not expect the Grand Dragon of the Ku Klux Klan to endorse Jesse Jackson's presidential candidacy or the president of the American Medical Association to recommend chiropractic care for his patients. Many social psychologists have argued that maintaining or regaining consistency between ideas or attitudes motivates us to change our attitudes or our actions (Festinger, 1957; Heider, 1958; Osgood & Tannenbaum, 1955). Because of the wealth of research on cognitive dissonance theory, the broad implications of dissonance findings, and the fact that Heider's balance theory is presented extensively in the chapter on interpersonal attitudes (attraction); our presentation of cognitive consistency theories will focus on cognitive dissonance theory (Festinger, 1957).

Cognitive Dissonance Theory

Cognitive dissonance theory was originated by Leon Festinger (1957). It has been one of the most influential theories in social psychology. The theory asserts that individuals find it discomforting to entertain two or more inconsistent but related ideas at the same time. *Dissonance* is an unpleasant, discomforting state that we are motivated to reduce. Secord and Backman (1964) stated the cognitive dissonance theory in the following equation:

$$\text{Dissonance} = \frac{\Sigma \, (\text{Dissonant cognitions} \times \text{Importance})}{\Sigma \, (\text{Consonant cognitions} \times \text{Importance})}$$

Clear as mud, right? The implications of this formula are that often more than two cognitions are involved in producing dissonance and that how important the ideas are to you influences how much dissonance is experienced.

Reducing Dissonance

Inconsistency between ideas creates cognitive dissonance, which the individual finds aversive and tries to reduce. The equation also implies how dissonance can be reduced. This dissonance can be reduced (1) by changing one of the two dissonant cognitions, (2) by adding cognitions that are consonant with one of the dissonant cognitions, or (3) by altering the importance of one of the dissonant cognitions mentally. The first way is to change one of the cognitions so that it is no longer dissonant with the other. People in most dissonance studies change one of their attitudes (cognitions) to reduce dissonance. For instance, an overeater may simultaneously have the cognitively inconsistent ideas, "I eat too much" and "Overeating shortens your life." One "easy" way to reduce dissonance is to quit eating so much. However, many people may reduce dissonance by denying the other cognition. Such a person may convince him- or herself that overeating does not really shorten lifespan by pointing out people like Tip O'Neill or actor Raymond Burr as evidence. He or she also may deny the second cognition in his or her case by arguing that only consumption of saturated fats, which he or she avoids, shortens life. Parenthetically, similar examples could be made with smoking, drinking alcohol, or using drugs. You might say that dissonance theory tells us how we become comfortable with our unhealthy habits.

Many of us reduce our dissonance about overeating in cognitive ways rather than by dieting.

The second dissonance reduction strategy is to think of other cognitions that are consonant or consistent with one of the dissonant ideas. By adding consonant cognitions, one increases the value of the denominator of the equation and thereby reduces the amount of dissonance experienced. In the overeater's example, he or she may think about friends, knowledgeable doctors, and professional athletes who also overeat and that realization is consistent with his or her overeating. He also may note that eating makes him or her feel content and relaxed and that attaining that state is consonant with his or her eating habits. One of the first dissonance studies, a participant observation study involving a doomsday cult (Festinger, Riecken, & Schachter, 1956), examined dissonance reduction by adding consonant cognitions. In that study, the investigators found that after the day of destruction came and went without catastrophe (creating much dissonance), cult members started energetically proselytizing for new members and

Table 6.3   A Summary of Cognitive Dissonance Theory

Motivation of Individual
To avoid or reduce inconsistency between ideas; To justify one's actions

Core Concepts
Changing attitudes can reduce dissonance

Focus of Theory
Effects of dissonance in affecting attitudes such as attraction, prejudice, preferences, and consumer decisions

Assumptions about rationality/awareness of people
Rationalizing, distorting

KUDZU

Cognitive dissonance theory portrays the rationalizing side of humans rather than the rational side.
KUDZU, by Marlette. © 1987. By permission of Doug Marlette and Creators Syndicate, Inc.

gaining media exposure. Festinger and his associates interpreted this behavior as getting others to believe in the preachings of their cult, which would be consonant with their keeping the faith. Studies of dissonance after decision making are also based on adding consonant cognitions (Brehm, 1956).

The third dissonance reduction tactic is to alter the importance of one of the discrepant cognitions. The overeater may acknowledge the original dissonant cognitions, but then observe that he or she would rather live a short, happy life eating what he or she wants than a longer, discontented one dieting all the time. This additional cognition reduces the importance of the "overeating shortens life" cognition and lowers the amount of dissonance experienced. (See table 6.3.).

It should be noted that dissonance theory presents a rationalizing or justifying view of mankind, rather than seeing humans as totally rational beings (Aronson, 1972). Attribution theories (Kelley, 1967) portray humans as rational information processors with a few irrational biases. Cognitive dissonance theory, on the other hand, sees humans as usually acting and thinking in self-protective or self-justifying ways so they can sustain the ideas that they are good and intelligent. In fact, this rational vs. rationalizing or self-enhancing distinction is an important feature of many of the opposing positions in social psychology.

Compliance and Attitude Change

An early classic study of cognitive dissonance examined the question of what happens when a person does something that is totally inconsistent with what he or she believes (Festinger & Carlsmith, 1959). In everyday life, a job, e.g., lawyer or flight attendant (Hochschild, 1983), or a role, e.g., debater, may make you do or say something that is the opposite of what you think or feel. In this experiment, the investigators gave every subject the same attitude rather than dealing with preexisting attitudes that may have been positive for some subjects and negative for others. They accomplished this by having every subject perform dull, monotonous tasks like turning pegs on a pegboard a quarter-turn again and again so that every subject had the same attitude toward the task—"This task is dull, dull, dull."

After they completed the tasks, the experimenter explained to them that they had participated in a study of the effects of expectancy or set on performance and that they had been in the control condition in which no expectations were given beforehand. However, the next subject in the waiting room was in the favorable expectation condition. Because the assistant who ordinarily gave expectations to subjects was unavailable, all subjects (except those in a real control condition) were asked if they could tell the next subject that the task was interesting and enjoyable. When they were given the choice to do this, half of these subjects were told that they would be paid $20 for this favor; the other half were told they would receive only $1.

After these subjects agreed to do the favor, each one did go into the waiting room and told the next subject (the experimenter's accomplice) the lie. Later, when they were asked about the experiment on an evaluation sheet, those who were paid $1 rated the task as more enjoyable than the $20 subjects or the control subjects did. The dissonance interpretation is that saying the opposite of what they believed aroused dissonance in the subjects. However, the situation did not arouse as much dissonance in the $20 subjects because receiving $20 was consonant with lying to the next subject. It is consonant for many of us to tell an innocuous lie for $20. The control subjects experienced no dissonance because they were not asked to, nor did they, talk to the next subject. The $1 subjects reduced their dissonance by changing their attitude about the task.

Originally, this type of study was called a counter-attitudinal advocacy experiment (because subjects said the opposite of what they believed) or a forced compliance experiment. *Induced compliance* is the more commonly used term now because it is imperative that subjects not feel that they were "forced" to comply with the experimenter's request for dissonance to occur. In the hundreds of induced compliance studies since 1959, several factors—many of which were varied or experienced by all subjects in the Festinger and Carlsmith experiment—have been shown to be important in obtaining dissonance effects. (See figure 6.6.)

Choice

If the individual does not perceive that he or she did the counterattitudinal action by choice, then he or she will not experience dissonance. *Choice,* as in the Festinger and Carlsmith study, is present when the experimenter asks rather than commands or demands a subject do an act. However, there is more to perceived

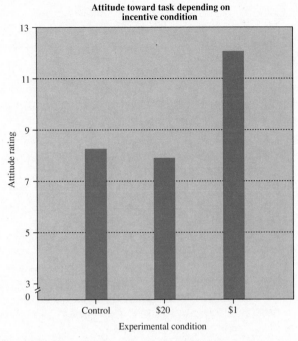

Attitude toward task depending on incentive condition

Attitude rating

Experimental condition

Figure 6.6
Subjects who told the "next subject" that the task was interesting for $1 became more positive toward the task than other subjects did.
(From Festinger & Carlsmith, 1959, Journal of Abnormal and Social Psychology, 58, 203–210.)

choice. If the subject is asked to act for a substantial sum of money, then perceived choice is low and attitude change due to dissonance will not occur (Cohen, 1962; Festinger & Carlsmith, 1959; Linder, Cooper, & Jones, 1967; Nel, Helmreich, & Aronson, 1969).

There are factors other than money that make the actor perceive that he or she did not have free choice. An early study showed that if subjects were induced to endorse a counterattitudinal position for the benefit of science, they perceived that they had little choice and did not change their attitudes like those who were not given the "science" justification (Rabbie, Brehm, & Cohen, 1959). In another study, persons who were induced to eat grasshoppers by a likeable experimenter did not adopt as favorable an attitude toward eating grasshoppers as did those who were induced to do it by an unfriendly experimenter (Zimbardo, Weisenberg, Firestone, & Levy, 1965). Therefore, doing something against one's attitudes for science or for a likeable person leads one to feel coerced and does not foster attitude change.

A case of failure to induce compliance is interesting in this context (S. Darley & Cooper, 1972). College students in this experiment were asked to write an essay endorsing dress codes for high schools, a position that all subjects opposed. However, in this study, conditions were set up so all subjects would refuse to write the essay. Half of the subjects were asked to write the essay for $.50 and half for $1.50. When subjects did not comply in this study, the amount of the inducement had an effect opposite to the effect in ordinary compliance studies. Those who were offered $1.50 (the larger inducement) to write the essay became more staunchly opposed to dress codes. Apparently, since subjects acted consistently with their attitudes, dissonance processes were reversed so that the more money

Figure 6.7
Subjects who resisted advocating a strict high school dress code when they were offered a high incentive to advocate it became most negative toward the dress code. These results demonstrate that persuaders must offer a strong enough incentive to make targets commit the act or they will get undesirable attitudinal effects (the boomerang effect).

(From S. Darley & Cooper, 1972, Journal of Personality and Social Psychology, 24, 324.)

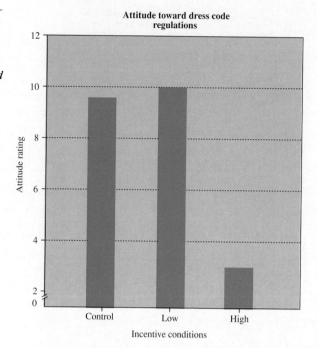

that was refused, the greater the dissonance experienced and the more the attitude was intensified. This result has implications for the application of dissonance principles in persuasion, which will be discussed later in this chapter. (See figure 6.7.)

Commitment

Publicly performing the counterattitudinal behavior (*commitment*) has been recognized as a very important element in the induced compliance situation since Festinger and Carlsmith's classic study. In their study, both the $1 and $20 subjects told the next subject that the experimental task was interesting. That act, because it was explicit, important, and irrevocable, made changing the cognition, "I said the task was interesting," virtually impossible (Kiesler, 1971). As a result, dissonance reduction must be accomplished through changing the earlier attitude toward the task. Some studies have shown that a sense of commitment is created by simply indicating that one will do the behavior without actually doing it. For instance, Rabbie et al. (1959) found that subjects showed the same attitude change if they agreed to write a counterattitudinal essay as did subjects who actually wrote the essay. One study clearly showed that if the subject publicly commits him- or herself to the counterattitudinal act, then he or she is more likely to change his or her attitude than if he or she writes an anonymous essay (Carlsmith, Collins, & Helmreich, 1966). Most investigators have found it effective in establishing commitment to have the subject identify him- or herself with the act publicly (on videotape) and to involve the subject in generating the details of the act (Nel, Helmreich, & Aronson, 1969).

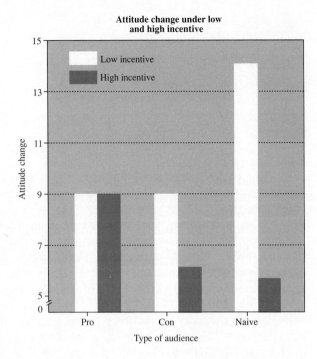

Figure 6.8
Antilegalization subjects changed their attitudes toward marijuana legalization most favorably after they had made a prolegalization videotape for a low incentive which they thought was going to be shown to a naive audience. The fact that such an audience would be easily misled surely aroused dissonance.

(*From Nel, Helmreich, & Aronson, 1969,* Journal of Personality and Social Psychology.*)*

The current dissonance position (Cooper & Fazio, 1984) is that a person's act must produce aversive consequences for someone else (and thus reflect poorly on the actor) for dissonance to be aroused in the induced compliance situations. Nel et al. (1969) varied the consequences of subjects' advocating the legalization of marijuana by describing the audience as staunchly for, staunchly against, or naive about legalizing marijuana. Only those who made a videotaped appeal for legalization to be shown to a persuasible, naive audience (and received minimal justification for making the tape) changed their attitudes favorably toward legalizing marijuana. So, only when the act was likely to produce negative consequences for someone did the dissonance effect occur. (See figure 6.8.) *Aversive Consequences*

In a replication of the Festinger and Carlsmith study, Cooper and Worchel (1970) varied whether the "subject" who was told that the experimental task was interesting was convinced or not. If the "next subject" was not misled by the subject's spiel (so there were no aversive consequences), then the subject did not change his or her attitude about the task. In a slightly different wrinkle on this study, Cooper, Zanna, and Goethals (1974) showed that if a person deceived a disliked person, then the expected attitude change toward the task did not occur. So, only if the outcomes are aversive to the subject—and they would not be if the subject caused bad things to happen to a disliked person—does the induced compliance situation create dissonance and attitude change. (See figure 6.9.)

If a person commits an act with free choice and he or she can foresee the aversive consequences of the action for someone else, then that person should feel personally responsible. It is when a person feels such responsibilty that dissonance should be aroused and attitude change occurs (Cooper, 1971; Wicklund & Brehm, *Personal Responsibility*

Figure 6.9
A model of cognitive dissonance arousal under induced compliance.

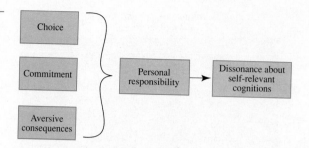

1976). The evidence indicating that dissonance arousal was closely associated with the individual feeling personally responsible for some harmful act led Bramel (1968) to argue that dissonance occurred in the induced compliance situation because the actor felt that he or she had acted immorally. One might say that what is really aroused is moral dissonance rather than cognitive dissonance (Kelman, 1974). The person's actions under the circumstances clash with his or her sense of morality. Aronson (1968; Nel, Helmreich, & Aronson, 1969) even argued that the dissonance in the Festinger and Carlsmith study was not between "the task was dull" and "I said that the task was interesting." Instead, he contends, the inconsistency lies between "I am a decent, truthful person," and "I misled another person into believing a falsehood." The previously mentioned Cooper and Worchel (1970) results and the Nel et al. (1969) results lend credence to this position.

Dissonance and Self-Relevant Cognitions

The view of dissonance as inspired by feelings of conflict about being responsible for an immoral act led Aronson (1968) and Bramel (1968) to emphasize the importance of self-relevant ideas. In the Nel et al. (1969) study, Aronson and associates assumed that dissonance would be aroused only when the person's actions produced consequences that were inconsistent with the person's self-concept. They found that attitude change only occurred when the videotape made by the subject under minimal justification ($.50) was to be shown to a naive, easily misled audience. Presumably, if the subjects in that study had been people who did not regard themselves as honest or moral, then dissonance would not have been aroused and attitude change would not have occurred as it did.

Steele and Liu (1981, 1983) also contended that it was the fact that the counterattitudinal behavior reflected negatively on the self, not just the cognitive inconsistency it instigated, which aroused dissonance. They reasoned that if a person who had committed an inconsistent act were given an opportunity to affirm some unrelated positive aspect of his or her self, then that person would not change his or her attitude to reduce dissonance. In the 1981 study, Steele and Liu found that subjects who wrote essays opposing more funding for handicapped facilities changed their attitudes to a more negative position on funding handicapped facilities unless they expected to be able to do a self-affirming behavior later, namely, help blind students. In the three later experiments (Steele & Liu, 1983), they showed that dissonance-reducing attitude change about raising tuition costs did not occur for those who were given the opportunity to express self-relevant values,

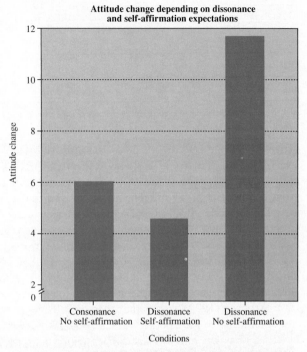

Attitude change depending on dissonance and self-affirmation expectations

Attitude change

Conditions

Consonance / No self-affirmation — Dissonance / Self-affirmation — Dissonance / No self-affirmation

Figure 6.10
Those subjects who wrote essays against aid for handicapped persons without the expectation that they could do self-affirming acts to help blind students changed their attitudes negatively toward aid. Those who expected to be able to act in a self-affirming way did not show the dissonance produced attitude change.
(From Steele & Liu, 1981, Personality and Social Psychology Bulletin, 7, 396.)

but attitude change did occur for those for whom the values expressed were not self-relevant. These studies suggest that when a self-relevant cognition is threatened, dissonance is most likely to occur. However, when self-esteem has been directly evaluated to see if immoral conduct generates more dissonance for high self-esteem persons, the expected results have not been obtained (Cooper & Duncan, 1971). Perhaps one's level of self-esteem is not a good indicator of who is likely to be most threatened by the implications of their own behavior. (See figure 6.10.)

The effects of dissonance on attitudes have also been examined in situations where restraint has been subtly or not so subtly induced. The principles of induced compliance and induced restraint seem to be similar except that minimal rewards produce the most dissonance in the compliance situation, while minimal punishments produce the most dissonance in restraint situations.

    A study with preschool children first examined the effects of getting someone to stop doing an activity on attitudes (Aronson & Carlsmith, 1963). The experimenter came to preschool several times to establish rapport with the young children. He then brought five different toys for the children to play with. He asked each child separately to indicate which toy he or she preferred of pairs of the toys until the child's favorability ranking of the toys was determined. Then, the experimenter told each child that he or she could not play with the child's second favorite toy while the experimenter was out of the room. Before leaving, he admonished half the children with a mild threat of punishment, "I would be a little

Induced Restraint

Table 6.4 Favorability Rankings of Forbidden Toy		
After mild threat	4	10	8
After severe threat	14	8	0
	Increased	Same	Decreased

From Aronson & Carlsmith, 1963, *Journal of Abnormal & Social Psychology:* 66, 586.

angry if you played with it." The other half received a severe threat of punishment, "I would be very angry; I would have to take all of the toys and go home and never come back again." After the experimenter left the room, he watched from behind a one-way mirror and discovered that none of the children played with the forbidden toy. Several minutes later, he came back and asked the child to rerank the toys. Aronson and Carlsmith found that the children who had been threatened mildly to restrain them from playing with the toy now devalued the toy. Those who had heard the severe threat did not devalue the toy. In a replication of this study, Freedman (1965) found that children who received a mild threat still would not play with a forbidden toy in a different context months later.

Aronson (1972) argues that these results demonstrate a very effective way to get children to incorporate values. When a person is disciplined very mildly but enough to get him to refrain from an activity, he or she will become disinterested in that activity to reduce dissonance. On the other hand, if he or she is threatened with severe punishment, he or she will desist only until the punisher is out of sight. (See table 6.4.)

Expended Effort and Dissonance

Suppose you and your friend Maude both wanted to join sororities. After open rush parties at separate sororities, both of you are equally excited about joining a sorority. Maude decides to join XXX; you join SOS. During the next few months of pledging, you and Maude have very different experiences. Maude gets calls all hours of the day and night from sorority sisters asking her to do favors for them. She has to participate in embarrassing skits and other public activities with other pledges. She has to collect signatures, work on the homecoming float, and do many more time-consuming activities to gain membership in the sorority. SOS, on the other hand, only requires you to attend an occasional party during the pledge period. Assuming that every sorority member in XXX had an identical twin who was a member of SOS and all other things were equal, would you or Maude treasure sorority membership more and develop closer friendships with members?

Cognitive dissonance theory has an answer to that question and related ones. Aronson and Mills (1959) created an experimental situation similar to these two sororities. Actually they made it so that every member of the "two sororities" acted exactly the same to every "pledge" by presenting the group members' talking on audiotape. In their experiment, female subjects were randomly assigned to a severe initiation condition like Maude's, a mild initiation condition like yours, or

**Liking for group members depending
on type of initiation**

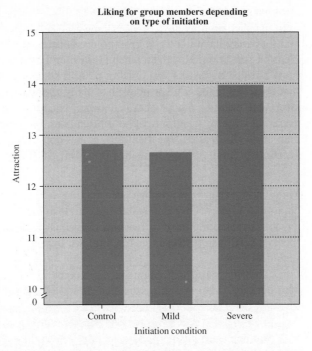

Attraction / Initiation condition

Figure 6.11
*Women who had to
read sexually explicit
words to get into a sex
discussion group
(severe initiation
condition) liked group
members more than
those who did not have
to work so hard to get
into the group.*
(From Aronson & Mills, 1959,
Journal of Abnormal and Social
Psychology, 59, *179.*)

a no initiation condition in order to gain membership into the group. The initiation was described as an embarrassment test used to see if they would be good participants in a sex discussion group. Severe initiation pledges read 12 risqué words and two vivid passages from *Lady Chatterly's Lover* to a male experimenter. Mild initiation "pledges" read 12 mild sex-related terms such as "petting" to the same male experimenter. All subjects passed the test, were introduced to the group members over a headset, and then listened to a boring, inane discussion about the sex characteristics of birds. Afterwards, all pledges were asked to indicate how well they liked the members of the group. (See figure 6.11.)

*Will their initiation
create a strong bond
among them?*

What do you think the results were? You've probably already guessed that the severe initiation pledges liked the group members best. That's right, but why? Aronson and Mills state that there would be dissonance for severe initiation pledges between "I worked hard to become a member of this group" and "The group members are boring, unlikeable people." Consequently, they came to believe that "The group members are interesting, likeable people," and that was reflected in their ratings of the group members. The mild and no initiation pledges did not experience such dissonance because they did not work hard to join the group. The self-relevant version of the dissonant cognitions might be "I'm a competent, intelligent person" and "It was stupid of me to work so hard to get into this group." One might say this is competence dissonance, rather than the moral dissonance of the induced compliance situations.

The basic principle is that if we expend more effort or other resources to gain something, then we will value it more. The "something" may be a bachelor's degree, a passing grade in statistics, a car, or someone's affection. The principle should apply if all other factors are equal beforehand. Some critics argued that

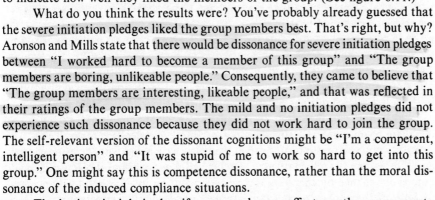

Aronson and Mills' experiment did not establish this principle because the severe initiation pledges may have been sexually aroused by reading the suggestive words, and they may have liked the group more because they were associated with this pleasant sensation. However, when Gerard and Mathewson (1966) obtained the same pattern of results while using painful shocks as the severe initiation rite, that criticism faded. The principle has many applications, which will be discussed later. One practice I hope that it does not encourage is intense *physical* hazing as part of fraternity and sorority initiation rites. I remember that a healthy young man in my dorm at college died during one such hazing rite, and there have been accounts of similar tragedies since (Cialdini, 1985).

Decisions and Dissonance

Many of us experience anguish over making decisions. Decisions are the turning points of our lives. They determine the course of our future. It should not surprise anyone that making hard, important decisions is stressful. Cognitive dissonance theory (Festinger, 1964) indicates that we experience dissonance after making such decisions.

The first published cognitive dissonance experiment (Brehm, 1956) dealt with decision making and dissonance. Women ranked eight household items as part of a marketing survey. Afterwards, a third of the women were given one of their favored items (the third-ranked item) for having participated. Another third of the women were given an easy choice between their third-ranked item and one of their least-favored items as a gift for helping. The other women were faced with the difficult decision of choosing between their third- and fourth-ranked items for their gifts. Then, the women were asked to rerank the items. For the women who just received a gift without a choice, there was no change in the rerankings of the items. For those who were given the easy choice, there was practically no change. However, the women who had to make the difficult choice ranked their chosen alternative higher and their unchosen alternative lower on the second ranking (described as "spreading of alternatives"). (See figure 6.12.)

According to dissonance theory, the positive features of an unchosen alternative and the negative features of the chosen alternative make the decision maker experience dissonance because they are inconsistent with the choice he or she made. So, seeing the chosen item in a more positive light after the decision and the unchosen one more negatively is a way of reducing dissonance. Such dissonance reduction only occurred in the difficult choice condition because the absence of an unchosen alternative and the presence of an unattractive alternative in the other two conditions did not arouse dissonance.

Couching the dissonance in terms of self-relevant cognitions, the operative dissonant cognitions are "I am a competent, intelligent decision maker" and "The relatively positive features of the unchosen alternative make my decision a stupid one." Spreading the alternatives, as Brehm's difficult decision subjects did, would reduce dissonance by changing the second cognition to "The relatively negative features of the unchosen alternative make my decision a competent one." Decision-making dissonance appears to arise from uneasiness about the competence implications of one's actions for if one did not see oneself as a competent decision maker, that person should not experience dissonance.

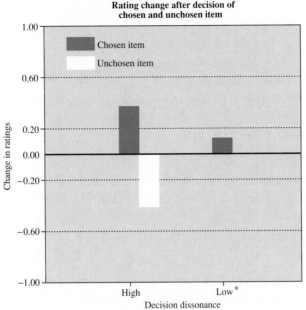

Rating change after decision of
chosen and unchosen item

*The unchosen item for low dissonance was 0.00.

Figure 6.12
*Women who had to
make a difficult
decision (high
dissonance condition)
about which gift to
take rated the chosen
alternative more
positively and the
rejected alternative
more negatively after
the decision. Those
who had an easier
decision did not show
postdecisional
spreading of
alternatives. In fact,
there was no pre- to
postdecisional change
in rating of the
unchosen alternative.*
(From Brehm, 1956, Journal of
Abnormal and Social Psychology,
p. 386.)

A study conducted at the Vancouver racetrack also demonstrated *postdecisional dissonance reduction* (Knox & Inkster, 1968). These investigators approached bettors as they approached or came away from the $2 bet window. They asked each subject to estimate their confidence that their horse would win the race. They were able to ascertain separately that the only difference between the prebet and postbet subjects was that the postbet subjects had crystallized their decision by betting. The postbet subjects indicated much more confidence in their chosen horse than the prebet subjects did. Another study replicated Knox and Inkster's findings convincingly using betting on games of chance at a fair instead of horserace betting (Younger, Walker, & Arrowood, 1977). So, making our decisions seem wiser occurs after the decision rather than before.

Do you always feel immediately comfortable about your decisions about clothing, a college, or a car? I know that the way I have dealt with clothing decisions may not be typical, but let me tell you anyway. I sometimes anguish a long time over two items of the same article of clothing, but I will usually decide to buy one. By the time I get to the parking lot, I'll look into the sack and say to myself, "That's the ugliest thing this side of Spuds MacKenzie." I usually experience considerable **regret** that I bought the item. Give me a few days, and I'll be wearing the ugly thing—my students will vouch for that!

A study by Elaine Walster (1964) suggests that these reactions after a decision are not so atypical. She had raw recruits at Ft. Ord, California, rank job assignments. They chose between two for their future assignment and then reranked the assignments, much like Brehm did with the household items. A key addition in her methods was that subjects did the second ranking of the job assignments either immediately, 4 minutes, 15 minutes, or 90 minutes after the

*After they have placed
their bets, these people
will be more confident
that their horse will
win.*

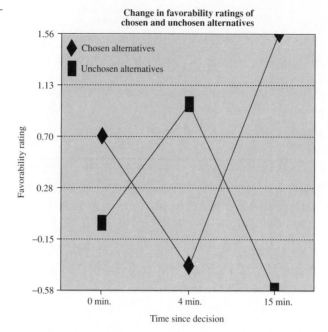

Figure 6.13
Army recruits showed a regret reaction (at 4 minutes) but later showed a typical dissonance-reducing reaction (at 15 minutes) toward job alternatives. Regret may often precede dissonance reduction after decisions.

(From Walster in Festinger, Conflict, Choice and Dissonance, 1964, p. 122.)

decision. The results indicated that four minutes after the decision these Army recruits were experiencing *regret* because they ranked the chosen job more negatively and the rejected job more positively than before. However, this regret phase was apparently short-lived because those who did the reranking at 15 minutes clearly showed the spreading of alternatives effect indicative of dissonance reduction. (See figure 6.13.)

Brehm and Wicklund (1970) characterized regret as reactance arising from the fact that making irrevocable decisions takes away a person's freedom to enjoy the unchosen alternative. **Reactance** is a tendency to value most those freedoms which are threatened or eliminated (Brehm, 1966). In the case of a decision, that freedom would be the opportunity to enjoy the unchosen alternative. In their study, Brehm and Wicklund found the same pattern as Walster did—regret followed by dissonance reduction. It seems that most of us eventually distort our perceptions to see our decisions most favorably. Perhaps there was so little time between races in Vancouver that bettors bypassed the regret reaction completely in order to reduce dissonance before the horses were off.

Other Explanations of Dissonance Effects

Not everyone thinks that the attitude change results we have described occur because of dissonance reduction. Daryl Bem (1965, 1972) has presented **self-perception theory** as a better explanation for this attitude change. He contends that if we observed someone work long and hard on a voluntary basis for a political candidate or a cause, we would infer that the person had a positive attitude toward the candidate or the cause. If we observed someone work long and hard for someone or some cause while being paid a very high salary for it, then we would be less sure of his positive attitude. In essence, we infer other people's attitudes from observing their *behavior and the circumstances* (rewards and costs) associated with the behavior. Bem argues that in many cases, we infer our attitudes in the same way—by observing our own behavior and the attendant circumstances. At the heart of this *self-perception* position is the assumption that we do not have good, direct awareness of our attitudes before we act. So, self-perception theory would not apply to attitudes toward attitude objects with which we had had much or significant experience (Fazio, Zanna, & Cooper, 1977; Taylor, 1975).

Bem (1965, 1967) conducted what he called interpersonal simulations of various dissonance studies, including Festinger and Carlsmith's induced compliance study. In these simulations, observer subjects were asked to predict the attitude of a subject in the earlier experiment after having had his or her behavior (telling the next subject that the task was interesting, for instance) and the attendant circumstances ($1 or $20 inducement) described to them. These observer subjects were able to predict the attitudes of Festinger and Carlsmith's subjects almost perfectly from these descriptions. These simulation results, according to Bem, show that cognitive dissonance, which the observer subjects did not experience, is not necessary to explain these results. He argues that the original subjects had not experienced dissonance and reduced it by changing their attitudes. Instead, they had inferred what their attitudes were from observing their own behavior, just as the observer subjects did later.

Many studies have been conducted to see which theory is better or to separate the appropriate domains of the two theories since Bem articulated self-perception theory. One study has convinced many people that dissonance theory applies better in some contexts and self-perception theory applies better in others (Fazio, Zanna, & Cooper, 1977). In this study, subjects were induced to agree to endorse a political position that was discrepant from their favored position under high or low choice. The discrepant position was either barely acceptable or barely unacceptable to them. To examine whether dissonance arousal occurred or not, half of the high-choice subjects were led to misattribute any tension they felt to being in an enclosed booth. The other high-choice subjects were not given a reason (other than dissonance) for their uneasiness. The idea was that if dissonance was aroused, it would be explained by the misattribution to the booth and changing one's attitude would not be required to reduce it. After they were committed to (agreed to endorse) the counterattitudinal position, subjects' political positions were assessed. The attitude change results are presented in table 6.5.

After endorsing the acceptable position, high-choice subjects changed attitudes and low-choice subjects did not, which is consistent with both theories. After endorsing the unacceptable (reject) position, only the high choice, no misattribution subjects changed attitudes, which is consistent with cognitive dissonance theory. The high-choice, misattribution results indicate that endorsing the

Self-Perception Theory

Research Trailblazers

Over the last two decades, Joel Cooper of Princeton University has been the most prolific dissonance researcher and theoretician. Much of his research has focused on whether dissonance occurs in induced compliance situations. A few of these studies by Cooper and his associates will be highlighted.

Zanna and Cooper (1974) used a misattribution procedure to establish the pattern of occurrence of dissonance first. If dissonance arousal were misattributed to an external factor, a pill, then attitude change due to dissonance should not occur. To test this idea, all subjects were given a placebo of powdered milk in a capsule. A third of the subjects were told that the pill would make them tense; a third were told that the pill would make them relax; and a third were told that the pill had no side effects. Shortly afterward, subjects were given a choice or not given a choice to write an essay in support of a ban on rabble-rousing speakers on campus (a curtailment of freedom of speech with which they did not agree). Then, they indicated their agreement with banning speakers from campus. Their results indicated that high-choice subjects changed their attitudes if they had

received the "relaxing" or "no-effect" pill. However, those subjects who believed they were tense because of the pill did not change their attitudes. These results suggest that a feeling of tension (dissonance) occurred in the choice conditions, and it produced attitude change unless it was misattributed to an external source. Bond (1981) attempted an interpersonal simulation (Bem, 1965) of this study and found that observer subjects could not estimate the attitudes of Zanna and Cooper's subjects, suggesting that dissonance was involved in their results. Another misattribution study (Higgins, Rhodewalt, & Zanna, 1979) indicated that a sense of tension rather than excitement describes the feeling of dissonance best. Other studies by Cooper and his associates have used the misattribution procedure to examine dissonance processes successfully (Fazio et al., 1977; Gonzales & Cooper, 1976). (See figure 6.A.)

Then, Cooper and colleagues (Cooper, Zanna, & Taves, 1978) asked whether there are drug effects that mimic or stifle dissonance arousal. This time they gave subjects either an amphetamine, a tranquilizer, or a placebo while telling them indirectly that it was a placebo. Then, under high- or low-choice

conditions, subjects wrote a counterattitudinal essay supporting the pardoning of Richard Nixon. Then, they indicated their attitude toward the pardoning. Placebo subjects showed the expected attitude change under high-choice conditions. Under high-choice conditions, subjects who had received the amphetamine showed great attitude change and subjects who received the tranquilizer showed no attitude change. Under low-choice conditions, amphetamine subjects showed attitude change! So, amphetamine arousal mimics or accentuates dissonance arousal and tranquilization counteracts dissonance arousal. These results suggest that cognitive dissonance has a physical effect on people.

Recently, Croyle, and Cooper (1983) attempted to measure dissonance arousal physically. First, they established that freely choosing to write a counterattitudinal essay in support of banning alcohol from the Princeton campus produced the expected attitude change and other conditions did not. Then, they replicated the conditions exactly except that they measured subjects' galvanic skin conductance as they went through the experiment. In this second experiment, they

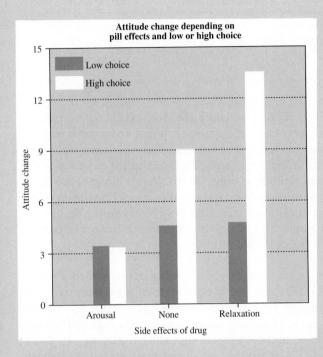

**Attitude change depending on
pill effects and low or high choice**

Legend: Low choice / High choice

(Bar chart. Y-axis: Attitude change, 0 to 15. X-axis: Side effects of drug — Arousal, None, Relaxation.)

Figure 6.A
Subject who expected no effects from a pill or expected to be relaxed by the pill showed a typical dissonance effect from induced compliance to support a speaker ban. However, those who thought the pill had aroused them did not show the dissonance effect. When the tension from dissonance was otherwise explained, attitude change did not occur.
(From Zanna & Cooper, 1974, Journal of Personality and Social Psychology, 29, 706.)

discovered that high-choice, counterattitudinal subjects displayed elevated arousal (via galvanic skin conductance measure) during a rest period following the essay writing. The other conditions did not produce the same sustained arousal. Clearly, there is evidence that dissonance arousal is a physical and psychological state involved in producing attitude change after induced compliance.

Cooper and his colleagues have been involved in the development of many other aspects of dissonance theory over the years (Cooper & Fazio, 1984). An example of one other area of interest is his therapeutic application of the effort justification approach (Aronson & Mills, 1959) in a weight-loss program (Axsom & Cooper, 1984). They had weight-loss candidates exert either high or low effort for five sessions over three weeks. The effort expended was not physical and it was totally unrelated to losing weight. Randomly assigned high-effort subjects spent more time doing a more difficult visual discrimination task than low-effort subjects. They also spoke for some time into a very distracting delayed auditory feedback (DAF) recording system, while low-effort subjects did not experience DAF. Certain intervals of delayed feedback of one's own voice make it quite difficult to count to ten, for instance. Zimbardo (1965) also used DAF to manipulate effort. Axsom and Cooper found that high-effort subjects lost more weight during this program and afterward than low-effort subjects did. Even a year later, they had maintained a substantially lower weight (about seven pounds)!

Table 6.5　Attitude Change after Induced Compliance (higher numbers, more change)

	Low choice	High choice, no misattribution	High choice, misattribution
Accept position	20.33	22.70	22.29
Reject position	18.77	21.14	18.89

From Fazio et al., 1977.

unacceptable position aroused dissonance (which was dissipated by the misattribution opportunity), but endorsing the acceptable position did not arouse dissonance. From this experiment, Fazio et al. concluded that endorsing a position within one's latitude of acceptance (one that is not too inconsistent with one's favored position) causes attitude change through self-perception processes, while endorsing a position in one's latitude of rejection (one that is inconsistent) leads to attitude change through dissonance arousal and reduction. They further contend that self-perception processes are most likely to operate during the formative stages of attitude development, and cognitive dissonance is more important in situations involving firmly established attitudes.

Dissonance Arousal　The debate about cognitive dissonance theory and self-perception theory places great importance on establishing whether or not a state called dissonance is actually aroused in the studies we have been discussing. Most dissonance studies have assumed that dissonance has been aroused and reduced when attitude change occurs. Bem's self-perception account of how this attitude change can occur without dissonance has made it imperative that dissonance researchers establish that dissonance actually exists. Recently, dissonance theorists have conclusively demonstrated that dissonance does occur.

One recent study has demonstrated a very interesting relationship between dissonance arousal and reduction and alcohol use (Steele, Southwick, & Critchlow, 1981). These investigators used the standard induced compliance procedure by asking subjects to write essays for a tuition increase for an important audience to create dissonance or against a tuition increase to create consonance. However, they added a twist. Subjects were given an opportunity to drink beer in a beer-tasting task either before or after indicating their attitude about a tuition increase in Experiment 1. In Experiment 2, subjects tasted either types of vodka drinks or different kinds of water after writing the counterattitudinal essay but before giving their attitude toward the tuition increase. Their results showed that drinking alcohol reduced dissonance and that dissonance arousal tended to make subjects drink more alcohol! These results suggest that dissonance is a negative emotional experience that people may try to eliminate with alcohol again and again. (See figure 6.14.)

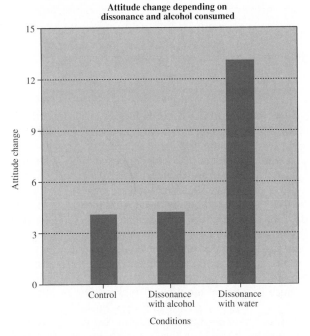

Attitude change depending on dissonance and alcohol consumed

Conditions

Figure 6.14
Drinking alcohol after writing a counterattitudinal essay reduced dissonance according to these attitude change results.
(From Steele, Southwick, & Critchlow, 1981, Journal of Personality and Social Psychology, 41, 840.)

Impression Management and Dissonance

We have just reviewed studies which indicate that dissonance arousal and reduction is involved in induced-compliance attitude change. While self-perception theory indicates that dissonance is not involved, proponents of impression management take an entirely different position. They insist that there is no real attitude change involved in the dissonance studies (Tedeschi, Schlenker, & Bonoma, 1971; Tedeschi & Rosenfeld, 1981). In their view, subjects just express attitudes consistent with their behavior in order to present or maintain a positive image with the experimenter or audience. Attitudes are expressed for self-presentational purposes; they do not represent true attitude change.

Some recent impression management approaches (Schlenker, 1980; Schlenker, Forsyth, Leary, & Miller, 1980) sound like revisions of dissonance that we have discussed. Schlenker and his associates contend that if a person's act is harmful and the person feels responsible for the act (because he or she did it with free choice and low inducement), then he or she will express attitudes consistent with the behavior to account for or justify the act. This description sounds similar to moral responsibility (Bramel, 1968) and self-relevant cognitions (Aronson, 1968) versions of dissonance theory except that the views disagree on the personal versus audience-oriented nature of the attitude.

The issue appears to turn on whether the attitude change is caused by feelings of inconsistency or self-presentation. Baumeister and Tice (1984) contend and have demonstrated that what they call dissonance can be caused by both. They demonstrated that if a person freely wrote a counterattitudinal essay under private conditions void of self-presentational concerns, that person changed his or her attitude. Also, if the person was forced (no choice) to write the essay under

A Question of Certainty

Aronson (1984) has presented what he calls "the psychology of inevitability" under the domain of cognitive dissonance. He states that when an unpleasant event or condition is considered unavoidable, a person will adjust his or her attitude to be more accepting of that event or condition. While I believe that this effect or phenomenon is real and important, I do not believe that it is a dissonance phenomenon. One of the central elements of dissonance arousal is choice. A distinct lack of choice to avoid it is part of what makes one perceive an unpleasant situation as inevitable. A person is also unlikely to feel responsible for something that is foisted upon him or her without him or her having a voice in the matter.

Whether it is dissonance or not, what happens when a person is faced with an unpleasant situation? There is some evidence that if the person sees it as inevitable, he or she will come to view it in a more positive light than if there is uncertainty about its occurrence. In the 1960's, government-provided health care for the aged, Medicare, was a controversial issue. While the Medicare bill was being debated in Congress but before its passage, a survey of medical doctors indicated that 62 percent of doctors opposed Medicare (Colombotes, 1969). However, after Medicare was passed but before it went into effect, the same researcher found that only 19 percent of the doctors surveyed opposed it. The only real difference between these two surveys was that at the time of the second survey, what had been seen as an unpleasant situation (by 62 percent of doctors) was going to occur. So over 40 percent of the doctors adopted a more positive attitude toward Medicare when they knew it was inevitable.

I tried to investigate the effects of certainty on attitudes toward another unpleasant event, serving in the U.S. armed forces, several years ago. At the height of the Vietnam war in 1970, the federal government instituted a draft lottery according to the birthdate of young men. The beauty of this lottery (if there was any beauty to it) was that the U.S. government randomly assigned subjects to (1) certain to serve, (2) uncertain to serve, and (3) certain not to serve conditions for me. I seized this opportunity to construct an attitude survey about military life, military discipline, military food and lodging, isolation from family and friends, and dangers of military life to administer to college seniors. My hypothesis was that men who were certain about having to serve in the armed forces (those with lottery numbers from 1 to 130) would have the most positive attitudes toward the elements of military life. Unfortunately, I was unable to get enough senior men who were not veterans, ROTC officers, or going to Canada to complete the questionnaire. One curious pattern I saw in the little data collected was that men with low draft numbers and no prospects of deferment indicated that they did not expect to be serving in the armed forces within a year. This denial of reality became more meaningful to me later.

A few years later, I heard about patterns of reactions to a prototypical unpleasant event, death (Kubler-Ross, 1969). Elisabeth Kubler-Ross noted in her observations of terminal patients and their families that people go through a common sequence of reactions to their own or loved ones' imminent death. She argued at that time

BLOOM COUNTY   by Berke Breathed

PC's apparently have some of the same reactions people do when facing a major loss.

BLOOM COUNTY, by Berke Breathed. © 1985 by Washington Post Co. Reprinted by permission.

that people in the grief process go through the following stages: (1) denial, (2) anger, (3) bargaining, (4) depression, and (5) acceptance. Current work in thanatology questions whether people always show the same pattern, whether or not they vacillate, and whether some of these reactions even occur for most people (Bowlby, 1980; Shneidman, 1973). Nevertheless, her first stage seemed to me to be what some of those senior men were displaying, and the last stage, acceptance, seemed to be what Aronson was writing about in his "psychology of inevitability."

To the extent that Kubler-Ross's stage model is correct and to the extent that death can be considered like other impending unpleasant events, we can assume that several negative reactions will precede positive attitude change toward unpleasant events. Extrapolating from Aronson's position and Kubler-Ross's perspective, I hypothesize that the speed with which a person proceeds through the negative reactions to acceptance and even whether a person progresses to ultimate acceptance is determined by his or her perceptions of the inevitability of the event. So, if a person perceives that a job loss, divorce, loved one's death, paraplegic condition, or loss of one's child in a custody battle is certain to occur or accepts that it has occurred; then he or she will become more accepting of that condition. To my knowledge, neither the validity nor generality of these speculations has been adequately tested.

public conditions with self-presentational concerns, then the person changed his or her attitude. If choice and self-presentation were both involved, then the attitude change was greatest. That attitude change occurred in the choice only, private conditions suggests that it was real attitude change. The fact that choice and self-presentation created similar changes suggests that self-presentational concerns can arouse dissonance. It appears that cognitive dissonance and impression management views of induced compliance are now less "dissonant" than they were.

Applications of Attitude Research

There are many kinds of attitudes that other people have which affect our daily lives. However, they usually exert influence only through behavior. Consequently, to apply attitude research meaningfully, we must be certain that the attitudes we assess are consistent with behavior. Strongly held attitudes are derived from direct experience, serve some important function for the person, are brought to his or her attention at an appropriate time, and are likely to be consistent with behavior. The applied psychologist must also assess the situation in which the behavior is to occur to assure that no situational pressures will countermand the influence of the attitude or to assess what those pressures are. Probably the best technique for using attitudes to predict behavior is Fishbein and Ajzen's (1975; Ajzen & Fishbein, 1980) approach to predicting reasoned action. They use several measures to evaluate the person's attitude *toward the behavior* of interest and several measures to evaluate the social norms operating in the situation. This approach has enabled them to predict several different kinds of behavior successfully.

Cognitive dissonance theory provides many approaches to practical attitude change. The counterattitudinal advocacy research clearly indicates that if you can get a person to act a particular way, then his or her attitudes will surely follow. However, this effect occurs only under certain conditions. The attitude change only occurs when the person commits the inconsistent act with perceived freedom of choice and with minimal inducement involved. Self-perception theory also indicates that perceived choice and minimal coercion or reward are necessary to make a person's attitudes follow his or her behavior.

Legislating Morality

The induced compliance studies indicate that "stateways can change folkways"; that is, laws can affect behavior which can change attitudes; but only under certain conditions. First, the laws must be enforced enough and carry heavy enough penalties to change the behavior of most people. However, the prosecution and penalties must be mild enough to be insufficient justification for changing the behavior so that dissonance will be aroused. The public accommodations portions of the Civil Rights Act of 1964 requiring that public eating and lodging establishments serve everyone regardless of race and the recent seat belt use laws are examples of laws which fit these criteria and have changed attitudes. The likelihood of prosecution under either of these laws was and is slight enough to be considered minimal inducement, yet the law was strong enough to get people to change their behaviors.

However, some laws have been unsuccessful in changing morality (attitudes). Laws prohibiting the use of alcohol and some other drugs are prime examples of such laws. The major problem with these laws seems to be that the probability of prosecution and the severity of the penalties were and are inadequate inducements to get people to change their behaviors in the first place. Possibly the positive attractions of alcohol and drug use are too great relative to the minor risks so that people have not changed their behavior. Susan Darley and Joel Cooper's (1972) study showing that failure to get behavior change creates boomerang effects suggests that illegal alcohol and drug users probably become more pro-alcohol or pro-drug in their attitudes because of the laws.

Of course, there are some laws which are unlikely to arouse dissonance. The primary purpose of most criminal laws is to reduce the incidence of the criminal behavior, and the effect on people's attitudes is not considered. After all, we want the probability of prosecution and the severity of penalties for murder to be strong enough that the law will act as a deterrent for potential murderous acts. We as a society are interested in compliance with the law, not attitude change. The attitudes of potential offenders are unlikely to be changed by severe prosecution of these laws.

Dissonance and Mass Communication

Using dissonance arousal and reduction to change attitudes is not a viable means of mass media persuasion. This is the case because what is minimal inducement (and dissonance-arousing) for one person may be inadequate inducement for another and excessive inducement for a third. We know from the $20 condition of Festinger and Carlsmith and the $5 conditions of Nel et al. that excessive inducement does not arouse dissonance or create attitude change. We know from Darley and Cooper's experiment that inducement inadequate to elicit the desired behavior produces attitude change in the opposite direction. If one presented the same inducement to a mass media audience, the message could possibly produce three different effects, two of which are undesirable. Unless the entire audience is of one mind, dissonance techniques must be individualized to be effective in persuasion applications.

Summary

Attitudes are evaluations of objects of thought. Our attitudes are derived from our beliefs and values. They are organized into networks, and that attitude organization may depend on the functions the attitudes serve. Cognitive consistency within these attitude networks affects how we react to new events and information.

Knowledge of one's attitudes helps us know how that person will behave. However, LaPiere's study on attitudes and behavior toward Chinese people showed that behaviors are not always consistent with attitudes. Attitude-behavior consistency is greatest when situational or social pressures on behavior are minimal, when the attitude is accessible and recalled before acting, when the attitude assessed corresponds closely to the behavior of interest, and when the person's transient mood state is not intensely positive or negative. Ajzen and Fishbein have been quite successful in predicting behavior by evaluating the person's attitude toward doing the behavior and the social norms about the behavior.

Our attitudes are formed through experiencing positive or negative sensations associated with the object of thought. Dramatic events or presentations shape our attitudes. Important historical events and figures during our youthful years can have great impact on our political attitudes.

The most prominent of the cognitive consistency theories has been Festinger's theory of cognitive dissonance. Dissonance is an unpleasant tension aroused when we are cognizant of inconsistency between ideas. We are motivated to reduce dissonance. Dissonance can be reduced by changing a dissonant cognition, adding a consonant cognition, or changing the importance of a dissonant cognition. In induced compliance studies, dissonance is reduced by changing one's attitude to fit with behavior. In induced compliance studies, dissonance is aroused when a person chooses to commit a counterattitudinal behavior which has negative consequences for someone. Dissonance is accentuated if the actor feels personally responsible for his or her action and the act is inconsistent with the actor's self-concept. The actor does not change his or her attitude to reduce dissonance if he or she is given the opportunity to do self-affirming behavior. Induced restraint using only mild threats of punishment can make people internalize desirable attitudes.

When a person expends great effort to attain something, she will experience dissonance if the attained status is not valuable. As a result, we come to value the things for which we have to strive more than things attained easily. When we make difficult decisions, we experience dissonance because the alternatives not chosen have positive features. We question the wisdom of our decisions. Eventually, we reduce dissonance by evaluating our chosen alternative more positively than we did originally, but in some cases, we regret our decision first.

Self-perception theory states that we infer our attitudes from our behavior and the attendant circumstances rather than experiencing dissonance and changing our attitudes to reduce it. However, Cooper and his associates have shown that we do experience dissonance in induced compliance situations. Self-perception processes apply most appropriately to situations wherein the behavior is consistent with one's original attitude. Impression management theorists assert that we express particular attitudes in order to present ourselves positively rather than actually changing attitudes. A compromise position suggests that both cognitive inconsistency and self-presentational concerns arouse dissonance.

The assertion from both cognitive dissonance and self-perception theories that behavior affects attitudes implies that we can legislate morality. If the legal sanctions are extreme enough to obtain the desired behavior but are not too extreme, we can affect people's attitudes through laws. The failures of alcohol and drug prohibition laws indicate that we cannot always legislate morality. Dissonance techniques are most successful in interactive persuasion applications that allow the persuader to individualize the inducements.

Social Influence and Group Dynamics

Social Influence

Persuasion

What is persuasion? **Persuasion** is a type of social influence in which a source tries to change the mind or actions of a recipient. Persuasion is being attempted whenever you see and hear actors or cartoon characters deliver messages about a product on television. The message may be simple, informative, logical, and delivered by an unseen person in a voice-over, or it may be delivered in a full-blown Michael Jackson video. The message may be frightening, humorous, appealing to your need for popularity, or boringly repetitious. Persuasion also occurs when you try to talk a friend into seeing a particular movie or when a lawyer tries to convince a judge or a jury that the defendant is guilty. Persuasion has many facets, many dimensions.

Persuasion involves overt attempts to change another person's attitudes or behaviors. Its explicitness makes persuasion different from other forms of **social influence,** such as conformity and modeling. However, a persuader is no more forceful or direct than an authority figure who commands obedience, as in the Milgram studies. Media advertising is the most common form of persuasion, but persuasion can involve simply one person trying to change another person's mind.

The Elaboration Likelihood Model

Recently, a new theory of persuasion, the **Elaboration Likelihood Model (ELM)** (Petty & Cacioppo, 1986), has become prominent. The basic idea is that the more able and motivated a person is to *elaborate* or think about and flesh out the issue-relevant arguments in a message, the more likely it is that rational or **central route persuasion** will occur. Central route persuasion occurs through focusing on the strength or logic of arguments. This mindful approach leads to enduring and strongly-held attitudes. If, because of personal or situational factors, the message receiver is unlikely to consider and elaborate on the information received; then issue-irrelevant or **peripheral route persuasion** will occur. Peripheral route persuasion occurs through focusing on irrelevant or peripheral cues, such as length of arguments, and this relatively mindless processing produces temporary and weakly-held attitudes. In this chapter, we will see that various source, message, channel, and receiver factors affect elaboration likelihood.

From the beginning of the social psychological study of persuasion, the field has been divided into (1) *Source* or communicator factors, (2) *Message* factors, (3) *Channel* or media factors, and (4) *Receiver* or target audience factors (Hovland, Janis, & Kelley, 1953). We will follow the same format.

Source or Communicator Factors

Expertise and Attractiveness

The earliest research indicated that the *perceived expertise* and *attractiveness* of the source greatly influenced the amount of persuasion accomplished (Hovland & Weiss, 1951). In that study, students in a Yale history class read several essays. The catch—and the manipulation of the independent variable—was that the same essays were attributed to two different sources in the versions the students read. For instance, the essay on the feasibility of nuclear-powered submarines in the 1950s was attributed to J. Robert Oppenheimer, the American atomic physicist, in one version and to *Pravda,* the Soviet newspaper, in the other version. Oppenheimer and similar sources proved to be more persuasive. The problem with these

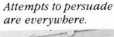

Attempts to persuade are everywhere.

findings is it is not known whether expertise or attractiveness made the source more credible and persuasive. Oppenheimer was undoubtedly a more attractive source to students than *Pravda* because he was an American, and he was a more expert source on nuclear issues because he was the leader in the development of the atomic bomb. Expertise and attractiveness appear to be hopelessly confounded in this study.

Subsequent research suggests that both perceived source expertise alone and source attractiveness alone affect communicator credibility. For example, Bochner and Insko (1966) found that an expert source was more persuasive than a nonexpert when both advocated an unexpected, unfounded position. (See figure 7.1.) Also, an expert on poetry was more convincing than a freshman English student when both took an extremely different position from the subjects' on poetry ratings (Aronson, Turner, & Carlsmith, 1963).

As for *source attractiveness,* some studies (Horai, Naccari, & Fatoullah, 1974; Dion & Stein, 1978) have shown that physical attractiveness per se enhances persuasiveness. Of course, features other than physical appearance affect our liking for people. Some of these features of communicators, such as speech content and style, nonverbal mannerisms, and information from other sources were discussed in chapter 4. Any of those characteristics, which would create a positive impression in the recipient, should enhance attractiveness and persuasiveness. Consequently, companies with established attractive reputations have better results from persuasive messages than new companies do.

Similarity between the *communicator* and the *recipient* makes the communicator more attractive and persuasive (McQuire, 1985). We like people who are like us in attitudes (Byrne, 1971), appearance (Murstein & Christy, 1976),

Figure 7.1
The sleep expert, the highly credible source, was more persuasive than the nonexpert when he advocated a ridiculously low number of hours of sleep needed each night. Expert sources are more persuasive, especially when they take extreme positions.
(From Bochner & Insko, 1966, Journal of Personality and Social Psychology, 4, 619.)

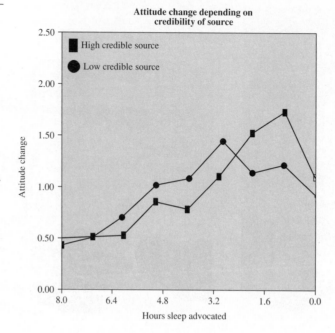

personality (Izard, 1963), ethnic background, age, and socioeconomic status (D. Buss, 1985). These similar people are more persuasive (Simons, Berkowitz, & Moyer, 1970). For instance, Stoneman and Brody (1981) found that food selections by same-age, same-race peers strongly influenced children's food preferences. Two experiments (Goethals & Nelson, 1973; Mills & Kimble, 1973) suggest that whether similar others are persuasive depends on the issue. The results of both studies indicate that similar others are more influential when the issue is a subjective matter of taste or values than when it is an objective matter of belief or knowledge. So, hidden camera interviews with ordinary people should make more convincing advertisements for coffee than for computer products. Since most advertising seems to address choices between different brands of the same product—a subjective judgment—capitalizing on source-recipient similarity is a viable advertising strategy. It even seems that in some businesses, subjectivity is maximized by obscuring information to the extent that intelligent comparison shopping is impossible.

Research evidence indicates that expert, attractive, and similar communicators are persuasive. However, an expert communication source is probably more effective than the other types of sources with certain issues or products. For example, "fifty-one percent of doctors surveyed chose acetaminophen for their pain" would be more effective than "fifty-one percent of glamorous movie stars surveyed chose acetaminophen for their pain." Attractiveness or similarity appear to be more effective in beer and soft drink ads. Of course, the advertiser must know who is attractive to the largest audience to maximize attractiveness and what kind of audience is likely to be watching and listening at the time in order to use communicator-audience similarity as a strategy. Petty and Cacioppo (1981) suggest that all three of these source factors use a peripheral approach to persuasion, which is most effective when the receiver of the message is uninvolved and not particularly mindful of the message—like a "couch potato." *Peripheral* persuasion is being attempted whenever factors irrelevant or unessential to the information or logical argument being presented are emphasized. Source characteristics are examples of such irrelevant factors.

The effectiveness of all advertisements in persuasion is undermined by the fact that we know that their purpose is to get us to buy the product. This knowledge makes us wary, skeptical, and resistant to their claims. The heart of the issue is probably trustworthiness, as the Hovland group at Yale originally thought. However, trustworthiness is based on more than expertise and attractiveness; it is based on the perceived honesty of the communicator. We just do not trust the claims that we hear and see in commercials on television and other media.

Creating Credibility through Trustworthiness

If a source can convince us that he, she, or it is being truthful, then the source's communication will be much more persuasive. Signs of trustworthiness can make a source, regardless of its expertise, attractiveness, or similarity, more credible. For example, suppose a doctor examined you and said, "You need to have your gall bladder removed." That statement would be perceived as trustworthy in certain circumstances and not in others. If that doctor were the surgeon who would remove your gall bladder, if another doctor had not given that diagnosis, and you had not been feeling any pain in that region, then you would likely think that he had made that diagnosis to make money, and you would probably hang onto your gall bladder. If another doctor were going to do the surgery, if a third doctor had diagnosed a gall bladder problem, and you had felt fierce pain in your chest, then you would probably think that he or she knew the symptoms and was telling the truth, and you would have your gall bladder removed.

To summarize, (1) if a communicator obviously had something to gain by sending a particular message, (2) if the message improved the speaker's self-interests, (3) if no uninvolved party endorsed the same position, and/or (4) the receiver's perceptions did not agree with the message, then the receiver would probably not be convinced by the message. If the opposite conditions existed, the receiver would probably be influenced by the message because the source would be seen as trustworthy.

Ample research evidence supports this trustworthiness perspective on communicator credibility. If a hardened criminal argues against his or her own self-interests, he or she is more persuasive than a judge (Walster, Aronson, & Abrahams, 1966). If a probusiness political candidate took a proenvironment, antibusiness position, he or she was more persuasive than a proenvironmental speaker was (Eagly, Wood, & Chaikin, 1978). (See figure 7.2.) When a person made statements while being unaware that an audience was listening—that is, the speaker could not have been trying to gain something by persuading the audience—the speaker was more persuasive than if the speaker talked directly to the audience (Walster & Festinger, 1962). Several studies (Allyn & Festinger, 1961; Hass & Grady, 1975; Kiesler & Kiesler, 1964; Petty & Cacioppo, 1979a)

Figure 7.2
A proenvironmental talk to a primary audience was most persuasive to a secondary audience when it was known that the speaker had a probusiness background or that the primary audience was probusiness. Such a speaker was apparently perceived as trustworthy.

(From Eagly et al., 1978, Journal of Personality and Social Psychology, 36, 429.)

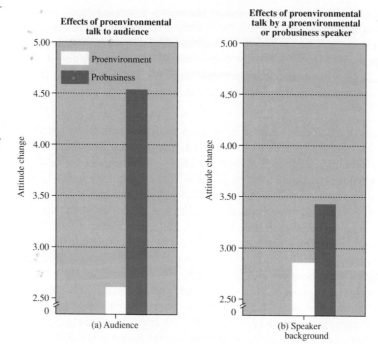

have shown that if a speaker clearly intends to persuade an audience, presumably to gain some reward, such a speaker is less persuasive than one whose intent to persuade is less clear. (See figure 7.3.) Finally, McGinnies and Ward (1980) found that when an author's associates viewed him as honest, sincere, and trustworthy and that information was passed on to the receiver; the author's message was more persuasive than if he were expert, but not so trustworthy. These research findings suggest techniques media advertisers might use to overcome their credibility disadvantage created by consumers' awareness of their intentions.

Message Factors

There are many conceivable types of messages. The content or style of messages may induce fear, create a positive mood, present logical arguments, or even appeal to the receiver's unconscious motivation. Of course, the first thing messages must do is get or retain your attention. Then you, the receiver, must understand the message. Given that you understand it, you must accept the message. Finally, for you to act on the newly-acquired attitude, you must store the message and retrieve it when it is time to act (Hovland et al., 1953; McQuire, 1985).

Attention

What messages get our attention? Unusual messages can grab our attention. If you have seen upside down signs, you realize they can get your attention. Words spoken very rapidly, as in some commercials, are unusual enough to get your attention. Vivid visual images (for example, bright colors, scantily clad people) can get your attention if they are in your visual field, and sounds (for example, loud sounds, music) can make you look toward their source. Studies have shown

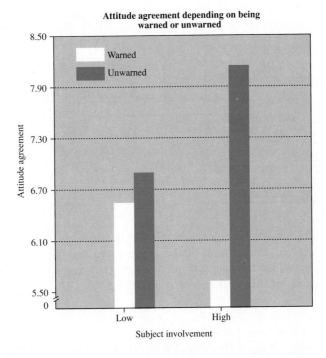

Attitude agreement depending on being
warned or unwarned

Figure 7.3
When the issue was important to the subject (high involvement) and the subject had not been forewarned of the speaker's persuasive intent, the greatest amount of persuasion occurred. The message was apparently seen as manipulative when forewarning of persuasive intent was given.
(From Petty & Cacioppo, 1979, Personality and Social Psychology Bulletin, 5, 179.)

that music, moving figures, and female voices can draw the attention of young children (Alwitt, Anderson, Lorch, & Levin, 1980). Generally speaking, unusual or potent visual or sound stimuli, which appeal to our distal senses, can elicit our attention. For some stimuli (for example, nude men), their attention value depends on the motivation of the audience and the acquired meaning of the stimulus.

However, attention is not the whole story. If no message is delivered after you attend to the source, persuasion will not occur. It seems that some attention-getting stimuli are so compelling that receivers don't attend to the accompanying message. It would be folly to use a powerful, provocative stimulus to gain a consumer's attention and then present a weak message unless the stimulus was the complete message. For instance, if a brand name were presented on the package in vivid color and it provoked retrieval of information about the product, that would be an appropriate use of an attention-getting stimulus.

Understanding the Message

When the receiver is attending, the communicator must send a clear, comprehensible message to be persuasive. Eagly (1974) demonstrated the importance of a clear communication by presenting arguments about how many hours of sleep are needed per night. A "sleep expert" presented good, understandable arguments indicating that people only need two, four, or six hours of sleep in some experimental conditions. In other conditions, the message was made less comprehensible by distorting the quality of the taped communication or by scrambling the words in the explanatory arguments. The poor comprehensibility messages were less persuasive than the understandable messages. Eagly speculated that subjects may have been upset by the poor-quality communications,

We are constantly being bombarded by persuasion attempts.

BLOOM COUNTY, by Berke Breathed. © 1987 by Washington Post Co. Reprinted by permission.

which made them less accepting of the message. So, there may have been more involved than simply understanding the message. Even though the subjects understood the poor communications, they may have been resistant to accepting them because of their annoying nature.

Drawing Conclusions

Another issue related to comprehension of a message is whether the communication should state conclusions explicitly or allow the receivers to infer the conclusions. Should you tell the listeners or readers what you want them to believe or should you encourage them to work through the arguments, think more, and perhaps persuade themselves? Much of the research indicates that explicitly stated conclusions are most persuasive (Hovland & Mandell, 1952; Fine, 1955; Thistlethwaite, de Haan, & Kamenetzky, 1955). The problem seems to be that most subjects do not work at understanding the communication in these studies because those few subjects who did understand the message were as persuaded by arguments without conclusions as those with conclusions. Also, one study showed that when comprehension was assured among all subjects, those subjects who had worked their ways through logical syllogisms (without explicit conclusions) were more persuaded than others who had simply read premises and conclusions (Linder & Worchel, 1970). Drawing conclusions explicitly was more persuasive in these studies because most subjects were not actively processing the information enough to infer conclusions.

Kardes (1988) used magazine advertisements for compact disc players to examine the effectiveness of messages with explicit or omitted conclusions. One ad gave information about three characteristics of the compact disc player and clearly stated the positive conclusions about the disc player. The other ad gave the same background information necessary to draw the conclusions about the disc player but did not state the conclusions. When the facts that subjects may be buying disc players soon and that there are good and bad disc players were made prominent to the subjects, subjects inferred the positive conclusions and formed more favorable attitudes about the disc player. These potential consumers

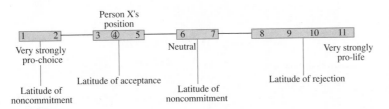

Possible positions on abortion

Figure 7.4
*An example of social
judgment theory.
According to social
judgment theory,
person X should accept
the attitude positions
within his or her
latitude of acceptance
and reject all positions
within the latitude of
rejection. Person X
would not take a firm
position on any of the
attitudes within the
latitudes of
noncommitment.*

could also retrieve their favorable attitudes more readily than subjects who read the conclusions directly. So, if consumers are motivated to understand the message, messages without conclusions are more effective.

If we hear a message over and over again, how are we likely to respond to it? With each repetition, we are more likely to understand the message and retrieve it readily when asked (Cacioppo & Petty, 1979). However, with each repetition, we are likely to attend to the message less because we already know it (Harkins & Petty, 1981c), and we are likely to be less accepting and think more negatively about the message (Cacioppo & Petty, 1979). If there are variations in the message (Grass & Wallace, 1969), if the message is presented by different sources (Harkins & Petty, 1981c), or if the repetitions are spread over time; the message can be effective even when used repeatedly. Even the "Tastes great! Less filling!" beer ads and the McDonald's jingle wear thin if they do not use some of these strategies.

Sometimes we attend to persuasive messages and comprehend their meaning, but we do not accept them. Actually, acceptance of messages into our attitude system and memory is often a more important issue than comprehension of the message. We may reject a message because it clashes with our existing beliefs and attitudes. **Social judgment theory** (Hovland & Sherif, 1961) begins with the view that a person's attitude on an issue can be located along a dimension of possible attitudes on that issue. Suppose that your position on the abortion issue were moderately pro-choice: you believe that abortions should be legal during the first trimester of pregnancy in most cases. Positions similar to yours endorsing the availability of safe abortions under certain circumstances would probably be acceptable to you and would fall into your "latitude of acceptance" (Sherif & Sherif, 1967). Strong pro-life positions would probably fall into your "latitude of rejection." Other positions, such as moderate ones or extreme pro-choice ones, would fall into gray areas of noncommitment. People with firmly-held attitudes typically have a narrow latitude of acceptance and a broad latitude of rejection on those attitude dimensions. (See figure 7.4.)

Social judgment theory suggests that messages should not be too discrepant from the receiver's position on the issue, or they will not be assimilated into the receiver's attitude system. Hovland, Harvey, and Sherif (1957) used attitudes and messages on what was a very controversial issue in Oklahoma at that time

Accepting the
Message

Figure 7.5
*The lower credibility
communicator (a
freshman student) was
only persuasive when
she advocated a
position moderately
discrepant from the
subject's position. The
high credibility
communicator, a
poetry expert, was
persuasive even when
he took a very
discrepant position.*
(From Aronson et al., 1963,
Journal of Abnormal and Social
Psychology, 67, 33.)

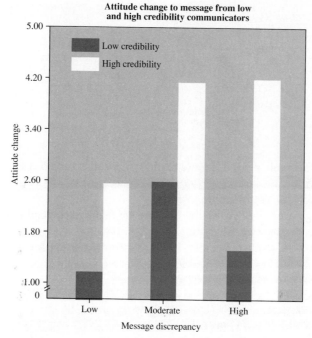

Attitude change to message from low
and high credibility communicators

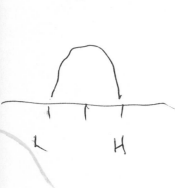

to test their ideas about message discrepancy and persuasion. The issue was whether or not the sale of alcoholic beverages should be legalized. After the investigators assessed these Oklahomans' positions on the issue, they presented to each subject a message tailored to be mildly, moderately, or extremely discrepant with the subject's position. The results showed that the moderately discrepant messages were most persuasive, apparently because the extremely different messages fell into subjects' latitude of rejection.

Some researchers have contended that whether the receiver will accept a very discrepant message or not depends on the credibility of the communicator (Aronson, Turner, & Carlsmith, 1963; Bochner & Insko, 1966). The cognitive dissonance position (Aronson et al., 1963) is that greater disagreement arouses more dissonance and that dissonance can only be reduced by changing one's attitude or denying the credibility of the communicator. If the communicator were perfectly credible, then the receiver could only change his or her attitude to reduce dissonance.

Using poetry ratings as the attitude dimension, Aronson and associates demonstrated that an expert communicator, T. S. Eliot, was persuasive when he registered great disagreement with the subject's position. Sherif and his colleagues could probably still claim that moderately discrepant messages are generally the most persuasive. Certainly, the Oklahoma subjects had much more invested in their positions on alcohol than the Harvard English students did in poetry ratings. It is possible that the Harvard students had no latitude of rejection for the poetry ratings. (See figure 7.5.)

Limited time offers induce reactance in consumers and promote sales.

The question of acceptance of arguments with explicit conclusions, as well as understanding of them, must also be considered. First, the communicator who draws conclusions for you is more likely to be seen as intending to persuade to gain rewards, which undermines the communicator's persuasiveness. Second, he or she may be perceived as threatening your freedom to decide on a position for yourself. When our freedoms are threatened, most of us react against the position espoused. This idea about the effect of threatened freedoms is the central tenet of **reactance theory** (Brehm, 1966).

Also, the directness or argumentativeness of the message style should affect your acceptance of the message. Reactance theory (Brehm, 1966, 1972; Wicklund, 1974) suggests that if forceful, arbitrary attempts are made to restrict your freedom, you are likely to change your mind in the opposing direction because you value freedom. So, messages containing statements such as "You can't do X" or "You *must* think Z" are likely to invoke reactance or "reverse psychology," and the receiver will not agree or comply. Recent research on speech acts (Holtgraves, 1986; Searle, 1975) suggests that indirect speech acts (Can you open the door?) are more effective than direct speech acts (Open the door.) in persuading people to do what you want. Perhaps indirect speech does not threaten the receiver's freedom as much. Also, research by Langer and her associates (Langer, 1989; Langer, Blank, & Chanowitz, 1978) on "mindlessness" and responses to requests suggests that offering explanations for one's behavior makes the message appear less arbitrary and unthreatening to the receiver's freedom. Therefore, requests with explanations—even meaningless explanations—are more persuasive than requests alone.

There is a way that a communicator can use reactance to his or her advantage (Cialdini, 1985). Instead of arousing reactance against the persuasion attempt, the communicator would use the message to inform the receiver that the opportunity to enjoy a product is being threatened. By stating, "Sale ends tomorrow" or "We have a very limited supply of Product X on hand," the source

This advertising uses humor to create a pleasant association with the product.

can arouse reactance in the receiver so that the receiver will value the product more. Cialdini (1985) refers to this technique as the *scarcity* principle of influence. In a similar way, censorship of a movie may cause us to value the movie more.

What other types of appeals are effective in persuasion? A message can have many kinds of content. One communication may have humor as its central characteristic. Another may be designed to provoke positive feelings in the listener. A third kind of message may be aimed at affecting your unconscious motives. Yet another may attempt to strike fear in the viewer. These four types of appeals are designed to gain the attention, acceptance, and retention of the message. Petty and Cacioppo (1981, 1984) would characterize all these messages as persuasion attempts using the peripheral route since none emphasize logical arguments in persuasion. Presentation of strong arguments encourage elaboration and typify the *central route* to persuasion (Petty & Cacioppo, 1986).

The evidence that humorous presentations are more persuasive than non-humorous ones is almost nil in systematic research (Markiewicz, 1974). Yet, nearly half of the four or more commercials in any two-minute break on television are intended to be funny and almost every speaker uses several funny stories to break the ice. Classical conditioning notions suggest that products associated with humor would come to evoke a pleasant response. However, that positive conditioned response may not be enough to get the consumer to buy the product. If costs and other factors were equal, perhaps you or I would be likely to buy a new product with a funny ad over one associated with a serious ad. In the real world, it is hard to establish that all other factors are equal. Clara Peller's "Where's the beef?" commercial poking fun at competitors in the hamburger business, did increase sales for that fast food company several years ago. However, ads by a similar fast food chain which poked fun at a fictitious customer, "Herb," fell on their face. This research area deserves more systematic study than it has received.

Commercials which provoke such positive feelings as warmth, exuberance, or sexual excitement are also based on classical conditioning principles. If the product becomes the conditioned stimulus for the positive feeling, then perhaps we consumers will buy it. Advertisements for soft drinks attempt to associate their products with excitement following this model. Another virtue of this type of advertisement is that it can highlight ways the consumer can improve him- or herself. If the product is involved in that means of improvement, then we surely will buy it so that we can enjoy the good life, right? Is it possible to classify such commercials into "classical conditioning" or "means of improvement" categories? It might be interesting to see if that is a meaningful classification system and if one type of commercial is more profitful than the other. There is not enough research in this area of persuasion either.

Unconscious Motivation

Unconscious motivation has been the focus of many advertising specialists (Dichter, 1960). There are at least two ways stimuli can affect a receiver without that person's conscious awareness. One, stimuli can be presented so rapidly or in

Sexuality is used to sell many products.

such a distorted form that they cannot be perceived consciously or stimuli can have implied meanings that are not recognized at a conscious level by the receiver.

The first form of appeal to unconscious motivation is represented in an advertising gimmick used in a New Jersey movie theater by James Vicary in 1956 (McConnell, Cutler, & McNeil, 1958). Ads for a soft drink and popcorn were superimposed on the movie screen for 1/3,000 second intervals, much too fast to be consciously seen. Yet, the customers consumed more popcorn and drinks than usual at those showings. Wild claims for the effectiveness of this subliminal advertising were made. However, appropriate comparisons to sales before and after that film and to sales during other seasons and under different circumstances were not conducted. The rapid exposure technique has been discredited as ineffective (McConnell et al., 1958). Even though a recent study (Robles, Smith, Carver, & Wellens, 1987) has shown that pictures presented at much slower (1/60 second) intervals during a videotape can affect our emotional reactions, there has been no demonstrations that subliminal advertising using this procedure affects buying behavior.

Another example of this type of subliminal appeal is evident in the presentation of satanic messages on records when they are played backwards. When these records are played normally, listeners cannot hear these messages (Thorne, 1984). Apparently, there is no reason for concern unless some listener is into manually rotating records backward around a turntable. Undesirable messages delivered at a conscious level should cause more concern.

Another type of unconscious appeal is based on Freudian psychology and is or has been endorsed by some advertisers (Dichter, 1960). Freud (1920/1965) believed that sexual features and activities are often represented unconsciously by other objects and events because they produce anxiety when we acknowledge them directly. He noticed that many sexual symbols are present in dreams. According to Freud, male sex organs and activities are symbolized by sticks, umbrellas, poles, knives, guns, water faucets, balloons, airplanes, and mechanical pencils. Female sex organs and activities are represented in dreams by doors, rooms, churches, ships, and boxes. Dancing, riding, climbing, and playing the piano in dreams are symbols of the sex act. These symbols might be used in persuasion to make consumers associate a pleasant sexual reaction with the advertiser's product. Cars and features of cars are often mentioned in sexual terms. According to some popular books (Key, 1973), unconscious appeals based on such symbolism are still commonly used. An advantage of the unconscious approach is that the persuader may be able to avoid the consumer's resistance to the sales pitch by using this indirect form of communication. However, there are no systematic studies in the social psychological literature showing that appeals to unconscious motivation work.

Fear Appeals and Persuasion

A fear appeal.

Fear appeals can also provoke resistance or reactance. Seat belt messages, and especially seat belt laws, are often resisted by receivers. Messages aimed at creating fear in the receiver are evident in many antidrug use and antismoking campaigns and in safe driving campaigns. I have a very clear memory of a "three-pack a day" man fainting as an antismoking film we were watching showed a vivid portrayal of lung surgery. What I don't remember is whether he stopped smoking.

Are fear appeals effective? An early study (Janis & Feshbach, 1953) presented low, moderate, and high fear-arousing messages to subjects about the consequences of poor dental hygiene. They found that the low fear appeal caused the greatest change in dental care practices. Subsequent investigations have emphasized the importance of clearly presenting remedies for the current maladaptive behavior (Leventhal, 1970; Rogers, 1975; Rogers & Mewborn, 1976). If you arouse fear in a person by telling him or her that there will be very severe consequences resulting from his or her mode of behavior, you must indicate a change in behavior that will prevent those consequences to persuade. If fear is aroused and no remedial action is presented, the fear appeal will not work. Rogers and Mewborn (1976) found that if the consequences of smoking, reckless driving, and venereal disease were presented as terrible and probable and the remedies were presented as effective, subjects were most likely to adopt the remedy. If the remedies were presented as ineffective, arousing subjects' fear was useless in persuading them. These studies point to the importance of presenting convincing evidence of the effectiveness of the recommended treatment in protecting life and health.

Remembering the Message

If the target person has attended to, understood, and accepted the message, that does not mean that he or she will act on the message. Many times, there is a long interval between receiving the message and acting upon it. That is certainly the case with most media advertising. Storage and retrieval of the message is crucial if the desired behavior is going to occur.

Attitude accessibility, the ease with which an attitude can be remembered upon cue, affects whether accepting a message will influence behavior (Fazio, 1986). One factor that affects attitude accessibility is repetition of the message (Fazio & Zanna, 1981). If you have seen a soap commercial for a particular brand many times, you are likely to remember that brand when it is time to buy soap. On the retrieval end of memory, it seems that the prominence or vividness of the cue (e.g., the brand name or symbol) when and where you are considering a purchase would be especially important.

Memory is important when a communicator has to decide when to present his or her message. A crucial factor is when the messages are delivered relative to when their persuasion effects are assessed (Miller & Campbell, 1959). If message A and an opposing message B were presented back-to-back and subjects' attitudes were measured after a delay, then message A had more persuasive impact (a **primacy effect,** what was presented first was remembered best). If message A was followed by a delay and then message B was presented right before attitude assessments, message B had more persuasive impact (a **recency effect,** the last presented message was remembered best). If there were no delays or there was a delay after each message, the messages had equal impact. It appears that the first presenter has the advantage if there is a considerable lag before action and that the most recent presenter has the advantage if action is immediately after that presentation. It would take a very astute and calculating lawyer or debater to take advantage of this memory effect within the prescribed courtroom format. A lawyer would have to know when his or her key points are going to appear in testimony and carefully arrange examinations (direct, cross, and redirect) relative to recesses. The points lost by upsetting the judge and jury would probably override any memory advantage gained. Sherrod (1985) has reviewed the effect of courtroom delays in light of some of this work on memory and persuasion.

Order of Presentation and Memory

Another memory effect in persuasion is the *sleeper effect* (Hovland, Lumdaine, & Sheffield, 1949). A message is said to have a **sleeper effect** when it has greater influence on attitudes after a long delay than it had immediately after presentation. Gillig and Greenwald (1974) did seven experiments trying to find more attitude change after a delay than immediately after presentation and failed to find the sleeper effect. However, Gruder, Cook, Hennigan, Flay, Alessis, and Halamaj (1978) demonstrated that the sleeper effect does occur. First, they presented a 1,000–word message which argued that the four-day work week would lead to worker dissatisfaction to subjects. Then, some subjects received a note indicating that the previous message was inaccurate and untrue. Those subjects who received the discounting note displayed the sleeper effect. Their initial attitudes were negative toward the message, but five weeks later, they agreed with the four-day work week message. It seems that these results occur because subjects remember the long message with stated and restated supportive arguments and forget the short contradictory note. This position is consistent with Kelman and Hovland's (1953) finding that the sleeper effect disappeared when the message *and* an untrustworthy source were restated after the delay so that the short source note would not be forgotten. Whenever the briefer, less emphasized source or discounting information is made resistant to forgetting, the sleeper effect does not occur. (See figure 7.6.)

The Sleeper Effect

Figure 7.6
The sleeper effect. The sleeper effect occurred in the condition where the message was followed by a short discounting note so that the message was more persuasive after a five-week delay than right after it was presented. The Message and Discounting condition produced the sleeper effect because the discounting note was forgotten during the delay and the message itself was retained.

(*From Gruder et al., 1978,* Journal of Personality and Social Psychology, 36, *1066.*)

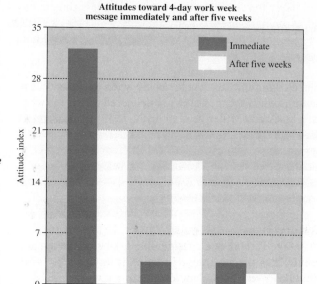

Attitudes toward 4-day work week message immediately and after five weeks

Immediate measure and after five weeks

Another interesting point in the context of memory and the sleeper effect is that the sleeper effect does not occur if the receiver is given the discounting information discrediting the message first (Greenwald, Baumgardner, & Leippe, 1979). Apparently, receiving the discounting information first casts the message into a different context for encoding by receivers (Mills & Harvey, 1972). Taken together, these results suggest that presenting weak evidence or inaccurate information to an audience will have delayed persuasive impact if the information is not discredited until later.

Media or Channel Factors

Messages can be communicated in many different ways. The more typical channels include: (1) *Verbally* in printed words; (2) *Spatially* through graphs, sketches, or pictures; (3) *Aurally* through spoken words; (4) *Visually* through moving pictures; or (5) a combination of channels. The print media, such as this book, are limited to the first two channels. Radio and telephones are constrained to the third channel. Television can use all channels, but typically uses only the third and fourth channels simultaneously. On television the aural and visual channels are often not redundant, but present different messages at the same time. Live presentations usually embody simultaneous aural and visual channels. Telephones and live presentations enable two-way communication, while the mass media, particularly print, allow minimal interaction. On the other hand, telephones limit the number of message receivers more than the other media do because only one person at a time usually listens on the phone.

Which channel is most effective in persuasion depends on the complexity of the message. Chaiken and Eagly (1976) presented easy or difficult messages in written, audio, or audiovisual form. The audio and videotape presentations

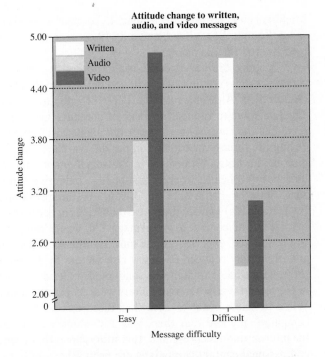

Attitude change to written, audio, and video messages

Message difficulty

Figure 7.7
Easy messages created more attitude change when they were presented on videotapes. Difficult messages produced more attitude change when they were presented in written form.
(From Chaiken & Eagly, 1976, Journal of Personality and Social Psychology, 34, 609.)

took seven minutes, and readers were allowed seven minutes to read the written message. They found that the easy message was understood equally well in all three channels and that the videotaped message was more persuasive than the written message. For the difficult message, they found that the written message was understood and recalled better than the audiotaped or videotaped message and that the written message was more persuasive than the other two. It seems that even though the exposure time was equal for all messages, subjects reading the written message could reread difficult passages so their comprehension was better than the other subjects, who heard the message only once. So, complex material is more aptly presented in print, but simpler material is more persuasive when presented on television. (See figure 7.7.)

Television is generally regarded as a more engrossing media because of its audio and video channels. It commands our attention better and is better liked than single channel (radio and print) media, especially more so than print (Andreoli & Worchel, 1978). Consistent with ideas about attention-capturing differences in media, it has been found that within the print media, pictures are more persuasive than words (Childers, Heckler, & Houston, 1986).

Over the years, social psychologists have found that *person-to-person* communication is more persuasive than *mass media* communication (Eldersveld & Dodge, 1954; Katz, 1957; Maccoby & Alexander, 1980). One study showed that voting patterns could be drastically changed through personal door-to-door canvassing, moderately affected by a mail campaign, and slightly affected by a local mass media campaign (Eldersveldt & Dodge, 1954). Their results showed that 75 percent of the voters who were contacted personally supported an Ann Arbor,

Personal versus Mass Communication

Michigan city charter amendment; 45 percent of those receiving persuasive messages through the mail did; and only 19 percent of those exposed only to the mass media voted for the change.

A more dramatic recent evaluation of the effects of personal persuasion versus the mass media was conducted in three small towns in northern California (Maccoby & Alexander, 1980). These investigators wanted to discover the most effective ways to reduce the risks of coronary heart disease. One town, Tracy, served as the control as no campaign about coronary risks was conducted there during the three-year evaluation period. Another town, Gilroy, was exposed to a multimedia blitz. A third town, Watsonville, not only received the mass media blitz but had health workers personally contacting most of their high-risk citizens. Both the media blitz (in Gilroy) and the media blitz plus personal contact (in Watsonville) yielded dramatic reductions in coronary risk among townspeople relative to the control town. Watsonville, where the personal contact campaign was conducted, experienced the most significant reduction in risk in the first year and ultimately reduced coronary risk factors by 30 percent. Gilroy, where only the mass media campaign was conducted, experienced the greatest improvement in the second year when risk factors were 25 percent lower than at the beginning. While it is important to note that there was no town with a person-to-person campaign only and that there was undoubtedly considerable variability in how the information was presented, this study shows that both mass media campaigns and personal contact campaigns are persuasive.

Despite the billions of dollars spent on television advertising and television political campaigns and the hours of television watching, there is minimal research evidence that television has much persuasive impact (McGuire, 1985). One of the most compelling arguments for the minimal persuasion effect is that opposing political and advertising campaigns cancel each other out. So, Pepsi's multimillion dollar ads minimize the effects of the multimillion dollar ads of Coca Cola and vice versa. The likely beneficiaries of these ad battles are other cola drinks, which have been made more salient to the buying public without spending the money. There is also evidence that new products or new political candidates (Patterson, 1980) benefit more from their mass media campaigns than older products or candidates do. The many problems with assessing the appropriate variables cleanly and isolating their effects from other factors in the "real world" must contribute to the ambiguous findings on the persuasiveness of television. Of course, many people literally and figuratively tune out attempts to get them to buy something or vote a certain way.

A clever recent study by Brian Mullen and a cast of thousands (Mullen, Futrell, Stairs, Tice, Baumeister, Dawson, Riordan, Radloff, Goethals, Kennedy, & Rosenfeld, 1986) points to the powerful influence of one aspect of television communication. These investigators videotaped the anchors of the three major networks as they spoke about Ronald Reagan, Walter Mondale, positive, negative, and neutral events on the evening news during the 1984 presidential campaign. (See figure 7.8.) Another study (Clancey & Robinson, 1985) had reported that there was no bias favoring Reagan in what was said in network news coverage during the campaign. Subjects' ratings of these videotaped clips showed

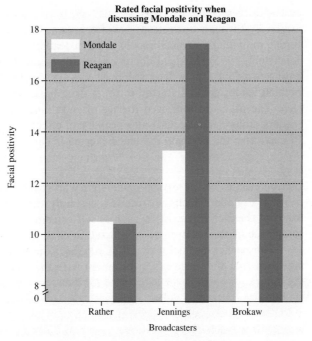

**Rated facial positivity when
discussing Mondale and Reagan**

Facial positivity

Mondale
Reagan

Rather   Jennings   Brokaw

Broadcasters

Figure 7.8
*Peter Jennings smiled
more when he talked
about Ronald Reagan
than he did when he
talked about Walter
Mondale during the
1984 presidential
campaign. Dan Rather
and Tom Brokaw
smiled about equally
when they talked
about the two
candidates. Can a
smile elect a president?*
(From Mullen et al., 1986, Journal
of Personality and Social
Psychology, 51, 292–293.)

that Peter Jennings of ABC smiled more when he referred to Reagan than to
Mondale and that the two other newscasters showed no nonverbal bias. By collecting data from voters around the country, Mullen and associates established
that a greater percentage of voters who had regularly watched ABC News during
the campaign voted for Reagan than did CBS or NBC viewers. They posed the
question: "Can a smile elect a president?" Given the correlational nature of these
studies and the presence of many other powerful influences, such as Reagan's
first term record, the best answer seems to be "Maybe it contributed to the result."

How does personal contact exert more influence than mass communication? First, it must be acknowledged that personal communication probably has
more impact per person contacted, but it has less overall influence than mass
media because the mass media reach so many more people. Personal communication is probably more influential because it is interactive and mass communication is not. An individual, face-to-face speaker can ask and answer questions
and present arguments that address the target person's concerns. Such persuaders can also show the receiver what at least one peer thinks about the issue
and that they care about the receiver's opinion. The persuader might also get the
receiver to commit him- or herself to a particular action. All of these factors are
advantages the person-to-person communicator has over the mass media because
of the ability to interact.

Since we know that person-to-person communication is more persuasive than
mass media communication, how can we maximize the impact of personal contact? Elihu Katz proposed the *two-step flow of communication* idea three decades ago (Katz, 1957). He stated that most people are influenced through a
second party. First, mass media or other sources disseminate information. Second,
some of the information receivers (opinion leaders) pass the information to the

rest of us in personal contacts. In this way, mass media sources affect most of us indirectly through our interpersonal contacts. In a particular community, different individuals are commonly opinion leaders on different issues (Katz & Lazarfeld, 1955). Medical doctors generally follow this two-step pattern in deciding to adopt a new drug (Menzel & Katz, 1956). For example, only a few opinion leader doctors started to use a drug based on pharmaceutical information. The other doctors used it only after talking with these leaders. Political leaders, union leaders, and sales people can effectively use this two-step process to maximize the personal influence exerted in support of their issues.

Receiver or Audience Factors

Characteristics of the person or persons who receive the message and the circumstances under which they receive it certainly affect whether persuasion occurs. Many of these characteristics, such as self-esteem, intelligence, age, gender, and confidence of the receiver, are discussed in chapter 8.

Our earlier discussion of social judgment theory (Sherif & Hovland, 1961) indicated that the receiver's involvement with the issue makes a difference. Receivers who are deeply involved with the issue are more resistant to persuasion than are uninvolved receivers. Reactance theory (Brehm, 1966) implies a similar reaction to persuasion attempts in that those who value the freedom to hold a particular attitude most should be most resistant to change.

Petty and Cacioppo (1979b; Petty, Cacioppo, & Goldman, 1981) used receiver involvement in a slightly different way to study persuasion. Involvement meant that the policy decision on the issue would directly affect the receiver or it would not. Involved receivers heard arguments for instituting comprehensive exams for seniors before they would graduate. Uninvolved receivers heard the same arguments for the same exams, but the exams would start long after they graduated. Involved receivers were swayed more by strong arguments, while uninvolved receivers were influenced more by the expertise of the source. According to Petty and Cacioppo (1981), the logical, informative aspects of a message constitute the central route to persuasion and such ancillary cues as source expertise and source attractiveness constitute the peripheral route to persuasion. Persuasion through the thoughtful central route has a more long-lasting effect and is directly related to behavior (Cacioppo, Petty, Kao, & Rodriguez, 1986). Personal involvement of the receiver promotes central route processing.

The Elaboration Likelihood Model, Involvement, and Need for Cognition

The Elaboration Likelihood Model (ELM) (Petty & Cacioppo, 1981, 1986) encompasses manipulated involvement and the receiver characteristic of need for cognition (Cacioppo & Petty, 1982; Cacioppo et al., 1986). The need for cognition work indicates that some people are prone to thoughtfully consider information presented to them and to develop or elaborate other ideas about the information. People low in need for cognition are considered cognitive misers (Taylor, 1981) and are likely to take shortcuts in making decisions (Eagly & Chaiken, 1984). The ELM predicts that receivers who elaborate on information presented to them either because of situationally-induced personal involvement or high need for cognition are more likely to be persuaded by central route factors, such as strength or logic of the arguments. Those receivers who are unlikely to consider and elaborate on the information are persuaded most by peripheral route factors, such as source expertise or attractiveness or length of the arguments. The many studies of this research team have generally confirmed these predictions.

The past experience and knowledge of the message receiver also affects the persuasion outcome. Evidence of this effect can be seen in children's naive acceptance of TV commercial claims (Adler, Lesser, Meringoff, Robertson, Rossiter, & Ward, 1980). Very young children are not experienced enough to know that the purpose of advertising is to get them to buy the products and that inexperience makes them easily persuadible. A few years ago, one of our elementary school age daughters presented me with a pre-Christmas list of 50 toys and games she wanted! You can guess where she first saw the requested items. On a more important but related issue, Patty Hearst's political naivete stemming from disinterest and lack of exposure made it easy for her Symbionese Liberation Army (SLA) kidnappers to brainwash her (Hearst, 1982).

Inoculation theory (McGuire, 1964) has shown one way in which experience with or exposure to persuasive messages can make receivers more resistant to persuasion. McGuire draws an analogy between being exposed to weak, refutable arguments for a position and being exposed to a mild form of a disease via smallpox vaccination. In one case, the body becomes more resistant to bacteria carrying the severe disorder; in the other case, the mind becomes more resistant to stronger arguments endorsing the position. McGuire and Papageorgis (1961) demonstrated that prior experience with arguments rebutting commonly accepted beliefs made receivers resistant to persuasion on the same topics later. One applied research effort has used the inoculation approach to give children experience so that they will be more resistant to TV toy ads (Feshbach, 1980). Another application of inoculation theory has been to expose teenagers to the kind of peer pressure to smoke they will face later, so they will be more resistant to that pressure (Evans, 1980).

Another receiver factor in persuasion is the presence or absence of other receivers and the characteristics of other receivers. We know from conformity research to be reviewed in the next chapter that if other people hear a message and publicly respond to it, the individual listener will be influenced by their opinions. If everyone responds in the same way, the listener will feel tremendous pressure to accept or reject the message as the others have.

Another possible effect of being in a group situation is that the individual may reduce his or her cognitive effort (Latané, Williams, & Harkins, 1979). Petty, Harkins, and Williams (1980) examined this possibility directly by making some receivers believe they were the sole evaluators of a message, while others were convinced they were one of ten evaluators of the same message. The basic message in favor of instituting comprehensive exams for seniors was presented with either strong, weak, or very weak supporting arguments. If the receiver was

Inoculation Theory

Children are very susceptible to influence via television.

Figure 7.9
*When evaluators
thought they were one
of ten evaluators, they
rated all messages
neutrally and about
the same. When they
thought that they were
the only evaluator,
they rated strong
arguments positively
and very weak
arguments negatively.
Evaluators were more
discriminating when
their evaluations
would not be lost in
the crowd.*
(From Petty et al., 1980, Journal of
Personality and Social Psychology,
38, 8.)

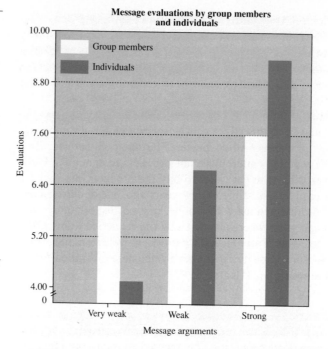

Message evaluations by group members and individuals

one of ten evaluators, he or she evaluated all the messages in a neutral, noncommittal fashion. If he or she was the only evaluator, the receiver rated the strong arguments message positively and generated many positive thoughts about it and rated the very weak arguments message negatively and generated many negative thoughts about it. So, the presence of other receivers means that you are unlikely to be attentive to and thoughtful about the message. Peripheral cues and cognitive shortcuts are likely to sway you in a nonresponsive group, not the compelling logic behind the message. The opposite pattern of persuasion should occur with lone receivers. (See figure 7.9.)

If you were a member of an audience who was bitterly and vocally opposed to the message being presented, conformity research indicates that you would not be persuaded either. What if you saw a message presented on television to an audience which bitterly and forcefully opposed it? You, as a member of this secondary television audience, might react quite differently. Studies that we discussed earlier in the context of trustworthiness of the communicator suggest that secondary audience members would be persuaded by the message (Eagly, Wood, & Chaiken, 1978; Mills & Jellison, 1967). Over a decade ago, Jimmy Carter stood before a meeting of the Veterans of Foreign Wars and announced that he was granting amnesty to draft evaders. The audience was very strong in its opposition. However, in the eyes of TV viewers, Carter's credibility grew greatly that day and many may have been convinced that granting amnesty was proper.

Brainwashing or indoctrination usually involves the use of many persuasion strategies to produce extreme changes in attitudes and behavior. The results of these indoctrination programs can be seen in the dramatic changes in the lives of concentration camp prisoners, religious group members, People's Temple members of Jonestown, and Patty Hearst, to name a few.

There are some very fundamental differences between these brainwashing situations and typical persuasion situations. The basic differences are that the indoctrinators in those situations have effect control and information control over the indoctrinatees (Crano & Messé, 1982). *Effect control* means that indoctrinators have the power to benefit or harm their victims through giving or restricting food, clothing, shelter, and rest or threatening or imposing physical and psychological harm. This kind of control was used by Chinese soldiers in the Korean War to destabilize the political beliefs of American prisoners (Schein, 1956). Patty Hearst was initially held in a dark closet, sexually assaulted, and fed in the closet irregularly to accomplish the same ends (Zimbardo, Ebbesen, & Maslach, 1977). Cult indoctrinations typically involve getting the potential recruits into isolated situations so the persuaders have complete control.

Information control means that the persuaders can censure or provide information at their whim. There is no other independent source of information. Adult victims must be isolated in order for their indoctrinators to have such control. The Chinese captors of American soldiers manipulated news from home in order to demoralize the prisoners (Schein, 1956). The Symbionese Liberation Army systematically misinformed Patty Hearst about her parents' response to their demands to make her feel abandoned (Hearst, 1982). On the day of the mass murder-suicide in Jonestown, Jim Jones misinformed his followers that they were doomed by Congressman Ryan's visit and an attack on the visiting group. One social psychologist commented that the most telling step made by Jim Jones in the events leading up to the poisonings was to move his group to the isolated Guyana jungle community, where he could exert such complete control (Cialdini, 1985). Parents usually have effect and information control over their children in their early years. It should not be surprising that children adopt some of the same attitudes, beliefs, and behaviors as their parents.

Only some people fall prey to these brainwashing tactics. Very few American POWs joined their captors and denounced America even when the prisoners were subjected to very harsh treatment. People who lack a firm ideology seem to be most susceptible to such tactics. Patty Hearst did not have well-established attitudes according to her own account. War prisoners show the same pattern. Being able to distract oneself through exercise, thoughts about faraway events, or mind games from one's current severe circumstances may have also played a role in resisting indoctrination (Schein, 1956).

However, different characteristics are probably important in the case of voluntary religious recruits. Lack of social support may play a key role. Once potential recruits with weak social support and community ties are found and

Brainwashing: The Ultimate Persuasion

Sophisticated and potent brainwashing techniques were used on Patty Hearst.

"Have a nice day"
aroused reactance
because of its
controlling aspects.

SHOE, by MacNelly. © 1987 by
Tribune Media Services, Inc.
Reprinted by permission.

isolated so they can be controlled, new religious beliefs may be fostered by dramatic presentations by charismatic speakers. At the same time, the offer of caring support from ordinary group members and the conformity among group members to the leader's will act to solidify the recruit's place in the new community.

Many influence techniques discussed in this and the previous chapter are evident in indoctrination programs. In addition to trying to isolate individuals and gain total control of them, indoctrination programs may use gimmicks to increase the credibility of leaders. They may try to get receptive target audiences, and they may capitalize on the conformity pressure exerted by other group members (Osherow, 1984). Getting new members more and more committed to the group by gradually escalating the demands on them appears to be a common tactic. With each agreement to a new demand, especially when the recruit perceives that the actions are undertaken voluntarily, the recruit becomes more closely attached to the group. After all of the compliant actions Jim Jones had evoked from People's Temple members, their compliance in poisoning themselves was just the next step.

Persuasion based on cognitive dissonance principles has also been used in indoctrinations (Zimbardo et al., 1977). After Patty Hearst had been kidnapped and abused, the SLA presented their political views to her repeatedly in talks/arguments. When they recognized they had made considerable headway with this politically naive person, the leader of the SLA told her that she was free to go if she desired. Giving her the illusion of choice when they knew she would not exercise it must have tightened her bond to the SLA. Later, she went so far as to fire shots in their behalf. The subtle tactics of the Chinese soldiers in making American POWs endorse positions they did not believe is another example of an influence technique consistent with cognitive dissonance principles.

Brainwashing involves the use of many different persuasion techniques. The feature that sets brainwashing apart from other attitude and behavior change programs is total or near-total control over the victim's well-being. If the SLA had just dropped in for some political bull sessions with Patty Hearst but had not controlled her comings and goings, they could not have had the effects they did. If People's Temple members had still lived in private residences in northern California and had only occasionally gone to worship services together when Jim Jones had told them to poison themselves, most of those 900 people would still be alive today. It is impossible to overstate the importance of force, threats of force, and isolation from other resources and people in indoctrination or brainwashing.

We have already presented many examples of how persuasion ideas can be or are being used in advertising and sales. There are many other examples of persuasion principles in advertising available in such journals as *Journal of Advertising Research, Journal of Consumer Research, Journal of Marketing, Journal of Marketing Research,* and *Advertising Age.*

Let us consider more subtle persuasions. More and more companies are selling or giving away shirts and other articles of clothing with the company product name and/or slogan on them. As we see people wearing one of these shirts, we are being exposed to a persuasion effort when our sales resistance is down. If we know and like the persons wearing the shirts, we are likely to be influenced even more to purchase the product. Such a sales technique may be quite effective because it is outside the ordinary advertising contexts.

Another form of persuasion is often present in the television program itself rather than in the commercial. Saturday morning children's programming with cartoon characters exactly like Transformers or other toys that the child (or parent) can buy is among the worst offenders. However, prime time can be offensive also. If a character wears a cap of an organization or uses a type of product (smoking cigarettes or drinking alcohol, for instance), the character and the program are implicitly endorsing the product. They are also creating an impression of what normal behavior is. Racial and ethnic groups, women, or other groups of citizens may be rightfully upset if television programs consistently portray them in false and disadvantageous ways. The messages within programs are more likely to be accepted by viewers because the persuasive intent is not so obvious (cf. Petty & Cacioppo, 1979a).

Defense attorneys and consultants should probably be sensitive to juror-defendant similarity in selecting jurors. In other words, it is a good idea to pick jurors who are similar to the defendant in as many ways as possible. We know from the research on communicator credibility that listeners who are similar to communicators are likely to believe the message more. Also, jurors who have similar backgrounds and experiences to the defendant might be expected to think "There, but for the grace of God, go I." The intuitive judgments of lawyers in picking jurors reflect this principle in some ways. Percy Foreman, a renowned criminal defense lawyer, once told a group of law students to pick jurors who can understand the defendant's situation. "If your client is accused of killing someone in a bar fight, you want jurors who have been in bars. If you are going to make an insanity plea, pick educated jurors who will appreciate and understand the subtleties of the case" (W. K. Kimble, personal communication, 1970).

Applications of Persuasion Principles

Persuasion in Nonadvertising Contexts

Persuasion in the Courtroom

Product-endorsing clothing has become prominent.

Of course, the credibility of the lawyer needs to be established with the jurors for him or her to be persuasive. We know from the research presented in the chapter that expert, attractive, similar, and trustworthy communicators are most likely to be believed. Lawyers need to establish that they have these traits in their presentations to the jury. In jury simulation studies conducted by many social psychologists, the characteristics and presentation styles of the lawyers have been neglected.

Lawyers could also use persuasion research on message characteristics to their advantage in the courtroom (Linz & Penrod, 1984). They could gain or maintain attention to the message by dramatic displays, asking jurors questions (MacLachlin, 1983), or vocal inflections. They should verbalize conclusions for jurors unless it is obvious they have the thoughtful attention of the entire jury (Kardes, 1988).

Attorneys might also avoid excessively dogmatic statements so they won't arouse reactance and resistance in jurors. One simulated trial study (Thompson, Fong, & Rosenhan, 1981) indicates that, at least in some situations, a judge's instructions to disregard particular testimony arouses reactance in jurors. The judge's admonition only served to highlight that testimony for the jurors. One might raise the question of whether a lawyer's objecting to parts of testimony frequently would have the same effect; that is, the jurors might weigh that testimony more than other testimony. If so, it would suggest three possible strategies for lawyers:

1. They could blurt out evidence that they know is inadmissible because it will only be highlighted by objections and admonitions
2. They could remain silent except when inadmissible evidence that is very injurious to their case is raised
3. They could ask that the jury be removed until a judge decides whether a line of questioning is admissible.

Even though there has been no direct research on this question, many trial lawyers have undoubtedly made intuitive judgments about these procedural strategies without any firm evidence on their effectiveness.

AIDS and Persuasion

The AIDS epidemic is now a societal health problem of massive proportions. How could social psychology help to alleviate the suffering and death produced by this epidemic? Obviously, the treatment for this awful disorder must be developed by medical researchers. However, there are many behaviors associated with the spread of AIDS that social psychologists could help to change. We know that anal-genital sex between males, sex with anyone whose sexual history is unknown to you, using hypodermic needles others have used, and receiving transfusions of contaminated blood are to be avoided. AIDS is especially burdensome for young people and others who have not had the opportunity to establish stable, dyadic sexual relationships (Brooks-Gunn, Boyer, & Hein, 1988), gay and bisexual men (Stall, Coates, & Hoff, 1988), and intravenous drug users (Des Jarlais & Friedman, 1988).

The location of such billboards near areas where risky behavior is likely is important.

One problem with these AIDS-related behaviors is that they have the characteristics of a *psychological social trap* (Platt, 1973). The sexual and drug use behaviors are one-person traps similar to smoking, drinking, and overeating. These particular traps are characterized by immediate pleasurable rewards and delayed—often for years—negative consequences. For example, immediate sexual pleasure will override, in most cases, consideration of the remote possibility of getting a deadly disease much later. Newspaper articles have described the despair of public health workers who attempt to educate people that if they adopt a particular preventive behavior, such as using condoms, today; the incidence of AIDS five or ten years from now will be less. The personal consequences are too remote for the message to have much impact.

Platt (1973) suggested ways to counteract these social traps affecting the well-being of individuals and future generations. One technique that social psychologists could potentially use is to make long-range consequences more salient to individuals now. This might be accomplished by placing billboards indicating the deadliness of AIDS near singles bars, gay bars, and known drug use dens. If such fear-arousing messages were used, social psychologists should be sure that remedial actions, such as using condoms, practicing abstinence, and/or avoiding unsterilized or used needles, were incorporated into the communication (Rogers & Mewborn, 1976). Another viable approach suggested by Platt would be reinforcing competing activities or highlighting other rewarding, pleasurable activities. This approach might entail emphasizing the pleasurable aspects of "safe" or non-AIDS spreading sex or the pleasing sensations arising from other noncontaminating activities. Still another approach would be to provide counselors who are capable of guiding clients in AIDS-related matters and in administering different reward-consequence contingencies (previously mentioned), which would promote behavior change. Social psychologists might also use persuasion techniques to educate the public to avoid risky practices and to be more humane to and less fearful of AIDS victims. The AIDS epidemic is so tragic and difficult to stop that the efforts, ideas, and techniques of social psychology as well as other disciplines need to be mustered to combat it.

In November, 1988, the American Psychologist presented a special issue on psychology and AIDS (Backer, Batchelor, Jones, & Mays, 1988). This informative issue indicated that participation of at-risk groups, such as the gay community in San Francisco, in community-level interventions has been one of the most effective ways of reducing risky sexual behavior (Coates, et al., 1988). Also, alcohol and drug use during sexual encounters was found to have made infection more likely because intoxicated people were less likely to take necessary precautions.

The AIDS pamphlet mailed by the Surgeon General C. Everett Koop to American households in 1988 was an informative and persuasive communication. The teenagers and younger people who got to see and read it must have been enlightened. The information may have prevented many from engaging in risky behaviors. Careful research on the success of this program needs to be done.

However, it seems likely that many high-risk people did not read the information. Many who were already engaging in risky behavior probably avoided reading the pamphlet. Even those who did read it may not have been persuaded by the message because they did not receive the message close enough to when they were deciding to engage in risky behavior. The personal timeliness of the communication is very important, and that timeliness might be improved through some of the techniques already mentioned.

Summary

Persuasive communications have been studied in terms of their source, message, channel, and receiver factors. Sources or communicators are more likely to be believed if they are seen as expert, attractive, trustworthy and similar to the receiver. Communicator credibility is greater when the communicator is not judged to be motivated by personal gain. Messages must be attention-getting, understandable, acceptable, and memorable to be effective in persuasion. For a message to be understandable, its arguments must be clear, its conclusions should be explicitly stated, and it should be repeated. For a message to be accepted by the receiver, it usually must not be too discrepant from the receiver's earlier position, or so direct and argumentative that it will arouse reactance, repeated too often, or too direct in stating conclusions. Messages which are humorous or otherwise provoke positive feelings associated with a product are sometimes persuasive. Fear-arousing messages can be effective if the remedies for the aversive condition are clearly stated. For simple messages, the audiovisual channels are most effective in persuasion. For difficult messages, written or printed communications are most effective. Several studies have shown that person-to-person communication is more persuasive than mass media communication. Of course, more people can be contacted through the mass media. Many audience factors such as their involvement with the issue, their previous experience with the information, and their tendency to think about and elaborate on the information affect whether the communication will be persuasive.

Brainwashing or indoctrination usually involves a combination of persuasion techniques. The most central characteristic of brainwashing situations is that the indoctrinators have effect and information control over their target persons. Persuasion research is clearly applicable in mass media advertising and courtroom presentations. Persuasion techniques should also be useful in combating the spread of AIDS.

CHAPTER 8

Social Influence

Obedience, Conformity, and Compliance

Every day many individuals and media sources attempt to influence us. Friends, family members, work associates, and others constantly try to sway our opinions or shape our behavior. Salespeople frequently try to get us to buy everything from Girl Scout cookies to cars in face-to-face interactions. Billions of dollars are spent annually on media advertising to influence us to buy products or to vote for political candidates. We, as consumers and as salespeople, advertisers, advocates, campaigners, and interpersonal influencers, can benefit from greater understanding of social influence principles.

There are many different terms used to describe social influence. **Obedience** is the term used to describe behavior initiated or changed in response to *commands* by authority persons, laws, and rules (Milgram, 1974). **Conformity** describes behavior initiated or changed in response to *implicit pressure* produced by the actions or stated positions of other people (e.g., Asch, 1951). **Imitation** describes behavior initiated or changed in response to *observing others'* similar actions without any implied pressure from others that the individual should act in the same way (cf. Bandura, 1977b). **Compliance** refers to behavior initiated or changed or positions taken in response to *direct requests* from others (e.g., Freedman & Fraser, 1966). Person-to-person sales techniques fall into the compliance category of social influence research (Cialdini, 1985). **Persuasion,** covered in the previous chapter, refers to attitude or behavior initiation or change produced by an active attempt by others to change the individual's mind through presenting information or arguments (cf. Petty & Cacioppo, 1986).

We have glossed over the distinction between attitudes and behaviors in our presentation of social influence so far and in our combining of conformity and persuasion. We have done so because even though persuaders focus on changing attitudes, they are ultimately interested in assuring that the behavior—buying or voting—inspired by attitude change occurs. Even though those promoting conformity emphasize behavior, they are often interested in the attitudinal underpinnings of the desired behavior in order to sustain the behavior over time. Most social psychologists (e.g., Crano & Messé, 1982) believe that attitudes are more stable, more long-lasting, more resistant to change, and more central to individuals' self-concepts than behaviors. Despite some of the problems of inconsistency between attitudes and behavior discussed in chapter 6 (cf. Fazio & Zanna, 1981; Wicker, 1969), we assume that behaviors stem from and reflect privately held attitudes. For instance, signing a petition is a behavior, but it is also an expression of an attitude, just as marking a number on a Likert scale under an attitude statement is a behavior expressing an attitude. So, many of the principles involved in effecting attitude change and behavior change are similar enough to encourage us to combine them while remaining cognizant of crucial distinctions between the two.

In the late 1930s and early 1940s, thousands of German soldiers participated in the systematic annihilation of 6 million European Jews under the orders of Hitler's Nazi regime. In the late 1960s and early 1970s, an unknown number of American soldiers in Southeast Asia followed orders in killing hundreds of noncombatants—old men, women, children, and babies. Documentation of the incident at My Lai indicates that several soldiers killed noncombatants under the orders of Lieutenant Calley after Calley had started the massacre by shooting many unarmed villagers allegedly under orders from superiors. In 1978, hundreds of People's Temple members poisoned their own children before drinking the poison themselves under the orders of Jim Jones at Jonestown, Guyana.

How could so many presumably ordinary people be made to commit such atrocious acts? In the early 1960s, about 20 years after the Holocaust and before the My Lai and Jonestown incidents, Stanley Milgram started the most dramatic research program ever conducted in social psychology to try to answer that question. Before he was done, Milgram had observed the behavior of almost 800 "ordinary people" under many different conditions to see when they would obey.

Milgram did not use soldiers indoctrinated into the military system or religious cult members enthralled with their leader as subjects. Instead, he recruited ordinary people—men in all studies except one—to participate in a teaching and learning psychology experiment at Yale University through a newspaper ad offering $4.50.

When these ordinary people arrived individually at Yale, they met an austere scientist in a white lab coat and a 50-year-old man who was also participating in the study. The authority figure with the serious demeanor (the experimenter) briefly introduced the study on teaching and learning. He permitted the two subjects to draw pieces of paper to see who would be the teacher and who the learner. The subject always discovered that his paper said "teacher." The experimenter allowed the teacher (the subject) to observe as he attached the wires to the learner's hand as the learner was seated in a separate compartment. The teacher next experienced a mild (45 volt) shock so that he knew what the learner would feel. The teacher then began the task. He read word pairs from a list to the learner. Next, he read the first word of the pair along with four alternative words, including the second word of the original pair. If the learner responded correctly, the teacher proceeded to the next word pair. If he made a mistake, the teacher was instructed by the experimenter to shock him with the 15–volt lever. With each mistake, the teacher was to move to the next higher voltage, which was 15 volts greater. It was evident from the shock apparatus that the shock levels continued all the way to 450 volts.

Every subject obeyed the experimenter until he reached the 300–volt level despite protests and screams from the learner at lower voltages. If the subject raised questions about the shocks, the experimenter verbally prodded him into continuing. When the learner quit answering, the experimenter indicated that no answer was an incorrect answer and that the teacher should continue to administer shock. If the subject asked who would take responsibility for harm to the

Social Influence

Obedience

learner, the experimenter invariably said that he would. Sixty-five percent of the subjects shocked the learner all the way to the 450–volt level—well after the learner had quit answering.

The behavior of the experimenter and the learner was pre-programmed. The learner, who was the experimenter's assistant or confederate, was never shocked; his answers, protests, and screams were prerecorded. The experimenter's prods and comments were planned and scheduled ahead of time.

With this study, Milgram knew that ordinary people like you and me were more obedient than most of us ever dreamed. At least under certain compelling circumstances, all of these people were capable of doing harmful and reprehensible acts at another person's command. Before you surmise that this finding applies only to males, the same percentage of women subjects (65 percent) also obeyed completely.

Victim Influence

What were the compelling factors that produced such obedience? Milgram did eighteen such laboratory studies to examine some of the important elements (Milgram, 1974). One factor that was examined in a series of studies was the remoteness vs. *immediacy* of the *victim*. In one variation, the learner was made more immediate by having an intercom system between the two rooms, so the teacher could hear the screams and protests more clearly. Also in this condition, the victim made more protests earlier and even complained about a heart condition. Hearing these protests had little impact on obedience; 62.5 percent of the 40 male subjects obeyed completely.

In two other studies, Milgram made the victim even more salient to the teacher by putting him in the same room, so he was visible to the subject. Making the victim visible did reduce the obedience rate to 40 percent. The other study in which the victim was in the same room required the teacher to be in even closer contact with the victim. At 150 volts, the learner refused to keep his hand on the shock plate, so the experimenter ordered the teacher to hold his hand down so that they could continue! In this most immediate condition, 30 percent of the subjects continued all the way to 450 volts. So, as the victim and his suffering were made nearer and clearer to subjects, they were less likely to obey the experimenter's commands. These results suggest that as the negative consequences of one's actions become more prominent in one's consciousness, fewer people will obey orders to act in that way. All other things being equal, a soldier should more readily obey an order to fire an artillery shell at a distant village than an order to shoot unarmed people at point blank range as at My Lai. (See figure 8.1.)

The Influence of Authority

The opposing force to the influence of the victim is the presence and *immediacy* of the *authority* person. One of Milgram's studies demonstrated that when the authority person—the experimenter—was not physically present but gave orders over a telephone, only 22.5 percent of the subjects obeyed fully in comparison to the basic 65 percent obedience rate. So, the more remote the person giving the orders is from the subordinate, the less likely the subordinate is to obey. Milgram also found that the experimenter's influence was also greater at Yale University than in a less prestigious setting (47.5 percent obedience in a downtown Bridgeport office).

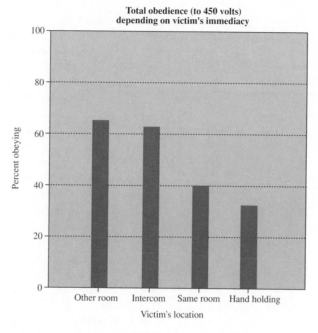

Total obedience (to 450 volts) depending on victim's immediacy

Percent obeying

Victim's location: Other room | Intercom | Same room | Hand holding

Figure 8.1
These studies of obedience show that "teachers" were more obedient when the victim was more remote. They were most obedient when the victim was in another room and could not be heard and least obedient when they had to hold the victim's hand to the shock plate.
(From Milgram, 1974, Obedience to Authority.)

These two studies examine different aspects of authority. The first addresses the impact of an authority depending on the immediacy of the person in charge. The second addresses how much authority a person is perceived to have depending on situational cues. The question of perceived authority was not addressed extensively by Milgram, but it is obviously a multifaceted and important topic. Were there aspects of the experimenter's behavior and style that affected his perceived authority? Certainly, there were factors, such as tone of voice and stern expression, that influenced the experimenter's authority, but these features were not systematically varied. Being in a scientific, experimental situation increased his authority; so much so that Orne (1962) and Baumrind (1964) have argued that the experimental "contract" was the overriding influence and that the results don't generalize outside the experimental situation.

The examples from Nazi Germany, Vietnam, and Jonestown suggest that the commander must have authority deriving from some source to be effective. A military environment in which there is a very explicit chain of command clearly gives authority to individuals of higher rank than the subject. Other organizations with clearly defined hierarchies also give such authority, and experience in them may produce obedient people. Jim Jones' case indicates that authority can be gained through acquiring the respect and admiration of others and through having the power to reward and punish others (cf. French & Raven, 1959). Another of Milgram's (1974) studies illustrated that if other group members disobey, the leader's authority can be undermined. When two confederates working with the subject in the teacher's role disobeyed, only 10 percent of the subjects obeyed to the end of the scale.

Obedience is expected when the sergeant barks orders.

Figure 8.2
*When observers could
see what was
happening to a shock
victim and they were
held responsible for the
shock, all of them
stopped the shock.
When levels of
feedback or
responsibility were
lower, very few of them
intervened.*

(From Tilker, 1970, Journal of
Personality and Social Psychology,
14, 98.)

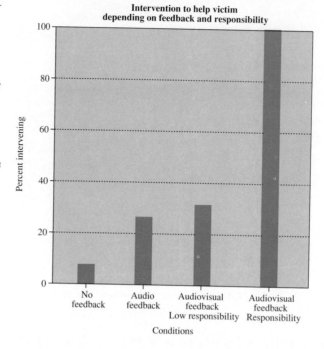

*The Issue of
Responsibility*

Most of Milgram's subjects asked who would be responsible if the learner were harmed. The experimenter was instructed to say that he would be responsible. Even though Milgram did not directly vary the extent of responsibility the subject bore, it is evident that responsibility was an important concern to subjects. Tilker (1970) created an experimental situation similar to Milgram's to assess the importance of responsibility for harm on obedience. In Tilker's study, the subjects performed the role of an observer, while two confederates served as the teacher and the learner. There were three levels of feedback from the learner and three levels of responsibility for the observer in this study. Some subjects could not hear or see the victim; some could hear the victim over an intercom; and the others could see and hear the victim. The observer either had no responsibility for continuing or stopping the shocks, shared responsibility with the teacher, or had total responsibility. The most striking feature of the results was that every subject who was given total responsibility and could see and hear the victim stopped the shocks quite early in the procedure. When consequences were salient and the subjects were held responsible, even though they did not administer the shocks, all subjects disobeyed. (See figure 8.2.)

One of Milgram's studies is relevant to the issue of responsibility. In one situation (cf. Milgram, 1974), the subject performed the more secondary task of reading the words as a confederate administered the shock. In such circumstances, 39 of the 40 subjects cooperated all the way to the end of the scale. It seems likely that the subjects felt diminished or diffused responsibility when they played a less central role, and that perception led to the high rate of obedience.

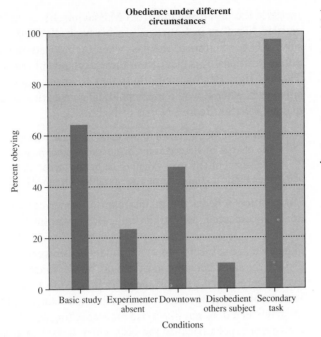

Obedience under different circumstances

Percent obeying

Basic study | Experimenter absent | Downtown | Disobedient others subject | Secondary task

Conditions

Figure 8.3
Subjects were least obedient when other "subjects" disobeyed the experimenter and most obedient when they performed a secondary task, rather than administering shock themselves. Also, few obeyed when the experimenter was not in the room.
(From Milgram, 1974, Obedience to Authority.*)*

We might expect that German soldiers who made Jews board trains for "unknown destinations" did so without compunction because of the noncentral nature of their role. (See figure 8.3.)

It is shocking that so many people—and, by implication, most of us—would obey an order to harm someone. Are we shocked that so many people drive on the right-hand side of the road? Are we shocked that so many people register with Social Security? Are we shocked that so many parents have their children vaccinated against certain diseases? No. These are simply the laws, rules, and regulations that require obedience for our society to run smoothly. If most people weren't obedient most of the time, we would have chaos. Some organizations, such as the military, could not operate without strict obedience. All of us have been in roles which require that we obey rules, regulations, guidelines, and orders. Consequently, it is easy to see why all of Milgram's subjects pressed the 15-volt lever. And, after all, the second mistake only called for a 15–volt increment in shock. If Milgram's experimenter had ordered a 100–volt shock for the first mistake and a 200–volt shock for the second error, many people probably would have disobeyed. Milgram's gradual escalation of shock levels probably committed subjects to continue more than a scale with abrupt increases would have (Gilbert, 1981).

Obedience is indoctrinated and ingrained into most people in most cultures of the world. It is necessary for societies to run smoothly and to ensure that unpleasant jobs are done. Milgram's results are so startling because they show that so many people will perform acts on command which are in conflict with universal standards of decency. It also demonstrates that even in America where individuality and independence is revered, obedience to authority is common.

Obedience and Disobedience

Conformity to Pressure

In 1955, the junior senator from Massachusetts, John F. Kennedy, wrote a book entitled "Profiles in Courage." In his book, Kennedy recounted the conduct of several U.S. senators of the past when their constituencies fiercely opposed their public positions. It is clear from these accounts of the behavior of Sam Houston, Thomas Hart Benton, and others that Kennedy regarded standing up for a position even when it would mean political ruin as the epitome of courage. Kennedy quoted Senator George Norris of Nebraska:

> I would rather go down to my political grave with a clear conscience than ride in the chariot of victory as a Congressional stool pigeon, the slave, the servant, or the vassal of any man, whether he be the owner and manager of a legislative menagerie or the ruler of a great nation (Kennedy, 1955, p. 168).

His position reflects the mainstream of American opinion. Stubborn independence is respected; conformity indicates cowardice.

Types of Responses to Social Influence Pressure

Conformity pressure didn't stop Kevin Wakefield from doing his own thing.

THE FAR SIDE, by Gary Larson. © 1987 by Universal Press Syndicate. Reprinted by permission. All Rights Reserved.

THE FAR SIDE   By GARY LARSON

Nov. 12, 1957: Kevin Wakefield, during snacktime, makes kindergarten history by selecting the soda cracker over the graham.

When we are subjected to social influence pressure, many of us may ultimately display the same behavior as others do, but for many different reasons. One driver may adhere to the 55 mph speed limit because he or she knows that there is a state trooper over the next hill. Another may not speed because his girlfriend or her boyfriend does not like to ride in a speeding car. A third driver may maintain a moderate speed because the boss whom he or she admires does not drive fast. Another does not drive at excessive speeds because she knows it is safer because the vehicle is easier to control at lower speeds. Yet another driver drives under 55 mph because he knows that the car will consume less gas at those speeds.

It seems evident that these different reasons for driving at legal speeds occur because the drivers are experiencing or have experienced different kinds of social influence pressures. Kelman (1958) would characterize these five motorists as having acted out of compliance, identification, or internalization based on their different reasons.

Compliance occurs when the behavior done or the attitude expressed is coerced by the power of an individual present at the time over the target person. The drivers who drive 55 mph to avoid the speeding ticket from the trooper or to avoid the anger of their passenger are displaying compliance. If the trooper or the girlfriend or boyfriend were not present, they would put the pedal to the metal (i.e., the behavior would not be sustained). Only if they were forced to drive at safe speeds many times might they become likely to sustain the behavior when not under surveillance. Under those circumstances, they might realize that there are other good reasons for driving more slowly (Aronson, 1984). However, when the behavior is motivated by something other than coercive power, it is no longer called compliance.

Conformity in Unambiguous Situations: Compliance   Solomon Asch (1951, 1952, 1956) did a classic series of studies in which conformity pressure from the group was pitted against objective reality. Seven to nine college men reported to a classroom for a psychology experiment on visual judgment. Their basic task was to

This subject in Asch's experiment is perplexed after the five previous "subjects" had chosen the incorrect length line.

indicate aloud which of three lines (a, b, or c) was the same length as a standard line. Different comparison and standard lines were presented on each of 18 trials. On each trial, one of the comparison lines was the same length as the standard line.

As they went around the room, each subject said the letter of the line he judged to be the same length as the standard. There was a catch: only the next to the last person to respond was a real subject; all of the others were confederates of the experimenter. After giving the correct answer on the first two trials, all six or eight confederates gave the same incorrect answer on 12 trials.

What did the perplexed subject do when everyone else gave an unbelievable response? He went along with the majority 36.9 percent of the time. About three-fourths of the men made at least one conforming error. These results occurred even though subjects who made the line judgments alone erred less than 1 percent of the time. It is evident that they said something different than they actually believed when they conformed.

How many peers does it take to exert maximum conformity pressure? Asch (1955) examined this question in his line judging situation by having one, two, three, four, six, seven, nine, or fifteen confederates unanimously assert that an incorrect comparison line was the same length as the standard. His results indicated that one confederate produced very little conformity (3.6 percent errors), two produced slightly more (13.6 percent errors), three substantially increased conformity (31.8 percent errors), and more than three confederates did not increase conformity significantly. In fact, 15 confederates produced essentially the same conformity as three confederates did (31.2 percent errors). So, a *unanimous group of three* opposing the obviously correct position created the maximum conformity effect and adding more people did not make any difference. (See figure 8.4.)

Does disagreement among group members affect the conformity rate? Asch (1955) found that if a confederate dissented by giving the correct answer or by giving the most incorrect answer, conformity errors dropped dramatically to 9 percent. Disagreement per se rather than the validity of the dissenter's response freed the subject to disagree also. Such a dissenter undermined the impact of the

Figure 8.4
Subjects answered with the incorrect line more often as group size was larger until three confederates were in the group. Adding more members to the unanimous majority beyond three did not produce more conformity.
(From Asch, 1955, Scientific American, 193, 33.)

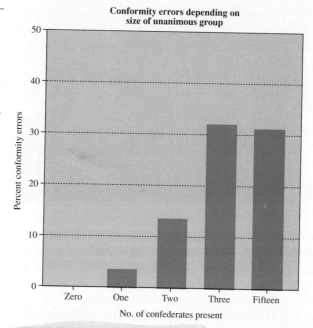

Conformity errors depending on
size of unanimous group

majority even when he was called out of the session early and the subject was left alone with the now-unanimous majority. Only one person taking a minority position reduces the majority's impact in the Asch situation.

Conformity in the Asch experiments is a good example of compliance. Other concepts have been used to describe these kinds of situations and actions. One could say that compliance occurs when behaviors or attitudes are under **normative influence** (Deutsch & Gerard, 1955; Kaplan, 1987). Both compliance and normative influence occur when a person behaves one way when potentially powerful others are present and another way when they are absent, as when Asch's subjects made different judgments about lines in a group situation than when alone. A person might also say that compliance is *extrinsically motivated behavior* (Bem, 1972). The person who acts only because he or she is being paid or because he or she will be punished if he or she does not do so is not motivated by enjoyment or value inherent in the activity itself. A worker in a boring job who stops working promptly at quitting time or the compliant drivers are both extrinsically motivated. One might also describe compliance as behavior under *impingement control* (Crano & Messé, 1982). That is, it is behavior that the person is forced to do by others.

Normative social influence appears to be the predominant feature of the Asch studies. *Normative social influence* occurs when an individual acts as others do to gain the approval or avoid the disapproval of other group members. Deutsch and Gerard (1955) characterized normative influence as conformity arising from the desire to live up to the positive expectations of others, but it seems appropriate to express the effect in terms of approval and disapproval of others. When subjects indicated their judgments in face-to-face situations where the others could identify their responses, they conformed more than when others did not know their responses (Deutsch & Gerard, 1955). The difference in conformity in these public and private situations is attributable to normative social influence.

What is behind normative social influence? The desire to create a favorable impression on the audience and to avoid embarrassment seems to be a pivotal factor (Baumeister, 1982). Schachter (1951) showed that groups generally dislike and reject a person who expresses a deviant position. On the other hand, groups like a slider, a person who originally expresses a deviant position but eventually moves to agreement with the majority position. To the extent that a person is aware of these common group reactions and knows that other group members will know his or her response, that person would be motivated to conform to the group norm to get along with the group. According to socioanalytic theory (Hogan, Jones, & Cheek, 1985), one of the two primary needs of individuals is to "get along"—to enjoy acceptance, approval, and popularity.

Normative social influence is most likely to occur when the influencing group can see or hear the individual's response and nonmembers cannot. This pattern occurs because influencing or persuading individuals perceive a person who yields to their pressure as intelligent, but impartial observers regard yielders as less intelligent than nonyielders (Cialdini, Braver, & Lewis, 1974). Consequently, individuals who hear a persuasive speech acknowledge the most yielding to influence when the persuader alone is also present and admit the least yielding to influence when an uninvolved observer alone is present (Braver, Linder, Corwin, & Cialdini, 1977). Normative influence is most prominent when an influencing group whose approval the individual wants to gain or maintain is present and can observe the individual's responses.

To Whom Do We Conform: Identification   **Identification** occurs when a person adopts a behavior or expresses an attitude because some person or persons whom he or she admires display that behavior or attitude (Kelman, 1958). The identifying person wants to be like the admired individual and acting like that person is one way to be like him or her. The behavior is motivated by respect for the other person and will be maintained for long periods without contact with the respected person. When the individual starts to respect someone else more and that person behaves or feels differently than the original respected person, then the individual will change behaviors and attitudes. One way that identification has been exploited occurs when advertisers get celebrities who are widely respected and admired to endorse their products. When that person is no longer popular, the advertisers stop using them.

The classic study of the identification process was conducted by Theodore Newcomb at Bennington College in the 1930s (Newcomb, 1943). Newcomb measured the political attitudes of Bennington College students, all of whom were women from wealthy, conservative families, throughout their college careers. From their freshman to their senior years, students' attitudes changed from conservative to liberal, especially among those students who developed strong ties with others on campus. The faculty and student body at this small liberal arts college in the 1930s was generally regarded as politically liberal to socialistic. New-comb's interpretation of this attitude change was that it occurred because the women's reference (or identification) group changed from wealthy family members and adolescent friends to members of the campus community as they went through college. Their attitudes changed to coincide with the attitudes of those with whom they identified. A follow-up study a quarter of a century later showed that the liberal attitudes formed during college through identification were still evident among most of the women (Newcomb, Koenig, Flacks, & Warwick, 1967).

Conformity under Ambiguous Conditions: Internalization   Internalization occurs when a person adopts an attitude or behavior because it is consistent with his or her existing network of attitudes and values (Aronson, 1984). Since the position taken is consistent with ideas already believed correct, the person sees the attitude or behavior as appropriate or correct and is likely to endorse it firmly and for a long time. The drivers who did not exceed the speed limit because maintaining such moderate speeds is safer or because they get better gas mileage have internalized the behavior. It is presumed that valuing life, limbs, and/or money is part of their existing network of values and attitudes. They are likely to continue driving that way until they are convinced that other modes of travel are safer or more cost efficient.

In 1935, Muzafer Sherif conducted a study to see how subjective reality evolves when there is no objective reality. He used the autokinetic effect to create an ambiguous situation for subjects. The *autokinetic effect* refers to the fact that when an individual focuses his or her vision upon a pinpoint of light in an otherwise completely dark room, the light will appear to move in a jagged, generally circular course around its original position. The light does not move; the individual's visual system makes it appear to move. It is extremely difficult to estimate how far the light "moves" because its course is jagged and curved.

Sherif asked lone subjects to estimate the distance that the light moved on several trials. Their first estimates were quite varied, but eventually these subjects developed an *individual norm*. Their later responses gravitated toward the mean of the earlier estimates and became less variable.

Then these subjects were placed in small groups to make their estimates. After a few trials, they developed a *group norm*. Subjects' estimates converged on an estimate that was basically the average of the individual norms represented in the group. By testing these subjects individually again later, Sherif discovered they had adopted the group norm as their own standard for estimation. Some subjects tested a year later made estimates concentrated around the group norm rather than their earlier individual norm. The group, in an interdependent way, had established a social reality where no objective reality existed.

Internalization is most likely to occur when the behavior or attitude stems from **informational influence** (Deutsch & Gerard, 1955; Kaplan, 1987). In ambiguous situations such as Sherif's, we look to others' behavior to see what to do. If their behavior seems consistent with our other knowledge about this situation and similar situations, we adopt it, we internalize it. Deutsch and Gerard assumed that kind of influence occurred when their subjects could see how others responded but others could not know how they responded. They found that in such private response conditions, conformity did occur even though feelings of pressure from the group were unlikely.

Other concepts are also similar to Kelman's ideas about internalization. One could also say that internalization has occurred when a particular behavior is *intrinsically motivated* (Bem, 1972). Before internalization, driving at legal speeds may have been due to extrinsic factors such as being fined or jailed; but when internalization has occurred, such driving is done because that way of behaving has value itself. Internalization may also be said to exist when a particular behavior or attitude is under **incorporation control** (Crano & Messé, 1982). Internalization and incorporation are synonyms that describe a process by which an action or an attitude, which is consistent with earlier attitudes and values, is assimilated into that existing body of ideas and buttressed or supported by them. Such internalized actions or attitudes are resistant to change and have long-lasting impact on the individual and his or her personal conduct.

Minority Influence

Asch's studies in which one confederate disagreed with the majority opens up the possibility that a minority in a group situation has a substantial influence on behavior. Certainly the dissenter had much more impact on the subject's behavior than he would have had as just one more member of the majority.

The focus of conformity research has been on the influence of an undifferentiated group of people on the individual until recent years. The French social psychologist, Moscovici (1985), and Charlan Nemeth (1986a and b) and her associates at the University of California have been most influential in reorienting the research toward the minority.

Moscovici (1985) has presented a three-category classification system of social influence processes: (1) normalization, (2) conformity, and (3) innovation. **Normalization** occurs when conflict between positions is resolved through compromise by all parties so that change toward consensus occurs gradually. The Sherif work on group norms where reciprocal influence among all group members occurred over time is a good example of normalization. **Conformity** occurs when conflicting positions are resolved in favor of the majority position. Asch's line judging situation involving a unanimous majority among the confederates is a good example of this process. **Innovation** is used to describe what happens when conflicts are resolved in favor of a minority position.

Can the few change the opinions and behavior of the many? Yes, at least some of the time and under certain conditions. Nemeth and Wachtler (1973a) showed that a person espousing a minority position is most influential when he or she chooses the "head" seat at the discussion table. Choosing this prominent seat indicates that the individual is confident. Generally, behavioral styles that exude *confidence* are likely to make such a dissenter more influential.

Another factor that enhances the influence of a minority person or subgroup is a consistent pattern of response (Moscovici & Faucheux, 1972; Moscovici, Lage, & Naffrechoux, 1969). If the minority maintains *consistency* that is not so repetitive that the pattern implies a mindless rigidity, then other group members

Is normalization, conformity, or innovation the likely outcome of this meeting?

will perceive that the minority is convinced of its position, and they are more likely to be swayed by the minority (Nemeth, Swedlund, & Kanki, 1974).

A third important factor in minority influence is the perception by other group members that the minority is endorsing the correct position (Nemeth, Wachtler, & Endicott, 1977). Asch's "ally" confederate obviously had the perception of *correctness* working for him when he chose the correct length line and the others did not. Objective reality is a great ally for majority and minority alike. Asch does not report any subject errors when the unanimous majority chose the correct length line. In their review of minority influence, Maass and Clark (1984) concluded that minority influence is more likely to be convincing and long-lasting than majority influence because it focuses other group members' attention on the reality of the judgment to be made and majority opinion does not cause that reevaluation. Nemeth and her associates have shown that the perception of correctness is also important in subjective situations involving color judgments.

In the next section, we will see that anything implying greater *strength* in Latané's (1981) terminology will enhance minority influence. If a minority person or persons have high status, expertise, or attractiveness, the minority will have greater influence than if they are low on these strength dimensions. Strength works in the same way for majorities.

General Principles of Social Influence

Social Impact Theory and Influence

Latané's (1981) **social impact theory** neatly summarizes some of the major factors involved in social influence. He states that the greater the *strength, immediacy,* and *number (SIN)* of the *influencing* group; the more the target individual will feel compelled to behave as the group indicates he or she should. These three factors affect social impact multiplicatively, which means that moderate values on all three factors may exert more impact than high value on one factor and low values on the other two, for example.

OLAF! YOU'RE NEVER GOING TO MAKE IT AS A *VIKING!*

YOU'VE GOT THE WRONG ATTITUDE!

The deviate is not always appreciated by other group members.
HAGAR THE HORRIBLE, by Dik Browne. © 1987 by King Features. Reprinted by permission.

Strength refers to "the salience, power, importance, or intensity of a given source to the target" as determined by "the source's status, age, socioeconomic status, and prior relationship with, or future power over, the target" (Latané, 1981, p. 344). There is ample evidence that the greater an influence source's expertise or status is, the more likely it is that he or she can influence a target person (Hollander, Julian, & Haaland, 1965; Strodtbeck & Mann, 1956; Tannenbaum, 1967). Lefkowitz, Blake and Mouton (1955) found that students at the University of Texas were more likely to walk across a street against the light if a neatly dressed man (high status or strength) started first than if a shabbily dressed man did. In addition, Jackson and Latané (1981b) found that more money was donated to older (higher strength) volunteers for the Leukemia Society than to younger volunteers. In the Milgram studies, the obedience shown to the commands of the high-strength authority figure (the experimenter) was much greater than the obedience shown to a peer who tried to assume the role of authority (65 percent vs. 20 percent). It seems clear that strength characteristics of expertise, legitimate authority, status, and attractiveness affect how influential a person may be.

Immediacy refers to "closeness in space or time and absence of intervening barriers or filters" (Latané, 1981, p. 344). The experimental evidence supporting the importance of nearness over long periods of time in conformity studies is so meager that Mullen (1985b) suggested that immediacy be discarded as a feature of social impact theory. For instance, Jackson and Latané (1981b) found that how far solicitors stood from subjects did not affect donations to leukemia research, while strength and number did.

Milgram's (1974) obedience studies provide some support for the notion that nearness of influence sources is important. You will recall that more subjects obeyed fully when the experimenter was close and the victim could not be seen or heard. When the experimenter was made more remote or the learner was made more immediate, obedience declined. The immediacy of both the experimenter and the learner had impact on obedience, but in opposing directions. It is impossible to determine which source had more impact in this complex situation because of the different features of immediacy manifested by the experimenter and the learner. Generally speaking, one would assume that one, immediate experimenter would have more impact than one, immediate victim because of the experimenter's greater "strength."

Table 8.1 A Summary of Social Impact Theory

Motivation of individual
To act in accordance with forces in one's environment

Core concepts
Impact = (Strength × Immediacy × Number) of influence source and influence target

Focus of theory
Group characteristics' effects on person's conformity, persuadability, decision making, and helping

Assumptions about rationality/awareness of people
Rational

One situation where the immediacy of an influence source has a substantial impact is in the home advantage. Schwartz and Barsky (1977) found that the home advantage was greatest in basketball and hockey, less in football, and least in baseball. They found that the home advantage increased with relative crowd size, as Hirt and Kimble (1981) also found. They use an *immediacy* argument to explain audiences' differential impact in different sports. That is, basketball and hockey crowds are closer to the players in enclosed arenas, and they are noisier more of the time than other kinds of crowds. Noise level to the players' position over the course of the game would be an index of immediacy in these cases.

Ironically, Mullen incorporated an aspect of immediacy into at least one of his recent studies (Mullen, 1985a). He demonstrated that individuals in your line of sight—they are more immediate—have more impact on your participation in a group discussion than individuals you cannot see readily. More research needs to be done on the influence of immediacy on conformity.

The third dimension of social impact theory, the *number* of influence sources, has been researched more extensively. Asch (1955) found that the size of a unanimous majority had a big impact on conformity, at least up to the magic number three. Conformity with a single erring confederate was quite low (3.6 percent); it increased significantly with two confederates (13.6 percent); and made its sharpest increase with three confederates (31.8 percent). Adding agreeing confederates to the group beyond three had no substantial impact. Latané (1981) formalized this pattern of conformity as a function of group size in his psychosocial law. The *psychosocial law* states that the first and earlier increases in number of influence sources create more conformity pressure than later increases do. Generally, conformity grows in proportion to the square root of majority size, assuming that the majority is unanimous and that there is some ambiguity in the stimulus situation (Latané, 1981). Latané assumes that the psychosocial law also applies to increments in strength and immediacy; but those dimensions are harder to quantify, and the empirical tests have not been conducted. (See table 8.1.)

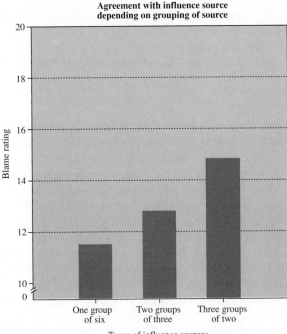

Agreement with influence source
depending on grouping of source

Figure 8.5
Jurors agreed more with the influence source in blaming the mother for her baby's injury if three groups of two people were the influencer than if one group of six individuals was the source. Mullen's self-attention theory predicts such a pattern of results.
(From Wilder, 1977, Journal of Experimental Social Psychology, 13, 263.)

Self-Attention Theory and Influence

Another approach to understanding the effect of group size on individual behavior is **self-attention theory** (Mullen, 1983). Basically, Mullen argues that conformity should be a direct function of Group Size—1 / Group Size (when there is only one target person). This other-total ratio (O-T ratio) equals .50 with one confederate, .67 with two confederates, .75 with three confederates, .80 with four confederates, and .83 with five confederates. By examining a dozen previous studies, including Asch's, Mullen (1983) demonstrated that this O-T ratio is a very good predictor of conformity. You should note that the O-T ratio rule indicates that conformity should be affected most by the first sources of influence, just as Latané's psychosocial law does.

A jury simulation study (wherein a subject is placed in the role of a juror but without deliberation with other jurors) by Wilder (1977) created an interesting problem for the number dimension of the social impact formula. The individual juror was to establish liability for damages to a baby burned by a vaporizer. One scenario presented to individual subjects indicated that six people agreed on who was liable. Two other scenarios indicated that two subgroups of three people and three subgroups of two people had come to the same conclusion. Subjects conformed most to the three subgroups, next most to the two subgroups, and least to the single group of six even though the social impact position indicates that there should be no difference because the number of influence sources is the same in all cases. (See figure 8.5.) One way to resolve the dilemma is to consider it a case of two or three independent influence sources versus one (Wilder, 1978). Perhaps a more complete model is presented by Mullen (1986b). He argues that an additive O-T ratio is most appropriate to predict conformity when distinct subgroups are recognized. Three subgroups of two would yield an additive O-T ratio of .67 + .67 + .67 = 2.0, and two subgroups would yield a .75 + .75 = 1.5, and the group of six individuals yields .85. This implies that the subgroups would be more influential as Wilder (1977) found. Of course, one must look beyond Mullen's O-T ratio rule for the basis for defining the two subgroups as separate.

Social Impact and Minority Influence

Sometimes we are not alone in facing a group united to influence us; we sometimes have allies. Asch's subjects who had another group member who disagreed with the majority were much less likely to conform to the majority position. A juror may also face a situation where there is a difference of opinion about guilt. In such situations, it is important to consider the strength, immediacy, and number of the target or minority group as well as the SIN of the influence or majority source. As a general rule, as the SIN of the target group increases, the influence source group has less impact on a target person.

Latané and Wolf (1981) have speculated about how these characteristics of two opposing groups influence individuals. The issue turns on whether you consider yourself a member of one of the groups or not. If you see yourself as a group member, then the social impact you should experience could be calculated by dividing the SIN of the other, influencing group by the SIN of your own target group. If you are not aligned with either group, as at the beginning of jury deliberations, then the social impact experienced would be determined by the difference between the SINs of the opposing groups [SIN majority − SIN minority]. In either case, the impact of the influencing group is diminished as the SIN of the target or minority group is greater. It should be noted that for a minority to be as influential as a majority, the minority must have greater strength and/or immediacy than the majority since their number is by definition smaller.

Moscovici (1976, 1980, 1985) has argued that *minority influence* is qualitatively different from majority influence. Instead of strength (status or expertise) being important in determining minority influence, he states that consistency of position over time, implying confidence and correctness, is important for minorities. However, the evidence is mixed on this issue. One study (Wolf & Latané, 1983) found that strength affected majority influence but not minority influence, but another (Wolf, 1985) showed that both majority and minority influences were affected by strength and neither was affected by consistency. Whether characteristics of sources other than strength, immediacy, and number affect conformity has yet to be clearly demonstrated.

The social impact characteristics of target groups has been shown to affect conformity in many different situations (Latané, 1981). The size of the target group has been studied extensively. One study showed that the more people who ate in a group at Columbus, Ohio restaurants, the smaller the tip was relative to the amount of the tab (Freeman, Walker, Borden, & Latané, 1975). The waiter's impact diminished as the number of the target group was greater, according to Latané's theory.

Another area where the number of people present has had a consistent impact on behavior is helping (Latané & Nida, 1981). If several people are available to help, the victim's plight will have less impact on each bystander and he or she is less likely to help than if she or he were the only bystander. This *bystander effect* will be discussed in chapter 12. It should be noted that the study of the impact of strength and immediacy of target groups has been neglected. Social impact theory suggests that, like number, greater strength and immediacy of others in your target group would mean that you would be affected less by an influence source.

The ambiguity of stimulus conditions contributes to conformity because informational social influence, as well as normative social influence, occurs in ambiguous situations. Only normative influence is likely to occur in unambiguous situations like Asch's line judging studies. When objective reality is clear, the pressure from the group must be greater in order to sway an individual's opinion. Of course, in cohesive or attractive groups, the individual may say, "What the heck—I want these people to like me. Who cares whether I'm right or wrong about these dumb lines?" However, in more ambiguous situations, the group's pressure does not have to overcome the force of reality. In the areas of clothing fashions, hair fashions, and many other domains, we would expect individuals to be affected by the tendencies of their friends and acquaintances more than in areas with clear-cut standards.

Stimulus Ambiguity

One analysis of social influence situations separates the influence of stimulus conditions from the influence of others' opinions (Kriss, Kinchla, & Darley, 1977). The results of a study testing their mathematical model of social influence showed that the opinions of others only affected subjects' perceptual judgments when subjects' sensory impressions of the stimuli were ambiguous. So, when objective reality is least, social influence is most likely to occur.

A factor that has been overlooked by the social impact position is how certain the individual feels about the judgment at hand. Social impact theory postulates that a person is more likely to conform as the strength (or expertise) of the influence source becomes greater and the strength of his or her target group becomes less. It says nothing about how the strength—or expertise or attractiveness—of the individual affects conformity. However, there is evidence from other research that as the strength factors of the individual (e.g., the self-perceived expertise) are greater, the individual is less likely to conform.

Personal Uncertainty

McGuire (1968a) has argued that there should be a complex relationship between two global strength factors, intelligence and self-esteem, and persuadability. He says that intelligence, for instance, should have mixed effects because high intelligence should make the individual both more able to understand and retain the message and more resistant to influence because he or she already knows the correct information. McGuire (1968a, 1985) contends that self-esteem works the same way, so moderate self-esteem people would be the most influenceable. Perhaps high self-esteem people see themselves as expert on many topics, which makes them less likely to acquiesce to other views; but simultaneously they may be unthreatened by and more open to other positions because of their feelings of certainty, which makes them more susceptible to influence. Low self-esteem people would not see themselves as experts, so other views would be credible, but they may be too threatened to fully consider those views. These competing factors would make low and high self-esteem individuals less influenceable than moderate self-esteem people.

Age is another potential "strength" factor that affects influenceability. Recall that Jackson and Latané (1981b) varied the strength of the influence sources by using younger and older solicitors for leukemia research. In terms of strength of the target individual, older people are more likely to perceive themselves as experts, and to be certain of their opinions. One study has shown that, among adults, older people are less likely to conform to pressure (Harris, James, Chavez, Fuller, Kent, Massanari, & Walsh, 1983). Another study indicated that older adults report themselves to be more assertive than younger adults (Kimble, Marsh, & Kiska, 1984).

Santee and Maslach (1982) investigated how global personality characteristics of the target person are related to the person's tendency to conform or dissent. They found that people who were high in self-esteem and individuation (the willingness to call attention to oneself) and low in social anxiety took dissenting positions more than people who scored in the opposite direction on those dimensions. Also, those low in individuation and high in social anxiety were more likely to conform with the majority position. These factors seem directly related to the target person's general feelings of certainty or confidence in his or her knowledge or ability.

Beyond these global factors which affect conformity, the individual's feelings of certainty or confidence in particular situations may affect susceptibility to influence even more. For instance, Deaux (1972) found that when chronically high self-esteem people were given negative personal evaluations—deflating their confidence at that time—they were more persuadable than any other group.

Sistrunk and McDavid's (1971) classic study on sex differences in conformity, presented in chapter 2, obtained results consistent with the idea that personal uncertainty in a particular situation creates conformity. They found that men conformed more to majority opinion on feminine topics and women conformed more to majority opinion on masculine topics. Instead of a systematic difference between the sexes in conformity, personal uncertainty or ignorance about the topic determined the pattern of response. Campbell, Tesser, and Fairey (1986) also found that self-doubt about ability to perform a dot estimation task led to greater conformity by subjects in that situation.

Intimidation to arouse personal uncertainty and thus gain conformity to standards of conduct seems to be a common ploy. It is used by senior members of groups and by authority persons to exact desired conduct. Deflating the confidence of new recruits or deviant members to gain conformity to group standards is a common practice in military units, football teams (Shaw, 1972), fraternities, sororities, gangs, prisons, and many other groups. Common threats call into question the individual's manliness, womanliness, morality or competence. Hazing is

Are these players being initiated into a world of unquestioning obedience?

one of the more blatant intimidation tactics. As Gary Shaw (1972) wrote in his exposé of life on a major college football team, "hazing initiated us into a world of unquestioning obedience." More subtle tactics may be used in more genteel groups, such as business and governmental organizations and academic circles.

Interactive Compliance Strategies

Compliance, as mentioned earlier in the chapter, refers to behavior undertaken or changed in response to direct *requests*. Many ways to make these requests effective so that the influence agent will make the sale or get the donation have been examined by social psychologists. These compliance strategies are different from mass media appeals, discussed in chapter 7, because they are interactive.

Reciprocity Demands and Compliance

Robert Cialdini (1985) reviewed many sales tactics in his interesting recent book, *Influence*. Some of these tactics work through the **norm of reciprocity** (Gouldner, 1960). The salesperson does something for a potential customer, which makes the target person feel obligated to return the favor. This feeling of being obligated to reciprocate makes the target person more likely to buy an insurance policy or make a donation to the influence agent's organization.

Here's how the technique works:

An insurance saleswoman prepared several different plans especially for you to consider, drove many miles to present the insurance plans to you, and spent two hours describing them to you. You feel that you should buy a policy to pay her back for all her efforts.

At the grocery store, a store employee is handing out freshly-cooked tidbits of a new food product while standing next to a display of the food. He graciously hands a sample to you and every kid in your entourage. Don't you feel like you should buy a package of the product?

The sales representative for Amway household products leaves a sample tray of six or seven products at your home for you to use for a few days at absolutely no charge or obligation. "No obligation," she says, so why do you feel compelled to buy something when she returns to pick up the tray?

The "free" sample. Shouldn't you buy the product?

A respected member of the White House staff suggests an elaborate, expensive plan to spy on and sabotage the Democrats' presidential campaign by using prostitutes and bugged pleasure boats at the convention. Gordon Liddy's bosses flatly reject the proposal. Some time later, Liddy proposes a more modest plan to bug the Democratic headquarters in the Watergate complex to these same superiors (Dean, 1976). In light of the fact that Liddy has made a major concession in modifying his undercover plans, his superiors okay the plan.

The vacuum cleaner salesman first demonstrates the quality of his hospital-type, $1,000 cleaner by getting dirt and grime from your "clean" couch and carpet. Since you indicate that the vacuum is a little out of your price range, he then suggests that the $75 model might be right for you. Since he has made the gesture to meet your needs, you feel pressure to return the favor and buy the $75 vacuum cleaner.

From the research in this area, there appear to be two primary ways to use reciprocity demands in persuasion. One way is to do something for or to give something to the receiver. If the receiver allows the influencer to benefit him or her, then the receiver will feel obligated to reciprocate. Even though Cialdini (1985) cites several real-life examples of this "free sample" approach and the first three scenarios exemplify this approach, there has been very little research verification of the effectiveness of this approach. However, Regan (1971) did show that if a person gave a soft drink to a receiver first, that person was able to sell more raffle tickets to the receiver than to a person for whom the person had not done a favor.

The other approach used to invoke reciprocity demands is to construct a plan of action that you would like the target person to accept and then to modify the proposed action in ways that are clearly beneficial to the target person. This willingness to negotiate to benefit the target person will often move the target person to reciprocate by accepting the modified plan.

One variation of this approach is called the **door-in-the-face technique** (Cialdini, Vincent, Lewis, Catalan, Wheeler, & Darby, 1975). This technique involves asking the target person to accept a very costly or demanding proposal first. After the target person slams the door in his or her face, the influencer suggests a more reasonable, less costly alternative. That more reasonable alternative is more likely to be accepted if it is presented as a concession after the rejection of a costly proposal than if it were presented alone. Cialdini and associates (1975) did find that they could get students to volunteer to chaperone some poor children on a trip to the zoo more easily if the students had heard and rejected a more costly request first (see Research Trailblazers box). The fact that the target persons of the request had slammed the door in the face of the requester might have made the target persons more agreeable to the second request out of guilt, especially since the other party was being conciliatory. Gordon Liddy and our vacuum salesperson in the previous examples used this approach.

A related compliance approach using the reciprocity principle is called the **"that's-not-all" technique** (Burger, 1986). This approach does not allow the target person to reject a more costly proposal first. The costly proposal is presented but the cost is lowered or additional benefits are mentioned before rejection occurs.

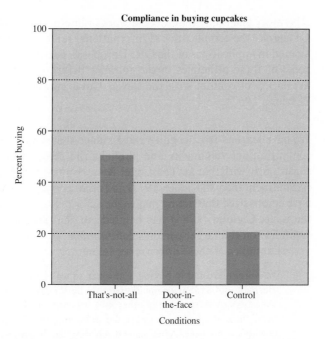

Figure 8.6
*More people bought
cupcakes when the
price was lowered
spontaneously (the
"That's not all!"
condition) than in the
other conditions. The
final price of the
cupcakes was the same
in all three conditions.*

(From Burger, 1986, Journal of
Personality and Social Psychology,
51, *282.)*

In several experiments, Burger (1986) had experimenters say that cupcakes at a bake sale cost $1.25 and then reduce the price to $1.00 or throw in a cookie for $1.25 before the subject could respond. Both of these that's-not-all techniques produced more cupcake sales than if the cupcakes were presented for $1.00, especially if the seller was presenting the lower price of his or her own accord. In one experiment, Burger (1986) showed that the that's-not-all technique (without rejection of the first offer) was slightly more effective than the door-in-the-face technique (with rejection of the first offer). Simply presenting the price as having been lowered to the customer's benefit causes the customer to meet the seller halfway. Perhaps this technique is being used when you see a price tag with a higher price on the tag with a line through it. (See figure 8.6.)

The reciprocity principle is also evident in a negotiation process recommended to assure world peace (Osgood, 1962). By using a process which he labelled **graduated and reciprocated initiatives in tension-reduction (GRIT),** Osgood believes that governments could achieve de-escalation of conflict. To start this process, a government would state its conciliatory intent and then demonstrate it by making a minor concession to its opponent nation(s). If the opposing nations reciprocate this action, the next step is to communicate and execute a slightly more important act of good will toward them. If opponents did not reciprocate initially, the government initiating this process could make a few more minor concessions after publicly announcing them. If opponents did not reciprocate eventually, then the process would stop or the initiating government might start different kinds of concessions. For example, instead of ceasing the supply of arms to the opponent's enemies, the initiating nation could start supplying scarce food products to its opponent. With each reciprocated action, the next conciliatory gesture could be a greater, more meaningful one until peace was assured. Negotiation simulation studies have indicated that this process is effective in the laboratory and imply that it could work in international affairs (Lindskold, 1981). Of course, the complexities of international relations would have to be fully considered in applications of the GRIT proposal. President Kennedy apparently used some of these principles in the summer before his assassination to start a de-escalation of conflict with the Soviet Union, which continued for several years (Etzioni, 1967).

Commitment and Compliance

We have learned from cognitive dissonance theory that if we can get a person to commit an act voluntarily and publicly, the person will come to think and act consistently with that act (Festinger & Carlsmith, 1959). From that background, commitment theory (Kiesler, 1971) and other perspectives (Jones & Gerard, 1967) have emphasized that acting makes the actor restructure his or her thinking about the issue. Cialdini (1985) has pointed out that several compliance approaches capitalize on the target person's *commitment*.

Examples of these approaches follow:

We were interested in buying a new car so we visited several dealerships. One salesman told us that he could give us a better price on the car we wanted than other dealers. After visiting other lots, we came back to that salesman. When it was obvious that we were interested in buying, the salesman checked with his boss about the price. After their discussion, the figures were within pennies of other dealers' price. Did we leave? Heck no, we placed an order for a new car with him. The salesman had gotten us committed, then he jacked up the price.

The insurance woman asks if you want the best for your family if something should happen to you. The inevitable answer is yes. "You want your kids to get an Ivy League education even if you kick off prematurely, don't you?" "Yes, of course." "What about the mortgage on your house if you should kick the bucket? Don't you want your wife to be able to pay off the mortgage and move to Hawaii if you keel over?" "Sure." "You do want any children you may have to have a secure start in business when you cash in your chips, don't you?" "Yes." "Then you obviously understand that you need this $$$$$$ policy?" "Yes." [If you accept all the premises, then you have to accept the conclusion to be consistent.]

During the Korean conflict, the Chinese persuaded American POWs to write or publicly make endorsements of communist practices or denunciations of American life (Schein, 1956). The evidence that they had taken these stands could then be shown to others. Commitment of these acts under fairly mild threats was an integral part of the Chinese brainwashing procedure.

Subjects in Stanley Milgram's obedience studies faced a number of escalating commands. Imagine their reactions. "Wrong answer. I'm supposed to shock him with 15 volts. OK. Fifteen volts isn't very much. Done." "Another wrong answer. Thirty volts won't hurt him.". . ."Missed again. 135 volts isn't much more than 120. No problem.". . ."No answer, wrong again. I've already used 435, might as well keep on going." Each act of obedience made it more likely that subjects would continue to shock the victim, especially since the increase was only 15 volts.

Back to the car sale. We placed an order for a car with certain internal and external characteristics, working and decorative features. The salesman calls, "I think we have just the car for you, buddy. It has so-and-so and so-and-so."

"Sounds good. One other thing, what color is the interior? [We did not want a dark interior because we already had suffered through too many summer days in a heat-collecting car.]"

"Oh, it's out on the lot; I think it's a buckskin."

"OK."

"We can close the sale tonight if you and your wife can make the money arrangements."

"I'll get the check from the credit union and we'll be there."

That night, with money in hand, we went to see the car. The interior was solid black! He lied. But did we refuse to buy the car? No, we suffered with that car for ten years because he got the commitment first and then increased the costs.

There are two major interactive compliance techniques based on commitment represented here: the foot-in-the-door technique and the low-ball technique. Freedman and Fraser (1966) introduced the **foot-in-the-door technique.** In one of their two studies, they had a man or a woman experimenter go to subjects' homes and request that they display a small sign or sign a petition supporting a safe driving campaign or a "Keep California Beautiful" campaign. A few weeks later, the other experimenter went to the same houses as a representative of Citizens for Safe Driving and asked the subjects to allow the group to place a large, unsightly sign saying "Drive Carefully" in their front yards. They showed subjects a picture of the poorly-lettered sign obscuring the front of a house. Control subjects were those people who were asked about the large sign, but had not been approached about the small sign or petition. The percentage of those agreeing to have the large sign put up are presented in figure 8.7.

These results show that if people are asked to and agree to do a small favor first; they are likely to agree to a larger, more costly request later, especially if the task and issue are similar (76 percent agreed). The effect occurred even when another person made the second request and the request was made weeks later. Freedman and Fraser believed that subjects who agreed to a request came to see themselves in a different way, and this new self-evaluation led them to agree again. Cialdini (1985; Cialdini, Petty, & Cacioppo, 1981) suggests that once a person has acted in a particular way, he or she agrees to the larger, second request simply to be consistent. The second agreement may be mindless and automatic and does not require self-redefinition in his view.

Since 1966, over 100 studies of the foot-in-the-door phenomenon have been conducted. While the technique is generally effective, it does not always work (Beaman, Cole, Preston, Klentz, & Steblay, 1983). The size or costliness of both requests seems to be important. The first request must be trivial enough that most people will do it but costly enough that subjects will remember the request and their acceptance (and perhaps reevaluate themselves) (Kernan & Reingen, 1985; Tybout, Sternthal, & Calder, 1983). Also, the second request must not be so costly to the subject that he or she would not agree to it under any circumstances. Perhaps the foot-in-the-door approach is unsuccessful in recruiting blood donors because donating blood is inordinately costly to some people (Cialdini & Ascani, 1976; Foss & Dempsey, 1979).

Figure 8.7
*The foot-in-the-door
effect. The largest
number of people
agreed to the ugly
"Drive Carefully" sign
in their yards if they
had been asked to and
had agreed to display
a small Safe Driving
sign first. Of those who
had not been
approached previously
(the control group),
few (17 percent)
agreed.*

(From Freedman & Fraser, 1966,
Journal of Personality and Social
Psychology, 4,)

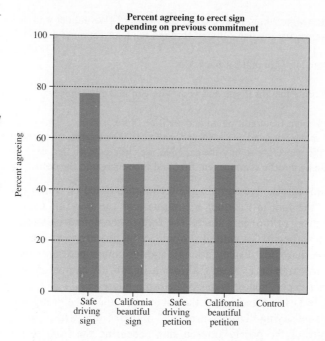

The insurance sales scenario and the Milgram obedience situation involve a whole series of "requests." They are not direct examples of the foot-in-the-door technique as it has been researched. All of the studies previously mentioned used only one small request and then a larger one. They have not examined an escalating series of requests or commands as in the Milgram studies or even a number of non-escalating questions as in the insurance sales scenario before the criterion request. Even though research has not been conducted directly on these types of situations, these examples seem to represent the way commitment and desire for consistency affect our behavior. Perhaps these issues will be studied systematically soon.

The two car sale examples described previously represent the **low-ball technique** (Cialdini, Cacioppo, Bassett, & Miller, 1978). In both cases, the salesman gained commitment from his customers and then increased the costs of the car purchase. In the first, typical scenario, the customers (the Kimbles) committed when they returned to the dealership to discuss price and the costs were increased by raising the price. In the second case, the customers committed when they arrived with the money and the costs were increased by presenting them with a car with undesired features for the same price. The salesman lied both times. The low-ball technique apparently entails withholding the truth, at least. The *commitment then costs* approach works better than describing all the costs before the decision is made. In the case of car sales, this advantage is probably greater because once the customers have worked through the decision process almost to completion, they are reluctant to abort the whole thing and start over—that would be more costly. The Cialdini et al. (1978) study of the low-ball technique is presented in the Research Trailblazers box.

Research Trailblazers

Robert Cialdini of Arizona State University and his coworkers have done a great deal of innovative research in many areas of social psychology. They have originated perspectives on how reinforcement affects attraction (Kenrick & Cialdini, 1977), how positive and negative moods affect prosocial behavior (Manucia, Baumann, & Cialdini, 1984), how people bask in the glory of others (Cialdini et al., 1976), and how feeling responsible for someone's plight makes us belittle them (Cialdini, Kenrick, & Hoerig, 1976), to name a few.

A prominent area of interest over the years has been how salespeople sell their products (Cialdini, 1985). In this fascinating book, Cialdini describes how people get others to do what they want them to do. The principles he outlines are based on much of his own research and astute observations of everyday life.

One sales technique that he brought from the everyday world into the laboratory for examination and clarification was the *low-ball* technique (Cialdini et al., 1978). The basic idea is that if you can get a person to commit him- or herself to an action, the person will do the action even if you raise the costs of the action. The idea is unabashedly borrowed from the practices of car salespersons described earlier.

To see if the low-ball procedure worked, Cialdini had a caller ask introductory psychology students if they would participate in an experiment. Half the students were told initially that the experiment was to be conducted at 7:00 A.M. before they accepted or rejected the opportunity to participate. The other subjects were asked if they were willing to participate before they were told about the early morning appointment time (the costly aspect of participation). Fifty-three percent of the second, low-ball group actually showed up at 7:00 A.M. Only 24 percent of the first, control group arrived. The low-ball technique of gaining commitment before introducing cost worked.

In a second experiment, Cialdini and his associates sought to see if a different kind of low-ball would work and how effective it was relative to a foot-in-the-door technique. In the low-ball condition, male graduate students who lived in the dorm were first asked if they would display two United Way posters on their window and door. When they agreed, they were told to pick up the posters at the desk downstairs within the hour (additional costs). Control subjects were told that they would have to go pick up the posters before they were asked if they were willing to display them. In the foot-in-the-door condition, after the subject agreed to display a window poster they were given, the experimenter explained that they could pick up the door poster downstairs. A day later, 60 percent of the low-ball subjects were displaying the poster on their door, while only 15 percent of the control and foot-in-the-door subjects had complied. The low-ball technique was more persuasive than the foot-in-the-door technique under these circumstances. Other investigators (Brownstein & Katzev, 1985) have found that the low-ball technique was more effective than the foot-in-the-door technique in securing museum donations. (See figure 8.A.)

In a third experiment, Cialdini and his associates assessed whether the low-ball effect is best explained by commitment theory (Kiesler, 1971), self-perception theory (Bem, 1967), cognitive dissonance theory (Festinger, 1957), or the idea that "behavior engulfs the field" (i.e., behavior is so prominent in our consciousness that it minimizes consideration of other elements of the situation) (Heider, 1958). In a voluntary low-ball condition, subjects were given a choice of tests to take after being told that they would receive two research credits for

(Continued)

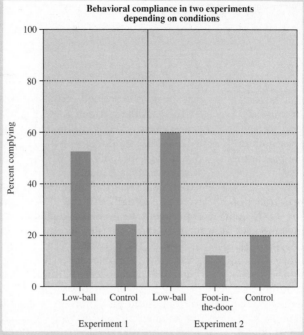

Figure 8.A
Cialdini and his associates showed in two different experiments that more people who commit to a request and are then told about additional costs (the low ball condition) comply than do people in other conditions.

(From Cialdini et al., 1978, Journal of Personality and Social Psychology, 36, 465, 467.)

taking one test and only one credit for taking the other. Then, the experimenter said that both tests only earned one credit. Subjects were allowed to choose again, and they rated the favorability of the tests again. Involuntary low-ball subjects first were only assigned to the two-credit test and then were given a choice after the credit was reduced to one. For control subjects, both tests were always presented as earning one credit. Voluntary low-ball subjects stuck with their initial decisions more than the other subjects did, but there were no attitude changes noted in the favorability ratings. Commitment theory supplies the best explanation for these results because dissonance and self-perception theories indicate that there should be attitude change as well as behavior change. The behavior engulfs the field

position implies that there should be no difference between the voluntary and involuntary conditions. Therefore, commitment freezes the individual to the choice even when the costs are changed.

In 1975, Cialdini and other associates (Cialdini, Vincent, Lewis, Catalan, Wheeler, & Darby) introduced the *door-in-the-face* technique. This procedure is based on the idea that if a person presents an outlandish request or position which is rejected by the target person, the persuader is more likely to gain agreement to a more modest request afterward than if the rejected position was never presented. Apparently, the fact that the persuader moderated his or her position made the target person feel that he or she should moderate the

intial position by changing from rejection to acceptance.

In their first experiment, the same person made both requests in the two-request conditions. In the door-in-the-face condition, the experimenters made the outlandish request that subjects they approached on campus volunteer as an unpaid counselor for two years at a juvenile detention center. When this was rejected, the experimenter asked them to volunteer to chaperone some of the same kids on one two-hour trip to the zoo. In an exposure condition, the experimenter presented the requests at the same time and asked if subjects would be willing to do either one. There was no rejection of the larger request and then moderating the favor in this condition. In a control condition, the experimenter only made the smaller request.

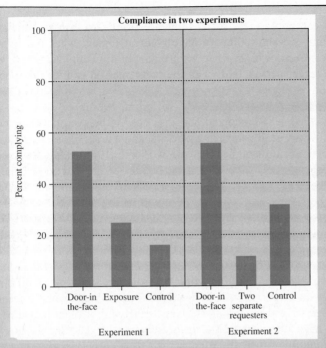

Compliance in two experiments

Experiment 1   Experiment 2

Figure 8.B
Two studies showed that when a person is approached with a large request which he or she refuses first and is then asked a more modest request (the door-in-the-face condition), the person is more likely to comply than in other conditions.
(From Cialdini et al., 1975, Journal of Personality and Social Psychology, 31, 209, 211.)

Half of the door-in-the-face subjects agreed to escort the kids to the zoo; one-fourth of the exposure subjects did; and only one-sixth of the control subjects agreed. Clearly, the large request-rejection-moderation strategy worked best.

In the second and third experiments, Cialdini and associates used essentially the same large and small requests. In the second experiment, a condition in which one experimenter presented the large request and another experimenter made the smaller request after the first was rejected was also conducted. This condition presented the contrast between the two favors, like the exposure condition in Experiment 1, without communicating that the first requester was making a concession. Again, the door-in-the-face condition produced the most compliance (55 percent). The two-requester condition produced the least compliance (10 percent). From these results, it is clear that the same person (or perhaps a representative of that person) must make both requests so that subjects will realize that the second request represents a concession. In the third experiment, the same experimenter made equivalent requests (two-hour chaperone jobs). The persuader didn't moderate the position by making the second request smaller. Over half (54 percent) of the door-in-the-face subjects agreed to chaperone, while one-third of the equivalent-requests subjects agreed. So, it is important that the persuaders adjust their positions to be more beneficial to the receiver if they expect the receiver to change from rejection to acceptance. (See figure 8.B.)

Besides these pioneering efforts in compliance, Cialdini and associates have looked at other features of the door-in-the-face technique (Mowen & Cialdini, 1980) and negotiation tactics (Cialdini, Bickman, & Cacioppo, 1979) in common sales situations. Another study has shown that saying "even a penny helps" increases donations significantly (Cialdini & Schroeder, 1976), perhaps by showing how agreeable the donation requester is. Other investigators (Reingen, 1978; Weyant, 1984; Weyant & Smith, 1987) have verified that it is harder to refuse someone who asks for small rather than large contributions.

In summary, Cialdini's contributions to the area of person-to-person or interactive influence have been substantial.

Applications of Social Influence Principles

The nurse will probably obey the doctor's orders without questions.

We can apply these social influence principles in many domains. As influence agents, we know that we have greatest impact when our expertise and/or attractiveness is high, when we are part of a unanimous group, when we are near the target person, and when the target person is uncertain about his or her position. Influence agents are also most powerful when there is a clear chain of command or status hierarchy (Milgram, 1974).

People in command positions need to be aware of their power and responsibility. A study involving doctors and nurses illustrates this point (Hofling, Brotzman, Dalrymple, Graves, & Pierce, 1966). The researchers had a doctor unknown to the hospital nurses on duty phone in a prescription for medication at a dosage that was twice the recommended maximum dosage according to a chart at the nurses' station. There were many reasons that the nurses should have disobeyed: (1) they did not know the doctor; (2) there was a regulation against taking prescriptions over the phone; (3) the dosage was too great; (4) they were unfamiliar with the drug, and (5) they were unfamiliar with the patient's case. Yet, 21 of the 22 nurses contacted administered the drug. The drug, of course, was a placebo. Like the Milgram situation and typical military situations, the high-status person was all powerful. Interestingly, when a scenario like this one was described to nursing students, nearly all of them indicated that they would not have administered the drug. Influence targets, like the hospital nurses, must be mindful of their situation as the action unfolds so that they will not be caught up in the conformity pressures.

Targets of conformity pressure or compliance attempts should consider the consequences of taking the actions influencers suggest to them. The elaboration likelihood model (Petty & Cacioppo, 1986) suggests that we can be wise consumers if we have a high need for cognition or if we can develop the necessary detachment from the situation to resist persuasion through unimportant or peripheral factors. Cialdini (1985) also encourages us to take a questioning stance as soon as we know someone is trying to influence us. If we do question what's happening, then we will know that if we buy the product or make the donation it will be for the right reasons.

Summary

We are often involved in social influence either as influence agents or targets of influence. Social influence includes the initiation or changing of attitudes or behaviors through obedience, conformity, imitation, compliance, or persuasion. Stanley Milgram's obedience studies showed that most people will obey orders to shock a man severely if the authority of the commander is strong, his or her responsibility for harm is evident, and the victim is remote from the subject.

The power to reward or punish produces compliance to the source's demands in the immediate situation. Attraction to the source produces long-lasting identification with the source's position. The verifiable expertise of a source can produce long-lasting internalization of the source's position if it is compatible with the target's network of attitudes and beliefs. The line-judging experiments of Asch indicated that even when making judgments about unambiguous stimuli, many people will publicly agree with a group's erroneous judgment if the group's opinion is unanimous and there are three or more people in the group. Sherif's autokinetic effect experiment demonstrated that in judging ambiguous stimuli, individuals look to others' judgments for information and accept the group norm as the long-term standard for their judgments. Recent work by Moscovici and others has shown that even when individuals are in a minority in a group setting, they can be influential if they display confidence and consistency of judgment.

According to social impact theory, the greater the strength, immediacy, and number of the source group; the greater will be the group's influence. The greater the strength, immediacy, and number of the target group; the less influence the source group will have on any particular target person. Ambiguity in the judgment stimuli and personal uncertainty in the target person also make conformity more likely.

The interactive compliance strategies, which can be used in person-to-person presentations, are often effective in sales. Some of these techniques, such as gift-giving, the door-in-the-face technique, and the that's-not-all technique, work by making the receiver feel that he or she should reciprocate the favor. Others, like the low-ball and foot-in-the-door techniques, work by making customers feel that they should live up to their commitments.

Group Processes

(a)

(b)

(a) An acting group; (b) a deliberating group.

We act, communicate, and make decisions in groups almost every day. People interact in many different kinds of groups often, and these interactions affect the course of our lives. To be considered members of a **group,** individuals must usually be in each other's presence and must interact enough to exert some influence on each other (Shaw, 1981). For instance, an exercise or aerobics class would be a group with only slight influence on each other. Members of a large lecture class may not be members of a group at all if they do not interact with each other. On the other hand, students in a seminar in which comments are directed to many different individuals are a group.

Other collections or bodies of people with whom we do not interact enough to be considered groups are also important to us. For instance, **reference groups** are collections of people with whom we identify, whose standards and values we adopt, even though we may seldom or never interact with them. Fellow ethnic group members, residents of various places (New Yorkers, Southerners, Californians), occupational groups, sports teams, or entertainers may be reference groups or reference persons for us. *Organizations* are typically made up of several groups that communicate with each other, but there are usually many people in an organization, such as a university, who never interact. *Collectives* are large numbers of people, such as crowds at entertainment events or political rallies or demonstrations, who act with each other (coact), but do not interact. Groups are the primary, but not the exclusive, focus of this chapter.

Groups differ not only in amount of interaction but in the desire of members to join the group and to be associated with it. A person may become part of a group at work only by necessity, but the same person may want to be a member of a sorority, a basketball team, a band, or a drama club. This difference in motivation influences how willingly and how well one performs in the group. Another motivational factor in group membership is the kind of need the group satisfies and how well it satisfies it. A person might join Weight Watchers, a therapy group, or a singles club to fulfill certain needs. If these groups improve his or her life, the individual is likely to maintain membership in the group.

How rewarding it is to belong to groups may depend on our status in the group and the group's status in the larger society. If others in society think highly of the group, members should readily and proudly acknowledge their membership and status in the group. Also, people who have higher status within a group are less constrained by group norms and rules (Hollander, 1964). Ecological psychologists (Barker, 1968; Barker & Gump, 1964; Wicker, 1979) have pointed out that the status a person enjoys in a group is often a function of how big the group is and how big the population is from which it recruits its members. The larger a group is, the less likely a particular individual is to attain a high-status position. Also, the larger the population from which the group is drawn, the less likely a particular person is to be recruited for membership and accorded a leadership position. Successful groups are less likely to seek and accept new members than are struggling groups (Zander, 1976); instead, they often have high standards and initiations.

Cohesive groups—groups with strong bonds among members—are also likely to have high standards for membership and are inclined to reject unattractive or deviant members (Schachter, 1951; Zander, 1976). Cohesiveness, one of the positive features of belonging to a group, seems to be related to group size. It is unlikely that strong interpersonal bonds can be maintained in large groups where person-to-person interactions among all members must be minimal. Large organizations must work hard to keep from splintering into smaller, close-knit groups or cliques.

Within the many kinds of groups, similar processes may operate. Social psychologists have generally examined processes presumed to be common to many kinds of groups. They have examined how the presence of others affects the behavior and thoughts of individual group members in positive and negative ways, how cooperation within groups and competition within and between groups affect individuals, how groups make decisions differently than individuals, how leaders emerge in groups, how leaders can effectively coordinate group efforts, and when and why individuals seek group membership.

The following are some examples of group situations addressed by social psychologists:

> Company Pseudorox has discovered that it has a faulty product on the market. The company must decide to remove the product from the market or to handle the problems that arise from the product on a case-by-case basis. The director of marketing thinks the company should keep the product on the market and take their chances. The popular director states that preference at the outset of the marketing committee meeting. Lo and behold, the committee decides to keep selling the product. A few months later, Company Pseudorox is named as defendant in a multimillion dollar class action products liability suit.
>
> A power failure has hit the city. Scores of people are breaking windows and looting in the shopping district. Honest John Valjean is trying to make it home from work in the dark. He notices the people scurrying around, the break-ins, and the absence of the police. He notices that someone has broken into the electronics store he passes every day. Several people are still in the store looting

as he peers in. He thinks, "No one will ever know," runs into the store, grabs a VCR and hotfoots it home. A few days later, he wishes that he'd gotten one with remote control.

Tracy "The Ace" Jackson has been the freshman sensation for the Flying Diablos basketball team all year. For the first time in 25 years, they are in position to win the conference championship and perhaps to go on to greater things. The situation is this: The Diablos have a one-point lead and the ball before a sellout home crowd when the rival Toads foul Jackson to stop the clock with 10 seconds left. As Tracy goes to the line, the crowd roars with the expectation of winning the championship. Jackson is not so sure; she's only hitting 62 percent from the line even though she has been a star of the team. The home crowd gets still and quiet as the freshman toes the line. The brick she throws up hits the back of the rim and bounces out to one of the Toads. A few dribbles, two passes, and a short shot later, the Diablos' championship is lost.

Keep these examples in mind as you read this chapter. See if you can identify the group processes operating in these situations.

Groups in Action

Individuals often perform in the presence of or in front of other people. What is the usual effect of having coactors or an audience?

The Presence of Others: Help or Hindrance?

The effects of the mere presence of other people on individuals' performance has been termed **social facilitation** (Zajonc, 1965). In his review of earlier research on the effects of someone watching the performer (*audience effects*) and of someone acting with the performer (*coaction effects*), Zajonc surmised that one general principle operates in both situations. That principle is that the presence of other people increases the performer's arousal and that arousal makes the individual likely to emit the dominant or preeminent response in his or her response hierarchy for the task. If the task has been mastered, the strongest response is likely to be the correct one. Therefore, the presence of others and the consequent arousal should improve performance. If the task has not been mastered, the dominant response tendency should hinder performance. So, the presence of others could either facilitate or impair performance, depending on the level of mastery of the performer.

Such audience effects could account for why basketball teams seek to foul the most inexperienced player on the floor or the poorest free throw shooter at the end of the game when the pressure and the arousal should be greatest. According to Zajonc's model, which is supposed to apply best to simple motor responses, such players should do worst in the clutch; while experienced, accomplished shooters should hit nearly every free throw in such situations. In fact, one recent study showed that good pool players become more accurate when they have an audience and bad players do worse when they are observed (Michaels, Blommel, Brocato, Linkous, & Rowe, 1982). (See figure 9.1.)

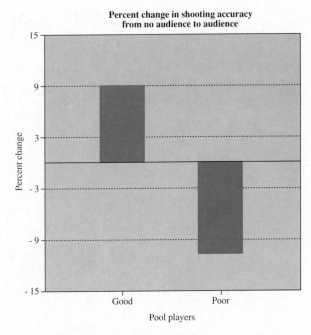

Percent change in shooting accuracy
from no audience to audience

Figure 9.1
*Good pool players
doing better before an
audience and bad
players doing worse
supports Zajonc's ideas
about social
facilitation.*
(From Michaels, et al., 1982,
Replications in Social Psychology,
2, 21–24.)

Of course, more than the mere presence of other people is involved in audience and coaction situations. Coactors, for instance, may distract the performer
(Sanders & Baron, 1975), they may be seen as competitors in that their performance may be compared to the performer's (Cottrell, 1972), and/or they may
reduce the performer's tension because the audience's attention may be perceived
as diffused among all the coactors (Jackson & Latané, 1981a). Audiences, on the
other hand, may distract the performer from the task (Sanders & Baron, 1975),
they may make the performer apprehensive because they may seem to be evaluating him or her (Cottrell, 1972), they may be supportive or not (Baumeister
& Steinhilber, 1984), they may communicate their expectations about the actor's
performance and thereby affect it (Baumeister, Hamilton, & Tice, 1985), and/
or they may affect the performer's self-consciousness by their sheer numbers
(Diener, Lusk, DeFour, & Flax, 1980; Jackson & Latané, 1981a). Coactors and
audiences can affect performers in different and complex ways.

Let us examine some of these effects, starting with the effects of coactors. One
consequence of having many coactors and virtually no audience is **deindividuation**
(Diener, 1980; Zimbardo, 1970). Situations which involve many people and much
unguided activity with minimal surveillance of individuals by an audience lead
individuals to feel *deindividuated* or "lost in the crowd." Very little attention can
be focused on the individual by others; therefore, the individual is unlikely to

Deindividuation
and Self-Attention

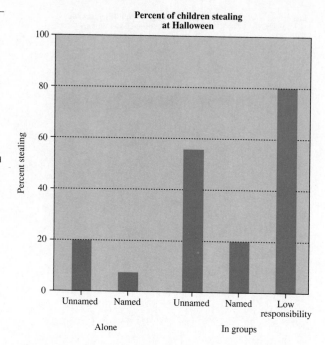

Figure 9.2
Lone, identified trick-or-treaters stole the least money and candy. Unidentified trick-or-treaters who were in groups and were not held responsible stole the most.

(From Diener, et al., 1976, Journal of Personality and Social Psychology, 33, *180.)*

focus attention or awareness upon her- or himself (Diener, 1980). This deindividuated state can lead to uninhibited behavior, which can have positive consequences (cf. Gergen, Gergen, & Barton, 1973; Johnson & Downing, 1979), but this uninhibited behavior is usually destructive or antisocial (e.g., Diener, Fraser, Beaman, & Kelem, 1976; Zimbardo, 1970).

One clever demonstration of the effects of deindividuation was conducted on Halloween night (Diener et al., 1976). When young trick-or-treaters went to 27 Seattle homes either alone or in groups, they became involved in an experiment. In their costumes and especially in groups, these children were anonymous and deindividuated. At the door, the hostess either increased or decreased their deindividuation or left it unchanged. Deindividuation was decreased (or individuation was aroused) by asking each child's name and address and repeating the name back to them. Deindividuation was increased for some groups by making the smallest—but unidentified—child responsible for stealing and thereby lessening responsibility for the other anonymous group members. The hostess told the children in all conditions that each child could have one piece of candy from a bowl and left the area. A hidden observer recorded whether the children took extra candy or took money from a nearby bowl of pennies and nickels. Figure 9.2 indicates the percentage of children who stole candy or money in different conditions.

Children who were in groups stole more than children who were alone, and children who were anonymous stole more than children who were identified. Those in the most deindividuated condition (anonymous groups with lowered responsibility) stole at the highest rate. Interestingly, two situations involving an audience (when a parent accompanied the children and when the experimenter remained in the room because a glut of seven or more kids came to the door at once) showed low transgression rates, 8.3 percent and 18.7 percent, respectively.

Diener and his associates also examined the effects of coactors and similar coactors on two aspects of deindividuation, self-consciousness and disinhibition of behavior (Diener et al., 1980). Lower self-consciousness is presumed to be an indication that one is deindividuated and more intense, unbridled behavior is supposed to be a consequence of deindividuation. In one experiment, subjects were asked to engage in some silly behaviors (acting like a chimp, etc.) either alone or with 1, 3, 7, or 15 coactors. The investigators found that subjects were less self-conscious as the number of coactors increased. However, they did not find the expected differences in disinhibited behavior. In another experiment, they had college women perform the same, potentially embarrassing behaviors with three male confederate coactors, two male and one female confederate coactors, or one male and two female confederate coactors. In this study, the women reported least self-consciousness and their behavior was observed to be most intense and uninhibited when more of the coactors were of the same sex. So, the more coactors there are and the more similar they are to the individual, the more indications of deindividuation the individual displays. In a similar way, performers in Greek Week song and dance skits at Ohio State reported less tension and nervousness as the number of coactors doing the skits with them was greater (Jackson & Latané, 1981a).

An archival study illustrates how deindividuation is greater in larger coacting groups and how deindividuation unleashes destructive behavior (Mullen, 1986a). The archival data in this study came from newspaper accounts collected in a book (Ginzburg, 1962) of lynchings of black victims by white mobs. These gruesome accounts were examined to see how the size of the mob and the number of victims had affected the atrocities committed by the mobs. Deindividuation research and Mullen's self-attention theory suggest that as crowd size increases and the number of victims decreases, the crowds' actions would become more destructive. An atrocity was scored as greater if hanging, shooting, burning, lacerating, and mutilating all occurred in the same incident and if the ordeal was prolonged rather than brief. The analysis indicated that there was more excessive destructive behavior as the mob size relative to the number of victims increased. The implication from the work of Zimbardo (1970) and others is that the way to defuse a mob situation is for an audience to individuate crowd members by calling them by name or otherwise focusing on their identities and increasing their self-attention.

Research Trailblazers

Brian Mullen of Syracuse University has presented an integrative theory of how groups affect individuals. Self-attention theory (Mullen, 1983) combines theories about focus of attention (Carver, 1979; Duval & Wicklund, 1972) with other theories of group behavior (e.g., Latané, 1981). Mullen (1983) states that when the number of people with whom you are associated (your self-group) is small relative to the number of people present in the group (the O-T ratio discussed earlier is large), you are likely to focus attention on yourself and evaluate yourself. This self-attention causes the individual to be self-conscious, and it makes one adhere to salient standards of conduct. When nearly everyone present is "with you" (your self-group is relatively large and the O-T ratio is small), you will be less self-conscious, and your behavior will be less inhibited. So, the number and classification of people in the immediate setting affects the individual's consciousness and behavior.

Self-attention theory, therefore, predicts that the O-T ratio will be positively correlated with self-focus, self-consciousness, conformity, and prosocial behavior; and negatively correlated with social loafing and antisocial behavior. How does Mullen evaluate this theory? In almost every case, he has examined previously conducted studies, calculated the O-T ratio for each condition, and correlated the O-T ratio with dependent measures collected by the earlier investigators. Using regression (correlational) statistics and meta-analysis, a technique used to combine and evaluate the results from several studies, Mullen (1983) found strong evidence that the O-T ratio is correlated with self-consciousness, conformity, prosocial behavior, social loafing, and antisocial behavior. Mullen (1983) also conducted an experiment which showed that the self-focus of men and women in groups do follow the principles of self-attention theory. The higher the proportion of women in the group, the lower the self-focus of women; and the lower the proportion, the greater the women's self-focus. Men reacted the same way.

Mullen has been very creative in using previous studies or archives to evaluate self-attention theory. He has taken very diverse data sources and has derived meaningful, comparable dependent variables from them so that the studies can be analyzed. To test the effects of group composition on individuals, Mullen has examined participation in religious congregations (Mullen, 1984), atrocities committed by lynch mobs (1986a), participation in discussion groups seated around rectangular tables (1986c), and the verbal dysfluencies of stutterers in groups. In all of these studies, the size of the subgroups whose members are operating in the same or different roles as the subject has had a striking influence on the behavior of the individual in precisely the ways that self-attention theory predicts.

One factor that varies from study to study is the way that the self-group and the other-group(s) are defined. Sometimes, the subgroups are operationally defined in straightforward ways, such as mob members vs. victims (Mullen, 1986a), men vs. women (Mullen, 1983, Study 2), and congregation members vs. ministers (1984). The lynch mob and religious group distinctions were clear and meaningful ways to draw the group lines. The sex distinction between self- and other-groups in Mullen (1983) had to be highlighted for it to affect individuals' self-focus. Presumably, any personal feature, such as sex, age, race, or student status, that is made salient by the situation or the experimenter could be the basis for distinguishing between self- and other-groups. For instance, in Mullen's (1986c) study on participation in group discussion, he defined people seated on the other side of the table from the subject and in his or her field of vision as members of one other-group, while

people on the same side of the table as the subject and out of the field of vision were ignored and were not included in calculation of the O-T ratio. So, there is some ambiguity in how subgroups should be defined from situation to situation.

Mullen distinguished between different other-subgroups in the stutterers study (Mullen, in press) and the group discussion study (Mullen, 1986c). In those studies, he calculated separate O-T ratios for each other-subgroup and added them together. The additive O-T ratios were more sensitive predictors of stuttering and discussion participation than simple O-T ratios, which ignored the subgroup structure. Careful distinction between different subgroups added complexity to the model, which enabled better prediction of individual behavior.

It could be argued that the theory needs even more complexity to capture usual behavior more precisely. For instance, what happens when other subgroups are exerting influence in opposing directions on the individual, as the

experimenter and the victim did in Milgram's (1974) obedience studies or as a divided jury might affect a juror? Would a subtractive O-T ratio be needed to represent the group's influence? Also, what about the status of group members? Might not a roomful of professors create greater self-attention in a new Ph.D. than a same sized group of high school seniors would? There is evidence that higher status audiences make performers more tense (Jackson & Latané, 1981b). Perhaps Mullen should not dismiss the strength or status component of social impact theory as readily as he has in a recent review of that theory (Mullen, 1985a).

Mullen has been very resourceful in using research archives and the information in them to test his theory. Self-attention theory represents a creative synthesis of interpersonal and intrapersonal elements to explain behavior in groups. Its clearly quantified features make it easily testable and, consequently, a good model for new researchers to follow.

Self-Attention and Social Impact

Two theoretical perspectives that have been used to explain these deindividuation effects and other coaction and audience phenomena are self-attention theory (Mullen, 1983) and social impact theory (Latané, 1981). *Self-attention theory* focuses on the effects of size of an individual's self-group relative to the size of an other-group on the individual's self-attention and behavior. Mullen uses an O-T ratio to calculate the expected effects of group composition on self-attention and behavior. The O-T ratio is equal to

# of Other-Group/# of Other-Group + # of Self-Group

Mullen (1983) proposes that as the O-T ratio increases, self-attention increases and behavior becomes more responsible or more adherent to the individual's ordinary standards for conduct. In the lynch mob study (Mullen, 1986a), the O-T ratio for the lynchers decreased as the relative mob size increased so that self-attention was lower and the behavior was more uninhibited. Mullen has been able to demonstrate that students participate more in discussions as the O-T ratio of teachers (other-group) vis-à-vis students (self-group) and teachers is greater (Mullen, 1986c). Church members participate more as the O-T ratio of ministers (other-group) relative to members (self-group) and ministers is greater (1984). Stutterers stutter more as the O-T ratio of listeners to speakers and listeners is greater (1985b), and performers are more self-conscious and inhibited as the O-T ratio of audience to performers and audience is greater (Mullen, 1983b). It should be noted that greater self-attention with higher O-T ratios can lead to positive (discussion participation) and negative (stuttering) behaviors, depending on which behavior is more "mindful" or readily accessible for the individual.

Social Impact and Deindividuation

Social impact theory, as discussed in the previous chapter, takes into account the strength, immediacy, and number (SIN) of both an influencing group and a target group (Latané, 1981; Latané & Wolf, 1981). The impact experienced by a member of the target group increases with the SIN of the influencing group and decreases with the SIN of the target group. The emphasis on group size and the acknowledgment of the importance of at least two different groups is similar in social impact theory and self-attention theory. Strength and immediacy are two distinctive elements of social impact theory (Mullen, 1985b). Despite Mullen's (1985b) contention that these two factors are unimportant, there is evidence that the age or status of an audience (i.e., strength) and the closeness of an audience do influence the reactions of a target person in some situations (Jackson & Latané, 1981b; Knowles, 1983; Latané & Harkins, 1976). Of course, it could be argued that you don't have a real group situation without high immediacy so that members can interact with and influence each other. Also, in some of Mullen's studies, the distinction between self and other groups seems to embody a strength or status difference (e.g., teachers and students, church members and ministers). So, strength and immediacy are of some importance in social influence situations.

How is social impact theory related to the mob violence discussed earlier? A person in a mob—a college spring break mob harassing young women or local proprietors, for instance—should experience less inhibiting impact as the SIN of his or her target group is greater and as the SIN of an audience is less. On the other hand, if the audience were a large (N), nearby (I), duly-authorized (S) police force; they should have a chilling effect on the mob members' activities. Again, we have characterized the deindividuation situation as one with an imposing set of coactors and an absent or unimposing audience.

Another phenomenon that occurs in situations where there are coactors and an unimposing audience is called social loafing (Latané, Williams, & Harkins, 1979). **Social loafing** refers to the tendency of individuals to exert less effort when participating in a group effort than when working alone. For social loafing to occur, the coacting individuals must be involved in a cooperative task, and the audience must be unimposing in that they must only have access to group performance, not individual performance.

Social loafing was first observed in a tug-of-war type situation where the pounds of pressure pulled by groups were substantially less than the sum of individual efforts. This poorer group outcome could have been partly due to poor coordination among group members such that all members may not have been pulling in exactly the same direction at the same time. However, one team of researchers showed that social loafing per se (less actual effort expended) was involved by measuring the pull of one individual when he thought he was pulling with a group versus when he knew he was pulling alone. They found that he pulled up to 18 percent less hard when he thought he was pulling with two or more others (Ingham, Levinger, Graves, & Peckham, 1974). (See figure 9.3.)

Social Loafing

Figure 9.3
(a) Ringelmann's (1913) data indicates that adding each additional rope puller reduces the effective performance of each performer. (b) When pullers thought others were pulling with them (they weren't), pullers reduced their effort. Large pseudogroups (4–6) didn't cause more reduction.

(a) From Kravitz & Martin, 1986, Journal of Social Psychology, 50, p. 938. (b) From Ingham, et al., 1974, Journal of Personality and Social Psychology, 10, 377.

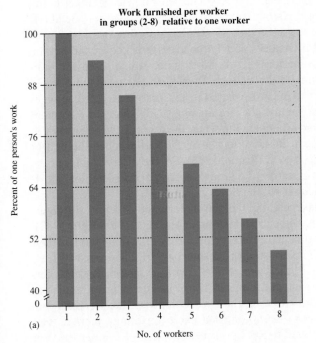

Work furnished per worker
in groups (2-8) relative to one worker

Percent of one person's work

No. of workers

(a)

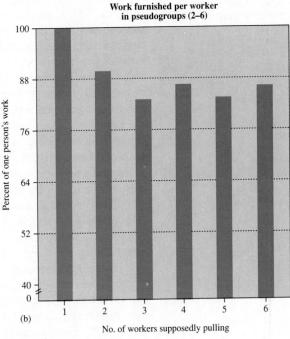

Work furnished per worker
in pseudogroups (2–6)

Percent of one person's work

No. of workers supposedly pulling

(b)

On what kinds of tasks is social loafing likely to occur? Steiner (1972) has provided a classification for different types of cooperative tasks. Steiner distinguishes between (1) sequential tasks in which individuals perform parts of the task in a prescribed order and simultaneous tasks in which individuals perform at the same time; (2) unitary tasks in which individuals do the same activity and divisible tasks in which there is a division of labor with different individuals doing different subtasks; and (3) maximizing tasks which demand maximum speed and effort and optimizing tasks which require accuracy and precision. Social loafing studies using rope-pulling, cheering, and clapping as tasks are evidence that loafing is most likely to occur on *simultaneous, unitary, maximizing tasks*. In fact, a study by Harkins and Petty (1982) showed that when a divisible task is used instead of a unitary one, the loafing effect disappears.

Other aspects of task performance are also important in affecting the loafing effect. Probably the most important feature affecting loafing is identifiability of individual performance. If the individual's performance is observable by the audience, social loafing does not occur (Williams, Harkins, & Latané, 1981). Individual performances are unidentifiable on what Steiner (1972) has called additive tasks. The additive feature refers to the fact that the group score is the sum of the individual performances. On these additive tasks, the subject is led to believe that the experimenter only obtains a measure of group performance and cannot identify individual performance. Apparently, this unidentifiability allows the person to get lost in the crowd and to loaf, especially if he or she believes that others are not giving maximum performance either (Jackson & Harkins, 1985).

Social loafing can occur on such factory tasks.

Other ways of computing the group score can also influence whether group members loaf or not. In compensatory tasks, the average of the group members' scores determines the group score (Steiner, 1972). Social loafing should occur on compensatory tasks, like additive tasks, if only the average is known and not the individual performances. In most cases, the investigator would learn the individual scores in order to compute the average. In such situations, loafing would be less likely to occur. Disjunctive tasks, where the best individual score becomes the group score, and conjunctive tasks, where the worst individual score becomes the group score, can both encourage loafing when the group is large enough or the individual's ability make it unlikely that he or she will produce the best or the worst score, respectively (Kerr & Bruun, 1983). So, the dispensability of the individual's performance in affecting the group's score affects social loafing. If it is indispensable, the individual will not loaf.

Two recent studies have highlighted the importance of equity in determining whether social loafing will occur (Jackson & Harkins, 1985; Kerr, 1983). Both studies indicate that individuals prefer to perform at the same level as their equal-ability peers; while the Kerr study also shows that individuals will free-ride on the efforts of another if they can get away with it. Jackson and Harkins showed that the social loafing effect disappears if the partner in a dyad indicates that she intends to exert high effort on the task. Otherwise, the worker's presumption seems to be that most people will not exert maximum effort if their performance products are unidentifiable. Consequently, the worker gives less than maximal effort so he or she is not taken for a sucker. Kerr demonstrated both the sucker effect and a free-rider effect in his study. The **sucker effect** refers to the fact that workers will reduce their efforts when they perceive that capable peers are not exerting full effort but are riding along on the workers' effort. The **free-rider effect** refers to the fact that workers will reduce their efforts when they see that their group score will not suffer because someone else is performing well. In workplace situations, these two mechanisms probably work in concert to yield submaximal performances. First, one person sees the opportunity to free-ride and does so. Soon the other workers realize they are being played for suckers and reduce their efforts also. Ultimately, the work yield may be sabotaged on a long-term basis.

How can social loafing be averted? There are several recommendations. One is to make each worker's performance identifiable and to otherwise maintain surveillance over each worker's efforts (Williams et al., 1981). Another is to communicate to workers that the top people in the workforce continually exert maximum effort so that hard work becomes the standard (Jackson & Harkins, 1985). Another recommendation is to make individuals' efforts indispensible by having them work on different, divisible aspects of the task and by eliminating redundancy with other workers' tasks (Harkins & Petty, 1982). Another is to promote friendships within the work group because cohesive groups do not loaf as much (Williams, 1981). Last but not least, attempt to assure that the task and its outcomes have personal relevance for the individual (Brickner, Harkins, & Ostrom, 1986). Some of the recommendations have apparently been taken to heart in some modern workplaces.

The Influence of Audiences

So far, the emphasis in this chapter has been on the influence of coactors in cooperative situations. Now, we will focus our attention on another prominent aspect of group action situations—the audience. Audiences or spectators present the possibility that they will evaluate the performance of the actor (Cottrell, 1972), which makes the actor consider him- or herself in competition with other performers. Martens and Landers (1972) showed that motor performance on a "roll-up" game, in which players try to roll a ball along two metal rods and drop it in circles of different score values, was poorer when direct evaluation was being conducted by the experimenter and the decrement was more pronounced as the number of coactors (implied competitors) increased. Audiences heighten the sense of comparison and competition even though rivals may not be present when the individual is performing. For example, lone runners increased their speed as they passed a woman on a park bench (Worringham & Messick, 1983).

Audiences may or may not be supportive. The assumption in most sports events (overt competitive situations) is that the audience is supportive of the home team and antagonistic to the visiting team. Therefore, the home team should win more often than the visiting team, especially in basketball (Hirt & Kimble, 1981). (See figure 9.4.) Hirt and Kimble proposed that the reason basketball showed the strongest home field advantage and baseball the least home field advantage among basketball, football, and baseball was because basketball fans could and

Figure 9.4
*All sports teams,
especially basketball
teams, enjoyed a home
team advantage.*
(From Hirt & Kimble, 1981,
Midwestern Psychological Assn.,
Detroit.)

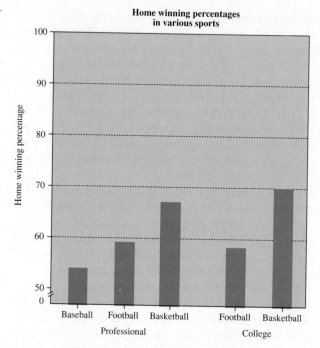

would make their presence felt more because (1) they yell more because there is more scoring, (2) they are closer to the players who are easily identified, and (3) their noise is louder to the actors in an enclosed arena (some arenas even display loudness meters at courtside). Of course, it is impossible to discount the possibilities that basketball's greater home advantage occurs because it is easier to intimidate officials (Greer, 1983) and officials' calls have more impact on the outcome in basketball, visiting teams may be more travel-weary in basketball, and familiarity with the playing area may be more critical. All of these factors and others may have contributed to the results. However, one result indicated that the audience had a substantial direct effect. The home team winning percentage was greater for teams that had the largest home crowds (relative to stadium capacity) in several sports. Some nay-sayers may say that the capacity crowds are the result of the team having been a winner in the past, rather than the crowds causing the current winning. That, of course, may be quite true. Such is the confusion that can occur when dealing with correlational, archival data collected in the real world. The only solution is to get more game tickets and collect more detailed data about the sequence of events in particular games.

*A Home Team
Disadvantage?*

There is probably not a sports fan or a gambler alive who believes that the home team does not have an advantage. Nevertheless, there appear to be some situations where the home team advantage disappears. Baumeister and Steinhilber (1984) took the self-presentational position that teams attempting to claim a new "desired identity" (Schlenker, 1980, 1982)—champions—before a home audience would feel more performance pressure and would be more likely to perform poorly (choke). They examined the records of World Series (1924–1982) and NBA semifinal and championship series (1967–1982). Football was not examined because the team with the better record is the home team throughout the playoff and the Super Bowl is played at a neutral site. In baseball, there is no relationship between a team's season record and whether they are the home team in particular Series games. In basketball, the team with the better record is the host for the seventh and final game. In series that went the full seven games in both sports, the home team won only 38.5 percent of the championships—a decisive home field disadvantage. Baumeister and Steinhilber thought that this failure in the decisive game represented home team choking because home team fielding in baseball and home team free throw shooting in basketball—two performance measures that would not be affected by the other team's performance—were poorest in the seventh games.

It should be pointed out that the home field disadvantage was clearest when the teams were otherwise equally matched; that is, when the series was tied 3–3 after six games. Other strong factors such as ability differences of the teams—Baumeister and Steinhilber excluded the 1960s Boston Celtics era in basketball and all four-game sweep series from their analyses—could be expected to overwhelm this home disadvantage. This disadvantage should not hold for defending champions since they are not trying to claim a new identity and should not experience as much pressure; however, these investigators did not present data on that point.

There is a home court disadvantage in NBA championship series.

Many times an audience has an adverse effect on performance. Laboratory studies have shown that individuals experience more tension and self-consciousness when they are performing before larger, more prestigious audiences (Diener et al., 1980; Jackson & Latané, 1981a; Knowles, 1983). Diener and his associates were able to demonstrate in a live audience situation that as the number of observers increased, the self-consciousness of the performers increased, and their memory for incidental information decreased. Kimble, Hirt, and Arnold (1985) found that when subjects were introduced to others in face-to-face interactions with an audience, their memory for the names of the people they had just met was poorer relative to the no audience condition. So, self-consciousness induced by an audience has a negative effect on memory.

Baumeister (1984) showed in six experiments that subjects' performances on motor tasks declined when they were put under pressure. One way that pressure was induced was through the presence of an evaluative audience. It appears that anything that makes the performer focus on the process of performance in an evaluative way will be detrimental to performance (Gallwey, 1974; Martens & Landers, 1972). In fact, Gallwey (1974), in his book on "inner" tennis, indicates that problems arise when players' consciousness is focused in a critical way on specific features of their performance and alters their natural responses. An audience could elicit such a self-evaluative focus. Arcade game performance by skilled players was much worse when a single person (audience) watched after asking players to do the best they could (Baumeister, 1984). This detrimental

Negative Audience Effects: All Those People . . .

Will an audience make this game player perform more poorly?

effect of an audience on performance was especially pronounced among teenaged players, who were perceived to be most self-conscious about their performance (Tice, Buder, & Baumeister, 1985).

Another important aspect of audiences is that they can communicate expectations about an individual's performance to that individual (Baumeister, Hamilton, & Tice, 1985). High expectations by an audience can be a source of added pressure instead of support. In one study, it was found that if the audience knew that a performer had previously succeeded at a task, the performer did worse than if the audience did not know (Seta & Hassan, 1980). This idea seems to contradict evidence of improved performance occurring when teachers communicate high expectations to students (Rosenthal & Jacobson, 1968). However, Darley and Fazio (1980) argue that self-fulfilling prophecy effects only occur when the performer or target person accepts the high expectations as valid or well-founded. Perhaps it was the teams who were not confident that the home crowds' high expectations were warranted that performed poorly in championship games in the Baumeister and Steinhilber (1984) study. Baumeister et al. (1985) found in two studies that subjects who expected to succeed when the audience did not expect them to succeed and subjects who were convinced by the audience that they would succeed solved the most anagrams (making words from scrambled letters). It is important to note that these expectations were experimentally manipulated. Therefore, it was not just those who believed that they would succeed because of their past history who succeeded.

Cooperation and Competition

We have discussed how certain effects such as social loafing are likely to occur in cooperative coaction situations where one can take advantage of another's efforts. We have also suggested that an evaluative audience can make a person perceive present and known, but absent, performers as competitors or rivals. However, we have not yet fully identified cooperative and competitive situations.

Cooperative interdependence exists when group members advance toward a goal together (Deutsch, 1949). When one person acts to advance toward a particular outcome, others in the group are also closer to attaining that outcome. *Competitive interdependence* exists when one person or group's advancement means that the other person or group is farther from attaining the goal (Deutsch, 1949). If someone wins, someone else must lose.

There are obviously many competitive situations in American society. There is competition for jobs, grades, mates, money, and victories on athletic fields. It is a prominent element of our national economy and culture.

Yet, cooperation is not alien either. Families, teams, and other kinds of groups and organizations work together for their mutual benefit. These social units often cooperate among themselves while simultaneously competing with other groups for resources. Business work groups, corporations, sports teams, communities, and ethnic groups exemplify such within-group cooperation and between-group competition. Along with individual competition, such group endeavors are probably the most common in our society.

Children's sports are often made too competitive by coaches and parents. Why?
SHOE, by MacNelly. © 1987 by Tribune Media Services, Inc. Reprinted by permission.

The performance outcomes of cooperative and competitive experiences depend on the nature of the task. In addition to the simple versus complex nature of tasks emphasized by social facilitation researchers (Zajonc, 1965, 1980), the maximizing or optimizing nature of the task is also important. In a *maximizing task,* the speed and intensity of response are most important. In an *optimizing task,* accuracy and precision of response are most important. A long time ago, Triplett (1897) showed that a coacting situation with implied competition improved the speed of reeling in a fishing line by children. Such speed tasks are clearly maximizing tasks where greater or faster output is emphasized. More recently, Wankel (1972) found that rivalry or competition improved performance on reaction time tasks, another example of a maximizing task. Running events in track are clearly maximizing tasks; and track records suggest that record-setting performances occur most often at the biggest, most competitive events (e.g., the Olympics), not on the practice field. On the other hand, optimizing tasks, such as the "roll-up" game (Baumeister, 1984; Martens & Landers, 1972) and solving anagrams (Goldman, Stockbauer, & McAuliffe, 1977), are usually performed more poorly under competitive pressure. Free-throw shooting in basketball is an example of an optimizing task, where precision rather than sheer output is important.

How much the task requires individuals to interact affects the impact of cooperation and competition. If each individual is acting alone and their outputs are simply being summed, then competitive interdependence brings out the best performances (Goldman et al., 1977). However, cooperation works best if the individuals' efforts have to mesh with each other (Goldman et al., 1977; Miller & Hamblin, 1963). Sports events have many situations involving much coordination among team members. The quarterback's beautiful pass will be to no avail if the receiver doesn't turn at the right moment; the blocker's powerful block will be fruitless if he and his ballcarrier are out of synch. This need for coordination suggests that it would be wise for coaches in such sports to emphasize the cooperative aspects of the game to those players.

What is it about very competitive situations that elicits superlative performances? In group efforts involving optimizing tasks in sports, academics, or business, it seems likely that the preparatory activities account most for the splendid performances. Knowing that the competition is going to be stiff can improve preparation and ultimately performance. On the other hand, if the individual or team does not believe the opponent is strong or does not realize it far enough ahead of time, then it is too late for preparation and defeat is likely. Mood and/ or motivation during preparation is crucial whether the competition is on "As Schools Match Wits" or the league softball championship. A big jolt of adrenalin at the beginning of the contest itself is probably more detrimental than beneficial in events involving optimizing tasks requiring precision. In effortful, maximizing events, an adrenalin surge may help early performance, but it will also tire the performer faster. Knowing that one is prepared will moderate the adrenalin surge.

Cooperation, on the other hand, with other group members has many beneficial features beyond victories for the group. In most team efforts, individuals develop communication skills, interpersonal relationships, feelings of camaraderie, and delight in the successes of others that cannot be achieved in individual efforts. The work of Muzafer Sherif and his associates (Sherif, Harvey, White, Hood, & Sherif, 1961) in summer camp settings has demonstrated that intragroup and intergroup cooperation, unlike intergroup competition, have many positive effects. Many other studies emphasizing intragroup cooperation in school classrooms have shown that it has positive interracial effects (Blaney, Stephan, Rosenfield, Aronson, & Sikes, 1977; DeVries, Edwards, & Slavin, 1978; Weigel, Wiser, & Cook, 1975). These studies will be discussed more fully in chapter 14. Negative aspects of intragroup cooperation are that (1) it can be overshadowed by the simultaneous intergroup competition and (2) the cooperative situation is, under some conditions, subject to detrimental processes such as social loafing.

The intergroup competition inherent in group efforts has certain strong detrimental features. Sherif et al. (1961) noted that it produced considerable intergroup animosity. Weigel et al. (1975) argued that intergroup competition limited the benefits of intragroup cooperation in their classroom study. The problem with competition is that one group loses in every contest, and nearly all groups lose some of the time. There are very few ultimate champions relative to the number of competitors. Greater emphasis should probably be placed on the joy of the activities per se rather than on being the best.

Discussion and Decision Making in Groups

Practically all of our discussions occur in groups (especially when you include dyads among groups), and most of our important decisions are made in groups. The activities that occur in committees, meetings, hearings, and other kinds of group deliberations are different from the behaviors we have discussed so far. In general, these group behaviors involve the exchange of ideas. They are less physical and more mental than the mob scenes and tugs-of-war discussed previously.

Some description of such situations seems appropriate. Usually, such groups meet regularly at a particular time and place, and they have a specific agenda. In these ways, they are behavior settings, as Barker (1968) defines them. They usually have an appointed leader who draws his or her authority from outside the group (Hollander, 1978). Otherwise, a leader emerges from the group and draws his or her authority from the support of the group members (Hollander, 1978). Examples of groups with appointed leaders are school boards, the Supreme Court, university courses, and the President's cabinet. These leaders may have emerged from larger groups (for example, the Chief Justice from a group of federal judges and the President from a field of politicians), but their talents were recognized and they were selected by groups other than the ones over which they preside. Even in such appointive leader groups, other individuals may emerge as leaders and exert influence. Sometimes they are officially recognized, and sometimes they are not. Club presidents, jury forepersons, and team captains are usually emergent leaders.

Often decisions, plans, and laws are made by groups because individuals want to have their input directly or through their representatives. When these groups make the decisions, the decisions are typically more widely accepted by constituents than if an individual made the decisions alone. A common assumption appears to be that group decisions are usually freer from bias than individual decisions. However, group deliberations are time-consuming and action may be delayed. For instance, the hierarchically-organized executive branch of the U.S. government can act more quickly than the legislative branch.

When unacquainted individuals are placed in groups, they typically make assertions more than they ask questions. They also tend to be positive and supportive of other group members more than they are disagreeable (Bales, 1970). Some members participate more than others. In newly-formed groups, two types of leaders usually emerge: a task-oriented person and an interpersonally-oriented one (Bales, 1950). Usually, the **task specialist** and the **socioemotional specialist** are two different people. Status characteristics, which are visible properties that individuals have upon entry to the group, such as sex, race, and age can affect participation roles taken in such groups (Berger et al., 1980). For instance, men may take a more central role when there is a strong task orientation (Strodtbeck & Mann, 1956), and women may take the central role when the group or interpersonal orientation is prominent (Dabbs & Ruback, 1984). By central role, I mean they talk more. Several investigators have shown that people who talk more are typically chosen as leaders, presumably because they have shown a willingness to share their knowledge with the group (Sorrentino & Boutillier, 1975; Stein & Heller, 1979). Those who talk first in groups are also likely to be chosen as leaders (Bass, McGehee, Hawkins, Young, & Gebel, 1953). There also appears to be a head-of-the-table effect in choosing leaders. People seated there are more likely to be chosen as forepersons of juries (Strodtbeck & Hook, 1961), and dominant people are more likely to choose such visible, central seats (Sundstrom & Altman, 1974). It seems likely that individuals in ongoing groups become more firmly entrenched in particular roles over time.

Some research has examined the importance of how groups interact. Ruback, Dabbs, and Hopper (1984) recorded talking and pausing patterns of five-person groups engaged in a brainstorming session. Talking was recorded from individual microphones using a computer program so they knew who talked when, when people talked at the same time, and whether a pause was within one person's speech or was a switching pause between speakers. They also obtained data on ideas generated and ratings of how much of a leader each person was and how

How Do Groups Interact?

Group meetings are sometimes frustrating.

DUFFY, by Howard. © 1986 by Universal Press Syndicate. Reprinted by permission. All Rights Reserved.

well liked each person was. Correlations indicated that the people who talked more were seen as more leaderlike, were liked better, and were rated as generating more good ideas. Most new ideas were introduced right after switching pauses between speakers as if the ideas had been incubated during the previous speaker's talking and the pause thereafter. Most ideas were generated early in the session. Surprisingly, there was no relationship between how evenly divided among the group members talking was (equally divided versus one person dominating the floor) and the groups' satisfaction with the session. One might expect that individuals would evaluate groups wherein participation time was more egalitarian more positively, but that was not the case.

Groups versus Individuals

As noted earlier, most people prefer that important decisions be made by groups rather than individuals because group decisions are viewed as more likely to be fair and free of bias. For example, jury trials were instituted many years ago as a check on the decisions of individuals—judges—who are likely to be more expert than jurors (Friedenthal, Kane, & Miller, 1985). For that reason, many decisions will continue to be made by groups even though research indicates that individuals perform better on some kinds of tasks. The call for democracy and fair representation will prevail, as it should. However, if we are going to insist that decisions be made by groups, we should examine the evidence to see if there are ways that group decisions can be improved. In some cases where bias is unlikely to be a problem, we may decide to let able individuals decide rather than groups.

There have been many studies comparing individual and group performances on different kinds of tasks (cf. Hill, 1982). Brainstorming is an approach
to generating ideas whereby individuals are encouraged to express any idea that
comes to mind. Others in the group are encouraged to spin off of these ideas with
their own thoughts, but they are not to react in critical or evaluative ways (Osborn,
1957). Presumably, a major benefit of brainstorming in groups is the possibility
that ideas expressed by one person will trigger thoughts by another that he or
she would not have generated alone. However, most of the research evidence indicates that brainstorming groups generate fewer ideas than the same number
of individuals generating ideas alone (Madsen & Finger, 1978; Taylor, Berry, &
Block, 1958). Two factors seem to account for these unexpected findings. First,
in brainstorming groups only one person at a time can effectively express ideas,
but individuals working alone can all be generating ideas at the same time (Hill,
1982). Second, individuals in groups can be distracted by what other members
are saying (Lamm & Trommsdorff, 1973). Perhaps you have thought of something as another person talked, but were inhibited from saying it because of the
group situation. By the time that person quit talking, you may have lost your
thought because you were also trying to follow what the speaker was saying. Such
distractions could partially account for the performance deficit by brainstorming
groups.

However, there are some situations in which brainstorming is beneficial.
Dunnette, Campbell, and Jaastad (1963) found that individuals who had first
participated in a brainstorming group generated more ideas on another topic
working alone than did individuals who had no previous brainstorming experience. A modified procedure called the nominal group technique consisting of individual brainstorming followed by group discussion and elaboration produced
(1) more ideas than a brainstorming group and (2) more satisfaction with the
process than the brainstorming group or a delphi procedure. In the delphi procedure, individuals did the same thing as the nominal group except the face-to-
face interaction (Van de Ven & Delbecq, 1974). It appears that group interaction
is most effective when it is combined with individual work and thought. (See
figure 9.5.)

One model for group problem solving suggests that group performance
should surpass individual performance because group members have abilities that
are not shared by other members, given that these abilities can be combined
(Steiner, 1966). If individuals of different relevant backgrounds, perspectives,
and abilities could be brought into group situations that promoted full expressions
of each person's ideas, then the best group problem-solving performance should
be achieved. Laughlin and Johnson (1966) did find that in heterogeneous-ability
groups, individuals working with someone of higher ability performed better than
if they worked alone or with someone of lower ability. However, a better test of
Steiner's model would be to combine people who have different kinds of ideas
and abilities rather than combining people of different levels of ability. The Steiner
model does point to the kinds of groups that should outperform any of its individual members.

Figure 9.5
*The nominal group
technique in which
individual
brainstorming was
followed by group
discussion produced
more ideas than the
noninteracting delphi
technique or the
interacting groups.*
(From Van de Ven & Delbecq,
1974, Journal of the Academy of
Management, 17, 616.)

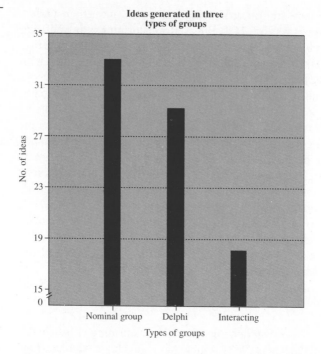

Ideas generated in three
types of groups

Types of groups

Problems in Group Decision Making

Groupthink

*Will groupthink
undermine the
decisions of this group?*

Irving Janis (1972) introduced the term, **groupthink,** to describe situations in which group members' desire to maintain solidarity and harmony in the group overrides members' ability to consider fully and independently all aspects of a problem. Cohesive groups with a respected leader are most likely to show *this conforming tendency to rush to a premature, ill-considered consensus.* Obviously, the tendency to jump on the leader's bandwagon is greatest when the leader promotes his or her preferred solution rather than encouraging careful analysis of possible alternatives.

Janis examined some important decisions made by American governmental groups for the presence or absence of groupthink characteristics. He indicated that the decisions to cross the 38th parallel in pursuit of the North Koreans in 1950, to support Cuban refugees' invasion of Cuba at the Bay of Pigs in 1961, and to escalate the Vietnam War in the mid-1960s were poor group decisions that showed characteristics of groupthink. On the other hand, the decisions to develop the Marshall Plan in 1947 and to handle the Cuban Missile Crisis in 1962 were presented as examples of well-considered decisions free of groupthink. Janis presented historical evidence from memoirs and records of the group meetings to illustrate the process of groupthink. It is interesting to note that many of the same capable people were involved in both groupthink and nongroupthink decisions. It is also interesting to consider some of the Watergate era decisions in the Nixon White House, decisions about the Iranian Hostage Crisis, and the decision to leave the Marines in Beirut until 240 of them perished as they slept from the groupthink perspective. However, it is so complicated because many

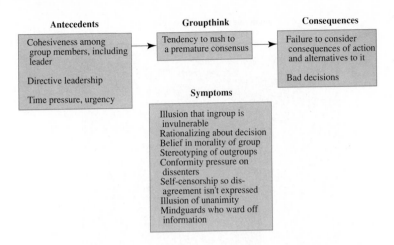

Figure 9.6
A model of groupthink processes.
(From Janis, 1972.)

factors other than groupthink affected these important decisions. Even different individuals were involved at different points in the same decision-making process. Such are the problems with doing retrospective analyses of real events.

Tetlock (1979) conducted content analyses of public statements of presidents and other individuals involved in the five important decisions previously mentioned to see if they exhibited characteristics of groupthink decisions. He obtained measures of (1) the integrative complexity of the statements; (2) the positivity of evaluations of their own group, nation, and allies; and (3) the positivity of evaluations of their opponents. (See figure 9.6.) Janis' (1972) view suggests that groupthink decisions should produce more simplistic statements, more positive evaluations of the U.S. and allies, and more negative evaluations of opposing nations, etc. Tetlock found that statements emanating from the three groupthink situations classified by Janis were more simplistic and more positive toward the American position than statements from the two nongroupthink situations. However, groupthink statements were no more negative toward the communist opposition than nongroupthink statements. Perhaps Janis has overstated the outgroup biasing effect of groupthink. One must interpret these findings with caution because these public statements are at best outgrowths of the group interaction processes. There is no complete record of these deliberations available to researchers.

Another approach to studying groupthink is to abandon the richness and complexity of the natural situation and construct an experimental situation to test the generality of the phenomenon (Flowers, 1977). Flowers assembled high-cohesive (acquaintances) and low-cohesive (strangers) groups with open or closed leadership to consider an urgent school administrative problem. This group situation was a role-playing or role-taking one for these college students. The closed (directive) leader situation produced some groupthink effects implied by Janis: fewer solutions proposed and fewer facts brought before the group. Group cohesiveness did not affect the results. Surely college acquaintances do not have

Figure 9.7
*Closed, directive
leaders stifled the
production of solution
alternatives, but the
cohesiveness of groups
did not affect the
expression of ideas in
this study on
groupthink.*

(From Flowers, 1977, Journal of
Psychology and Social Psychology,
35, 892.)

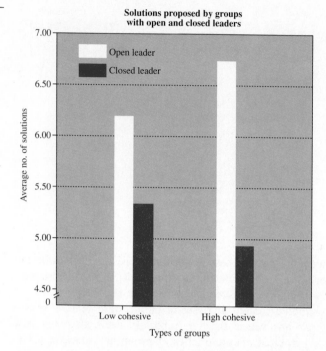

the cohesiveness of the presidential decision-making groups nor the same over-whelming respect for their leader. Also, the appointed leaders of the experimental groups were probably not the most influential persons in the group in their natural interactions. However, Flowers' study does illustrate the importance of the directiveness of the leader in producing hasty decisions. (See figure 9.7.)

Janis's suggestions for preventing groupthink pinpoint the importance of diluting the cohesiveness of the group and reducing the directiveness of the leader. The force of cohesiveness can be diluted by bringing in outside experts, having group members prepare for the meeting independently and record their ideas, breaking the group down into subgroups for separate deliberations, and emphasizing the importance of independence and "devil's advocacy" for opposing alternatives. The directiveness of the leader can be diminished by having the leader defer expression of his or her position until late in the proceedings, describe the problem instead of recommending a solution, encourage input from all members including dissenting positions. The interaction should be structured so the decision will be a bona fide group decision, not a single-minded one. These recommendations should be useful not only at the presidential cabinet level, but for parent-teacher organizations and for fraternities and sororities as well.

Group Polarization

A group process effect that has been examined much more than groupthink is *group polarization*. This extensive research began with the recognition of the tendency for individuals to endorse riskier decisions after engaging in a group discussion than they would have made without discussing the decision (Kogan

& Wallach, 1964; Stoner, 1961). The effect was called the *risky shift phenomenon,* and in ensuing years some reviewers argued that it occurred because risk-taking was valued more in our society than acting cautiously (Brown, 1965; Dion, Baron, & Miller, 1970). Then an embarrassing thing happened; investigators uncovered a tendency to shift toward caution after discussion of some dilemmas (Moscovici & Zavalloni, 1969; Stoner, 1968). At that point, the *risky shift effect* became known as **group polarization** because it was recognized that group discussion changed individuals' attitudes to more extreme positions in the same direction as they were originally inclined. The risky decisions became riskier and the cautious ones became more cautious.

Explanations of the risky shift had to be modified to accomodate choice shifts in both directions. From "risk is a value," some positions were changed to "stronger or more polarized positions are valued" (Levinger & Schneider, 1969; Myers, 1982). This class of explanations of the group polarization effect focus on the social and self-presentation aspects of the group discussion situation (e.g., Jellison & Arkin, 1977). At the risk of oversimplifying the picture and inadequately portraying important differences between positions, I will describe the choice shift process from these *social comparison* or *normative influence* perspectives (Brown, 1986; Kaplan, 1987; Lamm & Myers, 1978; Mackie, 1986; Sanders & Baron, 1977).

The discussion participant, holding a moderate position at the outset, soon discovers that everyone (or at least the vocal participants) in his or her group favors a choice in the same direction. At that point, the most extreme position in that direction seems most desirable perhaps because it is decisive, not wishy-washy. Then, when the participant is given an opportunity to endorse a position, he or she conforms to the desirable extreme.

There are many variations on this general theme. One interesting variation incorporating the role of group membership in the polarization effect was Diane Mackie's (1986) dissertation research at Princeton University. This work also illustrates that many researchers have eliminated live group discussions from their procedure for control purposes. She contends that the first step in the polarization process is identifying oneself as a member of a group. That ingroup's defining characteristic (in this case, their position on an issue) is stereotyped by the subject as more extreme than it really is. The ingroup's position is also considered more extreme than an outgroup's position or the position of a collection of separate individuals. The last step in the process is for the participant (group member) to conform to the stereotyped, extreme position of the group rather than to their actual position. In one experiment, Mackie's research strategy involved choosing individuals who mildly agreed with an issue statement as her subjects. Then, each one heard taped statements that were also mildly supportive on the same issue. These statements were presented as (1) discussion comments of a group the subject would soon join (the ingroup), (2) discussion comments on an unrelated group (the outgroup), or (3) isolated comments of separate individuals that had been pieced together by the experimenter. Results indicated that subjects did perceive

Figure 9.8
*When arguments were
presented as being
made by members of a
group the subject
expected to join, the
subject's attitudes were
most polarized.*
(*From Mackie, 1986,* Journal of
Social Psychology, 50, 722.)

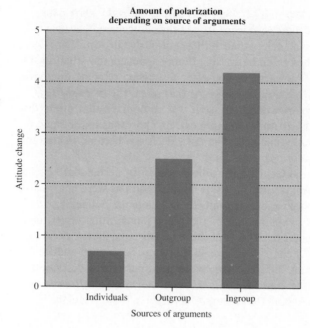

the ingroup's position as more extreme than it actually was and that those in-group subjects subsequently endorsed a position even more extreme than the group's perceived extreme position. So, Mackie's social identity variation of the social comparison explanation was supported. (See figure 9.8.)

The other major class of explanations for the group polarization effect is called the *persuasive arguments* (Burnstein & Vinokur, 1977) or *informational influence* (Kaplan, 1987) position. Within this perspective, the information presented in the discussion is more important than the social aspects of the situation. During the discussion, the participant is exposed to more arguments in the same direction than he or she would have generated alone. The fact that most of these new arguments are in the same direction polarizes the participant's position, independent of social motivation considerations. There is a substantial amount of evidence that when arguments are presented without the personal inclinations of the discussants to which the participants might conform, the participants' positions are swayed toward the advocated extreme (Burnstein & Vinokur, 1977; Clark, Crockett, & Archer, 1971; Myers, Bach, & Schreiber, 1974). Two recent studies (Stasser & Titus, 1985, 1987), however, indicate that in real group discussions, participants may not actually hear new persuasive arguments because there is a tendency to reiterate already shared information rather than introduce new, previously unshared information.

Kaplan (1987), arguing from an information integration perspective (Anderson, 1981), suggests that hearing persuasive arguments has a polarizing effect because individuals usually enter a decision-making situation with an unbiased or neutral initial impression and the discussion provides new information to be incorporated into the impression. Since the new information is nearly always on one side of neutral (all participants lean in the same direction beforehand), the polarization effect occurs.

It is likely that both informational (persuasive arguments) and normative (social comparison) features of discussion contribute to the group polarization effect in some situations. Kaplan (1987) has specified what conditions are likely to make normative influence and informational influence occur in group decisions. Normative influence is most prominent when socioemotionally-oriented people bent toward acceptance by the group consider a value-laden issue and give responses publicly. Informational influence is most prominent when task-oriented people bent on being correct consider a factual issue and give responses privately.

In ordinary life, we are usually uncomfortable with being indecisive and with appearing indecisive. A neutral or moderate position is an indecisive one in most people's eyes. Therefore, it seems reasonable that individuals would be motivated for both personal and social reasons to move to a more decisive position. So, it is understandable that group members would move to more extreme positions in one direction after hearing discussion indicating that nearly everyone favored a position in the same direction.

Some groups may have all their members line up on the same side of an issue. That appears to be what happened in the historical groupthink decisions (Janis, 1975). The conformity pressure toward an extreme or consensus in groupthink situations and group polarization are similar ones, but Janis's less scientifically rigorous approach places more emphasis on the influence of the leader. Juries may also exhibit such same-mindedness. In fact, Davis (1980) indicates that if eight or more of the 12 jurors in a jury trial initially favor a verdict, then that jury will usually arrive at that unanimous not guilty or guilty verdict. If there is less than two-thirds initial agreement, the jury will not arrive at a consensus decision. So, there appear to be some real-life parallels to group polarization in same-minded groups, but some extrapolation—some would say poetic license—is needed to draw the similarities.

Group polarization through discussion seems to contribute to both positive outcomes (verdicts rather than indecision) and negative outcomes (poor administrative decisions). Is polarization or depolarization desirable? Some degree of depolarization seems desirable since there are usually ample incentives to eventually decide on a course of action, which produce polarization. It would take longer to reach decisions in such situations, but they would be more amply considered ones.

How is depolarization achieved? Depolarization can be achieved by assembling heterogeneous groups—groups whose members are initially on opposing sides of the same issue (Burnstein, 1982). The effect of discussion is such groups is to moderate or depolarize the decisions of individual members. This depolarization effect is opposite to what happens when you make two separate groups of like-minded individuals discuss the same issue (Myers & Bishop, 1971). In that event, the two groups gravitate toward the extreme positions in the direction

Juries, such as this one, are susceptible to group polarization.

of their original leanings. Janis's (1972) suggestions that groupthink can be reduced by bringing in outside opinions and making sure that opposing positions are heard indicate that depolarization is desirable for groups being pressured to reach a quick decision.

Leadership

We have pointed out many of the pitfalls of coordinating the activities of groups. We have also mentioned the many ways in which groups can go awry so that their performances or decisions are inferior to the work of individuals. Assuring the productivity of the group, maintaining the satisfaction of group members, and avoiding the pitfalls that lead to poor group actions and decisions are responsibilities of a group leader.

What Is a Leader?

A leader is someone who attempts to influence how other members of the group think and behave. The motivation behind the leader's influence attempts is usually to improve the group's performance, conduct, and/or decisions. Accompanying this motivation are often the selfish motives of achieving one's own goals through the group's actions and making oneself look good to people outside the group.

Leaderless groups can perform very effectively under certain conditions. If group members are equally and highly able, experienced, trained, and independent and if the task is routine, unambiguous, repetitive; then, leaders appear to be unnecessary (Kerr & Jermier, 1978). These conditions serve as substitutes for leadership.

In leaderless groups, two different types of leaders tend to emerge: task-oriented leaders and socioemotional leaders (Bales, 1955). In some groups, they are the same person. A *task-oriented leader* is the person who gives the most information and suggestions, asks for the most information and suggestions, and makes the most task-relevant comments. A *socioemotional leader* is the person who acts the most friendly, laughs and jokes the most, acknowledges or responds to others the most, and makes the most task-irrelevant comments (Sorrentino & Field, 1986). One might assume that a stronger task-oriented leader would contribute to better performance, but there is no evidence that this is true in all conditions (Fiedler, 1971; Sorrentino & Field, 1986).

A leader has many potential sources of power to influence the group. French and Raven (1959) have categorized these bases of power: (1) legitimate power, (2) reward power, (3) coercive power, (4) referent power, (5) expert power, and (6) information power. People who have been elected or appointed to a formal position in the group have *legitimate power* in that they have been authorized by superiors in the larger organization or by an electorate. The higher their position in the organizational hierarchy or the larger their constituency, the more legitimate power they have. Other members of the group who have not been duly elected or appointed to a formal position do not have legitimate power. Their efforts to influence the group are often resented by other group members (Read, 1974). Perhaps one of the reasons Gerald Ford was one of the few incumbent presidents not to be elected was the fact that he had not been elected to the presidency and hence had little legitimate power. The lack of legitimate power may partly explain why Ferdinand Marcos of the Philippines abdicated his presidency shortly after seizing it unjustly. Leaders have *reward* and *coercive power* to the extent that they have hire-fire authority and influence over increases and cuts in pay.

Referent power is a different kind of power. It is the ability to influence others because they like and admire you. Referent power may be earned through benevolent treatment of group members or through establishing a reputation. Hollander (1964, 1985) has presented evidence that an individual must demonstrate that he or she is competent ("a good player") and loyal to group norms ("a team player") in order to emerge as a leader. Many a politician has established himself as presidential timber within his party by displaying loyalty and competence. Such emergent leaders are more likely to have referent power than appointed leaders. True emergent leaders like Gandhi and King have had substantial referent power.

Kelman's (1958) treatment of compliance, identification, and internalization (see chapter 8) indicates that referent power, which is based on identification, is more long-lasting than reward or coercive power. Which brings us to the age-old management question: Should I be their buddy or their boss? Is the demanding tyrant with reward and coercive power or the friend with referent power the most effective leader? The best answer may be that the person who can use all three kinds of power as the situation demands is the best leader. Whether more referent power or more reward/coercive power is better depends on the amount and frequency of interactions between leader and group members. Referent power should be used more in high-interaction groups where personal consideration can have more influence. A potential drawback of reward/coercive power is that allocation of resources within the group can raise questions of unfairness or inequity (Walster, Walster, & Berscheid, 1978). We will address the buddy vs. boss question again when we consider Fiedler's (1967) contingency model of leadership.

Expert power and information power are related, and they are important sources of influence for leaders to possess. *Expert power* is based on group members' perception that a person (the leader in this case) has expertise about the tasks which the group usually face. Since it is a perception or attribution about the leader, this reputation for expertise may extend beyond his or her actual expertise. The fact that talkative group members are more often chosen as leaders (cf. Stein & Heller, 1979) probably reflects that talkative people are seen as possessing expertise on the topic being discussed. *Information power* accrues from actually having more knowledge on a topic. Leaders and/or their lieutenants need to have superior knowledge about the tasks in order to maintain the respect of the group. Those who have such knowledge are most often chosen as leaders. The "idea men or women" in Ruback's et al. (1984) brainstorming groups were chosen as leaders more often. Stogdill (1974) characterized leaders as slightly more intelligent than the group average, which means that these leaders at least have the potential to have more knowledge about the tasks than do other group members.

The Research on Leadership

Great Leaders or Favorable Conditions?

Harry Truman once said, "Men make history; history doesn't make the man." That statement suggests that it is the convictions and qualities of people in leadership roles that shape events, not the technology or the sentiment of the times. Certainly, people in recognized leadership positions have power, but there are many leaders, and sometimes they and their groups conflict with each other. To the extent that groups have opposing goals, the power of their leaders are diminished. Within American government, if a president does not have an effective majority in Congress, his power to influence events is greatly reduced. You might infer that a particular president was not a great leader when the truth was that relatively unalterable conditions were unfavorable (e.g., Eisenhower being faced with a Democratic Congress throughout his administration). Other presidents probably will be judged as mediocre because of other powerful, uncontrollable forces during their administrations. Carter's administration being beset with economic woes partly because of the energy situation and OPEC is a good example.

The truth is that great leaders and favorable circumstances are both needed to yield great dynasties. Germany had to be in chaos for a Hitler to rise to power. Yet, no other person took advantage of the political and economic climate of Germany the way Hitler did. America was certainly ripe for change when Franklin Roosevelt came into office. However, if Herbert Hoover had stayed in office or someone else like John Nance Garner had won the nomination, it is doubtful they had the qualities to construct the powerful presidency Roosevelt did. When Rosa Parks refused to go to the back of the bus in Montgomery, the time was right for a young black clergyman to lead a movement. The force of Martin Luther King's personality allowed him to become the leader of the Civil Rights movement, while Ralph Abernathy did not have the necessary charismatic qualities and Andrew Young and Jesse Jackson were too young. It seems that the qualities of the man or woman and the social situation must fit well for history-making leaderships to occur.

The most extensively researched model of leadership holds that qualities of the individual and elements of the situation must mesh for optimal leadership effectiveness (Fiedler, 1954, 1964, 1967, 1978, 1981). Fiedler's approach is called the **contingency model of leadership** because certain personal and situational conditions must be met for effective leadership to exist. It should be emphasized that this work has focused on leadership of real groups in face-to-face contact rather than presidential leadership of nations or other noninteracting groups. For instance, high school basketball teams and military aircraft and tank crews were the kinds of groups Fiedler first studied.

In all of several hundred studies conducted by Fiedler and associated researchers, a personal characteristic of the leader and three elements of the group situation have been assessed and related to group performance. The leader characteristic is whether he or she is *person-oriented* or *task-oriented*. If a leader rates a self-generated **least preferred co-worker** favorably (high LPC), the leader is regarded as interpersonally or socially oriented. If a leader rates his or her imagined undesirable co-worker (LPC) unfavorably (low LPC), the leader is seen as task or productivity-minded. To use terminology mentioned earlier, a high LPC leader is a buddy-type or socioemotional leader, and a low LPC leader is a boss-type or task-oriented leader (Bales, 1955).

The three situational elements usually assessed are (1) affective leader-group relations, (2) task structure, and (3) position power of leader (Fiedler, 1964). *Leader-group relations* are assessed as good or poor by how popular the leader is with his or her co-workers or by the leader's rating of the group climate. The first, sociometric measure from co-workers' ratings seems methodologically superior because the group climate and LPC measures may be artificially correlated since both ratings are done by the same person. *Task structure* or ambiguity can be accurately judged by outside observers. A leader's *position power,* whether a leader has an official higher rank and has various kinds of power over group members, can also be accurately assessed by independent judges. These situational components are classified into good or poor relations, structured or unstructured tasks, and strong or weak position power for each group. (See figure 9.9.)

When the leader's LPC and the three situational elements are related to group performance, a pattern emerges. The considerate, group-oriented leader is most effective when situational factors are moderately favorable. The task-oriented leader is most effective when situational factors are either quite favorable or quite unfavorable. If leader-group relations are good, the task is structured, and position power is strong; a task-oriented leader will help produce the best group outcome. However, that type of leader also fares best when relations are poor, the task is unstructured, and position power is weak. These results boggle the mind. Another complication: Even though Fiedler (1964) states that the leader-group relationship is the most important situational component, in some cases leader-group relations do not make a difference. Good *and* bad relations generally favor task-oriented leaders as do globally favorable and unfavorable situations, and moderately poor relations favor the group-oriented leader as do

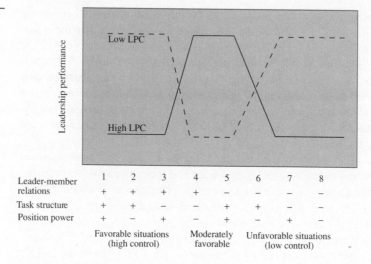

Figure 9.9
This model suggests that task-oriented leaders (low LPC) do better when situational factors are favorable or unfavorable. Group-oriented leaders (high LPC) do better when conditions are moderately favorable.

	1	2	3	4	5	6	7	8
Leader-member relations	+	+	+	+	−	−	−	−
Task structure	+	+	−	−	+	+	−	−
Position power	+	−	+	−	+	−	+	−

Favorable situations (high control)　　Moderately favorable　　Unfavorable situations (low control)

moderately favorable situations. So, the boss-type leader does well when leader-group relations are good *and* when the group is feeling mutinous. The buddy-type leader does better when leader-group relations are lukewarm or indifferent.

Nearly all the contingency model studies involve 100 percent correlational variables. The best supportive evidence for this complicated model comes from an experiment conducted at West Point (Chemers & Skrzypek, 1972). In this study, only the leader's LPC measure was a correlational variable; the situational components were manipulated. Their productivity results fit the Fiedler model very well with the low LPC leaders being most effective in the two most favorable situations and the most unfavorable situation. High LPC leaders shone most in the two moderate favorability situations. They also found that high LPC leaders were rated by their group members as displaying more relationship-oriented behavior and less task-oriented behavior than low LPC leaders. These results support Fiedler's ideas about what the least-preferred-co-worker measure means.

In consulting on leadership training, Fiedler, Chemers, and Mahar (1977) recommend that potential leaders be taught what kind of leaders they are (low or high LPC) so that they can manage the situational factors to be most appropriate for their style. For instance, a low LPC person should attempt to create good relations, structured tasks, and strong position power. A high LPC person should strive for good relations, unstructured tasks, and weak position power. Leaders trained to manage situations to fit their style are more effective than untrained leaders (Fiedler & Mahar, 1979). It appears to be easier to manage the situations than to change the leader's style.

Applications of Group Process Information

There are several possible application areas for social psychological information on groups. The first question to be answered follows: Is the group an action group or a deliberative or decision-making group? Of course, some groups do both—members serve in active performance roles and in deliberative roles. Leaders of such groups need to be attuned to both kinds of group processes. Acting groups are subject to social facilitation effects, deindividuation, social loafing, audience influences, the influences of cooperation and competition, and the motivational and training tactics of their leaders. On the other hand, deliberating groups are subject to the habitual or customary communication patterns of the group, groupthink, group polarization, and the status and directiveness of their leaders. Let us consider some kinds of groups in the world outside the laboratory.

There are many kinds of work groups that perform activities together or produce some product together. These teams or crews are subject to many of the problems of acting groups mentioned previously. One example of such work groups is cockpit aircrews. Group performance among such work groups has been scrutinized recently (Foushee, 1984). This review examined many of the group coordination and communication problems among flight crews with accounts of recent accidents and near-accidents. One of the major problems among flight crews is "captainitis," a tendency for flight captains to run the whole show independently and for other flight crew members and even air traffic controllers to submit to the captain's actions. A tragic example of this problem occurred on the Air Florida flight that went down in the Potomac in January, 1982. Recordings from the cockpit revealed that the copilot was not forceful enough in calling the captain's attention to icing on the wings, and the captain belittled the significance of the weather conditions until it was too late. Foushee (1984) indicated that this communication problem is quite common. The problem may stem from the fact that most skilled pilots got their early training in single-pilot, military aircraft. As a consequence, they have little team training experience, but both captains and subordinates have learned to respect the military chain of command and that respect may thwart necessary communications. The daring attitude and belief in their invincability often seen in top military pilots may also hinder safe group performance.

Work Groups and Performance

In the American legal system, juries are a very important deliberating group. Ironically, an extensive study of real juries led to the conclusion that most of the decisions were already made before the juries were sequestered for deliberation (Kalven & Zeisel, 1966). Because jury deliberations are closed meetings, investigators have not had direct access to how deliberations occur. As a result, jury studies have been limited to comparing initial votes with final verdicts as in the Kalven and Zeisel study or to examining the deliberation process of simulated juries.

Decision-Making Groups: Juries

One such simulated jury study showed that group polarization occurs in juries (Myers & Kaplan, 1976). If the preponderance of the evidence presented to these student juries indicated that the defendant was guilty, subjects gravitated toward the guilty verdict. If most of the evidence pointed to the defendant's innocence, student jurors moved toward an acquittal verdict during group deliberations. Group discussion did polarize these jury decisions, just as the early group polarization research indicated it would.

What is the role of leadership in the jury deliberation process? The foreperson is the formal leader of the jury. How forepersons are selected is different from court to court. In some jurisdictions, the judge appoints the foreperson (Hastie, Penrod, & Pennington, 1983); in others, he or she is elected by the jury; in still others, the first juror selected arbitrarily becomes the foreperson (Francis, 1979). In the first method, the judge can introduce his or her bias; in the second, the jury has its way; and in the third, the lawyers can exert their influence. Bias in selection of the jury's leader in terms of the sex, race, status, or occupation of the individual could occur unless the court had a truly representative jury pool, and the leader was chosen randomly from among the jury members.

Mock jury studies indicate that the foreperson is seldom the real leader of the jury (Hastie et al., 1983; Hawkins, 1960). In the Hastie et al. study, forepersons spoke more than other jurors, but their statements were primarily about legal issues and organization. That participation seems appropriate since the foreperson is typically charged with considering the evidence and seeing that every juror gets to speak to every issue presented. Forepersons actually made fewer verdict-related statements than other jurors. These formal leaders apparently served as arbitrators, a quite appropriate role in group decision making. The real leaders were the jurors who were most persuasive. According to persuasiveness ratings made by the jurors after deliberation, those leaders were members high in education level, income, social status, and occupational status (Hastie et al., 1983). Also, male jurors were rated more persuasive than female jurors.

Are Jury Minorities Persuasive?

Can minority subgroups within juries sway the rest of the jury to change its verdict? The conversion of all of the other jurors as Henry Fonda's character did in the movie, *Twelve Angry Men,* is a rarity. If the minority consists of four or five, then swaying the majority to their position is much more likely (Davis, 1980). For example, Maurice Stans was acquitted of charges in his Watergate trial because of the efforts of one very persuasive juror within a minority of four who originally favored acquittal (Wrightsman, 1978). As suggested by social impact theory and self-attention theory, there is strength in numbers even if your group's numbers are not as great as the other's.

Nemeth and her associates have examined this situation systematically. Nemeth (1986b) stressed that a minority must display consistency and confidence in order to sway a majority. If a person who disagrees with the majority takes essentially the same position consistently over time rather than waffling on the issue, he or she will influence others more (Nemeth, Swedlund, & Kanki, 1974). In another study, if a person who chose the seat at the head of the table later disagreed with the other group members, that person was more influential in getting others to change than someone who was assigned the head seat (Nemeth & Wachtler, 1974). The choice of the head seat was interpreted as important because it indicated that the individual was confident.

Even though the American legal system discourages "hung" juries—juries which don't arrive at a guilty/acquittal verdict—juries sometimes are not polarized enough to reach a verdict. Hung juries are more likely to occur in 12–member juries than in 6–member juries (Roper, 1980), and they are more likely to occur when a unanimous decision is required than when only a two-thirds majority is required (Hastie et al., 1983). These results are perhaps as you would expect them to be because the indecision occurs when it is required that more people agree on the same position in each of the two studies. However, these results do suggest that jurors are making independent decisions as they have been instructed, rather than just following like sheep in the larger, 12–member juries. In fact, Hastie and his associates (1983) found that the quality of deliberations was greater when unanimity was required of the 12–person juries. The use of such research findings to improve the legal system has been hampered by some obsolete principles used by the courts (Monahan & Walker, 1988).

Hung juries are not a major factor in our nation's courtrooms. Judges in nearly all jury trials give extensive instructions on continuing to deliberate until a verdict is reached (Committee on Model Jury Instructions of the 9th Circuit Court, 1985). Also there are many other ways to decide a case than just guilt or acquittal to a particular charge. For instance, a jury may compromise by convicting the defendant of a lesser charge. A few years ago, posttrial newspaper accounts stated that a jury was hung at 11–1 for a long time on an aggravated murder charge. A woman whose son was serving a prison term for a felony conviction was the juror who adamantly opposed the guilty verdict even though the evidence indicated that the defendant had killed two men, one in the course of a robbery and the other, a policeman, as he and another man were in flight. Ultimately, this case was resolved by the jury convicting the man on a lesser murder charge. Ironically, his cohort, who did not pull the trigger, was convicted of aggravated murder in another trial. Hung juries seem especially insignificant when you consider that only 10 percent of all criminal cases ever come to trial.

Of greater interest to defendants and lawyers is the probability that the defendant will be found guilty. In other words, if a person is charged with a felony, are his or her chances better if the defendant has a jury trial or is tried by the judge alone? After all, the right to a trial by jury is in the Bill of Rights. Data collected in the 1950s indicated that juries were more lenient in their verdicts than judges were (Kalven & Zeisel, 1966). However, data collected more recently suggests that lawyers would be wiser to advise their felony clients to be tried before a judge (Roper & Flango, 1983). In 1978 felony cases, judges found the defendant guilty in 58 percent of their cases, and juries convicted 72 percent of the defendants in the cases they heard. Trial by jury is not always the best alternative.

The Challenger accident highlighted the importance of communication in group decision making. The investigating commission headed by William Rogers pinpointed the ambiguities and flaws in the decision-making process (Report of the Presidential Commission on the Space Shuttle Challenger Accident, June 6, 1986). One of the communication problems in such massive projects is that the organization has so many different groups meeting in different locations that communicating vital information is difficult. The same group can have different members at different times, and they may need information from others outside

Group and Organizational Communication: The Challenger Accident

*Group communication
problems, as well as
engineering flaws,
contributed to the
Challenger disaster.*

the group. Knowing what has been communicated to whom under those conditions is hard to recall. With teleconferencing, which NASA uses extensively, the group members are often scattered around the country, and miscommunication can arise.

An example of problems from such an organizational morass occurred on the Challenger launch. A man named Ebeling with the subcontractor, Morton Thiokol, in Utah phoned a company representative in Florida to express concern about the effect of cold temperatures on the rockets' O-rings on the afternoon before the launch. It was a malfunction of an O-ring in a joint of the right solid rocket motor that caused the disaster. Ebeling urged a delay because of the expected cold temperatures the next day. The Florida representative of Morton Thiokol arranged to convene a meeting of representatives of contractors and NASA. The general consensus at the conclusion of that meeting was that a delay was recommended and that the message would be forwarded to the team leader of the ultimate go-no go decision-making group. Unfortunately, the NASA man who was to pass the recommendation on to the top level team leader did not do so. The failure to communicate the group's decision to the next level was disastrous. How many times have groups spent much time and effort to reach a decision and then the decision is not implemented because it is not communicated to others outside the group? Too many!

Beyond problems with communication from group to group within an organization, there are often problems arising from pressures within a single group, as Janis's (1972) groupthink work implies. Such a problem occurred during the final meeting of the Challenger's Mission Management Team. According to the Rogers Commission Report (1986), two Rockwell vice presidents were representing that company in a final meeting at Kennedy Space Center at 9:00 A.M. The Rockwell division president, who was in California at the time, later testified that he told his vice presidents to "make sure NASA understands that Rockwell feels it is not safe to launch" because of icy conditions on the launch pad and the unknown threats that the ice posed (Commission Report, 1986, vol. 1, p. 115).

Instead the Rockwell vice presidents said in the meeting that they could not give 100 percent assurance that it was safe to fly that morning. That statement is a far cry from "it is not safe to launch," and the NASA people did not perceive it as a no-go recommendation. The team leader later polled people in the room and in Houston, and all recommended that the launch proceed, as the Rockwell vice presidents listened. In the face of this pressure for consensus, one of the Rockwell vice presidents said that Rockwell would not give an unqualified go for launch. The NASA team leader did not interpret those statements as a no-go recommendation, so the launch proceeded. We can only hope that NASA attends to the group decision-making problems as much as they do to recommendations for reengineering the spacecraft. Such a massive project requires clear communication and a cooperative approach to work.

Much of our experience every day occurs in the presence of other people. Groups are individuals who interact with each other enough to exert influence on the thoughts and behaviors of each other. In acting groups, the presence of others affects the behavior of the individual. If the individual's task is a well-learned one, the presence of an audience is likely to help him or her perform better. However, if the task is new or complex to the individual, the presence of an audience will usually hinder that person's performance. The presence of coactors, people performing the same task as the individual, will usually help the individual's performance. Deindividuation occurs when there are many coactors, small audiences, and the individual perceives that he or she is unidentifiable. When he or she is deindividuated, the individual experiences low self-consciousness and displays uninhibited behavior, which is often antisocial. When individuals are working on cooperative tasks, the presence of coactors often leads to social loafing. Social loafing is the reduced effort individuals exhibit when they believe that their efforts are not discernible because they are being combined with others' efforts. Social impact theory and self-attention theory have been offered to account for deindividuation and social loafing.

Audiences often evaluate individuals. If they are openly supportive as crowds usually are of the home team, they promote better performance. However, home crowds can contribute to poorer performance if the pressure is otherwise great because the competition is important and the performer or performers are not confident of their ability to do well. If the audience convinces the performer that she or he can do well, performance is usually better. Cooperation among group members leads to better performance, especially if the group members have separate subtasks which require that they interact with each other. Cooperation promotes friendships among group members. Individual competition can elicit better performance, but it has negative personal effects because of failures and pressure to perform and discord among competitors. The intergroup competition of team sports produces positive personal and interpersonal effects because of the intragroup cooperation.

Decision making by groups is usually preferred over individual decision making because it is presumed that a group will have more ideas than an individual and because fair outcomes are more likely when different values and perspectives are considered. Group members are typically positive and supportive toward each other in their interactions. The most influential group members and those who emerge as leaders are the ones who talk the most.

Groups can make better decisions and solve problems better than individuals in some circumstances. If individuals are given time to brainstorm alone before they are assembled for group discussion, the group product is superior to the individual product. Groups are likely to perform better than individuals if diverse backgrounds, perspectives, and abilities are represented among group members. Groupthink, the tendency for groups to make poor, ill-considered decisions because of pressures for consensus, is most likely to occur in cohesive groups

Summary

with respected leaders. Groupthink can be avoided by emphasizing the independence of group members and diminishing the directiveness of the leader. Discussion of what might be called "one-sided issues" leads group members to take more extreme positions than individuals do. This group polarization is caused by conformity influences in the group discussion, exposure to persuasive arguments in the discussion, or both. Group depolarization can be achieved by having people who are initially on opposing sides of the issue included in the same group discussion.

Group leaders are members who try to influence other group members. They may have power through their election or appointment to the leader position, through their expertise on the topic, through their ability to reward or punish group members, and/or through their attractiveness to other group members. Leaders can emerge by demonstrating their competence and loyalty to the group. Leaders are most effective when their personal orientation toward the group and three elements of the group situation are congruent. A person-oriented leader should be most effective when leader-group relations are good, the task is unstructured, and the leader's position power is weak. A task-oriented leader should seek group situations with good relations, structured tasks, and strong position power.

The applications highlighted work groups, deliberating bodies, and communication within organizations. Aspects of air flight crew miscommunication and accidents, the deliberation process in juries, and the communication problems within and between groups involved in the Challenger accident were discussed.

CHAPTER 10

Communication

Harold goes out for a night of drinking and partying with friends. Later in the evening, Harold finds himself "glancing" several times at an attractive woman across the room. She looks back. All of a sudden, Harold finds himself in a headlock on the barroom floor. Apparently, the man who was with the target of his flirtatious glances took offense to his nonverbal behavior.

Our most communicative verbal messages seem to create comparisons. A person can be "as weak as a kitten," "as strong as horseradish," "as graceful as a gazelle," or "as lovable as a puppy," or he or she may "cry like a baby" or "run like the wind." A person can be a "kewpie doll" or a "snake." A situation can be "a powderkeg." A person's criticism can be "like the pot calling the kettle black." Such metaphorical expressions create meaning by tying vague or abstract conditions to concrete experiences. If the comparison is an outlandish one which still causes the receiver to conjure up a mental image, the expression will add impact to communication.

What is full channel communication? It is when every person can see and hear all of the verbal and nonverbal behavior of every other person and can be seen and heard by others. Every person can send and receive information. Full channel communication almost requires a live interaction situation, but a very sophisticated color video intercommunication system could provide full channel communication. There are, however, many media which provide some but not all channels, such as television, radio, books, and telephones. It is interesting to consider communication modes that do not use all of the communication channels. Do reduced channel media communicators attempt to compensate for the absent channels? Do radio broadcasters speak in more animated ways than TV broadcasters? Is the impact on the listener equivalent? Certainly the listener must be more active in conjuring up images to complement the radio broadcast. A skillful novelist can create profound images through the direct description of nonverbal acts. Again, the reader must be more active in producing these images than the TV viewer. Educators and education critics have bemoaned the tranquilizing effect of television viewing on young people in recent years on the grounds that it encourages inactivity and makes mental activity unnecessary and social activity unlikely. There are many questions about different types of communication yet to be answered.

Communication involves two or more people. There must be at least one sender and one receiver. The sender is said to encode a message and the receiver decodes it (Dittman, 1972). Studies can be classified as *encoding* or *decoding* studies depending on whether subjects are asked to enact messages or to interpret or judge the meaning of messages. There are several verbal and nonverbal communication channels: language, vocalizations, spatial behavior, touch, visual or gaze behavior, facial expressions, and body movements and postures. Behavior in these channels can be used to communicate power, status, influence attraction, or other emotions; to conceal emotions; to gain information; and to regulate the flow of communication (Kleinke, 1986).

Not all behavior is intended to communicate. Sometimes the sender may act a certain way when he or she says a message, and the receiver will see these nonverbal and/or paralinguistic acts as part of the total communication to be decoded even though the sender did not intend for those acts to communicate. Also more can be perceived in a verbal message than the words alone. That is, the receiver may wonder why a speaker said, "I just love pimento cheese sandwiches," or "I think your friend, Enrique, is a hunk" to him or her at that time and in that place. When you consider that participants often switch back and forth from sending to receiving rapidly; that listeners often make backchannel responses—smiling, nodding, or verbally agreeing—while the sender is speaking (Duncan & Fiske, 1977); and that there are so many simultaneous channels to be understood; you begin to appreciate the complexity of interpersonal communication.

A commonly asked question is "Are people more attentive to and more influenced by verbal or nonverbal behaviors?" Mehrabian (1972) concluded that most (55 percent) of the communication of emotion occurs through facial expression, 38 percent occurs through vocal expression, and only 7 percent occurs through verbal content. He is saying that 93 percent of the communication of emotion is through nonverbal channels. A few qualifications or limitations of this generalization should be noted. One is that Mehrabian is talking about the decoding of emotional communications, not all communications. Certainly, lecturers in academic settings would be dismayed to learn that no one is attending to what they say! Test performance by most students suggests that a lot of information, albeit nonemotional, is being conveyed and received through lectures. In fact, Friedman (1978) found that when a nonemotional judgment was being made, verbal comments were more influential than facial expressions in inconsistent communications.

Another point is that Mehrabian's generalization is derived from studies of inconsistent messages by Mehrabian and his associates (e.g., Mehrabian & Ferris, 1967; Mehrabian & Weiner, 1967). Inconsistent messages involve the expression of one emotion through one channel (e.g., the face) and expression of a contradictory emotion through another channel (e.g., the voice or verbal content). Creating normal inconsistent messages (such as sarcastic statements) required these investigators to severely limit the verbal comments sampled. To say some emotional statements in a positive or a negative emotional tone of voice would have seemed strange. Such verbal messages could not be used in their inconsistent messages studies. The verbal channel probably contributed only 7 percent to the message partly because it was so restricted. Two other studies (Argyle, Alkema,

Verbal and Nonverbal Communication

Do Verbal or Nonverbal Acts Have More Impact?

Is it what we say or how we say it that is most influential?

We can overinterpret nonverbal behavior.

BLOOM COUNTY, by Berke Breathed. © 1982 by Washington Post Co. Reprinted by permission.

Figure 10.1
*These results from
study 2 of Kraus and
associates (1981)
using videotaped
natural emotional
communication are
much different from
Mehrabian's (1972)
findings.*

(*From Kraus et al., 1981,* Journal
of Personality and Social
Psychology, *40, 317.*)

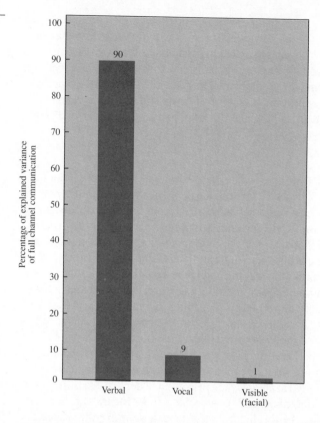

& Gilmour, 1972; Bugental, Kaswan, & Love, 1970) also showed that nonverbal channels were more influential than the verbal channels in reading emotional meaning from inconsistent messages. However, the limitation on verbal messages criticism also applies to those studies.

Other studies have shown that nonverbal channels are not so influential when *naturally* occurring, consistent messages are used. Krauss, Apple, Morency, Wenzel, and Winton (1981) examined how emotions are read from naturally occurring messages, and they broke the messages down into channel components. In two separate studies, they used videotaped positive and negative emotional segments from the Mondale-Dole vice presidential debate of 1976 and college women's responses from videotaped interviews to positive and negative questions. In both studies, they compared emotional or affective ratings of the full-channel videotaped segments with ratings of each of three isolated channels. The three channels were (1) video only, to evaluate the influence of facial expressions; (2) transcript, to evaluate verbal content; and (3) content-filtered audio, to evaluate vocal or paralinguistic characteristics. They found that the verbal transcript came closest to yielding the same emotional evaluation as the full-channel presentations did. Krauss et al. concluded that nonverbal behaviors are not the most important channels in our judgments of emotional communications. (See figure 10.1.) Another study (Ekman, Friesen, O'Sullivan, & Scherer, 1980) produced evidence supporting the same conclusion.

Humans engage in some confusing communication patterns. Some behaviors have multiple meanings and the specific meaning intended by the act is seldom made explicit. A set of verbal behaviors that are confusing in this way is our forms of address (Brown, 1965). A person may call another person by his or her first name or nickname if the speaker feels familiar with or close to that person. The speaker also may use the other person's first name if the speaker feels that he or she has higher status than the target person. Whether the form of address means closeness or dominance makes a big difference in some situations. Phyllis George conducted a post-Super Bowl interview with the parents of Marcus Allen, running back for the L.A. Raiders, a few years ago. During the interview, Ms. George addressed Mr. Allen as "Red" and Mrs. Allen as "Mama Allen," very familiar forms of address. A black man or a black woman might not have appreciated these lower-status names coming from a white woman from the South. Later, a sports talk show host offered excuses for Ms. George's conduct, saying that interviewers often try to establish familiarity with their famous interviewees and addressing them by first name was one way of implying familiarity. At least he was familiar with the double entendre problem of forms of address. The other side of this address phenomenon is that using Mr., Ms., etc. may connote unfamiliarity or higher status to the addressee. The following excerpt from a letter to a newspaper editor shows the importance of form of address:

> On a personal note in regard to editorial policy, your reporters give me the respect of using my full name in their articles, but the editorial writers persist in calling me "Art." While this may be an attempt to demonstrate friendship or familiarity, I would prefer that public references of this nature be Arthur ————.
>
> I find this use of "Art" as professionally insulting. While some acquaintances and associates might use that name in some instances, I view its public use as I would the use of the term "boy."

A nonverbal behavior that carries this same kind of ambiguity is touch (Henley, 1977). Touching someone, like using their first name, can indicate warmth or affection or it can indicate that the toucher feels that he or she has higher status than the recipient. Henley (1977) argues that touching someone or initiating touch is a sign of power more than it is a sign of affection. For instance, Henley (1973) reported that older people—older people, at least until they are in their 60s, have higher status in American society—intentionally touch younger people more than vice versa. She also found that men intentionally touched women more in public than vice versa. She interpreted this sex difference in touching as consistent with men's desire to dominate women (Henley, 1977). However, Stier and Hall (1984) reviewed over 40 studies and found that there was no consistent tendency for men to touch women more than vice versa. They also found that there was a slight tendency for females to initiate touch more than males in mixed-sex pairs. In most of the observational studies of touching, it is impossible to know if touching was motivated by a desire to show affection or power.

If we could know the relationship between the people involved, the situation, and the location and type of touch used, most of us could agree on whether it was a loving touch or a dominating touch (see Nguyen, Heslin, & Nguyen, 1975). One study that illustrates that different people may interpret the same

Figure 10.2
*The touch of a female
nurse before surgery
had a calming effect
on women patients
and a disquieting
effect on men patients.*
(From Whitcher & Fisher, 1979,
Journal of Personality and Social
Psychology, 37, 92.)

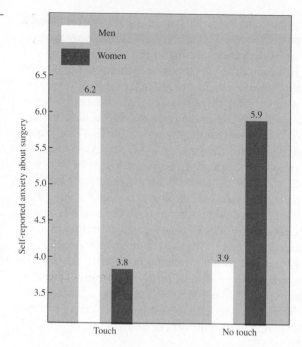

kind of touch differently was conducted in a hospital setting (Whitcher & Fisher, 1979). These investigators had female nurses touch half of their male and half of their female patients on the arm for a minute as they read a preoperational instructions booklet. As they left all patients, nurses extended a hand to see if the patient would "reach out and touch" them. Other dependent measures included a measure of anxiety about the operation, measures of attraction toward the nurse, and blood pressure readings taken in the recovery room. Males responded negatively to being touched by the nurse, while females responded positively to being touched. Touched females touched the nurse's hand more, perceived the nurse's touch to indicate interest, reported less preoperative anxiety, and tended to have lower postoperative blood pressure than the touched males and the untouched females. Males who were touched generally experienced the opposite reactions. Whitcher and Fisher (1979) interpreted the different response patterns of males and females to mean that women regarded the touch as a supportive and caring gesture and that men saw the touch as a sign of the nurse's power over them. It appears that the meaning of touch in some situations is ambiguous enough that the recipient's background and perspective determines the reaction to touch. (See figure 10.2.)

Communicating Intimacy: Too Much or Too Little

Two perspectives on communication have focused on the affection or intimacy aspect of communicative behaviors and have ignored the status or power function. Michael Argyle and Janet Dean (1965) of Great Britain proposed that in interactions most people try to maintain a constant level of implied intimacy with particular persons in certain settings. Both verbal and nonverbal behaviors contribute to the overall implied intimacy level. For instance, amount of eye contact, distance between conversation participants, positivity of facial expression (i.e., amount of smiling), and conversation topic all contribute to the intimacy implied toward one's conversation partner. The desired level of implied intimacy is different in different relationships (e.g., spouse vs. stranger) in different settings (e.g., public vs. private). When disequilibrium occurs (e.g., when a stranger is looking more, standing closer, smiling more, and/or talking about more personal topics than you deem appropriate), you will compensate by looking away, stepping back, or changing the topic of conversation to regain the appropriate level of intimacy (Aiello, 1977a; Argyle & Dean, 1965; Cappella, 1981; Russo, 1975). Rosenfeld, Breck, Smith, and Kehoe (1984) found that compensating by reducing one's gaze was especially likely if a male subject were in a listening role as a male stranger intentionally moved closer rather than sitting in a nearby seat. According to Argyle and Dean's **equilibrium theory,** *compensation* toward more implied intimacy would occur if a lover assumed a distant position, looked very little, and talked about impersonal matters in a private setting.

Will these two people maintain the implied intimacy level of their behaviors or change to a closer or more distant level?

Recently, Patterson (1976) has questioned whether we do always try to maintain a constant intimacy level with particular people. His **arousal model** of interpersonal intimacy suggests that if the other person's change in implied intimacy elicits a positive emotional reaction in the individual, he or she will respond in kind (*reciprocate*) to change his or her implied intimacy rather than to compensate and regain the previous level of intimacy. In the example given in the previous paragraph, if the stranger were extremely attractive to you, you would probably reciprocate the more intimate behaviors and change the intimacy level in the relationship. Those behaviors would entail coming closer, looking more, and talking about more personal topics. If the lover in the previous paragraph were one with whom you were currently disenchanted, then his or her distant behavior would elicit a positive emotional reaction, and you would reciprocate the distant behavior rather than compensating to reestablish the previous level of intimacy.

Some studies have shown that reciprocation, not compensation, does occur. Rosenfeld's (1967) finding that smiling by one person begets smiling in another is a reciprocity effect. Breed (1972) found that direct orientation, forward lean, and a high amount of direct gaze by a listening confederate caused subjects to rate the interviewer as interested and the interview as pleasant. These positive reactions were reciprocated as subjects leaned toward and looked at the "high intimacy" confederate more. Storms and Thomas (1977) demonstrated that fairly intimate nonverbal behavior by a stranger does elicit a positive emotional response as the Patterson model suggests. Patterson, Jordan, Hogan, and Frerker (1981) showed that nonverbal, intimacy-implying behavior does elicit an arousal change as the model suggests. However, they were unsuccessful in demonstrating the reciprocated behavior. In summary, the more differentiated model of Patterson has some explanatory advantages over Argyle and Dean's theory (cf. Heslin & Patterson, 1982). Judith Burgoon (1983) has proposed a somewhat similar arousal model wherein unexpected behavior arouses the recipient to make an adjusting response.

The Structure of Conversations

Perhaps you have seen and heard two people talk to each other simultaneously. Talking "at" each other might be a better description of two people speaking at the same time because it is doubtful that much information is being exchanged. Perhaps you have been in a situation where a speaker has maintained the floor so effectively (by ignoring others' throat-clearing or gestures) that it was impossible to enter the conversation. If so, you probably understand that conversations are ordinarily structured by speaker and listener roles, and there are various behavioral cues that participants use to move into and out of those roles.

Several investigators have examined turn-taking behavior in conversations (Duncan, 1972; Kendon, 1967; Rosenfeld, 1978). A common finding is that listeners look at speakers more than vice versa (Exline, 1963; Kendon, 1967). Speakers must look less because maintaining eye contact (and the visual information received) interferes with their thoughts and/or acknowledging the listener visually makes it easier for the listener to take the floor from them. When a speaker has finished expressing a thought, he or she will usually look toward the listener (Kendon, 1967), raise or lower the pitch of his or her last utterance and drawl the last syllable, terminate or relax hand gesticulations, and/or speak more softly as he or she says a stereotyped expression such as "you know" or "but uh" to indicate readiness to yield the floor (Duncan, 1972). The listener knows that he or she can start talking at that point.

This new speaker will now look away from the other person and may start gesturing with a hand (Rosenfeld & Hancks, 1980). In order to keep the floor when another person is attempting to take it, a speaker may gesture with a raised hand, hands, or finger—like a stop sign (Duncan, 1972); avoid the gaze of the other person; and/or keep on talking, filling pauses with some sound along the way. The listener's responses are called **backchannel responses** unless they are active attempts to take the floor (Yngve, 1970). Typical backchannel responses are smiles, nods, and verbal agreements, such as "uh-huh," to indicate attentiveness and understanding (Duncan, 1972). Use of these turn-taking cues reduces the number of interruptions and simultaneous talking (Duncan, 1972).

LaFrance and Mayo (1976) have made an interesting observation about turn-taking in interracial (black-white) conversations. They found that, relative to whites, blacks look at their interaction partner more while speaking and less while listening. They raise the possibility that this difference in turn-taking style could contribute to awkward interracial conversations. That is, when the white speaker looks to the black listener to indicate readiness to relinquish the floor, the black person may be looking away and not pick up the signal. The white person might also interpret the black person's looking at him or her while speaking as an indication that the white person should start talking when the look was not intended to be such a cue. No examination of the effects of this difference has been undertaken. It is possible that members of one racial group would adapt to the style of the other. It is also possible that turn-taking cues are so redundant that inappropriate signals in the visual mode alone would not cause miscommunication. These are questions yet to be answered. (See figure 10.3.)

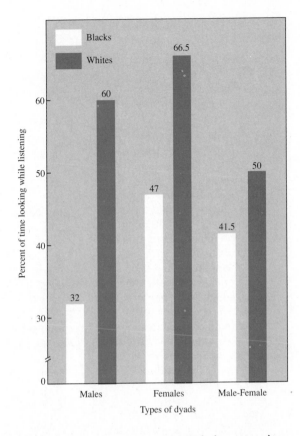

Figure 10.3
Blacks look at their interaction partners while listening to them less than whites do. Blacks' visual interaction pattern is more dominant.
(From LaFrance & Mayo, 1976, Journal of Personality & Social Psychology, 33, 550.)

Verbal communication has been assigned a back seat to nonverbal communication. This is unfortunate and misguided because most intentional communication is conducted verbally and nonverbal behaviors serve as accompaniments to amplify or accentuate the verbal acts.

Verbal behavior is probably central even in initial courtship encounters. Many recent popular authors (e.g., Givens, 1983) have emphasized the role of nonverbal behaviors in such encounters. These authors characterize the initial courtship sequence this way: (1) visual attention or orientation in conjunction with pleasant facial expressions, (2) conversation, (3) touch, and (4) further courtship, sex-related, or sexual activity. Such courtship sequences probably occur in only a few types of settings (e.g., singles bars, gay bars), and most courtship sequences occur over several days or weeks. Even if we accept this sequence as accurate, the linchpin in the sequence is the verbal rather than nonverbal ones. The verbal step must occur for relationships to develop and it cannot be skipped. So, verbal expression is important even in circumstances where nonverbal communication has been emphasized.

Are there magical words or phrases with which Martin Luther King, Jr., John F. Kennedy, Adolph Hitler, Mahatma Gandhi, Billy Graham, and Franklin D. Roosevelt influenced thousands of people? Probably not. In most cases, their rep-

Verbal Communication

Powerful Words

I Have a Dream

Rev. Martin Luther King, Jr.
August 28, 1963

. . . We have also come to this hallowed spot to remind America of the fierce urgency of now. This is no time to engage in the luxury of cooling off or to take the tranquilizing drug of gradualism. Now is the time to make real the promises of democracy; now is the time to rise from the dark and desolate valley of segregation to the sunlit path of racial justice; now is the time to lift our nation from the quicksands of racial injustice to the solid rock of brotherhood; now is the time to make justice a reality for all God's children. It would be fatal for the nation to overlook the urgency of the moment. This sweltering summer of the Negro's legitimate discontent will not pass until there is an invigorating autumn of freedom and equality. . . .

No, we are not satisfied, and we will not be satisfied until justice rolls down like waters and righteousness like a mighty stream . . . .

I have a dream that one day every valley shall be exalted, every hill and mountain shall be made low, the rough places shall be made plain, and the crooked places shall be made straight and the glory of the Lord will be revealed and all flesh shall see it together.

This is our hope. This is the faith that I go back to the South with.

With this faith we will be able to hew out of the mountain of despair a stone of hope. With this faith we will be able to transform the jangling discords

utations or high offices preceded them and contributed to the impact of their words. They expressed ideas that their audiences wanted to hear, and they expressed them with great fervor. Their enthusiastic, energetic styles created interest and arousal in their audiences, lending more impact to their words. In most cases, they spoke with high ideals and appealed to the nobler side of people. Perhaps the only way to assess the influence of particular words and phrases is to select forceful passages from sources unknown to readers and present altered and unaltered forms to the readers. If changing particular words or phrases changed the readers' reactions, one would know what words are powerful. Otherwise, it is difficult to separate the effects of the words from reputational or speaking style effects.

of our nation into a beautiful symphony of brotherhood . . . .

This will be the day when all of God's children will be able to sing with new meaning—"my country 'tis of thee; sweet land of liberty; of thee I sing; land where my fathers died, land of the pilgrim's pride; from every mountain side, let freedom ring"—and if America is to be a great nation, this must become true.

So let freedom ring from the prodigious hilltops of New Hampshire.

Let freedom ring from the mighty mountains of New York.

Let freedom ring from the heightening Alleghenies of Pennsylvania.

Let freedom ring from the snow-capped Rockies of Colorado.

Let freedom ring from the curvaceous slopes of California.

But not only that.

Let freedom ring from Stone Mountain of Georgia.

Let freedom ring from Lookout Mountain of Tennessee.

Let freedom ring from every hill and molehill of Mississippi, from every mountainside, let freedom ring.

And when we allow freedom to ring, when we let it ring from every village and hamlet, from every state and city, we will be able to speed up that day when all of God's children—black men and white men, Jews and Gentiles, Catholics and Protestants—will be able to join hands and to sing in the words of the old Negro spiritual, "Free at last, free at last, thank God Almighty, we are free at last."

Simple, straightforward words and expressions are have the most impact, the verbal styles of William F. Buckley, Jr. and Howard Cosell notwithstanding. The idea is to communicate, not to show off your vocabulary. Cosell's use of pompous phrases, such as "a veritable plethora of" to mean "many," was sometimes grating and obnoxious. Certainly, the language of King's "I Have A Dream" speech was simple, but powerful and exemplifies the creative use of metaphors. MacLachlin (1983) contends that concrete terms are remembered better and are more influential than abstract terms. Unadorned speech was most credible in the study of powerful and powerless speech styles described earlier (Erickson, et al., 1978).

Metaphorical speech has strong impact on the imagination.

THE FAR SIDE cartoon by Gary Larsen is reprinted by permission of Chronicle Features, San Francisco, CA.

THE FAR SIDE   By GARY LARSON

I got a bad feeling about this, Harriet.

On the other hand, metaphorical speech can be more vivid and colorful than straightforward speech. However, metaphors do not gain that vividness from complicated terms. Instead, it is the connection between previously unrelated circumstances that creates a lasting image. **Metaphors** point out relationships between concepts in interesting, creative ways. Dr. King's speech contained many metaphorical phrases that gave it vitality. The creation of both good metaphors and vivid images requires the use of specific rather than general words (MacLachlin, 1983). The phrase, "like a bull in a china shop," conjures up more vivid images than "like a large animal in a place with many breakable items." Many slang terms and terms in the language of many subcultures (e.g., language of urban American blacks) stem from metaphors. Humor is often achieved through the use of metaphorical language to draw outlandish comparisons.

Content of Conversations

The possible contents of conversations seem infinite. Conversational content has been categorized in studies of group communication. Robert Bales (1950, 1970) used a 12–category system for classifying statements and questions made in small group interactions. His four major categories were (1) answers, (2) questions, (3) positive actions, and (4) negative actions. Some of the 12 exclusive categories required interpretation, especially under the positive and negative action headings (e.g., shows solidarity or seems friendly). In 1970, Bales indicated that the most common communication acts in group discussions were (1) gives opinion (30 percent); (2) gives orientation, information (21 percent); and (3) agrees (12 percent). This pattern of results suggests that people make assertions more than they raise questions, and they tend to be positive and supportive more than they are disagreeable. It should be remembered that these acts were observed in groups. The pattern could be somewhat different in two-person conversations.

Ruback, Dabbs, and Hopper (1984) classified comments in group brainstorming sessions according to whether the statement introduced a new idea or not. They also electronically recorded the patterns of talking and pauses as these groups discussed ways to attract more tourists to the United States. The expression of new ideas occurred in clusters, and they usually occurred after silences

In discussion groups, new ideas are usually expressed after a switching pause between speakers.

(the switching pauses between speakers). The silent periods appear to have allowed the individual in the group time to form his or her idea, or the silence after the previous speaker was long enough to assure the idea person that he or she would have adequate opportunity to express the idea fully. Interestingly, the subjects in Ruback's et al. study rated the idea producers as good leaders; whereas group members in Sorrentino and Boutillier's (1975) study did not perceive people with good ideas as good leaders.

How much one says in conversation is more important than what one says (Sorrentino & Boutillier, 1975)! Confederates who talked a great deal in that study were rated as more competent, confident, interested, influential, and as better leaders by other group members than confederates who participated very little. The quality of his or her comments did not have nearly as much effect on the ratings. The results of Dabbs and Ruback's (1984) and Ruback's et al. (1984) studies also show that those who talked more were rated more positively and as better leaders. Sorrentino and Boutillier (1975) felt that the talkative people were regarded as better leaders because their active participation showed a willingness to share their ideas to the benefit of the group. Other studies have shown a positive correlation between talking time and leadership ratings (cf. Stein & Heller, 1979).

> Quantity of Speech

   An interesting sex difference in talking time appears depending on the nature of the conversation. Dabbs and Ruback (1984) found that women talked more, paused less, and enjoyed the conversation more when they engaged in get-acquainted, open conversations. On the other hand, Kimble and Musgrove (1988) found that men talked more than their women opponents in arguing, mixed-sex dyads. It appears that when conversations are more structured or task-oriented, men talk more than women. When conversations are open or interpersonally-oriented, women talk more than men (cf. Ruback et al., 1984; Strodtbeck & Mann, 1956).

Vocal and
Paralinguistic
Features

How statements and questions are made often has substantial impact on what is communicated. Paralanguage is the noncontent aspect of speech that occurs with the verbal content. They are nonverbal behavior technically, but they are presented here because of their connection with verbal behavior. In this section, we consider the pitch, loudness, rate, vocal assertiveness, and the filled and unfilled pauses that occur within speech.

Higher *pitch* has been associated with nervousness and attempts to deceive (Apple, Streeter, & Krauss, 1979; Streeter, Krauss, Geller, Olson, & Apple, 1977). Streeter et al. (1977) induced subjects to lie or tell the truth and found that the fundamental frequency (pitch) of the liars was slightly higher than the pitch of the truthful subjects. However, such pitch differences are usually hard to detect without electronic equipment.

Apple et al. (1979) taped speech of Columbia University men in interview sessions and electronically altered the pitch of the taped segments. They were able to raise or lower the pitch without changing other characteristics of speech. However, the altered speech did not sound quite normal. In three experiments, listener subjects rated higher-pitched voices as less truthful, less potent, and more nervous than normal, lower-pitched voices saying the same thing.

Apple et al. (1979) also electronically altered the *speech rate* of the taped segments without altering the pitch or loudness of the speech. Miller, Maruyama, Beaber, and Valone (1976) had talkers vary their speech rate, but this technique probably caused faster rate, louder speech, and higher-pitched speech to occur together so that it was unclear which characteristic produced their results. However, Cook (1969) has noted that the rate of normal speech is usually varied by longer or shorter pauses between words rather than the elongation or shortening the words themselves, which Apple et al. did. At any rate (pun intended), Apple et al. found that faster and slower speech were rated as less truthful than normal speech, slower speech was rated as more passive and more potent than the other two rates. Slower and faster speech (especially slower speech) were rated as less persuasive, fluent, and emphatic, and more nervous than normal speech. Miller et al. (1976) found that faster speech was more persuasive than slower speech as Apple et al. did, but they did not examine normal speech, which Apple et al. found the most persuasive rate of speech. So the fast-talking executive on the Federal Express commercials may not be the most persuasive speaker of all.

Speaking in a loud voice has been associated with expressions of strong negative feelings or attempts to dominate in our society. Speaking softly, on the other hand, may be an expression of meekness or affection (Scheflen, 1965). Costanzo, Markel, and Costanzo (1969) found that voices most characterized by *loudness* were associated with anger and contempt. Kimble, Forte, and Yoshikawa (1981) found that women spoke loudest when they were trying to express intense anger. Kimble and Musgrove (1988) found that assertive people talked louder than unassertive people, and men spoke louder than women in arguments between a woman and a man. Extroverts, who are socially dominant, speak louder than introverts (Scherer, 1972; as cited in Siegman, 1978). Also, louder speech indicates greater confidence in one's answers (Seidel & Kimble, 1989).

Vocal assertiveness is a rating of the global composite of speech sounds and patterns independent of verbal content. It is derived by having judges rate how dominant or assertive are voice samples which have been made content-free by a filtering system that cuts off all sound frequencies above approximately 500 Hz. Such a filtered voice retains all the inflection, rate, loudness, and other characteristics and changes in speech; but the words spoken cannot be understood. Bugental, Henker, and Whalen (1976) found that people who believe they control the events in their lives (i.e., internal locus of control) exhibit more vocal assertiveness than those who believe other influences control their lives (external locus of control). Kimble, Yoshikawa, and Zehr (1981) found that men are more vocally assertive than some women, but only in very limited circumstances (mixed-sex, structured discussions). Krauss et al. (1981) used such filtered voices to demonstrate that the voice alone does not contribute much to the emotional meaning of messages.

Pauses, filled ("Uh . . . well," "ah") and unfilled (silence), influence the perception of what is spoken. Fisher and Apostal (1975) found that when they interspersed tape recordings of simulated comments of clients with unfilled pauses, judges rated the comments as more self-disclosing than the same comments without the pauses. Apparently, the judges thought the silences indicated the clients were thinking more about revealing the subsequent information. Therefore, it must have been personal information. (See figure 10.4.)

Pauses

Another interpretation of the silent pause could be that it indicates great poise or composure, especially when one pauses to reflect in silence before a large audience. During my graduate days, one of my professors had the striking ability to stand silent in front of a large class that awaited his next utterance. He did not feel compelled to fill the silence with "uhs" and "ahs" or to rush into his next sentence. His ability to maintain that silence spoke volumes about his poise. There are no studies indicating that such silences are uncomfortable for speakers, but clearly people do get uneasy when a prolonged silence occurs in conversation and individuals feel compelled to fill the void. Weiss, Lombardo, Warren, and Kelley (1971) demonstrated that silent periods in conversation are unpleasant to those who are expected to reply. Periods of silences are awkward to speakers before audiences, especially large audiences. If a speaker creates such silent periods (unfilled pauses) rather than rushing to fill them, most of us would probably infer that the speaker is poised, not nervous or anxious.

It is quite a different story with filled pauses. Filled pauses are considered speech disturbances. Mahl (1956) divided these disturbances into two types: those containing the sound "ah" and those not containing the sound "ah." Non-ah disturbances include: correcting one's own sentence, leaving a sentence incomplete, stuttering, slips of the tongue, intruding unrecognizable sounds, omission of words or parts, and repetition of words. "Ah" disturbances surprisingly are related to conversation control and thinking, not to the speaker's anxiety. On the other hand, non-ah disturbances indicate transient or situational anxiety, as several studies have shown (Boomer, 1963; Cook, 1969; Kasl & Mahl, 1965).

Figure 10.4
Speakers were rated as more self-disclosing if there were unfilled (silent) pauses in their comments than if there were not.
(From M. J. Fischer & R. A. Apostal, 1975, Journal of Counseling Psychology, 22, 94.)

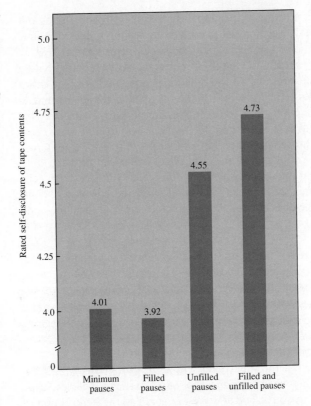

Nonverbal Communication

Some recurring themes will appear in this treatment of nonverbal communication. We will discuss nonverbal behaviors in relation to their implications for *relationships*, the portrayal of positive and negative *emotions*, the expression of status differences or *dominance*, and *deceptive communications*. Some other topics, such as the role of nonverbal behaviors in conversational turn-taking, have already been discussed.

Personal Space

Anthropologist Edward Hall (1966) first introduced the notion of personal space zones. He specified what kinds of interactions are ordinarily and comfortably conducted in eight distance ranges from a person. These distance zones are comfortable for face-to-face, standing or seated interactions among white, middle-class, adult Americans from noncontact European cultures living on the northeast seaboard of the United States. These generalizations might reasonably be extended to most Americans who do not live in isolated subcultures. The *relationship* between the interactants and the *setting* in which they are interacting determine which interaction distances are appropriate. For instance, the close, intimate zone described in table 10.1 would be comfortable for lovers in a private setting.

When people are forced into tight spaces with strangers, they seldom maintain eye contact, face-to-face orientation, or smile.

Table 10.1   Halls (1966) Personal Space Classifications

Category	Distance	Interaction activity
Intimate: Close	0–6 in.	Love-making and wrestling
Far	6–18 in.	Intimates talk in public
Personal: Close	1.5–2.5 ft	Peers, friends talk
Far	2.5–4 ft	Strangers, unequals talk
Social: Close	4–7 ft	Impersonal business
Far	7–12 ft	Formal business
Public: Close	12–25 ft	Formal presentation
Far	25 ft–outward	Famous person presents

It should be noted that people who position themselves too far away for a particular interaction arouse uneasiness in others just as surely as a stranger who positions him- or herself right under your nose. In chapter 2, we discussed the evidence that people from some cultures feel more comfortable at closer distances than Americans do. Other person variables affect comfortable interaction distances. For instance, two females typically interact at closer distances than two males do (e.g., Dosey & Meisels, 1969; Lott & Sommer, 1967; Pelligrini & Empey, 1970). Comfortable interaction distances for children of the same sex typically increase with age until they assume the typical interaction distances of adults in early adolescence (Aiello & Aiello, 1974). Personality traits also make a difference in interpersonal distances. External locus of control persons stand further from strangers than internal locus of control persons (Duke & Nowicki, 1972). Extraverts sit closer to others than introverts (Patterson & Holmes, 1966). Violent prisoners require a much bigger personal space cushion from all angles than nonviolent prisoners (Kinzel, 1970).

Other features of the interaction situation and other nonverbal behaviors also affect comfortable interaction distances. The presence of such barriers as desks should make distances that are ordinarily too close more tolerable (Hall, 1966). The bodily orientation of the two interactants also affects what distances are comfortable (e.g., Aiello & Aiello, 1974). People standing or sitting side by side and shoulder-to-shoulder probably would not find that close distance offensive unless they were strangers in an otherwise uncrowded room. Men friends in conversation would not feel uncomfortable within an inch of each other at the elbows if they were facing perpendicular to each other. In fact, a person who is approached face-to-face may turn during conversation to achieve the more comfortable 90 degree angle with the other person's body. It is only the face-to-face orientation that requires the 1.5–2.5 ft distance for interactants to be at ease in conversation with peers. Whether the interactants are sitting or standing also affects interaction ease at close distances. A person standing close to you is more threatening than one sitting close because he or she has more freedom of movement and position in standing than in sitting—at least when sitting in chairs. If there are many people in the room and loud conversation or music, closer interaction distances are more tolerated. As Argyle and Dean's (1965) intimacy equilibrium theory and Patterson's (1976) arousal model indicate, the extent of other nonverbal behaviors such as eye contact can also influence whether a particular interaction distance is discomforting or not. A great deal of eye contact makes a close distance more likely to be unsettling.

Touch

Touch obviously occurs only at the closest personal distances. Therefore, some of the same generalizations about relationships and settings that apply to intimate interaction distances apply to touch. In chapter 2, we noted that the United States is, generally speaking, a noncontact culture. Even though we all welcome touch by some people many times in our lives and regard those touches as signs of affection, some studies (e.g., Whitcher & Fisher's (1979) study of touches by nurses) indicate that touch is also a gesture of domination.

Other studies have demonstrated the positive, even therapeutic, effects of touch. Fisher, Rytting, and Heslin (1976) found that a simple touch on the hand by a stranger at the exit desk of a university library produced positive reactions toward that stranger and library services. This positive reaction occurred even though many of the people who were touched didn't realize it. Crusco and Wetzel (1984) found a similar effect in restaurants. They found that when waitresses touched men or women customers on the hand or shoulder when they presented the check, customers left bigger tips than when waitresses did not touch customers. (See figure 10.5.) Pattison (1973) found that when male and female counselors touched female clients at a university counseling center six times on the shoulder, arm, or back during an initial 45-minute interview, these clients were more self-disclosing than clients who were not touched. In this case, touching was beneficial to the therapeutic relationship; but it should be remembered that

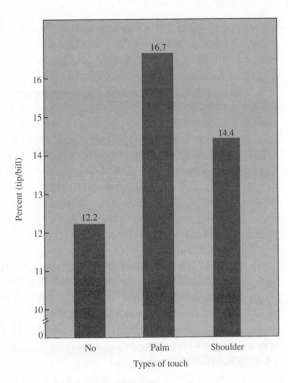

Figure 10.5
Tipping percent depending on whether a waitress touched customer on palm, shoulder, or not at all before the tip.
(From Crusco & Wetzel, 1984, Personal and Social Psychology Bulletin, 10.)

the study was conducted only with female clients. Women are touched more often than men (Stier & Hall, 1984), and apparently they are more positively disposed to being touched in such settings than men (cf. Whitcher & Fisher, 1979).

Heslin and Boss (1980) studied touch in a public setting where it is quite common—airports. They developed a scale of touch ranging from 0 (no touch) through handshakes to 5 (extended embrace or kiss). Then, they observed as passengers arrived and departed and coded the touches between them and those who met them. After observing and presumably with their health insurance paid up, they approached the individuals and asked them how they were related to each other. Analyses revealed that most relationships between travelers and others were intimate, and 60 percent of these airport dyads touched each other. In mixed-sex pairs, the older person initiated touch more than the younger person. Pairs of men shook hands more than pairs of women, and pairs of women touched more intimately (on the head, arm, or back) than pairs of men. The most frequently occurring categories were no touch (40 percent) and kiss on mouth (40 percent). The least common categories were handshake (10 percent—surprise), extended embrace (10 percent), and extended kiss (3 percent). As expected, those who were most closely related touched each other in more intimate ways.

Airplane arrivals and departures are emotional events often punctuated by embraces and other touching.

Eye Contact

Direct gaze would probably be a better description for this type of nonverbal behavior because many studies in this area only examine one person's visual behavior while having a confederate act in prescribed ways. Of course, two people gazing at each other are required for mutual eye contact.

Such visual behavior has long been considered an important indicator of affection, other emotions, and honesty. A person who will "look you right in the eye" is a person who can be trusted (Hemsley & Doob, 1978). Eye contact has also been taken to indicate interest in initial encounters (Scheflen, 1965) or affection in relationships. People do look more at approving confederates than at disapproving ones (Exline & Winters, 1965; Fugita, 1974). Observers infer that dating couples love each other when they look at each other often relative to those who don't look at each other often (Kleinke, Meeker, & LaFong, 1974).

However, the proposition that more looking means more liking is made questionable by several studies on the stare (Ellsworth, Carlsmith, & Henson, 1972; Elman, Schulte, & Bukoff, 1977; Greenbaum & Rosenfeld, 1978; Werner & Reis, 1974). Staring or prolonged continuous gaze is a high amount of eye contact (if reciprocated). Yet, all of these studies indicate that staring evokes negative reactions and avoidance, not positive reactions. For instance, Ellsworth et al. (1972) found that motorists drove away from an intersection faster when a stranger standing on a street corner stared at them than when he did not. Most of us do not believe a stare means that the starer likes us unless it is accompanied by a pleasant facial expression.

Ellsworth (1975) contends that more direct gaze signifies more intense feelings, negative or positive, rather than more positive feelings. Ellsworth and Carlsmith (1968) found that more direct gaze by evaluators caused recipients to dislike negative or disapproving evaluators more and to like positive evaluators more. Apparently, the recipients took the evaluator to be more involved in his evaluation, to mean what he said more, if he looked at them a lot while saying it. At least, more gaze led to more intense reactions, positive and negative, than less gaze.

Kimble, Forte, and Yoshikawa (1981) and Kimble and Olszewski (1980) examined whether eye contact indicates emotional *intensity* or *positivity*. We attempted to see how people act when they are asked to express positive and negative messages intensely or weakly. The question was "Do people look more when they portray positive emotions or when they express either kind of emotion intensely?" In the Kimble et al. (1981) study, female subjects were asked to learn and perform positive or negative messages four times, with strong and weak intensity and to a camera and to a man (a trained assistant they had just met). The direct gaze proportions and the average glance durations are presented in figure 10.6.

These results indicate that a higher proportion of direct gaze is used when more intense emotion is being expressed, regardless of whether it is positive or negative. Longer glances were used when expressing intense negative emotion. These longer glances appear to be like stares, which are long glances, in that both are associated with negative emotions. So, amount of eye contact or gaze is used

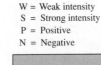

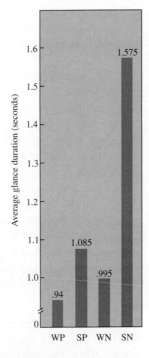

Figure 10.6
*Percent of direct gaze
and average glance
duration depending
on intensity and
positivity of emotion.
Stronger intensity of
emotional expression
produced higher
percentages of direct
gaze. Strong, negative
emotional expression
produced longer
glances.*
(From Kimble, Forte, & Yoshikawa,
1981, Journal of Personality, 49,
278.)

to express intensity of emotion, not positivity. What nonverbal behaviors do express positive feelings? Shorter glances or more frequent looks away are associated with positive communications in this study. Also, what seems to differentiate the malicious stare from the flirtatous glance, besides length of a single look, is the facial expression that accompanies the look. Pleasant facial expressions signify more liking.

Visual behavior, like some other behaviors we have already discussed, has been related to dominance or status. Exline, Ellyson, and Long (1975) noted that people with high status relative to their interaction partners (e.g., ROTC officers) and people with dominant personalities display the visual dominance pattern more than others do. A person displays the visual dominance pattern when he or she looks at his or her interaction partner often while speaking and, relatively speaking, looks very little while listening to one's partner. The following is a way of couching this behavior so that high values indicate high dominance:

$$\text{Visual Dominance Pattern} = \frac{\text{Time Spent Looking while Speaking/Speaking Time}}{\text{Time Spent Looking while Listening/Listening Time}}$$

To illustrate how this behavior communicates dominance, let us consider a common encounter. Imagine the interaction between a volatile baseball manager like Billy Martin and an umpire when the umpire makes a controversial call.

Staring and yelling is one way to dominate.

What happens? The manager tries to dominate by staring into the umpire's face and yelling at close range. What does the umpire, who is constrained to listen at this time, do? He looks away and attempts to ignore the manager by walking away, cleaning the plate, etc. When he can ignore the manager no longer, the umpire will glare and yell back at the manager. So, you can see how looking a lot while speaking and looking a little while listening are both dominant behaviors.

Exline and others (Ellyson, Dovidio, Corson, & Vinicur, 1980; Exline et al., 1975) have shown that men and women with high status and men and women with dominant personalities display high visual dominance ratios in same-sex dyads relative to people low in status or personal dominance. We (Kimble & Musgrove, 1988) had dyads consisting of an assertive or an unassertive man and an assertive or an unassertive woman argue an issue as we videotaped them. In these mixed-sex dyads, assertive women had slightly higher visual dominance ratios than unassertive women. However, the only factor that affected the men's visual patterns was the assertiveness of their female partners. Men paired with assertive women had lower visual dominance patterns than men paired with unassertive ones. So, the assertiveness of the woman in these mixed-sex dyads determined how both participants acted visually. The fact that women engage in more eye contact than men do (Exline, 1963; Exline, Gray, & Schuette, 1965) may contribute to their visual dominance in these situations.

Facial Expressions

The face is a complex anatomical area which could potentially assume over a thousand different appearances in a very short time (Ekman, Friesen, & Ellsworth, 1972). Therefore, the face is a very potent communication channel. Ekman et al. (1972) identified seven primary emotional expressions of the face that can be expressed and accurately interpreted all over the world. These emotional expressions are happiness, surprise, fear, sadness, anger, disgust/contempt, and interest. Ekman and Friesen (1975) reduced their list of primary emotions to six, excluding interest as too subtle and variable to appear on the universal list. LeResche (1982) identified a characteristic expression of pain with lowered brow, closed eyes, muscles around eyes contracted into a squint, and horizontally stretched, open mouth. This expression can probably be universally identified as well. With a little practice before a mirror, most of us could construct a prototypical face for each of the six basic emotions. Ekman and his associates argue that these emotions are genetically arranged in the nerves and muscles of all human faces and do not have to be learned. The eyebrow flash (Eibl-Eibesfeldt, 1972) and even the eye flash (Walker & Trimboli, 1983)—raising the lids without involving the brow—which are used in greetings and acknowledgments and to add emphasis to words, are universal facial expressions also.

Facial expressions, including eye movements, are the most informative nonverbal channel of communication (DePaulo, Zuckerman, & Rosenthal, 1980; Ekman & Friesen, 1969). While verbal statements are more influential, especially with more cognitive communications (Noller, 1985), facial expressions are more informative than tone of voice or bodily cues (DePaulo et al., 1980). However, Ekman and Friesen (1969) argue that the greater sending capacity of the face means that it can be more effectively controlled by the individual and less subject to leaking information about emotions and deception unintentionally. In fact, Zuckerman, DePaulo, and Rosenthal (1981) reviewed several studies on detecting deception and found that subjects were least effective in detecting lies when they received facial information only. Subjects were slightly more effective when they saw the body (except for the face) and much more effective when they only heard speech. Interestingly, subjects were more effective at detecting lies when they saw the body, heard the speech, and did not see the face than when they received information from all three channels. Apparently, seeing the face distracted the subjects and gave them misleading cues about the truthfulness of the statements.

The only facial behaviors that liars exhibit more than honest people are blinking and dilated eyes (DePaulo, Stone, & Lassiter, 1985). Several verbal cues are associated with lying: more negative statements, more irrelevant information, and less verbal "immediacy" (here and now, personal, direct statements). Vocal cues related to lying include higher pitch, more speech hesitations and errors, and shorter responses. A bodily cue strongly associated with lying was more self-adaptors (touching one's own body with hand). Although those trying to detect deception believed that liars looked less and smiled less at their questioners and shifted postures more, there is no evidence that liars act in those ways more than people telling the truth.

Men and women act and react differently to facial expressions. Many studies have demonstrated that women are better than men at decoding nonverbal cues (cf. Fugita, Harper, & Wiens, 1980; Hall, 1978). However, women rely on facial channel information more than men do; men use the vocal channel more often (Noller, 1980). Because of this difference in focus, women's decoding advantage over men disappears when they are trying to decode deceptive communications as nonfacial channels become more prominent (Rosenthal & DePaulo, 1979). Rosenthal and DePaulo (1979) argue that women follow a politeness strategy and purposely do not attend to the leakier channels (body and tone of voice) where deceptiveness might be unintentionally betrayed. Apparently, women also send deceptive messages facially more than men do because detection of lies told by women only occurs reliably when their faces are visible (DePaulo et al., 1985). It must be that women do not hide the emotions in the face as often as men.

Smiles have been regarded as a major component of facial expression (Ekman et al., 1972). Smiles have also been studied as a means for a listener to communicate positive reactions to a speaker (Duncan & Fiske, 1977; Rosenfeld, 1967). Kraut and Johnston (1979) examined the intriguing question of whether the smile is basically a response of happiness or a means of maintaining friendly contact. To examine this question, they observed people behaving as they experienced success, which should evoke a happy response, or as they interacted with friends, which should evoke a social response. They observed bowlers facing the pins after a successful ball (a strike or a spare)—the observer was actually behind the pins with binoculars—and while returning to their companions in the pit.

Figure 10.7
*Being in a social
interaction unit and
observing a good
outcome for one's
team produced more
smiling among hockey
fans. The social unit
effect was slightly
stronger than outcome
effect.*
(From Kraut & Johnston, 1979,
Journal of Personality and Social
Psychology, 37, 1546.)

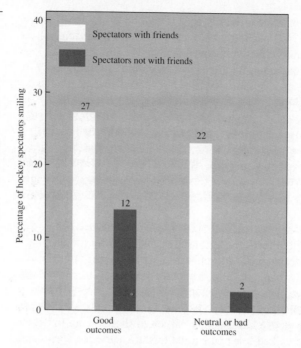

They took photos of Cornell hockey fans right after favorable, unfavorable, or neutral events occurred for the Cornell team on the ice. They also classified whether or not these fans were in a social unit from the photographs. (See figure 10.7.) In another study, they observed people who were or were not involved in social interactions as they walked outside on pleasant and unpleasant days. Bowlers rarely smiled while facing the pins, but they smiled often while facing their friends. Fans smiled both after the team's successes and as they were engaged in conversation. (See figure 10.8.) Pedestrians smiled while they were interacting with others and did not smile much when they were not interacting regardless of the weather. Except for the hockey study, these results point to the smile as a social response, rather than an emotional one. However, Kraut and Johnston acknowledge that there are different kinds of smiles. Closed-mouth smiles are more social and open-mouth smiles reflect a more emotional reaction.

Body Movements and Postures

What does it mean when a person slumps back in a chair rather than sitting upright or leaning forward? What does it mean when a person is constantly fidgeting, touching his or her body or clothing? These questions about body movements and postures have been examined by several psychologists.

Mehrabian (1972) found that relaxed backwards or sideways leaning body postures were associated with higher status or greater dominance in an interaction. He also implicated asymmetrical leg and arm positions as indicators of dominance. Conversely, the upright, symmetrical, attentive posture was associated with lower status in the interaction.

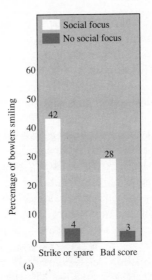

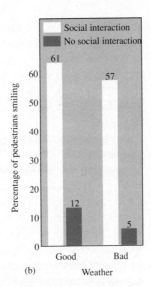

Figure 10.8
Smiling is a social response. (a) Getting a strike or spare did not evoke more smiles from bowlers but interacting with friends did.
(b) Likewise, pleasant weather did not evoke more smiles from pedestrians, but interacting with friends did.
(From Kraut & Johnston, 1979, Journal of Personality and Social Psychology, 37.)

Forward lean and a face-to-face orientation are behaviors that communicate even greater *immediacy* or involvement in interactions (Mehrabian, 1972). Trout and Rosenfeld (1980) found that forward lean led to the judgment of greatest rapport between clients and therapists presented to observers on videotape. Congruent body positions where the arm and leg positions of one participant were the carbon copy or mirror image of the others' positions also contributed to perceptions of perceived rapport. Harrigan, Oxman, and Rosenthal (1985) found supportive evidence through observations in a natural setting. They found that family practice doctors who established good rapport with patients exhibit more forward lean while interacting with patients than did doctors with poorer bedside manners.

As mentioned previously, liars make more frequent body-focused movements or self-adaptors (touching body or clothing with hand or hands) than those who tell the truth (DePaulo et al., 1985). These results might lead us to believe that these self-touches indicate nervousness or situational anxiety. There are other studies that substantiate this conclusion. Barroso, Freedman, and Grand (1980) found that taking the Stroop color test, which is known to induce stress, elicited more frequent body-focused hand movements than the control condition. Kenner (1984) compared the frequency of body-focused hand movements by 10 one-year-olds during rest, a mental arithmetic task, and a taped talk. He found that these movements occurred twice as often during the talk as during the other two conditions, which were not different from each other. LeCompte (1981) studied self-touching durations by people in stressful and nonstressful settings in Turkey. The stressful settings included hospital waiting rooms and a study room before an exam; the nonstressful settings included parks and theater foyers. In two large observational studies, people in stressful settings touched themselves on the face or body more than people in nonstressful settings. One interesting sidelight was that nonsmokers in stressful settings had higher hand-body contact rates than smokers did. It is unclear whether that occurred because smokers had one less hand with which to touch themselves (one was occupied holding the cigarette) or because smoking relaxed them. In one study, people in stressful settings smoked more than those in nonstressful situations, but that relationship did not occur in the other study. Most of us would assume that people would smoke more in stressful conditions than in unstressful ones, but that was not a stable finding in this research.

Preening behavior is a type of self-touch that is not associated with anxiety or nervousness. *Preening* is behavior aimed at making one's appearance more attractive and is interpreted as a sign of courtship readiness or interest (Scheflen, 1965). A study done in restrooms of restaurants and bars in Austin, Texas, measured the time spent preening (grooming hair, straightening clothes, and looking at oneself in mirror) by women and men (Daly, Hogg, Sacks, Smith, & Zimring, 1980). After one observer recorded the behavior, another person asked subjects who was with them in a questionnaire. If the person was accompanied by a spouse or a close friend, that person spent much less time preening than if he or she was out with someone for the first or second time. There was a direct relationship between familiarity of the relationship and preening time. This result is another illustration that settings and relationships between interactants influence a great deal of our nonverbal behavior.

Applications of Communication Research

Some nonverbal behaviors indicate how others react to us and are potentially applicable in understanding our relationships. All indicators of immediacy—close distance, high eye contact, forward lean (if seated), face-to-face orientation, and pleasant facial expression—vary with the *relationship* and the *setting*. Consequently, they may be useful signs of others' feelings toward us. Hall's (1966) personal space distances are useful guidelines in that regard. In another book, Hall (1959) indicated that the time other people spend interacting with us is a sign of their respect or esteem. If a person makes us wait a long time to see him or her or spends very little time with us, it indicates disregard.

Nonverbal analyses of a person's actions can be useful in other contexts too. During the summer of 1988, the Boston Herald asked me to go to a rally attended by Michael Dukakis, John Glenn, and Howard Metzenbaum to see if Dukakis' nonverbal signs indicated that Senator Glenn would be his vice presidential choice. Despite some reservations, I went to the rally and observed Dukakis' actions and reactions to the presence and mentions of John Glenn closely. My report to the paper was that, based on some forced smiles and half-hearted expressive gestures by Dukakis toward Glenn, "If Governor Dukakis has made a vice presidential choice (covertly), John Glenn is certainly not that choice (Dickson, Boston Herald, July 2, 1988, p. 1)." So, close observation and analysis of nonverbal behaviors may be useful in many public settings.

Being able to communicate one's feelings, needs, and aspirations to significant others in one's life has been recognized as important to mental health (Jourard, 1971; Mowrer, 1968). Jourard indicated that people who are unwilling

Michael Dukakis's nonverbal actions at this meeting indicate that John Glenn was not his vice presidential choice.

to reveal information about themselves not only conceal themselves from others, but they cannot attain the full understanding of themselves that others' reactions and two-way communication would provide. Mowrer suggests that revealing personal feelings to intimate others especially reduces tension and keeps negative feelings from building. Ideally, assertiveness is one way to communicate one's feelings and needs positively and inoffensively. Assertive communications are direct messages about our needs and desires presented to appropriate persons, and they should be useful in preventing and correcting misunderstandings.

Pennebaker (1989; Pennebaker, Hughes & O'Heeron, 1987) has offered some evidence of the mental health benefits of communication. He has demonstrated that talking about one's problems into a tape recorder—he calls it thought removal—at bedtime promotes sleep among insomniacs. Talking about previously undiscussed traumatic events has the physical health benefits of lowering one's arousal and blood pressure. On the other hand, just thinking about the painful experience and not talking causes negative physiological changes (Pennebaker & O'Heeron, 1984). Those who are high-level revealers in writing about everyday problems have fewer physical health complaints than low-level revealers do. All of these therapeutic effects stem from talking or writing about one's thoughts and feelings with minimal response and no therapeutic intervention.

The importance of communication in relationships is hard to overstate. The nature of what is communicated in close relationships will be discussed again in chapter 11. Noller (1980, 1981, 1982) has done extensive research on communication patterns between spouses. She has suggested that marital counselors should attempt to improve the communication skills of husbands because husbands' communication skills are one difference between happily married and unhappily married couples.

Applications of communication principles to persuade others and to get them to act in compliance with your wishes are discussed in chapters 7 and 8.

Husbands are less communicative than wives.

THE LOCKHORNS, by Bill Hoest. © 1987 by King Features. Reprinted by permission.

THE LOCKHORNS

"WHAT DO YOU MEAN WE DON'T COMMUNICATE? YOU'RE CERTAINLY AT LIBERTY TO WRITE ME A MEMO ANY TIME YOU HAVE SOMETHING ON YOUR MIND."

Summary

At least one sender and one receiver are required for communication to occur. Ordinarily, individuals alternate sender and receiver roles. Nonverbal channels convey the most meaning in emotional communications involving discrepant messages in different channels. However, in less emotional, consistent communications, they are less influential than the verbal channel. Forms of address and some nonverbal behaviors constitute ambiguous communications in that they may imply affection or domination. The combination of behaviors, such as interpersonal distance, eye contact, and content of conversation, imply a certain intimacy level between the interactants. Changes in implied intimacy may be welcomed with reciprocated acts or avoided with compensatory acts. Turn-taking cues, such as changes in speaking pattern, looking, and gesticulation, enable speakers and listeners to change roles comfortably.

The verbal content of messages and how much one says are both influential in communicating to audiences. Paralinguistic factors also contribute to the receiver's understanding of the message. The pitch, rate, and loudness of speech affect how messages are interpreted. Pauses filled with non-ah speech disturbances indicate that the speaker is anxious or nervous. Americans conduct different kinds of interactions at particular distances. Departures from appropriate distances make the interactants uneasy. Touching elicits positive responses from the recipient if the touch is appropriate for the setting and the relationship. Amount of direct gaze indicates the emotional intensity of the verbal message. Looking often at the listener while speaking and looking very little while listening indicate personal dominance or high status. Certain facial expressions seem to be universal within the human race. Because facial expressions can be controlled better than some other communication channels, they betray deception less than tone of voice and body movements. Relaxed body postures convey dominance. Body-focused hand movements occur more when people are in stressful situations.

Better understanding of communication can be useful in assessing relationships. Communicating more, and more accurately, can help sustain close relationships and promote mental and physical health.

Social Relations

CHAPTER 11

Interpersonal Attraction

Friends and Lovers

At the very beginning of this book, we mentioned that interpersonal relationships can be great sources of joy and anguish. In this chapter, we will present the social psychological research on relieving the anguish of negative relationships and on initiating and preserving positive relationships.

Relationship Problems: Have You Ever Been Lonely?

There is ample evidence that poor interpersonal relationships cause distress for individuals in our society. The yearly divorce rate in the United States relative to the number of marriages has been 47 percent (U.S. Bureau of the Census, 1989) or higher since 1975. That is about one divorce for every two marriages every year. These figures do not begin to tell the story of the personal anguish experienced by the spouses and children involved. For instance, there are thousands of child kidnappings by the noncustodial parents from broken relationships. Premarital and nonmarital breakups also take emotional tolls that can probably be measured in dollars and cents and productive effort lost. We have not even mentioned ongoing unsatisfactory relationships that make life miserable.

Yes, you say, but everybody picks up the pieces, new bonds are formed, and life goes on. Not everybody survives! Did you know that at least 20 to 25 percent of all murders every year in the U.S. involves one family member killing another? The assault rate among family members is even higher (Federal Bureau of Investigation, 1986). A student once told me that she had to miss class to attend the funeral of a high school friend. He had been helping his mother remove a refrigerator from the family home when his father arrived and shot him on the front porch. Spouse abuse and child abuse are so common that they now have names and social service organizations addressing them where none existed before.

Loneliness and Shyness

Social psychologists have been investigating two conditions, loneliness (Middlebrook, 1980; Peplau & Perlman, 1979; Perlman & Peplau, 1982) and shyness (Jones, Cheek & Briggs, 1986; Zimbardo, 1977), which are closely linked with inadequate interpersonal relationships. According to these authors, nearly all of us have felt lonely and/or shy at some time in our lives. **Loneliness** is an emotional reaction (1) to being unable to establish close relationships with others, (2) to being unable to communicate hopes and fears to those you feel close to and receive an adequate response, and (3) to being separated from friends and loved ones.

Shyness, on the other hand, suggests anxiety and reluctance in initiating interactions with others. When people are shy, they talk and smile very little, avoid eye contact, show few facial expressions, and they respond slowly in conversations (Cheek & Buss, 1981). Shy people are perceived as relatively unfriendly, unassertive, nervous, and tense in initial conversations with strangers. Zimbardo (1977) has implied that overcoming the reluctance to start interactions leads to interpersonal successes and reduces the anxiety of shyness in the future. He has recommended some social skills training exercises initially involving low risk and low self-consciousness to overcome shyness. For instance, one might be encouraged to make an impersonal phone call to a stranger in a

Relationships affect us: "One is the loneliest number . . ."

formal role (e.g., calling an apartment manager about rates and accommodations) in early training. It should be remembered that shyness is a transient feeling that only occurs in some situations interacting with certain kinds of people. If one can reduce the number of situations and the number of people who elicit anxiety, she or he is coping with shyness.

One might expect that people who are shy most of the time are usually lonely. That would be true unless the shy person has mentally adjusted to having few close interactions. The experience of loneliness occurs only when and where one's desired level of interaction is greater than his or her attained level of interaction (Peplau & Perlman, 1979). One recent investigation (Solano, Batten, & Parish, 1982) has shown that lonely people display some of the characteristics of shy people. That is, lonely people disclose less personal information about themselves to opposite-sex friends than nonlonely people do, and they use inappropriate levels (too intimate or too impersonal) of self-disclosure in initial interactions. Scores on the UCLA Loneliness Scale (Russell, Peplau, & Cutrona, 1980) and Mehrabian's (1970) Affiliative Tendencies Scale, which measures nonshy tendencies, are negatively correlated ($r = -.452$; Russell et al., 1980), indicating shy people are lonely and vice versa.

Middlebrook (1980) indicates that extremely lonely people may become depressed and suicidal. Many of us are familiar with suicides and suicide attempts of people rejected by a loved one or family member, or a person who has lost a close relationship through death or other circumstances. These acts are additional instances in which unsatisfactory interpersonal relationships cause distress for people. It is not an overstatement to say that relationship problems have caused more and longer human suffering than heart disease. If social psychological research can shed light on interpersonal relationships and indicate ways to make them better, it would be a service to all of us.

The Study of
Interpersonal
Attraction

Certainly, people do not want investigators meddling in their interpersonal affairs. Protection of individuals and their relationships is a legitimate concern. There have been instances in which the observation and study of relationships may have harmed the relationships. For instance, Rubin and Mitchell (1976) have reported that having both the man and the woman of dating couples complete extensive questionnaires and answer interview questions separately and confidentially had substantial impact on their relationships. Apparently, participating in the study and, in many cases, discussing it with their partners outside the study setting affected participants' perceptions of each other and their relationships and changed the development of relationships in positive and negative ways. Since many marriage therapists conduct joint interviews with couples and provide feedback about their partner's perceptions to the couples, Rubin and Mitchell's confidential procedures appear to constitute minimal meddling. One might also argue that it is beneficial for dating couples to discover how compatible they are before making long-term commitments. Nevertheless, Rubin and Mitchell suggest that ethical standards require that the researchers offer premarital counseling for the couples as well as discussing the possible impact of their participation.

Such ethical issues limit how interpersonal attraction research can be conducted. Research on existing couples is usually limited to self-report, correlational studies, such as Zick Rubin's (1970) early research to distinguish liking and loving. Less typical because of their possible intrusiveness in the relationship are observations in a natural setting, such as Christensen's (1979) time-sampled audio recording of family interactions in the kitchen and family room and structured observations, such as Raush, Barry, Hertel, and Swain's (1974) observations of couples working on conflict-resolution tasks. The experimental study of relationships in the sense of randomly assigning certain individuals to date and mate specific other individuals is obviously not ethical.

The many experimental studies of interpersonal attraction in this chapter usually investigate interaction processes that foster attraction. Experimental studies are simplified and controlled using operations and situations investigators hope are analogous to real-life situations. These studies also typically involve interactions among strangers meeting for the first time or no true interaction at all. Levinger and Snoek (1972) have argued that such artificial aspects of these experiments make them virtually useless in understanding relationship development. Proponents of experimental research counterargue that these core variables must be teased out of their complex natural circumstances, isolated, and investigated under simpler conditions if we are going to understand them.

Friends, Lovers,
and Family

Attraction researchers have defined interpersonal **attraction** as one person's positive or negative *attitude* toward another person (cf. Hendrick & Hendrick, 1983). Too often the difference between liking and loving is obscured by this approach. A prevalent assumption is that if a process or a condition has a particular effect on feelings between strangers or friends, it will have the same effect between potential lovers. Also, if it works that way early in a relationship, it will work that way 20 years into the relationship. I disagree. As indicated by the chapter title, we will consider attraction among friends and attraction among lovers as being different in many ways. Of course, some factors affect both types of attraction the same way. *Friendship* is conceived as attraction not involving sexual interest or behavior. *Love* is conceived as attraction involving sexual interest and/or behavior (K. Davis, 1985). If a factor affects friendship and love similarly, that factor will be presented in the section on friendship.

Another form of attraction is attraction between members of a family other than spouses (e.g., sister-sister, mother-son) which we will refer to as the kinship or sociobiological bond. Sociobiologists (Wilson, 1975) imply that kinship bonds should be strongest among those who are most alike genetically. For example, identical twins should be more attracted to each other than cousins are. All other things being equal, attraction is greater between same-sex siblings than opposite-sex siblings and between siblings closer in age than those more distant in age (Koch, 1960). Tesser (1980, 1985) indicates that a person's sibling's relative performance level, the relevance of the sibling's performance to the person's self-esteem, and closeness in age and proximity between the two siblings affects sibling attraction. There has been very little attraction research done on kinship bonds, so it will not be discussed further here.

Friendship

The study of factors that affect friendship can be divided into the study of ways of behaving that will endear one person to another and the study of attributes or characteristics of persons that will endear. We will discuss endearing behaviors first.

Social Rewards

Learning research has taught us that if a behavior of a bird, rat, or person is followed by an event pleasurable to that organism (e.g., getting food), the organism is likely to repeat the behavior (Skinner, 1938). So, if Sue talks to Mary and Mary says or does something that Sue regards positively, Sue will probably talk to Mary again. If Mary also regards Sue's reactions as pleasant, a friendship will probably ensue. Skinner has also shown us that conditions or situations can be arranged so that the initial behavior will be emitted so it can be reinforced and shaped. Bandura's (cf. Bandura, 1977b) work on observational learning and imitation indicates that showing a person someone else doing the behavior can provoke the initial behavior. Skinner has also taught us that if some person or condition is associated with a primary reinforcer (e.g., food), that person or condition will become a secondary reinforcer. A *secondary reinforcer* is any person, condition, or event that has become rewarding or pleasurable by itself so that its presence will now increase the rate of a behavior that it follows. If a person is a secondary reinforcer for us, we are said to like him or her. Lott and Lott (1960) demonstrated that people like individuals who are associated with their being rewarded, even when those individuals are not the source of the reward or in any way enable them to get the reward. However, providing the reward or helping a person get the reward would make that person more attracted to you.

Byrne and Clore (1970) have presented a reinforcement-affect model of attraction that is based on classical conditioning concepts. They contend that a positive event (the unconditioned stimulus in classical conditioning) elicits a positive feeling (the unconditioned response) in the person. Likewise, a negative or unpleasant event serves as an unconditioned stimulus for negative reactions. A person, originally a neutral stimulus in the classical conditioning paradigm, will become a conditioned stimulus for positive feelings if he or she is paired with the positive event. As a result, people come to like individuals who are associated with positive or rewarding events and to dislike those associated with negative events. Kaplan and Anderson (1973) see shortcomings in this classical conditioning approach. They argue that events and descriptions associated with a person provide positive or negative information about the person. In their view, we like people more if most important information about them is positive.

The upshot of both of these reward theories of attraction is that we should provide rewards or be associated with rewards to people we want to like us. So, if we bought someone a ticket to an enjoyable concert or shared a pleasant experience, such as sailing with someone (even if we didn't provide the boat), she or he should like us more. The problem in creating such conditions is knowing what is rewarding to the particular individual in particular situations (Aronson, 1969). Arnold Buss (1983) has attempted to identify what the primary social rewards are. In doing so, he expands on Foa and Foa's (1974) six interpersonal reinforcers categories: money, goods, services, information, love, and status. All of these resources could constitute rewards in the theories discussed previously, but Buss regards the first four as economic rewards and considers love and status as the only true social rewards. Buss (1983) makes a distinction between process rewards and content rewards. **Process rewards** occur naturally and are part of the process of social interactions. **Content rewards,** on the other hand, are particular responses that one person can offer another. According to Buss, others can provide process social rewards by (1) their presence, (2) paying attention to you, (3) responding or reacting to you, and (4) initiating a social interaction with you. There is a catch; if these process social rewards become excessive, they will be unrewarding and aversive. At some times and in some situations, a person can have too many people too close to him or her; too much attention can be focused on him or her; the responses can be stronger than expected or desired; or a social interaction can be intrusive.

Buss's content social rewards are elaborations of Foa and Foa's love and status categories. They are, from least to most intense: deference, praise, sympathy, and affection. Generally, these content social rewards cannot become excessive and be aversive, but the expression of sympathy and affection is appropriate only with those who are already at least good friends. Homans (1961, 1974) has also indicated conditions under which social actions will be more or less rewarding. Social actions will be less rewarding to the recipient if the actor has done them for the recipient many times recently. The more scarce a social activity is, the more rewarding it is. The harder a person has worked for a particular social reward recently, the less likely he or she will work for the same reward again soon.

Working too hard for approval saps the meaning from any approval received.

Reprinted by permission of UFS, Inc.

Ingratiation

E. E. Jones (Jones, 1964; Jones & Pittman, 1982; Jones & Wortman, 1973) has demonstrated some social actions that are likely to be rewarding to the recipient and increase attraction to the actor. Ingratiating behaviors, as Jones refers to them, are designed to make the ingratiator more attractive to the target person of the acts. Jones and Wortman (1973) indicate that ingratiating acts are likely to be less endearing if the target person detects that the actor is insincere. Consequently, they suggest that people use ingratiation tactics sparingly and only in certain situations. However, Dickoff's (1961) study showed that positive evaluations of subjects led to more attraction to the evaluator even when ulterior motives were obvious. So complimenting someone may win you points even if it is obviously flattery. This is probably true because by using flattery the ingratiator shows that he or she is interested in getting on the target person's good side. Another dilemma an ingratiator faces is whether he or she wants to win approval of his or her true self or approval of the ingratiating behavior. A person who acts in an ingratiating way to gain approval does not know whether the approval is of the person (his or her unvarnished self) or of the ingratiating behavior (Kimble & Helmreich, 1972). Similarly, a person who "fishes for" a compliment will not receive a meaningful one.

Jones has studied four types of ingratiation tactics: (1) complimentary other-enhancement, (2) self-presentation, (3) opinion conformity, and (4) rendering favors. *Complimentary other-enhancement* is often called flattery or some other, more negative, term. It usually involves building the other person up by saying positive things about him or her. Implausible compliments are usually ineffective. Jones and Wortman (1973) indicate that if a person can establish him- or herself as a discerning, knowledgeable judge, rather than a consistent flatterer; then that person's compliments will carry more weight. Salespeople appear to be at a distinct disadvantage in establishing their compliments as sincere. If you don't believe that, note your reaction the next time a salesman remarks on your obvious intelligence or good looks. One way a person could make his or her compliments more effective is to know the target person's aspirations and praise the target person on those characteristics. Kleinke, Staneski, and Weaver's (1972) study suggests that another way is to address the target person by name at appropriate times and not in excess. Indirect compliments, such as positive comments about one's alma mater, one's favorite sports team, musical idol, or children, should be particularly effective.

Self-presentation is a strategy by which one presents one's characteristics and abilities in a favorable light. In a recent theoretical review (Jones & Pittman, 1982), this tactic was called self-promotion and was presented as a self-presentation category separate from ingratiation. Self-promoters try to project competence, while ingratiators try to demonstrate likability. However, since successfully projecting competence may win you affection as well as respect, self-presentation is being included with ingratiation strategies as Jones and his associates did earlier. The optimum way of presenting oneself also depends on the target person's perspective. It would be best to emphasize your hard-working nature to some potential employers, but other employers would be most impressed by your easy-going disposition. It is important to know the values of the people you are trying to impress. Jones, Gergen, Gumpert, and Thibaut (1965) found that when they varied the personal values of a supervisor with whom subjects were working, subjects did present themselves in ways congruent with the supervisor's values. Positive self-presentation can be achieved by means other than bragging. Displaying good taste in attire, friends, music, art, or general demeanor in the target person's presence may be more subtle and effective ways to present one's positive characteristics. Having someone else highlight your accomplishments to the target person should also be quite effective (Jones & Pittman, 1982). In general, modest, even self-deprecating, presentations are very effective if the target person already knows about your virtues.

Opinion conformity is the tactic by which the ingratiator agrees with the target person. Byrne (1971) and others have demonstrated that people like others who agree with them more than those who disagree. Anyone who seeks to gain favor can use this information to improve his or her position. Presidential aides (e.g., Reedy, 1970) have commented that presidents have a particularly difficult time finding appointees and other subordinates who will openly and honestly disagree with them on issues. Such yea-sayers certainly contribute to the unwise, ill-considered decisions presidential cabinet groups sometimes make (Janis, 1972). Jones, Gergen, and Jones (1963) indicate that subordinates who want to gain favor do not and should not agree on everything with their superiors. In a study involving Navy ROTC officers and subordinates, they found that the lower-status subjects agreed more with their superiors on "important" items and disagreed with them on "unimportant" items. These subjects apparently wanted to increase their credibility by showing that they weren't undiscerning "yes-men" to their superiors.

Performing favors for someone is Jones and Wortman's last major ingratiation tactic. They show evidence that the recipient must perceive that the favor was intended to benefit the recipient (Greenberg & Frisch, 1972), that the favor was appropriate to the situation and the relationship (Schopler & Thompson, 1968), and that the favor-doer doesn't have ulterior motives in order for the recipient to like the favor-doer more. That is, favors can be such obvious attempts to curry favor that they can be ineffective in gaining attraction. Also, they may make the recipient feel so obligated to return the favor that they dislike the favor-doer.

Asking someone to do a favor for you may be a more effective way of gaining that person's esteem than performing favors for him or her. There is an anecdote about Benjamin Franklin that describes how he gained a friend by asking that person to do a favor for him (Rosenzweig, 1972). Apparently, Franklin was not on civil speaking terms with a fellow member of the Pennsylvania Assembly. After their relationship had gone on this way for some time, Franklin approached the man to ask him if he could see a rare book that the man had in his personal library. The man agreed to do the favor and lent Franklin the book. Thereafter, the man was much friendlier to Franklin. Why would such a request have so positive an effect on their relationship? Perhaps it communicated to the man that Franklin knew the man had a valuable resource that Franklin did not have and that Franklin trusted the man to share the resource. How would this relate to other favor-asking, such as asking for directions or asking someone to help you study? There has been one study derived from cognitive dissonance theory that examined the effects of favor-asking on attraction. Jecker and Landy (1969) found that when an experimenter asked subjects to do a small favor for him, the subjects liked him more than subjects who had not been asked to do the favor. There are still many questions to be answered about this area and other aspects of ingratiation.

Self-Disclosure

Exchanging personal information with another person can be mutually rewarding to both parties and is an important element of friendship development. Altman and Taylor's (1973) social penetration theory suggests that self-disclosure between close friends covers more topics and is more intimate than self-disclosure between more casual acquaintances. The kinds and amounts of self-relevant information being exchanged affect the closeness of relationships and is not just the product of the relationships (Kimble, 1972, 1974). Kimble (1972, 1974) contends that if a casual acquaintance discloses information about her- or himself (or initiates other approach behavior) that is appropriate for the next closer acquaintanceship level or "friend" and that disclosure is reciprocated, soon both parties will perceive themselves as friends and behave accordingly. In my view, friendship usually progresses through different levels as one person violates the norm for the current level by self-disclosing at the next closer level and the other person accepts the closer level by reciprocating disclosure. If two people have many opportunities to interact and they continue to interact at the same level, their relationship will stagnate at that level whether the level is "speaking strangers" or "close friends."

Derlega and Chaikin (1975) described **self-disclosure** as the process by which one lets oneself be known by another person, either verbally or nonverbally. Jourard (1971) contended that self-disclosure is important to mental health, and Rogers (1959) suggests it is especially therapeutic when the recipient is accepting of the self-disclosure. Chelune (1975) has characterized the basic features of self-disclosure by the (1) amount, (2) intimacy, (3) duration, (4) affective manner of presentation, and (5) flexibility of disclosure patterns. The flexibility of disclosure is typically assessed by examining the variability of disclosure due to different experimental conditions. To evaluate the other four features validly requires that the investigator collect at least audiotapes, and preferably videotapes, of live disclosures. A typed script of the disclosures would allow an investigator only to assess the amount of disclosure validly. The intimacy of self-disclosure is typically the most important measure of disclosure. Jourard (1973) and Taylor and Altman (1966) have scaled many topical statements for intimacy for use in self-report questionnaires about past disclosures. Morton (1978) has developed a two-dimensional intimacy scoring system. Self-disclosures can be low or high in descriptive intimacy, which is defined by the privacy of facts presented about oneself, and in evaluative intimacy, which is defined by the depth of emotion, judgment, and opinion one expresses. So, disclosure statements can be judged to be high in intimacy by independent raters by virtue of expressing very private facts or by expressing one's anxieties or affections. Besides these two dimensions, judgments about disclosure intimacy are probably affected by the following variables:

1. The topic discussed (implied by Taylor & Altman's 1966 scales) with sexual practices being judged more intimate than hobbies,
2. The negativity of the disclosures with one's suicidal feelings being judged more intimate than the exhileration experienced when the Detroit Tigers won the World Series,
3. The time of the conditions with disclosure of current problems being judged more intimate than disclosure of past, now solved problems.

The most consistent finding in self-disclosure experiments, even those involving strangers, is that if one person discloses at a particular level of intimacy, his or her partner will reciprocate by disclosing at the same level (Cozby, 1972; Ehrlich & Graeven, 1971; Jourard & Jaffe, 1970; Worthy, Gary, & Kahn, 1969). Many investigators (Cozby, 1972; Levin & Gergen, 1969) have expected that when a stranger disclosed at a high intimacy level, the other subject in the experiment would not reciprocate at such a high level. However, these studies have uniformly obtained the reciprocity effect at all levels. Why? Lynn (1978) has demonstrated that disclosure reciprocity in experiments may occur because the first discloser sets a standard for appropriate disclosure in an ambiguous situation and the second discloser follows it. Also, the first discloser creates a demand for equal disclosure through an equitable exchange norm that most people follow in conversations. The knowledge that one is participating in a psychological study may also make second disclosers likely to reciprocate earlier disclosures because they think personal disclosures are expected in such studies (Rubin, 1975).

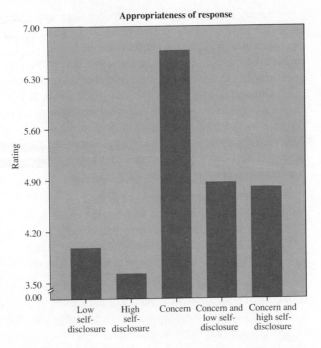

Appropriateness of response

Figure 11.1
*Expressing concern
was seen as the most
appropriate response
rather than
reciprocating self-
disclosure to the first
speaker.*
(From Berg & Archer, 1980,
Journal of Personality, 48, 252.)

There is at least one study that suggests that if disclosures occurred outside a structured setting, the first listener might not self-disclose at all. Berg and Archer (1980) did not study naturally occurring self-disclosures; instead, they had subjects read disclosures and rate the appropriateness of the first listener's response. The first speaker made a low self-disclosure comment, ". . . everyone is so into getting drunk . . . that's all some friends talk about," or a high self-disclosure comment, ". . . everyone is so into getting drunk . . . my father is leaving my mother because she's an alcoholic." The listener responded with the following statements:

1. Low self-disclosure, "I've just left a really interesting class . . . if I keep my grades up. . . ."
2. High self-disclosure, "I'm really strung out. My boyfriend just broke off with me . . . It's really hard. . . ."
3. Concern, "I'm really sorry. It's probably hard for you to concentrate on your work and stuff, isn't it? . . . I'd sure be willing to listen. . . ."
4. Concern followed by low self-disclosure
5. Concern followed by high self-disclosure.

As the accompanying figure 11.1 shows, the subjects who read the disclosures regarded the expression of concern as the most appropriate, regardless of the initial disclosure.

These results suggest that in real-life conversations self-disclosures are seldom reciprocated immediately. In fact, when one of our masters thesis students (Opeil, 1976) had a confederate make self-disclosures in a "spontaneous" conversation, subjects seldom self-disclosed in return. Instead, they typically asked questions to get the confederate to elaborate on her experiences.

Deborah Davis's work (Davis, 1982; Davis & Perkowitz, 1979) on responsiveness is pertinent to these self-disclosure phenomena and to interpersonal attraction in general. Davis and Perkowitz (1979) found that people who were responsive to their interaction partner's comments were liked better than those who were not. Davis (1982) states that communicative behaviors carry with them the following implicit demands for response:

1. The other person must respond
2. The response must address the content of the preceding communication of the other interactant
3. The response must represent the appropriate degree of elaboration (e.g., one word or an extended discourse)

Except for the concern condition, all of Berg and Archer's responses were unresponsive because they included comments irrelevant to the first communicator's statements. Responsiveness is probably the important factor underlying the perception that the concern response was most appropriate. It is also probably the reason that Opeil's (1976) subjects asked the confederate questions about her statements rather than interjecting irrelevant comments of their own. Reacting responsively is one way to provide a social reward to one's interaction partner according to Buss's (1983) system and is an aspect of behavior that endears one to that person.

There are studies which indicate that friends do disclose more personal information to each other more than strangers do (Rubin & Schenker, 1977; Taylor, 1968). Rubin and Schenker found that the closer the friendship among dormitory inhabitants, the more intimate were the disclosures they had exchanged. However, Altman (1972) theorized that the demand for reciprocity of disclosure is probably stronger early in a relationship than it is later. Apparently, people in established relationships can take longer balancing the books on disclosure than those who are more tenuously related. Derlega, Wilson, and Chaikin (1976) confirmed this reasoning in a laboratory study in which they had friends and strangers exchange self-disclosures in writing. They recruited one of the friends of each pair as a confederate to write either a low- or high-intimacy disclosure message to be given to her partner. They also used these messages written by such confederates as the messages given by one stranger to another. This method enabled them to make the messages credible among friends and to ensure that the same message content was exchanged in both types of pairs. They found that strangers matched the intimacy level that they received, but that friends did not. (See figure 11.2.) It is possible that friends thought they could always get even later, and did not disclose before a third party (the experimenter). Morton (1978) also found that spouses do not reciprocate disclosure intimacy immediately. (See figure 11.3.) Both studies support Altman's idea that immediate reciprocity is unimportant in established relationships.

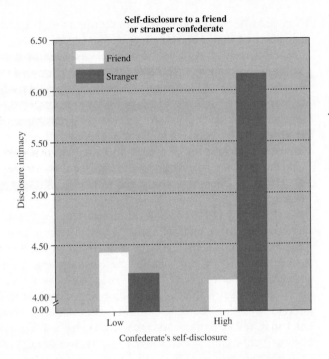

**Self-disclosure to a friend
or stranger confederate**

Figure 11.2
*Strangers disclosed
back to the
confederate at the
same level he or she
had first disclosed, but
friends did not
reciprocate the high
self-disclosures.*

*(From Derlega, Wilson, & Chaikin,
1976,* Journal of Personality and
Social Psychology, 34, 581.)

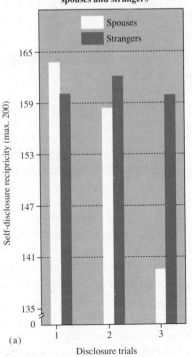

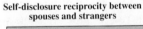

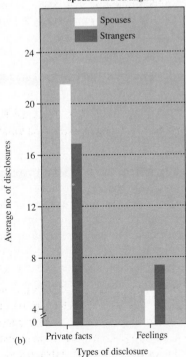

Figure 11.3
*(a) Spouses
reciprocated self-
disclosure much less in
later conversation, but
strangers followed the
reciprocity norm
throughout the
conversation.
(b) Spouses stated
private facts more in
self-disclosure;
strangers expressed
emotional feelings
more.*

(From Morton, 1978, Journal of
Personality and Social Psychology,
36, 77.)

Nonverbal Behaviors

There are also nonverbal behaviors that promote friendship. Mehrabian (1972) has indicated that a cluster of nonverbal behaviors communicate "immediacy" and are perceived positively by recipients. *Immediacy* behaviors include assuming a close position to one's interaction partner, leaning toward the other person, making a high degree of eye contact, assuming a direct, face-to-face body orientation, and touching or reaching toward the other person. All of these behaviors communicate a positive reaction toward the other person in ordinary conversation. Both Argyle and Dean's (1965) intimacy equilibrium model and Patterson's (1976) arousal model, presented in chapter 10, concerning nonverbal behaviors and interpersonal emotional reactions suggest that any of these behaviors can be done excessively and would be offensive in some friendship situations.

Rosenfeld (1966) took an interesting and different approach in studying nonverbal behavior and attraction. He told one member of same-sex dyads to imagine that they were attracted to their partner and wanted to get him or her to like them or to imagine that they were not attracted to their partner and wanted to get him or her to dislike them. Then, he observed these approval-seeking and approval-avoiding subjects as they interacted with a naive partner. Relative to approval-avoiding subjects, approval-seekers smiled more, made fewer negative head nods, talked more, made more utterances of acknowledgment or recognition such as "um-humm," and women approval-seekers made more hand and arm gestures. Approval-avoiders minimized conversation and acknowledged their partner's existence and actions as little as possible. You may recognize that as the "cold shoulder." The approval-seeking results indicate some ways that we typically behave nonverbally to promote friendship.

Proximity

Nearness, not absence, makes the heart grow fonder. Proximity, at least, makes it possible for attraction to grow stronger. The most prominent study of the effects of proximity on attraction in social psychology was conducted by Festinger, Schachter, and Back (1950) among MIT married student housing residents. When these residents were asked to indicate their three best friends, they most often chose next-door neighbors, then neighbors a house away, then neighbors in the same courtyard area, and so on. For most of the residents, friendship and proximity were linearly related with closer residents being more likely to be designated as friends. Exceptions to this rule were those whose houses faced the street rather than the other houses in the courtyard. These "social isolates" had less than half as many friends in the project as did those whose houses faced the courtyard. On the more popular extreme were those residents whose houses were near entrances, exits, mailboxes, or any area where the traffic was heavy. This general finding and the two exceptions suggest that architectural arrangements that afford more opportunities for contacts and interactions increase the likelihood of making friends.

People who work closely together often become friends.

Proximity appears to operate by providing the opportunity for more interactions, which enable relationships to become closer. Acquaintanceship theory (Kimble, 1972, 1974) indicates that many interactions are necessary for a friendship to develop because it is rare for people to become much closer in a single interaction. One person may make a strong approach in order to make a big change in the relationship at once, but the other person will likely reject that overture. This probability of rejection makes people change their relationships more slowly, so many interactions are required. Milgram (Tavris, 1974) discussed one type of situation wherein many interaction opportunities did not make the relationship closer. He recounted that a barrier grew between himself and "familiar strangers" whom he saw on a daily basis at a commuter train station for many years. In this case, the many interaction opportunities that were not taken to change their acquaintanceship level may have petrified them as strangers. Each interaction opportunity that occurs without any gesture to make the relationship closer solidifies the relationship at that acquaintanceship level, whatever it may be (Kimble, 1974). That may be why longtime friends find it hard to become lovers.

One investigation (Nahemow & Lawton, 1975) studied the effect of proximity on friendship in a public housing project for middle-income families in Manhattan. The adult residents interviewed were diverse in age and race with about 36 percent elderly, 22 percent middle-aged, and 41 percent young and 50 percent black, 33 percent white, and 17 percent Puerto Rican. They found that 88 percent of the first-chosen friends lived in the same building and about half lived on the same floor as the interviewed resident. Considering all three choices by respondents, 60 percent were in the same age category, 72 percent were of the same race, and 73 percent were of the same sex. Many more of the first-chosen friends who differed from the respondent in age or race lived on the respondent's floor than did similar friends. So, proximity had a potent impact on friendship; in some cases, it overrode the tendency to make friends with people similar to us. Other investigators (Athanasiou & Yoshioka, 1973; Byrne, 1961; Caplow & Forman, 1950) have also found friends usually live nearby.

It will probably not surprise you to find that we also love those who are near. Bossard (1932) found that 45 percent of the residences reported on marriage licenses in Philadelphia were within five blocks of each other. Of course, that could only indicate that we move close to the ones we love rather than closeness contributing to love. However, Clarke (1952) found that over half of a sample of Columbus, Ohio married couples lived within 16 blocks of each other at the time of their first date, suggesting that closeness does contribute to love. It seems evident that interaction opportunities are also necessary for love to grow.

Absences, or even the anticipation of absences, affect love relationships negatively. They probably have a more negative effect on love than on friendship. This devastating effect is probably traceable to the sexual aspects of love, which are not a part of friendship. A residence hall assistant once told me that January was a particularly trying time in the freshman dormitory wings because the freshmen usually broke up with boyfriends and girlfriends back home during the Christmas break. Apparently, the semester's absence and/or events that occurred during that time made the couples aware that they had to see each other more than was possible to sustain the relationship. There doesn't seem to be any empirical research on the effects of such separations or separations during wartime, etc. Certainly, situation and relationship factors affect whether such separations break the relationship or not. It seems safe to say that long periods of absence do not make the heart grow fonder.

Similarity

As Nahemow and Lawton's (1975) study indicates, we usually make friends with people who are similar to us in many observable characteristics such as race, age, and sex. One not so visible area of similarity that has been demonstrated to affect interpersonal attraction strongly is *attitude similarity*. Newcomb (1961) studied friendship development in housing for two groups of 17 incoming students at the University of Michigan. In this longitudinal study, Newcomb found that attitude similarity did lead to stronger friendship among these men. Banikiotes, Russell, and Linden (1972) also demonstrated the effect among well-acquainted individuals. Donn Byrne (1961, 1971) and his associates demonstrated that attitude similarity causes interpersonal attraction in many laboratory studies using different subject samples, attitudes, and dependent measures. Most of these studies used a bogus stranger technique in which the subject rated his or her liking for another person based on reading the person's attitudes but without meeting, seeing, or interacting with the person. In fact, the experimenters simply made up the fictitious person's attitudes to be similar/dissimilar to the subject's attitudes. Using many different degrees of similarity between 0 and 100 percent similar, they consistently found that the greater the attitude similarity, the more attracted the subjects were to the bogus stranger. Some investigators (e.g., Wright, 1971) have questioned the validity of this research because subjects do not interact with a real person, and the only information they have about the person is his or her attitudes. Demonstrations that the effect does occur in situations involving face-to-face interactions (Banikiotes et. al., 1972; Byrne, Ervin, & Lamberth, 1970; Newcomb, 1961) gives us greater confidence in the validity of the effect.

However, there are several theories about why attitude similarity leads to attraction. Clore and Byrne (1974) have summarized the reinforcement-affect model based on classical conditioning that was described earlier. Byrne and Clore (1967) argue that having someone agree with you is reinforcing because it offers you consensual validation of your view of events in the world. Satisfaction of the need to interpret one's world correctly and to deal effectively with one's environment, which is provided by consensual validation, gives rise to positive affect (the unconditioned response). Disagreement, on the other hand, gives one information invalidating one's opinions and causes negative affect. Therefore, you like someone who agrees with you because he or she makes you more confident of the correctness of your ideas. Information integration theory (Kaplan & Anderson, 1973) gives a less tortured, but similar account for the similarity effect. Agreement simply supplies positively-valenced information and disagreement, negatively-valenced information for making a judgment. Therefore, the more agreement, the more attraction.

Other authors (Berscheid & Walster, 1969; Davis, 1981; Santee, 1976; Werner & Parmelee, 1979) contend that something other than consensual validation is involved. They contend that another person having attitudes similar to yours indicates that interactions with that person would be pleasant, so you like him or her. This explanation should hold only if the attitudes were activity-related. That is, attitudes about large parties, watching football games, dancing, or camping indicate the kinds of activities you might enjoy together, but attitudes about defense spending or the existence of life in outer space give no information about future activities. Davis (1981) found support for this theory when she found that the attitude similarity-attraction relationship was stronger when the attitudes that a bogus stranger endorsed were activity-related than when the attitudes were not. (See figure 11.4.)

Another explanation of the attitude similarity-attraction effect is that we like agreeing others because agreement, in the absence of other information, makes us believe that the others would like us. Aronson and Worchel (1966) argued that if subjects had direct information that their partner liked or disliked them, then the similarity of their attitudes would have no effect on attraction. To test this idea, they had a confederate indicate agreement or disagreement with the subject's attitudes and give a positive or a negative personal evaluation to the subject. They found that subjects liked the confederate when he or she gave a positive personal evaluation, regardless of whether he agreed with them or not. Byrne and Griffitt (1966) countered that they had never contended that personal evaluations would not also increase attraction and that the reason that Aronson and Worchel had not gotten a similarity effect was that they had not used strong enough agreement and disagreement. Byrne and Griffitt made disagreement/ agreement stronger in their study (0 percent vs. 100 percent attitude similarity) and found that evaluations did not overwhelm the effect of similarity, but both evaluations and similarity affected attraction. However, they had to acknowledge that direct personal evalutions had three times as much impact on attraction as did attitude similarity. A recent experiment (Condon & Crano, 1988) showed that a stranger's similar attitudes led subjects to infer that the stranger liked

Figure 11.4
*Attitude similarity
affected attraction
most when activity-
related topics and
values were expressed.
Similarity of attitudes
about politics or
factual information
did not increase
liking.*
(From Davis, 1981, Journal of
Personality and Social Psychology,
17, 110–113.)

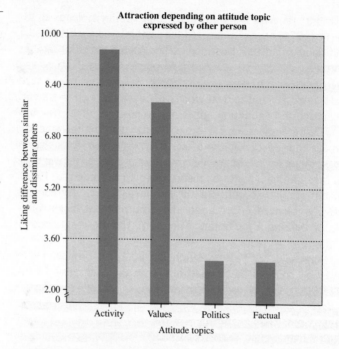

them and the inferred liking led to attraction to the stranger. Whenever attitude similarity did not produce inferred liking, the subjects were less attracted to the stranger, supporting Aronson and Worchel's position that attitude similarity has its effect through inferred liking.

Perhaps it is the expression, not just the possession, of similar attitudes which leads individuals to infer that someone likes them. Given that people seldom tell others that they like them directly, a person may infer that agreeing comments and other positive behaviors indicate liking and disagreeing comments and other negative behaviors indicate disliking. Gonzales, Davis, Loney, LuKens, and Junghaus (1983), using Byrne's bogus stranger technique, found that people do infer that strangers who agree with them would like them. Actors seem to use agreement to communicate liking and disagreement to communicate disliking rather than tell their interaction partners directly how they feel about them. Jones's (1964) work on opinion conformity as an ingratiation tactic indicates that agreement can imply liking. The active behavior of expressing one's agreement/disagreement is important in this context. If a person has an attitude, but does not express it, the attitude does not communicate anything interpersonally. Also, if a person expresses an attitude but does not know the target person's attitude, the attitude does not imply anything interpersonally. If one begins to hear a friend consistently express points of disagreement that had never been mentioned before, he or she might recognize a desire to cool the friendship. A steady stream of "you like to eat Kentucky Fried; I like Taco Bell" and "you're a Democrat; I'm a Republican" might soon be regarded as meaningful for the friendship. More research is needed in this area.

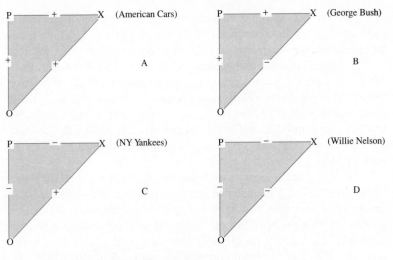

Figure 11.5
*Possible triads
illustrating balance.*

A = Balanced (Heider); positively balanced (Newcomb)

B = Imbalanced (Heider); positively imbalanced (Newcomb)

C = Balanced (Heider); nonbalanced (Newcomb)

D = Imbalanced (Heider); nonbalanced (Newcomb)

Balance theory (Heider, 1958; Newcomb, 1968) has been used to explain the attitude similarity effect also. **Balance theory** is a cognitive consistency theory that presents information from the perspective of one person, designated P. Other elements in this cognitive framework are another person, O, and any person, place, event, or concept, X. Between any two of these elements in person P's consciousness, there are positive or negative attitudes, called sentiment relations and/or ideas about whether one element belongs with or is part of another element, called unit relations. Sentiment relations have been emphasized in the balance research on interpersonal attitudes. When the three attitudes or sentiment relations among the elements are balanced, person P is in a cognitively consistent state of mind. When the three attitudes are imbalanced, person P experiences cognitive inconsistency and is motivated to change his or her attitudes. Figure 11.5 shows some possible triads to illustrate balance.

Balance Theory

Heider (1958) indicates that balance exists in any triad in which the product of the three sentiment relation signs is positive, as in the cases of American cars and the New York Yankees shown in figure 11.5. If the product is negative, imbalance exists and it exerts pressure on person P to change one of the signs to attain balance or cognitive consistency, as in the cases of George Bush and Willie Nelson in figure 11.5. Which attitude is likely to be changed may be a matter of which sentiment relation was formed first, is stronger or more polarized, and/or how many other triads a particular element is involved in. The last condition would favor keeping the P/O sentiment relation unchanged because if person O is well known to P, O is probably involved in other triads in P's thoughts.

Newcomb (1968) has made an important extension of Heider's theory. He contends that the P/O sentiment relation is primary, and if it is negative, P may be disinterested enough that an O/X sentiment relation is not formed. In Newcomb's system, triadic relationships involving positive P/O sentiment relations can be positively balanced (as in the American car triad) or positively imbalanced (as in the George Bush triad). However, triads with negative P/O sentiment relations are nonbalanced (as in the New York Yankees and Willie Nelson triads). Crano and Cooper (1973) have shown that Newcomb's distinction about P/O sentiment relations is related to the subjects' ratings of the stability of different triads.

How is balance theory used to explain the attitude similarity-attraction relationship? By using the balance theory notion that people prefer balance to imbalance and assuming you know two people's attitudes, you should be able to predict whether they will like each other. If both hold negative attitudes toward several things and positive attitudes toward several other things, such as American cars, then balance theory implies that they will like each other. If one holds negative attitudes toward certain things and the other holds positive attitudes toward those same things, such as the New York Yankees, they have dissimilar attitudes, then balance theory implies they will dislike each other. In fact, Tashakkori and Insko (1981) have characterized the P/X sentiment relation as an attitude, the O/X sentiment relation as person perception, and the P/O sentiment relation as interpersonal attraction. So, cognitive consistency considerations suggest that we should like those who agree with us.

There are definite limits to the relationship between attitude similarity and attraction. Banikiotes et. al. (1972) found that the attitude responses of best friends led to lower attraction ratings than a bogus stranger's similar attitudes did. In real life, other aspects of the person or interactions with him or her probably dilute the impact of attitude similarity. Aronson and Worchel (1966) have demonstrated that direct personal evaluations of the subject diminish the impact of similar attitudes. Folkes and Sears (1977) (see figure 11.6) have indicated another factor that can counteract attitude similarity. They have demonstrated that people like individuals who respond positively to persons, places, events, or things more than individuals who respond negatively. People who have a positive, optimistic, rosy outlook are liked more than those who don't. These positive people are liked even by those who don't share their positive outlook, i.e., people who have dissimilar attitudes. So, being positive is more important than being similar.

The role of personality similarity in friendship has been studied less than attitude similarity. However, Izard (1960, 1963) found that when freshmen were given the Edwards Personal Preference Schedule at the beginning of the year and were later asked to indicate who they liked most and disliked most, their personality profiles were more similar to those they came to like than those they disliked. Banikiotes et al. (1972) found that subjects liked those who were similar to them in extraversion-introversion and neuroticism. Hendrick and Page (1970) found that people like others who have the same level of self-esteem as they do. Demographic similarity (sex, age, race, religion, and socioeconomic status) also contributes to friendship (Byrne, Clore, & Worchel, 1966; Nahemow & Lawton,

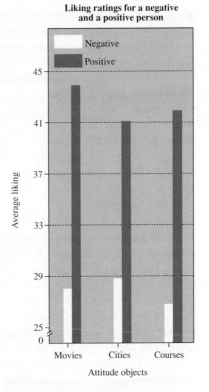

Liking ratings for a negative and a positive person

Average liking — Attitude objects (Movies, Cities, Courses)

Negative / Positive

Figure 11.6
Regardless of the topic, people who expressed positive attitudes were liked better than those who expressed negative attitudes.
(From Folkes & Sears, 1977, Journal of Personality and Social Psychology, 13, 513.)

1975), possibly because we interact with such people more. Similarity in interests, regional background, living habits, and life style are probably important in roommate compatibility. After all, "The Odd Couple" of theater and film who had incompatible living habits was always at odds!

Love

Describing Love

How is love different from friendship? Love involves sex and friendship does not. Keith Davis (1985) has identified a **passion cluster** of characteristics involved in love, but not in friendship. That cluster consists of (1) sexual desire, (2) fascination, and (3) exclusiveness of the relationship. Except for this cluster and a caring cluster, which consists of wanting to do things for and speak out for one's partner, Davis and his subjects see love as being the same as friendship. Earlier, Berscheid and Walster (Hatfield) (1974) had identified fascination or much fantasizing about the loved one as a central characteristic of love that distinguished it from liking. In fact, they say that the reason passionate love is fleeting is that reality replaces fantasy when interactions become frequent and routine so that it is difficult to conjure up one's dashing knight or fair damsel.

Tennov (1979) has attempted to capture the passion of love in her descriptions of a state of mind called **limerence.** Her account overlaps with Davis's three characteristics with additional emphasis on the intensity of feelings and the great need for the "limerent object," loved person, to reciprocate those feelings. According to Tennov, there is persistent thinking about, longing for, and idealization of the limerent object [fascination]; concoction of imagined scenarios of gratification [sexual desire]; and the inability to be limerent toward more than one person at a time [exclusiveness]. When the limerent object appears to reciprocate the feelings, the person in love feels buoyant or "on cloud nine," a reaction Buss (1973) called a boost in self-esteem. The intensity in Tennov's limerence is reminiscent of Peele and Brodsky's (1974) description of love as an *addiction* with characteristic physical reactions, such as increasing tolerance (the addict needs more love to get the same high) and withdrawal symptoms. Rubin's (1973) components of love, attachment, caring, and intimacy [exclusiveness], concentrated on Davis's care cluster and deemphasized sexual desire—perhaps it was assumed to be a given of love.

A triangular theory of love (Sternberg, 1986) indicates that love consists of three components: (1) intimacy, (2) passion, and (3) decision/commitment. **Intimacy** refers to feelings of closeness and warmth toward another person. This intimacy grows out of being able to count on the loved one, being able to communicate and self-disclose with the loved one, and experiencing happy times with the loved one. This definition of intimacy is not to be confused with sexual intimacy; rather, it is the essence of the closeness between good friends. **Passion,** on the other hand, does refer to the sexual desire component of relationships as described by Davis and Tennov. Sternberg calls passion the hot component of love, while intimacy is called the warm component of love. **Decision/commitment,** the cold component, refers to deciding that one loves another and becoming committed, sometimes through public acts such as marriage vows, to maintaining the relationship. This component is sometimes the glue that holds relationships together when intimacy and passion are at a low ebb.

Sternberg has fashioned a classification of relationships based on the presence or absence of these three components. See table 11.1. Liking, characterized by the presence of intimacy alone, was the focus of the friendship section of this chapter. The present section focuses on infatuated or passionate and romantic love, and companionate and consummate love are the focus of a later section.

Lee (1973) indicates that there are many ways to love. His six styles of love are called eros, ludus, storge, mania, pragma, and agape. An *erotic* lover expects physical attraction and sex with intense emotional involvement with the loved one. A *ludic* lover views love as a game to be played with many partners and little commitment. A *storgic* lover considers love similar to friendship with little excitement and sexual activity and a lot of shared activities and gradual building of the relationship. A *manic* lover approaches love romantically with all the attendant pathos and pain. Hendrick and Hendrick (1983) suggest that the manic lover is much like Tennov's limerent person with intense emotional swings depending on the relationship. A *pragmatic* lover is practical in wanting a compatible partner with whom a stable relationship can grow without an emotional roller coaster ride. Their style of love is like Berscheid and Walster's (1978) concept of companionate love, which many couples experience after the passion dies out. An *agapic* lover emphasizes caring for the loved one without sexuality for

Table 11.1   Taxonomy of Kinds of Love

Kind of love	Component		
	Intimacy	Passion	Decision/commitment
Nonlove	−	−	−
Liking	+	−	−
Infatuated love	−	+	−
Empty love	−	−	+
Romantic love	+	+	−
Companionate love	+	−	+
Fatuous love	−	+	+
Consummate love	+	+	+

Note: + = component present; − = component absent. These kinds of love represent limiting cases based on the triangular theory. Most loving relationships will fit between categories, because the various components of love are expressed along continua, not discretely.

From Sternberg (1986), *Psychological Review*, 93, 123.

pleasure. This is a rare love style stressing spirituality over sexuality. There was a Shaker religious society in the 1800's in the Northeast and Midwest United States which practiced agapic love with celibacy (Archer, 1985). You guessed it, the Shaker society is no more. Certainly, the sex and procreation attitudes of other religions have greater survival value for the group!

Sex roles affect how males and females interact with each other. LaFrance and Mayo (1978) state that males are expected to act in proactive ways and females are expected to act in reactive ways. That is, the male initiates activities and the female reacts to his behavior. In traditional dating situations, the boy asks and the girl accepts or rejects. Of course, that view ignores the interactions that preceded his "initiating" behavior. Wilson (1975) and other sociobiologists contend that these social roles and behaviors are dictated by biological and evolutionary factors. Sociobiologists believe that much social behavior is determined by a primary motivation of individuals to have their genes represented in future generations as much as possible. The optimal action to achieve "genetic immortality" for men would be to procreate with as many women as possible. In this view, women must be selective because time lost during pregnancies and childrearing and limited reproductive years mean that they can have few children. So, women must select mates who will probably produce hardy, healthy, surviving children. This primitive view ignores the fact that a stable family environment probably increases the survivability of the next generation. It also ignores the fact that more people these days are not so genetically motivated, having no or few children.

    Whatever the reason, males and females do act differently when they interact with each other. Abbey (1982) has shown a sex difference that has grown out of the different sex roles and expectations about behavior of women and men.

Sex Roles and Love

Figure 11.7
Men rated the same actions by the same female actor as more promiscuous and seductive than women did.

(From Abbey, 1982, Journal of Personality and Social Psychology, 42, 834.)

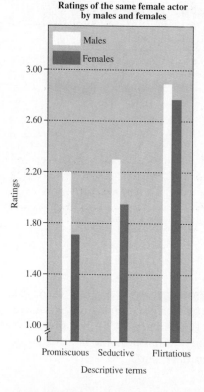

Ratings of the same female actor by males and females

She found that men are more likely to misinterpret women's friendliness as sexual or courtship interest than women are to misinterpret men's friendly behavior. (See figure 11.7.) You might want to discuss the validity of those observations with friends and discuss how these misinterpretations are related to sex roles and interpersonal behaviors.

Recent research (Muehlenhard & Hollabaugh, 1988) suggests that the traditional sexual script also dictates that men take the sexual initiative and women act resistant to sex. As a result of these expectations or norms, over 39 percent of the college women in this research study reported that they had offered token resistance to sexual advances by saying no when they really meant yes. Over 60 percent of the sexually experienced women reported that they had offered token resistance to sex. Both men and women need to be acquainted with the sex role expectations of their particular culture and their specific partners in order to avoid miscommunication and misbehavior. How prevalent is the double standard that men should be interested in sex and women should not in a person's particular social circles?

In less sexual matters, LaFrance and Carmen (1980) found that women smile more while listening to conversation partners and look more at their partners while speaking than men do. Kimble and Musgrove (1988) found that women look more at their partners in mixed-sex dyads whether they are speaking or listening than men do. Both of these behaviors seem to be reactive in nature;

backchannel smiling, as smiling while listening is called by Duncan and Fiske (1977), communicates receptiveness to the speaker and looking indicates that they are attempting to read the other person's response more. Rosenthal and DePaulo (1979) have found that women are more sensitive to nonverbal cues than men are. Verbally, women are expected to be more expressive and self-disclosing than men (Chelune, 1976; Derlega & Chaikin, 1976), and there is some evidence that they do disclose more intimate information (Levinger & Senn, 1967; Morgan, 1976; Morton, 1978).

As Jones's work on ingratiation has indicated, one of the best ways to endear oneself to another is to say positive things about the other person. Aronson and Linder (1965) conducted a study that demonstrated that *when* those positive statements are made makes a difference in how much attraction is engendered. A particular subject heard one of four possible evaluation sequences:

The Gain and Loss of Esteem

1. A *positive* evaluation sequence in which all evaluations were positive from beginning to end
2. A *negative* evaluation sequence in which all evaluations of the subject were negative
3. A *gain* evaluation sequence in which the first two evaluations were negative, the middle evaluations changed gradually from negative to positive, and the last two evaluations were very positive
4. A *loss* evaluation sequence in which the evaluations went from positive to negative just as the gain sequence had changed.

Aronson and Linder (1965) found that subjects liked the gain evaluator best, the positive evaluator better than the other two, and the negative and loss evaluators least.

Aronson and Linder thought that the gain evaluator represented a gain in esteem to the subject; therefore, she was liked most. Aronson and Linder (1965) and Aronson (1969) also indicated that the compliments of the positive evaluator lost their rewarding impact because they were so consistent and expected. However, investigators have had a difficult time replicating the gain effect. Tognoli and Keisner (1972) attempted to replicate the Aronson and Linder procedures exactly and found that the positive evaluator was liked better than the gain evaluator. Kimble and Moriarty (1979) also found that the positive evaluator was liked better. Berscheid, Brothen, and Graziano (1976) did obtain the gain effect in their study. They set out to examine Aronson's (1969) "law of marital infidelity." Aronson had compared an admiring stranger to the gain evaluator and a husband to the positive evaluator in discussing the Aronson and Linder results. In that discussion, he said that a compliment by a stranger, which would represent a gain in esteem, would thrill a woman; while the same compliment from her husband, because it was expected, would leave her yawning. So the seeds of infidelity would be sown! In the Berscheid et al. study, one or two evaluators were presented on a television monitor as they evaluated the subject after purportedly

Figure 11.8
*When only one
evaluator was
presented to subjects,
the gain evaluator was
liked better. When two
evaluators were
presented to the same
subjects, the positive
evaluator was liked
better.*
(From Berscheid, Brothen, &
Graziano, 1976, Journal of
Personality and Social Psychology,
33, 714.)

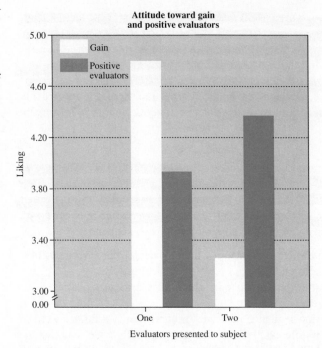

reading information she had written about herself. In the two evaluator conditions, the subject could see and hear only one evaluator at a time by holding down one of two buttons. In the conditions of interest to us, subjects in the one evaluator conditions heard either a gain evaluator *or* a uniformly positive evaluator. Subjects in the two evaluator condition heard a gain evaluator *and* a positive evaluator. When the subjects heard only one evaluator, they liked the gain evaluator better. When the subjects heard both evaluators, they liked the positive evaluator better. Subjects in the Aronson and Linder study had heard a gain, a positive, a negative, or a loss evaluator. So, Berscheid et al. got the gain effect in the conditions that were most like the Aronson and Linder conditions. However, Aronson's law of marital infidelity was refuted by the results of the two evaluator conditions. The positive evaluator was liked better when both types of evaluators were present in the same context. To carry the analogy to the marital situation, the husband would be liked better than the stranger if both were available at that period of time to be compared. (See figure 11.8.)

Is There a "Hard-to-Get" Effect?

Walster, Walster, Piliavin, and Schmidt (1973) also believed that a person who was initially disinterested or negative toward the target person would be liked better than someone who was positive from the beginning. After trying to demonstrate this "hard-to-get" effect five times using gain evaluation sequences, they had no significant results to support this idea. For instance, they had had men telephone prospective dates (confederates) who would refuse the first suggested date and then accept the second suggestion during the same phone call in the

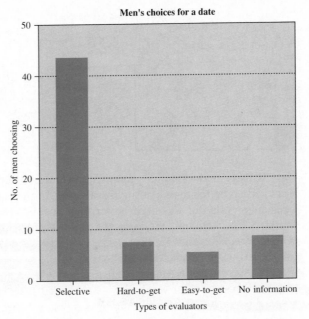

Men's choices for a date

Types of evaluators (x-axis): Selective, Hard-to-get, Easy-to-get, No information

No. of men choosing (y-axis): 0 to 50

Figure 11.9
Men found the woman who was interested in them but not interested in other men the most attractive.
(From Walster, Walster, Piliavin, & Schmidt, 1973, Journal of Personality and Social Psychology, 26, 118.)

hard-to-get condition. This sequence of refusal then acceptance is like the gain sequence of negative then positive evaluations. However, Walster et al. failed to show the hard-to-get phenomenon.

In their last experiment, they changed their approach. They had college men who had given some preliminary information about themselves for a dating service examine information folders of five women who were also participating in the dating service. Two of the folders contained only background information about the women. The other three folders also contained the woman's ratings of her interest in dating five of the men, including the subject, on a scale ranging from -10 to +10. The easy-to-get woman had rated her interest in all five men as +8 or +9, including the subject who was rated +8. The hard-to-get woman had rated her interest in all five men as +2 or +3, including the subject as +2. The "selectively hard-to-get" woman had rated her interest in four of the men as +2 or +3, but had rated her interest in the subject a +8. It may not surprise you to learn that the selective woman was rated more positively than the others on a number of personal characteristics and that she was chosen as the preferred date by 42 of the men, which was seven times as many men as those who chose the easy-to-get woman or the hard-to-get woman.

Walster et al. argued that the selective woman was preferred because she embodied characteristics of both of the other types, being hard-to-get for other men and easy-to-get for the subject. It should be emphasized that they did not demonstrate that someone whose approval is hard to win, who is hard-to-get, is liked better than someone who is easier to impress. The hard-to-get effect was not demonstrated to exist! (See figure 11.9.)

*Roz understands the
benefits of presenting
oneself as selectively
positive toward one
person—or five people.*

SHOE, by MacNelly. © 1987 by
Tribune Media Services, Inc.
Reprinted by permission.

Walster et al. essentially found in the first five studies, that a gain evaluator was liked no better than a positive evaluator. In the last study, they proved that a selective evaluator was liked better than nonselective evaluators. Kimble and Moriarty (1979) found that a selective evaluator was also liked better than a gain evaluator and contend that the selective woman in Walster's et al. study was liked best because she reacted more favorably to the subject than to other men. She was probably perceived by the subject as acting more favorably to him than other women would. In other words, it was the *exclusiveness* of her positive behavior that made it particularly meaningful. Just as exclusiveness is an important part of established love relationships (Davis, 1985), exclusive behaviors are also important in the initial development of such attraction. Kimble, Arnold, and Hirt (1985) and Kimble and Kardes (1987) have examined positive interpersonal behaviors from an attributional perspective and have found that exclusive positive behaviors do cause the most attraction in heterosexual interactions.

Arousing Situations and Passionate Love

Berscheid and Walster (1974) introduced a two-factor theory of *passionate love,* based on Schachter and Singer's (1962) approach to emotion, which indicates how behavior in certain situations can inspire affection. They stated that a person will experience passionate love when (1) he or she is physiologically aroused, and (2) situational cues indicate that "love" is the appropriate label for his or her current feelings. This theory has been called a misattribution theory of love because Berscheid and Walster have suggested that people sometimes experience arousal that is caused by something irrelevant to love and because of cues present in the situation, they incorrectly label their emotion as love. In Schachter and Singer's study, a confederate's anger served as a cue for the subject's anger only when the subject was aroused by a drug and had no ready explanation for the arousal. Usually, arousal caused by irrelevant factors should not inspire love. However, Berscheid and Walster suggest that arousal caused by fear-provoking situations, rejection by others, frustration, exciting events, parental interference, and sexual gratification can all contribute to passionate love if the cues are right.

Dutton and Aron (1974) conducted studies on two bridges and in a laboratory in Vancouver, British Columbia, which show that fearful situations can produce sexual attraction. In the first study, they had a male or female interviewer accost male subjects on a fear-arousing bridge or a nonarousing bridge. The fear-arousing bridge was a 450-foot-long, wood and cable bridge that swayed

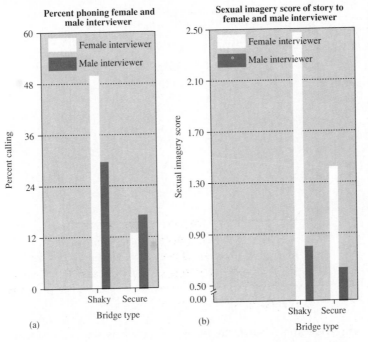

Percent phoning female and male interviewer

Sexual imagery score of story to female and male interviewer

(a) Bridge type

(b) Bridge type

Figure 11.10
(a) More men called the woman interviewer if she had interviewed them on the unstable, fear-arousing bridge.
(b) Men interviewed by a woman interviewer on the unstable bridge told stories with more sexual imagery in them than men in other conditions.
(From Dutton & Aron, 1974, Journal of Personality and Social Psychology, 30, 513.)

and tilted 230 feet above rocks and rapids. The nonarousing bridge was wide, firm, and 10 feet above a small stream. The interviewers approached subjects on the bridges and asked them to write a story about a picture of a distraught young woman. The interviewers also gave subjects their name and phone number and invited them to call if they wanted to talk more. The results indicated that when the subjects were interviewed by a woman on the fear-arousing bridge, their stories had more manifest sexual content, and they called the interviewer's number more than did subjects in the other three conditions. According to Berscheid and Walster's theory, the bridge aroused the subjects and the female interviewer served as a cue that what they were feeling was love. Another study by Dutton and Aron (1974) essentially replicated the bridge study results using the anticipation of shock to produce fear. (See figure 11.10.) White, Fishbein, and Rutstein (1981) also found support for the idea that irrelevant arousal does contribute to experiencing love under appropriate circumstances.

Byrne, Allgeier, Winslow, and Buckman (1975) helped specify what situational elements can be cues for love. They inferred that certain real-life situations, such as natural disasters, festive occasions, and stressful workload situations, can break down ordinary barriers between people and make them less inhibited and more affiliative. They also inferred that the common elements of those situations were (1) physiological arousal, (2) doing out-of-role behaviors, and (3) sharing the experience of arousal and behavior. They demonstrated in an experiment that attraction toward a stranger increased only when all three elements occurred together. Note that arousal is the common element of this

Figure 11.11
*Only when all three
factors (arousal, out-
of-role behavior, and
sharing the
experience) were
present and the other
person had dissimilar
attitudes was
attraction toward the
other person changed
positively.*

(From Byrne, Allgeier, Winslow,
& Buckman, 1975, Journal of
Applied Social Psychology, 5,
1–15.)

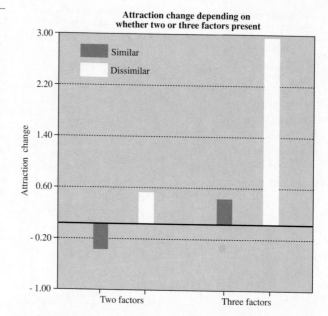

approach and misattribution theory. Assimilating these theories suggests that sharing unusual behaviors with someone provides the situational cues for love. So, experiencing unusual, dangerous, or exciting situations together provides a better backdrop for love than sitting together in a lecture class! (See figure 11.11.)

*An Alternative
Explanation of
Arousal and Love*

Kenrick and Cialdini (1977) argue that all of the evidence presented for misattribution theory can be more simply explained by reinforcement theory. They state that when someone provides a reward or is associated with a reward or terminates an aversive condition or is associated with such termination, the beneficiary of the reward or relief will like that person. In our earlier discussion of rewards and attraction, we neglected another form of reinforcement—negative reinforcement. Kenrick and Cialdini emphasized the role of negative reinforcement, which occurs when an unpleasant situation or condition is terminated or reduced, in explaining how aversive circumstances enhance attraction. For instance, they contend that the female interviewer in the Dutton and Aron (1974) study on the unstable bridge who administered a questionnaire and seemed oblivious to the fact that the bridge swayed reduced the male subjects' fear most and provided negative reinforcement. They further argue that the mistakes of attribution, which Berscheid and Walster say occur frequently, are very rare. Whether you believe misattribution theory or reinforcement theory, some of the implications for passionate love are the same. Both imply that arousing experiences and emotional roller coaster rides fuel passion more than ordinary experiences.

Physical attractiveness is an important factor in initial attraction in love relationships. David Buss (1985) has found that males value physical attractiveness in mates more than females do. The first study examining the role of physical attractiveness in dating was conducted by Walster, Aronson, Abrahams, and Rottman (1966). They randomly paired freshmen men and women for a dance. As the couples entered, the man and the woman of each couple was rated on attractiveness. After several dances, the music was stopped and everyone was asked to indicate how interested he or she was in dating his or her partner for the evening later. Walster et al. also collected personality, intelligence, and attitudinal information on each person to see how those variables were related to attraction. It turned out that their partners' appearance was the only factor related to interest in their partners. The more attractive the person's partner, the more that person was attracted to him or her, regardless of that person's own attractiveness. You may correctly point out that appearance was the only thing the subjects knew about at the time; so, it had the most impact on attraction. It does seem unlikely that they had inferred much about the person's personality, attitudes, or intelligence in the course of the evening. However this study does show that appearances are very important in forming first impressions. Otherwise, appearance too would not have been significantly correlated with initial attraction.

This pattern of results was a surprise to Walster and some of her colleagues because they thought those couples who were most similar to each other in attractiveness would have been most attracted to each other. However, even those who were unattractive themselves were more attracted to the partners who looked like Tom Cruise or Brooke Shields than to less attractive partners. So, the **matching hypothesis** that people will seek their equals in appearance for dates or mates was not upheld. More recent studies have yielded results more consistent with the matching hypothesis. Berscheid, Dion, Walster, and Walster (1971) did find that unattractive subjects chose slightly less attractive dates than attractive subjects did. Huston (1973) did not find a difference in the dating choices of unattractive and attractive subjects, but when acceptance of the date was assured, all subjects chose more attractive dates. Shanteau and Nagy (1979) found that women most often chose the most attractive prospective dates when acceptance of the date was assured, but when acceptance was unlikely, they showed no preference for attractive dates. In two other studies in which subjects were only shown pictures of dates and were not given probability of acceptance information, Shanteau and Nagy found that most women estimated that more attractive men were less likely to accept dates, and most women chose moderately attractive men for dates. Probability of acceptance was related to choice of date in that the most attractive person who was regarded as quite likely to accept the date was chosen most often. As a result, estimates of probability of acceptance appear to underlie the tendency to choose someone of equal or near equal attractiveness.

Physical Appearance and Love

The Matching Hypothesis in Appearance

Attractiveness is an important factor in close relationships.

Figure 11.12
*Couples who were engaged or married were most similar to each other in physical attractiveness, as expected.
Unexpectedly, cohabiting couples were not very similar in attractiveness.*
(*From White, 1980,* Journal of Personality and Social Psychology, 39, 665.)

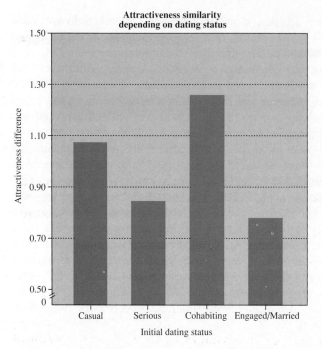

Attractiveness similarity depending on dating status

Correlational analyses have supported the matching notion that people who are more similar in appearance are more compatible with each other. Murstein and Christy (1976) found a correlation of +.60 between the attractiveness ratings of photos of married couples. Cavior and Boblett (1972) found a correlation of +.72 between rated attractiveness of married couples versus a correlation of only +.19 between attractiveness of dating couples. White (1980) related attractiveness to courtship progress. He found that serious daters, engaged couples, and married couples were more similar in photographed attractiveness than were casual daters and couples living together. Also among casually and seriously dating couples, those who broke up during the nine months of the study were less similar than those who stayed together. Apparently, inequality of appearance can put strain on a relationship. (See figure 11.12.)

The Matching Hypothesis in General

The matching hypothesis, however, does not require that couples be equal on each attribute, such as appearance. The basic idea is that the two should be equal on total social attributes (Goffman, 1952). So, one partner might bring wit, intelligence, warmth, or wealth to a relationship to exchange for beauty. Harrison and Saeed (1977) examined the content of 800 lonely hearts ads and found that attractive people sought attractive partners, but good looking women also sought wealthy men. They also found a positive correlation between the overall social desirability of assets offered and the desirability of assets sought. So, there is evidence for the matching of overall social attributes and for exchange of different kinds of assets (e.g., beauty for money). Berscheid, Walster, and Bohrnstedt (1973) assessed questionnaire data from 2,000 readers of *Psychology Today* and found evidence that different kinds of resources or inputs are exchanged. They found that if one partner was more attractive than the other, the less attractive partner was wealthier, more loving, and/or more self-sacrificing.

Sigall and Landy (1973) did a study which indicates that the general public believes that couples do match on total social attributes. They had two confederates and subjects wait together before an experiment started. The female confederate was made to appear attractive in half the cases and unattractive in the others. In half the cases, she and the male confederate were obviously going together, and in the other half, they were apparently strangers. When the experiment began, the real subject was asked to rate the male confederate on a number of personal characteristics. When the man was presented as going with the attractive woman, he was rated to have more positive traits than in any of the other three conditions. Obviously, he had a lot going for him if he was paired with such a beautiful woman! Bar-Tal and Saxe (1976) had subjects evaluate couples on the basis of photographs and found that unattractive men married to beautiful women were judged to be richer and more successful than other men and women. The ratings of the woman were not affected by the attractiveness of her mate.

Mate Selection

David Buss (1985) has reviewed patterns of mate selection and has found that we also match within a particular characteristic. In addition to the tendency to choose someone similar in appearance described earlier, he found that we usually choose a partner similar in age, education, race, religion, and ethnic background. We tend to match less strongly on such factors as attitudes and opinions (typical correlations around $+.50$); intelligence ($r = +.40$); socioeconomic status ($r = +.30$); height, weight, and eye color ($r = +.25$ to .30); and personality variables ($r = +.20$ to .25). This presents the distinct impression that we are likely to marry someone who is like us on many dimensions.

However, many investigators have suggested that we are likely to mesh better with those who have opposite personality characteristics to our own (Kerckhoff & Davis, 1962; Winch, 1958). Dominant people should get along better with submissive people, extraverts with introverts, and masochists with sadists rather than with their own kind. The preponderance of the evidence is that this attraction of opposites idea is not true. Meyer and Pepper (1977) tested well adjusted and poorly adjusted married couples on a number of personality dimensions. They found that similarity in needs for affiliation, aggression, autonomy, and nurturance were positively related to marital adjustment, but they found no evidence that being opposite or complementary on any need was related to marital adjustment. Other investigators have obtained similar results. One exception to this pattern is David Buss's (1984) finding that if one spouse was dominant, the other was likely to be submissive.

Companionate Love

Walster and Walster (1978) distinguished between passionate love and companionate love. Passionate love involves strong and fluctuating emotional states, sexual desires, and fantasies. This type of love is also assumed to be short-lived because mundane reality erodes the desires and fantasies, and because positive,

The experience of companionate love— after the fire has gone out.

THE LOCKHORNS, by Bill Hoest. © 1978 by King Features. Reprinted by permission.

"I FORGET. IS TOMORROW OUR WEDDING ANNIVERSARY OR THE DAY I TAKE OUT THE GARBAGE ?"

helpful acts become expected and not novel (Bercheid, 1983). Passionate love must be complemented with companionate love if marriages and other close relationships are to last. Walster and Walster (1978) regard companionate love as much like friendship in that both are based on reinforcement and don't involve very strong emotions. Companionate love is assumed to contribute to the stability and durability of the relationship.

Kelley (1983) uses the term *commitment* to describe all stable factors that maintain relationships. According to Kelley, commitment includes the following elements:

1. Companionate love (the positive, rewarding features of interaction with one's partner)
2. Common investments of the couple such as property, children, and effort put into the relationship
3. Public ceremonies and behaviors which indicate that individuals are a couple (e.g., marriage vows)
4. Social costs of terminating the relationship (loss of reputation)
5. Unavailability of attractive alternative relationships
6. Private pledges of loyalty to the relationship

All of these elements contribute to the interdependence of the two people and the longevity of the relationship.

Marital Satisfaction

Another view of long-term relationships is afforded by research on marital satisfaction. The most common finding in sociological work on marital satisfaction is that it is high during the early years, declines during the middle years, and then increases during the later years of the relationship (Rollins & Cannon, 1974; Spanier, Lewis, & Cole, 1975). The decline in marital satisfaction has been related to raising children. Childless couples, especially the wives, are more satisfied with their marriages than are couples with children (Glenn & McLanahan, 1982; Rollins & Galligan, 1978), and those couples with fewer children are happier than those with many (Antill, 1983). It is not hard to see how the advent of children would reduce the satisfaction of women more than men because they bear the brunt of childrearing responsibilities. Burr (1970) reported that marital satisfaction is at its lowest ebb during the children's elementary school years after the carefree years of early childhood. This is true even though the actual workload on parents, especially mothers, should be reduced when the child enters school. How do you account for this? Also, the increase in marital satisfaction in later years, especially for mothers, was associated with the children leaving home (Glenn, 1975; Skolnick, 1981). The "empty nest" doldrums, assumed to occur when the kids leave home, does not occur in most cases.

Perhaps Walster and Walster (1978) were too hasty in their contention that passion is less prominent later in relationships. Howard and Dawes (1976) demonstrated that sex plays an important role in marital satisfaction. They found

Companionate love makes our later years happy and fulfilling.

that couples who reported having sexual intercourse often and seldom having arguments were the most satisfied with their marriages. So the extent to which the positive passions are still ablaze does affect wedded bliss for years.

Antill (1983) looked at how the sex-role characteristics of husbands and wives affected the marital satisfaction of the couples. Husbands and wives in Antill's Australian sample were classified as masculine, feminine, androgynous, or undifferentiated according to how they answered items on the Bem Sex-Role Inventory (Bem, 1974). It should be noted that androgynous individuals are those who indicate they have both masculine (e.g., aggressive) and feminine (e.g. compassionate) characteristics and undifferentiated individuals indicate that they have neither masculine nor feminine characteristics. Antill's results indicate that both husbands and wives who had partners who were high in femininity (feminine or androgynous) were most satisfied with their relationships. It might surprise you to find that wives are most satisfied with feminine husbands. However, to quote Antill (1983): ". . . it is understandable that in an interpersonal situation such as marriage, it is people who describe themselves as sensitive to the needs of others, compassionate, and warm [which feminine and androgynous people do] that make such relationships successful" (p. 153). It also appears that the husband's feminine characteristics are especially conducive to the wife's marital satisfaction after the couple has been married for a while and have two or more children. This result also makes sense in light of the fact that one of the feminine characteristics is "loves children." (See figure 11.13.)

Another study (Wills, Weiss, & Patterson, 1974) used a method more closely related to the couples' behaviors and found results consistent with Antill's. They had couples rate each other's behaviors as task-related or emotion-related and pleasurable or displeasurable for two weeks. Pleasurable behaviors that were affectionate (e.g., giving flowers) were important to the wives' satisfaction. So husbands who were good at expressing affection, as Antill's feminine husbands should be, made their wives most satisfied with their marriages.

Equity in Close Relationships

Equity theorists (cf. Walster, Walster, & Berscheid, 1978) have applied the theory to interpersonal relationships. The matching hypothesis, whereby committed couples are assumed to match on inputs, is an offshoot of equity theory. We have already mentioned the fact that prospective marital partners do match on social attributes, such as physical attractiveness and intelligence. Equity theory also implies that most newlyweds see their relationship as equitable or fair at the time of their wedding. Whether the relationship remains equitable is seen as important to the continued happiness of the couple.

Relevant inputs or contributions to newlyweds in the equity equation could be giving love, praise, sympathy, or status to one's partner or paying attention to, responding to, or initiating a social interaction with one's partner (Buss, 1983; Foa & Foa, 1976). These are all effortful inputs instead of attribute inputs, but they may be even more important among married couples than the relatively static attributes. Outcomes can be anything that the person receives or has done for him or her such as money, approval, praise, services, gifts, etc. In close relationships, the effortful inputs done by one person may be the most important and relevant outcomes the partner receives.

Hatfield, Traupmann, Sprecher, Utne, and Hay (1985) have argued that equity or equality between the outcomes/inputs ratios of the two people is particularly important in intimate relationships. Walster, Walster, and Traupmann (1978) classified dating men and women as overbenefited, equitably treated, or underbenefited in their relationships based on their self-reports. They found that people involved in equitable relationships were more likely to be moving toward

Figure 11.13
(a) The happiest couples were those in which husband and wife were feminine or androgynous. By far the unhappiest couples were those in which the husband was undifferentiated, or, low in masculinity and femininity, and the wife was masculine. (b) The happiest couples were those in which both wife and husband were high in femininity, classified as feminine or androgynous.

(From Antill, 1983, Journal of Personality and Social Psychology, 45, 150.)

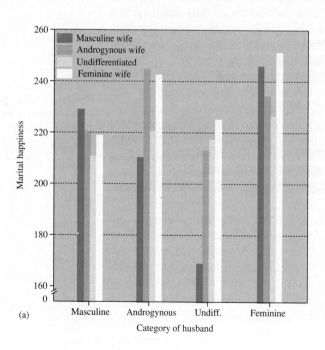

(a)

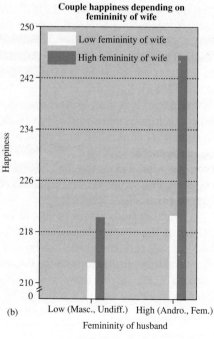

(b)

Equity Theory

Equity theory was first introduced in the 1960s by J. Stacy Adams (1963, 1965). The core of equity theory is the notion that a person prefers to be treated fairly and to treat others fairly. Equity theory is a theory about inputs and outcomes. *Outcomes* can be anything a person receives such as money or praise. *Inputs* can be anything a person is or does such as the person's physical beauty or the amount of work done. A state of fairness or equity exists when a person perceives that the ratio between the outcomes he or she receives and the inputs he or she has or contributes is equal to the outcomes/inputs ratios of other people. That is, equity exists when person A or anyone else evaluating the situation sees this state of affairs:

$$\frac{\text{Person A's Outcomes}}{\text{Person A's Inputs}} = \frac{\text{Other Person's Outcomes}}{\text{Other Person's Inputs}}$$

If these ratios are not equal, person A (especially) is motivated to regain equity. Person A may regain equity by (1) changing person A's or the other person's actual outcomes or Person A's own inputs, or (2) reevaluating person A's and/or the other person's inputs and/or outcomes. The first equity restoration technique mentioned involves restoring real or objective equity; the second involves regaining psychological or subjective equity (Walster, Walster, & Berscheid, 1973). It should be noted that the other person's inputs can't be changed by person A; they can only be reevaluated. Walster et al. (1973) contend that people prefer real equity over psychological equity unless real equity is difficult to attain or discomforting.

Equity considerations are thought to be important in business, interpersonal, and even international transactions. It seems evident that persons who feel they have been slighted in business or social interactions and representatives of countries or governments that have been victimized in international matters would be motivated to take steps to reduce the inequity.

Table 11.A   A Summary of Equity Theory

Motivation of individual

To act or think so that fairness prevails in one's personal world

Core concepts

A's Outcomes/Inputs $<$, $=$, or $>$ B's Outcomes/Inputs

Focus of theory

Relationships between individuals and groups of people

Assumptions about rationality/awareness of people

Rationalizing, distorting

Interestingly, Austin and Walster (1974) found, as equity theorists predicted, that subjects who were overpaid—i.e., who received outcomes greater than the amount they considered fair—also experienced more negative moods after the transaction than the underpaid subjects did. So inequity creates uneasiness in beneficiaries and exploiters as well as victims; therefore, the overbenefited should be motivated to reduce inequity as well as the underbenefitted. (See table 11.A.)

more intimate relationships than overbenefited or underbenefited people. Equitably treated people were also happier and more content with their relationships than inequitably treated people. The most noteworthy aspect of these results is that people who benefited from the inequity, who received more than they gave, were unhappy in the relationship. Hatfield et al. (1985) also report that equitable relationships are more stable than inequitable ones and that people in equitable relationships are more faithful to their partners longer.

Hatfield et al. (1985) hypothesized that changes in people originally in equitable relationships lead to inequity and attempts particularly by the disadvantaged partner, to regain equity. They and Walster, Walster, and Berscheid (1978) pointed out that equity can change to inequity through (1) one partner learning new information about the other's personal characteristics or behaviors, (2) actual changes in one partner or the other over time, or (3) changes created by environmental influences or events. For instance, the newlywed may discover that her husband snores, eats his mashed potatoes with his hands, and slurps his coffee from the saucer. The bon vivant fiancé may become the irritable recluse who only wants to watch television for entertainment, the steady mate for many years starts to show the ravages of Alzheimer's disease, or the newlywed may gain or lose a lot of weight. The poor medical student may become the rich doctor, the good breadwinner may lose his or her job, or the young athletic husband may be paralyzed in a car wreck. Hatfield and her associates assume that the person disadvantaged by the change may be less affectionate, less self-sacrificing, or less well-groomed to try to reestablish real equity. He or she will desert the relationship if equity cannot be regained. Hatfield et al. (1985) present some anecdotal evidence for these mechanisms from Komarovsky's (1971) work on adjustments that occurred in Depression era families when the husband lost his job. There were some strong changes in the behavior of husbands and wives and shifts in decision-making power in these traditional families. Hatfield et al. argue that these changes were attempts to restore equity in the relationships.

Types of Marriages

The individual perspectives that the husbands and wives bring to the marriage can affect equity. The same relationship can be equitable in one partner's assessment and inequitable as the other person sees it. If the two people held different views of the equity of the relationship, there would be much potential for discord unless the two communicated their views well and amicably to each other. One factor that should affect perceptions of equity by the two mates is their perception of appropriate marital roles. Peplau (1983) has categorized marriages as traditional, modern, or egalitarian. In traditional marriages, the husband is more dominant than the wife, the husband and wife have specialized roles, the wife doesn't hold a job outside the home, and there is little emphasis on joint activities and shared interests. In modern marriages, the husband is less dominant over the wife than in traditional marriages, there is less role specialization (i.e., the husband may help with the home and kids), the wife may have a job outside the home which is secondary to the husband's, and there is emphasis on togetherness and companionship. In the rare egalitarian marriages, there is no husband dominance or sex-typed role specialization, both have careers which are equally important, and there is emphasis on shared activities and companionship. It seems obvious that if the husband were a traditionalist and the wife became an egalitarian, they would view the equity of their relationship differently and conflict would occur. It also seems evident that the dual career situation of egalitarian couples would cause more conflict over job and residence location, educational priorities, and career decision making. In this vein, Ickes (1985) notes that there is often conflict between Maslow's needs for love and affection and his higher needs for independence, self-development, and self-actualization. Historically, women have been denied opportunities for self-actualization so that they can fulfill men's social needs and enable men to achieve self-actualization!

Clark and Mills (Clark, 1984, 1985; Clark & Mills, 1979; Mills & Clark, 1982) have presented evidence that equity may not be applicable in intimate relationships. Their position is that strict, immediate reciprocity of exchange is appropriate for "exchange relationships" between strangers and acquaintances, but that it is inappropriate for "communal relationships" between close friends and loved ones. Clark (1985) points out that they have demonstrated that prompt repayment for favors or services, tit-for-tat exchanges, requesting repayment, and keeping each individual's task inputs separate are inappropriate behaviors for close relationships. Self-disclosure studies which indicate that spouses (Morton, 1978) and friends (Derlega, Wilson, & Chaikin, 1976) do not reciprocate self-disclosure immediately, while strangers do are also supportive of their distinction between communal and exchange relationships.

Communal and Exchange Relationships

However, Clark and Mills' work on types of relationships does not directly dispute Hatfield, Walster, and Berscheid's notion that people strive for equity and pay attention to inputs and outcomes in intimate relationships. Clark and Mills deal with different kinds of inputs and outcomes than Hatfield and her associates do. Clark and Mills use work done or help given on a task as their relevant inputs and money or extra credit points as their outcomes. Hatfield and her associates use much more interpersonal inputs and outcomes, such as love, understanding, acceptance, appreciation, physical affection, and sex given to and received from one's partner (cf. Walster, Walster, & Berscheid, 1978, pp. 236–41). Considering the distinction between kinds of inputs and outcomes, both sets of observations appear true. Close couples ignore or avoid balancing the books on impersonal inputs and outcomes, but they keep close tabs on interpersonal inputs and outcomes.

Equity theorists (e.g., Hatfield et al., 1985) contend that when inequity becomes too great in marital relationships, separation and divorce is likely. Another social exchange theory, Thibaut and Kelley's (1959) theory of interdependence, offers many insights into the breakup of relationships. Outcomes (rewards-costs) that a person receives from a particular interaction partner are compared to that person's **comparison level (CL)** and his or her **comparison level for alternatives.** A

The Disintegration of Relationships

person's CL is the standard by which a person evaluates the attractiveness of a relationship with another person. It is the average outcome level a person expects to get from a relationship based on his or her past experiences and observations of other's experiences, such as his or her parents' marital outcomes. If a person's current outcomes from a relationship are above CL, that person is satisfied with the relationship. If a person's current outcomes are below CL, that person is dissatisfied or unhappy. The greater the difference between outcomes and CL, the more satisfied or dissatisfied the person will be. However, many people stay in unhappy relationships; battered wives are a prominent example of such people and circumstances.

What determines when a person will leave an unsatisfactory relationship? According to Thibaut and Kelley, a person will leave a relationship when his or her outcomes fall below his or her CL for alternatives. A person's CL for alternatives is the lowest level of outcomes a person will accept in the light of current available alternative opportunities. These current alternatives are not necessarily another dyadic relationship but can be just about any other living circumstances. Many factors must be considered. The battered wife has to weigh what alternative income sources are available, what housing is available for her and her children, and what family and friends are available for emotional support. Of course, the alternative may be another available, attractive partner. Thibaut and Kelley (1959) also stated that the extent to which your current outcomes in a relationship are greater than your CL for alternatives determines your dependency on the relationship. That is, if your current outcomes are not much better than your possible alternatives, you are not very dependent on the relationship. Waller and Hill (1951) related dependency to power in that the partner who is least dependent on the relationship can dictate that things be done his or her way.

An Extension of Interdependence Theory

Caryl Rusbult and her associates (e.g., Rusbult, Zembrodt, & Gunn, 1982) have done several studies, using some perspectives from interdependence theory, on how people in unsatisfying relationships react. Rusbult et al. (1982) have stated that the intent and tendency to act to maintain a relationship can be computed thus:

$$\text{Commitment} = \text{Satisfaction} + \text{Investments} - \text{Alternatives}$$

So, if a person were currently dissatisfied with a relationship, he or she should act to sustain the relationship if prior satisfaction were high, common investments were high, and currently available alternatives were low. He or she would react more destructively if satisfaction had been low, investments were low, and alternatives were high. Rusbult et al. (1982) have characterized possible responses to declining relationships in the following way:

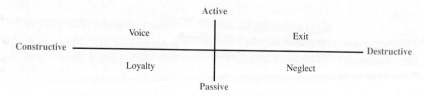

The active destructive response, *exit,* is to leave the relationship, leave the residence, or tell partner to leave, separate, and/or seek a divorce. The active constructive response, *voice,* is to discuss problems, compromise, seek counseling, attempt to improve elements of the relationship, and/or attempt to solve problems. The passive constructive response, *loyalty,* is to hope and pray for improvement in the relationship and/or wait patiently for partner to resolve his or her problems with the relationship. The passive destructive response, *neglect,* is to ignore one's partner, to avoid interaction, to avoid discussion of problems, and/ or to treat one's partner badly without directly addressing the relationship.

In experiments and correlational studies, Rusbult et al. (1982) examined the effects of prior satisfaction, investments, and alternatives on responses. They found that high prior satisfaction and investments led to constructive responses (voice and loyalty), and low satisfaction and investments led to destructive responses (exit and neglect). Surprisingly, alternative quality derived from Thibaut and Kelley's CL for alternatives ideas had a weaker influence on responses, but the influence was generally in the expected directions: poor alternatives promoted constructive responses and good alternatives promoted destructive responses. The active-passive dimension was not meaningful according to these results because the exit and neglect results were essentially the same, as were voice and loyalty. Stronger relationships, such as marriage, may have manifested different patterns of response than the hypothetical situations and dating relationships in these studies did. For instance, alternative quality may have more impact on marital relationships. In fact, Rusbult (1983) found that subjects who initiated termination of a dating relationship did so after experiencing an increase in alternative quality.

One aspect of unsatisfying relationships that Rusbult and her associates have not addressed is the relationship outcome. It seems clear that when both partners adopt a destructive response (exit or neglect), the relationship will ultimately end. On the other hand, the relationship should survive and flourish if both partners adopt constructive postures (voice or loyalty). What happens when one partner takes destructive action and the other partner takes a constructive stance? Will the destructive response prevail, or will an active response, either constructive or destructive, prevail over a passive response? To answer these questions, longitudinal, unobtrusive studies of both partners' actions and reactions in real relationships must be conducted. Levinger (1983) indicates that while "it takes two to tango," it only takes one to break up a marriage. That is, if one partner takes a destructive response according to Rusbult's typology, the relationship will probably end. However, Levinger (1979) found that one-fifth of the divorce applications of parents of young children were withdrawn by the applicants and that most of those couples were together several months later. One difference between the dismissers and a divorced sample was that the dismissing couples had higher husband incomes and lower wife incomes than the divorced couples. Since wives initiate divorce proceedings more often, these results may stem from the dismissing wives having lower CL for alternatives than the divorced wives. Also, the dismissing couples were more often living together at the time of the filing than the divorced couples. So, the dismissing couples were more interdependent and shared more investments in Rusbult's terms than the divorced couples.

Tolstedt and Stokes (1984) thought that depenetration should occur among distressed couples just as social penetration does in friendship formation (Altman & Taylor, 1973). **Social penetration theory** refers to the increasing breadth and depth of mutual self-disclosure between people who are becoming closer friends. *Depenetration* is the shrinking breadth and depth of disclosure presumed to occur between people who are growing apart. They obtained measures of current intimacy or closeness and breadth of self-disclosures from tapes of the individual couples charting and discussing their relationships. They found that couples who were less intimate at the time talked about fewer topics (lower breadth), which confirmed one aspect of depenetration. However, the discussion data yielded an entirely different picture. When they were asked to discuss their relationships, the couples who were no longer close said a lot of personal (deep), negative comments to each other. Closer couples disclosed more positive information. So, indications of a deteriorating relationship are communication over fewer topics and more negative communication when discussion is unavoidable.

Miller (1982) asked 20 divorced couples to discuss the breakup of their marriages. For most of the couples, there was first a drop in their attraction toward their mates caused by consistent indications of negative traits of their spouses or by some change in situation or status, such as moving or changing jobs. Then, the person began to attend to costs or problems in ending the marriage. Finally, he or she focused on the availability and attractiveness of alternatives. In most cases, disaffection toward the spouse occurred before attention turned to Harry or Harriet down at the office.

A drop in affection for one's spouse may grow out of frequent conflict. If one's spouse frequently interferes with that person's plans, goals, and actions, soon that person will see him or her as having undesirable characteristics or traits. Peterson (1979) found that four types of acts precipitate conflicts among couples. The first category, *criticism,* occurs when one partner says or does something that is seen as a put-down or demeaning by the target partner. Negative comments or action about one's appearance, cooking skills, home repair abilities, or habits are examples. *Illegitimate demands* are another category. They occur whenever one spouse asks or tells the other to do something that the other spouse sees as unfair or beyond his or her control. Asking someone to care for the children all the time without help or asking one's partner to clean three days of dishes because she or he had not done them are examples. A third category, *rebuff,* occurs when one partner is unresponsive to inviting behavior of the other partner in conversation or affection. The fourth category, *cumulative annoyance,* occurs when one partner does something unpleasant several times or does not do something desired several times. Rands, Levinger, and Mellinger (1981) found that young couples respond to such conflict-initiating events by ignoring them, confronting the actions constructively, or confronting the actions aggressively or destructively. The highest marital satisfaction was reported by those couples who confronted the problems without aggression and coped with them in an understanding way without escalating the conflict.

Negative interactions and conflicts make relationship partners ask and answer attributional questions about why their partner acted the way he or she did more than positive interactions do (Holtzworth-Munroe & Jacobson, 1985; Orvis, Kelley, & Butler, 1976). Unfortunately, there are some attributional biases that operate when a person searches for causes of behavior that contribute to the deterioration of relationships. First, there is a self-serving bias (Bradley [Weary], 1978; Zuckerman, 1979) by which a person is likely to see his or her actions as justified and positively motivated and the actions of the opposing partner in a more negative light. The actor-observer bias (Jones & Nisbett, 1972) of which the "fundamental attribution error" (Ross, 1977) is a part, makes each partner more likely to see his or her actions as caused by situational factors and the opposing partner's actions as caused by his or her traits or dispositions. When acts are interpreted as emanating from a person's traits, they are seen as likely to recur and less changeable. So, these two attributional tendencies suggest that in a conflict situation, each partner is likely to blame the problem behavior on negative, stable characteristics of the other partner. Weiss (1975) found that divorced persons do develop accounts of their marital problems that place blame on their exspouses. Orvis et al. (1976) contend that once the cognitive work of attributing causes has been done and the other person is seen as directly responsible, conflicts are even harder to resolve.

> Conflict and
> Attributions

Misperceptions that arise from or contribute to relationship conflicts have been studied by other attribution researchers. Harvey, Wells, and Alvarez (1978) found that males and females who were going together disagreed on what kinds of conflicts were likely to create relationship problems, and they misperceived their partners' views as similar to their own. Men saw sexual incompatibility and disloyalty as important areas of potential conflict and thought their partners did too. Women saw financial problems and work or education-related stress as important areas and misperceived that their partners did too. The failure to realize what kinds of conflicts are most important to avoid could create relationship problems in the future.

Other investigators (Fincham & O'Leary, 1983; Jacobson, McDonald, Follette, & Berley, 1985) found that happily married couples make relationship-enhancing attributions about their partner's behavior, and distressed couples make distress-maintaining attributions. Happily married persons saw their partner's positive behavior as dispositionally caused and stable and their partners' negative behavior as situationally caused and rare. Distressed persons saw their partner's positive behavior as rare and caused by the situation and their partner's negative behavior as stable and caused by their partner's disposition. It appears that these attributional tendencies arose from their current emotional reactions to their partners. However, our earlier discussion suggests that the act of attributing causes for their partners' behavior, especially in conflict situations, may make the emotional reactions to their partners negative or more extremely negative.

We have reviewed the sociopsychological research on relationship development from initiation to termination. We have examined factors that affect friendship and love. In an ideal world, friendships and love relationships would last forever, and everyone would be on positive terms with everyone else. In the real world, many relationships do last. Other relationships do not last because of internal conflicts or environment-related factors, such as geographic moves. It is best for the individual's well-being for old friends and lovers to be replaced by new ones.

Applications of Attraction Research Findings

As Cialdini (1985) has pointed out, the best way to get someone to buy a product from you is to get them to like you. To quote Willy Loman in *Death of a Salesman,* "Be liked and you will never want." Anyone who sells a product or a service could profit by applying some of the attraction principles. Doctors and lawyers build and keep their clientele through their friendly manner and interest in the clients as much as through their expertise. Cialdini (1985) notes that sales people often emphasize commonalities of background and interests in order to get prospective customers to like them and buy from them. Politicians are familiar with this technique; for instance, John F. Kennedy's "Ich bin Berliner" statement certainly touched a responsive chord with the Germans. A vice-presidential candidate tried to establish accord with voters of upstate New York in a deceitful way. Upon returning from his father's funeral in the western U.S., the candidate told voters at every stop how much his father had loved and admired the people of Poughkeepsie, Syracuse, Rochester, Binghamton, etc. It is unlikely that his father had known anything about those communities.

French and Raven (1959) referred to the type of influence by which one person can socially reward another as reward power. People who have established themselves as friends can also have coercive power (French & Raven, 1959) because it can be quite unpleasant and punishing to refuse the sales pitch of a friend. Some sales organizations exploit friendship by arranging for friends or relatives of the customer to make the sale. Behaving in some of the socially rewarding ways described in this chapter can be very beneficial for everybody from job-seekers to presidential candidates.

How else can attraction principles be used? They can be useful to ordinary citizens in attempting to overcome shyness and loneliness; in forming, developing, and maintaining close relationships; and in detecting warning signs of problems in existing relationships. The attraction findings related to proximity and similarity suggest that to initiate relationships one should immerse oneself in the activities of groups of people who share your interests. Such groups could be recreational, religious, or political groups. These activities would enable a person to meet people who have similar interests and would afford him or her enough opportunities to interact to establish relationships. Knowing how to act in socially rewarding ways and what is appropriate to disclose about oneself should help in forming relationships. Recognizing indications of inequity or conflict and realizing that it is best to address them quickly and directly should enable individuals to get over bumpy spots in relationships. Much of the attraction literature should be helpful to individuals in dealing with personal relationships.

Marital counselors, premarital counselors, and other psychotherapists need to have a good understanding of attraction research. Relationship problems create considerable anguish and often lead the individuals involved to seek counseling or therapy. Therapists should understand what makes couples compatible and incompatible and effective ways of reducing conflict and inequity. My impression is that many therapists evaluate and try to improve the mental health of the client, and improving the workings of the relationship is ignored. If the couple winds up in the divorce court, such is life, and the therapist continues to counsel the individual. Many relationships should end in divorce. However, if the couple has been happy in the past and no one is being abused, efforts to salvage the marriage should probably be made, especially if children are involved. Therapists need to know how dyads interact in order to improve those relationships.

Summary

The study of interpersonal attraction is important in understanding problems in initiating relationships (shyness) and problems resulting from poor relationships (loneliness, aggression within families, and divorce). Investigators must be scrupulous in examining close relationships so they won't disrupt them. Behaving in socially rewarding ways by being sympathetic, responsive, and praising are important in building friendship. Ingratiation tactics, such as flattering the other person and presenting oneself in a positive light, can also engender attraction. Reciprocating self-disclosure and being responsive in conversations is also helpful in forming friendships. Positive nonverbal behaviors, such as smiling and eye contact with a pleasant expression, also elicit positive reactions. Living or working near someone and the many interaction opportunities it affords make it likely that you and that person will become friends. Attitude similarity also produces attraction. Such agreement has been seen as attraction-producing because (1) it is reinforcing, (2) it indicates pleasant activities the individuals can share, (3) it indicates that the agreeing person likes the target person, or (4) it requires that the person like the agreeing person to maintain cognitive balance.

Love is distinguished from friendship by fascination, sexual desires, and relationship exclusiveness. Men are expected to take the initiative in heterosexual interactions; women are more reactive and selective in such interactions. Women are expected to be and are more expressive than men. Individuals who are initially lukewarm or negative and then become more positive toward a person are sometimes liked better than a uniformly positive person. Selectively positive persons are consistently liked better in mixed-sex encounters than nonselective persons. Physiological arousal and appropriate cues can make a person feel passionate love toward an appropriate other person. We may be most attracted to beautiful people, but fear of rejection and matching considerations make us gravitate toward people equal to us in attractiveness. For relationships to endure, it is important that both partners make equal contributions to and get equal benefits from the relationship. It is important that both partners have similar views of marriage whether they be traditional, modern, or egalitarian. Even though marriages are communal relationships, it appears important that equitable exchange of some resources be maintained. If one person becomes dissatisfied in a relationship, he or she will act to end the relationship if his or her earlier satisfaction was low, the partners' common investments in the relationship were small, and he or she has good alternatives to the relationship. Many conflicts in a relationship often lead to negative attributions toward one's partner and these attributions contribute to the deterioration of the relationship. These attraction research findings should be useful and applicable for sellers of goods and services, counselors and therapists, and ordinary people trying to establish and maintain relationships.

Altruism and Helping

Life and death matters abound in the news. Natural and man-made catastrophes of enormous proportions in terms of human lives are common. The famine in Ethiopia; the nuclear accident and the earthquake in the Soviet Union; the hurricanes, tornadoes, earthquakes, and floods in the United States; and the Union Carbide poisonous gas leak in India—all affect many lives. The survivors need help. The response in terms of money, food, clothing, health care, and shelter is equally enormous. People care. Many give their time, effort, and resources. For many of us, helping is easy. We call a number flashed on our TV screens and pledge money to the relief program at hand.

Other types of crises do not have such life and death dimensions. The motorist stranded by car problems or weather conditions, the person who suffers a seizure in our midst, the blind woman in unfamiliar surroundings, the student who is struggling with statistics or rejection in a personal relationship, the person who asks for directions, the person in a wheelchair faced with physical barriers, the young man who breaks his leg playing softball, the person who falls on the subway—all of these victims need our help. Social psychologists have examined helping in such emergency situations in many studies.

The fact that these situations occur frequently and require swift action by ordinary citizens justifies the focus on helping in emergencies prevalent in social psychology. Crimes against persons, such as attempted murders, rapes, assaults, and armed robberies, create some of these emergencies. Auto accidents, drownings or near-drownings, and health problems such as heart attacks and drug overdoses create many other crises demanding quick responses. Considering the number of these events that occur every year, a person would have to be quite fortunate not to witness at least one of these emergency situations in a lifetime.

People often help, sometimes at great risk to themselves.

Often the response in these real-life dramas is quite heroic. The flight attendant on the plane hijacked to Beirut in 1985 who saved the life of one Navy man and probably other passengers was certainly heroic. Joe Delaney, a star football player for the Kansas City Chiefs, gave his life for others when he tried to rescue three young boys from a construction-site water hole a few miles from his Louisiana home in 1982. Delaney jumped in even though he did not know how to swim. The government worker who rescued a woman from the icy Potomac when an Air Florida flight went down acted heroically. A man who was a passenger on that flight gave his life towing others to a helicopter hoist until he could stay afloat no longer. Many people acted with great bravery and skill in rescuing toddler Jessica McClure from an abandoned well shaft in Midland, Texas. Tom Brokaw saved John Chancellor, the man whom he eventually succeeded as anchor of the NBC Nightly News, from choking by using the Heimlich manuever when many others had not seen or had not acted. A man in Dayton, Ohio jumped out of his car and saved three young children who were being swept away by a stream swollen out of its banks. Accounts of other heroic efforts could undoubtedly fill several books.

How do we decide when someone's behavior is heroic, noble, or altruistic? **Altruism** is the *motivation* for acts that reflect an unselfish concern for the welfare of others (Batson & Vanderplas, 1982). **Helping** is *prosocial behavior* that may be altruistically or selfishly motivated. When is behavior seen as unselfish and, therefore, altruistic? It is when the behavior may be costly or dangerous to the helper and when the helper does not expect to receive material or social rewards for the action (Walster & Piliavin, 1972).

Costs, Rewards, and Altruism

What is meant by *costly*? It means that when a person knowingly and willingly gives up a great proportion of his or her time or resources, that person will be seen as motivated by altruism. If one is willing to jeopardize one's ultimate resource—one's physical well-being or even one's life with full awareness of the possibility of injury or death—then that person is judged to be acting altruistically. In the previous examples, it is evident that Joe Delaney, the plane passenger, and the flight attendant would be perceived as acting altruistically.

What about rewards and altruism? If a person helps in order to get the praise, esteem, or money of others, that person is not perceived to be behaving altruistically. However, if someone works only for the self-reward of feeling good, there is disagreement about whether altruism is the motivation or not. Whether a person receives an extrinsic reward or not is irrelevant; it is only one's expectations about being rewarded for helpful actions that are relevant to judgments of altruism. So, if a person risked incurring some costs *and* did not expect to receive *extrinsic* rewards, then his or her action is presumed to be motivated by altruism.

Others disagree:

> Even heroes and martyrs can benefit from their acts of apparent selflessness. Consider the soldier who saves his comrades by diving on a grenade or the man who dies after relinquishing his place in a rescue craft. These persons may have acted to escape anticipated guilt and shame for letting others die. Or they may have acted to gain rewards—the admiration and praise of those left behind or the benefits expected in a life to come (Batson, 1987, p. 66).

In this case, the benefits to others and the costs to self are so great and the rewards to self so small and uncertain, that a strong desire to benefit others (called *altruism*) would have to be a major motivational factor. Recently, Dan Batson and associates (Batson, 1987; Batson, Dyck, Brandt, Batson, Powell, McMaster, & Griffitt, 1988) and Robert Cialdini and associates (Cialdini, Schaller, Houlihan, Arps, Fultz, & Beaman, 1987) have argued about whether helpful behaviors are altruistically or egoistically motivated. Batson and his colleagues have contended and produced evidence for the position that only actions aroused by *empathy*, an other-oriented emotional response to another person's plight, are truly altruistic in nature. All other acts, they contend, have some selfish motivation. Cialdini and his colleagues contend that even empathy-based helpfulness is selfish in nature. Their recent study (Cialdini et al., 1987) showed that help

(in right margin)

Altruism

Defining Altruism

Figure 12.1
Subjects agreed to help a victim more only when they had empathic concern and when their negative mood was changeable. The investigators concluded that the helping was egoistically, not altruistically, motivated by the desire to alleviate the subjects' negative mood.

(From Cialdini et al., 1987, Journal of Personality and Social Psychology, 52, 756.)

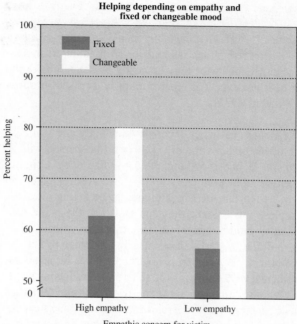

Helping depending on empathy and fixed or changeable mood

was rendered to alleviate the helper's personal sadness (a selfish motive), not empathy. (See figure 12.1.) Taken together, these positions, which include actions taken to make the helper "feel better" as selfishly motivated, indicate that there is no altruism in human hearts. Your author's opinion is that helpful acts done to alleviate personal distress *caused by another's plight* and intended to improve the other's condition are altruistically motivated. What do you think?

Bystander Nonintervention

Unfortunately, there are other accounts of events which illustrate the meaner side of human nature. The 1964 slaying of Kitty Genovese, which was seen or heard by 38 unresponsive people, instigated the research on helping behavior discussed in this chapter (cf. Latané & Darley, 1970). The terrible aspect of these bystanders' inaction was that the assault lasted over a half hour and occurred in three separate knife attacks by the same man so that intervention would have saved her life. Latané and Darley (1970) cited some situational factors peculiar to that incident that contributed to the bystanders' unresponsiveness.

Another incident which illustrates how unhelpful people can be occurred in Fairborn, Ohio a few years ago. Two boys, 6 and 10 years old, abducted a two-year-old girl while she was out of her babysitter's sight, and committed an awful crime. They disrobed her, beat her, and threw her into a pond. When two men happened by, the boys ran to them saying that there was something wrong with that girl over there and ran away. The two men discovered the girl floating face down in the water. One or both of the men went to a house nearby and called an ambulance. When the paramedics arrived, the two men and about twenty other people were standing by the water where the little girl was. The paramedics pulled her out of the water (which was only 3 or 4 feet deep!) revived her, and took her to the hospital where she died several hours later. In the newspaper account, one of the paramedics was absolutely outraged that none of those people had taken the child out of the water.

Certainly, many readers were almost as appalled at the bystanders' behavior as they were at the behavior of the 6- and 10-year-old boys. That reaction was probably similar to New York City readers' reaction to the unresponsive witnesses of the Genovese killing. However, in retrospect, there were some situational factors present in the drowning which could make the bystanders' inaction more understandable. For one thing, the first two men were visitors from out of state who were unfamiliar with how much or how little danger lurked in the standing water. The appearance of the infant may have made them think that the time for action was already past because she was dead. If they had arrived as the boys were throwing her in the water or while there were some signs of life, their response may have been much different. All of the cues to the subsequent bystanders, including the first two men's inaction, must have suggested that the emergency was over. So the unknown water depth and the cues from the child's condition and the behavior of others could have contributed to the bystanders' unresponsiveness.

There are some situations in which it is too costly to help. This judgment of the rewards and costs of helping has been used as a theoretical framework for estimating the likelihood that help will be given in particular situations (Piliavin, Dovidio, Gaertner, & Clark, 1981; Walster & Piliavin, 1972). This model suggests that bystanders weigh the probable rewards and costs of helping or not helping before they decide to intervene. Because emergencies occur unexpectedly and require quick action, it is reasonable to assume that these judgments are made very quickly and only the most salient potential rewards and costs to the helpgiver are considered. Costs to the victim are not included in this model. Personal danger and lost time are examples of potential costs of helping; self-congratulations and praise and admiration of observers are potential rewards; self-blame and public censure are examples of potential costs for not helping; and saved time and effort are potential rewards for not helping. The model has been couched only in terms of costs, but it is assumed that the rewards of helping have the opposite influences as the costs of helping and that the rewards of not helping have the opposite effects as the costs of not helping.

The Rewards and Costs of Helping

Most likely response as a function of costs

		Costs for direct help	
		Low	High
	High	Direct help	Indirect help or excuses to enable escaping situation
Costs for no help to victim			
	Low	Variable: Depends on (a) personality and (b) perceived norms	Leaving the scene, ignoring, denial

Most of us would probably use a model like this to explain bystander non-intervention in the Genovese case and other cases; to help would be too costly and not very rewarding. A few points about the model should be made. The model indicates that situational factors determine the potential helper's response, not the bystander's personal characteristics. The model also explicitly indicates that excuses or disparaging the victim (in the upper right cell) allows the bystander to leave the situation more easily.

Second, the model suggests that truly altruistic responses are very unlikely. We have already stated that helpful acts are regarded as altruistic when the perceived costs are high and the rewards are low (i.e., when conditions in the right half of the model exist). When both types of costs are high (the upper right cell in the model), indirect help like that of the two men in the drowning incident is the best one can expect to occur. Piliavin et al. (1981) have indicated even indirect help is rare when both types of costs are high. Truly altruistic acts involving risking one's life are uncommon. Saving someone's life as Tom Brokaw did with little cost to oneself (unless you regard potential embarrassment as high cost) is more common, as the model suggests (upper left cell). Putting oneself in jeopardy when the costs of not rendering aid are low (lower right cell) would be foolish or daredevilish, and we can only hope that it is as uncommon as the model suggests.

Third, the model is not presented in a vacuum; i.e., factors that do not conveniently fit into the model are considered. For instance, Piliavin and her associates assume that an emergency has been perceived and that the onlooker is aroused by the situation. Walster and Piliavin (1972) also consider the onlooker's judgment of the equity or fairness of the victim's predicament among other factors.

Empathy and Altruism

Batson and his associates (e.g., Batson, Duncan, Ackerman, Buckley, & Birch, 1981; Toi & Batson, 1982) suggest that this reward-cost model applies when the onlooker experiences only personal distress, not empathic concern. Batson and Vanderplas (1982) regard empathy as an important instigator of altruistic responding. Empathy involves focusing on the victim's experience and reactions, and empathic concern can only be reduced by knowing that the victim is no longer suffering. Only the costs to the victim, not the helper, are relevant. Escaping the situation can reduce personal distress, but it cannot eliminate empathic concern. If a person were *personally distressed,* he or she would be alarmed, disconcerted, disturbed, upset, anxious, and worried; if the person experienced *empathic concern,* he or she would be moved, touched, empathic, concerned, and compassionate (Coke, Batson, & McDavis, 1978).

Krebs (1975) showed that observers do empathize with victims who are similar to themselves and that when they are empathically aroused, they act altruistically. He also demonstrated that those who watched a similar victim being shocked experienced the most physiological arousal. Gaertner and Dovidio (1977) also found that those who had the greatest heart rate change at others' plight helped the fastest. So, those who "felt with" the victim most, both physically and by self-report, acted the most altruistically.

The reward-cost model suggests that we only help when the price is right. We do not behave altruistically. However, Stotland (1969), Krebs (1975), and Batson and his associates suggest that those who are induced to react empathically act in truly altruistic ways. Other investigators have suggested that egoistic motives rather than altruistic motives cause helping (Cialdini, Darby, & Vincent, 1973; Cialdini & Kenrick, 1976; Piliavin, Callero, & Evans, 1982). These researchers say that helpers are often selfishly motivated.

Piliavin et al. (1982) have argued that donating blood is sometimes done for selfish reasons rather than altruistic ones. They apply the opponent process theory of motivation of Solomon and his associates (Hoffman & Solomon, 1974; Solomon, 1980; Solomon & Corbit, 1974) to the experience of giving blood. **Opponent process theory** states that when one emotional reaction starts, the brain and nervous system initiates an opposing emotional reaction that eventually brings the person back to a neutral, stable state. First-experienced pleasant emotional states are followed by a short, mild unpleasant reaction and vice versa. After many experiences of an emotion, the opposing emotional reaction which follows becomes longer and stronger as the primary emotion becomes weaker and shorter. The opponent process model has been applied to the experiences of novice and experienced parachutists (Epstein, 1967) and joggers to explain why veteran jumpers and runners derive more pleasure from the experience than new ones do. It might also be used to explain why experienced drug users require more of a drug to sustain positive feelings than new users.

Piliavin et al. proposed that first-time donors would experience strong negative emotional reactions before and during blood-giving followed by a weak, positive reaction afterwards as the opponent affect (positive emotion) took over. With each successive donation experience, the donor's negative feelings should become weaker and shorter as the positive opponent affect becomes stronger and starts earlier. The overall experience should become more pleasurable with each successive blood donation.

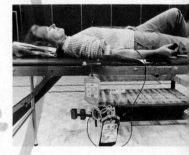

Blood donors may give to help others and to experience the "warm glow."

Piliavin and her associates were able to show that experienced donors at the University of Wisconsin reported more strong, positive feelings after donating than novices did. They note, however, that the pattern of results was not strong enough to argue that the "warm glow" was the main motivation for frequent donors. Also, this explanation of giving blood based on hedonism or gaining pleasure does not explain the motivation of first or second-time donors since their reactions should be quite miserable. In fact, Jane Piliavin (personal communication, 1986) believes that going from a first-time donor to a veteran donor requires some altruistic motivation.

Giving blood and giving coupons for other students (Cialdini & Kenrick, 1976) are not instances of helping in emergencies. Because emergencies demand fast actions, other, less selfish considerations may affect responses in emergencies. Hoffman (1981), in arguing that altruism is part of human nature and that empathy inspires altruistic action, commented that when helpers are asked why they helped, they invariably reported that they helped because the victim obviously needed help or that they helped without thinking. They did not report thinking about themselves or their distress at all. In these rapid action situations—several studies show that helpers respond in 10 seconds or less if they respond at all (e.g., Latané & Darley, 1968)—helpers do not think selfish thoughts. As Hoffman (1981) notes, just because a person feels satisfied after a helpful act does not mean that he or she was motivated to act benevolently for that self-reward. Rapid action in emergency situations appears to be more altruistically motivated.

Sociobiology and Altruism

Sociobiologists contend that there are only two types of altruism: (1) **kinship altruism** (Hamilton, 1964), whereby an individual risks himself or herself for the benefit of others who are genetically related to the individual; and (2) **reciprocal altruism** (Trivers, 1971), whereby an individual helps an unrelated individual with the expectation that the benefited party will return the favor in the future. Inclusive fitness or survival of one's genes is the presumed motivation for these helpful acts. In that the individual is seen as acting only to benefit oneself or one's kin in both cases, it seems that such helpful acts are not altruistic.

Helping one's relatives is governed by how closely related they are to the individual, their reproductive prospects, and how much risk is involved for the individual. According to these sociobiological tenets, a woman should not lay down her life even for her identical twin sister if her sister is beyond her reproductive years. Ginsberg (1977) demonstrated the importance of reproductive future in a study in which he asked grandparents whether they would save their children (50 percent genetically similar) or their grandchildren (about 25 percent similar) in a crisis. More grandparents said they would save their children with the exceptions occurring when their children were beyond their reproductive years! In those cases, they chose grandchildren. Don't even ask about saving in-laws (0 percent similar) relative to children! It would make good sociobiological sense for the woman to risk her life for two of her twin's children. Since her twin has the same genetic makeup as she does, her two children would represent the helper as much in the next generation as the helper does in the present one. If their reproductive future is good and one's own possibilities are dim, it makes sense to sacrifice all for several cousins. If the helper has to give up only a modest amount of one's own resources, helping relatives through parental care or getting them jobs should be common.

Freedman (1979) makes some interesting observations about Japanese society and altruism. He notes that Japan has a very homogeneous population. It has been an isolated society with much in-breeding so that everyone is related to everyone else, at least a little. He feels that these shared genes account for some of the altruistic features of Japanese society. Japanese workers have volunteered to take pay cuts which will benefit all of their "relatives" in the company. Schoolchildren are attuned to maximizing the gross national product, which will ultimately enhance the biological fitness of all. National and organizational allegiance seems to have the quality of family ties. Kamikaze pilots in World War II and other types of altruistic suicide may be common because of the genetic similarities in the society. Adoptions of nonrelatives are more common in Japan than anywhere else in the world. Adopting someone and providing for them are certainly helpful acts which are more understandable when there are blood relationships throughout the society. Freedman does not contend that this kinship-related altruism abounds independent of cultural influences. He only indicates that the presence of many shared genes correlate with, and may contribute to, the occurrence of these "altruistic" patterns. Rushton (1988) contends that kinship altruism is likely to be extended to similar others if there is recognition of genetic similarity in these nonrelatives.

Freedman (1979) noted that the Navajo have extended the umbrella of close relations in that they have no words for cousin, aunt, or uncle. All such distant relatives are regarded as brothers, sisters, mothers, or fathers. He notes that helpful behavior, such as providing food and lodging, is extended throughout the Navajo "family" network. This conduct represents truly extended kinship altruism, as advocated by Batson (1983).

Reciprocal altruism, helping others with the expectation that they will benefit you in the future, fits nicely with the selfish gene of sociobiology (cf. Dawkins, 1976). Such helping would be extended only to people who recognize you, who are likely to be near enough to have ample opportunities to reciprocate the aid, and who will have ample resources or capabilities to help in the future. Also, you would not help if the situation were too dangerous, because you would not be around to receive help in the future. Except, by combining kinship and reciprocal altruism, one might predict that a person would jeopardize his or her life if the recipient was expected to benefit the helper's relatives in the future. Otherwise, sociobiology paints a bleak picture for helping strangers in emergencies.

Equity and Helping

If a person is being victimized when he or she should not be, equity theory shows that we would usually help that person (Walster & Piliavin, 1972; Walster, Walster, & Berscheid, 1978). When we see that what happens to a person (that person's outcomes) is much more negative than what that person's characteristics or contributions (that person's inputs) indicate they should be, we whose outcomes and inputs are much more congruent will attempt to improve the victim's outcomes. Berkowitz (1972) has used the idea of a *norm of social responsibility* to explain why we help those in need. The norm of social responsibility is invoked when inequity is perceived; that is, when someone else is not enjoying benefits they deserve as much as you are. If we feel personally responsible for others' plight because we, not some third person or organization, reduced their positive outcomes in some way; we are especially likely to help those victims.

Even the abundant research on the fact that being in a good mood makes it more likely that a person will help others (e.g., Isen, 1970; Isen, Clark, & Schwartz, 1976; Isen & Levin, 1972; Weyant, 1978) seems to be compatible with an equity position. When people are made aware that everything is going their way by receiving a gift or experiencing success, they might be expected to act to benefit others to bring these victims' inputs and outcomes into equity with their own. (See figure 12.2.)

Figure 12.2
People who were put in a positive mood helped by volunteering to collect donations more than people in a neutral mood did. They also helped more than people in a negative mood except when the benefits of collecting were high and the costs were low for the negative mood people. Positive mood uniformly enhanced helping; negative mood did so only under limited circumstances.

(From Weyant, 1978, Journal of Personality and Social Psychology, 36, 1173.)

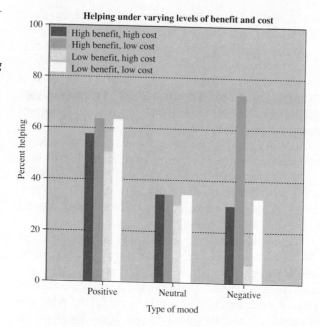

Systems of equity in our cultures seem to be part of the social evolution that Campbell (1975) felt was necessary to overcome humans' basic selfish nature. Walster et al. (1978) note that humans are motivated to maximize their material rewards in their basic propositions of equity. However, they contend that this selfish impulse is constrained by groups developing social rewards for those who act equitably—take only their fair share—and social punishments for those who don't restrain themselves. Socialization using these rewards and punishments apparently makes people feel guilty when they are overbenefited. So, some of our sociobiological selfishness has been curbed by equity demands made by groups to which we belong, starting with the family.

Reciprocity, doing unto others as they have done to you, seems to be a special case of equity. In reciprocity, the only inputs that are relevant are those that contribute to the outcomes of another person. If person A acts to enhance the outcomes of person B, then person B is expected to benefit person A in return. Gouldner (1960) argued that reciprocity is a very powerful norm. It seems to be the cultural component that makes reciprocal altruism suggested by sociobiologists possible.

However, some aspects of equity lead to greater victimization rather than helping. Our belief in a just world (Lerner, 1980) leads us to view a victim more negatively when we know very little about that person (Lerner & Simmons, 1966). However, when we can help and do, we do not denigrate the victim (cf. Lerner & Simmons' "reward" condition). (See figure 12.3.) In that situation, we seem to have reestablished real equity by improving the victim's outcomes and do not need to distort our perceptions to attain psychological equity. Many situations,

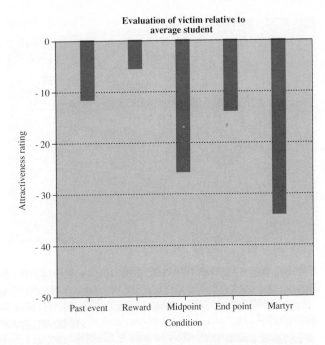

Figure 12.3
The victim of electric shocks (she wasn't really shocked) was rated most negatively and most deserving of being shocked when observer subjects didn't help her and were going to continue to see her suffer (midpoint and martyr conditions). When observers did help alleviate her suffering (reward condition), they rated the victim most positively.
(From Lerner & Simmons, 1966, Journal of Personality and Social Psychology, 4, 208.)

however, constrain us not to help, and we feel the need to believe that the victims deserve their fate. Equity has other implications for helping when we perceive that particular others have minimal inputs; that is, they got themselves into that fix. If we perceive them as unworthy of aid (whether it is true or not), we will not help, and we may even resent third-party (e.g., governmental) intervention for those "deserving" victims.

A five-stage decision model for helping in emergency situations has been proposed by Latané and Darley (1970). They state that in order for someone to render aid in an emergency, that person must do the following:

1. Notice that something is happening
2. Interpret the event as an emergency
3. Decide that it is his or her responsibility to act
4. Decide what form of assistance to give
5. Implement the action

These five steps are supposed to occur in this sequence, and if one of the steps does not occur, none of the subsequent choice points will be considered and help will not be given. Incidentally, Piliavin et al. (1981) and Schwartz and Howard (1981) do not believe that the process unfolds in such discrete, sequential steps; instead, they contend there are different or more complicated sequences. Let us consider each of these stages in sequence.

A Model for Helping in Emergencies

The helping rate on the New York City subway was quite high in one series of studies.

Noticing an Event

We are most likely to notice that a significant event is occurring if (1) the setting is familiar, uncrowded, and otherwise uneventful; (2) all of our senses are working; (3) we see the event or consequences of the event; and (4) we hear sounds from the event. Milgram (1970) contended that people on crowded, hectic city streets are unlikely to notice many events because of *sensory overload*—the bombardment of our senses by too many people and events. It seems likely that many people on the outskirts of the crowd waiting for a Who concert at Cincinnati's Riverfront Coliseum in December 1979 never realized a significant problem had developed. Nearly a dozen people were killed by the crush of that crowd.

If our sensory capacities are permanently impaired or temporarily diminished because we are inebriated or sleepy, we will also be unlikely to notice important events. Because of the necessity of seeing and/or hearing the event, noise and darkness can reduce the probability that a person will notice the event. Sounds are more likely to be heard than sights are to be seen because seeing requires one to be oriented in a particular direction and hearing does not. So, a shooting would be more noticeable than a knifing.

However, the most important factor in noticing an event seems to be when one arrives on the scene. If a person is present when an event transpires, he or she is more likely to notice and to help than if that person arrives later and sees only the aftereffects of the event. It is certainly more dramatic, arousing, and noticeable if a person falls in front of you or a car skids off the road nearby than if a person is lying on the ground or a car is resting in a ditch. Staub and Baer (1974) found that pedestrians were more likely to help someone whom they saw fall clutching his knee than someone who was already on the ground when they saw him. Piliavin, Piliavin, and Broll (1976) found that subjects helped victims only 1 time out of 8 when they saw the aftermath of an accident, but they helped 8 times out of 9 when they saw the whole incident. It is likely that the high percentage of helping observed when a man fell in a New York City subway car (Piliavin, Rodin, & Piliavin, 1969) was due to the fact that many people noticed the event. The falls were staged in a subway car that was familiar to the passengers, relatively uncrowded (the falls occurred during nonrush hours), at an uneventful time (eight minutes before the next stop), and during the daytime when everyone would be alert and able to see and hear the fall. Other factors undoubtedly affected the helping rate, but they contributed only because the observers noticed the event first.

Is that man at the head table gagging on his steak? Will he be able to cough it out by himself? . . . Is that healthy-looking young man laying on the couch seriously ill? Have any of those other people called an ambulance? . . . Is that guy twisting that woman's arm just fooling around or is he trying to hurt her? Do they know each other? . . . Is anyone in that car up on its side? Did it just happen or has it been there for weeks?

Perceiving an Emergency

After a person has noticed an event, he or she must decide whether it is an emergency or not. Shotland and Huston (1979) state that *emergencies* have five basic qualities:

1. They happen suddenly and unexpectedly
2. They impose harm or a threat of harm on the victim
3. The threat or harm increases with time
4. The victim cannot extricate him- or herself from the situation without someone's help
5. Effective intervention must be possible.

The likelihood of serious harm and its increasing with time were the most important factors in defining a situation as an emergency in their research.

What makes a person decide that an emergency is occurring? In some situations there are obvious physical cues, such as blood, loss of consciousness, cessation of breathing, or abrupt, high impact crashes. In other situations, the physical cues are more ambiguous, and we are dependent on others' reactions for information. If others are acting nonchalantly, we may be reluctant to energetically initiate mouth-to-mouth resusitation. Latané and Rodin (1969) found that when a woman had a bookcase fall on her in an adjoining room, lone subjects came to her aid about 70 percent of the time; but when a nonchalant, passive confederate was also present, only 7 percent of the real subjects helped.

Was the inaction caused by failure to interpret the event as an emergency or by deciding not to help because the embarrassment costs of helping were too high? It appears that two types of social influence—informational and normative—are operating here. You may recall from chapter 8 that *informational influence* occurs when an observer uses another's behavior as a basis for making judgments about events, while *normative influence* occurs when the observer acts like another to follow a norm in order to avoid embarrassment or to gain approval (Deutsch & Gerard, 1955). It seems likely that the passive confederate in the injured woman study exerted normative social influence on the subject, not informational influence. However, interpreting a situation as an emergency (Stage 2) would involve informational influence. (See figure 12.4.)

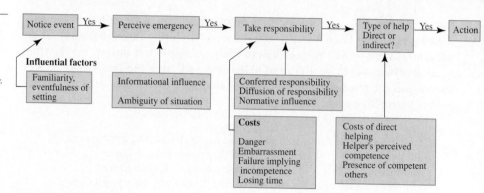

Figure 12.4
*A Decision Model of
Helping in
Emergencies.*

*(Adapted from Latané & Darley,
1970.)*

Other investigators have been more successful in teasing out the effects of these two types of social influence on helping. Darley, Teger, and Lewis (1973) had Princeton men seated either face-to-face, back-to-back, or alone sketching a horse when a workman had a partition fall on him nearby. When the pairs of subjects could see each other when the crash and groans occurred, they helped almost as frequently as lone subjects did (80 percent vs. 90 percent). However, when pairs of subjects could not see their partners' startled reaction at the crash, they helped only 20 percent of the time. Darley et al. contended that seeing the other's reaction provided cues—a form of informational influence—that the ruckus was indeed an emergency. Also, Latané and Rodin's (1968) finding that more pairs of friends (70 percent) helped the injured woman, and they did so faster than pairs of strangers (40 percent helped) was obtained, at least in part, because friends communicated their reactions to each other more than strangers did. Informational influence is most important at this second stage.

Schwartz and Gottlieb (1976) used a complicated method to examine facets of subjects' reactions to a fellow student who had a tape recorder stolen forcefully from him. Using an intercom system and separate rooms, they were able to manipulate a particular subject's awareness of other bystanders' reactions to the theft/attack (*informational influence*) and the other bystanders' ability to hear the subject's reaction to the theft/attack (*evaluation apprehension* or *normative influence*) separately. They also had a condition in which no other bystanders were present to overhear the attack (to assess *diffusion of responsibility*). The time until helping occurred results indicated that the subject's awareness or unawareness of others' reactions affected helping first. That is, subjects checked others' reactions to the situation first if that information was available. So, informational social influence does appear to occur earlier—at Stage 2—than other types of reactions. The two other factors—diffusion of responsibility and evaluation apprehension (or normative social influence)—exerted their influence later, presumably during Stage 3 of the Latané and Darley model.

A sobering example of how others' reactions can affect people's judgment in an emergency situation occurred at the Beverly Hills Supper Club in northern Kentucky in the late 1970's. It was very warm at the club one night as patrons awaited John Davidson's performance, but everyone reacted as if the cooling system was not working by removing coats, etc. That was the first case in which others' reactions were misinformative. After a while, a young busboy interrupted a comedy team by grabbing the mike and saying, "There is a fire in the kitchen [it had been smoldering in the walls for some time]," and pointing out several appropriate exits. Unfortunately, the comedy team initially reacted as if the busboy were part of their skit. Apparently, their reaction confused many people about the seriousness of the situation—more misinformation from others' reactions. Over 160 people died in that fire. Reports were that victims had been too slow vacating the room (perhaps because they were confused?) rather than showing the more typical pattern of clogging the exits.

Deciding to Take Responsibility

Should I help? . . . What is going to happen to him if I don't help? Will someone else help? . . . What is going to happen to me if I help? Will I get hurt? Will I have to take her to the hospital? . . . Will I make a fool of myself giving CPR to him?

Piliavin's reward-cost calculations model assumes awareness of an emergency (and arousal evoked by it) somewhat like Latané and Darley's early steps. Most of the evaluations of rewards and costs in her model seem to occur during this decision stage about taking responsibility. However, the costs to the victim are not specifically included in the Piliavin et al. (1981) model even though it appears to be an important feature in deciding to take responsibility.

Costs: Danger

What does affect whether we will take the responsibility to help? First, let us consider some cost factors. What about physical risk or danger? Most of us respond quickly that fear for their lives was probably a major determinant of the 38 bystanders' failure to rescue Kitty Genovese. Certainly, it must be a major factor in why poor swimmers seldom try to rescue drowning victims and why people seldom confront gunmen. Nevertheless, Piliavin et al. (1981) point out that there are situations that evoke "impulsive helping" (nearly all observers help and they do so quickly). Some of these situations involve grave danger. In one study, 100 percent of the subjects helped when an electric wire present would have killed them if it had been live (Clark & Word, 1974). Some theft studies (e.g., Moriarity, 1975; Schwartz & Gottlieb, 1976) also involved implied physical danger, and they also evoked high rates of helping. Apparently, the suddenness and clarity of the emergency and other involving aspects of the situation or the victim's plight lead these helpers to ignore the dangers. Again, the victim's costs seem to be an important neglected factor in Piliavin's basic model. Many of the heroic actions described at the beginning of this chapter could be described as instances of impulsive helping.

One study that showed a strong effect of implied physical danger on helping was conducted on the New York City transit system (Allen, 1972). In the physical threat condition, three actors participated. One actor, the misinformer, was a muscular fellow seated on the bus reading a muscles and health-type magazine. Another actor pretended to trip on the first actor's feet. The misinformer clenched his fists and told him to watch where he was going. Then, the third actor, the tourist, climbed on the bus wearing Bermuda shorts and a camera around his neck. Eventually, he asked the misinformer whether the bus was going uptown or downtown and the hefty, belligerent fellow misinformed him. The subject was whoever was seated next to the misinformer, and he could help the tourist by correcting the misinformer. Only 16 percent of the subjects helped in this physical threat condition as opposed to 82 percent who corrected a misinformer who did not pose a physical threat. Since investigators are not encouraged to brandish guns or knives or beat up on people in experiments, this is probably the most dramatic demonstration of the effects of danger on helping.

Costs: Embarrassment

Another kind of cost which deters people from assuming responsibility in a helping situation is embarrassment. To me, it is the main reason that only one-tenth as many subjects who were seated with the passive confederate helped the injured woman in the Latané and Rodin (1969) study as lone subjects did. This is the same normative social influence effect mentioned earlier. People will not take action when all those around them are acting as if no action is necessary. The embarrassment would be too great. It is at the heart of the **bystander effect**— the tendency for individuals to help less when other bystanders are present than when they are alone (Latané, Nida, & Wilson, 1981).

The desire to avoid embarrassment is why normative social influence occurs. That desire motivated many of Asch's (1952) subjects to say that the wrong length line was the same length as the standard line. It is also why many people do not help when they are in a public setting with many others present.

Any situation in which it may be inappropriate to rush to someone's aid could lead to embarrassment. Helping should occur less frequently in those situations. A study by Clark and Word (1972) illustrates the effects of uncertainty about the appropriateness of action on helping. In the clear emergency, they made it sound as if a workman had fallen off a ladder nearby, and the workman groaned in pain, said, "Oh, my back, I can't move," and a little later, "Help." In the ambiguous situation, the subjects only heard the sounds of the fall. All subjects in the clear emergency situation came to the workman's aid; only 30 percent came to his aid when the situation was ambiguous. The cry for help must have eliminated any concerns about the inappropriateness of helping. (See figure 12.5.)

Schwartz and Gottlieb (1976) showed that normative social influence can encourage helping rather than inhibiting it. Recall that they had subjects overhear a theft over an intercom in various experimental conditions. When Schwartz and Gottlieb's (1976) subjects heard the theft occurring over the intercom and they knew others could overhear their reaction, they helped more than if the other bystanders could not know how they responded. However, this evaluation apprehension effect (as they and Latané et al., 1981 call it) did not affect behavior as quickly as the previously mentioned informational social influence and diffusion of responsibility did. This temporal pattern of results appears to verify that evaluation apprehension or normative social influence occurs during the responsibility-taking period rather than earlier. As noted earlier, in this particular situation the embarrassment threat made subjects more likely to help. Usually, others' awareness of the bystander inhibits helping (e.g., Latané & Darley, 1976).

Where is the good Samaritan when we need him? There are many reasons why people don't help.

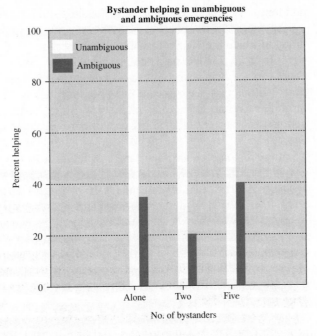

Bystander helping in unambiguous
and ambiguous emergencies

Percent helping

□ Unambiguous
■ Ambiguous

No. of bystanders

Figure 12.5
Bystanders always helped the fallen workman in the unambiguous situation (100 percent). They seldom helped in the ambiguous situation. The number of bystanders had little effect on helping.
(From Clark & Word, 1972, Journal of Personality and Social Psychology, 24, 397.*)*

Another example of the inhibiting effects of possible embarrassment is the classic subway helping study done by Piliavin, Rodin, and Piliavin (1969). In one case, the man who fell in the subway carried a cane; in the other, he was carrying a bottle in a brown paper bag and reeked of alcohol. On the "cane" trials, the victim received help from someone in the car 95 percent of the time before 70 seconds had elapsed. On the "drunk" trials, he received help within 70 seconds less than 25 percent of the time. Other factors, such as the belief that the drunk brought his problems on himself, probably contributed to his being helped much less than the weakened or crippled person. It seems certain, however, that the potential embarrassment from the unpredictable way a drunk might react to offers of assistance inhibited helping.

Many people might not help because they fear that they would make a mistake. This type of fear would be more likely to inhibit helping if the injury seemed serious and others who were more competent or better trained were available or could be summoned. Another subway study provided evidence that the seriousness of the problem can inhibit helping (Piliavin & Piliavin, 1972). In this study, the investigators had a white man with a cane fall on a Philadelphia subway car. In half the cases, the man bit a vial of red liquid as he fell, making it appear that he was bleeding from the mouth. In the other instances, the fall was the same as in the earlier study. The bloody victim was helped in 60 percent of the cases compared to over 90 percent for the victim who did not bleed. They also found that fewer people came to help, and those who did responded slower in the cases of the bloody victim when there was a medical intern present relative to when

Costs: Failure Implying Incompetence

no intern was present. Another experiment (Staub & Baer, 1974) showed that a victim who has a very serious health problem is not always helped. In the condition in which they had a man clutch his chest and fall to the ground across the street from an onlooker on a neighborhood street, not one of 20 onlookers helped! Onlookers did help if he grabbed his knee before falling! The extreme results for heart victims may have been a fluke because they reported that 5 of 12 helped in similar circumstances in another study. Still it seems that those who need our help most are often shunned because of our feelings of inadequacy.

Costs: Losing Time

The time lost can be an important cost factor that inhibits helping. If you are rushing to an important engagement, you would be less likely to stop and help someone. At least, that is what the results of a well-known experiment by Darley and Batson (1973) suggest. Princeton seminary students who were to give a talk on the parable of the Good Samaritan or on types of ministerial vocations were sent to another building to have the talk recorded. They were told that (1) they were late and had to hurry, (2) they should go right over, or (3) they had plenty of time to get to the recording. The seminarians discovered a sick man in the alley between the two buildings. The time pressure variable affected helping rate most with 10 percent of those in a real hurry helping, 45 percent of those in a moderate hurry helping, and 63 percent of those in no hurry helping. In a replication study, Batson and associates (Batson, Cochran, Biederman, Blosser, Ryan, & Vogt, 1978) found that only 10 percent helped if they were in a hurry to get to an important experimental task, while 67 percent of those not in a hurry or not involved in an important matter helped. Batson et al. (1978) contended that failure to help did not represent callousness but was motivated by a desire to do the most good for the most people. Presumably, if the person in distress were in greater need than he or she appeared to be in these studies, most of us would disappoint those counting on our timely arrival and help.

Conferred Responsibility

Nearly all of us help if someone has asked us to assume responsibility for his or her belongings. We are also more likely to take responsibility if it is difficult to escape the situation. Moriarty (1975) found that people are very willing to take responsibility for looking after another's belongings. In two studies, everyone who was asked to do so took that responsibility. The first experiment conducted on Jones Beach, New York, involved a man or a woman stealing a blaring radio from a person's beach blanket while he or she was away. The eventual victim placed his or her beach material near another person or persons' blanket. After a few minutes, the victim asked those on the adjacent blanket to "watch my things" or for a cigarette light and walked away to the boardwalk. Soon the thief picked up the radio and walked quickly away. Nineteen of 20 (95 percent) of those who had been asked to watch helped by trying to stop the thief, while only 20 percent of those who had been asked for a light helped.

The second experiment was conducted in a more hectic place where the thief could have been carrying a weapon in his clothing—a midtown Manhattan vending machine cafeteria. A young woman sat down with lone subjects at a

A theft might go unnoticed at this beach, but it did not at Jones Beach, New York.

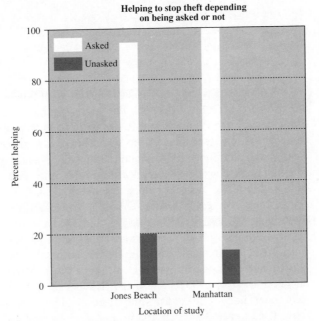

Helping to stop theft depending on being asked or not

Percent helping

□ Asked
■ Unasked

Jones Beach   Manhattan

Location of study

Figure 12.6
If subjects had responsibility conferred on them by having the victim ask them to look after his or her belongings, nearly all of them helped, regardless of the setting. Asking for help had a tremendous effect on helping.
(*From Moriarty, 1975,* Journal of Personality and Social Psychology, *31, 373, 375.*)

table. After a few minutes, she asked him or her for a light or to watch her overnight bag on the table and went to get her food. Soon a man stole the suitcase. All of those who had agreed to watch the bag stopped the thief. Only 12.5 percent of those who had not been asked to take responsibility helped. These results are dramatic evidence that we will be our "brother's keeper" if we are only asked. (See figure 12.6.) Austin (1979) reported that a preliminary study indicated that they had to ask subjects to look after their things in a library or subjects would be totally unresponsive to a theft right under their noses.

Figure 12.7
People who were put "in charge" of a group discussion over an intercom went to the aid of a choking man much more often than a mere group member did.
(From Baumeister et al., 1988, Personality and Social Psychology Bulletin, 14, 19.)

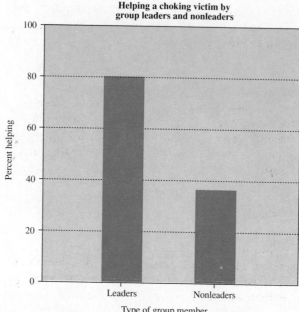

Helping a choking victim by group leaders and nonleaders

Responsibility can also be conferred by staging the incident so that it is difficult to escape the situation. The high helping rates in the subway studies conducted by the Piliavins and Rodin were so high partly because the falls occurred in an enclosed place from which there was no exit for several minutes. Also, Staub and Baer (1974) found that only 42 percent of the individuals helped when an apparent heart attack victim on the other side of the street from them collapsed, but 87.5 percent helped if he fell in front of the bystander on the same side of the street. So, if responsibility for another's well-being is imposed on us, most of us will not shirk that responsibility. That is probably why most people who are "in charge" in a particular situation (e.g., managers in restaurants or stores, teachers in classrooms, desk clerks in hotels) will interrupt the proceedings to help someone in distress. In fact, a recent study (Baumeister, Chesner, Senders, & Tice, 1988) showed that leaders in an unrelated group interaction were more likely to leave the study to respond to an emergency than nonleaders were. (See figure 12.7.) In 1985, an American and a Soviet doctor who were receiving the Nobel prize in medicine interrupted the ceremony to revive a Soviet journalist striken by a heart attack.

Diffusion of Responsibility

Diffusion of responsibility occurs in situations where several people could potentially help so that the brunt of responsibility for helping is shared, rather than concentrated on one person. It can be considered the opposite of the concentration of responsibility (cf. Wegner & Schaefer, 1978) on individuals just discussed. Latané and Darley (1976) and Latané et al. (1981) regard it as one of the three factors contributing to the *bystander effect*, the observed tendency for individuals who are among other onlookers to help less than those who are alone. The other two factors which contribute to the bystander effect are informational social influence and evaluation apprehension or normative social influence.

Often, it is hard to separate the effects of these three factors. Schwartz and Gottlieb (1976) successfully isolated them in their "theft over the intercom" study and found that 92 percent of the lone subjects intervened versus 45 percent of the subjects who knew that someone else heard the attack but did not know how other bystanders had responded. Temporally, the diffusion of responsibility effect appeared to start after the informational social influence effect and before the normative social influence effect. Latané and Darley (1976) also isolated the diffusion of responsibility effect in a study in which the experimenter accidentally received a very severe shock and found the effect to be weaker (95 percent of lone subjects vs. 84 percent of subjects together but not communicating helped). Where there was full two-way communication between subjects, only 50 percent helped. It seems that in real life, all three factors affect the helping rate, as in this full communication condition. The Genovese case appears to be one of those rare cases where diffusion of responsibility was the most important factor, because the bystanders could not tell whether others helped or not. If you can see how others react or others can gauge your reaction, then diffusion of responsibility is not the only factor operating.

Social impact theory has been used to account for the bystander effect (Latané, Nida, & Wilson, 1981). Social impact theory implies that as the number of bystanders increases, the emergency's impact on a particular bystander to help should decline. The change from 0 to 1 other bystander should cause the greatest decline in helping rate; the change from 1 to 2 should be next greatest, etc. The expertise and immediacy of the other bystanders should also affect helping. If you were a medical reporter in a room full of eminent cardiologists when a person collapsed, you would probably not feel compelled to rush to that person's aid. It should be noted that the social impact position is applied to the bystander effect where all sorts of social influence may be operating, not just diffusion of responsibility.

The Bystander Effect and Social Impact Theory

The bystander effect is related to the tendency for diminished helping by one person in a crowd relative to when he or she is alone. What are a victim's chances of getting help from one onlooker versus any one in a crowd of onlookers? There are some prominent studies that have shown that groups as small as two are just as likely or more likely to help a victim than a lone observer. Piliavin et al. (1969) found that size of the group in the subway car did not affect the helping rate. Clark and Word (1972) found that two- and five-person groups were just as likely to help the fallen workman as lone subjects were. Staub (1970) found that pairs of young children (kindergarten through second grade) were more likely to help another child in distress than single subjects were, but pairs of older children were as inhibited as lone subjects were. These studies indicate that the bystander effect inhibiting helping by people in groups does not always occur.

Figure 12.8
Strong, assertive leaders eliminated the bystander effect in the group and increased helping, regardless of whether they were elected or appointed.

(From Firestone, et al., 1975, Journal of Personality and Social Psychology, 31, 348.)

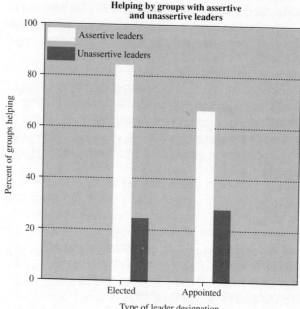

Latané et al. (1981) reviewed studies comparing subjects alone with those in real groups and concluded that single subjects were slightly more helpful than groups of subjects. However, the one person versus a group bystander effect is not strong, and it might not manifest itself in real groups that were acquainted or had one person who was "in charge." For instance, Firestone, Lichtman, and Colamosca (1975) found that groups that had a popular elected leader intervened in a medical emergency faster and more frequently than groups which did not have such a leader. (See figure 12.8.)

Direct or Indirect Helping

Should I go in the fire myself or should I call the fire department? . . . Should I call a doctor or start administering CPR immediately? . . . Should I leap in myself or should I yell for the lifeguard? . . . Should I try to stop the robber myself or should I call the police?

When one has decided to take responsibility, he or she must decide how to intervene (Latané & Darley, 1970). When two or more people are working together, one can summon the authorities and the other can help directly. In fact, Staub (1971) found that when one adult volunteered to go get help and suggested that the other intervene directly, all subjects did help directly. A person alone experiences a dilemma between helping and getting help. Piliavin et al. (1981) suggest that indirect help is more likely than direct help if the costs of helping are high. If the person does not feel competent to improve the victim's condition

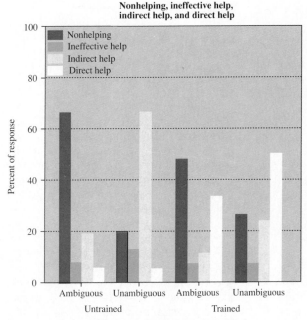

Nonhelping, ineffective help,
indirect help, and direct help

- Nonhelping
- Ineffective help
- Indirect help
- Direct help

Percent of response

Ambiguous Unambiguous   Ambiguous   Unambiguous
Untrained   Trained

Training of students and situation ambiguity

Figure 12.9
Bystanders who had first aid training were most likely to give direct help to a man with a bleeding leg, especially if it was an unambiguous emergency. Untrained bystanders most often gave indirect help if it was a clear emergency, but they were unlikely to help at all if the situation was ambiguous.

(From Shotland & Heinold, 1985, Journal of Personality and Social Psychology, 49, 352.)

safely and successfully, then the costs are high. Consequently, the person who is a poor swimmer or untrained in CPR will probably summon aid (indirect help). For instance, Shotland and Heinold (1985) found that students who had completed a Red Cross first aid course were much more likely to give direct help to a workman with a severely bleeding leg wound than those who were just starting the course. Other studies (e.g., Harris & Huang, 1973a; Midlarsky & Midlarsky, 1976; Schwartz & Ben David, 1976) have shown that those who felt competent to handle a particular emergency were more likely to help directly than others. John Sirica (the Watergate judge), among many others, must have been thankful that someone who felt competent to administer CPR was present when he had a cardiac arrest. (See figure 12.9.)

However, if a person were not able to summon aid quickly, then the person might reconsider and help directly. In reviewing 14 studies where type of help was specifically examined, Piliavin et al. observe that indirect help was common only when the means for summoning aid were made very salient. Apparently, the bias in fast-breaking emergencies is to help directly.

Once the dilemma of which type of action to take has been resolved, there are no more decisions to be made. Helping as effectively as possible is the final step (Latané & Darley, 1970).

People who know cardiopulmonary resuscitation techniques are more likely to help in emergencies.

Research Trailblazers
The Many Facets of Helping

Mary B. Harris and her associates at the University of New Mexico have been studying helping behavior in natural habitats for many years. Most of these observational studies have been true field experiments with certain variables being selectively manipulated.

Harris's studies are remarkable for the number of topics, requester characteristics examined, theoretical questions asked, methods used, and settings sampled. She and her students have studied whether going to confession at a Catholic church affects donations (Harris, Benson, & Hall, 1975), whether the accent of a caller making a wrong number phone call affects the response she received (Harris & Klingbeil, 1976), and whether a "feminine" request—asking for help with a stuck shopping cart—affected the helping rate (Harris & Bays, 1973). These helping studies have been done in many settings—on a college campus (Harris, 1977; Harris & Ho, 1984), in college classes (e.g., Harris, 1972), in shopping centers (e.g., Samerotte & Harris, 1976), at subjects' homes and over the telephone (Harris, Liguori, & Stack, 1973), in restaurants and a library (Harris & Samerotte, 1976), at a state fair (Harris & Baudin, 1973),

and at a church (Harris et al., 1975), as well as in the laboratory (Harris & Huang, 1973a and b).

Harris and her associates have focused on a few theoretical themes, and they have used a large number of clever methods to study these ideas. We will focus on a few of the central theoretical questions and findings. One question they have studied is whether helping one time will increase the likelihood that a person will help again, as in the foot-in-the-door research of Freedman and Fraser (1966), and if so, why? They have found that if the subjects look after the requester's belongings for a few minutes, subjects will donate more money to him later than they would have otherwise (Harris & Samerotte, 1976). If subjects give the time or directions to a requester first, they were more likely to give him or her a dime than if the first request had not been made (Harris, 1972). If subjects had written letters to prospective students on behalf of the university first, they were more likely to volunteer to lobby for the university to the legislature (Harris, 1972, Experiment 2). If subjects agreed to fill out an ecology survey, they were more likely to give a dime to another person (Harris & Samerotte,

1975). Harris's interpretations of these results suggest that greater later helping was caused neither by a change in one's self-concept to "I am a helper" nor by the rewards or thanks subjects received because they helped even when they received a negative response to the first favor performed. Instead, she favors the idea that the first experience makes a norm of social responsibility (Berkowitz & Daniels, 1963) salient to the subject when the second request is made.

One related theoretical theme is the role of rewards in instigating helping. Several of the studies on the foot-in-the-door effect involved the subjects receiving a positive, a negative, or a neutral response to their helpful acts. In those studies, the type of response received by the subject did not affect their subsequent helping one way or the other. So, a reward after helping did not have a reinforcing effect on later helping in Harris's work. In another set of studies, Harris, Ligouri, and Stack (1973) compared the effectiveness of a reward offered beforehand (a bribe) with requesting a favor as in the foot-in-the-door studies in eliciting help. Both of these techniques are common sales ploys, as discussed in chapter 8. When subjects were

These churchgoers should be more generous than those who have already been to services.

given a tree-shaped cookie as a bribe and when they were asked to do the favor of evaluating the taste of the cookie, both groups of subjects agreed to contribute to an Ecology Club bake sale more than subjects who were not offered the bribe nor asked the favor. So, small rewards offered beforehand do arouse helpfulness in some situations—especially if the rewards are tasty.

A second related theoretical area is the effect of guilt or guilt reduction on helping. One facet of the Harris and Samerotte (1976) study was to induce guilt in some subjects by asking them to look after a person's belongings and then having a confederate steal a radio from among the belongings. In another condition, subjects were also asked to look after the belongings, but the theft was so obvious that these subjects

stopped it and, therefore, did not feel guilty. Those who felt guilty because they had allowed the theft were more than twice as likely to donate money to the victim or another person for food than those subjects who had stopped the theft. In a related study, Harris, Benson, and Hall (1975) found that Catholics were more likely to donate to the March of Dimes before confession than after confession. Apparently, parishioners who had already confessed felt less guilty than those who had not, just as those who had stopped a thief did not feel as guilty as those who felt responsible for a theft. Guilt must make individuals feel more obligated to help; whereas, the absence or reduction of guilt frees people from the obligation to help.

Harris and her associates have done several studies

examining the effect of mood on helping and the effect of helping on mood. These studies generally have not supported the idea that one's mood affects that person's helpfulness, unlike several studies which indicate that positive mood promotes helping (cf. Isen, 1970; Isen & Levin, 1972). Caldwell and Harris (1979) found that mood did not influence the tendency to help by confronting a thief. Harris and Siebel (1975) found that thinking different kinds of thoughts did not affect third graders' tendency to share balloons with others. Harris and Smith (1975) found that feeling good at first was positively correlated ($r = .29$) with time spent helping. The idea that being helpful will elevate a person's mood (cf. Manucia, Baumann, & Cialdini, 1984) fared only slightly better. Subjects who were induced to

(Continued)

(*Research Trailblazers Continued*)

help another felt nicer than those who did not help (Harris & Smith, 1975). Helping a woman search for a lost piece of paper made helpers report a more positive mood than those who did not have the opportunity to help, but other helpful acts had no effect on mood (Harris, 1977).

Other interesting research studies on helping done by Harris and her associates include a study demonstrating that if a subject realizes that the arousal he or she experiences when seeing a woman in pain is attributable to feeling sympathy for her, then such a subject is more likely to help her than one who misattributes his or her arousal to something else (Harris & Huang, 1973b). This finding is particularly compatible with other researchers' emphasis on the importance of empathy in promoting helpful actions. Other studies have found that altruistic models are not a very effective way of eliciting helping (Harris, Liguori, & Joniak, 1973; Harris & Samerotte, 1975). Still other studies have examined the effects of the dependency, responsibility, ethnicity, and dress of the person needing help on likelihood of receiving help (Harris & Baudin, 1973; Harris & Ho, 1984; Harris & Klingbeil, 1976; Samerotte & Harris, 1976). It is evident that Harris's research program has been productive and creative in studying altruism.

Who Helps Whom?

Personality Factors

Generally speaking, the evidence concerning relationships between personality traits and helping behavior is mixed. One reason for this confusing situation may lie in the different types of helping situations studied. Situational factors are so strong in most emergencies that it is unlikely that personality characteristics could make a difference (Latané & Darley, 1970; Piliavin et al., 1981). However, other kinds of situations that call for helping someone with homework, sharing resources, or giving to charities are not determined so much by situational demands, so personality differences should influence behavior. However, most studies of traditional personality traits find that they are unrelated or minimally related to helping (Krebs, 1970). Some studies have shown that certain personality traits are related to some types of helping, but they are unrelated to other types (Gergen, Gergen, & Meter, 1972; Staub, 1974). For example, a recent investigation showed that high self-esteem people and people high in empathic concern were helpful when they could not easily escape the situation, but only later-borns helped out of altruism (Batson, Bolen, Cross, & Neuringer-Benefiel, 1986).

What about some factors that common sense tells us should be related to helpfulness? What about those with high moral standards or strong religious beliefs? Some investigators have examined the relationship between persons' stage of moral development (Kohlberg, 1969) and their helping behavior. Several researchers have found that adults who have a higher level of moral reasoning are more likely to help in a variety of helping circumstances than those lower in moral reasoning (Eisenberg-Berg, 1979; Krebs & Rosewald, 1977; Staub, 1974).

Batson and Ventis (1982) reviewed several studies on the relationship between religious involvement and moral standards. Seven of the eight studies reviewed indicated that religious people had higher moral standards than less religious people did. The interesting exception was a study which showed that religious people scored lower on Kohlberg's levels of moral reasoning (Haan, Smith, & Block, 1968).

Do religious people help more than nonreligious people do? If you believe what they say, they do. That is, Batson and Ventis (1982) found that all of the studies they reviewed indicated that church attenders self-reported that they were more helpful than low attenders reported they were. Unfortunately, in studies that examined their behavior, they did not help as much as they said they did. None of the five studies reviewed by Batson and Ventis reported any differences in helping rate between religious and nonreligious people.

Wilson (1976) looked at personality differences derived from Maslow's hierarchy of needs in relation to helping behavior. Using a sentence completion test developed by Aronoff (1970), Wilson divided his subjects into safety-oriented, esteem-oriented, and mixed categories. *Esteem-oriented* individuals are seen as higher on Maslow's growth hierarchy and could be characterized as independent, confident, competent, and dominant. *Safety-oriented* people are seen as lower on the hierarchy and could be characterized as dependent, anxious, and passive. These subjects were filling out a questionnaire either alone or with two confederates when they heard a loud crash/explosion and sounds indicating that the experimenter had been hurt coming from an adjacent room. Nearly all (96 percent) of the esteem-oriented subjects rushed to the experimenter's aid when alone, and 71 percent came to his aid when the two confederates were passive. Only 55 percent of the safety-oriented subjects helped when alone, and only 17 percent helped when the confederates were passive. Clearly, these confident, assertive types of people were more helpful than the meeker individuals. This result is consistent with the observations that Christians who helped Jews during Nazi terrorism and Carnegie hero award winners who endangered their lives for others could be primarily characterized as "adventurous" (Staub, 1974).

Tice and Baumeister (1985) uncovered another personality variable that is related to helping: masculinity. Many of us may have guessed that femininity would be related to helping. That is, feminine people are empathic and sensitive among other things; therefore, their empathic capacities should make them more likely to help, right? These authors hypothesized that another possibility is that masculine people are especially sensitive to embarrassing themselves by acting inappropriately; therefore, they should help less. You will recall that embarrassment is an important cost factor in helping situations.

To test these ideas, 47 subjects who had been classified as masculine, feminine, androgynous (high in both masculinity and femininity), or undifferentiated (low in both) participated individually in simulated group sessions over an intercom. The male victim started choking on a doughnut as he was speaking over the intercom. Only 9 percent of the subjects high in masculinity (masculine and androgynous subjects) helped, while 76 percent of those low in masculinity (feminine and undifferentiated) did. On the other hand, 44 percent of the high feminine subjects helped and 45 percent of the low feminine subjects helped. Why did masculinity have the expected effect and femininity did not? The major reasons apparently were that the helping situation was an emergency that held many possibilities for embarrassment from overreacting and, at the same time, did not allow time for reflection on the victim's plight that might inspire empathy. The femininity-empathy position could perhaps be tested better in another type of situation. Again, the impact of personality variables can be quite different from one type of situation to another.

Sex Differences in Helping

Who helps more, men or women? The research indicates that men help more overall (Eagly, 1987; Eagly & Crowley, 1986). Alice Eagly contends that the reason the helping literature indicates that men are more helpful is that most research studies have examined helping strangers in emergency situations. Men have been socialized to render that kind of aid, while women have been taught to give nurturant, supportive aid in long-term relationships. For example, consider the typical *social roles* of females—nurse, teacher, babysitter, and mother—and the kinds of help they promote.

However, as Eagly and Crowley have shown, which sex helps more often depends on the situation. In their exhaustive, meta-analytic review, men were more likely to help if the situation was regarded as dangerous more by women raters than by men and if men were confident that they had the skills needed for the task. For example, men are more likely to help if the intervention demanded by the situation is of a direct, physical nature. That is, if the situation clearly indicates that helping requires lifting a person or large object, men help more. For instance, Piliavin et al. (1981) reported that in the subway fall studies, almost 90 percent of the helpers of the fallen men were men even though roughly 50 percent of the subway passengers were women. Shotland and Heinold (1985) found that women helped the man with a cut leg less than men did. Also, when the victim was a stranded motorist and the aid might require changing a tire or mechanical work, men acted much more frequently to help than women did (Bryan & Test, 1967; West, Whitney, & Schnedler, 1975). Also, men helped women pick up their dropped groceries more than other women did (Wispé & Freshley, 1971).

Even though Latané and Darley (1970) casually wrote that "coping with emergencies is a male duty" (p. 102), some studies indicate that women sometimes respond to emergencies even at their own peril. Moriarty (1975) found that women acted to intervene in the theft at the automated cafeteria just as readily as men did. On a Phil Donahue show, Moriarty said that if women had agreed to look after the beach belongings, they often physically detained the male thief. In a study in which subjects were asked to look after another student's belongings in the corridor of a university building, women were much more likely to stop a thief who was stealing someone's calculator than men were (Austin, 1979). Apparently women took the responsibility conferred on them by others as seriously or more seriously than men did even though intervention could have been dangerous. These findings are consistent with Eagly and Crowley's review finding that women were just as likely as men to help if a direct request was made, but not as likely if a need was just presented.

Another factor that is important in helping, perhaps because of sex role expectations, is the sex of the person needing help. Latané and Dabbs (1975) found that the most common aid configuration involved a man helping a woman

 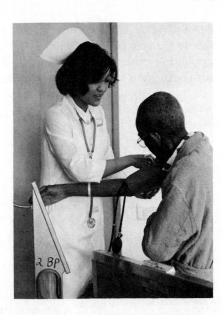

Women are more helpful in long-term care and supportive aid.

in picking up dropped objects. This man-helping-woman result was most common in the South (Atlanta), where traditional sex roles may still have more influence than in other areas. Bryan and Test (1967) and West et al. (1975) also found that male drivers more readily came to the aid of female motorists than male motorists. In fact, males helping females is the most common occurrence in all the helping literature (Eagly & Crowley, 1986), probably because of the teaching of social roles.

Women may be inhibited from helping men by their sex-role beliefs about how men and women should behave. For instance, women who had their belongings stolen were helped more than men were, especially by female helpers (Austin, 1979). So, women helped women more than they helped men. In Shotland and Heinold's (1985) emergency situation, women helped less than men did; but perhaps they were inhibited because the victim was a male and intervention would require direct physical assistance to him. However, Darley and Latané (1968) found that women helped a man who was having an epileptic seizure just as readily as men did. One can only speculate that he inspired more empathy than the fallen workman or that less drastic physical intervention was implied by the situation.

Many of the classic emergency studies (Clark & Word, 1974; Darley & Batson, 1973; Latané & Rodin, 1969; Schwartz & Gottlieb, 1976) used only men as subjects. The reason for this practice seems to be that these investigators thought that men would be more likely to render aid in emergencies requiring physical intervention. On the other hand, helping studies involving manipulations of empathic concern in nonemergency situations are more likely to employ women subjects (e.g., Toi & Batson, 1982). These investigators' choices are reasonable barometers to how social psychologists believe men and women behave in different situations. Women are usually more sensitive, empathic, and responsible toward the plight of others (cf. Schopler, 1967).

Intraracial and Interracial Helping

Do most of us only help people of our own race or ethnic group? Every one of the heroic acts described at the beginning of this chapter involved same-race helping except the Austrian-American TWA flight attendant who saved the black-American Navy man. Did this occur because we are race-biased in helping, because we are ignorant and fearful of the reactions of other-race help recipients, or because the world's races are so segregated that we are unlikely to have the opportunity to intervene directly for someone of another race? Probably all three factors stifle interracial helping. Certainly, campaigns like USA for Africa have fostered much indirect interracial helping.

Sociobiology suggests one reason why Joe Delaney tried to rescue three black boys or the Dayton, Ohio man pulled three white children, one of whom "reminded [him] of [his] daughter" about the same age, out of the raging water. People who are of the same racial group share some genes with us. However, the similarity is hardly more than 0 percent unless we are members of an isolated, geographically close group. However, the appearance of the individual may make us think and act as if the genetic similarity is greater, and such children are the genetic future of any race. Consequently, kinship altruism could be invoked to explain intraracial helping. However, there are too many psychological, cultural, historical, and other nonbiological factors involved for kinship altruism to be an important proximal cause for intraracial helping.

Some social psychologists have studied the prevalence of interracial and intraracial helping in everyday life. The first subway helping study (Piliavin, Rodin, & Piliavin, 1969) examined it by having black and white confederates play the part of the "drunk" and the man with the cane. More helpers of the drunk were of his race than were helpers of the man with the cane. Only when subway passengers would be expected to be leery and unsure of the help recipient's response (in the drunk condition) did race of the victim make a difference. Gaertner and Dovidio (1977) found that white women rushed to aid a black woman who had chairs fall on her just as readily as they did a white victim if they were alone. However, if other bystanders could also help, these women showed a higher rate of intraracial helping than interracial helping. The subjects' level of prejudice did not affect the helping rate.

Noncrisis situations have been examined also. Wispé and Freshley (1971) had a black woman and a white woman break and drop a bag of groceries as a black or white man or woman approached. Among whites, there was slightly more intraracial helping than interracial helping. Among blacks, there was no difference between interracial and intraracial helping. Black women helped either the black or white dropper least of the four categories of potential helpers.

West et al. (1975) observed how long it took for black and white male and female motorists to get help in black and white residential neighborhoods. In the first study, blacks were helped faster in black neighborhoods and whites were helped faster in white neighborhoods, indicating that intraracial helping was more common. The same pattern of intraracial helping was also found in white neighborhoods in a second study, but that bias did not appear in black neighborhoods in Tallahassee. Intraracial helping was also prevalent in neighborhoods near predominantly white and black college campuses.

It had been expected that interracial helping would have been more common near the liberal white college campus. This idea, which was not supported, came from an earlier study examining the interracial helping of Liberal and Conservative Party members in New York (Gaertner, 1973). White Liberals, especially young ones, were more willing to make a phone call for a black caller (who had called the wrong number) than Conservatives were. Perhaps the higher rate of interracial helping by liberal whites occurred in this study and not the West et al. study because no face-to-face contact with the black man or woman was required in the Gaertner study.

Katz, Cohen, and Glass (1975) have found that closeness of contact with the individual does affect interracial helping. They theorize that white Americans are generally ambivalent toward blacks and that these mixed feelings lead them to bend over backwards for blacks in some situations and to discriminate against them in others. In a phone survey study done in New York City, they found that white men were more helpful to black callers (who referred to themselves as Negroes) than to white callers. They also found that when the survey questions were introduced face-to-face on subway station platforms, interracial helping (to the black questioner) was more common than intraracial helping. When black and white confederates asked for change for a quarter on these subway platforms, the bias favoring interracial helping disappeared. It seems that the more remote the interaction is, the more likely it is that interracial helping will occur. When the interaction is too close, the tendency to appear egalitarian disappears. Uncertainty about how the recipients will react to cross-racial brotherly gestures may also inhibit person-to-person helping. These results may partly explain how the same person can contribute generously to Ethiopian relief and still shun his or her black neighbors.

Urban and Rural Differences in Helping

Who is more likely to help others in need, urban dwellers or people who live in small towns? Do the characteristics of the help-seeker affect helping by these two groups? *Where* are you most likely to be helped, in the city or the country? What aspects of situations affect helping?

Most of the social psychological research indicates that small town residents are more likely to help strangers than city dwellers are. One reason that small town people help more is that they are less threatened by strangers in their environment. Certainly, the rate of crimes against persons is much higher in cities than in small towns. Milgram (1970) reported a study in which men and women asked if they could enter a person's house to use the phone in New York City and in several towns on Long Island. Only about 30 percent of the New Yorkers helped the help-seekers, while about 70 percent of the town residents allowed them into their homes to make a call. The fact that men were allowed in much less than women were in both towns and the city is evidence of the threat factor. As a result, this type of situation may not be the best way to study helping tendencies in cities and towns.

Figure 12.10
*People in very small
towns were more
helpful than residents
of large cities in
Australia in every
situation except in
picking up dropped
envelopes.*
*(From Amato, 1983, Journal of
Personality and Social Psychology,
45, 579.)*

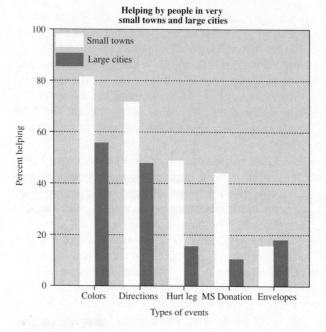

There are many other studies involving different kinds of help which also indicate that it is easier to get help in a small town than in a large city. For instance, Korte and Kerr (1975) found that people in small towns in Massachusetts were more likely to help people who called the wrong phone number, to give back overpayments to customers, and to mail lost letters than Bostonians were. Several other studies reviewed by Korte (1981) also found townspeople more helpful.

The most impressive evidence for the city-town difference comes from a study done in several localities and involving several types of helpfulness in Australia (Amato, 1983). Five of the six helping incidents were staged on the downtown sidewalks of several eastern Australian municipalities. Subjects could be helpful by (1) writing their favorite color on request, (2) stopping to help a man in pain with a bloody, bandaged leg, (3) buying greeting cards from the Multiple Sclerosis Society, (4) helping to pick up dropped envelopes, or (5) correcting inaccurate directions. A sixth measure of helpfulness was the return rate of national census forms from communities of different sizes. The population level categories ranged from communities of less than a thousand people to Sydney with three million inhabitants. Of the five field observation helping measures, all except picking up envelopes indicated that people in smaller communities were more helpful. The helping rate started declining in towns and cities larger than 20,000. The census results were atypical in that people in the smallest villages and the largest cities, Sydney and Brisbane, were more unresponsive than people in intermediate size communities. Overall, Amato again demonstrated that small town dwellers are more helpful than urban dwellers toward strangers. (See figure 12.10.)

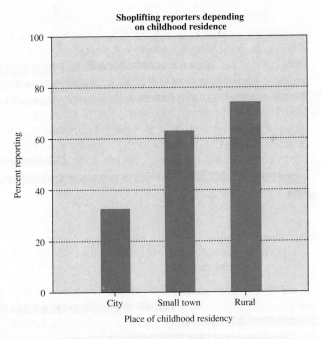

Shoplifting reporters depending on childhood residence

Percent reporting

Place of childhood residency

Figure 12.11
Customers who grew up in small towns or rural areas reported a shoplifter more often than customers reared in urban areas did.
(From Gelfand, et al., 1973, JPSP, 25, 282.)

A study conducted in the Netherlands suggests that the reason for this urban-rural difference is because there are more noisy and busy areas in cities than in small towns (Korte, Ypma, & Toppen, 1975). When they investigated helpfulness in low- and high-input areas in terms of noise and activity in both cities and small towns, they found that helpfulness was least in high-input areas. It did not matter whether the high-input areas were located in large cities or small towns. The fact that there are more high-input areas in cities than in towns could explain the differences found in other studies.

We might assume that people who grew up in rural areas would be more helpful than people from cities even when they are in a different environment. After all, shouldn't a person who grew up in a non-threatening environment where most people were familiar and where most activities required cooperation to be accomplished be more helpful than others? A few studies have shown that people from rural backgrounds do help strangers in nonrural environments (Darley & Latané, 1968; Gelfand, Hartman, Walder, & Page, 1973). (See figure 12.11.) Darley and Latané (1968) found that subjects who came from smaller communities were more likely to help a seizure victim than were subjects from larger communities. Gelfand et al. (1973) found that people with rural backgrounds were more likely to help the management of Salt Lake City drug stores by reporting a shoplifter than urbanites were. Parenthetically, the low rate of reporting shoplifters in that study and others (e.g., Bickman & Rosenbaum, 1977) suggests a "diffusion of consequences" effect may occur to the detriment of chain department stores. That is, it may be hard for consumers to perceive who the victims are and to empathize with them in such settings.

Townspeople and City People

Another study on helping seizure victims (Schwartz & Clausen, 1970) and another study on reporting shoplifters (Bickman & Rosenbaum, 1977) found no differences in helping rate between people with urban backgrounds and those from rural areas. A study done in Hawaii, which required subjects to leave their assigned experimental task if they helped a victim of a fall, showed that city-background subjects were more helpful than rural-background subjects (Weiner, 1976). This checkered pattern of results suggests that there are diverse early living experiences within small town environments and within urban environments and that the demands of the immediate helping situation also affect how urban people and rural people react in them. So, the number of people who lived in your hometown alone does not have a powerful influence on how helpful you are.

Will the Next Generation Be Helpful?

Better questions might be: How will the next generation become helpful? What can this generation do to assure that they will help appropriately? What will motivate their helping?

Children probably acquire the tendency to help others the same way that they acquire other behaviors. Children usually acquire behavior that leads to (or is followed by) reinforcement (cf. Skinner, 1938). In addition, children are likely to behave in ways that they have seen others behave, especially if they observe that those others have been rewarded for behaving that way (cf. Bandura, 1977b). Rushton (1980) and Staub (1971) point out that children will often behave the way they have been told they should.

What can adults do to assure that children will help appropriately? Adults can reward children when they behave in helpful, friendly, or cooperative ways. In a study involving adults, Moss and Page (1972) demonstrated that when people are rewarded for helping one person, they are much more likely to help the next person who needs it. They had a confederate ask for directions in downtown Dayton, Ohio, and then act rudely, courteously, or indifferently to the subjects' replies. Then, a second confederate dropped a bag in front of the subjects. Those who had been rewarded (treated courteously) for helping helped the second confederate more than the other two groups of subjects did. Many other studies have shown that reinforcing generous or cooperative acts by children increases future helpful acts (e.g., Altman, 1972). Rushton and Teachman (1978) showed that the positive effects of reinforcement on helping by children endured over time. Another strategy for adults would be to focus the child's attention on the positive consequences of their helpful acts. It might not be obvious to a child that another child's happiness or kindness occurred because he or she helped first.

The observational learning theory of Bandura indicates that adults can promote children's prosocial behavior by acting in generous and humane ways in the presence of children and by exposing them to other people who act in prosocial ways. Rice and Grusec (1975), for example, demonstrated that children who have seen an adult model donate to the poor will imitate those donations. Part of exposing children to others who act prosocially involves influencing what they see on television or at the movies. Several studies involving exposure to prosocial programs from "Lassie," "Mr. Rogers' Neighborhood," "The Brady Bunch," and "Father Knows Best" have demonstrated that children act more prosocially after watching such programs (Ahammer & Murray, 1979; Collins & Getz, 1976; Friedrich & Stein, 1975; Sprafkin, Liebert, & Poulos, 1975). Despite many negative commentaries about TV programming, some episodes from current and recent programs seem to promote prosocial behavior.

Telling a child how he or she should behave is another effective way to make children more helpful unless it is overwhelming and makes children believe that it is a behavior that is being forced on them by others (Walters & Grusec, 1977). It appears to be important that children internalize norms for helping. If they see their helpful conduct as externally caused, they are unlikely to internalize helpfulness (Grusec, Kuczynski, Rushton, & Simutis, 1978). Many studies have shown that "preaching" to children has a substantial and long-lasting effect on their giving to others (Grusec, Saas-Kortsaak, & Simutis, 1978; Rice, & Grusec, 1975; Rushton, 1975).

What will motivate children to help? From the perspectives just presented, the motivation for helpful behavior by adults of the next generation will be carryover or generalization effects from their earlier reinforcement experiences, observational learning, and moral instruction by others. These earlier experiences would presumably lead to internalized values for helping and these individuals would feel good when they help others (a form of self-reward). If many people had such helpfulness-promoting experiences as children, help would be more freely given.

According to another perspective (Batson, 1987), such prosocial, even self-sacrificial, behavior would not be altruistic. According to Batson, only behavior that is done to relieve the distress of another is altruistically motivated. So, our hypothetical next generation, which would learn to help in order to feel good or to relieve their own distress, would not be acting altruistically.

In the view of Batson and other empathy theorists (Krebs & Russell, 1981), the way to make the next generation act more altruistically is to increase their ability to take the emotional perspective of others. In this way, they will be able to empathize with the plight of others, and they will be motivated to reduce others' distress. However, Krebs and Russell (1981) review several studies which indicate an inconsistent relationship between role-taking by children and altruism.

While increasing the sensitivity of people to others' plights may increase altruistic action, it is not the only way to increase helpfulness. It is enough that people are more helpful; the purity of their motivation is secondary. If a person sacrifices some of his or her resources in order to benefit another without the expectation of monetary reward or other recognition, that person is acting benevolently and altruistically.

In fact, a few good words for those who help with the expectation of monetary gain or other recognition seem appropriate. Many people enter professions that require them to help others daily: lawyers, physicians, nurses, paramedics, firefighters, police, teachers, social workers, therapists, child care workers, auto

*People in the helping
and rescue professions
deserve our respect.*

People in the helping and rescue professions deserve our respect.

mechanics, and many others. They relieve the distress of many other people. To the extent that they could have chosen other, equally lucrative occupations or could operate in a less directly helpful role within their profession and do not do so; their motivation should be considered partly altruistic. Observing whether they render more or less aid than their job-role demands would give one a better sense of how altruistically motivated particular individuals are. Amato (1985) has advocated more study of planned helping, and he has found that those in helping professions do engage in more planned helping than others do. Of course, to the extent that one is handsomely compensated for his or her helpful acts, we would be likely to attribute little of that person's motivation to altruism.

Applications of Helping Research

There appear to be four major questions that knowledge of helping research can answer:

1. How can I get help when I need it?
2. How can I help others?
3. How can we get people to help others in need?
4. How can we train our children to act benevolently toward others?

How Can I Get Help When I Need It?

The most obvious answer is: Ask for it! If you yell for help, it will clarify the nature of the situation and place the burden of responsibility on those who hear. The cry for help of Clark and Word's (1972) workman showed just how effective such a cry can be (80 percent increase in helping). Directly requesting help is effective in getting others to help as demonstrated by Moriarty's (1975) theft victims on the beach and in the cafeteria.

Neighborhood watch programs to prevent crime are a means to apply the finding that conferring responsibility on people nearby makes them more likely to help. People in organized groups such as Neighborhood Watch are more likely to respond when the home of a group member is jeopardized.

Applying sociobiological theory suggests that a person should seek help from relatives and neighbors. In the sociobiologists' eyes, blood is certainly thicker than water. Neighbors should be approached for help after relatives. Neighbors are likely to help because you would reciprocate help the neighbor rendered. Because people are very likely to reciprocate help, it would be wise to seek help from someone you have helped in the past. Latané and Darley (1970) described different studies which showed that bystanders who are friends are more likely to help a victim than bystanders who don't know each other; and bystanders who have met the eventual victim are more likely to help than bystanders who haven't met the victim. These studies suggest that it is better to seek aid from a friend or group of friends than from a stranger. Also, Meindl and Lerner (1983) have found that a person will confront someone who has offended an assigned partner or fellow team member more readily than someone who has insulted the subject directly. So, a person should seek help from a relative, a neighbor, a friend, or a fellow team member first.

If such people are not available, you should seek help from someone who is similar to you. The Piliavin et al. (1969) subway studies suggest that you should seek help from someone who is racially similar to yourself. Krebs (1975) showed that people are more inclined to empathize with and help someone who is similar in personality and values than someone who is dissimilar. This research suggests that if one must seek help from a stranger, he or she should approach a similar stranger.

The bystander effect (Latané & Nida, 1981) suggests that a person seeking help should approach individuals rather than groups for assistance. Latané and Darley's (1970) decision model for helping and research on city-town differences (Korte et al., 1975) indicate that these helpseekers should approach those individuals in sparsely populated, low-activity settings. Darley and Batson's (1973) results also suggest that helpseekers should not approach individuals who appear to be in a hurry.

The most important thing a person can do to be helpful in emergencies is to develop competence in dealing with physical crises. A great inhibitor of direct helping for most people is not having the knowledge or the skills necessary to help the victim (cf. Eagly, 1987). Training in cardiopulmonary resusitation, use of the Heimlich maneuver, basic first aid, swimming and water safety, and recognizing problem conditions such as poison overdose give the trainee the confidence needed to render first aid to victims of emergencies.

Awareness of factors that may inhibit helping in emergencies should free the potential helper to act appropriately. Physical danger is a real cost in some emergencies and one might appropriately help indirectly by calling the police rather than jumping into the fray. A person should not be expected to act so altruistically that his or her life is jeopardized. However, it is realistic to expect a person to be sensitive enough to others' needs that the person will tolerate possible embarrassment and loss of time to help emergency victims. Knowledge that observers in groups have a tendency to let someone else help should sensitize potential helpers so that they may attempt to mobilize the group to action.

How Can I Help Others?

As for noncrisis helping, we can be helpful to others in our everyday environment by being sensitive to their direct or indirect requests for help. Support groups made up of people who have been through the same experience seem to be particularly effective in bolstering members' spirits. Alcoholics Anonymous, groups of people who have cancer or other maladies, groups of widowed people, groups of parents who have lost young children, and many other support groups testify that similarity of experience and the resulting empathy are important components of beneficial therapy. Acting in surrogate relationship roles such as Big Brothers and Big Sisters can be comforting to others. Doing things for dependents in our own families such as young children and aging parents are necessary and important types of noncrisis helping. Amato (1985) has pointed out that people in certain helping professions do more planned helping than other people do. Perhaps service-oriented people should be encouraged to enter such occupations.

At the same time, would-be helpers should be aware that sometimes help can pose a threat to the recipient's self-esteem (Fisher, Nadler, & Whitcher-Alagna, 1983). Letting people do what they can for themselves and encouraging them can be the most appropriate prosocial actions in such situations.

There are also limits to how much help a helper should give. A person can be too self-sacrificing. Much of the stress experienced in the health care professions and in social welfare work may come from excessive self-sacrifice. Many overburdened care-givers may become jaded and show some of the distancing behavior that Lerner (1980) has discussed in his "just world" work. No one should be expected to exhaust their energies and resources for the benefit of others.

How Can We Persuade People to Help Others in Need?

One approach would be to try to elicit empathy for the plight of the victims. British television was very successful in creating empathy for the starving in Ethiopia through a documentary that vividly portrayed their plight. Another strategy for inducing empathy derived from the work of Batson and Krebs is to highlight the similarity between the victim and the potential helper. "There but for the grace of God go I" seems to be a powerful motivator for prosocial behavior.

A recent development has been the multistar concerts and benefits by entertainers to call our attention to the problems of famine, flood, and earthquake victims; American farmers; victims of AIDS; and others. These performances attempt to personalize these problems and have been successful in showing people how they can help people in nearby and remote places. Giving feedback to the public about benefits of their giving should promote more benevolence.

The sociobiological approach suggests that we should emphasize family ties to increase helping. This link has been effectively used to gain voluntary aid for young people. Go to any place where children are receiving training or help, and you will invariably find that the helpers have a child in the group. Girl Scouts, Boy Scouts, Little League baseball, youth soccer, and various school groups all fit this description. The helpers are also helping other people's children as much as their own. So, this help generated by blood ties is also extended to others.

The research based on learning perspectives suggests that we should reinforce our children's helpful acts, we should be prosocial models for them by behaving in helpful ways in their presence, and we should expose them to other prosocial models in our daily surroundings and in the media. Teaching them societal norms of equity or fairness and social responsibility should also ensure that these children will become benevolent adults (cf. Rushton, 1980). Work on empathy and altruism suggests that we should teach them to be other-oriented to the extent that their capacity for empathy will be increased (cf. Krebs & Russell, 1981).

How Can We Train Our Children to Act Benevolently toward Others?

Summary

There are many occasions when others need our help. In life-threatening situations, they need our help quickly and desperately. Such emergency situations have been the focus of most social psychological research on helping.

Altruism is motivation presumed to exist when a person acts out of unselfish concern for the welfare of others. We assume that a behavior is altruistically motivated when the action may be costly or dangerous to the helper and the helper does not expect to be rewarded for the action. Some investigators state that we evaluate the costs of helping and not helping in particular situations and that we are most likely to help when the costs to us for helping are low and the costs for not helping are high. It seems that very little altruism is expected from humans.

Batson and his associates believe that altruism is most likely when the person feels empathy with the victim. Similarity to the victim and focusing on the plight of the victim can arouse empathy and inspire altruistic acts. Sociobiology suggests that we are most likely to help those who are most similar genetically to us and those who are likely to reciprocate the assistance. In these ways, we can increase our own and our relatives' survivability. Equity theory implies that we are likely to help those who are unjustly underbenefited relative to ourselves.

Latané and Darley (1970) state that an individual must notice an event, decide it is an emergency, decide that he or she is responsible to act, and decide what kind of help to give before he or she will help. The helping process can break down at any one of these steps. Informational influence, normative influence, the presence and actions of others, and various cost factors affect how individuals decide at different steps in this decision model. Conferring responsibility on a potential helper by asking him or her to be responsible for one's belongings is a potent facilitator of helping.

There is much debate about whether personality factors affect whether a person helps another. People higher in moral judgment or stronger in religious beliefs are no more helpful than other people. Masculinity detracts from helpfulness. Men are more likely to help women than vice versa in the types of studies that social psychologists conduct. However, in some nonemergency situations, women may be more helpful. We are more likely to help someone of our own race than someone of another race in most cases. City dwellers are not as helpful as inhabitants of less populous places. However, the evidence is mixed on whether people who grew up in small towns are more helpful than urban dwellers.

Adults can contribute to making the next generation more helpful by rewarding helpful behavior, providing helpful models for children to observe, instructing children to be cooperative and helpful to others, and increasing children's sensitivity to the plight of others.

Helping research suggests that the best ways to get help are to ask directly for help from relatives, friends, or neighbors and to ask lone individuals rather than groups. To be helpful, we should develop our competencies so that we are able to help in emergencies, be aware of factors that inhibit our helping, be sensitive to calls for help, and know when not to help. To encourage others to help people in need, we should attempt to arouse empathy for the plight of unfortunate people and take advantage of existing blood ties and other links between the needy and the potential helpers.

Antisocial Behavior

There had been a lot of drinking on the train from Liverpool to Brussels, authorities said. The fans from Liverpool, England and Turin, Italy eagerly anticipated the European Cup Final soccer match. So much so that heated words were exchanged between opposing fans in crowded adjacent sections of the stadium. The Liverpudlians threw rocks and bottles into the Italian section. Suddenly, the Liverpool fans broke down an 8-foot-high wire barrier between the two groups and rushed into the opposing fans' section. The fans from Turin tried to escape, but many were pinned against a concrete wall with such force that the wall collapsed. Thirty-eight people died and 437 were injured *before* the soccer match began (*Time,* June 10, 1985).

A young man walks home from his parents' house to his apartment in the same neighborhood. He is attacked and left for dead by unknown assailants, presumably other young men or boys in the neighborhood. The victim sustains severe head injuries and is unconscious for some time (Davis, *Dayton Daily News,* March 7, 1987).

Three generations of a family gather at an elderly woman's house on Easter Sunday. Before the day is done, the woman's son, a bachelor in his early 40's, has shot and killed her, his brother, his sister-in-law, and their eight children.

One semester I had several police and other criminal justice officers in an evening social psychology class. One of these students was a man who worked for the U.S. Treasury Department in a division charged with regulating the sale of alcohol, tobacco, and *firearms*. Less than a year later, I read in the newspaper that he had been killed in a shootout. He had been killed by a fellow alcohol, tobacco, and firearms officer in the Federal Building in an exchange of gunfire after a minor argument!

In 1974 at the state prison in Huntsville, Texas, a drug dealer serving a long prison term and two other prisoners gained control of the prison library and took two women librarians hostage. After a few days of negotiation, a car by which the prisoners were to escape the country was parked outside the library. The prisoners made a Trojan Horse of mobile blackboards with books strapped to them to effect their escape to the car. As the armed prisoners and their hostages moved within the protective Horse, a Texas Ranger-led group of law enforcement officers opened fire. Two hostages and two prisoners were killed in the barrage. The third prisoner was killed a moment later as he lay wounded on the ground.

Aggression is common.

The news media remind us daily of the violent world in which we live. Much of that violence comes from such "senseless" aggressive acts as those just described. Muggings, terrorist attacks, sexual assaults, barroom fights, and domestic quarrels are just a few of these aggressive acts.

It is evident that the United States continues to be one of the most violent nations on earth in terms of criminal aggressive acts. For Americans who regard our nation as just, peaceful, and moral, the national statistics on the violent crimes of murder, assault, rape, and robbery must be a source of concern (see box on page 400.)

Aggression is any *act* done with the *intent to harm* another living being, either physically or psychologically. Other social psychologists have presented more elaborate definitions of aggression (e.g., Baron, 1977), but at the heart of most definitions is the intent to harm another individual. The aspect of intent rules out destructive accidents, but some observers might say that blatant carelessness, as exhibited by drunk drivers, implies a lack of concern about harming others. In 1988, a drunk driver, driving the wrong direction on a divided interstate highway, ran into a bus, killing 27 people aboard. The driver had been seen driving in the wrong direction toward cars earlier in the evening. Was that aggression? Behavior which is intended to harm but has no harmful effect, like some assassination attempts, is aggression. The definition of aggression as behavior excludes smoldering rage or anger; aggression is not an unexpressed internal feeling. In this sense, aggression is like helping in that both are behaviors, and harmful intent is like altruism in that both are motivational concepts.

What Is Aggression?

Aggression is evident in the chapter-opening examples, but there are many situations which are hard to classify as aggression or nonaggression. For instance, suicide would only be classified as aggression if the suicidal person intended to harm *another* person through the self-destructive act. Also, what if the person's job or role called for him or her to act in destructive ways? A soldier, a parent, a hockey player, a police officer, or a football player may be expected to commit harmful acts in the line of duty. When are they being aggressive? We would probably conclude that they intended to harm another person when their actions go beyond the rules or laws for their roles. One study showed that observers regarded a person's actions as aggressive when he gave another person a shock more severe than the prescribed level in that situation (Kane, Joseph, & Tedeschi, 1976). Excessive force is a standard applied to determine when a police officer is acting aggressively. When a soldier knowingly attacks noncombatants, he is acting aggressively. Other situations are harder to judge. For instance, does the boxer's role legitimize his attempting to knock his opponent unconscious as nonaggression? I don't think so, especially if he voluntarily chose the boxer's role.

The boxer's situation highlights another factor in defining destructive actions as aggression. A boxer is in a competitive interaction, and he will be knocked unconscious if he does not hit his opponent. Self-defense is generally recognized by laws as justification for acting destructively toward another person. Bernhard Goetz used self-defense as an argument to justify his shooting four menacing young black men on the New York City subway. Ordinary observers endorse the idea that self-defensive, harmful actions are not aggressive (Kane et al., 1976). In the Kane et al. article, observers only regarded actors who initiated or escalated destructive action as aggressive. Those who only reciprocated earlier harmful actions were not seen as aggressive. Of course, these results still cast Goetz's actions in a murky light in that he escalated destructive actions when he fired a gun. The four-against-one confrontation complicates judgments even more. The consequences of Goetz's actions—one young man was left partially paralyzed—in this real-life example would not affect our judgment about aggression, but it would affect judgments about the offense in a trial. (See figure 13.1.)

Self-Defense

America's Aggressive Crimes

Every year, the United States has more aggressive crimes than any other stable nation not involved in war. We outstrip the rest of the world in murders, rapes, assaults, and robberies. Table 13.A shows the rates per 100,000 population for these crimes in 65 nations, including the United States, from 1970 to 1975 and in the U.S. in 1985. Bear in mind that the world crime rates cited are inflated by the U.S. figures for those years. For many countries, the murder rate, for instance, is less than one-tenth of the U.S. rate.

Other interesting patterns in the U.S. crime statistics of 1985 (Federal Bureau of Investigation, 1986) indicate that the homocide rate is higher in metropolitan areas (9 per 100,000) than in cities and towns outside metropolitan areas (5) and in rural areas (6). The percent of black murder victims (42 percent) is about 3.5 times the proportion of blacks in the U.S. population. Ninety-four percent of black victims were slain by blacks; 88 percent of whites were killed by whites. About 80 percent of the murders were committed with a gun or a knife, with 60 percent done with a firearm and 43 percent with a handgun. Overall, the homocide rate was 19 percent lower in 1984 and 1985 than it was in 1981.

Men were about three times as murderous as women in 1985. Ninety percent of the female victims were killed by males. Thirty percent of the females killed were killed by husbands or boyfriends, while 6 percent of the males killed were slain by wives or girlfriends. Seventeen percent of murders were committed by relatives and 41 percent were by acquaintances.

Murders and robberies were down by 19 percent from 1981; but rapes of females by males were up 2.5 percent. Aggravated assaults, which involve the use of weapons, were up 5 percent from 1981.

Why are Americans so much more aggressive than other nationalities? It is probably not our overall standard of living which is high in relation to the rest of the world. Our aggressiveness may have its roots in the differences in standard of living between our richest and poorest subcultures. Perhaps our high-pressure, competitive way of life is a factor. We will explore these and other factors in this chapter.

Copyright 1989 United Feature Syndicate, Inc. Reprinted by permission.

Table 13.A   Aggressive Crimes in 65 Nations

	United States	World
Murder	8	4
Rape	71	24
Assault	303	184
Robbery	209	46

From the Uniform Crime Reports, 1986 and the United Nations Report of the Secretary-General, 1977 (cited in Wilson & Herrnstein, 1985).

Perhaps we are not that much more aggressive than the rest of the world. Perhaps we are just more destructive because of the availability of weapons. Certainly a threatened or angered person with a gun is much more dangerous than a person in the same state of mind with only his or her bare hands. In 1980, the handgun homocide rate in the United States was 5 per 100,000 people. That year, for every 500 Americans killed by handgun, there were 1 Englishman, 7 Japanese, 22 Swedes, 37 Swiss, 3 Australians, 3 Canadians, and 59 Israelis killed by handguns. It seems undeniable that the availability of weapons takes a heavy toll in American lives without even counting suicides and accidents.

GEECH®   **by Jerry Bittle**

GEECH, by Bink. © *1986 by Universal Press Syndicate. Reprinted by permission. All Rights Reserved.*

Self-defense is not aggression.

Figure 13.1
Self-Defense and Aggression. If the second person to respond delivered a high level of shock to his opponent, he was not rated as aggressive if he was reciprocating his opponent's high level (self-defense). But if the first person had not delivered a high shock first, the second person was regarded as aggressive.

(From Kane, Joseph, & Tedeschi, 1976, Journal of Personality and Social Psychology, 33, 669.)

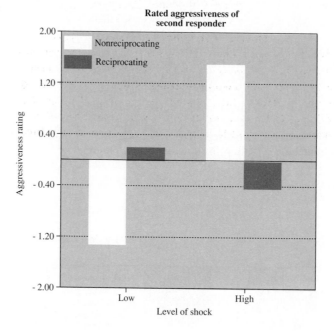

Rated aggressiveness of second responder

Table 13.1   Human Aggressive Acts

		Types of aggression	
		Physical	*Verbal*
Active	*Direct*	Hitting a person	Insulting a person
	Indirect	Practical joke; (taking chair from under a person sitting down)	Malicious gossip
Passive	*Direct*	Obstructing passage; (a strike action)	Refusing to speak
	Indirect	Refusing to perform a necessary duty; (not doing dishes when it's your turn)	Refusing consent

Examples are given in parentheses. From Buss (1971).

Two different kinds of aggression are hostile or angry aggression and instrumental aggression (Buss, 1961). **Hostile aggression** occurs when a person is irritated or upset and acts to harm another person. It is an expression of the person's anger and the clear-cut goal of the action is to harm another person. While hostile aggressions occur in the heat of passion, **instrumental aggressions** are cold-blooded. These aggressive acts are "instrumental" in achieving some goal other than harming the target. Zillman (1979) has described instrumental aggression as incentive-motivated, while he sees hostile aggression as annoyance-motivated. Examples of instrumental aggression are gangland slayings done to gain control over certain territory or criminal enterprises, professional boxers fighting to get the bigger purse, or a military unit bombing an enemy position. The aggressive acts are simply means to some other end.

Human aggressive acts have also been categorized as physical or verbal, direct or indirect, active or passive (Buss, 1961, 1971). See table 13.1. Most observers and investigators are concerned most with physical, active, direct aggressive acts such as punching, knifing, or shooting someone because they are very destructive acts. However, the other forms of aggression, even verbal ones, cannot be ignored because they often precipitate physical aggressions in hostile interactions (Toch, 1969). Of course, for these particular acts to be considered aggressive, there must be verifiable evidence of the intent to harm another individual instigating the act.

Biologists classify aggression in a much different way, according to the context in which it occurs. Table 13.2 shows Wilson's (1975) categories of aggression among animals, including humans.

Kinds of Aggression

Table 13.2	Types of Animal Aggression
Territorial	Actions to repulse intruders from an area claimed by an individual
Dominance	Actions to claim or maintain status in a group and to maintain access to resources associated with status
Sexual	Threats and attacks by males on females for mating and to keep them from straying
Parental—disciplinary	Actions by parents on young offspring, usually to improve survivability of young
Weaning	Actions by parents, usually mothers, on mammalian young to keep them from nursing beyond when they need that nourishment
Moralistic	Punishing acts to enforce community standards
Predatory	Actions to kill prey, typically members of other species
Antipredatory	Fear-induced, defensive actions by potential prey, often in groups, to ward off or kill predators

The last two forms of aggression are more life-threatening than the other forms. Territorial and dominance aggression usually occurs between males as they fight for resources, including possible mates (Moyer, 1971). As we will discuss in the next section, biologists assume that aggression improves the fitness of the attacker and/or his or her kin.

Biological and Evolutionary Views

Why are we aggressive? **Ethologists** and **sociobiologists,** who study the behavior of animals in their natural habitat, tell us that aggression has been instilled in our nature over time. Their evolutionary perspectives indicate that if aggression did not aid in survival, such behavior would no longer occur. Lorenz (1966) contends that aggression helps to perserve the species in three ways:

1. Fighting causes members of the same species to spread out over the available environment so the animals will not overtax the resources in one place
2. Fighting associated with mating assures that the strongest animals will reproduce more, making the offspring hardier
3. Strong, aggressive parents can defend the young better, helping them survive to maturity.

The Ethological View

Konrad Lorenz (1966) considers *aggression* as an *instinct* manifested in fighting against members of the same species. An **instinct** is a behavior that is biologically preprogrammed into the individual, and it should occur whenever there is an adequate triggering stimulus. In lower animals, instinctive behavior is expressed simply, directly, and without hesitation in a "fixed action pattern" (behavior performed the same way every time) as the male stickleback fish will attack any object which has a red spot on its underside. A red spot serves as a triggering stimulus for this attack response apparently because male sticklebacks develop such a spot on their underbellies during mating season (Tinbergen, 1952).

The ethologist, Lorenz, believes that there is a *spontaneous buildup of aggressive energy* that must be discharged to avoid explosive aggression. He cites as evidence of the spontaneity of aggression the behavior of cichlid fish, Ute Indians, and his elderly aunt. Cichlids, in an aquarium with other cichlids, are so aggressive that one male-female couple will drive the other fish, injured, into the corners of the tank. If these other fish are removed, Lorenz says, the female of the couple will soon be floating belly-up because the male comes to discharge his aggression against her. The solution is to put two pairs of the fish in the same tank on opposite sides of a glass partition so they can clash harmlessly with the same-sex fish on the other side of the partition. However, Lorenz says that the fishkeeper must be careful to keep the weeds down so that the fishes will not lose sight of their "scapegoats" or aggression against one's partner will occur.

Lorenz regarded the cichlids' behavior as stemming from the same wellspring as his widowed aunt's behavior toward her maids. She would hire a maid and things would go well for a short time. Relations grew gradually worse until his aunt had a violent outburst and fired the maid. Then, she would hire a new maid and repeat the process. Lorenz felt that this pattern of behavior occurred because his aunt's aggressive energy built up, and it had to be dissipated eventually. He also stated that when aggressive energy has been accumulated and not discharged, minimal provocation is adequate to trigger aggression.

Lorenz cites work by Margolin (undated) with the Utes of North America to illustrate the effects of pent-up aggressive energy. Historically, the Utes were a raiding, warring tribe, but reservation life has not allowed them to express their aggression recently. Margolin found that they are chronically ill, neurotic, and accident-prone in cars (where they may be venting some of their aggressive drive, Lorenz says). Lorenz states that present-day civilized humans suffer greatly from insufficient opportunity to discharge aggressive energy.

Among many animals, aggression is linked with reproduction and territoriality. Fighting will occur if another same-sex member of the species trespasses on the individual's home area during mating season, but a potential mate is allowed entrance. Some animals don't establish territory, but for them aggression is still linked with reproduction and the battle for other resources (food) through dominance hierarchies. When an animal has established status in a "pecking order," no animal lower in the hierarchy will try to gain the higher animal's mate or resources or fighting will occur. So, territoriality and dominance hierarchies assure that the most powerful animals reproduce and get the best resources and that peace and order prevails. While some psychologists have argued that humans do not display territoriality, Edney (1974) has shown that we often do gain, mark, and defend territory. After all, what are wars, home ownership, and trespassing laws all about? John Dean (1976) recounted how territoriality and status seemed to be combined in the Nixon White House. He said that staff members strived to get as much office space—painted in their color—as close to Nixon's office as possible. It was such a status symbol that if an office space change were made, the painters would be called back to apply the new color even if the old paint was hardly dry.

Territoriality

THE FAR SIDE, by Gary Larson. © 1986 by Universal Press Syndicate. Reprinted by permission. All Rights Reserved.

THE FAR SIDE   By GARY LARSON

"Out! Everyone out! ... I've had it with this 'symbiosis' baloney!"

Lethal Aggression in Humans and Other Animals

Sports activities may discharge aggressive urges in less injurious ways, according to Lorery.

According to Lorenz, these territorial and dominance fights seldom result in death for the loser among animals. The loser typically goes through an appeasement ritual and is spared by the victor. Humans, because they are born without any naturally lethal weapons, do not have instinctive inhibitions against deadly aggression against their own kind. Lorenz contends that because of this lack of inborn inhibitions and the weaponry we've acquired, humans are more murderous than other animals.

Lorenz has little faith in humans' ability to eliminate destructive aggression by eliminating all stimulus situations that might elicit it or by trying to inhibit aggression by "moral veto" or legal punishments. Our spontaneous aggressive nature would overwhelm those measures. Instead, he recommends redirecting and discharging aggression on substitute objects, rechanneling "militant enthusiasm" toward good causes or occupations, and building personal friendships between members of rivalrous groups. In this vein, he sees sports as useful "in the cathartic discharge of the aggressive urge" (Lorenz, 1966, p. 271). He also sees humor and laughter as beneficial in redirecting and expressing aggressive impulses, and building friendships among the young of different groups and nations as antithetical to aggression between groups.

Sociobiological Amendments

The sociobiologist, Wilson (1975), has added perspectives to and suggested changes in the ethological view expressed by Lorenz. The sociobiological position has emphasized the reproductive fitness of an individuals' kin (inclusive fitness mentioned in chapter 4) as well as the fitness of the individual in expanding on Lorenz's evolutionary view. That addition means that the individual is likely to aggress against genetically dissimilar individuals to protect those who share genes with him or her. It also implies that aggression against one's kin would not be lethal and would serve to help them survive.

The role of competition for food, shelter, and mates in instigating aggression is emphasized even more in the sociobiological position (Wilson, 1975). Competition highlights the importance of environmental factors in governing aggression. The number of competitors of the same and similar species present, the amount of physical resources available, and the number and quality of potential mates would affect the aggression displayed by a particular individual. Different levels of aggressiveness are adaptive for different species. If an animal is too aggressive, it is nonadaptive because those actions may be inadvertently directed against unrecognized kin, and the individual will spend time and energy aggressing when the animal should be doing other survival tasks such as courting.

Wilson notes that the experiences of an animal can affect the form and intensity of its aggression. In essence, he is taking more of an environmental emphasis and less of an instinctive emphasis than Lorenz. Unlike the fixed action patterns of instinctive behavior described by earlier ethologists, Wilson notes the many forms of aggression within the same animal. For instance, Barlow (1968) has described the different reactions of a rattlesnake, depending on its opponent. Two male rattlers will intertwine their necks and wrestle but never bite. Rattlesnakes attack small prey from many positions without rattling. With animals large enough to pose a threat, such as humans, the snake coils, raises its head in a striking position, and rattles. With a king snake which preys on other snakes, the rattler coils, hides its head, and slaps a coil at the predator.

Wilson disagrees strongly with Lorenz on the idea that man is more murderous than other animals. He argues that we simply have more observation hours and records of man's murderous activities. If we had comparable observation time of lions, gulls, hyenas, and some primates, we would see as much killing within those species as we see in humans. It is interesting to note that it took several years of observation before Jane Goodall discovered that chimps kill other chimps. Then, she found infanticide by one female and her son against other mothers' offspring and groups of adults killing another adult in a short period of time. Wilson (1975) also notes that lions and hyenas, like humans, kill more prey than they need to eat.

Aggressive actions, especially life-threatening or deadly ones, against spouses, children, siblings, and parents are hard to explain from the sociobiologists' position. Such aggressive behaviors are too common, according to crime statistics. Incidents like the chapter-opening example in which a man eliminated his genetic future by killing all of his blood relatives are very difficult to understand. The Japanese custom whereby women who have been sexually betrayed by their husbands may drown their children and themselves is also a sociobiological puzzle. Perhaps it is the ultimate spite to eliminate the husband's genetic future. There must be other strong motivational factors to account for such familial violence.

In further disagreement with Lorenz, Wilson believes that we can structure our environment and reduce aggression. He is optimistic that we can reduce our population densities and design our social systems to make aggression less adaptive.

Freud's Views

The Freudian or *psychoanalytic* position on aggression is included with biological perspectives because the foundations of Freud's approach are biological. His unique idea is that humans have a self-destructive or death instinct called *Thanatos* (Freud, 1933). Before World War I, Freud thought that we had only life instincts consisting of *eros*, the sex instinct, which sustains the species, and *ego* instinct, which preserves the life of the individual. World War I convinced Freud that the self-destructive instinct, Thanatos, was also part of human nature. The suicidal urge, Thanatos, must be deflected from oneself and provides the force behind destructive actions against others, aggression. Aggression seems more primary, more instinctive, and certainly more adaptive or species-preserving than suicide. Evolutionary biologists, like Lorenz and Wilson, imply that suicide would be a more secondary, derived, and aberrant urge rather than a primary instinct as Freud sees it.

Regardless of the impetus for aggression, Freud and the later biologist and fellow Austrian, Lorenz, agreed on the basic instinctive features of aggression. They both endorsed the idea that *aggressive urges build up spontaneously* over time and that they must be expressed in order to relieve the accumulated tension.

Catharsis or tension relief can be achieved through direct aggression or some alternative activity in Freud's view. If aggressive impulses are bottled up too long, highly explosive aggression is likely. *Overcontrolled aggressors* (Megargee, 1966), quiet people who live calmly for years in the face of many agitations before having a violent outburst, seem to be an example of what Freud described. Of course, there are surely numerous, but uncounted, people who live their entire lives without lifting a hand against another person.

Freud also linked sex and aggression, but in a different way. Both are behaviors that society restricts. Sexual and aggressive impulses are often expressed in other forms because of the repression of these behaviors. In Freud's system, the ego copes with this repression by using defense mechanisms to rechannel the urges. Displacement and sublimation are two common **defense mechanisms** by which aggressive impulses are given different forms of expression. In displacement, aggression is expressed against another person or object that is less threatening to the actor. For example, an angry mother may yell at her child to pick up his toys. Rather than hitting his mother, the boy may kick the dog. Rather than biting the boy, the dog may attack the cat. Also, terrorism against noncombatants appears to be another example of displaced aggression. Targets of such displaced aggression may wonder what they did to deserve such an attack. *Sublimation* involves expression of aggressive impulses in activities that are accepted by society, perhaps through participating in an aggressive sport.

Other Biological Approaches

Brain Centers

Biological research on aggression has also focused on how physical events or conditions are associated with and may cause aggression. For instance, electrical stimulation or tissue damage to various areas of the brain has been linked to aggressive behavior. Stimulation of one spot in the hypothalamus, a part of the midbrain in the approximate center of the head, of cats causes an undirected, rage reaction; while stimulation of a nearby point elicits directed, instrumental aggression (Delgado, 1969; Flynn, 1967). Lesions or tissue damage to the amygdala, brain structures located in the midbrain toward the sides of the head, are also associated with aggression (Egger & Flynn, 1962). Some distinctly different parts of the brain are associated with aggression, but activation of most brain areas does not affect aggression.

The **limbic system,** located in midbrain regions, contains pleasure and pain centers. Stimulation of some nerve cells in this region cause pleasurable reactions in humans, primates, and rats (Olds & Milner, 1954). Stimulation of other points mixed among these pleasure cells induces pain (Delgado, 1954). It is interesting to note that the autopsy of Charles Whitman, the man who gunned down dozens of people from atop the Main Tower at the University of Texas in August, 1966, showed that he had a tumor in that region of the brain. It is impossible to know if the tumor impinged on some of those pain points or otherwise caused irritating pressure by its size and contributed to his violent reaction.

Sex hormones have also been linked to aggression in animals. Castrated male rats are more docile than normal male rats (Connor & Levine, 1969). When these castrated rats are injected with testosterone, a male hormone, their aggressiveness increases (Bean & Connor, 1978). Also, when female mice are injected with testosterone, they become more aggressive (Edwards, 1968). Higher testosterone levels in the blood of male rhesus monkeys is associated with more aggressiveness (Rose, Holaday, & Bernstein, 1971). In humans, the use of anabolic steroids, which increase the level of testosterone in the blood, is reported to increase aggressiveness in athletes. While hormones probably don't influence behavior as directly in humans, experimental behavioral studies of aggression show that men generally respond more aggressively than women (Eagly & Steffen, 1986).

Hormones

Certainly, imbalances in a person's biochemistry could affect aggressive behavior (Moyer, 1982). These imbalances could occur through intake of food and drugs or through pathological conditions within the individual. One condition which could be affected in both of these ways is blood sugar level. Hypoglycemia or hyperglycemia, too little or too much blood sugar, could be caused by a physical problem in producing or regulating insulin or temporarily by too much or too little intake of carbohydrates.

Body Chemistry, Diet, and Drugs

There have been a few systematic studies on the effects of low blood sugar level on aggression (Benton, Kumari, & Brain, 1982; Bolton, 1976). There is also information in the public domain which suggests that excessively high or low blood sugar contributes to irritability and aggressiveness. Nutritionists believe that eating too many sugar-laden foods contributes to aggressive behavior. An Ohio judge placed several teenagers with behavior problems in foster homes to curb their carbohydrate intake and reported drastic improvements in their behavior (*Dayton Daily News,* AP, Newark, Ohio, July 6, 1982). The Los Angeles County jail system has started a program to replace sweets with healthier foods in the hope of reducing antisocial behavior. The "Twinkie defense" was used by Dan White in his trial for having killed Mayor George Moscone and City Supervisor Harvey Milk of San Francisco over a decade ago. He pleaded that eating too much sugar-laden junk food had made him temporarily insane.

Heavy alcohol comsumption often leads to aggression.

On the other hand, low blood sugar also seems to affect irritability and aggressiveness. Anyone who has been around someone on a rigorous diet knows that they can be moody and irritable. Also, people who have been without food for six or seven hours can be quite testy. Diabetics, who at some times have too much sugar in their blood and other times (after insulin injection) have too little, sometimes behave aggressively.

Drugs affect the aggressive responses of individuals. Amphetamines and PCP, originally a tranquilizer for horses, may directly affect aggressiveness through their chemical actions. Other drugs may create aggressiveness indirectly because of addicts' high need for them. The effects of two drugs, alcohol and marijuana, on aggression have been studied experimentally by Stuart Taylor and his associates.

Research Trailblazers

Stuart Taylor and his associates at Kent State have contributed to the methods of study in aggression as well as increasing our understanding of the effects of drugs on aggression. They have established an experimental procedure by which on each trial, subjects set a shock level for an opponent if he should lose, compete with the opponent to get a faster reaction time, receive feedback about the shock level set for them and whether they won or lost, and receive shock if they lost (Epstein & Taylor, 1967; Taylor, 1967).

This procedure has several advantages. It seems quite natural for opponents on a competitive task to set punishment for each other. Two-way interactive aggression situations such as this also seem more common in the real world. Unlike some other procedures, subjects know that they are harming the opponent, not helping him by setting high shock levels. Tedeschi (1983) argues that procedures that lead subjects to believe they are benefiting their victims by shocking them are not assessing aggression validly. Their shock setting for the opponent on a particular trial seems to be a particularly valid measure of physical aggression because subjects believe that their opponent is being shocked when he loses because the subjects have been shocked when they lost. Also, the responses of the opponent can be programmed to see how subjects react to different types of counteraggression strategies (Kimble et al., 1977; Pisano & Taylor, 1971). The extent to which the subject loses can also be manipulated to see whether it is the level of shock received or the opponent's intent that affects aggression. It is the opponent's intent which is more important (Epstein & Taylor, 1967).

Obviously, the procedure also lends itself to examining how traits, such as prejudice (Genthner & Taylor, 1973), and states, such as drunkenness, of the subject affect physical aggression. In their studies of alcohol, Taylor and his associates have found the following results about alcohol consumption:

1. High doses of alcohol relative to individual body weight produces more physical aggression than low doses (Shuntich & Taylor, 1972; Taylor et al., 1976).
2. Purer alcohol (vodka, which is free of congeners, production by-products) produces stronger aggression effects in high doses than does less pure alcohol (bourbon) (Taylor & Gammon, 1975).
3. High dose subjects responded more aggressively if the opponent posed a threat than if he or she stated a pacificist position or an observer suggested nonaggression (Taylor & Gammon, 1976; Taylor, Gammon, & Capasso, 1976; Taylor, Schmutte, Leonard, & Cranston, 1979).

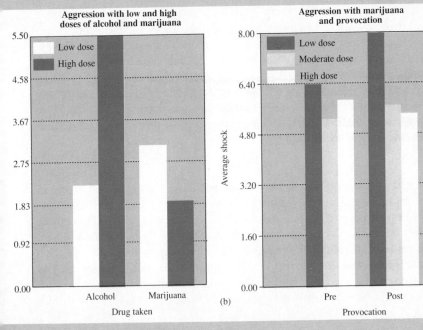

Aggression with low and high doses of alcohol and marijuana

Low dose
High dose

5.50
4.58
3.67
2.75
1.83
0.92
0.00

Alcohol   Marijuana

Drug taken

Aggression with marijuana and provocation

Low dose
Moderate dose
High dose

8.00
6.40
4.80
3.20
1.60
0.00

Average shock

Pre   Post

(b)

Provocation

Figure 13.A
(a) Subjects receiving a high dose of alcohol acted aggressively; marijuana subjects did not. (b) Subjects who had been provoked by their opponent and had received a low dose of marijuana acted aggressively. Those given a moderate or a high dose did not act aggressively.

*(a. from Taylor et al., 1976,
Aggressive Behavior, 2, 158;
b. from Myerscough & Taylor,
1985, Journal of Personality and
Social Psychology, 49, 1544.)*

From these results, Taylor and Leonard (1983) argue that the pharmacological or arousing effect of alcohol alone does not cause aggression because intoxicated subjects don't act aggressively unless provoked. On the other hand, the THC of marijuana stifles aggression even in the presence of provocation (Myerscough & Taylor, 1985;

Taylor et al., 1976). (See figure 13.A.)

Gantner and Taylor (1988) have recently examined the effects of diazepam on aggression. Diazepam is the generic name for the prescription drug, Valium, which is a tranquilizer used to treat anxiety. Like alcohol, diazepam is a depressant.

Subjects who had received diazepam an hour earlier were much more aggressive on the reaction time task than were placebo subjects.

Taylor and his associates have given us a concrete picture of the aggressive effects of these drugs.

Both of these drugs were studied in a single experiment (Taylor, Vadaris, Rawitch, Gammon, Cranston, & Lubetkin, 1976). Subjects, who had used the drugs before, were given low or high doses (relative to subjects' weights) of alcohol or THC, the active ingredient in marijuana. A fifth group of subjects received no drug. All subjects received the drugs in a drink of ginger ale and peppermint oil to disguise the content. Individually, subjects played a competitive reaction time game with a preprogrammed confederate in which the opponents set shock levels for each other on each trial and the loser was shocked. The average shock level each subject set for his opponent was the aggression measure. The results showed that only the high dose of alcohol produced more aggression than the control condition. This a clear demonstration of the direct effects of alcohol consumption on aggressive behavior. Stronger doses of THC tended to reduce aggression in this study, and a recent study confirmed that THC consumption does reduce aggression (Myerscough & Taylor, 1985).

Environmental Perspectives on Aggression

So far, we have discussed viewpoints which emphasize that aggression is part of human nature. That is not the whole story. Many psychologists take exception to the positions of Lorenz, Wilson, and Freud (e.g., Berkowitz, 1978). They object most to the ideas that biology dictates behavior completely in the strongest instinctive positions; that humans operate in the same ways as lower animals, such as fish and birds; and that aggressive drives must be expressed periodically to reduce later aggression. Investigators like Berkowitz have emphasized *the role of environment and experience on aggressive behavior.*

Frustration and Aggression

In 1939, a group of Yale scholars introduced the idea that *frustration causes aggression* (Dollard, Doob, Miller, Mowrer, & Sears, 1939). They believed that **frustration**—blocking a person from achieving a goal—created an instigation or urge to aggression and it was the only factor that caused this urge. These statements almost sounded like an instinctive approach with frustration the universal triggering stimulus for aggression, but one of the group (Miller, 1941) made it clear that they did not assume that these response tendencies were innate or learned. Over the years, the focus has been on the environmental factors that frustrate us or otherwise cause us to act aggressively.

Motivation to Aggress: Frustration

The book by Dollard and his associates opened up the study of aggressive motivation. They stated that you would be most motivated to aggress when (1) the goal being blocked is a very important one, (2) the response is totally blocked, and (3) a number of goal-directed responses have been thwarted (Dollard et al., 1939). These conditions produce the highest magnitude of frustration. Many studies have been conducted which show that high frustration alone, without verbal insults or shocks, usually increases aggression (Berkowitz & Geen, 1967; Burnstein & Worchel, 1962; Geen, 1968; Harris, 1974). One clever study (Harris, 1974) showed that when confederates, especially males, produced a higher magnitude of frustration (by breaking in front of the second person in a waiting line), they elicited more aggression than when they caused less frustration (by breaking in front of the twelfth person). Several studies have shown that children, the more primitive, natural versions of ourselves, respond with greater aggression when they have been frustrated (Barker, Dembo, & Lewin, 1941; Mallick & Mc-Candless, 1966). However, other investigators (A. Buss, 1963, 1966; Kuhn, Madsen, & Becker, 1967; Taylor & Pisano, 1971) have shown that frustration often does not produce aggression. Verbal and physical attacks produce more aggression. Also, one of the foremost researchers in aggression, Leonard Berkowitz (1962, 1965), typically used verbal insults and/or shocks, not frustration, to produce anger.

Frustration is most likely to produce aggression when it is intense and when it is unexpected or arbitrary (Baron, 1977; Worchel, 1974). For example, verbal aggression against an experimenter was greatest when he arbitrarily and unexpectedly gave subjects their least attractive reward instead of the most attractive one (Worchel, 1974).

Some of the mixed results of these frustration-aggression studies may come from failing to use truly frustrating events or failing to establish whether individual subjects were frustrated. For example, there is a difference between being jilted by your fiancee at the altar and being rejected by a first date. There are many different features of frustration that are not captured by saying that frustration is the blocking or thwarting of goal-directed activities.

The Nature of Frustration

Frustration might be fruitfully defined as *expectations* minus *outcomes*. We develop expectations about what we deserve and what we can expect to attain by examining what has happened to us in the past and by what has happened to other people with similar backgrounds, talents, and efforts. Information in the mass media may influence the expectations that we form. Fictional and real depictions of life styles on television have broadened the experience and affected—some might say distorted—the expectations of most of us.

If we get about what we expected in a particular realm of our lives, frustration is minimal. If there is a drastic, unexpected drop in the benefits we receive or our expectations increase greatly because of new information or experience, we are likely to be very frustrated.

One theory about the collective aggression of revolutions has shown historically that frustration works in the way just described (Davies, 1962, 1969). Davies found that major and minor rebellions occur after periods of social reform, not when the citizens' outcomes are at their lowest level. These eras of reform apparently led citizens to expect better outcomes, but slow progress after the reforms led to discontent and revolutions. Davies analyzed five different revolutions or rebellions, including the Russian revolutions of 1915–1917, and found a consistent pattern suggesting that failure to meet rising expectations contributed to the revolutions. The American and French Revolutions seem to have followed similar patterns to this nonhistorian.

It is interesting to consider the riots in black communities around the U.S. in 1966 and 1967 from this perspective. Those riots did not occur when the plight of blacks in this country was worst, but after an era of social reforms and improvements. Beginning with the landmark Supreme Court decision to desegregate the schools in 1954 and continuing through the Civil Rights Act of 1964, the Voting Rights Act of 1965, and Lyndon Johnson's War on Poverty and Great Society growing from the Martin Luther King-led black civil rights movement, the status and conditions of blacks in America improved. Expectations also rose and the difference between them and the real conditions of many blacks' lives apparently produced frustration and riots. Of course, many other factors contributed to this explosive situation. It is hoped that this viewpoint does not encourage government officials to ignore the problems of disadvantaged subgroups for fear of raising the groups' expectations. Instead, they should attempt to fulfill the promises they make.

Reformulations of Frustration

Some investigators have argued that frustration should be streamlined because what has been called frustration often included verbal and physical attacks (Baron, 1977; Buss, 1963). It is important that we recognize attacks, other aversive conditions, inequitable conditions, and other arousing events as being capable of instigating aggression. We will discuss these factors later.

Berkowitz (1962, 1965, 1980, 1983, 1984) has reformulated the frustration-aggression hypothesis. He says, among other things, that current aggressive cues are needed to carry frustration into open aggression. Frustration is one motivational factor that creates a readiness for aggressive responding. *Motivation* or drive, in conjunction with *aggressive habits* which are learned, combine to make the individual ready to aggress (Berkowitz, 1980). Aggressive cues precipitate aggressive action. These *aggressive cues* are words or objects associated with aggression (Berkowitz & Geen, 1966; Berkowitz & LePage, 1967; Geen & Berkowitz, 1966). These cues, which may be provided by aggressive movies or TV programs, prime aggressive thoughts and give the person ideas for aggression (Berkowitz, 1984). If the person seeing or hearing the cues is frustrated or habitually aggressive, he or she is more likely to act aggressively.

The sight of weapons is an aggressive cue (Berkowitz & LePage, 1967). These investigators found that angered men who were in a room containing weapons acted more aggressively toward their antagonist than similar men in a room with other objects. This has been a very controversial finding because the weapons were not used in the aggression and cues to the experimental hypothesis may have been too great. Other investigators have failed to replicate the effect (Buss, Booker, & Buss, 1972; Page & Scheidt, 1971). Buss et al. failed to observe the effect in five laboratory experiments. It does seem far-fetched that seeing two guns laying in the room would make subjects shock their antagonist more times unless you believe that seeing them sets off a whole string of aggressive thoughts, as Berkowitz (1984) suggests. However, one study showed that motorists honk more at a pickup with a rifle in the gun rack and an aggressive sticker on the bumper than at other pickups (Turner, Layton, & Simons, 1975). Another showed that carnival-goers threw more wet sponges at a target person if guns were nearby (Turner, Simons, Berkowitz, & Frodi, 1977). The availability of weapons to use seems to be a stronger influence on aggression than weapons as cues.

In Berkowitz's revision, frustration makes people angry, and anger is the central instigator of impulsive, angry aggression. Other events such as insults and being shocked can also provoke anger. What else can provoke anger?

Attacks and Anger   We know that verbal attacks can make the victim angry and aggressive (Berkowitz, 1965; Buss, 1961; Toch, 1969). In real aggressive encounters, Toch found that violent crimes usually stemmed from verbal barbs and taunts that made both parties angry. Likewise, it is no surprise that physical attacks provoke anger and aggression (Geen & Berkowitz, 1966; Taylor & Pisano, 1971). Like an animal threatened by a predator, most humans become very aroused and ferocious when they are attacked. Most of the attacks in the laboratory are done by electrical shocks, which are not life-threatening but are painful.

Other Motivators

Inequity, Anger, and Aggression   *Inequity* or unfair treatment seems to be a very much overlooked motivator of aggression. Unfair treatment from a mild interpersonal affront to long-term abuse or exploitation angers many people and if the conditions are ripe, such inequity leads to aggression. When a person or group is not receiving what they feel they deserve based on their contributions, they may retaliate to restore equity (Walster et al., 1978). Inequity was one of the foremost causes of the ghetto riots of the 1960s, and it is surely centrally involved in the strife in South Africa. Many major and minor spats in our work environments and in our home lives stem from our perceptions that we are being treated unfairly. For instance, when a man is treated unfairly by being excluded from conversation by a man-woman dyad, he apparently becomes jealous and aggresses strongly (with shocks) against the other man (Thompson & Richardson, 1983). In only a very general way can these inequitable conditions be interpreted as frustration. Much more research needs to be done on this topic. (See figure 13.2.)

The Self, Anger, and Aggression   Threats to or disparagement of the self can arouse anger and aggression. Such threats may come in the form of verbal attacks on our ancestry or something else about us. It does seem useful to distinguish between self-relevant insults and other verbal attacks, which were discussed earlier. Toch (1969) characterized some of the offenses of violent criminals he interviewed as being done to defend their reputations, to defend their self-images, or to promote their self-images. James Tedeschi (1983) also contends that many aggressive acts are committed to create or enhance particular self-images. He regards much of the theorizing on aggression as being too mechanistic, too stimulus-response, and not attending to the social meaning of actions to the actors. Suppose a teenage boy stole a purse from a little old woman and injured her in the process. Other theorists might say that his pent-up aggressive energy needed to be expressed or that the accumulated frustrations of his everyday life impelled him to do it. Maybe the real reason, according to Tedeschi, was so that he could

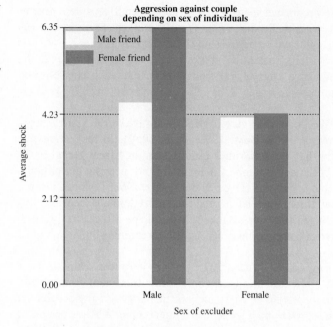

Figure 13.2
Men who had been excluded from a conversation with a woman who had acted friendly to them by another man were the most aggressive against the excluder and the woman.
(From Thompson & Richardson, 1983, Personality and Social Psychology Bulletin, 9, 420.)

Did John Hinckley Jr. shoot President Reagan to become famous?

show the purse and tell about the incident to his peers and enhance his "macho" image. Tedeschi recounts how Arthur Bremer, who tried to assassinate George Wallace during the 1972 presidential campaign, appeared to be motivated by the desire to gain notoriety. There was evidence that he had trailed Richard Nixon, George McGovern, and Hubert Humphrey before shooting Wallace. Obviously, the political inclinations of the victim made no difference to him; all that mattered was that the shooting would give him national attention.

Competition and Aggression Again   In competitive interactions, when one person or group gains, the opponent loses. In a sense, the winner frustrates the loser by blocking the loser from attaining his or her goal. Beyond that, it may be useful or "instrumental" for competitors to injure or distract their opponents through aggression. Some games or competitions provide greater opportunities for direct physical blocking of an opponent or for physical aggression than others. For instance, golfers and pole vaulters have little opportunity to impede their opponents, but basketball and soccer players do. Football, hockey, and wrestling provide contexts for direct physical exertion against opponents and make aggression easier.

How much hostility is inspired may depend on whether or not the participants see their interaction as competitive. Many situations can be construed as competitions. The insurance saleswoman wants to sell you as big a policy as she can collect; you as customer want adequate protection at the cheapest rate. The president wants to present a positive image to the public; the press wants to get interesting news about presidential quirks or wrongdoings. Two kids want to play

The strong sense of competition in soccer may provoke aggression.

with the same toy. Two people love the same third person and want the exclusive love of that person. The list is endless. People who take sides often act aggressively if the opportunity arises.

Let's consider the fans at the soccer game in Belgium. Soccer is not as aggressive a game as football or hockey, for instance, so it is hard to make the case that viewing aggression released their aggressive tendencies. Especially since the riot occurred *before* the game. There were undoubtedly many factors involved, such as alcohol consumption and the anonymity of the spectators. A central factor had to be that the Italian fans were defined as the enemy by the competition. Apparently, an extremely aggressive sport is not required for such violence to occur, only identifying with one side in the conflict is necessary.

Frustration and competition also contributed to another gruesome crowd situation that resulted in aggression and death before a concert by The Who in Cincinnati, Ohio, in December 1979. Frustration contributed to the 11 trampling deaths because the crowd had to wait for hours before the gates were opened to Riverfront Coliseum. Then, only a few gates were opened. The competition that caused the crush was for choice seats because all seating was first come, first served. Similar competition for choice viewing spots was involved in the soccer crowd crush that killed 96 people in England in 1989. It should be noted that the aggression in these incidents was instrumental, unlike the hostile aggression of the soccer crowd at Brussels. While the fans certainly did not intend to harm other fans; their zealous pursuit of choice seats did produce a disregard for others' safety.

Aversive Conditions as Motivators   Unpleasant or aversive conditions that put the individual in a negative mood can create readiness for aggression (Berkowitz, 1987). One condition that promotes irritability is pain. In animals, painful experiences, such as being shocked, elicit furious attacks on other animals present (Ulrich & Azrin, 1962; Ulrich, 1966). Azrin (1967) and his associates have found that birds, reptiles, amphibians, and mammals show this instaneous, apparently

Figure 13.3
*Temperature and
collective aggression: A
curvilinear
relationship. This
investigation of riots in
black areas in the late
1960s and early 1970s
showed that the
number of riots
peaked between 80
and 90 degrees and
then declined.*

(From Baron & Ransberger, 1978,
Journal of Personality and Social
Psychology, 36, 356.)

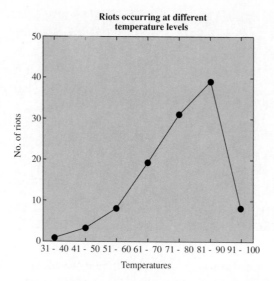

instinctive attack reaction when they are shocked. This team of investigators has also shown that cutting off reinforcement when it is expected—that is, extinction after reinforcement—elicits attacks (Azrin, Hutchinson, & Hake, 1966). It is tempting to call this type of aversive situation frustration. Pain seems less directly linked to aggression in humans.

Heat is another aversive condition that motivates people to aggress. Ulrich and Azrin (1962) also showed that heat causes an attack reaction in animals. In humans, high temperatures have been linked to crime (Anderson & Anderson, 1984) and riots (Baron & Ransberger, 1978; Carlsmith & Anderson, 1979). Baron and Ransberger (1978) correlated local temperatures with the occurrence and duration of 102 riots primarily in black communities in 1967–1971. We should note that many other factors contributed to the occurrence of the riots, including the assassination of Dr. Martin Luther King in April 1968. However, they found that riots typically started at the beginning of a heat wave (higher than normal temperatures). The longer and hotter the heat wave, the longer the riots lasted. They also found that when the temperature was very high, riots were less likely to occur. (See figure 13.3.) However, a later analysis of the same data showed that the higher the temperature, the more likely it was that a riot would occur (Carlsmith & Anderson, 1979). The reason for the few riots at the highest temperatures was that there were very few days with temperatures above 95 degrees in the riot locations, which were concentrated in the Northeast, Midwest, and West instead of the hotter South and Southwest. The lack of large black communities in the Southwest and the police forces of the South who were stricter with blacks at that time probably stifled riots in those areas. It should be noted that heat is not only an aversive condition, but it also encourages outdoor interactions and alcohol consumption, which also make aggression more likely. (See figure 13.4.)

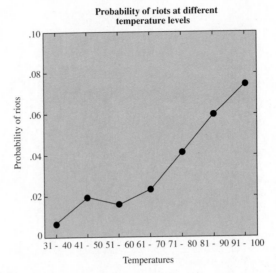

Probability of riots at different temperature levels

Probability of riots

.10

.08

.06

.04

.02

0

31 - 40 41 - 50 51 - 60 61 - 70 71 - 80 81 - 90 91 - 100

Temperatures

Figure 13.4
Temperature and collective aggression: a linear relationship. This reanalysis of the same data shows that the hotter it is, the more likely riots are to occur. This analysis used conditional probabilities rather than actual riot occurrences to correct for the fact that there were very few days in the affected cities when the temperature was over 90 degrees. Percentagewise, there were more riots in those hottest days.
(From Carlsmith & Anderson, 1979, Journal of Personality and Social Psychology, 37, 340.)

Arousal and Aggression Surprisingly, stimulating events which make you angry are not the only events that make you aggressive. Any stimulating event may cause aggression. Any exciting event which activates the sympathetic nervous system, the half of the autonomic nerves which prepare the body for "fight or flight," can make a person more aggressive (Zillman, 1983). This arousal or excitation may account for the riotous behavior exhibited by fans of winning teams after sports events. Such conduct is certainly not caused by frustration. However, Zillman (1983) contends that **excitation transfer,** whereby arousal from one event causes stronger reactions to unrelated events, depends on some separate provocation or instigation to aggression to produce aggression unless arousal is extremely high. He also suggests that if the individual correctly attributes the arousal to the irrelevant source, the aggressive response will not be energized by the arousal. In many ways, this excitation transfer model is similar to the misattribution theory of passionate love (Berscheid & Walster, 1974), only the situational cues are different.

Zillman and other investigators have shown that if a person is provoked while being in an aroused state from vigorous exercise, watching a sexually explicit movie, or watching a violent action movie, that person will respond more aggressively than if he or she were in an unaroused state. With a few exceptions (e.g., Jaffe, Malamuth, Feingold, & Feshbach, 1974), only provoked subjects acted more aggressively. So, it appears that *arousal typically intensifies aggressive behavior* instigated by some other factor.

Sexual Arousal If you are sexually excited, will you act aggressively? The research just discussed suggests that you will if you are provoked, cued, or have learned to be aggressive in such situations. In view of the statistics on rape and partner abuse, we should focus on male aggressiveness in sexual situations.

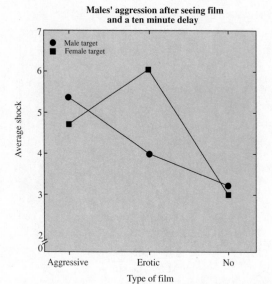

(From Donnerstein & Hallum,
1978, Journal of Personality and
Social Psychology, 36, 1274.)

Figure 13.5
*After a brief delay,
men who had just seen
an erotic movie were
more aggressive (with
shock) toward women.
Usually, after seeing
an aggressive movie in
this experiment, men
are more aggressive
against men. Sexual
arousal contributed to
greater aggression
against women in this
study.*

First, we might think that expressing tender affection would be incompatible with aggression. In fact, there is experimental evidence that exposure to mild erotica seems to make the excitation transfer occur away from aggression and reduces the aggression of angered subjects (Baron & Bell, 1977). However, there is also evidence that very arousing erotica causes angered subjects to act more aggressively (Donnerstein & Hallum, 1979; Zillman, 1971; Zillman, Hoyt, & Day, 1974). (See figure 13.5.) Unprovoked subjects almost never act aggressively after viewing similar erotica (Cantor, Zillman, & Einsiedel, 1978; Russell & Kimble, 1978). It is the combination of anger and sexual arousal that causes aggression. However, remember that the aggressive response in these studies is administering shock. More sex-related forms of aggression such as rape, which obviously cannot be studied in laboratory experiments, may be affected differently. (See figure 13.6.)

Erotic movies have become more prevalent recently, and they often contain aggressive scenes. Rapes are depicted more often, and you may recall that several years ago, there were reports of a "snuff" movie being circulated in which an actress was actually killed on film. These movies present both aggressive cues and sexually arousing material; they even portray women as ultimately enjoying being raped. They are exploitative of women in that they may set up women to be victims in real life.

Evidence collected by Neil Malamuth and his associates indicates that this aggressive erotica does make ordinary men more likely to have rape fantasies, to be more sexually aroused, to have less sensitivity to rape, and to be more likely to accept rape myths and violence toward women (cf. Donnerstein, 1983). Another study indicates that aggressive erotic movies elicit more overt aggression

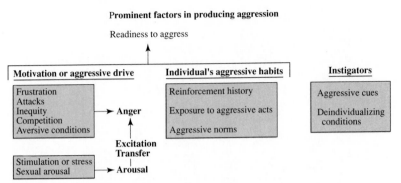

Prominent factors in producing aggression

Figure 13.6
*Both motivational
factors and a person's
aggressive habit
strength contribute to
the person's readiness
to aggress. Some
motivational factors
make the person angry
in a direct fashion.
Other factors arouse
the person and
augment a preexisting
angry reaction via
excitation transfer.*

than do nonaggressive erotic movies (Donnerstein, 1980). It seems that seeing the combination of sex and aggression does affect sex-related aggressive tendencies in many men.

Social (Observational) Learning

The theories of aggression presented so far have emphasized the motivational bases of aggression. The **Social Learning Theory** of Albert Bandura (1973, 1983), in contrast, examines and explains how we learn to be aggressive. Its focus is decidedly on the environmental influences on the acquisition and performance of aggression. Also in contrast to animal research of the biologists and the research with adults by Berkowitz, Buss, Baron, and most other social psychologists; Bandura's work has examined the behavior of young children.

Basic Studies of Social (Observational) Learning Theory

Stanford nursery school children saw an adult model act aggressively or nonaggressively toward toys in the three basic studies (Bandura, 1965; Bandura, Ross, & Ross, 1961, 1963). Other children in control groups did not observe the adult models. In the aggressive model conditions, the man or woman punched, pummeled with a mallet, kicked, sat upon, and cursed an inflated Bobo clown doll either live or on film. The nonaggressive model played quietly with tinker toys. All children were then frustrated by letting them play with attractive toys a few minutes and then taking them to a room containing a Bobo doll, mallet, tinker toys, and other toys. In the first study (Bandura et al., 1961), imitative and nonimitative physical and verbal aggression by boys and girls after watching a man or a woman live model were scored. In the second study (Bandura et al., 1963), the same behaviors were observed after watching models live, on film, or dressed as a cartoon cat. In the third study (Bandura, 1965), the behaviors were recorded after watching a filmed aggressive male model who was either praised and rewarded with a drink and candy (**vicarious reinforcement**), criticized and spanked (**vicarious punishment**), or left alone (control). Vicarious reinforcement or punishment means that the child experienced reinforcement or punishment second-hand because it was the model, not the observing child, who received reinforcement or punishment. (See figure 13.7.)

Figure 13.7
These results indicate that children do learn aggressive acts when they see them (positive incentive conditions). They also indicate that children are less likely to imitate an adult model if they see him being punished for acting aggressively.
(From Bandura, 1965, 592.)

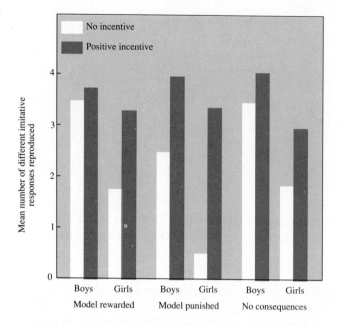

Figure 13.7
These results indicate that children do learn aggressive acts when they see them (positive incentive conditions). They also indicate that children are less likely to imitate an adult model if they see him being punished for acting aggressively.
(From Bandura, 1965, 592.)

The first study showed that children are more aggressive after seeing adult aggressive models than after seeing nonaggressive models or no model. Boys were especially aggressive physically after seeing a man act aggressively. The second study showed that live, film, and cartoon models created more aggression by the children than a no-model control condition. The third study indicated that boys imitated the aggressive man model more than girls did. It also showed that seeing the model punished inhibited the children's imitative aggression, but seeing him rewarded did not increase aggression over the level of the control (no consequences for model) condition. A separate test in which Bandura offered the children rewards for reproducing the model's behavior indicated that all the children had learned the aggressive behavior even though some of them had not acted aggressively spontaneously. For Bandura, this result pinpointed the difference between learning and performance and demonstrated the great impact of simply seeing someone else act aggressively.

Learning from Seeing and from Doing

Social learning theory suggests that young people learn to act aggressively in two ways: (1) by seeing others act aggressively and (2) by being rewarded for acting aggressively. Learning aggressive habits through direct experience follows the principles of operant conditioning. The more times you have acted aggressively and been rewarded, the stronger your aggressive habits become. Bullies and chronic violent offenders have strong aggressive habits and a high readiness for aggression. It doesn't take much to set them off.

There are many potential rewards for acting aggressively. For one, if you hurt your opponent badly enough, your opponent will retreat and you can go on to more pleasant activities. This is a common source of reward in nursery school

DOONESBURY, by Gary Trudeau. © 1987 by Universal Press Syndicate. Reprinted by permission.

encounters, especially if there is no adult intervention (Patterson, Littman, & Bricker, 1967). For the child who is frequently successful in overwhelming other children, being a good fighter may become part of his or her self-image.

Another type of reward for aggression is approval from others. There are many subcultures, especially male teenage gangs, in which aggressive acts are widely approved by one's peers. Team members in aggressive sports are usually very supportive of violent actions. Even adults in the community are often likely to praise fighters. I remember an incident during my sophomore year in high school that illustrated this fact of life to me. As my dad and I were walking to our car after a junior varsity football game, we saw a crowd of people circled into a small area between cars. As we came closer, it was apparent that two of my schoolmates were squared off, and the crowd containing many solid citizens ("backbones and pillars of the community") was encouraging them to fight. As the fight started and the two slammed into a car, my dad stepped forward and broke up the fight. It was a good thing he did because banging into cars could have been dangerous. You can imagine my embarrassment in school the next week as word got around that my dad stopped a fight. Such aggressive subcultures abound in our society!

Even if an aggressive child does not gain the approval of others in the situation, he or she is likely to receive a great deal of attention. We will see later that social learning advocates (Brown & Elliot, 1965) consider ignoring aggression as one of the most effective ways to reduce it. By implication, paying attention to a child who is otherwise starved for attention can be quite rewarding. The main problem arises from the fact that we are often unaware that we are rewarding undesirable behavior when we pay attention to an unruly child. Aggression certainly commands our attention! When I worked as an attendant on a children's mental hospital unit one summer, a 15-year-old, 6'1", 180 lb boy who loved to beat up eight- and nine-year-olds received more attention than any five other children, who were more mentally disturbed than he. These kinds of rewards can become a strong incentive for aggression.

Other researchers do not believe that we learn specific aggressive habits. Huesmann (1987) stated that what young children learn and retain in later years are aggressive programs or scripts (Schank & Abelson, 1977). **Scripts** are patterns of behavior we learn to display when we recognize certain cues in our environments. These scripts enable the individual to know what kind of aggression to use when certain conditions exist. Such scripts are learned by observing events in one's environment and in the media.

Bandura (1977b, 1983) has come to view learning by direct experience as a special case of observational learning. From this perspective, the individual evaluates his or her past actions and their consequences much like the individual observes others' behavior and assesses its viability as a course of action for himself or herself. The past reinforcing or punishing consequences of the individual's past actions provide information about the suitability of particular behaviors just as vicarious punishment or reinforcement operate in observational learning.

Observational Learning

Bandura (1983) argues that we learn most of our aggressive behaviors through observing and imitating others. The prominent sources for modeled aggression are family members, the subculture including schoolmates and teachers, and the mass media.

Parents and siblings who fight in the presence of children provide striking models for aggression. If they beat on the youngster, particularly in unjustified or illegitimized ways, they also provide strong models for aggression. Even well-controlled spankings under the auspices of parental discipline provide fodder for future aggressive thoughts and behavior. Live, vivid, painful assaults occurring regularly within a child's household have the most profound effect on a child's development.

There is ample evidence that an abusive home life produces aggressive children and aggressive adults later. Young children who have been beaten by their parents get into trouble in school and with the law as teenagers more than other children do (Bandura & Walters, 1959; Eron, Walder, & Lefkowitz, 1971). People who were abused as children become parents who abuse their own children (Straus, Gelles, & Steinmetz, 1979). Also, children who observe their parents fight or see their fathers physically abuse their mothers often become abusers and victims in their own marriages. One memorable case of this cycle of violence was presented on "Sixty Minutes" several years ago. The story of a woman who had hired someone to kill her husband after he had abused her and the kids for years was being told. In an interview, Mike Wallace asked a son who had loathed the abusive father if he had beaten his new bride. With her at his side on national television, the young man admitted that he was following the pattern of his loathsome father. Certainly, many factors were involved in producing that aggressive outcome, but observing abuse in the home had to have been a very central cause.

Violence comes into even peaceful homes via television. Many social psychologists, including Bandura and Berkowitz, contend that, based on their own research, aggressive acts on television provide aggressive models and cues and make our children more aggressive. One 10-year longitudinal study showed that viewing a lot of violent television in the third grade caused boys to be more aggressive 10 years later (Eron, Huesmann, Lefkowitz, & Walder, 1972). Eron et al. assert that early viewing *caused* later aggression because they took multiple measures of both variables and used a sophisticated statistical procedure, a cross lag panel design, to establish causality with this correlational data. That is an impressive long-term effect of TV violence when you consider all of the intervening experiences that could have wiped it out.

Television and Models for Aggression

We all know that kids, and adults for that matter, watch a lot of television. Most television programs present violent acts. In past years, there have been about seven violent acts an hour in prime time television and about eighteen per hour in Saturday morning kids' programs (Gerbner, Gross, Morgan, & Signorielli, 1980). With the proliferation of cable television and VCRs, there is even greater potential for viewing violent acts. Our five-year-old son seems to be able to find humanoid characters firing laser guns at each other at any time, day or night. At the same time, it does appear that the major networks have moved the more violent prime time shows to a later hour (Gerbner et al., 1980). From the Central Time Zone west, those shows start at 8:00 P.M., when even the youngest viewers are still awake.

Controversies have sprung up about the assessment of TV violence and its effects on behavior (Bergreen, *TV Guide,* November 5, 1977; Blank, 1977; Gerbner et al., 1977; Gerbner, Gross, Morgan, & Signorielli, 1981a, 1981b; Hirsch, 1980, 1981a, b; Wober & Gunter, 1986). The first issue concerns whether too many events are being included in the measurement of violence. Pies in the face, boulders dropped on Wiley Coyote with minimal injurious effect, and accidents are included along with knifings and shootings. In this case, violence has a much broader definition than we have given aggression. Some types of violence, such as reckless driving or cartoon violence, cannot be imitated by young children. So, even though children's cartoons display the most violent acts, one might question the impact of these unreal characters and acts on children. Even though one study showed that seeing an aggressive cartoon did increase natural interpersonal aggression among first graders (Ellis & Sekyra, 1972), Hapkiewicz (1979) characterized the evidence that cartoon violence increases aggression as inconsistent and fraught with methodological problems.

Children may be made fearful by violent television.

The second controversial issue that has arisen is whether heavy television watching distorts viewers' perceptions of the world so that they see it as a meaner and more dangerous place (Gerbner et al., 1981a). Hirsch (1981a, b) argues that this **cultivation effect** of television whereby heavy viewers are more fearful is not supported by the Gerbner group's data. Wober and Gunter (1986) did not find a cultivation effect among British viewers. Other investigators (Slater & Elliot, 1982) contend that the cultivation effect only occurs with very realistic programs. It is also interesting to note that other investigators (Cline, Croft, & Courrier, 1973; Drabman & Thomas, 1974) have found an opposing effect in experiments; that is, viewing media violence made their subjects more jaded or indifferent to real-life aggression. One possible conclusion suggested by these and other studies (e.g., Singer, Singer, & Rapaczynski, 1984) is that young children may be made more fearful by violent television, while older people are less likely to be affected by violent programs.

The Bottom Line on Media Violence and Aggression

Recently, a renowned social psychologist, Jonathan Freedman (1984, 1986), has taken the position that we have not convincingly demonstrated that viewing violent television causes aggression. He dismissed laboratory experiments as ungeneralizable to real life because their aggression measures are artificial, their designs tip off participants to their purposes, and the studies only expose subjects briefly to a short film or tape before measuring aggression to get maximum effect. He does make some valid criticisms of these experiments that others have also made, but his standards for natural aggression measures are too high given the ethical standards we must maintain. It is easy to say that hitting a Bobo doll, pushing a "hurt" button, or even pushing a "shock" button or lever are not natural forms of aggression and that intent to harm someone is not clear in these actions. However, we cannot set up experiments wherein a subject can punch, stab, or shoot someone else. To ask for natural aggression against a real person is asking too much.

It is somewhat like the Florida judge's question in the Zamora case in which the defense was based on the argument that TV violence led the young boy to kill an elderly woman. After removing the jury, he asked Margaret Hanratty Thomas, an expert witness, if there were any experiments which showed that watching violent television caused people to commit murder. Of course she had to answer "no" because we cannot conduct experiments in which "killed victim" is a dependent measure. Before Dr. Thomas could elaborate, the judge excluded her testimony from the case. Freedman's standard is not that high, but it seems unrealistic.

Freedman dismissed correlational studies as having weak results or as being unable to satisfy the statistical requirements to prove causality. So he concentrated on field experiments as the best possible way to demonstrate that TV violence affects aggression in the real world. He notes that some of these field experiments produced no effects or effects in the opposite direction (Feshbach & Singer, 1971). Two other TV researchers (Friedrich-Cofer & Huston, 1986) have presented reasonable arguments for why Feshbach and Singer's field study obtained these unexpected results. The group forced to view unaggressive programming may have been very frustrated and angered by the restrictions on their viewing.

A field experiment conducted in Belgium by a research team including Leonard Berkowitz (Leyens, Parke, Camino, & Berkowitz, 1975) provides some of the most convincing evidence that media violence fosters aggression. This study satisfied many of the conditions necessary to generalize the findings to the real world in that naturally-occurring physical and verbal aggression was observed at several times after exposure to five complete movies. It was also important that these Belgian teenage boys in a foster care setting did not have access to or expect to see certain entertaining TV shows, unlike Feshbach and Singer's subjects. The behavior of these boys was observed in premovie, movie, and postmovie weeks in the evenings (right after seeing the movies during movie week) and after noon of the next day. Two cottages of boys saw five blood-and-guts American movies like *Bonnie and Clyde,* and two other cottages of boys saw five unaggressive French romantic comedies. Results showed that the boys who watched the aggressive movies were more physically aggressive right after the movie during movie week and more verbally aggressive into the next day and into the postmovie week. Increased physical aggression was quite short-lived. Of course, one does not have to be in an aggressive state too long to injure or kill someone. Verbal aggression was elevated for a longer time. Another team of researchers (Parke, Berkowitz, Leyens, West, & Sebastian, 1977) have found similar results in similar field experiments in the United States. These and other studies provide convincing evidence that TV and movie violence contributes to aggression among viewers.

Evidence that people do mimic or, at least, loosely reproduce what they see in the media is abundant. John Hinckley, Jr. shot President Reagan after he had seen an aggressive movie called *Taxi Driver* about a dozen times. In the last scene in that movie, Robert DeNiro was arming himself to shoot a politician who was speaking outside the building. A man in Boston was doused with gasoline and

Other Instances of Imitation

burned to death within weeks after such a scene had been depicted on a TV cop show. A girl was sexually assaulted with a blunt instrument by other girls after Linda Blair of *The Exorcist* fame was abused in a similar way on a TV movie. An Omaha boy killed a family of six next door after seeing part of *The Texas Tower Killings,* a TV movie about Charles Whitman's shooting rampage. These and other incidents are vivid testimony to the fact that media presentations of aggressive behavior inspire aggressive acts by some people in the audiences.

There is also evidence that a contagion effect involving many people occurs to produce a rash of incidents. Bandura (1983) points out that airline hijackings in copycat fashion produced a wave of these incidents in the late 1960s and early 1970s. Terrorist actions seemed to come in flurries in 1985 and 1986. One investigator (Philips, 1982, 1983) has shown that television suicides are followed by a temporary increase in suicides nationwide and closed-circuit boxing matches are followed by a jump in murders a few days later. Food and drug tamperings and poisonings seem to have come in bunches after the initial Tylenol poisoning in Chicago. In the spring of 1977, an Indiana man held another man hostage for hours with a shotgun aimed at his head before releasing him. Within two weeks, there had been about a dozen hostage-taking incidents in the northeast quadrant of the U.S., many of them resulting in death for the gunman and/or his hostage.

These instances of acting in similar ways to the publicized actions of a model cannot be construed as instances of observational learning. These people were not acquiring aggressive habits through imitation like children. They had probably just been given ideas by observing the actions of others. While Bandura (1973) characterizes the model's actions as disinhibiting (unleashing) the observer's aggressive tendencies, Berkowitz (1984) claims that because the observer's actions are not exact replicas of the model's, the action serves instead to prime certain aggressive thoughts. This priming may lead to a chain of thoughts, especially in habitually aggressive people, which may lead to behavior different from the model's actions. Both processes probably operate to produce this adult imitative behavior, which is somewhat different from the aggression acquisition process in children.

Normative Influences on Aggression

Most of us probably aggress very rarely. Why? We have learned that people in our environment will dislike us, chastise us verbally, confine us, or even punish us physically if we aggress. From our early experiences, we have learned the standards or norms for conduct, even aggressive conduct. We have learned at home and/or at school that we should not hit people who are smaller than us, that males should not hit females, and that we should not hurt anyone badly.

Reciprocity and Aggression

There is a *reciprocity norm* in harming others as well as in helping others as exemplified in the biblical prescription of "an eye for an eye, a tooth for a tooth." Surely you have seen it used in interpersonal and international affairs. The warring factions in the Middle East, for instance, use the past atrocities of their

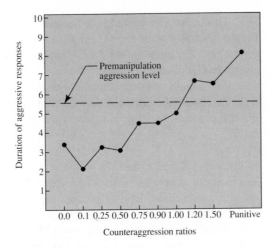

Figure 13.8
Adjusted cell means of aggression responses for counteraggression strategies combined across Blocks 2, 3, and 4 compared with the adjusted premanipulation aggression level. These results indicate that a person acts as aggressively (1.0 ratio) or more punitively than his or her opponent (1.2 ratio up), then he or she will receive sustained or increased aggression. Less aggressive reactions reduce aggression through the norm of reciprocity.
(From Kimble, Fitz, & Onorad, 1977, Journal of Personality and Social Psychology, 35.)

enemies as the reason for their own hostile actions. One experiment even showed that in interpersonal situations, at least, such a matching or "getting even" strategy can reduce your opponent's aggression toward you (Pisano & Taylor, 1971).

Kimble, Fitz, and Onorad (1977) were skeptical about this matching strategy finding. We decided that one way a person might use this reciprocity norm to his or her advantage is to act less aggressively than his or her opponent. To follow the norm, the opponent would have to reduce his or her later aggression level. To test this idea and others, we had a confederate use one of ten strategies in setting durations of noise bursts to be delivered to the ears of his opponent, the subject, if the subject should lose a competitive reaction time task. The subject did lose 13 of the 25 trials and received the noise blast prescribed by his opponent on those trials. The subject's noise duration setting for the confederate was the measure of aggression. The results showed that subjects followed the norm of reciprocity scrupulously. If their opponent set longer noise durations than they had on a trial, subjects responded more aggressively on subsequent trials. If he set shorter durations than subjects had on a trial, they responded less aggressively on later trials. If he matched their level (1.0 ratio on the figure nearby), they remained as aggressive as before. It appears that matching (1.0 ratio) and punitive (maximum noise settings by confederate) strategies are not effective in reducing aggression toward oneself. (See figure 13.8.)

Usually, our knowledge of these norms and the punishments for violation of them keep us from acting aggressively. Sometimes all that is required is that the offender be made very aware that he or she is operating in an antinormative or illegal way. That awareness may partially explain why Minneapolis police found that the repeat offense rate for domestic violence dropped dramatically when each offender was arrested and jailed overnight (Sherman & Berk, 1984). The night in jail probably made the assailant aware that his actions were a serious offense.

Of course, if we lived in a home or a culture where these norms were not taught, then we would be less inhibited about aggressing. When young children go out into the broader world of school, they learn norms of conduct as well as the three R's. There are some differences between homes, classrooms, and playgrounds in their socialization of norms against aggression. There are some settings that prescribe different norms about aggression. Violent sports and military groups, especially during war, have rules and norms that restrict aggression very little.

Deindividuation and Aggression

In chapter 9, I mentioned that when a person feels deindividuated, he or she is less likely to adhere to norms of conduct (Zimbardo, 1969). *Deindividuation* or low self-awareness is likely to occur when individuals are in the midst of dense, active crowds (Diener, 1980; Mullen, 1983; Prentice-Dunn & Rogers, 1983). In those situations, they feel unrecognizable and unaccountable for their conduct. They do not evaluate their conduct and are not inhibited by norms as they usually would be. It has been shown that in such conditions people act more aggressively (Mullen, 1986; Zimbardo, 1969).

Applications of Aggression Research

How can we assure that our children will not be too aggressive? How can we avoid being victims of aggression? How can we control our own aggressive urges? How can societies reduce aggressive crime? These are the basic questions to be answered by aggression research and related work.

Rearing Unaggressive Children

You may ask, "Would I want my children to be unaggressive?" Given the fact that they must be able to compete for their places in the world, you might decide "No." However, if one considers what we have defined as aggression, most of us would desire that our children be physically unaggressive, at least.

Social learning advocates recommend that parents ignore children's minor acts of aggression in order to extinguish those responses (Brown & Elliot, 1965). In conjunction with this extinction, these behavior modifiers recommend that parents reward desirable behaviors incompatible with aggression. Even though the extinction technique has been demonstrated to be effective with young children, it is sometimes hard to do, especially if someone else is being hurt by the aggressive acts.

However, attending to a child right after he or she acts aggressively, even to punish the child, can serve as positive reinforcement for the aggression (Bandura, 1971). The best alternative seems to be "time-out from positive reinforcement," which means that the parent would remove the child from the situation in which the child aggressed for a short period (Azrin, 1961; Tyler & Brown, 1967). This quiet time alone in the child's room or elsewhere usually calms child and parent alike.

The hard part can be carrying these recommendations out. For instance, I recall seeing a videotape of a kindergarten teacher who inadvertently reinforced the unruly behavior of two boys while "punishing" them. I'm sure she saw the problem when she heard the second boy on the tape say, "Me too, me too," as she started "punishing" the first boy by making him sit on her lap as she read a story to the class. Also, I had a painful and embarrassing experience when I tried to use "time-out" with our daughter (who was three at the time). I grabbed her by the wrist to take her to another room as she was hitting her one-year-old brother. When I did, she threw her weight in the other direction and dislocated her elbow. After a restless night, unsuccessful treatment at an emergency room, and a painful day, we got an appointment with our pediatrician. He popped the elbow back in place, and everyone, especially I, breathed a sigh of relief. As we left the building, we bought her a drink for her bravery. By the time we got to the car, Lauren was hitting Daniel on the head with the drink can, using her restored "good right arm." Nevertheless, we still use the time-out procedure, and it usually has the desired effect.

Social learning theorists also advise that parents shouldn't model aggression through their own conduct or provide aggressive models through exposure to media violence. Parents can model aggression through fighting between themselves, beating other children, or directly punishing the child physically. Spanking or otherwise hitting a child can also frustrate, annoy, and arouse the child, which we know from motivational research is likely to make the child more aggressive. For these reasons, physical punishment is not recommended (Baron, 1977). Selectivity in the TV shows and movies children see is also recommended.

The normative perspective suggests that parents would be wise to use rule-setting to teach children society's norms about aggression. Overt, simple articulation of these standards of conduct may effectively replace physical punishment as a means of teaching these norms or restrictions on behavior. Setting rules which anticipate later problem behaviors may prevent those behaviors and the need to discipline the child. Prevention seems to be the idea behind norms and law enforcement. Knowing about them and the potential punishments from violations of these standards may keep most of us from speeding in our cars, robbing banks, or hitting someone.

From the FBI statistics on aggressive crime, the best advice to avoid becoming a victim is to avoid situations where weapons are likely to be present and may be used on people. Such advice is especially true when individuals are likely to be aroused or angry (Berkowitz & LePage, 1967). Aggression involving weapons is much more injurious than aggression with one's bare hands.

Avoiding Victimization

Again, this is a recommendation that is hard to follow. Knives and pistols are very easy to conceal. Many people have weapons in their homes for protection. Too often these weapons are used in domestic violence, suicides, or accidental shootings rather than against intruders. One should be leery about entering such homes uninvited and sometimes even with an engraved invitation. There have been so many killings with weapons in and around schools in recent years that some schools have periodic searches. Seriously, rental of airport metal detectors might be a good idea for some school systems.

Guns in homes often lead to murders, suicides, and accidental shootings.

There are ways of recognizing volatile situations involving weapons. There are many convenience stores that should be avoided, especially late at night. Many parties and drinking places should be left early in the evening. Drug dealers and other such unsavory characters involved in illegal enterprises often carry weapons and should be avoided, especially in isolated, dark settings.

Even without weapons, it can be dangerous to get involved with someone who has drunk too much alcohol in a very short time. We know this can be dangerous from the work of Stuart Taylor and associates on alcohol and aggression and police records indicating that violent crimes often are associated with too much drinking (e.g., Wolfgang & Strohm, 1956). This information indicates that we should avoid late-night, weekend parties where too much alcohol has probably been consumed. This drinking problem is especially severe in drinking establishments where the patrons may be carrying weapons. Even in the Old West, many saloons had the good sense to disarm people at the door. Also, research by Malamuth, Donnerstein, and others suggests that women should avoid areas where aggressive erotic films are shown.

If someone acts aggressively toward you in an interpersonal confrontation, there are several ways you can react to reduce your opponent's aggression. If you had the strength or resources to overwhelm your opponent, you could reduce his or her aggression by direct attack. Unfortunately, individuals (and nations) tend to overestimate their ability to overwhelm an opponent, and they incur greater aggression in retaliation to their attacks (Kimble et al., 1977). A better strategy suggested by the Kimble et al. study would be to counteraggress less and less over the course of the interaction (some counteraggression may be necessary to protect your interests) and thereby induce your opponent to aggress less. In interpersonal confrontations, there is ample evidence that it is best to keep verbal aggression to a minimum because it escalates physical aggression (Straus, 1974; Toch, 1969).

Other means of blunting aggression are suggested by several experiments by Baron (1977, 1983). His work indicates that if one can arouse reactions incompatible with anger and aggression, that person is much less likely to be victimized. He suggests that nonhostile humor, pain cues to arouse empathy, and mild sexual arousal are incompatible with anger and can reduce aggression in certain situations.

If you are confronted by an armed person or a group of threatening people, the best advice seems to be to do as you are told. There have been too many situations where individuals gave up their lives or health for their money when they challenged an armed robber. A few years ago, a man named Alton Coleman and his girlfriend went on a murder spree in the Midwest. At one point, they accosted a man, took his car, and took him hostage. The newspaper accounts indicated that the man obeyed their commands and was eventually found in his trunk unharmed. The twosome killed several other people. Thomas Moriarty (1974) stated that we should stand up for our rights more against muggers. That is unwise advice, especially if there are more than one mugger and/or if they have weapons.

If the criminal has you in an isolated area, you may be better off to fight or flee. One strategy would be to make the situation public. In the same crime spree previously mentioned, one woman managed to escape the murderous duo by causing a car wreck in heavy traffic. Creating a scene can be effective in escaping an aggressor. Several years ago, one of our graduate students used the strategy of gaining others' attention to escape a terrifying situation. As she got into her car in an isolated area of a shopping center parking lot one evening, a man rushed her from behind, pushed her across the driver's seat, and tried to gain control of the car. She screamed so loud and flailed at her assailant so much that he gave up and fled.

It has already been mentioned that many people have guns for protecting households from intruders. Perhaps they can provide protection without problems if they are kept unloaded in a safe place away from children. However, there are many mishaps that can occur with guns. In addition, if you display a weapon, an intruder may be more likely to use his weapon than if you had no weapon. Instead, deadbolt locks, lights, alarm systems, and dogs should be used for protection. The locks are to keep anyone from entering; and lights, alarms, and dogs call attention to the intrusion and prevent it. Dogs can be very effective because they know familiar from unfamiliar people, and they recognize unusual situations. I know that the spine-chilling growl of a dog we owned discouraged three teenage boys from entering our unlit home one night. It could have been coincidental, but a few months later three boys entered a house the same way ours had been approached and beat a couple, killing the woman. They later acknowledged that they had burglarized homes throughout the metropolitan area. Suffice it to say, I am a great believer in using dogs, not trained killers but ordinary pets, for protection.

Controlling our aggressive impulses is another problem. If it were possible, we might be well-advised to avoid provocative circumstances that motivate aggression. However, it is not always in our control to avoid frustrating, competitive, inequitable, irritating, or painful situations. To the extent that we can avoid these aversive conditions by changing jobs, etc., we would be happier and less aggressive if we did take control of our lives.

Controlling Aggressive Urges

One suggestion for controlling aggression from Lorenz, Freud, and the frustration-aggression tradition (Dollard et al., 1939) is to achieve catharsis. *Catharsis* occurs when a person experiences a reduction in aggression-producing tension by expressing one's aggressive urges. Several studies have examined whether catharsis can be achieved through direct physical aggression, displaced aggression, verbal aggression, fantasy aggression, and nonaggression (see Geen & Quanty, 1977; Hokanson, 1970 for reviews). Most of the evidence indicates that people do experience tension reduction in terms of systolic blood pressure after direct physical or verbal aggression against the person who offended them, but not after displaced aggression or fantasy aggression (e.g., Hokanson & Burgess, 1962). However, most studies reveal that one aggressive act against a person intensifies later aggression (Buss, 1966). Even though tension is reduced, this

Catharsis does not seem to work as a means of controlling aggression.

Reprinted by permission of UFS, Inc.

SURE, WAR IS VIOLENT... BUT IT'S THE ONLY THING THAT STOPS SOCIETY FROM RESORTING TO ICE HOCKEY,

cathartic effect does not reduce subsequent aggressive behavior. Beating on an inanimate object as suggested by Lorenz does not reduce aggression either (Ryan, 1970). Nor does vigorous exercise, aggressive play, or watching aggression reduce aggression by the participant. Catharsis does not seem to work as a means of controlling aggression.

Dwelling on an inequitable or otherwise disturbing situation tends to sustain or reinstate one's anger and is likely to make one more aggressive (Berkowitz, 1984; Zillman, 1979). So, thinking about other matters or considering justifying reasons for the offender's provocative act may be a way to control one's aggressive urges. In their review of catharsis, Geen and Quanty (1977) state that aggression will usually cease when equity is restored. This implies that if we convince ourselves that the offensive condition was justified, then we would cease our aggression.

Talking about the incident with a third person who is likely to discourage aggressive action might be an effective way to reduce arousal (Pennebaker, Hughes, & O'Heeron, 1987). Even though exercise may create excitation transfer to anger (Zillman, 1983), the aftermath of exercise is commonly a calmer, less aroused state. Any action that would reduce arousal without providing aggressive cues, such as removing or distancing oneself from the situation physically or mentally, should reduce aggression.

Reducing Aggressive Crime

One way to reduce crime is to keep weapons from the hands of potential offenders. Weapons give the holder an advantage over unarmed persons. Practically all of the violent crimes reported at the beginning of the chapter, except rape in some cases, involved the use of a weapon. Aggravated assault is defined by the FBI as assaults involving use of a weapon, and armed robbery obviously involves weapons. Burglaries, auto theft, and other crimes of stealth do not involve use of weapons and are classified as nonaggressive, property crimes. Cross-national comparisons suggest that murders, assaults, robberies, and even rapes would decrease drastically in the U.S. if weapons were less available to give offenders the advantage over the rest of us. Of course, the weapon of choice in most criminal activities is the handgun because it is concealable yet deadly.

So far, it has not been politically feasible to institute effective gun control laws. "Cooling off periods" for gun sales, which might help in cases of impulsive aggressive or suicidal tendencies, are rarely instituted or observed for anything except new gun sales at retail stores. Felons, who are not allowed to buy guns legally, have ample access to them anyway. Handgun laws are usually on a local, rather than statewide, basis unless the laws are restrictions on carrying unlicensed handguns. Such cases also seem to be rarely enforced or prosecuted unless the gun was used in the commission of a crime, and by then the damage is already done. There seems to be little hope for reducing the availability of weapons, but here are a few ideas:

1. More restrictions on and less production of certain kinds of ammunition
2. Gun buy-out programs by which governments would buy and destroy used guns from pawnshops and citizens rather than having them recycled
3. Greater use of metal detectors at entrances of high crime spots like convenience stores, perhaps even with an alarm system attached
4. Encouragement of the use of signs publicizing alarm systems and other crime prevention devices and programs, such as "Police patrol this area 24 hours."

Other approaches to crime reduction have been to increase the costs of crime and the rewards of legal activities for potential offenders (Wilson & Herrnstein, 1985). In many ways, this is an application of social learning principles to adults. Wilson and Herrnstein (1985) point out that such behavior modification programs are more effective than other types of therapeutic intervention, especially when family and community environments can be made more rewarding when the program is over (see Patterson, 1982). To increase the costs of crime, governments need to make possible criminals realize that detection, arrest, prosecution, conviction, and incarceration for their offenses are swift and certain. To increase the rewards of legal activities, prisons must become rehabilitation and job training centers rather than aggressive subcultures for further involvement in crime. Lengthy terms without parole are only appropriate to keep proven incorrigibles from aggressing against law-abiding citizens again. Zimbardo (1974) recommended more rewards for constructive inmate behaviors, less rewards for aggressive behavior, and better pay for the correctional people administering rewards appropriately. Greater job opportunities for less skilled workers may prevent the low incomes that encourage criminal activities.

At national and international levels, there are many crime problems to be addressed. The regulation of drug trafficking is a problem that must certainly be handled at an international level. Some illegal drugs certainly create many desperate and disoriented people who commit many crimes. Trafficking in those drugs is a big and lucrative business. Drug use, which contributes to so many of society's problems, must be attacked at both the supply and demand end. Stifling the supply is a major international economic issue that will require cooperation between nations. The personal reasons for drug use were addressed briefly in chapter 3.

Generally, the secret to reducing crime at national and international levels lies in restoring or maintaining equity or justice for groups and individuals. The individual who feels that she is being unfairly treated relative to others is motivated to aggress against others. Groups of people who feel that their living conditions are poor or their rights are being abused are likewise motivated. Unfortunately, two or more individuals or groups sometimes desire the same resources, creating competition and conflict. The only equitable solutions in those cases seem to be to create new equivalent resources for one of the parties, to have them share proportionately in the existing resources, or to reduce one party's interest in those resources and interest them in other resources. The most reasonable solution may vary from case to case. Governmental agencies, legal systems, and even the United Nations or other groups of nations must address some of these issues of inequity.

Summary

Aggression is defined as any act done to cause physical or psychological harm to another living being. Angry aggression is behavior primarily intended to injure or harm another, while instrumental aggression is action done as a means of attaining some other resource. Aggressive acts can be physical or verbal, direct or indirect, and active or passive. The sociobiologist, Wilson, categorized aggression according to the context in which it occurred.

Lorenz, the ethologist, regarded aggression as the fighting instinct which aided in the preservation of the species. He believed that it resulted from aggressive energy that spontaneously builds up and needs to be dissipated. Aggression was seen as important in gaining mates and other resources. Wilson amended some of Lorenz's ideas by saying aggression is instrumental in improving the reproductive fitness of the individual's kin as well as the fitness of the individual. Wilson also highlighted competition, the environmental context, and the flexibility of aggressive responding more than Lorenz. Earlier Freud had viewed aggression as stemming from a self-destructive instinct. He believed that aggression could be rechanneled to be more acceptable to society. Freud, like Lorenz, believed that catharsis of aggressive energy was necessary. Biological approaches to the study of aggression have emphasized the role of pain centers, hormones, and body chemistry in affecting aggression.

The frustration and aggression hypothesis started the study of aggressive motivation and a focus on environmental influences. Frustration has more recently been related to the disparity between one's outcomes and expectations. Frustration is now seen as one motivator; along with attacks, inequity, competition, and aversive conditions; of anger that leads to aggression. Arousal, including sexual arousal, intensifies aggression through excitation transfer. The social learning perspective emphasizes that we learn to be aggressive through evaluating our actions and their consequences and observing the actions of others. Home, school, and media violence can serve as models for aggression. We also learn social norms for when aggression is appropriate or inappropriate. The norm of reciprocating harm—harming another just as she or he has harmed you—is a strong standard for conduct. We usually do not follow the norms for non-aggression when we are in deindividuating situations.

Social learning theory has taught us that children will be less aggressive if we (1) ignore or (2) use time-out with their aggressive acts, (3) reward other behaviors, (4) do not act aggressively with them, and (5) do not provide exposure to media violence. As adults, we may avoid being the victims of aggression by (1) avoiding situations where weapons are present, (2) avoiding people who have drunk heavily, (3) doing as armed or otherwise threatening people say, and (4) if isolated with an offender, trying to call others' attention to your plight.

To control our aggressiveness, we should avoid and reduce our exposure to anger-provoking and arousing situations, think about things other than the provoking situation, and talk to a dispassionate third party. Unfortunately, catharsis does not reduce later aggression, so it is not a useful technique for reducing aggression. The most promising approaches for reducing aggressive crime seem to be for society to reduce the availability of weapons to potential offenders and to increase the costs of crime and the rewards for legal activities for potential offenders.

CHAPTER 14

Prejudice and Discrimination

An Anglo policeman was summoned to a Mexican-American district in southeast Austin, Texas, in the middle of the night. When he arrived at the convenience store, he discovered that a window had been broken, and he saw a figure fleeing in the dark. He fired on the figure climbing a fence. A young boy died of the gunshot wound to the back of the head. He had been carrying sandwich makings in his hands as he fled. Would the policeman have fired if he had been summoned to some other neighborhood?

In the ghetto riots of 1967 in Newark, a black man used the chaotic situation to steal a case of beer. In vivid, chilling pictures presented in *Life* magazine, one can see what happened next. A white policeman with a rifle killed the man. Why was petty theft a capital offense in this case?

In India, while a woman, Indira Gandhi, was the head of state, many young wives were killed in appallingly torturous ways by their husbands or other family members. Why? Their dowries had not been lucrative enough to satisfy their husbands.

In American society, women are often physically abused. Spouse abuse in America is clearly one-sided. Men abuse women much more than vice versa. Women are more frequently subjected to sexual harassment on the job than men are. Date rape has just recently been recognized as a common problem. The sexual abuse of children, both girls and boys, is also being recognized as a more common traumatic experience than was realized before.

By 1972, nine soldiers from my home county of about 20,000 people had died in the Vietnam War. All nine were Mexican-American. About 55 percent of the county's population at that time was Mexican-American. Also, almost a fourth of the combat casualties in Vietnam were black soldiers, while the black population of the United States is only about one-eighth of the entire population. Poor employment opportunities and excessively stringent college admission standards are some of the discriminatory factors that contributed to these lopsided figures.

What is Prejudice?

Surely you have been a victim of prejudice. Has anyone ever shunned you or slighted you for impersonal reasons? Maybe you thought this treatment was due to your sex, religion, appearance, or ethnic identity. Maybe it was because you were a sorority member or maybe it was because you were not. Maybe they belittled you because of your major. Regardless of the reason, it is usually unpleasant to be the butt of these snap judgments, which may be expressed in snubs, avoidance, ridicule, or even overt aggression.

Prejudices are privately-held *attitudes* by which we judge individuals based on their group membership. Black, white, Mexican, Italian, American, foreigner, Arab, Jew, Catholic, man, woman, gay, straight, Democrat, Republican, jock, intellectual, Communist, Nazi, aged, young, rich, poor—these are some of the group membership categories that make a difference to us. Any of these labels may be outgroups toward whom prejudice is displayed. These attitudes toward groups other than our own are usually negative in comparison to evaluations of members of our own group. We are **ethnocentric,** which means that our group

Members of many groups are targets of prejudice.

forms the standard for evaluation of correct conduct and thought (Brown, 1965). So, **prejudice** is a negative evaluation of an individual based on a single aspect of the individual—group membership, as defined by the beholder. It is prejudgmental in that such an attitude exists before knowing anything about the individual to whom it is applied.

Prejudices are associated with stereotypes. *Stereotypes* are *beliefs* that members of certain groups have particular characteristics. Some examples of stereotypes follow: men are obstinate, whites are dull, blacks are religious, teenagers are defiant. If those characteristics are judged to be bad, then the attitude toward that group is negative. Negative evaluations (prejudices) may lead to generation of negative beliefs (stereotypes) or these beliefs may create negative evaluations. Both causal chains probably occur. Devine (1989) contends that stereotypes are usually established before attitudes are. Normally, we believe that members of particular groups have positive, negative, and neutral traits. Our beliefs about groups are not as one-dimensional as the previous examples suggest. However, if most of the central traits a person ascribes to a group are negative, then we would judge him or her to be prejudiced against that group. These beliefs are often untrue for individuals in the group. To the extent that we think and act toward those individuals mainly on the basis of their group membership, we are treating them unfairly.

Prejudices are also associated with discrimination. **Discrimination** occurs when someone or some institution acts unfavorably toward a person based on that person's group membership. Discriminatory behavior is presumed to stem from prejudice, and prejudiced people usually behave disfavorably toward outgroup members (Stephan, 1985). Discrimination, the manifestation or expression of prejudice, encompasses everything from social slights to murder of outgroup members. When nearly all of the nontenured English composition instructors at a university are women and nearly all of the tenured English faculty are men, we might assume that sex discrimination has occurred. When blacks and hispanics are vastly overrepresented among U.S. combat fatalities in the Vietnam War, we can assume that race discrimination has occurred.

Types and Targets of Prejudice

Dominative racists were involved in the Howard Beach incident.

Some types of prejudice have already been implied. Racism, sexism, nationalism, religious prejudice, ageism, and sexual-orientationism (one dimension of this bias is homophobia, the fear of homosexuals) cover the most common categories. More than one outgroup label was mentioned for each type of prejudice to indicate that usually the fear and the hatred are not one-sided. However, in many situations one group enjoys a power advantage over another group in control over valuable resources. Many of these advantaged-disadvantaged relationships have a long history of enslavement, imprisonment, and/or annihilation. Also, in most cases, the members of the target groups have little or no choice about being a member of the disadvantaged group. Hence, most of the research and writing on prejudice and discrimination has focused on men's exploitation of women, whites' prejudices and biased reactions against blacks, and gentiles', especially Nazis', treatment of Jews. This does not mean that all men, whites, or gentiles are bigots who discriminate, or that there are not many other hurtful prejudices that could be considered. Nor does this focus imply that women, blacks, or Jews are the only oppressed people. Many of the effects of sex roles and sexism were discussed previously in chapter 2.

Many distinctions have been drawn of the forms of prejudice. For instance, Kovel (1970) distinguished between dominative and aversive racists. **A dominative racist** is one who is willing to overtly discriminate against members of the target group. They are willing to act aggressively to maintain their presumed superiority. The apartheid of South Africa and the "Jim Crow" segregation laws of the South of the past suggest that these societies are and were controlled by dominative racists. **Aversive racists** are much more subtle in expressing their feelings. They avoid members of the outgroup and behave "properly" in enforced interactions. They are not openly hostile, but in the privacy of the voting booth, for instance, they will discriminate on the basis of race or ethnic group.

Other researchers have indicated that the aversive racist may be affected by **ambivalence** toward the outgroup (Dutton & Lennox, 1974; Frey & Gaertner, 1986; Gaertner, 1973; Katz, Wackenhut, & Glass, 1986; Kinder & Sears, 1981). (See figure 14.1.) Aversive or modern racists may feel admiration or sympathy and fear or dislike for the outgroup at the same time. They are also motivated by a desire to appear nonprejudiced. Apparently, the subjects in Sigall and Page's (1971) study who acknowledged prejudiced attitudes under "bogus pipeline" conditions but not under normal self-report conditions were aversive racists (see chapter 6, p. 144). So, depending on the presumed attitudes and reactions of the audience present and the deservingness of the victim, white modern racists are likely to help a black more readily than a white. If there is no evident reason other than race to react in a negative way, ambivalent racists bend over backwards to behave positively toward outgroup members. However, if there is some other issue, such as forced busing to pin the behavior on, ambivalent racists will express negative attitudes toward the target group (Kimble, 1980; McConahay, 1982). In both of these studies, whites expressed negative attitudes toward busing even though they did not have children being bused to school. However, Kimble (1980) found that whites endorsed, as enthusiastically as blacks, the benefits of

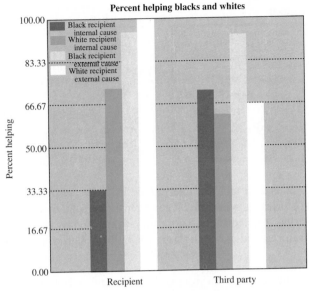

Percent helping blacks and whites

Legend:
- Black recipient internal cause
- White recipient internal cause
- Black recipient external cause
- White recipient external cause

Y-axis (Percent helping): 0.00, 16.67, 33.33, 50.00, 66.67, 83.33, 100.00

X-axis (Person who asked for help): Recipient, Third party

Figure 14.1
Ambivalent racism. If the white subjects were asked to help by a third party or if the problem was caused by external factors, they helped blacks just as much as whites. But if a female victim had brought the problem on herself (internal cause) or she asked for help herself, subjects helped blacks less than whites.

(From Frey & Gaertner, 1986, Journal of Personality and Social Psychology, 50, 186.)

racial integration. Ambivalence seems to characterize the interracial feelings of many Americans as we enter the last decade of the century. It is interesting to consider whether there are similar ambivalent attitudes toward the other sex and similar overt and covert types of sexists.

Jones (1972), a black social psychologist, considered other aspects of racism. He distinguished among individual, institutional, and cultural racism. By *individual racism,* he referred to the prejudiced attitudes and discriminatory behavior of the individual. It seems, however, that he considered only Kovel's dominative racists. He also specified that such racists believe that the different traits of various races are biologically based and are, therefore, less susceptible to change. Perhaps you can see some parallels here between racist beliefs and sexist beliefs.

Institutional racism is not defined by attitudes of the prejudiced individual, but by the disadvantage it creates for the members of a particular race. The focus here is on discriminatory practices rather than what is in the hearts and minds of men and women. Whether the segregation is de jure (by law, which the Supreme Court has prohibited) or de facto ("naturally" occurring, which means that housing patterns developed spontaneously) is unimportant, both are instances of institutional racism. It does not matter whether college administrators intended to bar certain groups from their schools by adopting certain admission standards, unequal opportunities have been created by such decisions. It is such racist practices and similar sexist practices that affirmative action laws are designed to counteract.

Cultural racism is a failure by individuals and groups of people to recognize the contributions of particular racial and ethnic groups. Individual racism and cultural racism seem to go hand in glove. Persons who are bigoted are unlikely

Much hatred and aggression is engendered by individual and group allegiance to their own religious beliefs.

KUDZU, by Marlette. © 1986. By permission of Doug Marlette and Creators Syndicate, Inc.

KUDZU

to attend to and are likely to belittle the contributions of groups they dislike. Historically, white missionaries to foreign lands failed to recognize that civilizations existed there before they came. Today, there are many educational programs aimed at highlighting the cultural heritages of our many subgroups.

Effects of Prejudice and Discrimination on Targets

Living with the awareness that you are maltreated on the basis of your group membership affects your mental and emotional status. The effects of constantly being put down was first studied systematically by Clark and Clark (1947). They tested over 250 young (3–7 years old) black children in Arkansas and Massachusetts by showing them two brown dolls with black hair and two white dolls with yellow hair. They asked individual children to indicate which doll was like a black person (racial identification), which doll looked like the child (self-identification), and which doll the child would prefer to play with (racial preference). They found that although the vast majority of the children could make the racial distinction, a third of them responded incorrectly in identifying themselves, and over half of them preferred to play with the white doll. The Clarks interpreted these results to mean that these very young children had already learned to devalue themselves and their racial group from their early experiences in American society. This study was influential in the 1954 Supreme Court decision to abolish segregation in the public schools.

It seems unlikely that black children would choose white dolls today.

    Another influential psychologist of that era, Gordon Allport, wrote very perceptively about the effects of being the target of discrimination in his classic book, *The Nature of Prejudice* (Allport, 1954). He stated that no one can be indifferent to the obvious prejudices and discriminations that often occur to members of some groups. Some oppressed people become hypersensitive to the verbal slights and biased treatments. Others attempt to deny their group membership by changing their appearance or their language and by not associating with other group members. These two diverse reactions seem likely to foster two different clusters of behavior patterns. The hypersensitive individuals seem likely to do the following:

1. Strengthen ties with their ingroup
2. Display prejudice against outgroups
3. Become militant in their protests
4. Sympathize with people of other oppressed groups
5. Voluntarily segregate to avoid the attacks of prejudiced others.

On the other hand, those oppressed persons who desire to dissociate themselves from the group may do the following:

1. Identify with the dominant group and display self-hate
2. Aggress against their own group
3. Mock or belittle their group traits by caricaturing those traits
4. Have different public selves and private selves
5. Display different public selves depending on the presence of ingroup and outgroup members.

These two clusters of five reactions I have distilled from Allport's undivided list of 10 reactions seem to go together in forming two types. There are few systematic studies to support these observations.

The most likely reactions to mistreatment by other groups in the society are voluntary segregation or avoidance of the oppressive group and resentment toward that group for the unfair treatment. Avoidance of the prejudiced group allows one to avoid the mistreatment, to avoid unfavorable comparisons, and to avoid having his or her consciousness directed to that negative experience. Resentment seems to be a natural reaction to the negative treatment and the apparent unwillingness of members of the dominant group to change the situation.

There is some evidence that prejudices are powerful expectations that are sometimes confirmed in the behavior of the target person. They may even override other expectations that the prejudiced individuals are given. For instance, studies examining elements of the Pygmalion effect in the classroom have shown that it doesn't work the same way for black students as it does for whites (Chaikin & Derlega, 1978; Rubovitz & Maehr, 1973). Both of these studies looked at how individuals placed in a teaching role treated "bright" (as labeled by experimenters) blacks and whites. Both examined climate or warmth factors, which are seen as ways self-fulfilling expectations are communicated to the target, so they may be fulfilled (Rosenthal, 1974). Consistent with earlier findings, whites who were labeled "bright" to the teachers were treated better than control whites in terms of attention, praise, and positive nonverbal behaviors received. It did not work that way for black students. Generally, the "bright" blacks were treated worse than the control blacks and all the whites in these interactions. What happened? Apparently, these white "teachers" had preconceived ideas about what kind of students blacks were supposed to be, and those who disconfirmed those expectations were not treated the same way as similar whites. (See figures 14.2 and 14.3.)

Two studies conducted with white subjects at Princeton University indicate that these prejudiced expectations are translated into action and those actions influence the behavior of the target persons (Word, Zanna, & Cooper, 1974). In the first study, they had white subjects in the role of job interviewers interact with a black or white applicant. Both of the applicants were confederates whose behavior was preprogrammed and standardized. Subjects interacting with the

Prejudice as a Self-Fulfilling Prophecy

Figure 14.2
"Bright" white students received more eye gaze from their teachers. "Bright" black students did not benefit from the Pygmalion effect, however. Similar results were obtained on positive head nods and smiles.

(From Chaikin & Derlega, 1978, Journal of Applied Social Psychology, 8, *122.)*

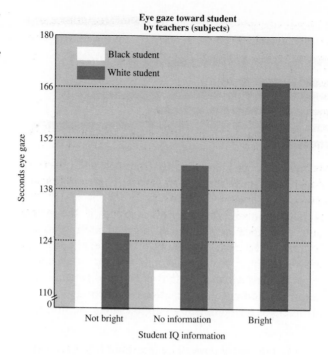

Figure 14.3
Teachers paid more attention to "gifted" white students, but not to "gifted" black students. Overall, the white teachers paid more attention to white students.

(From Rubovits & Maehr, 1973, Journal of Personality and Social Psychology, 25, *212.)*

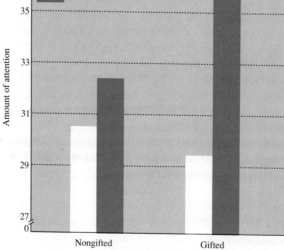

black applicant displayed less eye contact, forward lean, and face-to-face orientation toward him than subjects who interacted with the white applicant displayed. They also gave the black applicant less interview time. So their racial reactions were translated into behavior.

Does such discriminating behavior affect the reactions of the target person? To answer this question, Word, Zanna, and Cooper reversed the roles for the white subjects in the second study. Now they were in the role of the job applicant. Trained (white) interviewers treated half of them as the black applicant had been treated in the first study. They treated the other subjects the same way the white applicant had been treated. Those subjects who received negative nonverbal treatment (as the black applicant had) reported more nervousness in the interview and performed less adequately than the other subjects did. So, the prejudiced expectations produced their own fulfillment in the conduct of the target persons. In this way, prejudice and discrimination can, through subtle means, create greater disadvantage for members of target groups.

The prejudiced attitudes and discriminatory behavior of others limit where one can comfortably go and what one can comfortably do. There are jobs members of oppressed groups can't do and places they cannot go because members of more powerful groups disapprove. In fact, a target person may feel most at ease if he or she never has to interact with groups of people who are likely to be prejudiced. That is a factor in "voluntary" segregation. Conflicts arise because members of those other groups have valuable resources. Members of those groups may have a job to offer, they may have knowledge that one needs to get ahead, they may be potential customers, or they may have many votes needed for a political candidate to gain office. In order to gain those resources, the member of the oppressed group must interact with people of other groups.

For women and girls, competition with men and boys for advancement is one of those interaction situations they must learn to handle. Achievement in education and careers for women requires them to compete with men. However, their earlier experience has taught them to act harmoniously with others, especially men, if they want a happy social life. Matina Horner (1970) argued that this conflict between enacting the feminine role and competing with men creates a "fear of success" in achievement situations. In the 1960s, she did find that women showed strong psychological reactions to being placed in such a conflict situation (as discussed in chapter 2). Although this fear of success effect has not been convincingly demonstrated in recent years, it seems certain that women still experience more conflict between their careers and their social lives than men do. These psychological effects, even beyond overt prohibitions, constrain the opportunities of women greatly. Generally, the contraints put upon the conduct of oppressed individuals of various groups can take a strong psychological toll.

Constraints on Behavior and Internal Conflicts

HAZEL, by Ted Key. © 1987 by King Features. Reprinted by permission.

HAZEL

"Rule number one: let the male of the species score occasionally. And if he OWNS the ball..."

Female executives often experience more conflict between business and social life than male executives do.

Explanations of Prejudice

Developmental Views on Prejudice

There are many theories of prejudice that address directly or indirectly the formation of prejudice in children. The assumption seems to be that for attitudes to be so strongly held and resistant to change as some prejudices are, they must have developed quite early (Katz, 1976). Devine (1989) suggests that stereotypes are established in young children's minds before they are capable of critical evaluation and that they become automatic responses to outgroup members that remain with us into adulthood.

For children to develop prejudice, they must be able to tell the difference between their own groups and other groups. This principle is implied by theories which emphasize ingroup favoritism and outgroup bias (Brewer, 1979; Tajfel, 1982). Identifiability, in terms of appearance and/or language, plays a role in defining ingroups and outgroups and initiating bias, especially among children. Children must have sufficient experience and cognitive ability to identify their own groups and other groups. Three-year-old children can define ingroups and outgroups on the basis of sex and ethnic group in cases of racial or ethnic groups which are clearly different in appearance (Goodman, 1952; Kohlberg, 1966). Ethnic group identification based on more subtle traits, such as language, occurs at an older age and is probably more dependent on exposure to such groups.

Positive attitudes toward one's own group and negative attitudes toward other groups don't develop until school age even though the distinctions between groups can be made at the age of three (Goodman, 1952). It also seems likely that distinguishing members of the other sex and adults as outgroups and developing outgroup bias against them does not develop early because children interact with them every day in their "primary" ingroup—the family. On the other hand, outgroup bias toward groups readily identifiable as not one's group and groups with whom the child does not live (i.e., blacks and whites) may develop earlier.

The young boy who is brought to the KKK rally in his personalized robe and hood by his father is certainly being exposed to direct instruction in prejudice. Such cases appear to be unusual. Studies examining the agreement in attitudes between parents and young children generally find little evidence of such direct training (e.g., Byrne, 1965). It is more likely that a young child will learn prejudices through observation of parents' behavior and events on television. The fact that one's parents and siblings do not associate with members of certain ethnic groups could communicate to the child that such an arrangement of one's life is appropriate.

Learning Prejudices

Kenneth Clark, the black psychologist who studied the effects of a racist environment on young black children, has argued that the manifestations of institutional racism affect the attitudes of young children profoundly (Clark, 1963). The young white child who sees many blacks working in hard, low-paying jobs does not realize that this circumstance exists because of years of racist practices. He or she is likely to conclude that blacks must deserve such poor jobs, especially when he or she consistently sees such differences between the status of blacks and whites. So, conditions observed frequently in everyday life provide the underpinnings for the development of prejudice.

Thus far, we have been discussing the cognitive features of the development of prejudice. Now, what would motivate a young child to dislike a whole group or groups of people? In 1950, Adorno and his associates established a perspective on how prejudice is motivated by the experiences of young children. They established that authoritarian adults are more prejudiced against other groups than nonauthoritarian adults. Their position was that authoritarianism, which describes a large set of personality traits, develops from the individual's early experiences. Using a Freudian perspective, Adorno and associates believed that children who have tyrannical, punishing parents during the time when they are resolving their Oedipal complexes (ages 5–7) become authoritarian. These children develop an uncritical submission to authority, respect for power, rigid adherence to conventional values, opposition to subjective approaches to life, cynicism about human nature, and aggressiveness (traits of the **authoritarian personality**) through "identification with the aggressor" (their fathers) (Brown, 1965). There is some evidence that children reared in such households are more prejudiced than others (Triandis & Triandis, 1962; Weatherley, 1963). Others have argued that it is the lowered self-esteem, not the authoritarian values, of the mistreated child that makes them put other groups down (Rosenberg, 1965; Stephan & Rosenfield, 1978; Wills, 1981).

The Authoritarian Personality

Young children seldom display racial bias.

Even though I have focused on the very early years in examining the development of prejudice, it seems evident that very young children are not very hateful toward members of other groups. As I observed at an elementary school in its first year of desegregation several years ago, extensive play and voluntary association at lunch and recess between blacks and whites was very common among children of the first four or five grades. Segregation by race was evident only in the upper elementary grades. It seems that the interracial attitudes and behaviors of *young* children can be most affected by positive interracial experiences.

Frustration and Downward Comparison

The idea that frustration causes aggression (Dollard et al., 1939) has been used to explain prejudice. The argument is that frustration produces hostility that cannot always be expressed in direct aggression toward a frustrator. In fact, our frustrations are often produced by unidentifiable or inaccessible groups or organizations, not by persons. In such cases, one's fury may be displaced toward other, safe targets. These targets of displaced hostility are called **scapegoats.** Scapegoats are commonly members of groups that members of your surrounding subculture derogate. This theory has been used to explain why Jews became targets of hatred, persecution, and unspeakable atrocities in economically depressed and frustrating Germany; why Southern whites lynched more blacks during periods of low cotton prices (Hovland & Sears, 1940; see reanalysis by Hepworth & West, 1988); and why people of low social status display more prejudice than others (e.g., Smedley & Bayton, 1978).

The **downward comparison** theory has been used to explain some of these phenomena (Wills, 1981). This theory states that people feel better when they can compare themselves to "inferior" others. The people who are most likely to engage in such downward comparisons are those who have been frustrated and know no remedy, those with chronically low self-esteem, and those whose self-esteem has been recently threatened by a decrease in subjective well-being. Downward comparison can be achieved by attending to those who are less fortunate, verbally derogating another person, or actively harming another to make him or her less fortunate. Such a threatened individual would presumably be upset when members of an "inferior" group were becoming rich and famous as sports or entertainment stars. Downward comparison theory provides a more general motivational framework for understanding when prejudice will occur than frustration-aggression theory does. A recent study (Crocker, Thompson, McGraw, & Ingerman, 1987) showed that some people whose self-esteem has recently been threatened do derogate outgroups more, but partially contrary to Wills' (1981) theory, it was high self-esteem people who responded this way. (See figure 14.4.)

Competition and Prejudice

Another theory of prejudice is competition or **realistic group conflict theory** (Levine & Campbell, 1972). It states that we are most likely to become prejudiced toward groups that compete with us for resources. When we perceive that a group of people pose a threat to our livelihood and well-being by gaining valuable commodities we desire, we become hostile toward them. For example, when a group of Vietnamese fishermen were taking away from their catch a few years ago, fishermen on the Texas Gulf Coast reacted negatively. When the competition is fierce, we are also likely to rally around other members of our ingroup. The classic field experiment demonstrating the effects of competition on intergroup feelings was conducted at a boys' camp in Robbers' Cave, Oklahoma (Sherif,

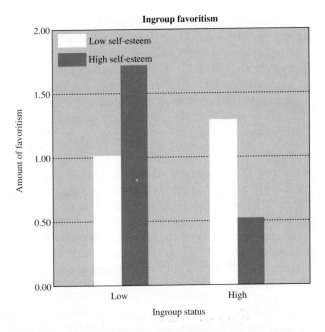

Ingroup favoritism

Figure 14.4
Downward comparison. Women who were members of a low-status sorority and who were high in self-esteem themselves showed the most ingroup favoritism.
(From Crocker, et al., 1987, Journal of Personality and Social Psychology, 52, 918.)

Harvey, White, Hood, & Sherif, 1961). The study showed that when boys were arbitrarily divided into groups and pitted against each other in contests where one group won and the other lost, the two groups became hostile toward each other and became quite creative in initiating new competitions and expressing their hostilities.

In everyday life, there are many situations in which one individual or group gains by taking something from another person or group. Losses create anger toward the ones who took the resource. Prejudice exists when the loser generalizes his or her hostility to others like the winner. There are undoubtedly many instances in which prejudice increased because the individual perceived that he or she was losing a valuable commodity, such as a job or a marriage partner, to someone who was different from him or her.

One situation in which the perceived competitive threat is likely to be great is when there are many members of the threatening subgroup present in one place. If animosity toward a group already exists, the perceived competition from the presence of many group members increases the prejudice. Pettigrew (1961) noted that the greatest upheaval about school desegregation in the South occurred where blacks made up a large portion of the population. My impression growing up was that the greatest prejudice in my hometown was against Mexican-Americans who constituted a large part of the population there; while prejudice against blacks, who made up only 1 or 2 percent of the population, was slight. I recently read that a now well-known black TV evangelist from my hometown held the same opinion (Kinchlow, 1985). We seem to be threatened most and are most prejudiced against the largest other group. The size of other ethnic groups in a location is an important factor in "white flight" from schools and neighborhoods.

Realistic group conflict theory is congruent with downward comparison theory in some ways. The perceived competitive threat to people of low status or low self-esteem is likely to be exaggerated, according to downward comparison theory (Wills, 1981). The personal insecurity of the individual heightens the sense of competition. The negative effects of conflict seem to occur if the individual construes the situation as a competitive one even if it is not. We will see later that a proposed remedy to prejudice is to place groups in cooperative rather than competitive interactions.

Social Identity Theory: Ingroups and Outgroups

In recent years, social psychologists have shown great interest in the fact that people divide other people into social categories readily (see Brewer, 1979; Stephan, 1985 for reviews). This tendency to divide people into ingroups and outgroups on the basis of trivial distinctions (differences in dot estimation, aesthetic preferences) has several consequences. We favor ingroup members over outgroup members (Billig & Tajfel, 1973; Tajfel & Billig, 1974; Tajfel, Billig, Bundy, & Flament, 1971), apparently out of a sense of competition (Brewer & Silver, 1978). We judge that outgroup members are very similar to each other in attitudes (Linville, 1982), even members of outgroups with whom we have frequent contact like the other sex (Park & Rothbart, 1982). This judgment that "they're all alike" makes it very easy to generalize traits of one member of the outgroup to the entire group (Quattrone & Jones, 1980).

Henri Tajfel, the late British social psychologist, and his associates (Tajfel, 1982; Tajfel & Turner, 1986) have constructed **social identity theory** from these and related findings. Their basic idea is that when one's personal identity is threatened or diminished, she may seek to enhance her sense of well-being by improving her social identity. **Social identity** is "that part of the individual's self-concept which derives from their knowledge of their membership of a social group together with the value and emotional significance of that membership" (Tajfel, 1982, p. 915). Someone who feels low is likely to put value on the group's identity relative to other groups in order to enhance his or her self-concept. This idea is akin to the idea that people bask in the reflected glory of sports teams to elevate their self-esteem (Cialdini et al., 1975). There is some evidence to support the social identity idea that we tend to define ourselves in terms of our group memberships when we feel insignificant. For instance, a recent study showed that English-speaking Canadians who had been embarrassed rated French-speaking Canadians more negatively than if they had not been embarrassed (Meindl & Lerner, 1985). Again, ingroup favoritism and outgroup derogation seem to go together.

Sociobiology and Prejudice

Sociobiology suggests that distinctions between some groups in our world are natural. The focus of sociobiology is on maximizing inclusive fitness, which was defined earlier as the reproductive success of the individual and all of his or her genetic relatives. This tendency to perpetuate oneself genetically in future generations leads to favoring one's kin or nepotism. A sociologist who espouses sociobiology, van den Berghe (1981), states that we are therefore programmed to

SHOE, by MacNelly. © by Tribune Media Services, Inc. Reprinted by permission.

behave favorably or altruistically toward those in whom we recognize ourselves. He also indicates that ethnic groups are recognized as kin because of their appearance or linguistic similarity. Consequently, they are appropriate targets for favoritism or kinship altruism (discussed in chapter 12). It should be pointed out that his position really extends the idea of kinship because most members of the same ethnic group share very few of the same genes even though they are more similar than people of different ethnic groups.

In a similar way, sociobiology can be used to explain the prevalence of **homogamy,** the practice of marrying individuals who are like us. Each individual who reproduces only contributes half the genes to the child. In order to ensure that the offspring looks like ourselves, we are inclined to mate with someone who looks like us. Hence, the increased separation of ethnic groups during courtship ages may be partly inspired by the desire to perpetuate ourselves in the appearance of our children.

Wilson (1978) points out that each reproduction represents an opportunity to bring diversity into the family tree. Greater diversity is adaptive because deadly or debilitating recessive genes are unlikely to occur together in an offspring if the parents were dissimilar. Inbreeding, the mating of individuals who are related, is discouraged in order to avoid the birth of such unhealthy offspring. In fact, there are disorders such as Tay-Sachs syndrome and sickle cell anemia, which are more likely to occur when both parents are of the same ethnic group than if they are not. Outbreeding appears to be biologically advantageous and socially advantageous for breaking down the distinctions and prejudices between groups. A psychologist, Freedman (1979), who has researched human sociobiology extensively, sees intermarriage between people of different racial and ethnic groups as the only solution to the "natural" antagonism between groups.

Sociobiology also presents the different sex roles as natural (Wilson, 1978). Elsewhere, I have presented their view that it is reproductively advantageous for males to be aggressive, promiscuous, undiscriminating, and fickle in sexual matters. For the females who must bear, feed, and rear the young for years, it is best to be selective for the male with the best genes who will help in rearing the child. Wilson (1978) argues that the sexual double standard, the sexual division of labor, and male dominance are natural. He does not, however, argue that such is the way it has to be. Instead, Wilson argues that these biological constraints have to be addressed in order to create more equal, more just societies. The facts that having children now only requires women to be away from their careers a very short time—as short as a month, if desired—and that men seem to be accepting more family responsibilities seem to be steps in the right direction.

The Reduction of Prejudice

Allport's Recommendations

In 1954, Gordon Allport wrote:

> Prejudice (unless deeply rooted in the character structure of the individual) may be reduced by equal status contact between majority and minority groups in the pursuit of common goals. The effect is greatly enhanced if this contact is sanctioned by institutional supports (i.e., by law, custom or local atmosphere), and provided it is of a sort that leads to the perception of common interests and common humanity between members of the two groups (Allport, 1954/1979, p. 281).

These words have come to be known as the **contact hypothesis** for reducing prejudice. The assumption is that close, prolonged contact of a fairly intimate nature between groups leads to greater understanding and to the undermining of fallacious, overgeneralized beliefs (stereotypes) about the opposing group and its members. The contact hypothesis has been examined in the contexts of young Arabs and Jews in Israel, Germans and foreigners in Germany, blacks and whites in South Africa and the United States, whites and various other races in Britain,

Protestants and Catholics in Northern Ireland, French and English in Quebec, and workers and managers in industry in a recent book by Hewstone and Brown (1986). It could presumably be examined in the context of males and females also. The effects of contacts between blacks and whites in America has been examined and reviewed extensively (Cook, 1978, 1984; Pettigrew, 1961, 1971; Stephan, 1978).

It is apparent that contact alone is not enough to reduce prejudice. Otherwise, the desegregation of the public schools would be an unqualified success in increasing interracial understanding. Most of the research indicates that school desegregation has not been so successful in breaking down racial barriers (Gerard & Miller, 1975; St. John, 1975; Schofield, 1986; Stephan, 1978). Likewise, the increase of women in the labor force would have led to harmony between the sexes in the workplace; such harmony does not appear to be universal. Also, neighborhoods would be stable, integrated communities rather than the racially segregated inner cities and suburbs that we see all around us (Winsberg, 1986).

One part of the problem is that most of these situations don't involve *voluntary contact* between people of equal status. In most studies, equal status has meant equal status in one particular context, not in society as a whole (Amir, 1976). For instance, Deutsch and Collins (1951) defined equal status in terms of equal numbers of blacks and whites among residents and among management staff in housing projects in New York City. They found that racial attitudes in integrated housing in New York City were much more positive than comparable segregated housing in Newark, New Jersey. That is one bit of evidence indicating that equal status contact, rather than noncontact, reduces prejudice.

A field experiment in a summer camp provides more evidence of the positive influence of equal status contact (Clore, Bray, Itkin, & Murphy, 1978). These investigators arranged for an equal number of black children and white children to live at various campsites under the supervision of a black camp counselor and a white camp counselor. When the children arrived for their week stay, their racial attitudes were evaluated in subtle ways. Campers were asked who they would like to get to know better, and the proportion of their choices which were of an other-race person were recorded. They played games of Duck, Duck, Goose; and their proportion of other-race choices for Goose were recorded. They were each given a box camera and a roll of film to take pictures; and after the films were developed, the number of other-race people relative to the total number of people pictured was recorded. After the week's activities, the same measures with minor variations were taken again. The proportion of other-race choices (black child-white choices and white child-black choices) on all three measures were greater after the week of contact than before. A nice feature of this study was that it employed unobtrusive measures of natural, meaningful behavioral choices which clearly reflected the children's racial attitudes. (See figure 14.5.)

One of the pioneers of prejudice research, Stuart Cook (1970), showed that when prejudiced white women worked under a black and a white supervisor—the black woman had equal status with the other supervisor, higher status than the subjects—for an extended period, most of them displayed less prejudice. Of

**Equal Status
Contact**

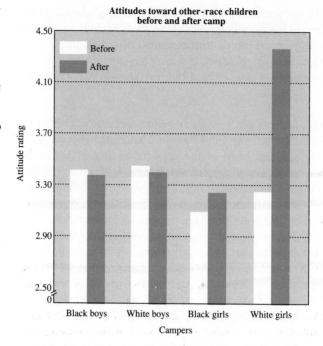

Figure 14.5
Equal status contact. Girls, especially white girls, showed the most positive interracial attitude change after a week in camp with blacks and whites. Boys started camp with more positive interracial attitudes. Other measures also showed the benefits of equal status contact.
(From Clore et al., 1978, Journal of Personality and Social Psychology, 36, 110.)

course, there is always the possibility that when equal status contact brings about a positive interaction with a member of an outgroup that the outgroup member will be regarded as atypical of the group. In such cases, the benefits of such contact for the reduction of prejudice toward all outgroup members may be minimized. Wilder (1984) investigated such a situation.

Students at two state colleges held stereotypic views of the women students at the other college. Women at one college were regarded as conservative and excessively concerned with their appearance and with making good grades. Women at the other college were regarded as liberal, more interested in partying than grades, and unkempt in their appearance. Wilder had women from both colleges participate with a confederate supposedly from the other college on a cooperative task. The confederate acted pleasantly or unpleasantly in the interaction, and she presented herself as typical or atypical of women at the other school. Subjects' attitudes toward women at the other college were most positive when the woman was typical of the outgroup and the interaction was pleasant. The results shown in table 14.1 suggest that if we have pleasant experiences with a member of another group who we cannot regard as atypical of the group, then we are likely to develop a more positive attitude toward the entire group.

Contact in Schools

Equal status contact in the schools has not been easy to achieve. When desegregation has been mandated in some communities, alternative schools have often developed. Sometimes families have moved to different suburban school districts where there are few black or hispanic residents. Even in a model desegregated

Table 14.1 Evaluations of the Outgroup College

	Pleasant contact		Unpleasant contact		
	Typical	Atypical	Typical	Atypical	Control
Quality of education & students	5.93	4.60	4.24	4.31	4.71
Recommend college	6.57	5.37	4.86	4.63	5.06

Note: Higher numbers indicate more positive attitudes.

middle school, Schofield and her associates (Schofield, 1979; Schofield & Sagar, 1977) have found that black and white children segregate themselves and are segregated in the classroom by educators.

One recent investigation conducted in elementary schools in northern California pointed out the importance of equal status—in terms of equal numbers of both groups—contact in the classroom (Hallinan & Smith, 1985). They examined friendship choices of black and white children in classrooms that ranged from 17 percent to 89 percent black. They found that racially balanced classrooms (close to an equal 50 percent split) maximized the interracial friendliness of blacks and whites alike. In classrooms where the majority of students were black or white, the friendliness of the minority race toward the majority was reduced. In light of the fact that interracial friendships are an important element in reducing prejudice, it seems unfortunate that most schools do not maintain a stable racially balanced composition.

Contact in Housing

Today, there is evidence that contact in neighborhoods does not remain equal status long enough to improve harmony. The dominant pattern seems to be minimal uneasiness among white residents when one black family moves in. If one or two resident families move out, they are likely to be replaced by blacks interested in the better housing. As the number of black families mount, more white residents become concerned about the value of their homes, etc. and move out (Farley, Schuman, Bianchi, Colasanto, & Hatchett, 1978). Eventually, the white neighborhood becomes a black neighborhood. Many times the determining attitudes are not social prejudices, but economic ones. Yet, it doesn't seem logical that a black family who could afford to buy into the neighborhood should drive property values down.

One suggestion offered to prevent the decline of neighborhoods in what have become predominantly black areas is to enforce a quota of a particular race or socioeconomic level in federal housing projects (Newman, 1980). There are areas in many cities where federal housing has become practically 100 percent minority, and the surrounding area has even been economically blighted. Newman argues that we can have stronger communities if we integrate people by race and socioeconomic level and segregate them by age or life-style. He contends that such integrated communities can be maintained by varying rent schedules according to income level so long as the proportion of poor or minorities is restricted to a certain quota (about 30 percent). He states that the real problems arise when singles, childless couples, families, and the elderly live in the same neighborhoods. That is why he recommends segregation by life-styles.

Voluntary Contact

Some of the problems arising in contact in schools and housing occur because the contact is involuntary. Because of the constrained contact, many people minimize their interactions with members of the other group rather than developing friendships which are likely to reduce prejudice. In Quebec, where the French and English live together with very little conflict, the preponderance of conversations are with ingroup members and even French-speaking students attending English-speaking universities have very few interactions with English-speakers (Taylor, Dube, & Bellerose, 1986). In American public schools, there is much voluntary segregation among older students and grouping by educators according to abilities segregates classmates even more (Schofield, 1986). High schools being represented by predominantly black football, basketball, and track teams and by predominantly white soccer, baseball, golf, and tennis teams is quite common in many cities. Participation on these teams seem to present a golden opportunity for equal status contact in pursuit of common goals, but only the most talented athletes, like Sen. Bill Bradley or Larry Bird in pro basketball, are likely to be minority participants.

In Pursuit of Common Goals

The Robber's Cave Study

What should one do if he or she had two groups of boys at a summer camp constantly at each other's throats? That is a question that was examined by Sherif and his associates (Sherif et al., 1961). It should be noted that Sherif and his associates were responsible for the groups becoming bitter rivals in the first place. They had accomplished that by treating one group better than the other some of the time and by pitting the groups against each other in competitive contests. The groups of boys (the Red Devils and the Bulldogs in one camp and the Eagles and the Rattlers in another) took it from there and invented their own competitions.

How did they dissolve the disharmony between the groups? They did it by doing what Allport had recommended. They created several situations where the members of one group alone could not accomplish the task. The groups of boys had to work together to fix the camp water supply, to get to see a movie, and to help get a truck started. These tasks with superordinate goals forced the two groups to cooperate across group boundaries to accomplish them. This pursuit of common goals apparently caused the boys to cease identifying with their own ingroups and identify with all the other campers as a single unit. This study is regarded as a classic demonstration of the discord that can be produced by competition and the healing properties of cooperation.

In many school systems, desegregation has failed to produce equal status contact for many children (Schofield & Sagar, 1977), and it has failed to produce an atmosphere of cooperation among the children of different groups. Aronson and his associates (Aronson, Blaney, Stephan, Sikes, & Snapp, 1978) noted that most classrooms are structured so that students compete with each other. They compete for the teacher's attention, and they compete for good grades. They may compete so much that they hope other students do poorly. These competitions may foster ingroup-outgroup divisions along racial lines.

Cooperation in the Schools

These investigators created what they called the "jigsaw classroom" in order to see how cooperative classroom interactions affect interracial attitudes. They broke the classrooms down into groups which contained members of all three ethnic groups (blacks, anglos, and Mexican-Americans) present in the school. Each student in a group was given a separate bit of information about the day's topic. For instance, if Eleanor Roosevelt was the topic of the day for social studies, then one student's piece of the jigsaw puzzle might be "the White House years" and another student might get "philanthropy in her later years." With teachers only acting as facilitators, the students learned the material from the other students in their group. This procedure, which encouraged cooperative interactions across racial lines, proved to be beneficial for individuals' self-esteem, liking for school, and development of interracial friendships. One problem these investigators had was maintaining control classrooms for comparison purposes because the scuttlebutt in the teachers' lounge about the procedure was so positive that many teachers instituted the technique on their own. Unfortunately, as recently as 1986, Aronson reported that this peer teaching technique involving multiracial groups had not been adopted on a long-term basis by any school systems.

Other teams of investigators (Cook, 1978; DeVries, Edwards, & Slavin, 1978; Weigel, Wiser, & Cook, 1975) have generally found that interracial cooperative groups in the schools have positive effects on interracial attitudes. In addition, Cook (1985b) investigated the effects of being helped by a black peer on a cooperative task on the attitudes of prejudiced Air Force enlistees. The central question was whether the person helped would be so embarrassed, threatened, or offended by being helped by an outgroup member that he or she would not like the helper. Results indicated that if the help was rendered voluntarily in a cooperative role, these prejudiced subjects liked and respected a black helper as much as a white helper. So, cooperative situations provide a context in which prosocial behavior among group members is likely to be appreciated and such behavior may counteract prejudices. Cook and others (e.g., Worchel, Andreoli, & Folger, 1977) have emphasized that cooperative arrangements which lead to pleasant, successful outcomes are most likely to have beneficial effects on attitudes.

This element of prejudice reduction is important in determining whether general tolerance or prejudice will prevail. Pettigrew (1961) contended that many people who express prejudice do so because the dominant public attitude in their locale

Institutional Supports

Reprinted by permission of UFS, Inc.

The 1963 march on Washington was effective in getting political action.

is a prejudiced one. These people act prejudiced in order to conform to what the important people in their lives believe. Pettigrew (1961) saw evidence of the effects of institutional supports in the course of desegregation in southern cities and towns:

> That is, violence has generally resulted in localities where at least some of the authorities give prior hints that they would gladly return to segregation if disturbances occurred; peaceful integration has generally followed firm and forceful leadership (p. 105).

The effects of institutional supports can be observed at a national level as well. When the Supreme Court makes a decision on school desegregation or affirmative action or equal rights for women, it has a substantial effect on the behavior and attitudes of Americans. When the Congress passes a civil rights or voting rights act or integrates the armed forces, it has many repercussions around the country. I state this even though racially identifiable public schools are evident in many places 35 years after the 1954 Brown decision.

Simply getting people to behave a certain way goes a long way in changing attitudes, and strong institutional supports make the behavior occur. In addition, when a different pattern of behavior is instituted, people come to see it as normal. For instance, when an authority person's decision breaks down a racial barrier, such as allowing Jackie Robinson to play major league baseball; events that had never occurred before happened, and they were expected and seen as normal after a time.

At the same time, whether the institutional supports will materialize or not may depend on predominant public opinion at the time and place. Most of our politicians are sensitive to what most of the people believe at a particular time; therefore, it is usually important for oppressed groups to express their displeasure publicly. Demonstrations like the 1963 March on Washington involving over 100,000 people can be very effective in getting politicians to act. Even though Allport did not recommend coalesing into large identifiable groups as a means to reduce prejudice, it appears that it is an important way to gain power in the public arena and muster institutional support. Such consciousness-raising activities may increase the awareness of undesirable conditions for members of oppressed groups and prejudiced groups alike.

The activities discussed previously should lead to the perception of common interests and common humanity, according to Allport. This idea implies that it is desirable to emphasize the similarities in interests, beliefs, values, and goals between the groups in conflict. Rokeach and his associates (Rokeach, 1960, 1968; Rokeach & Mezei, 1966) have presented the idea that if someone is of a different ethnic group, we assume that they have dissimilar beliefs. In their experiments on race and belief similarity, they presented a different-race person who expressed similar beliefs to the subjects. The other combinations of race similarity and belief similarity were also presented, sometimes in live face-to-face interactions. When beliefs were made explicit, subjects liked and preferred individuals with similar beliefs regardless of their race. The only occasions when race was more important than beliefs were when intimate relationships like marrying and dating were at issue (Hendrick, Bixenstein, & Hawkins, 1971; Mezei, 1971). One reason activities promoting perceptions of common interests and humanity are influential is in debunking notions that people who are dissimilar to you in race, for instance, have different values and beliefs. (See figures 14.6 and 14.7.)

Another reason that emphasizing commonalities is important lies in reducing the salience of intergroup distinctions (Worchel, 1986b). As we have seen, even trivial bases for identifying ingroups and outgroups can cause ingroup favoritism and outgroup hostilities. Anything that blurs the lines between groups or reduces our awareness of distinctions between groups, like cooperating across group lines as in the Sherif et al. (1961) boys camp study, should improve our treatment of others.

There are at least two sides to this issue. One side argues that we should decategorize people, so we may be better able to tell outgroup members apart and treat them as individuals (Brewer & Miller, 1984). Yet others think it is important that we recognize a person's group membership and that he or she is a typical group member in order for our more positive feelings to generalize to the outgroup as a whole (Brown & Turner, 1981; Hewstone & Brown, 1986; Pettigrew, 1986). In addition, others believe that it is very important to emphasize the positive distinctive qualities of the subgroups as well as the fundamental similarities between the groups (Stephan & Stephan, 1984). In other words, we should not go so overboard in focusing on "we are one" that we fail to recognize the positive qualities and contributions of our various subgroups. In America, perhaps we should strive for a "stew" culture wherein distinctive ingredients flavor each other rather than a "melting pot" wherein the brew is completely homogeneous.

Common Humanity

Figure 14.6
Belief versus race similarity. Subjects liked videotaped black and white actors who expressed similar attitudes about the war more than those with dissimilar attitudes. Race had no effect on liking. Blacks and whites were liked equally by these white subjects.

(From Hendrick et al., 1971, Journal of Personality and Social Psychology, 17, 254.)

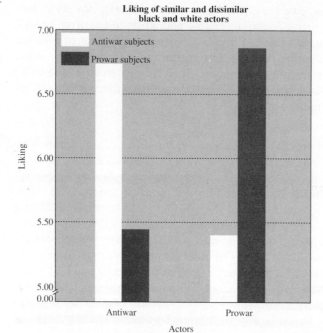

Figure 14.7
White subjects said that they would like videotaped black and white actors as speaking acquaintances almost unanimously. Fewer of them endorsed having a black actor date their sister.

(From Hendrick et al., 1971, Journal of Personality and Social Psychology, 17, 255.)

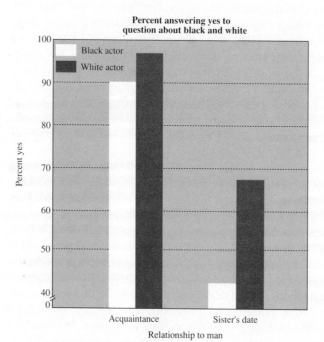

We have arrived at a more political or philosophical question than a social psychological one. However, at least two prominent social psychologists have addressed this question directly in the context of American black-white relations (Pettigrew, 1971; Taylor, 1973, 1984), and many others have addressed it less directly. The 1954 Brown decision ruled that public schools must be desegregated because separate is inherently not equal. The ruling was made to assure that blacks got educational opportunities equal to those available to whites, not to assure integration of the races. Any benefits or problems from blacks and whites going to school together were secondary to the improvement of educational opportunities for blacks. In this light, the Supreme Court intended to give more power to blacks, not to integrate American society with the ruling.

Pettigrew and many other social psychologists believe that racial integration should be a goal of American society. He wrote:

> [T]he attainment of a viable, democratic nation, free from personal and institutional racism, requires extensive racial integration in all realms of life as well as vast programs of ghetto enrichment. To prescribe more separatism because of discomfort, racism, conflict, or the need for autonomy is like getting drunk again to cure a hangover. The nation's binge of *apartheid* must not be exacerbated but alleviated (Pettigrew, 1971, p. 327–28).

Pettigrew made that pronouncement when black radicalism and black separatism were at their zenith, but he has not recanted on his position.

Taylor disagreed then and later. His goal for America is **pluralism,** where there is power equally divided among all groups. He thinks that black Americans and other disenfranchised groups must develop power first before true racial justice can be achieved. So equality, not integration, is what Taylor desires, unlike Pettigrew.

Integration may mean sacrificing the positive distinctive qualities of their subculture to Taylor and other members of minority groups. Certainly, that is what assimilation and integration has meant to many groups which are asked to give up their linguistic heritage in order to communicate with the majority group. Religious groups should be especially resistant to giving up their beliefs to join the dominant culture.

On the other hand, when people are isolated from other modes of living, as people are in segregated societies, they are culturally and intellectually deprived. Different groups should be able to coexist without acting, feeling, and thinking in the same ways. The sad fact is that segregation and lack of power go hand in hand in societies around the world. The question remains: Does integration produce equal power or does equal power produce integration? Both seem to be desirable goals. The contact hypothesis social psychologists have espoused implies that the key to understanding and equal power lies in integration among diverse groups.

Pluralism versus Assimilation

Integrated situations like this one are needed to promote interracial harmony.

Applications of Prejudice Research

There are many situations in which understanding of the causes, consequences, and cures of prejudice could be applied. Activists representing aggrieved groups should learn the mechanisms of prejudice and its reduction. Individuals in government should be prepared to understand and reduce prejudice and discrimination rather than exploit them. All of us should be aware of when we respond to someone on the basis of his or her group membership rather than on a personal level.

On a societal level, the emphasis has been on reducing discrimination and segregation. Laws exist to eliminate discrimination, but the execution of those laws has not always been faithfully fulfilled in all parts of our country or in all presidential and gubernatorial administrations. Eliminating discrimination is especially important because cognitive dissonance theory (cf. Aronson, 1984) tells us that once people behave in desirable ways, their attitudes will usually follow.

Segregation in our society has been addressed most overtly in the desegregation of the public schools. Stephan (1978) reviewed the evidence on the effects of school desegregation available at that time and concluded that desegregation had accomplished only one of the four goals mentioned in the 1954 decision and associated papers. It had not reduced the prejudice of blacks toward whites or whites toward blacks, nor had it increased the self-esteem of blacks, but it had improved the educational achievement level of blacks. As we get away from the initial turmoil of desegregation in a locale and if we examine its effects among young children, the picture looks brighter. However, there is no denying that resegregation in residences and resegregation in the schools themselves (Schofield, 1986) undermine the whole process. In addition, the failure to create cooperative, pleasant interaction situations in the schools has hindered progress in improving race relations (Aronson, 1986; Cook, 1984).

The problem for women and girls, unlike many groups, is not the lack of opportunities to interact with the other group (men and boys), with whom they interact as they grow up in their families. Instead, it is the unequal status involved in most of these contacts. In the workplace, there is much intersexual

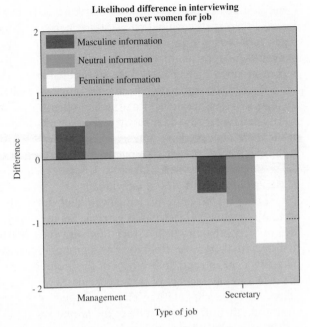

Likelihood difference in interviewing men over women for job

Masculine information
Neutral information
Feminine information

Difference

Management   Secretary

Type of job

Figure 14.8
Business professionals were uniformly more likely to bring a man in for an interview for a sales management position and a woman in for a secretarial position. Counter-stereotypic information (masculine interests of women, feminine interests of men) did not appreciably affect this sex discrimination.
(From Glick, Zion, & Nelson, 1988, Journal of Personality and Social Psychology, 55, 182.)

contact but often it involves the unequal status of a boss and his secretary, for instance. We know that unequal status contact will often reinforce biases rather than undermine them. Even today, business professionals practice sex discrimination in hiring. They are much more likely to hire a woman for a secretarial job than a sales management job even if they know she is qualified (Glick, Zion, & Nelson, 1988). Legal pressure may be the best way to eliminate these discriminatory practices. (See figure 14.8.)

The work on the effects of competition and cooperation on intergroup attitudes suggests that acting in easily identifiable groups against other groups is unlikely to reduce prejudice. A rainbow coalition, to borrow Jesse Jackson's term, seems to be the best approach for activist groups. Boys against the girls or teenagers against parents or black against white competitions are likely to lead to further division. Competitions with people of diverse groups working together on the same side are likely to engender more respect across group lines.

Programs that do not require intergroup contact may also be helpful in reducing prejudice (Pettigrew, 1986). Such programs may not have the impact of interpersonal contact, but they have the advantage of people being more willing to voluntarily participate in them. Social influence techniques which do not involve contact, such as various mass media persuasion techniques, can aid in convincing bigots of the common humanity of members of other groups. Some television shows, such as the "Bill Cosby Show," emphasize the commonality of humankind and seem to be quite beneficial. Documentaries have emphasized the common humanity of homosexuals and heterosexuals and various other groups which are often at odds with each other. The mass media can be a source of substantial positive influence.

Summary

There is much evidence of prejudice around us in our everyday lives. This evidence is seen in discrimination or biased behavior which is associated with the negative attitudes toward members of some groups, which we call prejudice. Stereotypes are overgeneralized, often one-dimensional beliefs we hold about members of groups which are the targets of prejudice.

Racism, sexism, nationalism, and religious prejudice are some of the most common kinds of prejudice. Racism, and other prejudices, can be expressed very overtly and forcefully (dominative racism) or more subtly (aversive racism). Ambivalent racists, who have both positive and negative feelings toward racial outgroups, will only act in overt prejudiced ways when there is an explanation other than race for their actions. Racism also occurs on institutional and cultural levels as well as in the attitudes of individuals.

Being the target of prejudice can have devastating effects on individuals', especially young children's, self-esteem. Some oppressed people react to prejudice by strengthening their association with their ingroup. Others may attempt to dissociate themselves from their own group. Prejudices are expectations which may affect the intergroup behavior of the prejudiced person and may even affect the reactions and feelings of target persons. Several studies have shown that prejudices do have self-fulfilling effects. Targets of prejudice are sometimes constrained in their actions because of the prejudices of others; these constraints can create internal conflicts, such as between femininity and displaying competence in women.

Several explanations of prejudice have been offered. As children develop awareness of differences between themselves and other people, they may learn biases from their family and their subculture. Theorists of authoritarianism argue that it stems from punishing childrearing practices. Others contend that frustration or the desire to see oneself as better than others provides the impetus for prejudice. Competition and the perception of competitive rivalries and threats for one's resources are at the heart of prejudice, according to realistic group conflict theory. Social identity theory suggests that ingroup-outgroup distinctions are accentuated when one's personal identity is insecure and such reactions feed prejudice. Sociobiologists contend that intergroup biases are based on reproductive and kinship considerations and are dictated by human nature.

The contact hypothesis has been presented as the best way to reduce prejudice. Equal status, voluntary contact in schools, housing, and recreational settings—in those instances where it has been achieved—does have beneficial effects. The reduction of competition through cooperative efforts involving both groups also minimizes prejudice. It is important that legal and other institutions of our society support these activities, fostering intergroup contact for them to be successful. If the commonalities of diverse groups can be stressed without sacrificing the positive, distinctive qualities of each group, greater brotherhood and sisterhood may be achieved.

CHAPTER 15

The Physical Environment and Social Behavior

by James Rotton

Imagine a world of long lines and short tempers—a world where you begin your day stuck in a five-mile long line of traffic, where you later wait in lines for simple amenities, such as food and drink, and where it's so easy to get lost you need a map. It's a world full of people, nearly all of them strangers, elbowing each other as they wait in those long, interminable lines. They stand so close that you can feel the heat from their bodies, and your nose detects odors that perfumes and colognes can't mask. Their voices and music blaring from a loudspeaker make it hard to hear periodic announcements, asking the crowd to form another line and, please, be patient. . . .

Where is this place? New York City during a rush hour? One of the futures that authors of science fiction seem to favor? The first week of classes at your school? Our answer may surprise you: What we have presented is a slightly skewed view of a day at Disney World! It is a place that attracts a million tourists each year with commercials that ask, "Why can't every day be like a day at Disney World?" However, as our opening suggests, even the "imagineers" at Disney World fail when they try to design an environment that satisfies every person's wants and needs.

Social psychologists have had a long and continuing interest in how the environment affects relations between people. Shortly after the second World War, for example, a team of social psychologists (Festinger, Schachter, & Back, 1950) looked at the effects of physical distance on friendships in a student housing project. We mentioned their research in chapter 11. Festinger and colleagues found that one of the best predictors of friendship formation was *physical proximity*. When wives were asked to list their three best friends, more than a third named somebody in the same building; of those named, two-thirds lived on the same floor.

A day at Disney World.

Similar results have been obtained in social psychological research on friendship patterns in classroom and suburban environments (e.g., Ebbesen et al., 1976; Oxley et al., 1986). But social psychologists aren't the only ones who have looked at relations between the physical environment and behavior. Much of what we know about the environment's impact is based on work presented at interdisciplinary conferences (Wener & Szigeti, 1987), which attract sociologists, anthropologists, and members of the design professions (e.g., architects, city planners). In this chapter, we will borrow heavily from the research of environmental psychologists (e.g., Fisher et al., in press). Doing so is appropriate because most environmental psychologists received their training in social psychology (Proshansky & Altman, 1979), and a good number think of themselves as applied social psychologists (Aiello et al., 1982).

Environmental Psychology is a multidisciplinary field that can be defined as the study of reciprocal relations between the physical environment and human behavior. The reciprocal nature of these relations is captured by a line from one of Winston Churchill's memorable speeches: "We shape our buildings, and afterwards our buildings shape us." As you might guess, environmental psychology is a problem-oriented field. Noise, crowding, litter, and crime on city streets are some of the problems that interest environmental psychologists.

However, only a cynic (who knows the price of everything and the value of nothing) can deny that the environment is a source of delight as well as concern. In this chapter, we look at people's behavior at theme parks which, despite our opening paragraph, are fun places. Of course, in choosing this setting, we run the risk of leading you to expect a Mickey Mouse chapter. There are several reasons why we're willing to take this risk. First, it's only when we find ourselves in a novel environment, such as a theme park or a foreign country, that we pay much attention to our surroundings (Nahemow, 1971). This point can be appreciated by thinking back to your last trip from your home to classes. How many buildings, signs, and individuals can you recall? The answer, in all probability, is not many (McGill & Korn, 1982). It is for this reason that this chapter opens with a section on *environmental perception and preferences*.

Second, the popularity of theme parks is in some ways paradoxical because results of studies show that familiarity produces attraction (Moreland & Zajonc, 1979). On the one hand, we travel great distances to spend a day in novel and unusual environments. On the other hand, most of us feel more comfortable in places we occupy on a day-to-day basis. We use the term *place attachment* in this chapter's second section to describe how we feel after a long trip and say, "It's good to be home."

Third, it's hard to think of a more *social* place than a theme park. Everybody's with somebody—friends, lovers, children, grandparents, mothers and fathers, etc. However, another paradox of human behavior is that there are times when we want to be alone. This chapter's third section takes up the twin topics of *privacy and sociability*. It sets the stage for a section that looks at people's behavior in offices, stores, and other *interior settings*. These places are designed for and by people, which brings us back to the idea of reciprocal relations between environment and behavior. Building on this idea, our last section looks at ways we can apply information from environmental psychology to improve our surroundings.

Environmental Perception and Preferences

The idea of building the first theme park came to Walt Disney as he watched his daughters ride the merry-go-round at an amusement park (Corliss, 1986). Disney was bothered by the park's cheap, decrepit, and generally tawdry appearance. Why not place rides in an attractive setting? These perceptions led Disney and, later, others to design parks that are physically attractive as well as fun places to spend the day.

Environmental perception is concerned with how individuals apprehend and experience their surroundings. This area differs in several important respects from other approaches to perception, including how we perceive others (see chapter 4). Research on perception has traditionally been concerned with how individuals detect, recognize, and discriminate between small objects in space (Ittelson, 1976; Ittelson et al., 1974). However, a moment's thought should convince you that every object is a part of a larger (molar) environment. What is behind you is as much a part of your environment as what you happen to be looking at. As a consequence, it's only by moving through an environment that we can understand

Figure 15.1
*A Perceived
Environmental
Quality Index (PEQI).
Instruments like this
are used to obtain
perceptual-cognitive
appraisals. Descriptors
are based on material
in Kasmar (1970) and
Danford et al., 1979.*

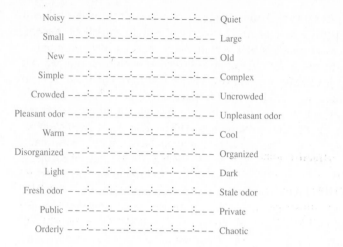

Noisy	Quiet
Small	Large
New	Old
Simple	Complex
Crowded	Uncrowded
Pleasant odor	Unpleasant odor
Warm	Cool
Disorganized	Organized
Light	Dark
Fresh odor	Stale odor
Public	Private
Orderly	Chaotic

and appreciate its features. It has been estimated that it takes at least three days of walking to see everything that Disney World has to offer. Of course, visitors do not wander aimlessly through the Magic Kingdom. The first thing that small children do is head for Cinderella's Castle in Fantasy Land; older children make a beeline to Space Mountain. Their parents show more interest in finding a good restaurant and, toward the end of the day, a place to sit down and relax. As these examples suggest, movement through the environment is purposeful. It is guided by plans and a desire to reach certain goals (Gärling et al., 1986). Finally, the environment involves all of our senses. What you smell, hear, and touch is as much a part of the environment as what you see (Anderson et al., 1983; Porteous, 1985). A theme park would lose much of its appeal if you were deprived of the sound of children laughing, fireworks exploding, and music blaring from loudspeakers!

Environmental Appraisals: "Pee-Kwees"

Think back to the last theme or amusement park you visited. How would you describe it? There are a lot of ways to answer this question. One way to describe a setting is in terms of its ambient or objective properties (e.g., pollution, decibel, and light levels). Characterizations based on objective measures are called *environmental quality indices (EQI)* (e.g., Thomas, 1972; von Gierke & Harris, 1987). However, it may have occurred to you that we usually reserve the word *quality* for things that are subjective. If you're interested in quality, it makes sense to ask people how they feel about their surroundings (Craik & Zube, 1976). This can be accomplished by having them complete a **perceived environmental quality index** or **PEQI** (pronounced "pee-kwee"). The PEQI in figure 15.1 is similar to ones that have been developed to assess the environmental and scenic quality of city streets, rivers, coastlines, and forests (e.g., Craik & Feimer, 1987; Stewart, 1987; Zube, 1980).

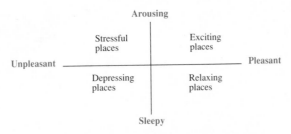

Figure 15.2
Emotional reactions to environmental settings. Settings can be characterized by how much pleasure and arousal they produce.
(Based on date in Russell & Snodgrass, 1986.)

Unlike PEQIs, **affective appraisals** are designed to measure individuals' subjective evaluations or attitudes toward environments. One of the most surprising findings to emerge from research on affective appraisals is that they vary along no more than two dimensions (Russell, 1979; Russell & Snodgrass, 1987). One dimension is evaluative (pleasant-unpleasant); the other reflects varying degrees of arousal. The model in figure 15.2 is based on data obtained from 329 individuals. Each person was interviewed in a different setting—downtown streets, stores of all sorts, a nightclub, an emergency waiting room, a hairdresser's salon, a Japanese park, and even a nude beach (Russell et al., 1981).

In order to understand and predict how a person will judge a particular environment, we have to draw a distinction between an environment's content and structure. *Content* refers to specific objects or elements, such as grass and trees, while *structure* describes the pattern that emerges when elements are combined.

Environmental Aesthetics: Eye of the Beholder

Content: Finding the Pieces of the Puzzle

What kinds of environments do people like? As you might guess, people show a strong preference for familiar scenes (Herzog et al., 1982; Sonnenfeld, 1966). To take a *familiar* example, the Eiffel Tower was called grotesque when it was completed in 1889 (Harrison, 1977). It is now the most frequently photographed object in the world. People also like scenes that contain water (Ulrich, 1983). This may be a part of a more general preference for smooth surfaces. For example, even lawns receive higher ratings when they're mowed than when they look scruffy (Kaplan, 1983). It's also been found that individuals prefer forests with spaces between trees over ones that are so overgrown that they appear impenetrable (Kaplan, 1977).

However, none of these factors are as important as one that has been termed *nature.* There is almost no overlap in judgments when individuals rate natural and built scenes (e.g., Kaplan, 1983; Herzog & Smith, 1988). However, saying that people like nature raises as many questions as it answers (Wohlwill, 1983). What is nature? While there is no easy answer to this question, research in this area suggests that most individuals equate nature with greenery. People value grass, bushes, shrubs, and trees (Kaplan, 1985). This preference is so strong that trees counteract the negative evaluations that urban areas usually receive (Herzog et al., 1982). Conversely, most of us react negatively when we encounter telephone poles and signs in what should be a natural or an unspoiled setting (Evans & Wood, 1980; Kaplan, 1977).

Table 15.1　Effects of View on Need for Analgesics

Analgesic strength	View	
(Daily doses per patient)	*Wall*	*Trees*
Strong (addictive)	2.48	.96
Moderate (e.g., Percodan)	3.65	1.74
Weak (e.g., aspirin)	2.57	5.39

Source: Ulrich (1984).

Quite a few people believe that "getting back to nature" helps them unwind and deal with the stresses of modern life. Recent studies suggest that there's more than a kernel of truth in this belief. In one interesting study, Ulrich (1981) monitored electroencephalograhic (EEG) activity while subjects looked at slides of forested areas, small bodies of water, and urban scenes. His dependent variable was *alpha,* which is a measure of a relaxed but attentive state of consciousness. As Ulrich predicted, more alpha was recorded when subjects looked at vegetation than urban scenes, and his results suggested that scenes containing water are also relaxing. In a more recent study, Ulrich (1984) looked at the effects of greenery on recovery rates. His subjects were patients who were wheeled back to one of two rooms following surgery. Half of the patients could see a small strand of trees from the window in their room. The other half could only see the brick walls of an adjoining wing of the hospital. (It should be noted that which room a patient got was a matter of chance.) From the results shown in table 15.1, it can be seen that patients who could see trees from their room required fewer painkillers. Also, their stay in the hospital was shorter, and ward notes revealed that they were more cooperative than patients whose window faced a brick wall.

Structure: Putting the Pieces Together

Water, greenery, and even nature do not depend on other elements in a scene. We do not have to worry about familiarity and openness when we measure greenery, for example. All we have to do is count the number of trees, bushes, and shrubs in a setting (Im, 1984; Schroeder & Daniel, 1980). How about novelty and complexity? These are collative variables which can only be understood when elements are brought together (as in "collating sheets on an exam") and compared. Collative variables derive their power from the conflict they produce (Berlyne, 1960; Rotton et al., 1983). Novelty, for example, describes conflict between present and past experiences (i.e., events are novel when they conflict with what you've encountered in the past). The monorail at Disney World was once novel, but it seems to have lost its appeal for visitors who come from cities with modern transportation systems.

Complexity is a function of the number of elements in a scene and their diversity. Disney World is considerably more complex than nearby theme parks in Orlando, Florida, which feature no more than one or two types of attractions (e.g., animals *or* water sports). As a general rule, we prefer moderately complex environments (Mehrabian & Russell, 1974; Wohlwill, 1976). Too much complexity is confusing; too little is boring. However, there are exceptions to this rule

(Nasar, 1983; Ulrich, 1986). For example, high levels of complexity do not reduce our enjoyment when we find ourselves in a natural setting. It is only when we are in an urban environment that high levels of complexity are not enjoyable.

> Proper attire is required. Shoes and shirts must be worn at all times in the Magic Kingdom and aboard all transportation vehicles. No flash photography, eating, drinking, or smoking is allowed in any Magic Kingdom attraction. Food or drink may not be brought into the Magic Kingdom.

Place Attachment and Territoriality

As this sign suggests, you're on Mickey's turf when you enter the Magic Kingdom. The mouse makes the rules. Turf is another name for an animal's or human's *territory*, which can be defined as the area an individual controls. It follows that **territoriality** is behavior that establishes control over an area. This definition highlights the interdependent nature of transactions between the environment and behavior. Without a territory, there would be no territoriality, and without territoriality there would be no territories (Carpenter, 1958).

It is easier to document territoriality in fish, birds, and insects than primates and other mammals (Howard, 1948; Wilson, 1975). You know that fish swim upstream to spawn, and you have probably heard about swallows coming back to Capistrano. How about the buzzards that return to Hinckley, Ohio, on March 15 of each year? Nobody's written a song about their return ("Will you still love me when the buzzards come back to Hinckley?"), but another one ("Where the Boys Are") reminds us that birds aren't the only species that migrates. The second week in March is also the time that thousands of college students head for Florida's beaches.

Animal Territoriality: Beasts of the Fields and Fields of the Beasts

Whether or not an animal is territorial depends on a number of factors, but the most important is one's definition of territoriality. If we follow the lead of popular writers (e.g., Ardrey, 1966) and consider territoriality to be synonymous with aggressive defense of an area, we have to conclude that very few primates engage in anything resembling territorial behavior (Cook, 1975; Crook, 1973; Vine, 1974). To take one example, troops of gorillas evidence little concern when they meet and may even bed down together at night. To take another example, when one troop of chimpanzees encounters another, members greet each other with a considerable amount of excitement and glee, which is sometimes followed by an orgy of mate-swapping (Reynolds & Reynolds, 1965). However, if territoriality is defined as attachment to a specific place, then we have to conclude that many primates are territorial. For example, chimpanzees view their foraging areas as exclusive preserves (Nishida & Kawanaka, 1972).

At first glance, it might seem that territorial behavior of humans does not differ from that of other animals. Territories provide animals, including humans, with a reliable place in which to eat, sleep, and mate (Edney, 1974). Also, humans as well as other animals group together to defend their territories. There are some (e.g., Lorenz, 1966) who interpret patriotism as a form of territoriality and regard wars as an incursion into another's territory. Moreover, there appears to be a reliable relationship between an individual's rank in a group and the size or value of *his* territory (Edney, 1976; Sommer, 1969). As the pronoun in the preceding sentence suggests, it is usually the male of the species that engages in territorial defense. Males of our species claim larger territories than do females (e.g., Mercer & Benjamin, 1980; Smith, 1981). Finally, humans as well as lower animals use *markers* to personalize the territories they inhabit and keep others from trespassing. Just as animals vocalize and leave bodily deposits to claim territories, humans leave personal objects (e.g., books, coats, scarfs) when they step away from a table or chair.

However, these similarities are dwarfed by a number of important differences between humans and other animals (Edney, 1974). First, an animal's territoriality is usually limited to the area it is occupying. But most of us would object if somebody entered our bedrooms or offices while we are away. Second, as this example suggests, while most animals stay in one place for long periods of time, humans occupy a number of areas (e.g., bedrooms, automobile, your seat in class) during any day, all of which they feel belong to them. Humans also feel territorial about objects (e.g., diamond rings) and ideas (e.g., patents), whereas an animal's territory is limited to the areas it occupies. Finally, as Edney notes, humans entertain others of the same species on their territories; other animals limit their welcome to mates and offspring.

These differences suggest that it is useful to regard territoriality as the behavioral component of a more general attitude, which has been termed **place attachment** (Shumacher & Taylor, 1983). This attitude's affective component corresponds to what Tuan (1974) has called *topophilia* (love of place), which consists of the emotional bonds we form for the places we inhabit ("home sweet home"). These bonds are stronger than is commonly realized. When an urban renewal project forced residents to move out of a run-down neighborhood in Boston's West End, for example, a number of residents evidenced symptoms usually associated with grief for a loved one (Fried, 1963). It's also been found that elderly individuals suffer health problems and may even die at an earlier age when they're forced to move from one nursing home to another (e.g., Markus et al., 1972). We might caution that social ties are also severed when individuals are forced to move. Consequently, some of the effects of forced relocation might be due to loss of social support (see chapter 16).

Attachment's cognitive component has been termed **place identity** (Proshansky, 1978; Proshansky et al., 1983). The best way to grasp this concept is to think back to the last time you had to stand up and say a few words about yourself. You probably began by saying, "Well, I grew up in Indiana (or Ohio or Texas), so I guess you could call me a Hoosier (or a Buckeye or Texan)." The places you name are part of your self-identity. You are not *just* someone who lives in a particular locale—you are an American or a Canadian. You are not *just* a student—you are a student who attends a particular college or university. Territories define and support the roles we play. Try to imagine a doctor without an office, a judge without a court, or a grocer without a store!

Table 15.2 Three Types of Territories

Type	Permanence	Centrality	Degree of control
Primary (e.g., home, office)	Permanent; long-lasting	Central to self-concept of occupants	High
Secondary (e.g., neighborhood bar)	Temporary but recurring	High for regulars; low for others	Unofficial and ambiguous
Public (e.g., library, restaurant)	Transient	Low or nonexistent	Limited to length of stay

Types of Territories

It would take us too far afield to describe all the schemes that have been devised for classifying the territories that humans occupy (e.g., Goffman, 1971; Lyman & Scott, 1967). One prominent theorist (Altman, 1975) has simplified matters by linking territorial behavior to membership in primary, secondary, and reference groups (see table 15.2). According to Altman, a **primary territory** is a relatively permanent space central to people's lives, for example, a home-owner's house or a student's dorm room. A **secondary territory** is a temporary space occupied on a recurring basis by individuals who rarely exert official or legal control over what happens, for example, a tavern, clubhouse, or a gang's street corner. Finally, a theme park is a good example of a **public territory.** This is a place occupied for brief periods of time, and it doesn't play an important role in our everyday lives. Also, it is only while we are occupying a public territory (e.g., a table at a library or a spot on the beach) that we determine what happens on it; that is, control is limited to the duration of our stay.

Altman's taxonomy has received mixed support. On the one hand, residents report spending the greatest amount of time in primary territories (e.g., bedrooms, bathrooms), less time in secondary territories, and the least amount of time in public territories, such as neighborhood stores (Taylor & Strough, 1978). On the other hand, Altman's typology does not capture the nuances of home life. Sebba and Churchman (1983) found that residents draw a distinction between *individual* and *shared areas*. One member of the family decides what happens in individual areas (e.g., a child's bedroom, father's study), while two or more decide what happens in bedrooms that children and parents share. On the other hand, living rooms and hallways are typically *public areas,* which belong to everybody in the family, while the kitchen is a *jurisdiction,* where one person has the final say (e.g., you can use the kitchen as long as you don't get in the cook's way).

Similar problems arise when we try to identify secondary territories. Is the lobby in a dormitory a secondary territory, or is it a public territory? How about the sidewalk in front of your home? The answer depends, in part, on where you live. There are a number of interesting cross-cultural differences in territorial behavior (Altman & Chemers, 1980). For example, individuals living in Greece draw a clear distinction between the areas they do and do not own. By way of contrast, Americans are more likely to regard the land between their property's edge (usually the sidewalk) and the street as an area they control. This includes

Figure 15.3
*Effects of culture and
type of property on
responses to territorial
contamination. Home
owners in Greece
draw a sharp
distinction between
public and primary
territories, whereas the
territorial behavior of
individuals living in
the United States
extends to public areas
around their homes.*
*(Based on data in Worchel &
Lollis, 1982.)*

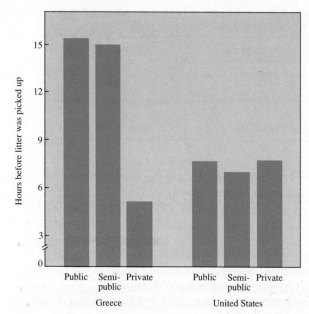

Figure 15.3
Effects of culture and type of property on responses to territorial contamination. Home owners in Greece draw a sharp distinction between public and primary territories, whereas the territorial behavior of individuals living in the United States extends to public areas around their homes.
(Based on data in Worchel & Lollis, 1982.)

a strip of land that the city owns but the homeowners have to mow. These observations led Worchel and Lollis (1982) to hypothesize that Americans are territorial about all of the area around their homes, whereas Greeks would only protect the land they owned. They tested their hypothesis by dropping plastic bags filled with dry litter, such as newspapers and cans, in front of people's homes. One-third of the bags were dropped, in yards, at least 20 feet from the street; another third were dropped on the sidewalk; and a final third were dropped on the street's edge. (For obvious reasons, the drops were made early in the morning, and the investigators collected the bags that residents had not picked up.) As you can see from the graph in figure 15.3, it was only when litter was dropped in their yards (between their house and the sidewalk) that Greek home owners picked it up. However, Americans were just as quick to pick up litter on public as private property.

Territorial Claims: Land Grabs and Range Wars

The old buildings, water troughs, and hitching posts at theme parks conjure up images of a crusty old miner, perhaps a Forty-niner, who came out west to strike it rich. To do so, he had to "stake a claim." This image provides a useful device for organizing what is known about how individuals acquire, mark, and defend territories.

Territorial Acquisition: Squatter's Rights

It doesn't take much effort to establish control over an object or place. Sometimes all you have to do is touch something that you think should be yours. In a study conducted in a game arcade, for example, Werner and colleagues (1981) found that players would touch a machine they were going to play in order to ward off intruders, and those around them respected this nonverbal message of territorial

One way to prevent territorial intrusions.
SNUFFY SMITH, by Fred Lasswell. © 1978 by King Features. Reprinted with special permission of King Features Syndicate, Inc.

intent. It has also been found that individuals feel more territorial about places they have decorated (Edney, 1972b). Decorating takes time and, as you might expect, individuals also feel more territorial about places they have previously occupied (Edney, 1975; Edney & Uhlig, 1977). The longer a setting is occupied, the more territorial an individual feels (Sommer & Becker, 1969).

Markers and Personalization: Staking a Claim

Even today, prospectors lay claim to land by pounding a stake into the ground. As this example suggests, markers serve a preventive function. Some people rely on "Private Property" and "No Trespassing" signs to keep others off areas they have claimed. What sort of people do so? Edney (1972a) answered this question by knocking on doors of houses with signs in their front yards. He found that home owners were more likely to post signs than people who rented. Also, those with signs had lived at their residence for a longer time than those without signs. One of Edney's most interesting results was obtained when he timed how long it took residents to come to the door. A half minute elapsed when interviewers approached houses without signs. How long did it take when there was a sign in the front yard? Thirteen seconds!

While early research focused on the preventive functions of markers, more recent studies call our attention to their role in establishing and cementing relationships. People who decorate the outside of their houses know more neighbors and have more friends in their neighborhood than those who do not (Brown, 1987; Brown & Werner, 1985). This relationship probably stems from the fact that neighbors strike up a conversation when they are outside taking care of their property.

Markers serve a number of other functions. First, as we noted, individuals leave coats, scarfs, and other items when they want others to know that a table or chair is occupied. It has been found that these and other items (e.g., notebooks, umbrellas) are very effective *place-holders* (Gal et al., 1986; Shaffer & Sadowsky, 1975). Second, we use markers to express ourselves. This function has been termed **personalization.** Photographs, posters, calendars, and trophies are some of the items we have in our homes and offices to let others know who we are and what we like (Hanson & Altman, 1976; Konar et al., 1982). However, you don't have to enter a person's home to draw conclusions about what he or she is like (Cherulnik & Wilderman, 1986). A flag in the front yard conveys one message; a welcome mat conveys another (Greenbaum & Greenbaum, 1981).

Perhaps the most obvious example of personalization are bumper stickers and signs in the rear windows of automobiles, which tell us who's "on board" and what they would rather be doing.

Territorial Invasions: Claim Jumping

What would you do if you found somebody sitting in your seat when you walked into class? Although it is commonly assumed that people aggressively defend their territories, Haber (1980) found that most students go out of their way to avoid territorial disputes. Only 27 percent of the students in her study asked for their seat when they found a stranger sitting in it. Interestingly, these individuals stood around for a considerable amount of time before they worked up the courage to ask for their seats back. From what we have written about the importance of prior occupancy, it should come as no surprise to learn that students were more likely to engage in territorial defense if they had been sitting in the seat before a class break than if they encountered the invader at the beginning of class.

A territory's value or worth also determines if it is defended. In a library, for example, a carrel with walls around it is more valuable than a table that seats several persons. What happens when a library patron returns to find that somebody has taken his or her seat? Taylor and Brooks (1980) found that only 50 percent of those who had left a marker on a table asked the intruder to move, but every person who had left items at a carrel did so.

Privacy and Sociability

As we noted, theme parks are attractive places. Since they contain facilities that allow us to satisfy our basic needs, such as hunger and thirst, it would be easy to conclude that they are "the best of all possible worlds." Unfortunately, theme parks aren't very private places.

Privacy is one of those words that means different things to different people. For some, it is being alone; for others, it is not being seen; for still others, it is being able to withhold information (Hunter et al., 1978; Marshall, 1974; Pedersen, 1982). However different these views may be, they have two things in common. First, privacy has something to do with *withdrawing* from social contact. We use such words as *solitude* and *seclusion* to describe our desire to get away from others. Second, most attempts to define privacy consider people's attempts at *withholding* information about themselves—things that are just "too private" to discuss, such as when we are alone with a lover (a "private affair"), what we do behind closed doors ("private offices"), and our bodies ("private parts").

These apparently conflicting views can be integrated by defining *privacy* as "*selective control of access to the self and one's group*" (Altman, 1975, p. 18). As this definition suggests, privacy can be achieved by withholding information about ourselves. What about withdrawing from social interaction? Altman answers this question by suggesting that we rely on *interpersonal boundary control* (IBC) processes, such as personal space and territoriality, to pace and regulate interactions with others. These processes include environmental barriers, such as walls and doors. As the diagram in figure 15.4 suggests, we use doors to maintain

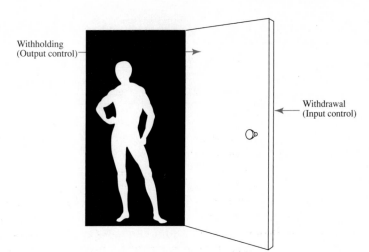

Figure 15.4
This door swings both ways. Interpersonal boundary controls (IBCs) include doors which enable us to obtain the privacy we desire by withdrawing information about ourselves (output control).

(*Based on material in Altman, 1975.*)

control over environmental inputs by withdrawing from social interaction. Doors also let us withhold information about ourselves (output control). One of the beauties of a door is that it permits *selective* access. We use doors to keep some people out, and we rely on them when we want to be sure that "our words won't go beyond this room."

It's useful to think of privacy and sociability as lying on opposite ends of a continuum. While there are times when we want to be alone (*apart* from others), there are also times when we desire social contact (to be *a part* of a group). This view is consistent with responses that were obtained when students living in a dormitory were asked what they did when they desired privacy. Vinsel and colleagues (1980) found that students who took steps to avoid unwanted contacts were more likely to remain in school than those who did not (see table 15.3). Compared to the drop-outs, students who stayed in school were more likely to close the doors to their room, take walks by themselves, and find a quiet place to study. However, students who remained in school also engaged in activities that increased their chances of coming into contact with others when they *wanted* to be with others. Sadly, those who dropped out would do things like go to the student lounge, which is known to be a place for studying rather than meeting people, when they desired company.

There are other reasons why it's useful to regard privacy as the opposite of sociability (Knowles, 1980). One of them stems from the fact that individuals differ in their need to be with and affiliate with others. As you might suspect, affiliative tendencies affect choice of living arrangements. This suspicion is supported by responses on a questionnaire given to students who had to move out of their dormitory after their freshmen year. Switzer and Taylor (1983) found that students who scored high on a measure of need affiliation chose social living arrangements (e.g., fraternities and shared bedrooms), whereas those who scored low on their measure chose more private accommodations (e.g., an apartment for singles).

Table 15.3 Use of Privacy Mechanisms in a College Dormitory

Obtaining privacy	Percentage using each mechanism	
Mechanisms used to avoid contact with others	*Freshmen staying in school*	*Freshmen dropping out of school*
Shut dormitory room door	92	84
Went for walk alone	54	37
Arranged room for privacy	19	11
Tuned out noise and slept	61	53
Tuned out noise and studied	54	47
Prepared for bed at quiet time	22	0
Used bathroom at quiet time	17	0
Obtaining companionship		
Mechanisms used to seek interpersonal contacts		
Opened dormitory room door	70	47
Visited someone's room	74	63
Invited others to own room	67	58
Phoned someone	76	68
Studied in busy place	33	21
Used bathroom at busy time	11	5
Played music to attract others	22	16

Source of data: Vinsel et al. (1980).

A more practical reason for regarding privacy as the opposite of sociability stems from the following fact: Settings that insure privacy usually do so by discouraging interaction. Conversely, it is hard to obtain privacy in a setting that encourages social interaction.

Public Places and Private Spaces

Several years ago, a psychiatrist named Humphrey Osmond (1957) coined the term **sociopetal space** to describe places and furniture arrangements that bring people together and encourage interaction. Its opposite is a **sociofugal space,** which keeps people apart and makes it hard for them to converse and interact. As the photographs in figure 15.5 suggest, chairs around a table in an outdoor cafe are sociopetal, while chairs in airline terminals tend to be sociofugal.

Interest in the effects of sociopetal and sociofugal spaces can be traced to an inadvertent experiment whose unfortunate "subjects" were women living in a home for the elderly (Sommer & Ross, 1958). Administrators at this home had gotten a windfall grant to remodel a dayroom on one of the wards. They did their best to turn the room into a pleasant place. For example, they hung curtains, put new tiles on the floor, installed fluorescent lights, and bought new furniture. Regrettably, when Sommer arrived at the geriatric ward, he found the women sitting in their chairs without talking with each other, "like strangers waiting in a

(a)

(b)

train station for a train that never came" (1969, p. 79). He guessed that their isolated and passive behavior stemmed from the room's sociofugal arrangement. Most of the chairs were lined against the wall. Others had been set back-to-back in the center of the room. Sommer transformed the dayroom into a sociopetal space by grouping chairs around tables and putting conversation items (e.g., magazines, sewing material) on the tables. It took some time for the women to get used to this new arrangement. However, after about two weeks, they were engaging in nearly twice as much conversation.

Figure 15.5
Sociopetal and sociofugal spaces. Some furniture arrangements bring people together, while others keep them apart.

The results obtained in this and subsequent studies (Holahan, 1976; Holahan & Saegert, 1973) have been so impressive that it is easy to jump to the conclusion that institutional settings should be sociopetal. While this view is quite prevalent among administrators and members of the design professions, a recent survey reveals that people living in institutions prefer sociofugal arrangements (Duffy et al., 1986). Their preference stems from the fact that privacy is a scarce commodity in most institutions. Indeed, it has been found that psychiatric patients withdraw and avoid social contact when they cannot get away from others (Ittelson et al., 1970).

In short, it is a mistake to assume that a sociopetal arrangement is desirable just because it promotes interaction, nor should we assume that sociofugal arrangements are always bad because they curtail interaction. As Altman's model of interpersonal boundary control processes suggests, there is a time and a place for each. For example, most of us desire a private (or sociofugal) place when we're studying at the library (Eastman & Harper, 1971; Sommer, 1966), but many students like to study in groups. Obviously, libraries need to provide both kinds of spaces—sociopetal ones for couples on "study dates" and sociofugal ones for students who don't want to mix pleasure with work.

Proxemics:
Designing for
Privacy—and
Sociability

Proxemics can be defined as the study of how people use space—and how spaces use people. This field was founded by anthropologist E. T. Hall (1966), who drew a distinction between fixed-feature and semifixed-feature space. *Fixed-feature space* refers to areas with environmental elements, such as walls and partitions, which resist change. As we shall discuss, *semifixed-feature space* describes areas with elements (usually furnishings) that people can move.

*Fixed-feature Space:
"Good Fences Make
Good Neighbors"*

One of Robert Frost's poems begins by suggesting that "there is something that doesn't like a wall." That may be true, but we depend on walls when we desire visual privacy. For example, the best predictor of satisfaction with privacy in an office is the number of walls around one's desk. The more sides on which a worker's desk is enclosed, the more private it seems (Sundstrom et al., 1982). The importance of visual privacy is illustrated by the fact (Kira, 1976) that there is frosting on the glass of the public restrooms high atop the Eiffel Tower!

We rely on doors, walls, and partitions for auditory as well as visual privacy. The importance of auditory or acoustical privacy is illustrated by results Kuper (1970) obtained when he interviewed individuals living in a housing project in England. The apartments in this project were separated by thin partitions (so-called party walls). Residents reported that they were embarrassed by conversations that passed through the walls. As one of Kuper's respondents observed, "You can sometimes hear them say rather private things, as, for example, a man telling his wife that her feet are cold. It makes you feel that *you* must say private things in a whisper" (p. 249, italics in the original). This led residents to avoid activities that might bother their neighbors. For example, parents would go out of their way to make sure that their children did not make too much noise.

Visual privacy corresponds to what Westin (1970) has termed **solitude.** Table 15.4 summarizes Westin's taxonomy. You can see that there is a difference between solitude and social isolation. Solitude is freely chosen, whereas isolation is forced on us (Suedfeld, 1982). Westin has suggested that solitude is necessary for creative enterprises. His suggestion is supported by research that has found that those engaged in technical and managerial work value privacy more than typists do (Sundstrom et al., 1982).

With its emphasis on "protected conversation," Westin's *intimacy* is close to what we have termed auditory privacy. His **anonymity** can be defined as freedom from identification and surveillance in a public setting (i.e., "lost in a crowd"). It's interesting to note that Taylor and Ferguson (1980) found that students choose public territories (e.g., parks, libraries) when they want to get away from people they know. Finally, Westin's **reserve** describes all of the verbal and nonverbal mechanisms (e.g., reduced eye contact) we use to withhold information about ourselves. In a sense, reserve is the opposite of self-disclosure, which was discussed in chapter 11.

It might be thought that reserve is such a stable characteristic that it would be impervious to changes in the environment. However, Chaikin and colleagues (1976) found that students are more reticent when they are interviewed in austere than pleasant settings. This study is interesting because its "cold" (i.e., austere) room bore a striking similarity to psychological laboratories we have worked

Table 15.4	Four Types of Privacy	
Type	**Definition**	**Typical setting**
Solitude	Voluntary separation from others and freedom from observations (Visual privacy)	Studies; bathrooms; wilderness
Intimacy	Isolation desired by a couple, family members, and friends for protected conversation (Auditory privacy)	Bedrooms; private automobiles
Anonymity	Freedom from identification while in a public setting	Theaters; sporting events; busy streets
Reserve	Verbal and nonverbal channels that are used to withhold information about one's self	Almost anywhere that one's dignity is respected

Source: Based on Westin (1970).

in (e.g., bare cement block walls, overhead fluorescent lights, straightback chairs). After Chaikin and colleagues "softened" their room by installing indirect lighting, placing a rug on the floor, and adding comfortable furniture, they found that subjects were much more willing to talk and disclose private details about themselves.

It also has been found that a child's reserve is influenced by permeable barriers. Levitt and Weber (1988) used a low, open-lattice barrier to separate 2 1/2-year-old toddlers. Their "baby gates" separated the children, but they were permeable to visual, auditory, and physical contact. For example, one child could touch another by reaching through openings in the gate. However, Levitt and Weber found that the gate's presence curtailed interactions, including vocalizations and smiles, especially when one of the toddlers had toys to play with.

Semifixed-feature Space: Flexibility

The thing that distinguishes and, indeed, defines semifixed space is flexibility: Can the objects in a room be moved and rearranged to suit our needs and desires? The answer to this question may have implications for your social life if you live in a dormitory. An increasing number of dormitory rooms contain "built-in" furnishings. In some rooms, the only object that can be moved is the chair in front of the desks. High and Sundstrom (1977) found that inflexible arrangements reduce the amount of time students use their room for personal encounters. Surreptitious counts of guests also revealed that women living in flexible rooms received more visitors than those whose furnishings lacked flexibility.

The way furniture is arranged can tell us a lot about who talks to whom. The circular arrangement in figure 15.6, for example, encourages sociability (Hendrick et al., 1974; Mehrabian, 1976). However, if you record who talks to whom, you will find that the people sitting on the couch seem to be ignoring each other, and most of the conversation will be between individuals sitting across from each other. This finding has been observed in so many studies that it's earned a special name: the **Steinzor effect.** People address most of their remarks to whoever happens to be sitting across from them (Hearn, 1957; Mehrabian & Diamond, 1971a; 1971b; Steinzor, 1950). A corollary is that side-by-side seating inhibits conversation.

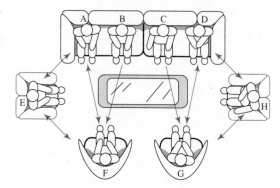

Figure 15.6
Conversational flow and furniture arrangement. As the arrows in this diagram suggest, individuals direct most of their comments to whoever happens to be sitting across from them except when there is a large distance between them. As a consequence, people sitting on a couch may feel limited in their choice of conversation partners, and what's been called a "conversational grouping" is composed of two separate groups of individuals.
(Adapted from A. Mehrabian, 1976, 92.)

What accounts for the Steinzor effect? Probably the best answer is given by the *expressive eye contact hypothesis*: We feel obliged to talk when somebody looks at us or "catches our eye" (Baker, 1984). Research on the Steinzor effect explains why leaders are usually chosen from whomever happens to be sitting at the head of the table (Howells & Becker, 1962; Silverstein & Stang, 1976). When you are sitting at a table, there are two people whose eye you can catch—the person across from you and whoever happens to be sitting at the end of the table. However, the person at the end of the table is the one that everyone else can see, too. So he or she will usually emerge as the group's leader.

The expressive eye contact hypothesis also accounts for frequently observed differences in participation during classroom discussions. From the diagram in figure 15.7, you can see that students sitting in the front and middle seats of a college classroom speak more often than those who sit in the back of the room (Sommer, 1969; Stires, 1980; 1982). This is because you are more likely to catch your instructor's eye when you are sitting in the front row. However, it is possible that the correlation between classroom seating and participation stems from personality factors, such as sociability and interest in the contents of a course (Levine et al., 1980; 1982). For example, it has been found that verbally fluent students are much more likely to take part in classroom discussions when they are assigned front row seats, but it doesn't seem to matter where shy or less fluent students sit (Koneya, 1976).

Personal Space: "At Arm's Length"

The distance we place between ourselves and others has been likened to an invisible wall, a portable territory, a shell, and "breathing room" (Sommer, 1969). It's usually termed **personal space.** However, a moment's thought should convince you that this space always involves another person. A more accurate term might be *interpersonal space* (Patterson, 1975). It doesn't make much sense to talk about personal space when we are alone.

Few topics have inspired as much interest as personal space. It's a topic that has generated more than 1,000 empirical investigations at last count (Hayduk, 1985). These studies leave little doubt that the best predictor of personal space is *acquaintance*—how well individuals know and like each other. At a theme park, for example, you will see parents holding their children, lovers hugging, friends

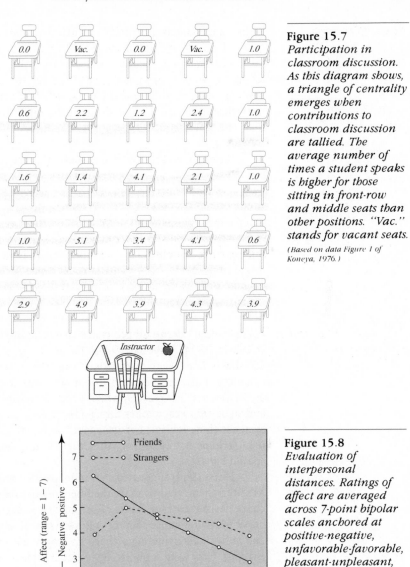

Figure 15.7
Participation in classroom discussion. As this diagram shows, a triangle of centrality emerges when contributions to classroom discussion are tallied. The average number of times a student speaks is higher for those sitting in front-row and middle seats than other positions. "Vac." stands for vacant seats.
(Based on data Figure 1 of Koneya, 1976.)

Figure 15.8
Evaluation of interpersonal distances. Ratings of affect are averaged across 7-point bipolar scales anchored at positive-negative, unfavorable-favorable, pleasant-unpleasant, bad-good, and fair-unfair.
(Adapted from Ashton, Shaw, & Worsham, 1980.)

standing next to each other, and nearly all of them shying away from strangers. Likewise, in laboratory studies (e.g., Ashton et al., 1980), it has been found that subjects feel uncomfortable when a stranger walks up to them. However, as the graph in figure 15.8 suggests, we are also uncomfortable when a friend chooses a distance that makes us wonder about our breath (Baker & Shaw, 1980; Thompson et al., 1979). When it comes to friends, the closer the better!

Sex Differences

It may not come as a surprise to learn that a man and a woman (i.e., mixed-sex pairs) like to stand and sit closer than pairs composed of members of the same sex, and women interact at closer distances than men. However, we wouldn't be telling the whole story if we didn't report that mixed results have been obtained in research on sex differences (Aiello, 1987). There is some reason to believe that the other person's sex or gender is more important than our own (Dabbs, 1977); that is, regardless of your own sex, you'll probably stand closer to a woman than a man.

Research on topic intimacy highlights the importance of the other person's sex. On the one hand, mixed-sex couples (i.e., a man and a woman) prefer closer distances when they are engaged in an intimate conversation than when they are talking about something like the best restaurant in town (Scott, 1984). On the other hand, men who don't know each other put a considerable amount of distance between themselves when conversation turns to sex. This is one of several findings that Worchel (1986) obtained in an important series of studies. Another is that individuals put more distance between themselves and strangers when they are told their conversation is being videotaped (and will later be viewed by a team of behavioral scientists) than when they are assured privacy.

Developmental and Cultural Trends

An individual's desire for personal space increases from 3 to 21 years of age (Aiello & Aiello, 1974; Hayduk, 1983). What happens after a person's 21st birthday? The few studies that have looked into the question suggest that interpersonal distances continue to expand (along with our waists) until we reach 40 years of age. However, for reasons which aren't entirely clear, elderly individuals stand and sit closer to each other than younger people (Heshka & Nelson, 1972). However, one thing is clear: Personal space is something we learn (Aiello, 1987). Thus, it is perhaps not surprising that there are a number of cultural differences in spatial behavior.

Hall (1966) suggested that individuals living in Arab, Latin American, and Mediterranean countries are members of **contact cultures,** whose interactions are characterized by high levels of intimacy. He contrasted their behavior with that of people living in **noncontact cultures** (specifically, Orientals, North Americans, and individuals living in northern European nations, such as Germany and Great Britain). How valid is Hall's suggestion? While nobody doubts that personal space depends on culture, early studies seemed to suggest that Hall's classification was too broad to be useful (e.g., Mazur, 1977; Shuter, 1976). However, early research did not take language into account. Anyone who speaks another language knows that one acquires a lexicon of nonverbal gestures as well as a vocabulary of foreign phrases and words. This fact led Sussman and Rosenfeld (1982) to hypothesize that interpersonal distances mirror the language an individual happens to be speaking. They tested their idea by recording how far Venezuelans and Japanese students sat from a confederate when they conversed in English or their native language. As they hypothesized, Venezuelans sat closer to the confederate when they spoke Spanish, whereas the Japanese students put more distance between themselves when they spoke in their native language than when they conversed in English.

An interesting thing happens when our classes meet outside on pleasant days. Although there's more room on the university's lawn, students sit closer to each other. This is consistent with results obtained in several studies: People stand and sit closer to one another when they are outdoors than when they are inside a building (Cochran et al., 1984; Pempus et al., 1975). This could be due to higher noise levels in outdoor settings. As you might guess, people stand closer to each other in noisy settings than in quiet settings (Mathews et al., 1974). However, it is also possible that individuals are compensating for the lack of room to move around when they are in a building. Indeed, people put more distance between themselves and others in small rooms than they do in large rooms (White, 1975). Consider how we maximize distances between ourselves and others on elevators, which are small rooms. It has also been found that individuals desire more space in long and *narrow* rooms, which place constraints on their movements, than they do in square rooms (Daves & Swaffer, 1971; Worchel, 1986). We are even influenced by the space over our heads! Individuals desire more space in rooms with low ceilings than when they are in rooms with high ceilings (Cochran & Urbanczyk, 1982; Savinar, 1975).

Enclosures: "Don't Fence Me In"

Most of us are uncomfortable when circumstances force us to invade another's personal space. Indeed, some people are so uncomfortable that they will even forgo the pleasure of taking a drink from a water fountain when they have to violate another's personal space to do so. Barefoot and colleagues (1972) found that fewer people stopped to take a drink when a confederate was standing next to the fountain than when he or she was five feet or ten feet away. The presence of another person has little effect, however, when a hallway is crowded (Thalhofer, 1980). Apparently, we assume that our actions won't be noticed and may even be excused when everybody's personal space is being invaded. From the results shown in figure 15.9, it can be seen individuals are more likely to ignore another's presence and take a drink when a water fountain is set in the wall (Baum et al., 1974). While this finding is somewhat pedestrian, it suggests one way to make life a little bit more comfortable and, in this case, refreshing.

Invading Another's Space: Some Refreshing Findings

Anxiety, annoyance, and anger are some of the emotions we experience when a stranger violates our personal space (e.g., Fisher & Byrne, 1975; Smith & Knowles, 1978). These emotions lead us to put distance between ourselves and those who get too close for comfort. For example, Konečni and colleagues (1975) had same-sex confederates stand one, two, five, or ten feet from pedestrians who were waiting at a light to cross a street. The closer the confederate stood, the faster individuals crossed the street when the light changed.

It does not seem to matter where one's personal space is invaded. People also put distance between themselves and invaders in libraries (Polit & LaFrance, 1977), hospitals (Felipe & Sommer, 1966), and amusement parks (Nesbitt & Steven, 1974). However, flight is usually a last-ditch effort to deal with an invader. Before individuals flee, they try to put psychological distance between themselves and the invader by averting their eyes, turning their bodies to one side, leaning away from the invader, and drawing in their arms and legs

Violations of Personal Space: Too Close for Comfort

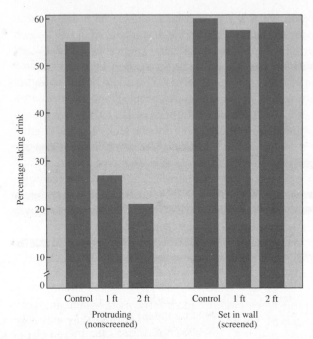

Figure 15.9
Reluctance to violate another's personal space. Fewer people take a drink from a water fountain when doing so forces them to violate someone's personal space, but the inhibiting effects of another person's presence can be overcome by screening (i.e., setting the fountain into the wall).
(Based on data in Baum et al., 1974.)

(e.g., Felipe & Sommer, 1966; Patterson et al., 1971). These are *compensatory behaviors,* whose aim is to reestablish a comfortable level of intimacy (Patterson, 1973). They are also indicative of emotional arousal—a fact that Middlemist, Knowles, and Matter (1976) confirmed by conducting a field experiment in a restroom. Their subjects were men who were standing in front of a urinal. Each man's personal space was invaded by a confederate who stood in front of an immediately adjacent urinal or left a urinal between himself and the unsuspecting subject. Middlemist and colleagues surreptitiously timed how long each man took to begin and finish urinating (proven measures of physiological arousal). These measures provided strong support for their hypothesis: The closer the confederate stood, the longer it took a man to begin urinating and the faster the act was completed.

You may recall that, in chapter 1, questions were raised about this study's propriety. Middlemist and colleagues (1977) dealt with most of them by pointing out that (a) pilot subjects did not object when they learned that their actions had been observed and (b) a lavatory is a public place where we are not surprised when our behavior is observed. We might add that this study's methods can also be defended by referring to research described in the previous section. As we noted, individuals are more likely to use a water fountain when it's screened. The results obtained by Middlemist and colleagues provide support for the practice of placing screens around urinals. This suggestion is based on the idea that "comfort station" should be something more than a euphemism.

While there can be little doubt that another person's close proximity is arousing, it is obvious that we do not always react negatively when people get close to us. (If we did, amusement parks would go out of business.) How we react depends on the label we apply to the arousal caused by another person's close proximity. As the diagram in figure 15.10 suggests, we choose negative labels (e.g., fear, anxiety) when we interpret another's approach as rude and intrusive. On the other hand, we choose a positive label (e.g., liking or love) when we interpret another person's approach as an attempt to gain our friendship. Further, as this model suggests, we reciprocate by trying to get closer to the person whose presence has produced positive feelings (Heslin & Patterson, 1982).

How much support has this admittedly complicated model received? Quite a bit! In one experiment, Schiffenbauer and Schiavo (1976) had a confederate take a seat two or four feet from a subject. They found that a confederate's close proximity led subjects to like him more when he complimented them, but it reduced liking when the confederate raised questions about the subject's abilities. This model is also supported by studies that have looked at people's willingness to lend assistance. On the one hand, several investigators have found that individuals are less willing to do favors for someone who has invaded their personal space (e.g., DeBeer-Keston et al., 1986; Glick et al., 1988). On the other hand, we are more willing to lend assistance when close proximity is accompanied by a verbal appeal for help. In one study (Baron, 1978), closeness was interpreted as a sign of distress. Subjects assumed that invaders needed help if they were ready to take the chance of causing offense by violating the target's personal space.

An Attributional Model of Intimacy and Interpersonal Distance

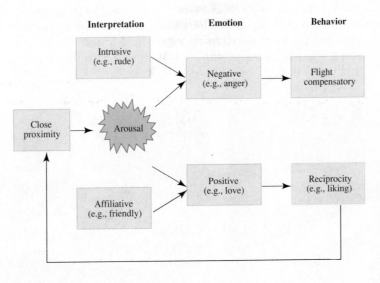

Figure 15.10
An attributional model of intimacy and interpersonal distance. When another person's approach is unwanted or intrusive, we use a negative label to describe the arousal that close proximity causes, which leads us to avoid further contact by fleeing and engaging in compensatory behaviors. However, when another person's approach is wanted, we choose a positive label to describe the arousal that close proximity causes, which leads us to engage in affiliative behavior.
(Based on diagrams in Patterson, 1976, 1982.)

Interior Settings: An Inside Job

No matter how much we enjoy the time we spend at theme and amusement parks, we know that we will have to go back to work when our holiday ends. Thus, it is only appropriate that we take a brief look at people's behavior in the workplace. This section focuses on open-plan or *landscape* offices. It also considers social interactions in stores, restaurants, and other indoor settings. It is perhaps worth noting that 90 percent of all activity occurs inside one interior setting or another (Koelega, 1987).

Open-Plan Offices

It is in some ways unfortunate that offices conjure up images of solitary individuals engaged in isolated activities—bent over a desk, pouring over annual reports—because most work in an office gets done in groups. For example, managers spend more than a third of their day in meetings (Gifford, 1987). It makes some sense to assume that their efficiency might be improved by removing barriers to rapid and efficient exchange of information. This assumption led the Schnell brothers, in Germany, and later the Quickborner Team in the United States, to advocate the **open-plan concept.** The thing that distinguishes an open-plan office is the absence of interior or floor-to-ceiling walls. Removing the walls that separate workers produces a "bullpen;" replacing them with shoulder-level partitions, storage cabinets, and indoor plants produces a "landscape office." Sundstrom and Sundstrom (1986) report that one-third of all office-workers are now employed in settings like the ones shown in figure 15.11.

There are several reasons why so many firms and corporations have embraced the open-plan concept. First, it costs less to build and renovate open-plan than traditional offices. Second, open-plan offices are energy efficient. It's easier to heat and cool a large space than several small offices. Third, it has been suggested that open-plan offices are sensitive to the changing needs of growing firms and corporations. Their flexible design makes it easy to move, expand, consolidate, and eliminate departments as the need arises. Finally, it has been argued that it is easier for a supervisor to spot difficulties as they arise in open-plan than traditional offices.

Figure 15.11
Bullpen and landscaped offices. While these offices are aesthetically pleasing, surveys indicate that workers prefer the privacy and lower noise levels found in traditional offices.

(a)   (b)

Unfortunately, some of these advantages turn out to be more apparent than real. For example, it has yet to be shown that supervisors benefit when they can see everything that's going on around them. As Sommer (1974) notes, managers know that problems will eventually land on their desks; and if they go out of their way to find problems, they won't have time for long-range planning and clients. To take another example, it's been argued that open-plan offices make it easier for workers to exchange information. However, while workers spend more time talking with each other in open-plan offices, they are no more likely to exchange information about work-related activities. Instead, employees spend most of their time talking about matters that have nothing to do with work (Wineman, 1982).

Very few workers like open-plan offices. Surveys indicate that most would rather work in a conventional office environment (e.g., Marans & Speckelmeyer, 1982; Sundstrom et al., 1982). These preferences stem, in part, from the fact that a co-worker's movements are often distracting. However, the thing that bothers workers most is overheard conversation (Hedge, 1982; Nemecek & Grandjean, 1973). There are two reasons why a co-worker's voice is not always music to our ears. One is that conversation grabs our attention and makes it hard to concentrate on what we are supposed to be doing (Rotton et al., 1978). The other is related to acoustical privacy: If we can hear our neighbors, they can hear us!

Aesthetics and Interior Design: "Neatness Counts"

After what we have written about open-plan offices, you are probably hoping that you will have an office that you can call your own. Have you given any thought to how you might decorate it? Campbell (1979) found that visitors feel more welcome and comfortable in offices that have been improved by the addition of art objects. In the same study, women evidenced more concern than men about how an office was decorated. Thus, it is perhaps not surprising that women are more likely to have aesthetically pleasing objects (e.g., paintings, works of art) in their workspace. Men, on the other hand, opt for objects that reflect family ties and professional achievements, such as certificates and trophies (Goodrich, 1982).

However, it appears that the objects in a room are not as important as its overall neatness. When it comes to impressing a visitor, "neatness counts." At the same time, we should caution that you run a risk if you're *too* neat (Morrow & McElroy, 1981; McElroy et al., 1983). From the graph in figure 15.12, you can see that messy and fastidiously clean offices are not as comfortable as ones that contain neatly organized piles of papers. This finding makes some sense if you think about Felix Unger's apartment in *The Odd Couple*. It is hard to feel at home when a place is so neat that anything you might do will spoil its appearance.

If your room isn't as neat as you might like, you might take some comfort in the fact that visitors will assume that you are a busy person (Campbell, 1979; Morrow & McElroy, 1981). However, there doesn't seem to be any relationship between how neat a place is and how much work gets done: People accomplish

Figure 15.12
*Effects of neatness on
judgments of a visitor's
comfort and
welcomeness. Offices
with neatly stacked
papers on a desk
receive more favorable
evaluations than
spotlessly clean rooms,
and the latter are
evaluated more
favorably than messy
rooms.*

(Based on data in Morrow &
McElroy, 1981.)

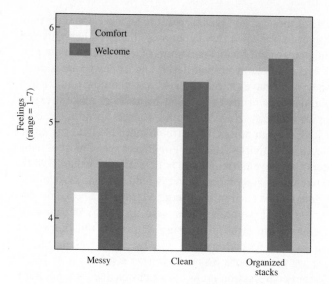

as much in messy and unattractive settings as they do in settings that are aesthetically pleasing (Krieger, 1972; Samuelson & Lindauer, 1976). Does this mean that we don't have to worry about a room's appearance? Not at all. More than a half of the work force in the United States is now employed in service industries, where "productivity" is measured in terms of client and customer satisfaction.

Results obtained by Maslow and Mintz (1956), in one of the earliest studies on environmental design, illustrate the effects of decor on social judgments. These investigators tested students in average, beautiful, or ugly rooms. Their "average" room was a neat but functional setting (actually a professor's office). The "beautiful" room was carpeted, well-lit, and elegantly furnished (e.g. mahogany desk, soft armchairs, sculptures, paintings on the walls, and carpet on the floor). By way of contrast, the "ugly" room's furnishings consisted of little more than straightback chairs around a small table, tin cans for ashtrays, and torn window shades. (Indeed, with boxes and papers on the floor, it resembled a janitor's storeroom.) Subjects were given the task of forming impressions of other students after looking at a number of photographs. As one might expect, students formed more positive impressions in the "beautiful" than the average room, and the "ugly" room's decor led them to be negative in their evaluations. It is interesting to note that the room's decor also affected the individuals who were given the task of interviewing subjects. Interviewers finished their task more quickly when they had to collect data in the "ugly" room (Mintz, 1956).

It has also been found that individuals express a greater desire to interact with others in pleasant than unpleasant settings (Russell & Mehrabian, 1978). A setting's appearance even affects how willing we are to respond to requests for help. In three separate studies, Sherrod and colleagues (1977) found that subjects were more willing to help an accomplice after they had looked at slides of attractive places than after they had looked at slides of unattractive environments. Pleasant surroundings also increase the probability that an individual will return a friendly greeting, engage in eye contact, and do small favors, such as picking up pencils that another person dropped (Amato, 1981). These effects are strongest in exciting (or arousing) settings. Amato and McInnes (1983) found that individuals engage in more affiliative behavior in pleasant *and* arousing settings than they do in settings that possess only one of these properties (i.e., are pleasant *or* arousing). Apparently, as these authors suggest, arousal intensifies the pleasure we feel when we find ourselves in a place we like.

There are many potentially important applications of principles that have been derived from research on the environment and social behavior. In this section, we will see how findings from this research can be applied to make our communities safer and cleaner places.

Applications of Environmental Psychology

Defensible Space: Crime Prevention through Environmental Design

Defensible space can be defined as a semipublic or secondary territory that has been brought under the control of residents (Jacobs, 1961). The best way to grasp this concept is to imagine yourself leaving your home. It takes some time for you to reach the public territory of the street if you live in a single-family house in the suburbs. In all probability, you have to step off your porch and walk down a long sidewalk that is surrounded by a lawn and perhaps a fence. By way of contrast, if you live in an apartment, you will find yourself in a hallway that may be a public territory when you open your door and step outside. All too often, the hallways, lobbies, and land around apartment houses are secondary territories that nobody controls (Yancey, 1972).

According to architect Oscar Newman (1972), crime can be reduced by transforming semipublic areas in public housing projects into defensible space. Newman bases this assertion on a study of crime rates in two housing projects in New York City. One of them was a group of apartments (Brownsville) whose spaces could be defended; the other was an adjoining project (named Van Dyke) that lacked the characteristics of defensible space. The projects housed about the same number of residents (approximately 6,000 people in all) and did not differ in levels of population density. However, as Newman notes, Van Dyke's overall crime rate was 50 percent higher than Brownsville; its robbery rate was three and a half times higher. Why? The photograph and diagram in figure 15.13 suggest a few answers. Note that the buildings in the Van Dyke project are twice as tall as the ones in Brownsville. Note also that the Van Dyke buildings are separated by large parklike areas, whereas Brownsville apartments are built around courtyards. The parks between the buildings in Van Dyke became "no man's lands," which were taken over by juvenile gangs. Building entries in Van Dyke building's served between 112 and 136 families. By way of contrast, no more than five or six families lived in each one of Brownsville's buildings. Consequently, Brownsville residents knew their neighbors. Newman reports that it wasn't unusual to see children playing outside their apartments in Brownsville. Indeed, the short corridors in this project provided an ideal spot for neighbors to meet and converse.

(a)

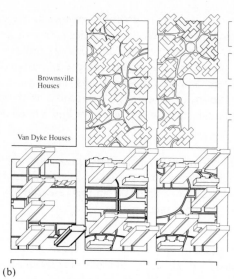

Brownsville Houses

Van Dyke Houses

(b)

Figure 15.13
Two housing projects. Aereal view and site plan of Van Dyke (top) and Brownsville (bottom). Felonies, misdemeanors, and offenses were 64 percent higher in the Van Dyke than the Brownsville project.

Not everybody agrees with this analysis. Several critics have pointed out that the people living in these projects differed on a number of other dimensions, including socioeconomic status and the amount of time residents had lived in each project (e.g., Hillier, 1973; Taylor, 1987). However, this criticism does not seem to apply to university residences, which attract similar and upwardly mobile young people. Sommer (1987) assessed the basic tenets of defensible space theory by comparing two types of housing on a campus in California. From the diagrams in figure 15.14, you can see that one of the dormitories consisted of a cluster of halls around an enclosed space; the other consisted of high-rise halls which were set off from each other and the surrounding neighborhood. Sommer found that the chances of being a victim of a serious crime (e.g., burglary, assault) were five times greater in the high-rise towers than the cluster arrangement of halls. He also found that students living in the high-rise dormitories were twice as likely as those living in the clusters to be a victim of minor incidents and civil offenses (e.g., pranks, disputes between neighbors).

What accounts for these differences? Newman (1972) has suggested that four factors or environmental features contribute to defensible space: zones of territorial influence, opportunities for surveillance, image, and milieu. Referring to figure 15.14, it can be seen that the fence linking buildings provides a clear *zone of territorial influence,* which tells outsiders that this area is under the control of individuals living in the cluster arrangement. The buildings in the cluster arrangement also make it easier to see and, more importantly, recognize outsiders (i.e., *opportunities for surveillance*). In addition, as Sommer (1987) notes, the cluster hall's architecture is similar to other buildings on campus. Thus, its *image* is that of the university with which it is associated. By way of contrast, it's hard to tell the difference between the tower halls and apartment buildings in a public

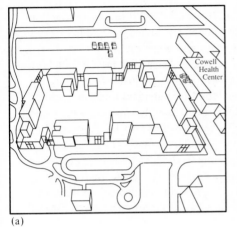 (a)

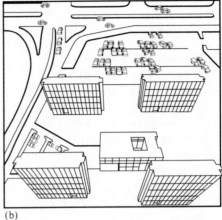 (b)

Figure 15.14
Exterior view of cluster and high-rise halls. Fewer crimes occurred in the cluster halls (left) *than the high-rise dormitories* (right).
(Sommer, 1987.)

(a)

(b)

Figure 15.15
Environmental cues and burglary. Which one of these houses is more likely to be burglarized? See accompanying text for answer.
(Brown, 1985.)

housing project. Finally, as you may know, *milieu* is the French word for "surroundings." From Figure 15.14, you can see that the high-rise towers are set in the middle of an empty field that is next to parking lots and a busy highway, while the the cluster halls adjoin other dormitories and campus pathways.

Now that we have described the defining features of defensible space, look at the two houses in figure 15.15. Which do you think would be among the 7,394,000 homes in the United States that are burglarized each year? An analysis of burglaries in Salt Lake City, Utah, suggests that the answer is the house portrayed in the lower diagram. Its design does not include three features that deter burglars: barriers, markers, and traces (Brown & Altman, 1983). Actual or *real barriers* are represented by the fence around the house in the top figure.

Barriers also include doors, walls, and gates. Newman (1972) drew a distinction between actual and *symbolic barriers,* such as open gates, hedges, and low curbs. These can be distinguished from *markers* (e.g., an owner's name on mailboxes and the side of one's house). It may surprise you to learn that markers include street signs (e.g., "25 mph sign in the bottom figure). Because these signs are directed at the public at large, burglars conclude that outsiders won't be noticed. In addition, these signs suggest that a street is more heavily traveled, which also reduces the chances that a burglar "casing" a house will be noticed. Fewer crimes occur on one-way streets and in a cul-de-sac, which is a fancy name for a dead-end street (Fowler et al., 1979). This may be due to the fact that there are fewer escape routes for criminals on such streets. However, a cul-de-sac may also deter crime by encouraging neighborly behavior. People living on one cul-de-sac spent more time with their neighbors than individuals living on through streets (Brown & Werner, 1985).

Traces are represented by the rake and sprinkler in figure 15.15. Other examples are lawn furniture, ornaments, and tools, all of which help a burglar decide if a house is occupied (Brower et al., 1983). It's also been found that garages deter burglars. As Brown (1985) notes, a garage makes it hard for a burglar to figure out if an owner is at home. Other kinds of traces are dilapidation, trash in vacant lots, litter, abandoned automobiles, and graffiti on walls. These are what Hunter (1978) has termed *signs of incivilities.* Their presence leads people to conclude that a neighborhood has a crime problem (Lavrakas, 1982; Nasar, 1981–1982). They may also invite crime by suggesting that residents don't care enough to defend the land around their homes. This conclusion is based on comparison of vandalized and nonvandalized schools in Houston, Texas. In this study, which controlled for grade levels and the ethnic background of each school's neighborhood, Pablant and Baxter (1975) found that maintenance and upkeep deterred vandals. Compared with schools that had been vandalized, the ones that had not showed signs of upkeep and attempts to beautify their grounds.

Encouraging Environmentally Responsible Behavior

You might think that litter would not be a problem if people paid attention to public service announcements on television. "People cause pollution," we are told, "people can stop it." Unfortunately, these campaigns are not very effective (Cone & Hayes, 1980), largely because of the weak link between attitudes and behavior described in chapter 6. For example, in one revealing study, Bickman (1972) asked people, "Should it be everybody's responsibility to pick up litter when they see it?" Over 94 percent of the people he interviewed agreed that it should be. What makes this study interesting is that Bickman strewed trash on the ground, so his respondents had to walk through or around it before they were interviewed. How many stopped to do what they said is everybody's responsibility? Less than 2 percent (8 out of the 516 respondents).

There are several ways to reduce the amount of litter in parks and on streets (Cone & Hayes, 1980; Geller, 1987). These procedures have a lot in common with procedures developed to encourage other types of environmentally responsible behavior, such as recycling (Burn & Oskamp, 1986) and energy conservation (Stern & Oskamp, 1987). One way to reduce litter is to motivate people to pick up after themselves and others. This is what Geller (1986) calls *unlittering*. It would not be necessary if we could get people to stop littering. Geller coined the work *antilittering* to describe procedures that have this aim.

Even children know that they should not litter, but we are not always mindful of our actions. It has been found that individuals are more likely to engage in responsible behavior after they see a model do so (Jason et al., 1979). Unfortunately, as was noted in chapter 13, people model inappropriate as well as appropriate behavior (Cialdini, 1985). If one person litters, those around him or her may conclude that they are in a setting (e.g., a football stadium) where littering is acceptable or at least tolerated.

Antilittering: Nipping the Problem in the Bud

A better way to increase the salience of the norm against littering is to use a *prompt*. As you might guess, this is a message or cue that suggests appropriate behavior. An example is the reminder on sandwich and beverage containers (e.g., "Please throw me in the trash container"). Investigators have devised several techniques for increasing a prompt's effectiveness. One is to ask individuals to engage in a simple or convenient action; for example, people are much more likely to heed a prompt when they are near a trash receptable (Durdan et al., 1985; Geller et al., 1976). Another is to make sure that a prompt's message is specific (e.g., "Please dispose of this cup in the green can at the front of the store"). This type of message is more effective than more general messages (e.g., "Please don't litter") found on many containers (Geller et al., 1976). You may have noticed that the earlier message was worded in a positive fashion: It lets people know what they should do. Positively worded messages produce more compliance than those that contain a negative word, such as "Please *don't* litter" (Durdan et al., 1985). This brings us to a third and very important principle: A prompt's effectiveness is greatly reduced when it contains language that threatens one's freedom. Indeed, it's been found that threatening and demanding messages arouse so much reactance that individuals will litter in an effort to restore their freedom. Imagine how you would react if someone gave you a flyer that said, "Don't you *dare* litter." Reich and Robertson (1979) found that more trash was left around a swimming pool when patrons got this message than a polite one that reminded them that "Keeping the pool clean depends on you."

It is worth noting that litter, itself, is a prompt. One of the best predictors of littering is the amount of trash already on the ground (e.g., Finnie, 1973; Robinson & Frisch, 1975); that is, as the saying goes, "litter begets litter."

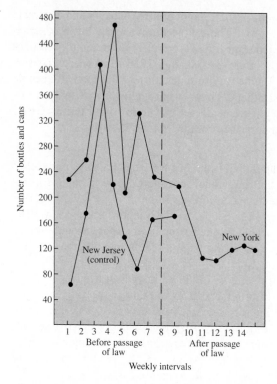

Figure 15.16
*Bottle laws work.
There was a sizable
decline in bottles and
cans left near highway
exits after New York
became the ninth state
to pass a bottle law.*
(Adapted from figure in Levitt &
Leventhal, 1986.)

*Unlittering:
A Clean Sweep*

Anyone who spends much time on the road cannot help but be struck by the fact that fines for littering jump from $25 to $500 when you cross some state lines. It is in some ways unfortunate that states have spent so much money on making and posting these signs, because punishment and negative reinforcement rarely stops littering (Geller et al., 1982). On the other hand, positive reinforcement has been shown to be an extremely effective means of getting people to pick up after themselves and others (e.g., Cope & Geller, 1984; Kohlenberg & Phillips, 1973; McNees et al., 1979).

A good example of a positive or an incentive approach is the passage of "bottle bills," which require manufacturers to place a small (usually 5 cent) deposit on beer and soda pop containers. At last count, nine states had passed such bills. To assess the effectiveness of one state's bill, Levitt and Leventhal (1986) counted the number of bottles left along highway entrances in New Jersey and New York. Since New Jersey had not passed a bottle bill, it provided a convenient control to assess the effects of New York's law. As you can see from the graph in figure 15.16, the law produced a dramatic and long-lasting decrease in the number of bottles on New York's roads.

It doesn't take a large incentive to get people to pick up litter. For example, in one study, Clark and colleagues (1972) told children that they would get a small prize if they brought a bag of litter to a collection center in a campground. The prizes consisted of ranger badges, comic books, and Smoky the Bear patches whose total cost was a little over three dollars. For these prizes, however, children collected more than 175 pounds of litter. It would have cost $55 to hire adults to do the same job. Another cost-effective approach, which works with adults as well as children, is a "litter lottery" (e.g., Bacon-Prue et al., 1980). People pick up as much trash when they are given a chance to win a prize as they do for fixed amounts of money.

Summary

Environmental psychology is a relatively young discipline that has attracted social psychologists and members from a number of other disciplines (e.g., sociology, architecture). Social psychologists have made major contributions to this field by identifying theoretical links between the environment and basic psychological processes, such as perception, preferences, territoriality, privacy, and personal space.

Environmental perception is an active and purposeful process that involves all of the senses. It includes affective as well as cognitive-perceptual appraisals of one's surroundings. Affective appraisals are determined by the amount of arousal and pleasure that a scene elicits. Cognitive-perceptual appraisals depend on a number of other factors, including familiarity, novelty, and complexity. For example, it has been found that individuals prefer familiar, natural, and moderately complex scenes.

Familiarity also contributes to place attachment. The cognitive component of this attitude is place-identity; its behavioral component is territoriality, which describes behavior that establishes control over an area. Although it is tempting to draw analogies between the territorial behavior of humans and other animals, only human beings exert control over ideas, claim objects, and feel territorial about places they inhabit on an irregular basis. The territorial behavior of humans includes personalization of primary territories and the use of objects (markers) to claim public territories.

Territories are one of several interpersonal boundary control (IBC) processes, which enable us to to achieve desired levels of intimacy and privacy. There is some reason to believe privacy and sociability lie on opposite ends of a continuum, because sociofugal spaces discourage interactions, whereas sociopetal spaces encourage sociability. Fixed-feature and semifixed-feature space, such as furniture arrangements, also enable individuals to regulate interactions and achieve privacy.

Interpersonal boundary controls include personal space, which describes the distance individuals place between themselves and others. A number of factors influence this distance, including a person's sex, culture, age, and topic of conversation. However, the primary determinant of personal space appears to be degree of acquaintance. In addition, people prefer small distances when they are outdoors, in noisy settings, and inside square rooms with high ceilings. They experience anxiety and usually retreat when strangers violate their personal space. Because spatial invasions are arousing, close proximity can lead to positive and affiliative as well as negative reactions.

Research on environmental aesthetics, privacy, and personal space has been applied to facilitate interactions in offices and other interior settings. As research on privacy suggests, most workers dislike open-plan offices. As might be guessed from research on environmental aesthetics, attractive settings exert a number of positive effects on social interactions.

We can make our residences safer by maximizing the defensible space in and around them. Defensible space can be achieved by establishing zones of territorial influence, providing opportunities for surveillance, using markers, improving an area's appearance, and relying on symbolic as well as physical barriers. We can make our environments cleaner through the use of prompts and incentive programs (e.g., bottle bills, "lotteries"), which are effective techniques for reducing litter.

CHAPTER 16

Stress

by James Rotton

You may have noticed that there is usually an outbreak of mononucleosis during exam periods. Mononucleosis is, for good reason, called "the lover's disease." Those who escape the virus that causes it when they're young, contract mononucleosis when they come into oral contact (kiss) with a carrier. But why does mono (as it's usually called) strike students during exam periods? The answer that many people give is that exams are stressful. Referring back to chapter 6, you will recall that stressful events bring people together (i.e., "misery loves company"). Perhaps young people are more likely to enter into liaisons, which usually involve oral contact, when they are under stress. We will, later in this chapter, examine research that has linked stress to affiliation and several other types of social behavior. It is also possible that stress reduces a person's resistance to disease. This possibility is supported by recent research on immunological reactions, which is described in the first section of this chapter. Unfortunately, research on physiological reactions does not explain why most students make it through exams without succumbing to infectious disorders.

Who gets mono? Kasl, Evans, and Neiderman (1979) found that it's only students who are worried about failing exams. This finding may not surprise you. Most of us experience stress when we are not as successful as we would like to be. However, there are also people who take failure in stride. Kasl and colleagues (1979) observed that failing students didn't contract mono when their desire to get a degree was low. It was only students who were failing despite their motivation and commitment that got mono.

What Is Stress?

As the preceding suggests, stress is a pretty slippery concept. The father of stress research, Hans Selye, began an article on his life's work by observing, "Everybody knows what it is" (1973, p. 692). It suggested that stress could be defined as "the nonspecific response of the body to any demands placed on it" (p. 693). This is a *response-based definition*. Not everybody accepts it, because there are times when we place demands on our bodies as a way of coping with stress. One of them is when we go for long walks to relieve tension; another is when individuals try to unwind by engaging in vigorous exercise. Unfortunately, response-based definitions leave us in the dark about what causes stress. Why is one activity stressful while another is relaxing? Attempts to answer this question have led to *stimulus-based definitions,* which place more emphasis on factors that cause stress. It is not unusual for television shows and magazine articles to begin with photographs of individuals in situations that most of us would regard as stressful (see figure 16.1). The biggest problem with this kind of definition is that it doesn't take individual differences into account. For example, while some people enjoy airplane trips, others talk about "white knuckle flights." Still others like to end a trip by parachuting from the plane (Epstein, 1967; Zuckerman, 1978).

Most investigators favor transactional and *mediational definitions,* which lead them to view stress as a process that describes relations between environmental factors (called *stressors*) and the responses they elicit:

$$\text{Stressor} \xrightarrow{\text{Stress}} \text{Symptoms of stress}$$

(a)

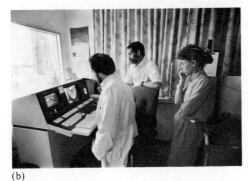
(b)

(c)

For those of you who might be asked to define stress (in 25 words or less), we offer the following definition: **Stress** is a process that is triggered by harmful or potentially harmful events. The crucial word in this definition is *process*. Its importance can be appreciated by thinking back to the last exam you took (e.g., the midterm in this course). It's our guess that you didn't give much thought to the exam at the beginning of the semester; but as time for the midterm approached, you probably began to feel apprehensive. It is interesting to note that most students (as many as 98 percent in one sample) report that they look on exams as challenges as well as threats to their well-being. Quite often, these mild emotions give way to anxiety—worry, arousal, and unpleasant symptoms—when students sit down to take an exam (e.g., Sarason, 1984; Smith & Ellsworth, 1987). Afterwards, students report they feel frustrated, angered, or relieved, depending on how well they did. However, when they are taking a full load of courses, students suppress these emotions so they can get on with their lives and deal with other problems. The point is that responses to threatening and harmful stimuli unfold over time. Indeed, the time may come—after you have left college and are worrying about getting or keeping a job—when you will look back and reminisce about your days in college the way retired soldiers do about the pressures of army life.

Figure 16.1
Life can be stressful. It is easy to think of situations that can cause stress, but stimulus-based definitions do not explain why some people fall to pieces while others seem to thrive on stress.

Figure 16.2
Diseases of adaptation. The frustration of being forcefully immobilized causes a rat's adrenals to swell (A), and thymus gland to shrink (B), and its lymph nodes to atrophy (C). In addition, ulcers develop inside the rat's stomach (D).

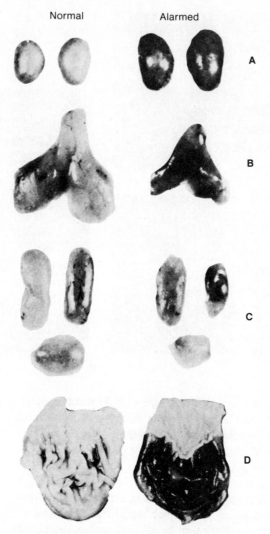

Normal   Alarmed

A

B

C

D

Systemic Stress: Life's a G.A.S.!

Stress is such a familiar concept that it might surprise you to learn that it is little more than fifty years old. Before 1936, most physicians subscribed to Pasteur's "germ theory of illness." Find a pathogen (germ, virus, or bacteria) and you would know what caused the disease. This view was changed by a serendipitous discovery made by Hans Selye who was investigating the effects of an ovarian hormone. He noticed that one of his extracts produced three symptoms in the rats he was using in the experiment: enlarged adrenals, gastrointestinal ulcers, and shrinkage of the thymus gland, which controls immunological reactions (see figure 16.2). As you might imagine, Selye was elated: "At the age of 28, I seemed to be already on the track of a new hormone" (Selye, 1956, p. 22). His joy didn't last long, however. The symptoms he had observed disappeared when he used better extracts. Much to his chagrin, they reappeared when he injected rats with

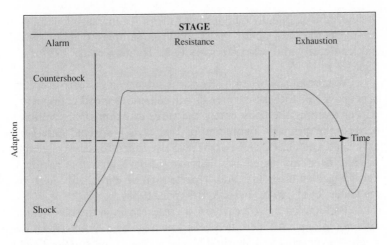

Figure 16.3
Temporal course of the General Adaptation Syndrome. The body's defenses pass through three stages, culminating in disease and death, when they fail to restore homeostasis.
(After Selye, 1956.)

placental and pituitary extracts. Why should symptoms disappear when one was careful and reappear when one used less pure extracts? It occurred to Selye that they might be caused by irritation. Almost in desperation, he injected rats with formalin (an irritating chemical), and the symptoms reappeared. This discovery led him to suspect that the body responds in the same fashion whenever it is exposed to noxious and irritating conditions. His suspicion was confirmed when subsequent experiments revealed that the same symptoms were produced by heat, cold, electric shock, and forcefully restraining rats in harnesses.

Systemic stress describes the body's reactions to noxious and aversive stimuli. However, Selye did not use the term *stress* in his first articles. Instead, he coined the term **general adaptation syndrome (G.A.S.)** to describe the body's attempt to defend itself against noxious agents. From the diagram in figure 16.3, you can see that this syndrome consists of three stages: alarm, resistance, and exhaustion. The *alarm stage* can, in turn, be divided into two phases (Selye, 1981). During the *shock phase,* there is a dramatic drop in temperature as blood rushes away from peripheral organs and muscles lose their strength. An individual may look like he or she has seen a ghost. This phase is replaced by *countershock* as the heart races, arterial pressure rises, muscles tense, and one begins to perspire. These and other reactions (e.g., dry mouth, pupil dilation, halted digestion) are adaptive. They are part of W. B. Cannon's (1932) "fight or flight reaction."

The body would quickly wear itself out if the alarm stage did not give way to a *stage of resistance*. During this stage, the inner portion of the adrenal glands produce hormones that return the body to its initial state of equilibrium. This desirable equilibrium state is called *homeostasis*—from the Greek words for same (homeos) and state (stasis). In order to restore homeostasis, the outer portion of the adrenal gland (i.e., the adrenal medulla) produces *epinephrine* and *norepinephrine*. (These used to be called adrenalin and noradrenalin, respectively.) Rather than describe how these hormones are transformed into neurotransmitters or chemical messengers, we will simply note that they are frequently used to determine if an individual is under stress. An increasing number of social psychologists routinely obtain blood and urine samples to assess the effects of population density and other stressors (e.g., Fleming et al., 1987; Schaeffer et al., 1988).

What happens when a stressor is prolonged or so severe that homeostasis is not possible? Either the adrenals will collapse, or another organ (e.g., the heart) will give out as the body enters the *stage of exhaustion.* We have already described the primary symptoms of this stage—adrenal enlargement, thymus shrinkage, and ulcers. These are what Selye called "diseases of adaptation." Stress has also been implicated as a factor in the development of rheumatoid arthritis, cardiovascular disorders, and hypertension or chronically high blood pressure (S. Cohen et al., 1986; Feist & Brannon, 1988).

Building on Selye's early work, researchers in the new field of *psychoneuroimmunology* have identified cells which act as a link between the general adaptation syndrome and physical illnesses. One of these is the T helper (Th) cell; another is natural killer (NK) cell activity. NK cells destroy tumors and viral infections, while Th cells increase resistance to disease. (Th is what victims of the acquired immune deficiency syndrome or AIDS lack.) There is some reason to believe that stress hormones suppress the development of these cells (Laudenslager & Reite, 1984). For example, it has been found that NK activity level is lower among women who have lost a spouse (Irwin et al., 1987).

| Cognitive Appraisal: "It's All in How You Look at Things" | It was once thought that only noxious and aversive stimuli triggered the general adaptation syndrome. However, anyone who has lain awake the night before an important test or job interview knows that anticipating an event can sometimes be as stressful as its occurrence. It turns out that the responses Selye thought were a consequence of stressful encounters (e.g., elevated levels of cortisol) are preparatory responses: They are observed *before* an individual encounters a stressor (Arthur, 1987). Indeed, individuals do not have to encounter aversive stimuli for them to experience stress. For example, individuals report discomfort and evidence signs of nervous tension (e.g., reduced eye contact) when they are told they will have to interact with several people in a small room (Baum & Greenberg, 1975; Baum & Koman, 1976). To take another example, individuals do poorly on cognitive tasks when they are led to believe they will have to plunge their hand in an ice-cold bucket of water (Spacapan & Cohen, 1983). This brings us to what Richard Lazarus, one of the leading theorists in this area, has called the catch-22 of stress research: "No environmental event can be identified as a stressor independently of its appraisal by the person" (Lazarus et al., 1985, p. 776). Lazarus has advanced a sophisticated theory that integrates much of what has been learned about the psychological effects of environmental and social stressors (Coyne & Lazarus, 1981; Lazarus, 1966; Lazarus & Folkman, 1984). His cognitive-phenomenological theory is outlined in figure 16.4. |

Lazarus defines *cognitive appraisal* as the evaluation of an event with regard to its significance for one's health and well-being. His definition calls to mind a line from Shakespeare's *Hamlet:* "There is nothing good or bad, but thinking

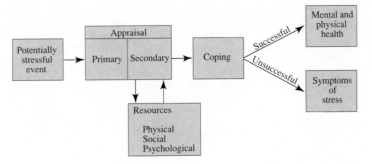

Figure 16.4
Cognitive-phenomenological theory of stress.
(Based on material in Lazarus, 1966 and Lazarus & Folkman, 1984.)

makes it so" (Act II, Scene 2, line 259). For example, you might chuckle when a child points a cap pistol at you. We are certain that you would respond in a different way if you knew that the youngster's mother was a police officer and saw the child pull the pistol from her holster.

As the diagram in figure 16.4 shows, there are two types of appraisal. **Primary** (or *stimulus*) **appraisal** describes an individual's assessment of an event: "Am I in trouble or being benefited, now and in the future, and in what way?" **Secondary** (or *response*) **appraisal** is an evaluation of one's resources or capabilities: "What, if anything, can I do?" These two types of appraisal go hand-in-hand. It is only when an event's potential for harm or injury exceeds our resources that we experience stress. *Resources* are what an individual brings to a situation—physical assets, social support, and psychological skills. You can get a feel for these by recalling advertisements for the Charles Atlas body-building course—"Are you a 98–pound weakling?" These ads suggested that the best way to deal with a bully who kicked sand in your face was to build up your muscles (a *physical resource*). You might also ask a friend to defend you (a *social resource*). Another way to cope is to rely on your persuasive skills (a *psychological resource*) and hope that the bully will listen to reason.

Coping can be defined as cognitive and behavioral efforts aimed at managing conditions that tax and might exceed our resources. As our diagram suggests, individuals will evidence one or more symptoms when these efforts are not successful. The primary symptoms of stress are negative affect, physiological arousal, impaired performance on cognitive tasks, and the presence of stress hormones (Baum et al., 1982). Negative affect is a general term that includes annoyance, anxiety, depression, and physical symptoms, such as headaches and heartburn (see table 16.1). It would take us too far afield to describe all of the tests that have been developed to measure these and related symptoms. For our purposes, it is enough to know that paper-and-pencil measures assess a general factor that has been termed psychological distress (Tanaka & Huba, 1984).

Secondary symptoms of stress include physical illnesses, negative forms of social behavior (e.g., hostility and aggression), nonverbal gestures (e.g., trembling, playing with objects), and social pathology. The last refers to psychiatric admissions, suicide rates, and other forms of undesirable behavior (e.g., crime and juvenile delinquency). Typically, social pathology is inferred from large-scale

Table 16.1   Symptoms of Stress

Primary symptoms	Secondary symptoms
Self-report measures Annoyance (e.g., discomfort, irritability) Psychological distress (e.g., anxiety, nervous tension, depression, demoralization) Somatic distress (e.g., headaches, heartburn)	*Physical illness* Cardiovascular disorders Hypertension Lowered immunology Gastrointestinal problems Other symptoms (e.g., colds, accidents)
Biochemical assays Corticosteroids (adrenal medulla) Catecholamines (epinephrine, norepinephrine) Free fatty acid Lymphocytes	*Epidemiological measures* Mortality rates Suicide rates Substance abuse Crime and delinquency Spouse and child abuse Psychiatric admissions
Psychophysiological measures Heart rate Increased blood pressure Respiration rate Muscle tension Elevated skin conductance (e.g., increased galvanic skin response)	*Interpersonal behavior* Increased hostility and aggression Reduced helping Social withdrawal Depersonalization of others Stereotyping
Task performance Reduced reaction time Decreased vigilance Memory deficits Lowered frustration tolerance Premature closure making decisions	*Nonverbal indicants* Vocal stress (e.g., pitch, speech faults, hesitancies, rapid speech) Gaze avoidance Defensive posture (e.g., arms/legs crossed) Automanipulative gestures (e.g., fidgeting, preening) Stereotype object play (e.g., tapping pencil)

After Evans and Cohen (1987).

or epidemiological analyses of data in police, hospital, and census reports (e.g., Rotton, Barry, & Kimble, 1985; Rotton & Kimble, 1989). Social pathology, aggression, and so forth are termed secondary because it is assumed that relations between stressors and behavior are mediated by physiological and cognitive states (i.e., the variables listed in the lefthand column of table 16.1).

Primary Appraisal: Clear Danger

The same event can be regarded as a threat, a challenge, or a loss, depending on time and circumstances. *Threat* describes future or anticipated injury, whereas *harm/loss* describes damage that has already occurred. This simple distinction is complicated by the fact that there is usually an element of threat when we suffer a loss. Think back to the last exam you took. A low grade is an obvious threat—reducing a student's chance of graduating on time—but if you're like most students, you also experience a loss in self-esteem when you do poorly on an exam. The difference between threat and *challenge* is a matter of emphasis or perspective. Threats lead us to interpret events in terms of the harm or damage they can inflict, whereas challenge appraisals lead us to pay more attention to

© 1987 King Features Syndicate Inc. World rights reserved

Examinations: Threat, loss, or challenge?

WHAT A GUY!, by Bill Hoest.
© 1987 by King Features.
Reprinted with special permission
of King Features Syndicate, Inc.

opportunities for mastery, gain, and growth. Lazarus and Folkman (1984) maintain that challenges as well as threats are stressful. After all, we wouldn't feel challenged if there weren't a chance that we might fail. As we noted earlier, most students report that they feel challenged as well as threatened before an exam (Folkman & Lazarus, 1985).

A number of other factors influence primary appraisal. One of the most important is *imminence* or nearness (Paterson & Neufeld, 1987). For example, most of us don't think about death, even though it is an event of considerable severity and certainty, until we see a car coming at us and are sure that a crash is imminent. You can get a feel for factors that influence primary appraisal by completing the Perceived Stress Scale in table 16.2. Note that its items describe conditions that most of us find stressful: overload, unpredictability, and lack of control over events in one's life. Scores on the Perceived Stress Scale predict depression, physical symptoms, and utilization of health services (Cohen, 1986; Cohen et al., 1983).

Secondary Appraisal: Taking Stock and Taking Charge

Quite a bit has been learned in recent years about how individuals take stock of their resources (i.e., secondary appraisal) and select coping strategies (e.g., Folkman et al., 1986a; 1986b). For example, we now know that coping serves two functions, and both are observed during examinations. One of them is thinking of a solution or right answer (**problem-focused coping**); the other is dealing with the stress that exams engender (**emotion-focused coping**). There is a tendency to regard emotion-focused coping as maladaptive or indicative of psychopathology. However, it is only after we have gotten a grip on our emotions that we can focus on problems (Lazarus & Launier, 1978). Thus, it is perhaps not surprising that Folkman and Lazarus (1985) found that most students engage in both kinds of coping before an exam.

To learn more about how people deal with stress, Folkman and Lazarus (1980) developed a 67–item scale called the *Ways of Coping Checklist (WCC)*. Some of the items on their scale are listed in table 16.3. As you can see, problem-focused coping includes instrumental actions, negotiation, and restraint (or cautiousness). Emotion-focused coping includes escapism, self-blame, seeking meaning, and efforts aimed at minimizing and denying one's problems (Aldwin & Revenson, 1987). The last of the strategies in this table—support mobilization—serves both functions. We turn to others for emotional support as well as advice when we have a problem (Dunkel-Schetter et al., 1987).

Table 16.2   Perceived Stress Scale

Instructions: The questions on this scale ask you about your feelings and thoughts during the last month. In each case, you will be asked to indicate *how often* you felt or thought a certain way. Although some of the questions are similar, there are differences between them and you should treat each one as a separate question. The best approach is to answer each question fairly quickly. That is, don't try to count up the number of times you felt a particular way, but rather indicate the alternative that seems like a reasonable estimate.

For each question choose from the following alternatives:

0 never
1 almost never
2 sometimes
3 fairly often
4 very often

1. In the last month, how often have you been upset because of something that happened unexpectedly?

2. In the last month, how often have you felt that you were unable to control important things in your life?

3. In the last month, how often have you felt nervous or "stressed"?

4. In the last month, how often have you dealt successfully with irritating life hassles?

5. In the last month, how often have you felt that you were effectively coping with important changes that were occurring in your life?

6. In the last month, how often have you felt confident about your ability to handle your personal problems?

7. In the last month, how often have you felt that things were going your way?

8. In the last month, how often have you found that you could not cope with all the things you had to do?

9. In the last month, how often have you been able to control irritations in your life?

10. In the last month, how often have you felt that you were on top of things?

11. In the last month, how often have you been angered because of things that happened that were outside your control?

12. In the last month, how often have you found yourself thinking about things you have to accomplish?

13. In the last month, how often have you been able to control the way you spend your time?

14. In the last month, how often have you felt difficulties were piling up so high that you could not overcome them?

Scoring: Because half of the scale are keyed in a reversed direction (with higher scores indicating lower levels of perceived stress), the easiest way to obtain a total is begin by subtracting scores on items 4, 5, 6, 7, 9, 10, and 13 from 28 and then adding the result to scores on items 1, 2, 3, 8, 11, 12, and 14:

A = sum of scores on items 1, 2, 3, 8, 11, 12, and 14
B = sum of scores on items 4, 5, 6, 7, 9, 10, and 13
Total score = $28 + A - B$

Source: Cohen, Kamarck, and Mermelstein (1983).

Table 16.3 Ways of Coping

These statements are a sample of items from a checklist developed by Folkman and Lazarus (1980). They are organized in terms of factors uncovered in analyses done by Aldwin and Revenson (1987).

Problem-focused coping

Instrumental action

I knew what had to be done, so I doubled my efforts to make things work.
I made a plan of action and followed it.
I was inspired to do something creative.

Negotiation

I tried to get the person responsible to change his or her mind.
I bargained or compromised to get something positive from the situation.
I did something that I didn't think would work, but at least I was doing something.

Caution (self-restraint)

I went over in my mind what I would say or do.
I tried not to burn my bridges, but leave things open somewhat.
I tried not to act too hastily or follow my first hunch.

Emotion-focused coping

Escapism

I had fantasies or wishes about how things might turn out.
I daydreamed or imagined a better time or place than the one I was in.
I wished that the whole situation would go away or somehow be over with.

Minimization (repression)

I felt that time would make a difference—the only thing to do was wait.
I tried to forget the whole thing.
I went on as if nothing had happened.

Self-blame

I blamed myself.
I made a promise to myself that things would be better next time.
I realized that I had brought the problem on myself.

Seeking meaning

I tried to discover new faith or some important truth.
I prayed.
I tried to discover what is important in life.

Problem- and emotion-focused coping

Support mobilization

I talked to someone about how I was feeling.
I talked to someone to find out more about the situation.
I accepted sympathy and understanding from someone.

Aldwin and Revenson, 1987.

Are some ways of coping more effective than others? Aldwin and Revenson (1987) found that individuals who engaged in instrumental (problem solving) kinds of coping evidenced less stress than those who did not. A riskier but sometimes effective means of coping with stress is negotiation. Having to negotiate is stressful, but those who put out the effort evidenced fewer symptoms than those who did not. Other ways of coping with stress are described in the Applications section at the end of this chapter.

Table 16.4   Types of Stressors

Extent/level	Magnitude (severity)	
	High	*Low*
Community (large numbers of people)	**Cataclysmic stressors** Combat Hurricane Three Mile Island	**Ambient stressors** Noise Heat Air pollution
Individual (small numbers of people)	**Life stressors** Divorce Death of spouse Job loss	**Microstressors (hassles)** Losing things Home maintenance Concern about weight

Based on Campbell (1983) and Lazarus and Cohen (1977).

Sources of Stress

Early research on stress focused on internal or intrapsychic states, such as guilt, frustration, and conflict. This list could be expanded to include dissonance (see chapter 6). More recent research has focused on situational factors that cause these emotional and cognitive states. While these factors vary along a number of dimensions, two of the most important are an event's severity and its scope (Evans & S. Cohen, 1987; Lazarus & J. Cohen, 1977). *Severity* describes the number of demands an event places on an individual. It is not generally realized that the American Psychiatric Association's (1980) *Diagnostic and Statistical Manual* contains an axis that asks for a 7-point rating of a stressor's severity, ranging from 1 (none) to 7 (catastrophic). *Scope* refers to the number of individuals affected by a stressor: Is a stressor's effect felt by a few individuals, or does it affect everybody living in a community or geographical area? Taking scope and severity into account, we can identify four broad types of stressors (see table 16.4).

This chapter builds on the classification scheme in table 16.4. After we examine the effects of *cataclysmic stressors,* we will review recent research on *life stressors,* such as unemployment, divorce, and death of a spouse. This review will set the stage for a consideration of *microstressors* (or "hassles"), such as missing appointments and getting stuck in traffic. As will become apparent, hassles turn into *ambient stressors,* such as crowding and traffic congestion, when they persist and bother a large number of people.

Cataclysmic Stressors

Wars, floods, tornadoes, and accidents at nuclear power plants share two things in common. First, they are events of overwhelming magnitude. Second, they affect everybody living in a geographical area. These two factors make them **cataclysmic stressors.** These are powerful events that affect large numbers of people. However, as attribution theories suggest, an event's outcome is not as important as its cause. From the time of Job to the present, victims have asked, "Why me? What did I do to bring on my suffering?" Answers to these questions determine how much stress individuals experience (Peterson & Seligman, 1984). Combat is probably the most stressful of all events, because victims know that their suffering was caused by the deliberate actions of other human beings. *Technological catastrophes* can also be traced to the actions of others; however, if one rules out sabotage, their cause is accidental rather than deliberate. This class of stressors includes dam failures, fires, industrial accidents, and toxic spills (Fisher et al., in press). By way of contrast, *natural disasters* are cataclysmic events that we cannot blame on others. They are what insurance companies list as "acts of God." Examples are hurricanes, droughts, floods, tornadoes, and earthquakes (Baum, 1987).

The idea that everybody has a "breaking point" received formal recognition in 1980 when the American Psychiatric Association added the *posttraumatic stress disorder (PTSD)* to its list of psychiatric problems. According to the *Diagnostic and Statistical Manual (DSM-III)*, this disorder is caused by events that "would evoke significant symptoms in almost anyone" (American Psychiatric Association, 1980, p. 238). The primary symptoms of the PTSD are (1) reexperiencing the event that caused the trauma (flashbacks) and (2) numbing of responsiveness as reflected by any one of the following: detachment, flattened affect, or diminished interest in current events. Other symptoms are guilt, hyperalertness, impairment of cognitive abilities (e.g., trouble concentrating), and nightmares.

War: The Posttraumatic Stress Disorder

It's been estimated that between 24 and 48 percent of the men who served in Vietnam showed some sign of the posttraumatic stress disorder (Solomon et al., 1987). While there are some who might dispute these figures, a recent review of the literature leaves little doubt that service in Vietnam exacted a heavy toll on the men who were sent overseas (Kaylor et al., 1987). As you might guess, this toll was highest among men who saw combat (Foy & Card, 1987; Foy et al., 1987). Further, men who took part in atrocities, such as the massacre at My Lai, show more symptoms than those who did not (Breslau & Davis, 1987). It is worth noting that severity of symptoms appears to be independent of premilitary levels of adjustment; that is, it was not just "emotionally unstable" men who had trouble adjusting after service in Vietnam. So, too, did men who appeared to be well-adjusted before they entered the service (Foy et al., 1987; Roberts et al., 1982).

Another factor that influences adjustment is social support. Solomon and colleagues (1986) found that soldiers who felt they received support from superior officers evidenced fewer symptoms than those who felt that such support was insufficient or lacking. **Social support** can be defined as the help or assistance we receive from others (Cohen & Wills, 1985). House (1984) has identified four types of social support:

1. *Instrumental aid.* A loan, help with housework
2. *Informational support.* Advice, suggestions, directions
3. *Appraisal.* Feedback about one's performance
4. *Emotional concern.* Empathy, caring, and understanding

Of these four types, emotional concern appears to be the most important (e.g., Cohen & Hoberman, 1983; Sarason et al., 1987). For example, the severity of posttraumatic stress disorders was less among combat veterans who felt they received support from friends and relatives than it was among men who were dissatisfied with the support they had received (Solomon et al., 1988).

It should be noted that these results are based on what individuals *say* they want from friends. Costanza and colleagues (1988) have found that there are times when we are better off when friends provide informational rather than emotional support. In this experiment, subjects had to confront a large tarantula on a specially constructed cart. They were told that their task was to pull the cart toward their face. Before subjects performed this frightening task, they were given a chance to talk with a friend. Some were encouraged to share their feelings, fears, and uncertainties. Others were led to view the task as a problem that could be solved. Costanza and colleagues found that subjects evidenced less anxiety and depression when they were encouraged to exchange information about the problem. In fact, subjects who were encouraged to talk about their feelings were more upset than individuals in a third group, who had been asked to talk about other matters. As Costanza and colleagues suggest, talking about one's fears and feelings is like putting them in a pressure cooker. In the long run, we may be better off with a friend who doesn't let us stew in our emotional juices.

Technological Catastrophes: Buffalo Creek and Three Mile Island

Few catastrophes have received as much attention as the collapse of a slag dam above the Buffalo Creek Valley, in West Virginia, which swept away several small towns. Among the symptoms observed after this catastrophe were nightmares, clinical levels of depression, gastrointestinal disorders, and alcoholism (Gleser et al., 1981). Some of these symptoms were evident two years after the flood. Their severity and duration can be traced to two factors. First, nearly every resident lost one or more loved ones. As a result, much of the community's social structure was destroyed. Second, most of the victims thought the disaster could have been prevented. This factor also played a role in reactions to the meltdown at Three Mile Island near Harrisburg, Pennsylvania.

On March 28, 1979, workers had to shut down one of the reactors at the Three Mile Island plant to prevent the escape of radioactive gases. A few days later, Pennsylvania's governor issued a warning and suggested that pregnant women and small children should evacuate the area. What makes this catastrophe interesting is that its threat was psychological rather than physical. No one was hurt, and none of the residents were exposed to harmful levels of radiation. However, Baum and colleagues (1982) found that individuals living near the reactor had more stress hormones in their urine than individuals living in other communities. Standardized measures also revealed that Three Mile Island residents suffered from a number of clinical symptoms, including depression, anxiety, and alienation (Baum et al., 1983; Fleming et al., 1982). It is sobering to note that these symptoms have persisted for more than four years (Baum, 1988; Dew et al., 1987). Apparently, this catastrophe caused a mild form of the posttraumatic stress disorder, which was described in the preceding section.

Figure 16.5
Three Mile Island. The cooling towers in the distance remind residents of the emergency that was declared when the nuclear plant had to be shut down. After more than four years, residents regard the plant as a threat to their health and well-being.

It is interesting to note that individuals who resorted to problem-focused coping have shown more symptoms than those who relied on emotion-focused strategies. This may be because the problem facing people in the community was an insoluble one. Collins, Baum, and Singer (1982) suggested that individuals felt even more helpless when they tried to solve it. These investigators also examined the effectiveness of denial and defensive reappraisal. They used the following statement to assess denial: "I refuse to believe what is happening." They measured defensive reappraisal by asking residents if they believed that "something good might come of this." Their results indicated that residents who look for the proverbial silver lining (defensive reappraisal) experienced less stress than those who tried to ignore the problem. Why didn't denial work? Figure 16.5 suggests one answer: The cooling towers outside the homes of residents are a constant reminder of the accident.

Natural Disasters: A Tornado Hits Xenia

It is commonly believed that disasters bring out the worst in people. However, contrary to popular opinion, individuals rarely panic, nor do they engage in antisocial activities such as looting and pillaging. (It is usually outsiders who try to take advantage of a community's vulnerability by looting.) It is true that a small number of individuals evidence what used to be called a *disaster syndrome*. Their initial response is shock and dazed behavior, which gives way to anxiety and obedient docility. But this response is limited to individuals who have lost a loved one, and it only occurs when a victim thinks that he or she could have done something to prevent the loss (Perry & Lindell, 1978; Vitaliano et al., 1987).

One of the best examples of the social effects of a natural disaster is provided by a tornado which swept through Xenia, Ohio, in 1974. More than a fifth of the houses in this working class town of 28,000 persons were destroyed. In its wake, the tornado left 33 dead and more than a thousand needing medical assistance (see figure 16.6). However, much to surprise of some, this disaster turned out to be "a mixed blessing." As Taylor (1977, p. 9) notes, a large proportion of

Figure 16.6
*A natural disaster.
Xenia, Ohio, after
tornado, April 3, 1974.*

the people living in Xenia "had *extremely positive reactions* to the disaster" (italics in original). For example, more than three-quarters of the residents reported that the experience had shown them that they could handle crises better than they had thought. A whopping 98 percent reported that they believed Xenia would be "a better place to live in the future as a result of the tornado." The disaster also strengthened community and social ties: More than a quarter of the people living in Xenia reported that they felt closer to their friends, and 28 percent said that their marriages had improved.

These perhaps surprising reactions can be understood in terms of the **shared stress hypothesis.** According to this hypothesis, individuals are more likely to engage in positive and affiliative behavior when they are facing a common threat, such as a hurricane or earthquake (Byrne et al., 1975; Rotton et al., 1978). Disasters are a powerful source of similarity, with everybody facing a common enemy. It has consistently been found that disasters bring people together. The first thing victims do is check with their neighbors to find out how others are reacting (Hoyt & Raven, 1973; Hansson et al., 1982). This is what social comparison theories and informational influence ideas would lead us to predict. Once they find that their experiences are not unique, survivors work together to help those whose distress exceeds their own. Later in this chapter, we shall describe how almost any stressor will increase liking when members of a group feel that "everybody's in the same boat."

Life Stressors

As we have seen, the detrimental effects of catastrophes and disasters are greatest when an individual has lost a loved one. The death of a spouse is one of several life stressors. Unlike cataclysmic stressors, which affect entire communities, **life stressors** are events we have to deal with as individuals. They can be defined as personal crises that require substantial amounts of readjustment (Dohrenwend & Dohrenwend, 1981).

Stressful Life Events

The scale in table 16.5 has shown up in articles with titles like "What's Your Stress Quotient?" and "Avoid Sickness—How Life Changes Affect Your Health" (Wolfe, cited in Kobasa, 1979). After going down the list of items and checking the ones that have occurred during the past two years, readers are told they can assess the likelihood of succumbing to physical illness by adding up the scores beside each item. The scores on the right on this scale are called *life change units*. They were derived by asking 400 individuals to rate each item in terms of the amount and duration of change it required (Holmes & Rahe, 1967). According to Holmes and Masuda (1974), you can rest easy if your total on their scale falls below 150 life change units; the probability of succumbing to a major illness is less than 4 percent. This number jumps to 37 percent if your score is between 150 and 199, 51 percent if it is between 200 and 299, and 79 percent if it is over 300.

Table 16.5 Social Readjustment Rating Scale

Rank Life event	Life change units
1. Death of Spouse	100
2. Divorce	73
3. Marital separation	65
4. Jail term	63
5. Death of a close family member	63
6. Personal injury or illness	53
7. Marriage	50
8. Fired at work	47
9. Marital reconciliation	45
10. Retirement	45
11. Change in health of family member	44
12. Pregnancy	40
13. Sex difficulties	39
14. Gain of new family member	39
15. Business readjustment	39
16. Change in financial state	38
17. Death of close friend	37
18. Change to different line of work	36
19. Change in number of arguments with spouse	35
20. Mortgage or loan for major purchase (home, etc.)	31
21. Foreclosure of mortgage or loan	30
22. Change in responsibilities at work	29
23. Son or daughter leaving home	29
24. Trouble with in-laws	29
25. Outstanding personal achievement	28
26. Wife begin or stop work	26
27. Begin or end school	26
28. Change in living conditions	25
29. Revision of personal habits	24
30. Trouble with boss	23
31. Change in work hours or conditions	20
32. Change in residence	20
33. Change in schools	20
34. Change in recreation	19
35. Change in church activities	19
36. Change in social activities	18
37. Mortgage or loan for lesser purchase (car, TV)	17
38. Change in sleeping habits	16
39. Change in number of family get-togethers	15
40. Change in eating habits	15
41. Vacation	13
42. Christmas	12
43. Minor violations of the law	11

Reprinted with permission from *Journal of Psychosomatic Research, 11,* T. H. Holmes and R. H. Rahe, "The Social Readjustment Scale," Copyright 1967, Pergamon Press plc.

Life change units are correlated with and predict physical illnesses, such as myocardial infarction and sudden death from heart attacks (Holmes & Holmes, 1970; Holmes & Masuda, 1974). As you might guess, psychologists have shown more interest in correlations between scores on life event questionnaires and psychiatric disorders (e.g., Dohrenwend & Dohrenwend, 1974; Vinokur & Selzer, 1975). Life change units are correlated with anxiety, depression, psychiatric admissions, and suicidal tendencies. Even grade point averages are lower when students accumulate a large number of life change units (Wildman, 1978).

However, studies that have used the scale in table 16.5 can be criticized for not taking the *meaning* of life events into account. For example, while most of us regard divorce as stressful, there are some who see it as the only way of solving the problem that is causing them distress. Even the death of a spouse can be seen as a blessing when one's husband or wife is suffering from an incurable or painful disorder, such as Alzheimer's disease (Thoits, 1983). There are a number of other problems with the life event questionnaires (Schroeder & Costa, 1984). For example, you may have noticed one of the items on Holmes and Rahe's (1967) scale is "personal injury or illness." But isn't this what we are trying to predict? Several other items on the scale could be symptoms of a physical ailment (e.g., sex difficulties, changes in sleeping habits). A considerable amount of effort has gone into devising scales that avoid these problems (e.g., Maddi et al., 1987; Sarason et al., 1978). Has this effort paid off? A recent study by Maddi and colleagues leaves little doubt that the answer is yes: Stressful life events do predict illness. One of the factors these investigators considered was desirability. You may be relieved to learn that desirable events, such as marriage and pregnancy, do *not* predict mental and emotional disorders (Suls & Mullen, 1981; Vinokur & Selzer, 1975).

Chronic Stress and Role Strains

It is easy to overestimate the effects of life events because they reflect commonly held stereotypes about what is and is not stressful. However, as Kessler and colleague (1985, p. 532) have observed, "the vast majority of people who are exposed to stressful life events do not develop emotional disorders." Correlations between scores on life event questionnaires and measures of psychological distress are usually low. This fact has led investigators to draw a distinction between acute and chronic stressors. The difference between the two can be appreciated by referring to "death of a spouse," which is always the first item on life event questionnaires. People sometimes faint when they hear that their spouse has died. This kind of news constitutes an acute stressor. It is followed by the chronic stress of learning to live alone. As this example suggests, *acute stressors* are)brief in duration, whereas *chronic stressors* persist for some time.

Individuals are remarkably resilient when it comes to brief or acute stressors. However, as Selye's work suggests, the effects of chronic stressors are usually debilitating (Baum et al., 1982; Fleming et al., 1984). For example, research has shown that most people get over the death of a spouse in 4 to 6 months (Clayton, Halikas, & Maurice, 1972). However, a careful study by Lehman and colleagues (1987) reveals that individuals continue to show serious signs of depression and grief (e.g., anxiety, hostility) three years after a spouse dies in an automobile accident. To take another example, being "fired at work" may be a frustrating and humiliating experience. However, a moment's thought should convince you that there is a world of difference between being fired and not having a job. Being fired is an acute stressor, whereas unemployment is a chronic condition.

It might be objected that retirement also ushers in a period of unemployment. Why then do most of us think that being fired is more stressful than retirement? The answer seems to be that "retired" is a respectable role in our society. Individuals don't blush when they say, "I'm retired." They do when they confess, "I'm unemployed right now." As you may have noticed, the most stressful episodes on life event questionnaires force individuals to accept roles that are not valued in our society. For example, the death of a spouse transforms a wife into a widow; imprisonment transforms a free citizen into a convict. These transformations place a tremendous *strain* on an individual's ability to adjust to the continued demands of chronic stressors (Pearlin et al., 1981). This strain is due, in part, to having to accept the undesirable roles that accompany unemployment ("bum"), poverty (shiftless and lazy), and hospitalization ("invalid").

Unemployment

One of the best predictors of well-being in the workplace is job security. Workers who lack security show much higher levels of distress than those who believe that their jobs are secure (Dooley et al., 1987). This correlation is consistent with what has been learned in recent years about the devastating effects of unemployment (e.g., Brief & Atieh, 1987; Kessler et al., 1987).

Several years ago, a sociologist, H. Harvey Brenner (1973), found that downturns in the economy were followed by increases in psychiatric hospital admissions. This correlation was strongest for men and individuals in their peak earning years. More recently, Brenner told a Congressional Committee that a 1 percent rise in unemployment is followed by a 1.9 percent increase in deaths (36,887 in all) from stress-related diseases over a six year period. Not everybody agrees with these estimates (Wagstaff, 1985). However, there can be little doubt that economic conditions are correlated with psychiatric problems, alcoholism, and suicide rates (Dooley & Catalano, 1984; Liem & Rayman, 1982; Stack & Haas, 1984).

Job Stress

It is hard to think of a more stressful job than monitoring and directing traffic into a major airport. Air traffic controllers have to contend with large amounts of information, which contributes to overload (see figure 16.7). At the same time, they know that their decisions can mean the difference between a safe landing and an event featured on the six o'clock news. Thus, it is not surprising that Cobb and Rose (1973) found that air traffic controllers were more likely to develop peptic ulcers than pilots and other groups on whom statistics were available. As this study's findings suggest, overload and responsibility contribute to stress in the workplace.

While a great deal of concern has been expressed for individuals (e.g., executives) who have to make difficult decisions, it is worth noting that many more workers have jobs that do not capitalize on their skills and talents. Ganster and

gure 16.7
*A stressful occupation.
Air traffic controllers
are at high risk for
ulcers.*

colleagues (1986) found that the best predictor of stress in one firm was *skill underutilization.* The fewer skills a job required, the more problems (e.g., depression, somatic symptoms) employees reported. This study's results also implicated role ambiguity and conflict as sources of stress.

Role ambiguity and conflict are usually assessed by having employees complete a 14–item scale developed by Rizzo and colleagues (1970). Individuals receive high scores on *role ambiguity* when they disagree with items of the following sort: "I know what my responsibilities are," and there are "clear, planned goals and objectives for my job." The following item taps *role conflict:* "I receive an assignment without the manpower to complete it." Scores on this scale have been found to predict somatic symptoms, psychological distress, and job dissatisfaction (Howard et al., 1986; Kemery et al., 1987). A recent study by Barling and Rosenbaum (1986) indicates that role ambiguity and conflict are also correlated with spouse abuse. These investigators found that men with high scores were more likely to be in a program for husbands who had abused their wives than men who reported high or low levels of satisfaction with their marriages.

Another consequence of job stress is **burnout.** According to Maslach (1982), the primary symptoms of this disorder are (1) emotional exhaustion, (2) low feelings of accomplishment, and (3) a tendency to treat patients or clients in an impersonal fashion (e.g., "the kidney in Room 609"). Maslach and Jackson (1984) have developed a 44–item inventory to measure these symptoms. Two of the items on their inventory are "I feel emotionally drained" and "I've become more callous toward people since I took this job."

As you may have guessed, burnout is most likely to be a problem for persons in the helping professions—social workers, teachers, physicians, lawyers, and police officers. Individuals typically enter these professions with zeal, high expectations, and a great deal of enthusiasm. They identify with their clients and believe they can help them. Their enthusiasm begins to wane when clients don't live up to their expectations. In time, disillusionment gives way to discouragement and cynicism, which leads individuals to set lower standards for themselves and their clients. Eventually, workers find themselves feeling alienated from their

Table 16.6 Items on the Hassles Scale

Hassle	Examples
Household	Preparing meals; shopping
Health	Physical illness; side effects of medication; concerns about medical treatment
Time pressure	Too many things to do; not enough time to do the things you need to do; too many responsibilities
Inner concerns	Being lonely; concerns about inner conflicts; fear of confrontation
Environmental	Noise; neighborhood deterioration; crime
Financial	Financial responsibility; concerns about owing money; responsibility for someone who doesn't live with you
Work	Job dissatisfaction; don't like current work duties; problems getting along with fellow workers
Future security	Concerns about job security; concerns about retirement; property, investments, and taxes

Abstracted from Kanner et al. (1981) and Lazarus et al. (1985).

jobs, worried about their health, and having family troubles because they take their problems home (Pines & Aronson, 1982; Russell et al., 1987; Shinn et al., 1984).

All of us have had days when everything seems to go wrong: First the clock doesn't go off when it should. Then, you can't find your keys. Next, the car won't start. These **microstressors** are not as severe as life stressors. However, what they lack in severity, they make up for in frequency. Because they are everyday occurrences, they've been termed *daily hassles* (Kanner et al., 1981; Lazarus, 1984). Kanner and colleagues report that, in terms of frequency, the top three hassles are "misplacing and losing things," "physical appearance," and "too many things to do." (Other hassles are listed in table 16.6.) Surprisingly, these investigators found that hassles do a better job of predicting depression and psychological symptoms than life events. DeLongis and colleagues (1982) obtained similar results when they looked at health and somatic symptoms: Apparent relations between life events and health vanished when they took hassles into account.

> You are not alone if you find it hard to believe that things like missed appointments and lost keys are more important than such major life events as divorce and unemployment. Dohrenwend and Shrout (1985) have pointed out that measures of hassles, like early life event scales, are confounded with existing symptoms of stress; that is, complaining about hassles may be a symptom rather than a cause of psychological distress. However, by using scales and procedures that avoid this problem, several investigators have found that hassles predict anxiety, depression, and somatic symptoms (Monroe, 1983; Nowack, 1986; Weinberger et al., 1987; Zika & Chamberlain, 1987).

Microstressors: The Little Things in Life

Why are we bothered by events that are so minor that we call them hassles? This question seems to have three answers. First, minor events take on added significance when we have other problems. It is one thing to find yourself stuck in traffic when you have plenty of time and are heading to the beach. It is something else when you are late for an important meeting. Kanner and colleagues quote a poem, by Charles Bukowski, that captures this view of hassles:

> It's not the large things in life that
>   send a man to the madhouse . . . .
> No, it's the continuing series
>   of small tragedies that send
>   a man to the madhouse
> Not the death of his love
>   but a shoestring that
>   snaps with no time left.

Second, hassles lead us to wonder if we are as competent as we would like to believe. It's easy to dismiss occasional hassles, such as losing one's keys. After all, "nobody's perfect." However, what if you discover that you have lost your wallet (another hassle) and forgot about an important meeting? You might begin to have doubts about your memory. As an aside, we should note that this point applies to stressful life events as well. We may be sympathetic when a friend gets a divorce, but we begin to wonder about our friend's ability to maintain intimate relationships when one divorce follows another.

Finally, it may have occurred to you that what makes a divorce stressful is the hassles it generates—hiring a lawyer, making a list of the family's assets, deciding who gets what and, if there are children, who will have custody. This view of hassles is consistent with results obtained by Eckenrode (1984) who found that most of the negative effects of stressful life events were mediated by hassles. For example, unemployment generates hassles, such as mailing out one's resume and dealing with creditors, which add to the strain of not having a responsible position in society.

Before we leave this topic, we would like to call your attention to an important difference between life stressors and hassles. There is rarely anything individuals can do to prevent or avoid major life events (e.g., death of a spouse, unemployment). However, there are ways to avoid and deal with hassles. Some of them are so obvious that we take them for granted—until we find them listed in books written for busy executives. They include disconnecting your phone when you have work to do and keeping a record of appointments. To take a more mundane example, if you are always losing your keys, you might follow a friend's lead: She bought a key ring that beeps when she whistles for it!

Ambient Stressors

Suppose you were asked to complete the following sentence: "A city is. . . ." What is the first word that comes to mind? Crowded? Noisy? Polluted? Noise, crowding, and air pollution are **ambient stressors.** They resemble hassles in that they do not place heavy demands on our ability to adapt. However, while hassles are discrete and usually unique events, ambient stressors are chronic or persistent conditions that affect everybody living in a community (Campbell, 1983). As a class, ambient stressors include heat, cold, and other weather conditions. "Everybody talks about the weather," we are told, "but nobody does anything about it." As this quote suggests, ambient stressors are typically accepted as intractable or beyond our ability to avoid and change (Jue et al., 1984).

Few stressors have received as much attention as population density. This probably stems from the fact that crowding conjures up images of getting caught in an elevator, locked in small rooms, and elbowed on subways (Epstein, 1982). A moment's thought, however, should convince you that there are also times when we're not bothered by high levels of density. For example—when we are enjoying a show in a crowded theater. Indeed, it is easy to think of times when a high level of density adds to our enjoyment. What would a sporting event be without the roar of a crowd? Would we enjoy parties and carnivals if they were not crowded? The obvious answer to these questions led Stokols (1972) to draw a distinction between population density (a physical condition) and crowding (a psychological state). Stokols defined **crowding** as the stress that *sometimes* accompanies high levels of population density.

Crowding and Population Density: A Sometime Stressor

As you probably know, density is a ratio that is obtained by counting the number of persons in a given amount of space. One way to vary density is to hold space constant while increasing the number of people in an area (e.g., four versus eight people in a room measuring 10 meters on a side). This is a manipulation of **social density** or group size. Another way to vary density is to hold group size constant and vary the amount of space in an area (e.g., four persons in a room that measures either 5 or 10 meters on a side). This would be a manipulation of **spatial density.** The reason we have drawn this distinction is that social density's effects are more detrimental and last longer than the effects of varying a room in size (Baum & Paulus, 1987). However, while there is good reason to worry more about the effects of social density, we would be remiss if we did not describe some of the intriguing results of studies that have looked at the effects of room size.

It may have occurred to you that it is hard to vary a room's size without forcing people to sit and stand close together. This suggests that the effects of spatial density might be due to violations of personal space. As we noted in chapter 15, close proximity is arousing (e.g., Nicosia et al., 1979; Walden & Forsyth, 1981). Building on the two-factor theory described in chapter 15, Worchel and Teddlie (1976) predicted that individuals would feel crowded if they attributed their arousal to the close proximity of others. This prediction received strong support. Worchel has, in a number of studies (e.g., Worchel & Brown, 1984; Worchel & Yohai, 1979), found that crowding is less when individuals are distracted and attribute their arousal to other factors, such as noise or an interesting movie.

Spatial Density: Make Room!

However, Worchel's two-factor theory does not explain why density is sometimes enjoyable. A theory that does so is the **density-intensity model.** Freedman (1975) has suggested that density intensifies initial predispositions. If you find yourself in a situation that elicits positive emotions (e.g., a theme park), density will increase your pleasure. However, if you find yourself in an unpleasant situation (e.g., standing in line), a high level of density will amplify your initially negative emotions. Freedman likens density to the volume control on a stereo. If you are listening to music you like, turning up the volume will increase your enjoyment; but if you are listening to a song you don't like, turning up the volume will make things worse. This model makes a great deal of sense. It has also received a considerable amount of support (Freedman et al., 1980; Morasch et al., 1979; Schiffenbauer & Schiavo, 1976).

The density-intensity hypothesis accounts for an interesting pattern of sex differences observed in studies that have varied room size. It has been found that males behave more negatively, competitively, and aggressively in small rooms than in large ones. This is what Freedman and colleagues (1972) had expected. However, these and other investigators (e.g., Epstein & Karlin, 1975; Leventhal & Levitt, 1979) found that females responded to high levels of density by behaving in a positive, affiliative, and accommodative fashion. How can we explain these reactions? Freedman answered this question by suggesting that men are predisposed to behave in an aggressive fashion, whereas women tend to be more affiliative than men. In Freedman's view, density intensifies these initial predispositions, leading men to behave more aggressively and women to behave in a more affiliative or accommodative fashion. Others have suggested that sex differences in this area stem from norms that govern the behavior of men and women (Karlin et al., 1976). This suggestion is supported by the fact that the usual pattern of sex differences is reversed when members of a group are given a competitive task (Marshall & Heslin, 1975). In this case, men seem to enjoy themselves (a form of "up-close fighting"), whereas women experience a considerable amount of discomfort.

Social Density: The Sometimes Maddening Crowd

While sex differences are observed in research on spatial density, it has been found that women as well as men respond negatively when they are surrounded by a large number of people. What follows is a brief summary of results obtained in research on social density. Hang on, we are going to "crowd" a lot of material into a small amount of space. First, as you might expect, individuals report that they feel annoyed, confused, anxious, and uncomfortable when they find themselves in densely populated settings (e.g., Evans, 1979; Griffitt & Veitch, 1971). Second, social density has negative effects on interpersonal attraction (e.g., Baron et al., 1976; Zuckerman et al., 1977). Indeed, earlier in this chapter, we noted that the mere *anticipation* of crowding causes tension and reduces liking. Third, high levels of density are physiologically arousing. The immediate effects of population density include increases in blood pressure, skin conductance, and heart rate (e.g., D'Atri, 1975; Evans, 1979). Fourth, these immediate reactions are followed by chronically higher levels of adrenalin secretions (Fleming et al., 1987; Schaeffer et al., 1988). Fifth, as Selye's work implies, there is a reliable correlation between the number of persons living in a dormitory and health complaints (Stokols et al., 1978; Weners & Keys, 1988). Stress-related illnesses and even death rates have been linked to crowding in penal institutions (Paulus et al., 1988).

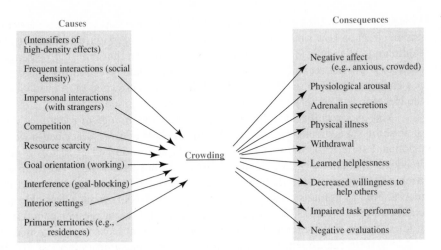

Figure 16.8
*Causes and
consequences of
crowding.*

Sixth, individuals are less likely to notice that another person needs assistance in densely populated settings (Cohen & Spacapan, 1978). This reduces helping and other types of prosocial behavior (Bickman et al., 1973; Jorgenson & Dukes, 1976). It has also been found that one of the most common ways of dealing with high levels of density is to withdraw and avoid social contacts (Baum & Koman, 1976; Baum & Valins, 1977; Ittelson et al., 1972). Finally, spatial as well as social density impairs performance on complex tasks, but the effects of social density are stronger than variations in roo   size (Paulus & Matthews, 1980; Paulus et al., 1976).

Figure 16.8 summarizes these effects, and also lists some of the conditions under which they are observed. The effects we have described are most likely to occur when: (1) individuals find themselves interacting with strangers rather than friends or acquaintances (McClelland, 1976; Rotton, 1987a); (2) interactions involve competition rather than cooperation, which usually occurs when resources are scarce (Smith & Connolly, 1977; Stokols et al., 1973); (3) individuals are working or studying as opposed to relaxing (Cohen et al., 1975); (4) one person gets in another's way and makes it difficult for him or her to accomplish a task (Heller et al., 1977; Sundstrom, 1975); (5) individuals are inside buildings or occupying primary territories, such as dormitories and family residences, rather than stores or public territories (Galle et al., 1972; Stokols, 1976). This last factor is worth emphasizing. It is the density inside a person's home rather than the number of people he or she meets in the neighborhood that predicts crime and other forms of social pathology (Rotton & Kimble, 1989).

Most of the effects we have described can be traced to two factors. One of them is **overload.** Referring again to chapter 2, you may recall that individuals experience overload whenever they have to deal with too many inputs (e.g., other people) in a short amount of time. The other factor is *perceived control*. Individuals are healthier, less likely to be depressed, and better able to tolerate frustration when they believe that events can be controlled (Rotton, 1983; Thompson,

*Conceptualizations
of Crowding*

Figure 16.9
Passengers who could reach the elevator's control panel did not feel as crowded as those without access to the buttons.

1981). Even something as minor as access to the button that controls an elevator has an effect on how well individuals cope with crowding. Figure 16.9 shows how Rodin and colleagues (1978) stationed confederates so that entering passengers could or could not reach the button for their floor. These investigators found that passengers who could reach the button didn't feel as crowded (and even viewed the elevator as roomier) than those who were kept from doing so.

You may recall that individuals experience *psychological reactance* when their ability to control events is threatened. In chapter 6, we described how this emotional state leads individuals to engage in actions aimed at restoring their freedom. What happens when these efforts are not successful? Wortman and Brehm (1975) suggested that reactance gives way to **learned helplessness:** Animals as well as humans give up when their actions fail to produce desirable consequences (Seligman, 1975). The strongest support for this suggestion comes from studies (Baum & Gatchel, 1981; Baum et al., 1978) that looked at the immediate and long-term consequences of dormitory design. The subjects in these studies were freshmen who had been assigned to one of two kinds of living arrangements. One was a corridor-style dormitory whose hallways made it difficult to avoid people living on the floor. The other was a cluster of suites, which placed a limit on the number of people that residents met when they left their rooms. As the diagrams in figure 16.10 show, students living in the corridor-style dormitory could meet any one of 30–33 neighbors, while those living in the suites rarely ran into more than four or five people. In an earlier series of studies, Baum and Valins (1977) had found that corridor residents felt more crowded than students living in the suites. For students living in the corridor-style arrangement, interactions with neighbors were frequent, unpredictable, and unavoidable.

During the first few weeks of the fall term, students living in the corridor-style dormitory tried to cope with crowding by organizing small groups on their floor. When these efforts failed, they retreated and tried to avoid social interactions. For example, they spent less time on the floor of their dormitory and kept their doors closed when they were in their rooms. This pattern of retreat generalized and affected the students' behavior in other settings. Using a game to assess competition and cooperation, Baum and Gatchel (1981) found that students living in the suites chose a cooperative style of play throughout the semester. By way of contrast, corridor residents began the semester by favoring competition over cooperation; however, after seven weeks, they reported that they did not care who won the game and chose, instead, a strategy that would allow them to avoid interactions by withdrawing from the game. Baum and colleagues concluded that the corridor resident's initially competitive style was indicative of psychological reactance, whereas their subsequent withdrawal and "giving up" were symptoms of learned helplessness.

Coping with Crowding

The research we have reviewed suggests several ways to reduce the effects of high-density living. For example, as we have seen, the detrimental effects of crowding are due to social rather than spatial density. This implies that it is better to increase the number of rooms in a building than it is to group individuals in single space, such as open-plan offices (see chapter 15). It has also been found

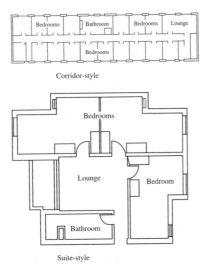

Figure 16.10
Two kinds of dormitories. Students living in corridor-style dormitories cope with frequent, unwanted, and avoidable interactions by spending less time in their residence and avoiding contacts with their neighbors.
(Baum & Valins, 1977.)

that crowding can be reduced by using doors to divide long corridors and painting walls a light color (e.g., Baum et al., 1974; Baum & Davis, 1980). Another factor that influences crowding is a room's shape (Desor, 1972). For example, it has been found that people are more likely to report that they feel crowded when walls are curved than when a room contains well-defined corners (Rotton, 1987a).

Of course, we rarely have much say about the design of the places we occupy. What can individuals do to cope with crowding in settings that others have designed? The research we have reviewed suggests you can avoid some of the negative effects of population density by getting to know the people with whom you interact, spending more time outside, and turning competitive situations into ones that involve cooperation and sharing. It has also been found that crowding is less when individuals form groups, which help members structure their interactions (Baum et al., 1975; Schopler & Walton, 1974). However, this only works when a group contains four or more people. It is almost always the case that a coalition forms when three students are crowded into a room that was designed to house two. Most of the negative effects of "tripling," as this living arrangement is called, occur when two roommates form a coalition, leading the one who is left out to feel like the proverbial third wheel on a date (Aiello et al., 1981).

Finally, it is worth noting that less crowding occurs when individuals receive information that lets them know that a setting is crowded and what to expect (Baum et al., 1981; Langer & Saegert, 1977). It appears that "forewarned is forearmed." Perhaps reading about the effects of population density, in this chapter, will help you cope with crowding and avoid that "hemmed-in feeling."

According to the Environmental Protection Agency, 70 million Americans live in neighborhoods where noise levels are high enough to interfere with communication and cause annoyance. Noise leads the list when residents are asked what they don't like about their neighborhoods (Cohen, 1981). But what is noise? Most

Noise: Sound Effects on Behavior

people would say a loud sound. It is true that there is a reliable correlation between a sound's intensity and the number of people that report that they are annoyed. Very few people object to sounds below 50 decibels (e.g., the hum of an air conditioner or refrigerator). Many more report they are bothered by sounds over 70 decibels (e.g., a vacuum cleaner). Nearly everybody is bothered by sounds over 110 decibels (e.g., a pneumatic drill). However, there is a lot more to noise than amplitude or intensity (Griffiths & Raw, 1987; von Gierke & Harris, 1987). For example, you may enjoy the music at a rock concert, although it is sometimes played at a level that could cause hearing loss (Dey, 1970; Lebo & Oliphant, 1968). But you would probably use the word "noisy" to describe a couple in a theater if their barely audible whispers kept you from enjoying a movie. As these examples suggest, one person's noise may be (and often is) another's music. It is for this reason that most investigators define *noise* as *unwanted sound*.

Health Effects

It has been estimated that more than 3 million Americans suffer from noise-induced hearing loss (Environmental Protection Agency, 1972). How can we be sure that this loss is caused by noise and not age? Rosen and colleagues (1962) answered this question by testing tribesmen who lived in a remote part of the Sudan, where sound levels rarely reached the level of the refrigerator in your home. Their tests revealed that individuals in this tribe did not lose their hearing as they grew older, while people in the United States did so.

Laboratory studies leave little doubt that loud, sudden, and unexpected noises are arousing. Loud noises cause people's hearts to beat faster, lead to higher levels of systolic and diastolic blood pressure, increase electrodermal activity (e.g., galvanic skin response), and raise levels of stress hormones (e.g., A. Cohen, 1977; S. Cohen et al., 1979; Kryter, 1972). However, most of these effects are short-lived (Cohen et al., 1986). It does not take individuals long to adapt to brief exposures of noise under laboratory conditions. But what happens when individuals are exposed to noise on a continuous or day-in-day-out basis? Studies conducted in factories indicate that cardiovascular and gastrointestinal disorders are more frequent in noisy than quiet factories (National Academy of Sciences, 1981). We should caution that these correlational results might stem from another factor, such as the danger of working in a factory whose machinery produces high levels of noise. However, similar results have been obtained in studies of people living near busy airports (Knipschild, 1977). For example, Cohen and colleagues (1980) found that children attending schools under the air corridor to the Los Angeles International Airport had higher systolic and diastolic blood pressure than students attending schools in quiet neighborhoods.

Aggression

Since noise is arousing, it is not surprising that several investigators have found that individuals behave more aggressively in noisy than quiet settings. However, this only happens after an individual has been insulted or watched a violent movie (e.g., Donnerstein & Wilson, 1976; Geen & McCown, 1984). In other words, noise-induced arousal does not cause individuals to behave aggressively, but it can strengthen initial response tendencies, as the model of excitation transfer (Zillman, 1988) suggests.

People living on noisy streets have fewer friends and are less likely to interact with their neighbors than people living on quiet boulevards (Appleyard & Lintell, 1972). However, it would be a mistake to conclude that noise was responsible for all the differences observed in this study. There is more traffic on noisy streets, which reduces the chances that a resident will walk across the street and get to know his or her neighbors.

More definitive conclusions can be drawn from studies that have manipulated noise levels. In one interesting study, Sauser and colleagues (1978) had undergraduate males play the role of a personnel manager who had to decide if an applicant should be hired. Half of the men in this study were exposed to loud (70–80 decibel) noises as they looked over each applicant's resume; the other half performed this task in a quiet (50–57 decibel) room. As you might guess, noise exerted negative effects on interpersonal evaluations. In fact, this study's results suggest that an applicant's starting salary will be $971 less if the person making the recommendation has to work in a noisy room. It has also been found that noise causes individuals to be more extreme and less differentiated (i.e., simpleminded) in their evaluative judgments (e.g., Rotton et al., 1979; Siegel & Steele, 1980).

However, there are also times when noise increases liking. How can this be? This question can be answered by referring to the *shared stress hypothesis,* which was mentioned in the section on natural disasters. Kenrick and Johnson (1979) obtained strong support for this hypothesis when they exposed women to loud (95 decibel) and raucous noises. Their subjects were given the task of evaluating two persons, one of whom they thought was also being exposed to noise. The other was described as a student who was not taking part in the experiment and would never be exposed to noise. From the graph in figure 16.11, you can see that the effects of noise depended on whether exposure was shared or not. Noise reduced liking when a subject thought that she was evaluating a stranger (i.e., "miserable people treat others miserably"). However, when the subjects thought that the other person was also being exposed to unpleasant noises, it increased liking (i.e., "misery loves company").

Interpersonal Attraction

Several investigators have found that noise reduces helping (e.g., Mathews & Canon, 1975; Page, 1977). Why doesn't this finding surprise us? "Well," you might say, "noise is annoying, and people are not going to go out of their way to help somebody when they're in a bad mood." However, it has been found that the effects of noise on helping do not depend on how a person feels (Yinon & Bizman, 1980). There are several other reasons why noise reduces helping. First, you may be so busy trying to get away from a noisy setting that you might not notice that somebody needs your help. Second, noise masks conversation. You are less likely to hear a request for assistance in noisy than quiet settings. But the most important reason appears to stem from the fact that noise is distracting. As overload theories predict, individuals pay less attention to social cues in noisy than quiet settings (Cohen & Spacapan, 1984).

Helping

Figure 16.11
*Effects of noise on
interpersonal
attraction. While noise
and other aversive
stimuli lead to
negative evaluations
of strangers, a fellow
sufferer's presence acts
as a negative
reinforcer, which leads
to more positive
evaluations.*
(Based on Figure 1 in Kenrick &
Johnson, 1979.)

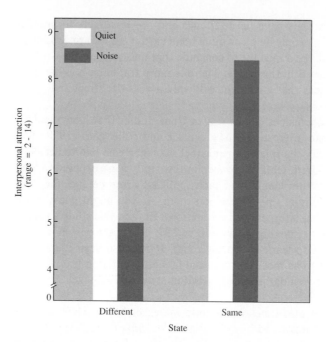

Thermal Stress:
A Heated
Controversy

There are some who believe that people living in warm climates move slower and are less energetic than people living in cool and cold climates. How valid is this belief? To find out, Rotton (1985) timed pedestrians as they walked 50 feet (a little over 15 meters) in warm and cool settings. Half of the pedestrians were observed in climate-controlled malls, where temperatures hovered around a comfortable 72° F, and the other half were observed in outdoor settings in Miami, Florida. Much to his surprise, Rotton found that people actually walked faster in the outdoor settings, where the temperature was an uncomfortable 82° F, than they did in the climate-controlled malls.

How can we account for these results, which run counter to common beliefs about the effects of heat? A moment's reflection suggests one answer: High temperatures are aversive. Most of the pedestrians in these studies were observed as they hurried to climate-controlled malls and air-conditioned automobiles. The faster they walked, the more quickly they would be able to escape the heat. However *pedestrian* these findings may be, they are consistent with our earlier remarks about "fight and flight" as being ways of coping with stress: People take steps (often very rapid ones) to escape conditions that threaten their well-being. However, Cannon's fight-or-flight reaction leaves us with a question: "When do people flee, and when do they fight?"

Baron and Bell (1975) answered this question by suggesting that moderately high temperatures produce emotional states (e.g., anger, irritability) that facilitate aggression, whereas high temperatures cause so much discomfort that individuals are more interested in finding a cool place to escape the heat. Because these are incompatible responses, Baron and Bell predicted that people engage

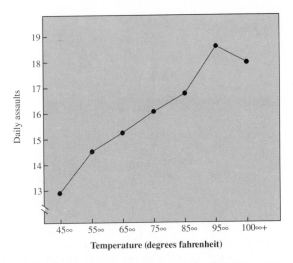

Figure 16.12
Ambient temperature and violent crimes. While laboratory studies suggest that very high temperatures reduce aggression, field studies have consistently found that more violence occurs on hot than warm days.
(Keith Harries, personal correspondence.)

in less aggression at high than moderately high temperatures. However counterintuitive this prediction may be, it is supported by results obtained in several experiments (e.g., Baron & Bell, 1976; Bell & Baron, 1976; Palamarek & Rule, 1979). On the basis of these results, Baron and Ransberger (1978) hypothesized that violent crimes reach a peak at moderately high temperatures (80–90° F) and then decline. From the data in figure 16.12, however, you can see this hypothesis has *not* been confirmed. For example, Harries and Stadler (1988) found that assault rates in Dallas, Texas, continued to rise after temperatures reached 90 degrees. There is a positive (and apparently linear) relation between outdoor temperatures and assaults, rapes, and other forms of violence and aggression in field settings (Anderson, 1989).

Despite the attention this topic has received, it is not clear why different results have been obtained in laboratory and field settings (Bell & Fusco, 1989). Rather than speculate, we will end this section by noting that research on heat and aggression is one of the "hottest areas" in social and environmental psychology. With several investigators pursuing this issue, it should not be long before someone comes up with an answer.

Air Pollution: Every Breath You Take

It might surprise you to learn that twice as many people die from breathing polluted air as are killed in automobile crashes each year. However, this estimate is based on a careful analysis of data on more than two million death certificates in a study that controlled for the effects of age, sex, marital status, population density, and geographical variations in temperature and rainfall. Mendelsohn and Orcutt (1979) concluded that air pollution accounts for more than 140,000 deaths each year—9 percent of all deaths in the United States.

Air pollution describes a number of sins—heavy metals, carbon monoxide poisoning, photochemical oxidants, and so forth. As a class, heavy metals include lead and mercury, which exert direct or neurological effects on behavior (Weiss, 1983). It is from the symptoms of mercury poisoning—headaches, convulsions, and uncontrollable tremors—that we get the phrase "mad as a hatter." Before

Figure 16.13
*Air pollution and
interpersonal
behavior. As this
diagram suggests, air
pollution exerts direct
and indirect effects on
behavior. The latter
are mediated by
negative emotional
states, such as
irritability and
annoyance.*
*(Based on material in Rotton,
1987.)*

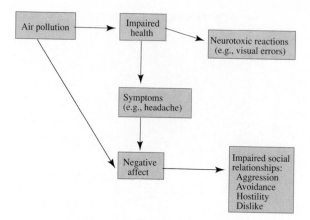

the turn of the century, haberdashers inhaled mercury vapors while they were curing animal pelts. However, as the model in figure 16.13 suggests, pollutants exert indirect as well as direct effects on behavior. Indirect effects can be traced to the annoying symptoms that pollutants cause: watery eyes, reduced visibility, a sore throat, inflamed nasal passages, and trouble breathing.

Social psychologists have developed sophisticated procedures for calibrating annoyance (Evans & Tafalla, 1987; Zeidner & Schechter, 1988). However, the task of linking air pollution to social behavior is much more difficult. For obvious reasons, investigators are reluctant to expose human volunteers to potentially hazardous chemicals (Rotton et al., 1982). One way to get around this problem is to use chemicals which are unpleasant but do not exert direct or neurotoxic effects. The chemicals that have received the most attention are malodorous pollutants, such as ammonium sulfide, whose rotten-egg smell you may recall from chemistry classes or the geysers at Yellowstone National Park. Research on maldorous pollutants suggest that their effects are similar to the ones observed in research on heat and noise pollution. For example, unpleasant odors reduce liking for others. However, as you might guess from research on noise pollution, this only occurs when individuals evaluate people they have not met previously. Unpleasant odors increase liking when individuals think that the person they are evaluating is also having to breathe polluted air (Rotton et al., 1978). To take another example, moderately unpleasant odors cause individuals to engage in aggressive behavior, but the effects of extremely unpleasant odors resemble ones observed in laboratory studies on heat and aggression. They cause so much annoyance that people try to escape the situation rather than engage in aggressive behavior (Rotton et al., 1979).

How general are these results? Are they relevant to the experiences of individuals living in cities who are more likely to complain about burning eyes, sore throats, and chest pains? To find out, Rotton and Frey (1985) tracked levels of real world pollutants and criminal behavior, in a midwestern city, over a two year period of time. They found that more assaults and family disturbances (a category that includes spouse and child abuse) occurred when pollution levels were high than when they were low. These results emerged from analyses that included statistical controls for day of the week, seasonal trends in violence, and a number of other factors, such as daily temperature and humidity levels. Similar results have been obtained in studies that have looked at psychiatric admissions. Pollution levels are correlated with psychiatric admissions and trouble with patients in mental institutions (e.g., Briere et al., 1983; Rotton & Frey, 1984).

We should caution that these findings are based on correlational data, which makes it difficult to rule out rival hypotheses. However, they are consistent with results obtained in a well-designed series of studies on the effects of smog in the Los Angeles basin (Evans et al., 1987; 1988; Jacobs et al., 1984). In one of these studies, Jacobs and colleagues found that perceived but not actual levels of photochemical oxidants predicted hostility and depression. This observation led Evans and colleagues (1987) to hypothesize that relations between air pollution and psychological symptoms would be stronger when individuals were facing other problems. This hypothesis received strong support. The principal element in photochemical oxidants (i.e., ozone) exerted few effects when individuals had low scores on a life events questionnaire; however, among those who had to deal with other stressors, high levels of ozone were associated with a variety of psychological symptoms (e.g., nervousness, depression, anxiety). Apparently, air pollution is not enough to precipitate a nervous breakdown, but a smoggy day may be "the straw that breaks the camel's back" when an individual has other problems.

Applications: Living with Stress

After reading about the causes and consequences of stress, you are probably wondering if there is any way to avoid the symptoms we have described. The following suggestions are based on findings reported in social psychological rather than clinical or psychiatric journals.

1. *Accept the fact that stress is a part of life.* It would be unfortunate if the reader came away from this chapter with the idea that stress is always bad. It isn't. As we noted, systemic reactions are adaptive. There is also some reason to believe that encountering stressors early in life is necessary for healthy development. That is, minor stressors serve the same function as weak attacks on our attitudes and beliefs (see chapter 7). Some stress may be necessary for immunological resistance (Aldwin & Stokols, 1988). Moreover, it is only by encountering threatening events (e.g., exams) that individuals can develop skills and traits, such as self-confidence, which will help them deal with the vicissitudes of life. This is another way of saying, "Nothing ventured—nothing gained." Life would be pretty boring, which is a symptom of stress, if there was no chance for failure (Martin et al., 1987).

2. *Ask for help.* After years of sometimes heated debate, there is now ample evidence that psychotherapy helps people deal with psychological problems (Smith et al., 1980). However, there is no evidence that one form of therapy is better than another: "Systematic evaluations of different kinds of counseling treatment

show that almost all of them are effective to some extent and no one of them is better than others" (Janis, 1983, p. 3; cf. Holland et al., 1981). Janis has suggested that social support accounts for most of the effects attributed to "talking cures" and groups (e.g., Alcoholic Anonymous) that help individuals overcome various kinds of addiction.

It is not entirely clear how social support helps people cope with stress (Jung, 1984). But one thing is certain: It is better to have one person you can count on than a lot of fair-weather friends (Levitt, in press). This conclusion is based on a study of elderly individuals living in a depressed area of South Florida. One of the groups of individuals in this study (Levitt et al., 1987) had outlived their spouses, relatives, and friends. It was this group's reactions that accounted for negative relations between social ties and problems: Those without social ties showed more signs of depression and dissatisfaction than those who had at least one important person in their lives.

3. *Count on companions.* Social support is one of the things we expect from friends; another is camaraderie or "companionship." Rook (1987) has defined *companionship* as the amount of time friends spend in leisure activities (e.g., dinner engagements, inviting friends for a game of cards). As part of a larger study, she found that social support helped people cope with major life events, such as loss of a loved one, but having a companion was more important when an individual had to contend with minor, everyday sorts of hassles. Rook suggests that companions help us keep things in perspective—very often by letting us know that we are taking ourselves too seriously. Think back to the last time you told a friend about something that was bugging you. In all probability, your friend responded with a joke that began, "You think you got problems. . . ."

4. *Lighten up!* There is ample evidence that laughter helps people cope with stress (e.g., Aiello et al., 1983; Nezu et al., 1986). Interest in the medicinal effects of laughter can be traced to a book by Norman Cousins (1979) who claimed that he overcame a crippling form of arthritis by taking a nightly dose of Marx Brothers comedies. However, studies by Lefcourt and Martin (1986) suggest that there is an important difference between appreciating and generating humor. It is one thing to be amused by a comedian (i.e., *humor appreciation*); it is another to come up with an amusing comment when things go wrong (i.e., *humor production*). Lefcourt and Martin found that individuals who could produce humor on demand (e.g., develop an amusing skit) showed fewer signs of stress than those who could not think of anything funny to say.

5. *Look on the bright side.* Why are children amused when they see a comic slip on a banana peel? The way we have phrased this question suggests an answer: Children derive a considerable amount of pleasure when an adult does something that they are too smart to do. Whether we like to admit it or not, we feel better about ourselves when we look down on others. This process has been called **downward social comparison.** The best way to be "one up" is to compare ourselves with somebody who is down (Wills, 1981). Downward social comparison explains the popularity of Pee-Wee Herman films and, unfortunately, some kinds of aggression and prejudice (see chapter 14).

However, this process does not always have to be destructive. For example, you have probably started to complain about things only to have a friend say, "Things could be worse." This comment is usually followed by a comparison with those who are less fortunate. Downward social comparison is one kind of *cognitive reappraisal.* As we have seen, the best predictor of whether an event is stressful or not is how you look at it. You will experience less stress if you can convince yourself that what appears to be a threat is actually a challenge. To illustrate, suppose that after several years of working for a firm you are transferred to an office in another city. This can be a threatening event ("Is the boss trying to get rid of me?"). It can also be viewed as an opportunity to discover what another city has to offer, make new friends, and even place yourself in a position where it is easier to climb to the top of the corporate ladder. It has been found that lawyers are healthier when they feel challenged by change than when they view it as a threat to their well-being (Kobasa, 1982).

6. *Work up a sweat.* Exercise is a challenge that a lot of us would rather not accept. It is easier to sit under a tree and watch somebody else work out. However, there is ample evidence that people who exercise are healthier than those who do not. For example, a study of Harvard alumni indicates that regular and vigorous exercise (2,000 or more kilocalories per week) adds about two years to one's life (Paffenbarger et al., 1986). But does exercise help people cope with stress? To find out, Kobasa and colleagues (1982) asked 137 businessmen how often they engaged in various forms of exercise. As you might expect, they found that men who exercised were healthier than those who did not. What is more important, the benefits of exercise were more pronounced when a man had to deal with a lot of stress on his job (see also Brown & Siegel, 1988). It has also been found that exercise increases a person's self-confidence and reduces depression (e.g., Brown & Lawton, 1986; Martinsen, 1987; McCann & Holmes, 1984). Thus, while more research needs to be done, enough is already known about the benefits of exercise to recommend it as a strategy for coping with stress.

7. *Learn to relax.* It has been found that individuals who describe themselves as having an easy-going disposition cope better than those who do not choose this descriptive label. Easy-going individuals are also less likely to be depressed and show signs of psychosomatic symptoms (Holahan & Moos, 1986; 1987). Of course, it is hard to take it easy when you have a problem and your world seems to be falling apart. Fortunately, several techniques have developed to help people learn to relax. The one that has received the most attention in recent years is *progressive relaxation.* It is accomplished by tensing groups of muscles (e.g. biceps, shoulders, neck) and attending to sensations as the muscles relax. Progressive relaxation has been found to be an effective technique for dealing with headaches, insomnia, hypertension (i.e., high blood pressure), and a number of other stress-related disorders (Feist & Brannon, 1988). It is worth noting that relaxation accounts for most of the effects attributed to meditation. In one study, for example, Holmes and colleagues (1983) compared the physiological reactions of highly trained mediators and individuals who were told to relax as best they could. Their measures included heart rate, respiration, and blood pressure. Not one of these measures revealed a reliable difference before, after, and during meditation (see also Holmes, 1984).

8. *Get some REST.* Lest you think we're repeating ourselves, we should note **REST** stands for *Restricted Environmental Stimulation Technique.* As the term implies, REST is accomplished by having individuals lie in a darkened, soundproof room for fairly long (12–24 hour) periods of time. As you may know, a few firms give individuals a chance to retreat by floating in tanks filled with an epsom salt solution of water (Forgays & Belinson, 1986).

   REST has been used to help individuals deal with high blood pressure, overcome phobic reactions, and lose weight (Borrie & Suedfeld, 1980; Suedfeld, 1984; Suedfeld & Clark, 1981). This has led some to suggest that the "T" in REST should stand for "therapy." This suggestion receives its strongest support from research that has looked at the effects of REST on addictive behaviors (Adams, 1988). Suedfeld and Baker-Brown (1986), for example, found that a brief (24–hour) REST session can produce a 55 to 86 percent reduction in the number of cigarettes individuals smoke. It is worth noting that this reduction persists. After twelve weeks, individuals who took part in brief sessions smoked fewer cigarettes than those who did not (Suedfeld & Ikard, 1973).

9. *Plan ahead.* It has been found that individuals show more signs of stress when events are unpredictable (Mineka & Hendersen, 1985). Probably the best way to avoid unpredictable events is to plan ahead. For example, if you are bothered by unexpected visitors, you might suggest that they are more likely to find you at home if they call first

(which is true). If you are bothered by a phone that rings when you have a job to do, you can disconnect it before you begin to work. To take another example, few things are as aggravating as getting stuck in traffic. Among the long-term consequences of traffic congestion are an increase in blood pressure and a reduction in one's tolerance for frustration (Schaeffer et al., 1988). One way to avoid this problem is to shift your work schedule: Leave for work before traffic begins to build up. Another way to avoid this stress, which requires *long-term* planning, is to find out which routes are most congested before you move into an apartment or buy a home. For example, if most of the traffic in your city runs along north-south routes, you would do well to find a home that is west or east of where you will be working.

10. *Don't put all your eggs in one basket.* This principle can be illustrated by considering the plight of two students. While one of them spends all of her time cramming for exams, the other is married, has children, belongs to civic groups, and plays a mean game of tennis. Who do you think would be devastated if she got a low grade in one of her courses? There are some who might argue that the second woman, who has several interests, is a prime candidate for burnout. As this argument goes, she has "spread herself too thin." However, a study by Linville (1987) suggests that the first woman's single-minded dedication to a single goal will cause depression and physical symptoms when she gets a failing grade. This woman is low on *self-complexity,* which can be defined as the sum of a person's roles, capabilities, and unique characteristics. She loses everything and, in a sense, defines herself out of existence if she gets a low grade. However, the second woman can say, "Well, I may not be much of a scholar, but I'm a good wife and mother. The world won't end if I have to drop out of school. I'll have more time to perfect my tennis game. Maybe I'll get good enough to enter a pro tournament." This student's reaction illustrates another trait— *dispositional optimism*—that seems to characterize individuals who are able to cope with adversity. It has been found that optimists are more likely to engage in problem-oriented coping, seek social support when they have a problem, and ignore the stressful aspects of social situations (Scheier & Carver, 1985; Scheier et al., 1986). Pessimists, on the other hand, run a greater risk of succumbing to illnesses (Peterson et al., 1988).

Two points should be borne in mind before you act on any of these suggestions. First, all of them involve risk. Second, when it comes to coping with stress, there is no strategy that works for all of the people all of the time. The first point can be illustrated by considering the benefits of exercise. "Work up a sweat" is good advice if you are healthy and have seen a doctor. It can be deadly if you have a heart problem. To take another example, although popular songs suggest that social support is a panacea, a lot of our problems are caused by the people we count on for social support (e.g., Pagel et al., 1987; Riley & Eckenrode, 1986). For example, drug addicts and juvenile delinquents get a lot of support from their friends. That's what gets them into trouble. As a final example, there are times when humor can add to your problems (e.g., when a state trooper pulls you over and asks if you know how fast you were going).

Our second point can be illustrated by referring to recent research on Type A behavior. This behavior pattern is characterized by a chronic sense of time urgency, a desire to control events, a competitive striving for achievement, and high levels of hostility and aggression. Early research suggested that Type A individuals could increase their chances of surviving a coronary by slowing down and learning to take it easy. This has given rise to therapeutic programs that consist of relaxation exercises and re-examining one's long-term goals (Haaga, 1987; Suinn, 1982). However, it is not a Type A's fast-pace and desire to get ahead that causes heart attacks. Recent studies suggest that it is only Type As who are hostile that end up in intensive care (e.g., Dembroski & Costa, 1987; Linden, 1987). The "A" in Type A does not stand for "achievement;" if anything, it stands for "anger." As research on Type As suggests, there is no universally applicable set of rules for dealing with stress.

Summary

Stressors are threatening or harmful events that trigger a process (called stress) that leads to attempts to adapt, overcome, and cope with adversity. It is customary to draw a distinction between the physiological and psychological effects of stressful stimuli, although the two are hard to separate. Systemic stress describes a whole-body reaction whose aim is to restore homeostasis. This reaction can be understood in terms of Selye's general adaptation syndrome, which consists of three phases or stages: alarm, resistance, and exhaustion. The psychological effects of stressors can be understood in terms of Lazarus's cognitive-phenomenological theory. According to this theory, individuals experience stress when they conclude that an event is a threat to their well-being (primary appraisal) and believe that it exceeds their ability to cope (secondary appraisal). The primary symptoms of stress are impaired performance, negative affect, physiological arousal, and elevated levels of stress hormones. Secondary symptoms are physical illness, nonverbal signs of tension, and undesirable forms of social behavior.

Cataclysmic stressors are powerful events that affect a large number of individuals, such as war, combat, technological catastrophes, and natural disasters. The long-term effects of war and technological catastrophes include a constellation of symptoms (the posttraumatic stress disorder) that reduces a soldier's ability to cope. These effects are less likely to occur when friends, relatives, and superiors provide social support. The effects of natural disasters are usually transient and, as the shared stress hypothesis predicts, include positive (e.g., affiliative) as well as negative behavior.

Life stressors are events of considerable severity whose impact is limited to a small number of persons. Events are most stressful when they are undesirable, persist for some time (chronic stressors), and cause role strain. The last includes role loss, ambiguity, and conflict in the workplace. It has also been found that workers are more likely to show signs of job stress and burnout when they feel their skills are not being utilized and their efforts are not appreciated.

Microstressors or daily hassles are frequent, annoying, and seemingly minor events. Although they do not require substantial amounts of adjustment, they can cause anxiety, depression, and physical symptoms when individuals are having to cope with other problems. There is some reason to believe that hassles are responsible for effects that are usually attributed to more serious life events.

Ambient stressors describe aversive and chronic conditions that afflict everybody living in a geographical area. This class includes population density, which is a necessary but not sufficient condition for individuals to experience crowding stress. It has been found that the effects of social density are more serious and last longer than the effects of room size or spatial density. Males but not females respond negatively to high levels of spatial density. Social density affects females as well as males. The long-term effects of social density or group size include chronically higher levels of stress hormones, physical illness, and withdrawal. The last of these effects is a symptom of learned helplessness. Social density also impairs performance on cognitive tasks, leads to negative evaluations of others, and reduces helping behavior. These effects are ameliorated when individuals believe there is something they can do to avoid and manage interactions in crowded settings. This belief has been termed perceived control. It also reduces the adverse effects of noise and other stressors.

Sounds are called noise when they cause hearing loss, interfere with conversation, and impair health. The social effects of noise include a facilitation of aggression, reductions in helping, and negative evaluations of other persons. Laboratory studies suggest that moderately high temperatures also facilitate aggression. However, for reasons which are not entirely clear, violence does not decline at high temperatures in field settings. Similar results have been observed in studies that have examined relations between air pollution, aggression, and violence.

Finally, there are several ways to cope with stressors. They include turning to others for social support, looking on the bright side, developing a sense of humor, learning to relax, and planning ahead. While these techniques are often effective, none of them is without risk.

Accessibility The ease with which an idea can be retrieved from memory.

Actor bias The tendency for people to overestimate the extent to which their behaviors are caused by external, situational factors.

Affective appraisals Assessments designed to measure individuals' subjective evaluations of environments.

Aggression Behavior committed with the intent to harm another living being physically or psychologically.

Altruism Unselfish motivation to do acts to benefit others; acts are sometimes at great cost to the actor and are done without expectation of gaining reward.

Ambient stressors Chronic or persistent conditions that affect everybody living in a community (e.g., air pollution).

Ambivalence State of mind in which a person may have positive and negative attitudes toward a group at the same time. It may make the person act in very different ways toward group members when circumstances are only slightly different.

Anchoring and adjustment heuristic The rule of thumb by which people make judgments which are influenced by their first (anchor) judgment. Bias occurs because people stick close to the anchor.

Androgyny Psychological trait of having many masculine and many feminine characteristics. Such persons may be simultaneously aggressive and warm or ambitious and compassionate.

Anonymity Type of privacy in which the person enjoys freedom from identification while in the presence of others—"lost in the crowd."

Archival research Investigations typically done on data that has been recorded by some organization before the individual investigator uses it.

Arousal model Theory about nonverbal behavior which suggests that a person will reciprocate or compensate for another person's actions depending on whether the other person's action elicits a positive or a negative emotional reaction in the individual.

Assimilation Process by which divergent groups are incorporated into the dominant culture. Some groups may have to sacrifice their distinctive qualities in the process.

Attachment The type of bond an infant forms with its mother during the infant's second year (1–2); attachment between primary caregiver and child can be secure, anxious/ambivalent, or avoidant.

Attitude A positive, negative, or neutral evaluative judgment about an object of thought, such as a person, group, event, or issue.

Attraction One person's positive or negative attitude toward another person.

Attribution Process by which we infer causes of events and behavior.

Audience Any person or persons who observe the actions of another.

Augmentation The tendency to attribute greater causal impact to a particular facilitating cause of an event or behavior when inhibiting forces are present.

Authoritarian personality A rigid, dogmatic type of personality. Authoritarian people are prone to display anti-Semitism and other types of ethnic prejudice.

Availability heuristic Assessment of the probability that an event occurs by using the ease with which instances of that event can be brought to mind as the basis for judgment.

Aversive racist A prejudiced person who acts very subtly in expressing animosity toward a racial group; such a person is likely to avoid members of the race and act "proper" but distant in interactions with them.

Backchannel responses Listener's responses supportive of the speaker which are not active attempts to take the floor. Typical back-channel responses are smiles, nods, and verbal agreements.

Balance theory Cognitive consistency theory which states that a person tries to achieve and maintain balance or consistency in the sentiment and unit relations perceived among oneself and persons and entities in the psychological environment.

Basking in reflected glory The tendency to identify with a winning sports team, entertainer, or famous person with whom we are remotely associated.

Behavioral self-handicapping The act of putting oneself at a disadvantage before a threatening event occurs to avoid negative attributions about oneself.

Behavioroid measure A measurement procedure related to behavior in that the subjects are asked to commit themselves to do certain behaviors, which subjects are never actually required to do.

Behavior settings The particular social/physical situations in which people regularly conduct programs with an agenda, functions, and roles to be executed. Behavior settings can be undermanned (having too few people to execute the program of events smoothly), optimally manned, or overmanned (having more people than needed).

Belief A nonevaluative thought about characteristics of an object of thought such as a person or group.

Bogus pipeline Technique investigators use to make subjects believe that they know ("have a pipeline into") their most secret attitudes so that subjects will respond honestly to attitude questions.

Brainwashing Indoctrination procedures in which the indoctrinators have virtually total control over their recruits' outcomes, and they use that control to effect drastic changes in their attitudes and values.

Burnout A condition common among helping professionals characterized by emotional exhaustion, low feelings of accomplishment, and impersonal treatment of clients.

Bystander effect The tendency for individuals to help less when other bystanders are present than when they are alone.

Cataclysmic stressors Powerful stressful events that affect large numbers of people (e.g., combat, tornadoes).

Catharsis A reduction in aggression-producing tension by expressing one's aggressive urges symbolically or directly; unfortunately, such expression of hostile urges does not reduce subsequent aggression.

Central route persuasion Persuasion that occurs when the receiver attends to the logic of the arguments in the message.

Classical conditioning A type of learning by which originally neutral stimuli or events can elicit strong emotional responses after they have been paired (and associated) with pleasant or unpleasant stimuli.

Coactors People who are doing the same thing at the same time as a performer. Coaction does not necessarily imply competition.

Cognitive dissonance theory Theory that we experience tension whenever we hold two ideas simultaneously which are inconsistent with each other, and that we are motivated to reduce or avoid this tension or dissonance.

Communication The process wherein a sender enacts or encodes a message and a receiver decodes or understands it.

Comparison level A standard derived from the person's past experiences by which a person evaluates the attractiveness of a relationship; if relationship outcomes are higher than the CL, the person will be satisfied with the relationship.

Comparison level for alternatives The lowest level of relationship outcomes a person will accept based on his or her current alternative opportunities; if relationship outcomes fall below comparison level for alternatives, the person will leave the relationship.

Competition Individuals or groups working against each other to win a contest or to achieve a higher status than one's opponents; usually involves situations where there is ranking of performances or determining a winner and a loser.

Compliance Initiation or change of behavior in response to direct requests. Behavior done to satisfy demands of a powerful other without any underlying attitude change.

Conditional approval Type of approval given when the person has to perform up to certain standards to receive it; regard is *unconditional* when the person receives approval regardless of how the person performs.

Confirmatory hypothesis testing A bias in cognition in which we tend to look only for information that will confirm, rather than disconfirm, our ideas.

Confluence model Theory to explain how family constellation factors such as family size and birth position are related to the family intellectual environment and intelligence.

Conformity   Initiation or change in behavior produced by the implicit pressure of other people's actions.

Contact cultures   Cultures where interactions have high levels of intimacy or physical closeness (e.g., Arab, Latin American, and southern European); *noncontact cultures* are more restrained in interactions (e.g., Oriental, American, and northern European).

Contact hypothesis   The idea that prejudice between groups can be reduced by involvement of minority and majority group members together in activities having equal status contact in the pursuit of common goals.

Content rewards   Particular kinds of responses a person can make in an interaction which will be pleasing to the other person and increase attraction to the actor.

Contingency model of leadership   A theory of leadership which indicates that group effectiveness depends on the leader's person or task orientation and situational factors including task structure, leader position power, and leader-group relations.

Cooperation   Individuals or groups working together to achieve a common goal; usually involves situations in which participants' outcomes are linked.

Coping   Cognitive and behavioral efforts aimed at managing conditions which tax or might exceed our resources; *problem-focused coping* is aimed at rectifying the problem condition, while *emotion-focused coping* is aimed at controlling our emotional reaction to the problem.

Correlational studies   Procedures in which investigators measure independent variables as they naturally occur, and subjects place themselves in different correlational conditions by how they respond to particular items or by their personal attributes.

Correlation coefficient   A statistic for determining whether two variables vary together (are related). The higher the absolute value of the number, the stronger the relationship.

Correspondence   In attribution theory, the degree to which one can infer a direct relationship between an observable behavior and an unobservable trait or disposition. It is affected by the *social desirability* of the act and the number of *noncommon effects* it has.

Counterfactualizing   The process of imagining how things could have been otherwise; a type of simulation heuristic.

Covariation principle   The method most people use to infer whether a person, stimulus, circumstance, or a combination of elements caused a particular event or behavior. *Covariation* between a behavior and one of the causal elements is determined from the consensus, distinctiveness, and consistency of the act.

Critical mass   A number of people with common interests in an activity adequate to sustain the activity. Cities provide more critical masses for more activities.

Crowding   Stress reaction that sometimes results from being in high population density conditions.

Cue similarity   A factor in impression formation that exists when someone looks or talks like a person the perceiver has known in the past.

Cultivation effect   The effect of heavy television viewing on viewers' perceptions of the world as a meaner and more dangerous place.

Cultural racism   Racial prejudice manifested in the failure by individuals and groups to recognize the cultural contributions of particular racial and ethnic groups.

Daily hassle   A minor but frequent, frustrating, and annoying event. Hassles are also called *microstressors.*

Debriefing   The session after dependent measures have been collected when the experimenter explains the study to the subject, answers questions, assures the subject of confidentiality, and puts the subject at ease about the experience.

Defense mechanisms   Means by which aggressive and other undesirable impulses are given different, more acceptable forms of expression (e.g., displacement and sublimation).

Defensible space   Semipublic or secondary territory under the control of residents because it affords adequate surveillance opportunities over entry into the area.

Deindividuation   A state of consciousness in which a person has low awareness of self, feels others are unaware of him or her, and feels little responsibility for one's actions; it is produced by the presence of many people, hectic activity, and minimal surveillance of individuals by an audience.

Demand characteristics   Cues in the experimental situation that may enable subjects to infer the hypothesis. Investigators try to minimize them.

Density-intensity model   The idea that high density conditions intensify or magnify our initial predispositions, whether they are positive or negative.

Dependent variable   *See* hypothesis.

Diffusion of responsibility   Perception that one is less obligated to help when several other people who could also help are present; opposite of *concentration of responsibility.*

Direct speech   Statements in which the sentence meaning is consistent with what the speaker wants to accomplish (e.g., "Get me a glass of lemonade.").

Discounting In attribution, the tendency to downplay the importance of a potential cause of a behavior to the extent that other potential causes of that behavior are also present.

Discrimination Behavior by a person or institution which produces unfavorable outcomes for a person based on that person's group membership.

Dominative racist Prejudiced person who overtly and even aggressively discriminates against members of a racial group.

Door-in-the-face technique Influence approach in which the influencer makes a demanding proposal, has it rejected, and then makes a more modest proposal. The second proposal is more likely to be accepted than if no outlandish proposal had been made.

Downward comparison theory Theory which states that people feel better when they can compare themselves to "inferior" others.

Elaboration Likelihood Model A theory of persuasion which states that whenever a person is able and motivated to fully consider the issue-relevant arguments in messages, the person will be persuaded by logical arguments.

Empathy An emotional reaction to the suffering of another person such that one feels compassionate or touched by the other's plight; this distress for the other produces altruistic motivation to help.

Emotional leakage When a person's nonverbal actions betray an emotional state that the person may wish to hide.

Environmental perception The study and measurement of how people apprehend and experience their surroundings.

Environmental psychology The study of reciprocal relations between the physical environment and human behavior.

Equilibrium theory An approach to nonverbal behavior which suggests that people like to maintain a stable level of implied intimacy in their interpersonal acts and that they will compensate for departures from that equilibrium level.

Equity theory Theory that people like to maintain equality between their outcomes/inputs ratio and the O/I ratio of others. Inequality between ratios implies an unfair condition exists and people are motivated to reduce such inequities.

Ethnocentrism Bias in favor of one's group such that the person holds up his or her own group as the standard for evaluation of proper conduct and thought.

Ethology The biological study of the behavior of animals in their natural habitat with an emphasis on instinctive behavior.

Excitation transfer The process by which arousal from one event energizes and causes stronger reactions to unrelated stimuli; it is how unrelated arousal intensifies aggressive responses.

Experimental realism A term describing the extent to which the procedures of a study actively involve the subject so that they have impact upon the subject's thoughts and actions.

Experiments Studies in which investigators manipulate levels of independent variables and randomly assign subjects to the different conditions.

False consensus effect In attribution, the tendency to assume that others share our beliefs, values, and preferences in the absence of evidence—"everyone thinks like I do."

Fear of success A reaction thought to be more prevalent in girls and women which occurs because others' expectations and their own internalized expectations create conflict for females between being feminine and achieving success.

Femininity Psychological trait of having many characteristics associated with females. Some feminine characteristics are cheerfulness, compassion, warmth, and understanding.

Field studies Investigations conducted anywhere people are doing their normal activities, unaware that they are being studied.

Filled pauses Speech disturbances between meaningful words or statements which may or may not contain the sound "ah." They fill periods of silence.

Foot-in-the-door technique Influence approach in which a person is asked to do a small favor first and then is asked to do a more costly favor. The person is more likely to agree to the costly favor if it was preceded by the small one.

Free-rider effect Loafing or reduced effort that occurs when a performer decides that he or she can depend on a co-performer's efforts to attain good outcomes for the group.

Frustration The blocking or thwarting of an individual from attaining a goal, which motivates aggressive acts; it is sometimes produced by a discrepancy between one's outcomes and what that individual expected to receive.

Fundamental attribution error Inaccurate judgment in which people overestimate the extent to which a person's behavior is determined by the person's characteristics.

Galatea effect The influence of the actor's self-expectations on the actor's performance.

Gambler's fallacy Gamblers' belief that their luck will change, that things will even out based on the erroneous assumption that the previous pattern of outcomes (the bad luck streak) affect the probabilities on the next play.

Gender roles Social roles applied to persons based on their gender, which affect males' and females' behaviors. The female role emphasizes communal qualities; the male role, agentic qualities.

Gender schemas Persons' beliefs about how male and female persons think and act.

General adaptation syndrome (G.A.S.) The sequence of bodily reactions to noxious stimuli consisting of (1) the alarm stage including shock and countershock; (2) stage of resistance when the body tries to recover; and (3) the stage of exhaustion when some bodily systems may collapse.

GRIT (graduated and reciprocated initiatives in tension-reduction) International conflict reduction proposal which states that a nation should make a minor concession first; and if it is reciprocated by the opposing nation, make larger and larger concessions until conflict de-escalation is achieved.

Group Any collection of people who are aware of each other's presence and interact enough to have influence on each other's thoughts and actions.

Group polarization The fact that individuals adopt a more extreme position in the same direction after engaging in group discussion than the position they held before.

Groupthink The tendency in some groups for members to conform to the prevailing opinion and rush to a premature decision without due consideration of alternative courses of action.

Helping Action taken that improves the welfare of another person.

Heuristics Rules of thumb or mental shortcuts commonly used to simplify the process of making judgments; they sometimes lead to errors of judgment because they are too simple.

Hindsight bias The tendency to overestimate the probability that one would have correctly *pre*dicted the correct outcome after the outcome has occurred—"I knew it all along."

Homogamy The practice of marrying an individual who is similar to oneself in terms of race, religion, social class, income, etc.

Hostile aggression Destructive acts that occur because a person is irritated and wants to harm another person.

Hypothesis An investigator's statement beforehand about how one factor (an independent variable) will affect another factor (a dependent variable).

Identification Process in which one adopts a behavior or attitude because some person or persons whom the actor admires displays that behavior or attitude.

Illusory correlation The tendency to overestimate the degree of association between two variables, to think that they are more closely related than they are.

Immediacy Nonverbal actions that imply involvement in interactions—close distance, high eye contact, forward lean (if seated), face-to-face orientation, and pleasant facial expression. Closeness in social impact theory.

Implicit personality theories An individual's ideas about what personality traits are likely to appear in the same person.

Impression formation The process by which perceivers make judgments about actors' characteristics.

Inclusive fitness An index of how successful an individual is in perpetuating his or her genes in future generations; it includes the number of offspring of the individual and of one's close and distant kin.

Independent variable *See* hypothesis.

Indirect speech Statements in which the speaker's intent is not obviously presented in words the speaker is saying.

Informational influence Process in which the individual examines others' behavior for information about the present situation and acts in accordance with the judgment made from the observation.

Information integration theory Description of how a perceiver processes information in a weighted averaging manner. It is important in impression formation.

Ingratiation The strategic use of social actions intended to be rewarding to the recipient and increase attraction to the actor; these actions are considered illegitimate because the actor has the ulterior motive of gaining favor.

Innovation Conflict resolution occurring in favor of a position taken by a minority of the group.

Inoculation theory Theory that exposing a receiver to weak, refutable arguments for a topic will make that receiver more resistant to persuasion on the topic.

Instinct Biological programming of the animal that manifests itself in inflexible behavior whenever an adequate triggering stimulus is present. Biologically based urges for death (thanatos), sex (eros), and preservation (ego).

Institutional racism Discriminatory practices by social institutions that create disadvantage for members of a particular race.

Instrumental aggression Destructive acts which occur when the actor is motivated to attain some other goal; such aggression is a cold-blooded means to achieving some end.

Internalization Process in which a person adopts a behavior or attitude because it is consistent with one's existing network of attitudes and values; synonymous with *incorporation.*

Intimacy Type of privacy in which a few people enjoy each other's company in a private setting.

Intrinsic motivation The amount of interest a person has in doing an activity for the rewards or enjoyment of the activity itself.

Kinship altruism Action taken to benefit others who are genetically related to the individual; it is not altruism in the strictest sense of the word. According to sociobiologists, it is motivated by the desire to perpetuate one's genes in future generations.

Labeling effect The influence of preliminary expectations about an actor on the way that a perceiver interprets subsequent behavior of the actor.

Laboratory study Investigation in a place arranged by the investigator for this particular study and in which the subject is aware that his or her actions or thoughts are being examined.

Learned helplessness Inactivity or unresponsiveness in an individual acquired through repeated failures to control personal outcomes in particular situations.

Least-preferred-coworker (LPC) measure A technique used in research on the contingency model of leadership designed to determine if the leader is interpersonally- or task-oriented. A high LPC score means the leader is interpersonally-oriented.

Life stressors Stressful events or conditions in one's life that may constitute personal crises that require substantial readjustments (e.g., divorce, job loss).

Limbic system The area in the brain where pleasure and pain sensations originate.

Limerence Intense feelings for a loved one and great need for the loved one to reciprocate those feelings.

Loneliness Sadness from being unable to establish close relationships, from being unable to communicate to close ones, or from being away from loved ones.

Low-ball technique Influence approach in which a person gains commitment from a customer to do something and then increases the costs of the action. If commitment is gained before the increase in cost, the customer is more likely to comply.

Masculinity Psychological trait of having many characteristics associated with males. Some masculine characteristics are dominance, self-confidence, and aggressiveness.

Matching hypothesis The idea that people are likely to seek and be attracted to someone who is roughly equal to them on the sum of several social attributes for a mate.

Microstressors Low severity stressful events in a person's life or "hassles" that take a toll if there are enough of them (e.g., losing things, car problems).

Misattribution therapy An approach to treatment which emphasizes that it is often beneficial to get the client to attribute problem thoughts and behaviors to external causes rather than internal causes.

Noncommon effects *See* correspondence.

Noncontact cultures *See* contact cultures.

Normalization Conflict resolution in which all parties move gradually to a consensus position.

Normative influence Process in which an individual acts as others do to gain the approval or avoid the disapproval of group members.

Norm of reciprocity The expectation in many societies that a person should repay an action done to or for him or her with an act of similar quality and magnitude; the idea that one should do unto others as they have done unto you.

Obedience Initiation or change of behavior in response to commands by an authority.

Observational learning The process by which a person's behavior may be changed after seeing another person perform a behavior the observer is capable of imitating.

Observer bias The tendency for people to overestimate the extent to which another person's behavior is caused by internal or dispositional characteristics of that other person.

Open plan concept Office or school design characterized by the absence of interior floor-to-ceiling walls.

Operant conditioning The process of change in an individual's behavior that occurs when actions of that individual are followed by *reinforcement, punishment,* or no action.

Operational definition Statement of what concrete measures or techniques are going to be used to determine levels of variables, typically described in the method sections of empirical articles.

Opinion conformity An ingratiation tactic by which a person seeks to endear oneself to a target person by agreeing with that person on issues.

Opponent process theory Motivational theory which states that when one emotional reaction starts, the body initiates an opposing physical response that makes the individual experience the opposite emotion after the first one.

Other enhancement An ingratiation tactic by which a person seeks to endear him- or herself to a target person by complimenting that person or commenting on his or her positive qualities to others.

Other-total ratio In self-attention theory, the number of people present who are not aligned with the target person divided by the total number of people present. The higher the O-T ratio, the greater the self-attention the target person experiences.

Overload Condition existing when there are too many objects, people, and events bombarding a person's senses for him or her to process everything.

Paralanguage Features of communication that are noncontent aspects of speech which occur with the verbal content. It is how statements and questions are made.

Passion cluster Qualities of love that differentiate it from friendship: sexual desire for partner, fascination about partner, and exclusiveness of the relationship.

PEQI's Measurement techniques in environmental psychology used to obtain subjective perceptual-cognitive appraisals of environments.

Peripheral route persuasion Persuasion that occurs when the receiver is unduly affected by issue-irrelevant factors, such as attractiveness of the source.

Perseverance effect The tendency to stick to a belief that has been disconfirmed.

Personalization The act of decorating or otherwise marking an area as a means of expressing one's identity.

Personal space Interpersonal distance zones around a person in which certain kinds of interactions are ordinarily and comfortably conducted.

Persuasion A form of social influence in which overt attempts are made to change another person's attitudes or behavior.

Physical attractiveness stereotype The belief that "what is beautiful is good"; that people who are attractive in appearance have other positive personal qualities.

Place attachment The emotional bonds we form for the places we inhabit.

Place identity The sense of identification we experience with places we have experienced; some places become part of our self-identities.

Pluralism A system in which power is equally divided among all involved groups.

Power The ability to influence others by means of rewards, coercion, recognized legitimate status, recognized expertise, or others' respect and admiration.

Powerful speech A way of speaking which is characterized as straightforward and succinct with no excess words.

Powerless speech Employs many qualifying words, such as intensifiers, hedges, and hesitation forms.

Prejudice An attitude by which one judges individuals based on their group membership rather than personal qualities; such an attitude exists before meeting the individuals to which it is applied and is resistant to change.

Primacy effect Influence on memory or persuasion whenever the first-presented message has the greatest impact; the *recency effect* is when the last-presented message has the greatest impact.

Primary appraisal An assessment of how much of a threat a particular situation or condition poses to one's well-being conducted before deciding how to cope with it.

Primary territory An area with relatively permanent features that is central to occupants' lives and over which they exert a high degree of control (e.g., home).

Priming Systematically exposing people repeatedly to judgment-relevant information about evaluation objects in order to affect ideas that the persons have in memory.

Privacy The process of selectively controlling access to one's self and/or one's group.

Process rewards Positive events or actions that occur naturally within interactions and serve to cement the relationship between the interactants.

Proxemics The study of how people use and are related to space.

Psychosexual stages Eras in a child's development in which *oral* sensations are most important to development first; later, *anal*-related and *phallic* or genital-related experiences are primary.

Public territory An area which people occupy only on a temporary basis, which is not central to their lives and over which they exert very little control (e.g., library).

Random assignment A procedure used by investigators in assigning subjects designed to assure that the different experimental groups are equivalent before the independent variables are introduced.

Reactance theory Theory which states that when a freedom that a person currently has is threatened or eliminated, that person will come to value the freedom to do that activity more.

Realistic group conflict theory
Theoretical position which states
that when members of different
groups are in competition with
each other for resources, prejudices
are likely to develop between the
groups.

Reciprocal altruism Helping an
unrelated individual with the
expectation that the benefited
person will return the favor in the
future. It is not altruism in the
strictest sense because it is
motivated by the desire to receive
more help later.

Reference group A collection of
people with whom one identifies
and whose standards and values
one adopts.

Regret In dissonance research, a
reaction occurring right after
making a decision characterized by
devaluing the chosen alternative
and valuing the unchosen
alternative more.

Representativeness heuristic The rule
of thumb that someone or
something is a member of a
category if it has the essential
features of the typical member of
that category. It produces bias if
the features considered are not
defining features of the category.

Reserve Type of privacy in which one
withholds information about one's
self and one's thoughts through the
use of verbal or nonverbal
messages, usually in public
settings.

Roles Positions or statuses most
people believe should be enacted or
fulfilled in particular ways.

Scapegoat Any person or group who
is the target of displaced hostility
because of their accessibility and
position in society.

Schemas Knowledge structures about
elements in our environments.

Scripts Patterned sequences of
behavior people display when they
recognize certain cues in their
immediate environment.

Secondary appraisal An assessment
of one's physical, psychological,
and social resources for dealing
with problems, which one conducts
when faced with a stressful
situation.

Secondary territory An area people
occupy on a temporary but regular
basis, which is central to the lives
of regular occupants, and over
which occupants have only
unofficial control (e.g.,
neighborhood park).

Self Two sets of personal features of
individuals: (1) how the person
interacts with his or her
environment and the people in it;
(2) how the person evaluates him-
or herself.

Self-adaptors The act of touching
one's own body with hand or
hands; this self-touching is
associated with anxiety.

Self-attention theory A theory about
the influence of a group on an
individual depending on how much
the group's presence makes the
individual focus on him- or herself;
the greater the self-attention, the
more responsibly the individual
behaves.

Self-attribution The cognitive
process by which we evaluate our
motives, abilities, and
performances; and by which we
understand why others treat us the
ways they do.

Self-awareness A temporary state of
consciousness wherein the
individual's attention is focused on
the self.

Self-complexity The extent to which
a person conceives him- or herself
as having few or many
independent or unrelated aspects.

Self-consciousness A term indicating
the amount of time a person
typically directs his or her
attention toward the self.

Self-disclosure The revealing of
personal information to another
person.

Self-discrepancy A theory which
relates one's self-cognitions to
different kinds of emotional
vulnerabilities.

Self-efficacy A person's belief that
he or she can master situations and
control events in particular
performance domains.

Self-esteem How one feels about
oneself in terms of being able to
succeed at important activities,
liking oneself, and feeling liked by
others.

Self-fulfilling prophecy The effect on
one person's behavior of another
person's expectations and beliefs
about that person; it occurs when
the expectations are communicated
to the target through climate,
feedback, input, and output.

Self-identity The description of
features of the person that are
important to the person; aspects of
the person that the person wants to
claim.

Self-monitors People who are
sensitive to social cues and control
and adjust their behavior from
situation to situation.

Self-perception theory A position
stating that we infer our attitudes
from considering our past
behaviors toward the attitude
object and the circumstances under
which the behaviors were done.

Self-presentation Acting in a way
that makes oneself appear
attractive to an audience; also
called *impression management*.

Self-reported handicaps Claims that
problem conditions or states of
mind exist and are hindering one's
performance in order to avoid
negative attributions about oneself.

Self-serving bias In attribution, the
tendency to see internal causes for
successes and to see external,
nonpersonal causes for failures.

Shared stress hypothesis The
proposition that individuals are
more likely to engage in positive
and affilitive behavior when they
view an event as a common threat.

Shyness Anxiety about and reluctance to interact with others.

Simulation heuristic Judgment of the likelihood of an event by using the ease with which one can mentally construct scenarios which would produce the event to make the judgment.

Sleeper effect Persuasion influence that occurs when a message has greater impact on attitudes after a long delay than it had immediately after presentation.

Social cognition The study of how people assign objects of thought to cognitive categories; how people judge social events.

Social density Comparisons of the effects of number of people per area in which group size is varied; *spatial density* involves comparisons of the same number of people in different size areas.

Social desirability *See* correspondence.

Social facilitation The enhancement or hindrance of performance produced by the presence of coactors and/or an audience.

Social identity Aspects of a person, such as age, sex, race, college, or religion, which establish the person's group memberships.

Social identity theory Theory about prejudice which states that when an individual's personal identity is threatened or diminished, the person emphasizes his or her social identity or ingroup membership, which can lead to discrimination against outgroups.

Social impact theory A theory about the influence a group has on an individual depending on characteristics of the group.

Social influence Any way actions of one person or group affects the behavior or attitudes of others; includes obedience, conformity, compliance, and persuasion.

Socialization A term used to describe how adults teach a society's rules to children through the adults' everyday actions and their treatment of the children to make those children fit into the society better.

Social judgment theory A theory of persuasion which holds that messages which are too discrepant from the receiver's initial position are unlikely to be persuasive.

Social learning theory *See* observational learning.

Social loafing The reduced effort exhibited by individuals who believe they are involved in a group effort.

Social penetration theory Theory which proposes that as friendship develops, the depth and breadth of self-disclosure increase between the two people; *depenetration* suggests that depth and breadth of self-disclosure decrease in deteriorating relationships.

Social psychology The study of the causes, consequences, and patterns of human interaction.

Social support Help we receive from others in the form of instrumental aid, informational support, feedback, or expressions of emotional concern.

Social trap Description of any condition or activity which provides immediate gratification, but in the long term produces negative consequences, such as death.

Sociobiology The theory that much social behavior occurs because we are motivated to ensure the survival of our genes in future generations.

Socioemotional specialist The person in a group whose actions are directed at promoting group harmony more than other group members' actions are.

Sociofugal space An area arranged so that it discourages interactions between people (e.g., furniture arrangements in airports).

Sociopetal space Space arranged to promote interaction (e.g., a circular dining table).

Solitude Type of privacy attained by physically separating oneself from others.

Spatial density A condition that occurs when the amount of space in a setting is restricted, regardless of the number of persons in the area.

Steinzor effect The tendency of people to attend to and interact with others who are most visually accessible; it partly explains why the head of the table is a position of power.

Stereotypes Beliefs about characteristics of members of a group.

Strength In social impact theory, the salience, power, importance, or intensity of an influencing person or group or target person or group on a target person.

Stress A process that is triggered by harmful or potentially harmful events.

Sucker effect Loafing or reduced effort which occurs when a performer realizes that other co-performers are free-riding on his or her efforts.

Task specialist The person in a group whose actions are directed at promoting group productivity more than other group members' actions are.

Territoriality The tendency to gain, mark, defend, and control an area or territory.

That's-not-all technique Influence approach in which an initial offer or position is reduced before the target person rejects it; conciliatory offer is made before pressure is exerted.

Theories Conceptual frameworks to aid in understanding facts and in uncovering new relationships.

Theory of passionate love   Theory that feelings of love develop whenever a person experiences physiological arousal and situational cues indicate that the arousal is caused by affection for the other person. Also called misattribution theory.

Theory of reasoned action   A theory which indicates that a person's behavior can be predicted best from knowing the person's *attitude toward doing the behavior* and the person's subjective norm.

Triangular theory of love   Theory that different kinds of relationships are characterized by the presence and strength of intimacy (warmth), passion, and decision/commitment.

Two-step flow of communication   Persuasion process in which the source of a message communicates to opinion leaders and, in the second step, they pass the message on to others.

Unconditional approval   *See* conditional approval.

Universal facial expressions   Displays of emotions such as happiness, surprise, fear, sadness, anger, and disgust/contempt recognized around the world.

Urban villages   Small communities within cities consisting of people with whom community members regularly interact; autonomous units within cities.

Value   Evaluation of the goodness or badness of objects of thought; a specific type of attitude.

Vicarious punishment   The experience of an observer who sees someone else criticized or physically punished for doing some behavior.

Vicarious reinforcement   The experience of an observer who sees someone else praised or rewarded for doing some behavior.

Visual dominance pattern   Visual behavior displayed by dominant people characterized by looking a lot at one's interaction partner while speaking and looking very little while listening to one's partner.

Abbey, A. (1982). Sex differences for friendly behavior: Do males misperceive females' friendliness? *Journal of Personality and Social Psychology, 42,* 830–838.

Abelson, R. P. (1988). Conviction. *American Psychologist, 43,* 267–275.

Adams, B. N. (1972). Birth order: A critical review. *Sociometry, 35,* 411–439.

Adams, H. B. (1988). Studies in REST: III. REST, arousability, and the nature of alcohol and substance abuse. *Journal of Substance Abuse Treatment, 5,* 77–88.

Adams, J. S. (1963). Toward an understanding of inequity. *Journal of Abnormal and Social Psychology, 67,* 422–436.

Adams, J. S. (1965). Injustice in social exchange. In L. Berkowitz (Ed.), *Advances in experimental social psychology* (Vol. 2, pp. 267–299). New York: Academic Press.

Adler, R., Lesser, G., Meringoff, L., Robertson, T., Rossiter, J., & Ward, S. (1980). *The effects of television advertising on children.* Lexington, MA: Lexington Books.

Adorno, T., Frenkel-Brunswik, E., Levinson, D., & Sanford, R. N. (1950). *The authoritarian personality.* New York: Harper.

Ahammer, I. M., & Murray, J. P. (1979). Kindness in the kindergarten: The relative influence of role playing and prosocial television in facilitating altruism. *International Journal of Behavioral Development, 2,* 133–157.

Aiello, J. R. (1977a). A further look at equilibrium theory: Visual interaction as a function of interpersonal distance. *Environmental Psychology and Nonverbal Behavior, 1,* 122–140.

Aiello, J. R. (1977b). Visual interaction at extended distances. *Personality and Social Psychology Bulletin, 3,* 83–86.

Aiello, J. R. (1987). Human spatial behavior. In D. Stokols & I. Altman (Eds.), *Handbook of environmental psychology* (Vol. 1, pp. 398–504). New York: Wiley.

Aiello, J. R., & Aiello, T. C. (1974). The development of personal space: Proxemic behavior of children 6 through 16. *Human Ecology, 2,* 177–189.

Aiello, J. R., Baum, A., & Gormley, F. B. (1981). Social determinants of residential crowding stress. *Personality and Social Psychology Bulletin, 7,* 643–649.

Aiello, J. R., Thompson, D. E., & Baum, A. (1981). The symbiotic relationship between social psychology and environmental psychology: Implications from crowding, personal space, and intimacy regulation research. In J. H. Harvey (Ed.), *Cognition, social behavior and the environment* (pp. 423–441). Hillsdale, NJ: Erlbaum.

Aiello, J. R., Thompson, D. E., & Brodzinsky, D. M. (1983). How funny is crowding anyway? Effects of room size, group size and the introduction of humor. *Basic and Applied Social Psychology, 4,* 193–207.

Ainsworth, M. D. S., Blehar, M. C., Waters, E., & Wall, S. (1978). *Patterns of attachment: A psychological study of the strange situation.* Hillsdale, NJ: Erlbaum.

Ajzen, I., & Fishbein, M. (1980). *Understanding attitudes and predicting social behavior.* Englewood Cliffs, NJ: Prentice-Hall.

Alba, J. W., & Hasher, L. (1983). Is memory schematic? *Psychological Bulletin, 93,* 203–231.

Aldwin, C. A., & Revenson, T. A. (1987). Does coping help? A reexamination of the relation between coping and mental health. *Journal of Personality and Social Psychology, 53,* 337–348.

Aldwin, C. A., & Stokols, D. (1988). The effects of environmental change on individuals and groups: Some neglected issues in stress research. *Journal of Environmental Psychology, 8,* 57–75.

Allen, H. (1972). Bystander intervention and helping on the subway. In L. Bickman & T. Henchy (Eds.), *Beyond the laboratory: Field research in social psychology* (pp. 22–33). New York: McGraw-Hill.

Alloy, L. B., & Abramson, L. Y. (1979). Judgment of contingency in depressed and nondepressed students: Sadder but wiser? *Journal of Experimental Psychology: General, 108,* 441–485.

Alloy, L. B., & Abramson, L. Y. (1982). Learned helplessness, depression, and the illusion of control. *Journal of Personality and Social Psychology, 42,* 1114–1126.

Alloy, L. B., Abramson, L. Y., & Viscusi, D. (1981). Induced mood and the illusion of control. *Journal of Personality and Social Psychology, 41,* 1129–1140.

Allport, G. (1954/1979). *The nature of prejudice.* Reading, MA: Addison-Wesley.

Allyn, J., & Festinger, L. (1961). The effectiveness of unanticipated persuasive communications. *Journal of Abnormal and Social Psychology, 62,* 35–40.

Altman, I. (1972). *Reciprocity of interpersonal exchange.* Paper presented at American Psychological Association convention, Honolulu, Hawaii.

Altman, I. (1975). *The environment and social behavior: Privacy, personal space, territory, crowding.* Monterey, CA: Brooks/Cole.

Altman, I., & Chemers, M. (1980). *Culture and environment.* Monterey, CA: Brooks/Cole.

Altman, I., & Taylor, D. A. (1973). *Social penetration: The development of interpersonal relationships.* New York: Holt, Rinehart & Winston.

Alwitt, L. F., Anderson, D. R., Lorch, E. P., & Levin, S. R. (1980). Preschool children's visual attention to attributes of television. *Human Communication Research, 7*, 52–67.

Amato, P. R. (1981). The effects of environmental complexity and pleasantness on prosocial behavior: A field study. *Australian Journal of Psychology, 33*, 285–295.

Amato, P. R. (1983). Helping behavior in urban and rural environments: Field studies based on a taxonomic organization of helping episodes. *Journal of Personality and Social Psychology, 45*, 571–586.

Amato, P. R. (1985). An investigation of planned helping behavior. *Journal of Research in Personality, 19*, 232–252.

Amato, P. R., & McInnes, I. R. (1983). Affiliative behavior in diverse environments: A consideration of pleasantness, information rate, and arousal-eliciting quality of settings. *Basic and Applied Social Psychology, 4*, 109–122.

American Psychiatric Association. (1980). *Diagnostic and statistical manual of mental disorders* (3rd ed.). Washington, DC: American Psychiatric Association.

Amir, Y. (1976). The role of intergroup contact in change of prejudice and ethnic relations. In P. A. Katz (Ed.), *Towards the elimination of racism* (pp. 245–308). Elmsford, NY: Pergamon.

Anderson, C. A. (1989). Temperature and aggression: Ubiquitous effects of heat on the occurrence of human violence. *Psychological Bulletin, 106*, 74–96.

Anderson, C. A., & Anderson, D. C. (1984). Ambient temperature and violent crime: Tests of the linear and curvilinear hypotheses. *Journal of Personality and Social Psychology, 46*, 91–97.

Anderson, L. M., Mulligan, B. E., Goodman, L. G., & Regen, H. Z. (1983). Effects of sounds on preferences for outdoor settings. *Environment and Behavior, 15*, 539–566.

Anderson, N. H. (1962). Application of an additive model to impression formation. *Science, 138*, 817–818.

Anderson, N. H. (1965). Averages versus adding as a stimulus combination rule in impression formation. *Journal of Experimental Psychology, 70*, 394–400.

Anderson, N. H. (1968). Application of a linear-serial model to a personality-impression task using serial presentation. *Journal of Personality and Social Psychology, 10*, 354–362.

Anderson, N. H. (1981). *Foundations of information integration theory.* New York: Academic Press.

Andreoli, V., & Worchel, S. (1978). Effects of media, communicator, and position of message on attitude change. *Public Opinion Quarterly, 42*, 59–70.

Antill, J. K. (1983). Sex role complementarity versus similarity in married couples. *Journal of Personality and Social Psychology, 45*, 145–155.

Antisocial activity curbed via diet, Ohio judge says. (July 6, 1982). *Dayton Daily News, 105* (299), 25.

Apple, W., Streeter, L. A., & Krauss, R. B. (1979). Effects of pitch and speech rate on personal attributions. *Journal of Personality and Social Psychology, 37*, 715–727.

Appleyard, D., & Lintell, M. (1972). The environmental quality of city streets: The residents' viewpoint. *Journal of the American Institute of Planners, 38*, 84–101.

Archer, D. (1985). Social deviance. In G. Lindzey & E. Aronson (Eds.), *Handbook of social psychology* (3rd ed., Vol. 2, pp. 743–804). Hillsdale, NJ: Erlbaum.

Archer, D., & Akert, R. M. (1977). Words and everything else: Verbal and nonverbal cues in social interpretation. *Journal of Personality and Social Psychology, 36*, 443–449.

Ardrey, R. (1966). *The territorial imperative.* New York: Dell.

Argyle, M., Alkema, F., & Gilmour, R. (1972). The communication of friendly and hostile attitudes by verbal and nonverbal signals. *European Journal of Social Psychology, 1*, 385–402.

Argyle, M., & Dean, J. (1965). Eye contact, distance and affiliation. *Sociometry, 28*, 289–304.

Aronoff, J. (1970). Psychological needs as a determinant in the formation of economic structures. *Human Relations, 23*, 123–128.

Aronson, E. (1968). Dissonance theory: Progress and problems. In R. P. Abelson et al. (Eds.), *Theories of cognitive consistency: A sourcebook* (pp. 5–27). Chicago: Rand McNally.

Aronson, E. (1969). The theory of cognitive dissonance: A current perspective. In L. Berkowitz (Ed.), *Advances in experimental social psychology,* (Vol. 4.) New York: Academic Press.

Aronson, E. (1972). *The social animal* (1st ed.). New York: W. H. Freeman.

Aronson, E. (1984). *The social animal* (4th ed.). New York: W. H. Freeman.

Aronson, E. (1986). Applications of social psychology. In symposium, *Communicating with the public,* at Society of Experimental Social Psychology meeting, Tempe, AR.

Aronson, E., & Carlsmith, J. M. (1963). Effect of the severity of threat on the valuation of forbidden behavior. *Journal of Abnormal and Social Psychology, 66*, 584–588.

Aronson, E., & Cope, V. M. (1968). My enemy's enemy is my friend. *Journal of Personality and Social Psychology, 8*, 8–12.

Aronson, E., & Linder, D. (1965). Gain and loss of esteem as determinants of interpersonal attraction. *Journal of Experimental Social Psychology, 1*, 156–172.

Aronson, E., & Mills, J. (1959). The effect of severity of initiation on liking for a group. *Journal of Abnormal and Social Psychology, 59*, 177–181.

Aronson, E., Stephan, C., Sikes, J., Blaney, N., & Snapp, M. (1978). *The jigsaw classroom.* Beverly Hills, CA: Sage.

Aronson, E., Turner, J. A., & Carlsmith, J. M. (1963). Communicator credibility and communicator discrepancy as determinants of opinion change. *Journal of Personality and Social Psychology, 67*, 31–36.

Aronson, E., & Worchel, P. (1966). Similarity vs. liking as determinants of interpersonal attractiveness. *Psychonomic Science, 5*, 157–158.

Arthur, A. Z. (1987). Stress as a state of anticipatory vigilance. *Perceptual and Motor Skills, 64*, 75–85.

Asch, S. E. (1951). Effects of group pressure upon the modification and distortion of judgment. In H. Guetzkow (Ed.), *Groups, leadership, and men.* Pittsburgh: Carnegie University Press.

Asch, S. E. (1952). *Social psychology.* Englewood Cliffs, NJ: Prentice-Hall.

Asch, S. E. (1955). Opinions and social pressure. *Scientific American, 193(5)*, 31–35.

Asch, S. E. (1956). Studies of independence and conformity: A minority of one against a unanimous majority. *Psychological Monographs, 70*, (9, Whole No. 416).

Ashton, N. L., Shaw, M. E., & Worsham, P. (1980). Affective reactions to interpersonal distances by friends and strangers. *Bulletin of the Psychonomic Society, 15*, 306–308.

Athanasiou, R., & Yoshioka, G. A. (1973). The spatial character of friendship formation. *Environment and Behavior, 5*, 43–65.

Atwood, R. W., & Howell, R. J. (1971). Pupillometric and personality test score differences of female aggressing pedophiliacs and normals. *Psychonomic Science, 22*, 115–116.

Austin, W. (1979). Sex differences in bystander intervention in a theft. *Journal of Personality and Social Psychology, 37*, 2110–2120.

Austin, W., & Walster, E. (1974). Participants' reactions to "equity with the world." *Journal of Experimental Social Psychology, 10*, 528–548.

Axsom, D., & Cooper, J. (1984). Reducing weight by reducing dissonance: The role of effort justification in inducing weight loss. In E. Aronson (Ed.), *Readings about the social animal* (4th ed.). New York: W. H. Freeman.

Azrin, N. H. (1961). Time-out from positive reinforcement. *Science, 133,* 382–383.

Azrin, N. H. (1967, January). Pain and aggression. *Psychology Today,* pp. 27–33.

Azrin, N. H., Hutchinson, R. R., & Hake, D. F. (1966). Extinction-induced aggression. *Journal of the Experimental Analysis of Behavior, 9,* 191–204.

Backer, T. E., Batchelor, W. F., Jones, J. M., & Mays, V. M. (Eds.) (1988). Special issue: Psychology and AIDS. *American Psychologist, 43,* 835–987.

Bacon-Prue, A., Blount, R., Pickering, D., & Drabman, R. (1980). An evaluation of three litter control procedures—trash receptacles, paid workers, and the marked item technique. *Journal of Applied Behavior Analysis, 13,* 165–170.

Baird, L. L. (1969). Big school, small school: A critical examination of the hypothesis. *Journal of Educational Psychology, 60,* 253–260.

Bakan, D. (1966). *The duality of human existence: An essay on psychology and religion.* Chicago: Rand McNally.

Baker, E., & Shaw, M. E. (1980). Reactions to interpersonal distance and topic intimacy: A comparison of strangers and friends. *Journal of Nonverbal Behavior, 5,* 80–91.

Baker, P. M. (1984). Seeing is behaving: Visibility and participation in small groups. *Environment and Behavior, 16,* 159–184.

Bales, R. F. (1950). *Interaction process analysis: A method for the study of small groups.* Cambridge, MA: Addison-Wesley.

Bales, R. F. (1955). Task roles and social roles in problem-solving groups. In E. E. Maccoby, T. M. Newcomb, & E. L. Hartley (Eds.), *Readings in social psychology* (2nd ed.). New York: Holt, Rinehart & Winston.

Bales, R. F. (1970). *Personality and interpersonal behavior.* New York: Holt, Rinehart & Winston.

Bandura, A. (1965). Influence of models' reinforcement contingencies on the acquisition of imitative responses. *Journal of Personality and Social Psychology, 1,* 589–595.

Bandura, A. (1971). *Social learning theory.* Morristown, NJ: General Learning Press.

Bandura, A. (1973). *Aggression: A social learning analysis.* Englewood Cliffs, NJ: Prentice-Hall.

Bandura, A. (1977a). Self-efficacy: Toward a unifying theory of behavioral change. *Psychological Review, 84,* 191–215.

Bandura, A. (1977b). *Social learning theory.* Englewood Cliffs, NJ: Prentice-Hall.

Bandura, A. (1982). Self-efficacy mechanism in human agency. *American Psychologist, 37,* 122–147.

Bandura, A. (1983). Psychological mechanisms of aggression. In R. G. Geen & E. I. Donnerstein (Eds.), *Aggression: Theoretical and empirical reviews* (Vol. 1, pp. 1–40). New York: Academic Press.

Bandura, A., & Adams, N. E. (1977). Analysis of self-efficacy theory of behavior change. *Cognitive Therapy and Research, 1,* 287–310.

Bandura, A., Adams, N. E., & Beyer, J. (1977). Cognitive processes mediating behavioral change. *Journal of Personality and Social Psychology, 35,* 125–139.

Bandura, A., Adams, N. E., Hardy, A. B., & Howells, G. N. (1980). Tests of the generality of self-efficacy theory. *Cognitive Therapy and Research, 4,* 39–66.

Bandura, A., Ross, D., & Ross, S. A. (1961). Transmission of aggression through imitation of aggressive models. *Journal of Abnormal and Social Psychology, 63,* 575–582.

Bandura, A., Ross, D., & Ross, S. A. (1963). Imitation of film mediated agression models. *Journal of Abnormal and Social Psychology, 66,* 3–11.

Bandura, A., & Schunk, D. (1981). Cultivating competence, self-efficacy, and interest through proximal self-motivation. *Journal of Personality and Social Psychology, 41,* 586–598.

Bandura, A., & Walters, R. H. (1959). *Adolescent aggression.* New York: Ronald Press.

Bandura, K., & Walters, R. H. (1963). *Social learning and personality development.* New York: Holt, Rinehart & Winston.

Banikiotes, P. G., Russell, J. M., & Linden, J. D. (1972). Interpersonal attraction in simulated and real interactions. *Journal of Personality and Social Psychology, 23,* 1–7.

Bar-Tal, D., & Saxe, L. (1976). Perceptions of similarly and dissimilarly attractive couples. *Journal of Personality and Social Psychology, 33,* 772–781.

Barash, D. (1979). *The whisperings within.* New York: Harper & Row.

Barefoot, J. C., Hoople, H., & McClay, D. (1972). Avoidance of an act which would violate personal space. *Psychonomic Science, 28,* 205–206.

Bargh, J. A., & Thein, R. D. (1985). Individual construct accessibility, person memory, and the recall-judgment link: The case of information overload. *Journal of Personality and Social Psychology, 49,* 1129–1146.

Barker, R. G. (1968). *Ecological psychology: Concepts and methods for studying the environment of human behavior.* Stanford, CA: Stanford University Press.

Barker, R. G. (1979). Settings of a professional lifetime. *Journal of Personality and Social Psychology, 37,* 2137–2157.

Barker, R., Dembo, T., & Lewin, K. (1941). Studies in topological and vector psychology: II. Frustration and regression. *University of Iowa Studies in Child Welfare, 18,* 1.

Barker, R. G., & Gump, P. V. (1964). *Big school, small school: High school size and student behavior.* Stanford, CA: Stanford University Press.

Barling, J., & Rosenbaum, A. (1986). Work stressors and wife abuse. *Journal of Applied Psychology, 71,* 346–348.

Barlow, G. W. (1968). Ethological units of behavior. In D. Engle (Ed.), *The central nervous system and fish behavior* (pp. 217–232). Chicago: University of Chicago Press.

Baron, R. A. (1977). *Human aggression.* New York: Plenum.

Baron, R. A. (1978). Invasions of personal space and helping: Mediating effects of invader's apparent need. *Journal of Experimental Social Psychology, 14,* 304–312.

Baron, R. A. (1983). The control of human aggression: A strategy based on incompatible responses. In R. G. Geen and E. I. Donnerstein (Eds.), *Aggression: Theoretical and empirical reviews* (Vol. 2, pp. 173–190). New York: Academic Press.

Baron, R. A., & Bell, P. A. (1975). Aggression and heat: Mediating effects of prior provocation and exposure to an aggressive model. *Journal of Personality and Social Psychology, 31,* 825–832.

Baron, R. A., & Bell, P. A. (1976). Aggression and heat: The influence of ambient temperature, negative affect, and a cooling drink on physical aggression. *Journal of Personality and Social Psychology, 33,* 245–255.

Baron, R. A., & Bell, P. A. (1977). Sexual arousal and aggression by males: Effects of type of erotic stimuli and prior provocation. *Journal of Personality and Social Psychology, 35,* 79–87.

Baron, R. A., & Ransberger, V. M. (1978). Ambient temperature and the occurrence of collective violence: The "long, hot summer" revisited. *Journal of Personality and Social Psychology, 36,* 351–360.

Baron, R. M., Mandel, D. R., Adams, C. A., & Griffen, L. M. (1976). Effects of social density in university residential environments. *Journal of Personality and Social Psychology, 34,* 434–446.

Barroso, F., Freedman, N., & Grand, S. (1980). Self-touching, performance, and attentional processes. *Perceptual and Motor Skills, 50,* 1083–1089.

Bass, B. M., McGehee, C. R., Hawkins, W. C., Young, P. C., & Gebel, A. S. (1953). Personality variables related to leaderless group discussion behavior. *Journal of Abnormal and Social Psychology, 48,* 120–128.

Batson, C. D. (1983). Sociobiology and the role of religion in promoting prosocial behavior: An alternative view. *Journal of Personality and Social Psychology, 45,* 1380–1385.

Batson, C. D. (1987). Prosocial motivation: Is it ever truly altruistic? In L. Berkowitz (Ed.), *Advances in experimental social psychology* (Vol. 20, pp. 65–122). New York: Academic Press.

Batson, C. D., Bolen, M. H., Cross, J. A., & Neuringer-Benefiel, H. E. (1986). Where is the altruism in the altruistic personality? *Journal of Personality and Social Psychology, 50,* 212–220.

Batson, C. D., Cochran, P. J., Biederman, M. F., Blosser, J. L., Ryan, M. J., & Vogt, B. (1978). Failure to help when in a hurry: Callousness or conflict. *Personality and Social Psychology Bulletin, 4,* 97–101.

Batson, C. D., Duncan, B. D., Ackerman, P., Buckley, T., & Birch, K. (1981). Is empathic emotion a source of altruistic motivation? *Journal of Personality and Social Psychology, 40,* 290–302.

Batson, C. D., Dyck, J. L., Brandt, J. R., Batson, J. G., Powell, A. L., McMaster, M. R., & Griffitt, C. (1988). Five studies testing two new egoistic alternatives to the empathy-altruism hypothesis. *Journal of Personality and Social Psychology, 55,* 52–77.

Batson, C. D., & Vanderplas, M. S. (1982). Helping. In D. Perlman & P. C. Cozby (Eds.), *Social psychology* (pp. 284–311). New York: Holt, Rinehart & Winston.

Batson, C. D., & Ventis, W. L. (1982). *The religious experience: A social-psychological perspective.* New York: Oxford University Press.

Baum, A. (1987). Toxins, technology, and natural disasters. In G. R. VandenBos & B. K. Bryant (Eds.), *Cataclysms, crises, and catastrophes.* Washington, DC: American Psychological Association.

Baum, A. (1988, April). Disasters, natural and otherwise. *Psychology Today,* pp. 57–60.

Baum, A., Aiello, J., & Calesnick, L. E. (1978). Crowding and personal control: Social density and the development of learned helplessness. *Journal of Personality and Social Psychology, 36,* 1000–1011.

Baum, A., & Davis, G. E. (1980). Reducing the stress of high-density living: An architectural intervention. *Journal of Personality and Social Psychology, 38,* 471–481.

Baum, A., Fisher, J. D., & Solomon, S. (1981). Type of information, familiarity, and the reduction of crowding stress. *Journal of Personality and Social Psychology, 40,* 11–23.

Baum, A., Fleming, R., & Singer, J. E. (1982). Stress at Three Mile Island: Applying psychological impact analysis. In L. Bickman (Ed.), *Applied social psychology annual* (Vol. 3, pp. 217–248). Beverly Hills: Sage.

Baum, A., & Gatchel, R. J. (1981). Cognitive determinants of response to uncontrollable events: Development of reactance and learned helplessness. *Journal of Personality and Social Psychology, 40,* 1078–1089.

Baum, A., Gatchel, R. J., & Schaeffer, M. A. (1983). Emotional, behavioral, and psychological effects of chronic stress at Three Mile Island. *Journal of Consulting and Clinical Psychology, 51,* 565–572.

Baum, A., & Greenberg, C. I. (1975). Waiting for a crowd: The behavioral and perceptual effects of anticipated crowding. *Journal of Personality and Social Psychology, 32,* 667–671.

Baum, A., Grunberg, N. E., & Singer, J. E. (1982). The use of physiological and neuroendocrinological measurements in the study of stress. *Health Psychology, 1,* 217–236.

Baum, A., Harpin, R. E., & Valins, S. (1975). The role of group phenomena in the experience of crowding. *Environment and Behavior, 7,* 185–197.

Baum, A., & Koman, S. (1976). Differential response to anticipated crowding: Psychological effects of social and spatial density. *Journal of Personality and Social Psychology, 34,* 526–536.

Baum, A., & Paulus, P. (1987). Crowding. In D. Stokols & I. Altman (Eds.), *Handbook of environmental psychology.* New York: Wiley.

Baum, A., Reiss, M., & O'Hara, J. (1974). Architectural variants of reaction to spatial invasion. *Environment and Behavior, 6,* 91–109.

Baum, A., Singer, J. E., & Baum, C. S. (1982). Stress and the environment. In G. W. Evans (Ed.), *Environmental stress* (pp. 15–44). New York: Cambridge University Press.

Baum, A., & Valins, S. (1977). *Architecture and social behavior: Psychological studies of social density.* Hillsdale, NJ: Erlbaum.

Baumeister, R. F. (1982). A self-presentational view of social phenomena. *Psychological Bulletin, 91,* 3–26.

Baumeister, R. F. (1984). Choking under pressure: Self-consciousness and paradoxical effects of incentives on skillful performance. *Journal of Personality and Social Psychology, 46,* 610–620.

Baumeister, R. F. (1986). *Identity: Cultural change and the struggle for self.* New York: Oxford University Press.

Baumeister, R. F., Chesner, S. P., Sanders, P. S., & Tice, D. M. (1988). Who's in charge here? Group leaders do lend help in emergencies. *Personality and Social Psychology Bulletin, 14,* 17–22.

Baumeister, R. F., Hamilton, J. C., & Tice, D. M. (1985). Public versus private expectancy of success: Confidence booster of performance pressure? *Journal of Personality and Social Psychology, 48,* 1447–1457.

Baumeister, R. F., & Steinhilber, A. (1984). Paradoxical effects of supportive audiences on performance under pressure: The home field disadvantage in sports championships. *Journal of Personality and Social Psychology, 47,* 85–93.

Baumeister, R. F., & Tice, D. M. (1984). Role of self-presentation and choice in cognitive dissonance under forced compliance: Necessary or sufficient causes? *Journal of Personality and Social Psychology, 46,* 5–13.

Baumgardner, A. H., & Brownlee, E. A. (1987). Strategic failure in social interaction: Evidence for expectancy disconfirmation processes. *Journal of Personality and Social Psychology, 52,* 525–535.

Baumrind, D. (1964). Some thoughts on ethics of research: After reading Milgram's Behavioral study of "obedience." *American Psychologist, 19,* 421–423.

Beaman, A. L., Cole, C. M., Preston, M., Klentz, B., & Steblay, N. M. (1983). Fifteen years of foot-in-the-door research: A meta-analysis. *Personality and Social Psychology Bulletin, 9,* 181–196.

Bean, N. J., & Connor, R. (1978). Central hormonal replacement and home-cage dominance in castrated rats. *Hormones and Behavior, 11,* 100–109.

Beck, A. T. (1967). *Depression: Clinical, experimental, and theoretical aspects.* New York: Hoeber.

Bell, P. A., & Baron, R. A. (1976). Aggression and heat: The mediating role of negative affect. *Journal of Applied Social Psychology, 6,* 18–30.

Bell, P. A., & Fusco, M. E. (1989). *Heat and violence in the Dallas field data: Linearity, curvilinearity, and heteroscedasticity.* Unpublished manuscript, Psychology Department, Colorado State University, Ft. Collins, CO 80523.

Belmont, L., & Marolla, F. A. (1973). Birth order, family size, and intelligence. *Science, 182,* 1096–1101.

Bem, D. J. (1965). An experimental analysis of self-persuasion. *Journal of Experimental Social Psychology, 1,* 199–218.

Bem, D. J. (1967). An alternative interpretation of cognitive dissonance phenomena. *Psychological Bulletin, 74,* 183–200.

Bem, D. J. (1972). Self-perception theory. In L. Berkowitz (Ed.), *Advances in experimental social psychology* (Vol. 6, pp. 1–62). New York: Academic Press.

Bem, D. J., & McConnell, H. K. (1970). Testing the self-perception explanation of dissonance phenomena: On the salience of premanipulation attitudes. *Journal of Personality and Social Psychology, 14,* 23–31.

Bem, S. L. (1974). The measurement of psychological androgyny. *Journal of Consulting and Clinical Psychology, 42,* 155–162.

Bem, S. L. (1975). Sex role adaptability: One consequence of psychological androgyny. *Journal of Personality and Social Psychology, 31,* 634–643.

Bem, S. L. (1979). Beyond androgyny: Some presumptuous prescriptions for a liberated sexual identity. In J. Sherman & F. Denmark (Eds.), *Psychology of women: Issues in psychology.* New York: Psychological Dimensions.

Bem, S. L., & Bem, D. (1970). Case study of a nonconscious ideology: Training the woman to know her place. In D. Bem (Ed.), *Beliefs, attitudes, and human affairs* (pp 89–99). Belmont, California: Brooks/Cole.

Bem, S., & Lenney, E. (1976). Sex-typing and the avoidance of cross-sex behavior. *Journal of Personality and Social Psychology, 33,* 48–54.

Benton, D., Kumari, N., & Brain, P. F. (1982). Mild hypoglycemia and questionnaire measures of aggression. *Biological Psychology, 14,* 129–135.

Berg, J. H., & Archer, R. L. (1980). Disclosure or concern: A second look at liking for the norm breaker. *Journal of Personality, 48,* 245–257.

Berger, J., Rosenholtz, S. J., & Zelditch, M., Jr. (1980). Status organizing processes. *Annual Review of Sociology, 6,* 479–508.

Berglas, S., & Jones, E. (1978). Drug choice as a self-handicapping strategy in response to noncontingent success. *Journal of Personality and Social Psychology, 36,* 405–417.

Bergreen, L. (1977, November 5). How do you measure violence? It depends on who is counting. *TV Guide,* 5–10.

Berkowitz, L. (1962). *Aggression: A social psychological analysis.* New York: McGraw-Hill.

Berkowitz, L. (1965). The concept of aggressive drive: Some additional considerations. In L. Berkowitz (Ed.), *Advances in experimental social psychology* (Vol. 2). New York: Academic Press.

Berkowitz, L. (1969). The frustration-aggression hypothesis revisited. In L. Berkowitz (Ed.), *Roots of aggression* (pp. 1–28). New York: Atherton Press.

Berkowitz, L. (1972). Social norms, feelings and the factors affecting helping and altruism. In L. Berkowitz (Ed.), *Advances in experimental social psychology.* New York: Academic Press.

Berkowitz, L. (1978). Whatever happened to the frustration-aggression hypothesis? *American Behavioral Scientist, 21,* 691–708.

Berkowitz, L. (1980). *A survey of social psychology* (2nd ed.). New York: Holt, Rinehart & Winston.

Berkowitz, L. (1983). The experience of anger as a parallel process in the display of impulsve, "angry" aggression. In R. G. Geen & E. I. Donnerstein (Eds.), *Aggression: Theoretical and empirical reviews* (Vol. 1, pp. 103–133). New York: Academic Press.

Berkowitz, L. (1984). Some effects of thoughts on anti- and pro-social influences of media events: A cognitive-neoassociation analysis. *Psychological Bulletin, 95,* 410–427.

Berkowitz, L. (1987). Mood, self-awareness, and willingness to help. *Journal of Personality and Social Psychology, 52,* 721–729.

Berkowitz, L. (Ed.) (1988). *Advances in experimental social psychology: Social psychological studies of the self* (Vol. 21). New York: Academic Press.

Berkowitz, L., & Daniels, L. R. (1963). Responsibility and dependency. *Journal of Abnormal and Social Psychology, 66,* 429–437.

Berkowitz, L., & Geen, R. G. (1966). Film violence and the cue properties of available targets. *Journal of Personality and Social Psychology, 3,* 525–530.

Berkowitz, L., & Geen, R. G. (1967). Stimulus qualities of the target of aggression: A further study. *Journal of Personality and Social Psychology, 5,* 364–368.

Berkowitz, L., & LePage, A. (1967). Weapons as aggression-eliciting stimuli. *Journal of Personality and Social Psychology, 7,* 202–207.

Berlyne, D. (1960). *Conflict, arousal, and curiosity.* New York: McGraw-Hill.

Berscheid, E. (1983). Emotion. In H. H. Kelley et al. (Eds.), *Close relationships* (pp. 110–168). New York: Freeman.

Berscheid, E., Brothen, T., & Graziano, W. (1976). Gain-loss theory and the "law of infidelity": Mr. Doting versus the admiring stranger. *Journal of Personality and Social Psychology, 33,* 709–718.

Berscheid, E., Dion, K., Walster, E., & Walster, G. W. (1971). Physical attractiveness and dating choice: A test of the matching hypothesis. *Journal of Experimental Social Psychology, 7,* 173–189.

Berscheid, E., Graziano, W., Monson, T., & Dermer, M. (1976). Outcome dependency: Attention, attribution, and attraction. *Journal of Personality and Social Psychology, 34,* 978–989.

Berscheid, E., & Walster, E. (1969). *Interpersonal attraction.* Reading, MA: Addison-Wesley.

Berscheid, E., & Walster, E. (1974). A little bit about love. In T. L. Huston (Ed.), *Foundations of interpersonal attraction* (pp. 355–381). New York: Academic Press.

Berscheid, E., & Walster, E. (1978). *Interpersonal attraction* (2nd ed.). Reading MA.: Addison-Wesley.

Berscheid, E., Walster, E., & Bohrnstadt, G. (1973, July). Body image. *Psychology Today,* pp. 119–131.

Bettelheim, B. (1943). Individual and mass behavior in extreme situations. *Journal of Abnormal and Social Psychology, 38,* 417–452.

Bickman, L. (1972). Environmental attitudes and actions. *Journal of Social Psychology, 87,* 323–324.

Bickman, L., & Rosenbaum, D. P. (1977). Crime reporting as a function of bystander encouragement, surveillance, and credibility. *Journal of Personality and Social Psychology, 35,* 577–586.

Bickman, L., Teger, A., Gabriele, T., McLaughlin, C., Berger, M., & Sunaday, E. (1973). Dormitory density and helping behavior. *Environment and Behavior, 5,* 465–490.

Billig, M., & Tajfel, H. (1973). Social categorization and similarity in intergroup behavior. *European Journal of Social Psychology, 3,* 27–52.

Blaney, N. T., Stephan, C., Rosenfield, D., Aronson, E., & Sikes, J. (1977). Interdependence in the classroom: A field study. *Journal of Educational Psychology, 69,* 139–146.

Blank, D. M. (1977). The Gerbner violence profile. *Journal of Broadcasting, 21,* 273–296.

Bochner, S., & Insko, C. A. (1966). Communicator discrepancy, source credibility, and opinion change. *Journal of Personality and Social Psychology, 4,* 614–621.

Bolton, R. (1976). Hostility in fantasy: A further test of the hypoglycemia-aggression hypothesis. *Aggressive Behavior, 2,* 257–274.

Bond, C. F., Jr. (1981). Dissonance and the pill: An interpersonal simulation. *Personality and Social Psychology Bulletin, 7,* 398–403.

Bonora, B., Linder, R., Christie, R., & Schulman, J. (1983). Selecting a jury. In B. Bonora & E. Krauss (Eds.), *Jurywork: Systematic techniques* (2nd ed.). New York: Clark Boardman.

Boomer, D. S. (1963). Speech dysfluencies and body movement in interviews. *Journal of Nervous and Mental Disease, 136,* 263–266.

Borden, R. J. (1980). Audience influence. In P. B. Paulus (Ed.), *Psychology of group influence* (99–132) Hillsdale, NJ: Erlbaum.

Borrie, R. A., & Suedfeld, P. (1980). Restricted environmental stimulation therapy in a weight reduction program. *Journal of Behavioral Medicine, 3,* 147–161.

Bossard, J. H. S. (1932). Residential propinquity as a factor in mate selection. *American Journal of Sociology, 38,* 219–224.

Bowlby, J. (1973). *Attachment and loss: Separation: Anxiety and anger (Vol 2).* New York: Basic Books.

Bowlby, J. (1980). *Attachment and loss: Loss, sadness and depression* (Vol. 3). New York: Basic Books.

Bradley, G. W. (1978). Self-serving biases in the attribution process: A reexamination of the fact or fiction question. *Journal of Personality and Social Psychology, 36,* 56–71.

Braginsky, B., & Braginsky, D. (1967). Schizophrenic patients in the psychiatric interview: An experimental study of their effectiveness at manipulation. *Journal of Consulting Psychology, 31,* 546–551.

Bramel, D. (1968). Dissonance, expectation, and the self. In R. P. Abelson et al. (Eds.), *Theories of cognitive consistency: A sourcebook* (pp. 355–365). Chicago: Rand McNally.

Braver, S., Linder, D., Corwin, T., & Cialdini, R. B. (1977). Some conditions that affect admissions of attitude change. *Journal of Experimental Social Psychology, 13,* 565–576.

Breckler, S. J., & Greenwald, A. G. (1981). *Favorable self-referent judgments are made faster than nonfavorable ones.* Paper presented at the Midwestern Psychological Association convention, Detroit, MI.

Breed, G. R. (1972). The effect of intimacy: Reciprocity or retreat? *British Journal of Social and Clinical Psychology, 11,* 135–142.

Brehm, J. W. (1956). Post-decision changes in desirability of alternatives. *Journal of Abnormal and Social Psychology, 52,* 384–389.

Brehm, J. W. (1966). *A theory of psychological reactance.* New York: Academic Press.

Brehm, J. W. (1972). *Responses to loss of freedom: A theory of psychological reactance.* Morristown, NJ: General Learning Press.

Brehm, J. W., & Wicklund, R. A. (1970). Regret and dissonance reduction as a function of postdecision salience of dissonant information. *Journal of Personality and Social Psychology, 14,* 1–7.

Brenner, M. H. (1973). *Mental illness and the economy.* Cambridge, MA: Harvard University Press.

Breslau, N., & Davis, G. C. (1987). Posttraumatic stress disorder: The etiological specificity of wartime stressors. *American Journal of Psychiatry, 144,* 578–583.

Brewer, M. B. (1979). In-group bias in the minimal intergroup situation: A cognitive-motivational analysis. *Psychological Bulletin, 86,* 307–324.

Brewer, M. B., & Miller, N. (1984). Beyond the contact hypothesis: Theoretical perspectives on desegregation. In N. Miller & M. B. Brewer (Eds.), *Groups in contact: The psychology of desegregation.* New York: Academic Press.

Brewer, M. B., & Silver, M. (1978). In-group bias as a function of task characteristics. *European Journal of Social Psychology, 8,* 393–400.

Brickner, M. A., Harkins, S. G., & Ostrom, T. M. (1986). Effects of personal involvement: Thought-provoking implications for social loafing. *Journal of Personality and Social Psychology, 51,* 763–769.

Brief, A. P., & Atieh, J. M. (1987). Studying job stress: Are we making mountains out of molehills? *Journal of Occupational Behaviour, 8,* 115–126.

Briere, J., Downes, A., & Spensley, J. (1983). Summer in the city: Urban weather conditions and psychiatric emergency-room visits. *Journal of Abnormal Psychology, 92,* 77–88.

Brodt, S., & Zimbardo, P. (1981). Modifying shyness-related social behavior through symptom misattribution. *Journal of Personality and Social Psychology, 41,* 437–449.

Brooks-Gunn, J., Boyer, C. B., & Hein, K. (1988). Preventing HIV infection and AIDS in children and adolescents: Behavioral research and intervention strategies. *American Psychologist (Special Issue: Psychology and AIDS), 43,* 958–964.

Brower, S., Dockett, K., & Taylor, R. B. (1983). Residents' perceptions of territorial features and perceived local threat. *Environment and Behavior, 15,* 419–437.

Brown, B. A. (1985). Residential territories: Cues to burglary vulnerability. *Journal of Architecture and Planning Research, 2,* 231–243.

Brown, B. A. (1987). Territoriality. In D. Stokols & I. Altman (Eds.), *Handbook of environmental psychology* (Vol. 1, pp. 505–531). New York: Wiley.

Brown, B. A., & Altman, I. (1983). Territoriality, defensible space, and residential burglary: An environmental analysis. *Journal of Environmental Psychology, 3,* 203–220.

Brown, B. B., & Werner, C. M. (1985). Social cohesiveness, territoriality, and holiday decorations: The influence of cul-de-sacs. *Environment and Behavior, 17,* 539–565.

Brown, J. D., & Lawton, M. (1986). Stress and well-being in adolescence: The moderating role of physical exercise. *Journal of Human Stress, 12,* 125–131.

Brown, J. D., & Siegel, J. M. (1988). Exercise as a buffer of life stress: A prospective study of adolescent health. *Health Psychology, 7,* 341–353.

Brown, P., & Elliot, R. (1965). Control of aggression in a nursery school class. *Journal of Experimental Child Psychology, 2,* 103–107.

Brown, P., & Levinson, S. (1978). Universals in language usage: Politeness phenomena. In E. Goody (Ed.), *Questions and politeness* (pp. 56–310). Cambridge, England: Cambridge University Press.

Brown, R. (1965). *Social psychology.* New York: Free Press.

Brown, R. (1986). *Social psychology. The second edition.* New York: Free Press.

Brown, R. (1987, October). *Politeness theory: An exemplary case.* Address presented at the Society of Experimental Social Psychology meeting, Charlottesville, VA.

Brown, R., & Turner, J. C. (1981). Interpersonal and intergroup behaviour. In J. Turner & H. Giles (Eds.), *Intergroup behaviour.* Oxford: Basil Blackwell.

Brownstein, R. J., & Katzev, R. D. (1985). The relative effectiveness of three compliance techniques in eliciting donations to a cultural organization. *Journal of Applied Social Psychology, 15,* 564–574.

Bruner, J. S. (1957). On perceptual readiness. *Psychological Review, 64,* 123–152.

Bruner, J. S., & Tagiuri, R. (1954). The perception of people. In G. Lindzey (Ed.), *Handbook of social psychology* (Vol. 2). Reading, MA: Addison-Wesley.

Bryan, J. H., & Test, M. A. (1967). Models and helping: Naturalistic studies in aiding behavior. *Journal of Personality and Social Psychology, 6,* 400–407.

Bugenthal, D. B., Henker, B., & Whalen, C. K. (1976). Attributional antecedents of verbal and vocal assertiveness. *Journal of Personality and Social Psychology, 34,* 405–411.

Bugental, D. E., Kaswan, J. W., & Love, L. R. (1970). Perception of contradictory meanings conveyed by verbal and nonverbal channels. *Journal of Personality and Social Psychology, 16,* 647–655.

Burger, J. M. (1986). Increasing compliance by improving the deal: The that's-not-all technique. *Journal of Personality and Social Psychology, 51,* 277–283.

Burgoon, J. K. (1983). Nonverbal violations of expectations. In J. M. Wiemann & R. P. Harrison (Eds.), *Sage annual reviews of communication: Nonverbal interaction* (Vol. 11). Beverly Hills, CA: Sage.

Burn, S. M., & Oskamp, S. (1986). Increasing community recycling with persuasive communication and public commitment. *Journal of Applied Social Psychology, 16,* 29–41.

Burnstein, E. (1982). Persuasion as argument processing. In H. Brandstetter, J. H. Davis, & G. Stocker-Kreichgauer (Eds.), *Group decision making* (pp. 103–124). New York: Academic Press.

Burnstein, E., & Vinokur, A. (1977). Persuasive arguments and social comparison as determinants of attitude polarization. *Journal of Experimental Social Psychology, 13,* 315–332.

Burnstein, E., & Worchel, P. (1962). Arbitrariness of frustration and its consequences for aggression in a social situation. *Journal of Personality, 30,* 528–541.

Burr, W. R. (1970). Satisfaction with various aspects of marriage over the life cycle: A random middle class sample. *Journal of Marriage and the Family, 32,* 29–37.

Buss, A. H. (1961). *The psychology of aggression.* New York: Wiley.

Buss, A. H. (1963). Physical aggression in relation to different frustrations. *Journal of Abnormal and Social Psychology, 67,* 1–7.

Buss, A. H. (1966). Instrumentality of aggression, feedback, and frustration as determinants of physical aggression. *Journal of Personality and Social Psychology, 3,* 153–162.

Buss, A. H. (1971). Aggression pays. In J. L. Singer (Ed.), *The control of aggression and violence.* New York: Academic Press.

Buss, A. H. (1973). *Psychology: Man in perspective.* New York: Wiley.

Buss, A. H. (1980). *Self-consciousness and social anxiety.* San Francisco: Freeman.

Buss, A. H. (1983). Social rewards and personality. *Journal of Personality and Social Psychology, 44,* 553–563.

Buss, A. H., Booker, A., & Buss, E. (1972). Firing a weapon and aggression. *Journal of Personality and Social Psychology, 22,* 296–302.

Buss, A. H., & Briggs, S. R. (1984). Drama and the self in social interaction. *Journal of Personality and Social Psychology, 47,* 1310–1324.

Buss, A. H., & Plomin, R. (1975). *A temperament theory of personality development.* New York: Wiley.

Buss, D. M. (1984). Marital assortment for personality dispositions: Assessment with three different data sources. *Behavior Genetics, 14,* 111–123.

Buss, D. M. (1985). Human mate selection. *American Scientist, 73,* 47–51.

Buss, D. M. (1988). The evolution of human intrasexual competition: Tactics of mate attraction. *Journal of Personality and Social Psychology, 54,* 616–628.

Buss, D. M., & Scheier, M. F. (1976). Self-awareness, self-consciousness, and self-attribution. *Journal of Research in Personality, 10,* 463–468.

Byrne, D. (1961). The influence of propinquity and opportunities for interaction on classroom relationships. *Human Relations, 14,* 63–70.

Byrne, D. (1965). Parental antecedents of authoritarianism. *Journal of Personality and Social Psychology, 1,* 369–373.

Byrne, D. (1971). *The attraction paradigm.* New York: Academic Press.

Byrne, D., Allgeier, A., Winslow, L., & Buckman, J. (1975). The situational facilitation of interpersonal attraction: A three-factor hypothesis. *Journal of Applied Social Psychology, 5,* 1–15.

Byrne, D., & Clore, G. L. (1967). Effectance arousal and attraction. *Journal of Personality and Social Psychology, 6,* Monograph Whole No. 638.

Byrne, D., & Clore, G. L. (1970). A reinforcement model of evaluative responses. *Personality: An International Journal, 1,* 103–128.

Byrne, D., Clore, G. L., & Worchel, P. (1966). The effect of similarity-dissimilarity on interpersonal attraction. *Journal of Personality and Social Psychology, 4,* 220–224.

Byrne, D., Ervin, C. E., & Lamberth, J. (1970). Continuity between the experimental study of attraction and real-life computer dating. *Journal of Personality and Social Psychology, 16,* 157–165.

Byrne, D., & Griffitt, W. (1966). Similarity versus liking: A clarification. *Psychonomic Science, 6,* 295–296.

Cacioppo, J. T., & Petty, R. E. (1979). Effects of message repetition and position on cognitive response, recall and persuasion. *Journal of Personality and Social Psychology, 37,* 97–109.

Cacioppo, J. T., & Petty, R. E. (1982). The need for cognition. *Journal of Personality and Social Psychology, 42,* 116–131.

Cacioppo, J. T., Petty, R. E., Kao, C. F., & Rodriguez, R. (1986). Central and peripheral routes to persuasion: An individual difference perspective. *Journal of Personality and Social Psychology, 51,* 1032–1043.

Caldwell, J. A., & Harris, M. B. (1979). The effect of mood and arousal on confronting a thief. *Journal of Psychology, 103,* 231–239.

Campbell, D. E. (1979). Interior office design and visitor response. *Journal of Applied Psychology, 64,* 648–653.

Campbell, D. T. (1963). Social attitudes and other acquired behavioral dispositions. In S. Koch (Ed.), *Psychology: A study of a science* (Vol. 6, pp. 94–172). New York: McGraw-Hill.

Campbell, D. T. (1969). Reforms as experiments. *American Psychologist, 24,* 409–429.

Campbell, D. T. (1975). On the conflicts between biological and social evolution and between psychology and moral tradition. *American Psychologist, 30,* 1103–1126.

Campbell, D. T., & Stanley, J. C. (1966). *Experimental and quasi-experimental designs for research.* Chicago: Rand McNally.

Campbell, J. D., Tesser, A., & Fairey, P. J. (1986). Conformity and attention to the stimulus: Some temporal and contextual dynamics. *Journal of Personality and Social Psychology, 51,* 315–324.

Campbell, J. M. (1983). Ambient stressors. *Environment and Behavior, 15,* 355–380.

Campos, J. J., Barrett, K. C., Lamb, M. E., Goldsmith, H. H., & Stenberg, C. (1983). Socioemotional development. In M. M. Haith & J. J. Campos (Eds.), *Handbook of child psychology: Vol. 2. infancy and psychobiology* (pp. 783–915). New York: Wiley

Cannon, W. B. (1932). *The wisdom of the body.* New York: Norton.

Cantor, J. R., Zillman, D., & Einsiedel, E. F. (1978). Female responses to provocation after exposure to aggressive and erotic films. *Communication Research, 5,* 395–411.

Cantor, N., & Mischel, W. (1977). Traits as prototypes: Effects on recognition memory. *Journal of Personality and Social Psychology, 35*, 38–48.

Caplow, T., & Forman, R. (1950). Neighborhood interaction in a homogeneous community. *American Sociological Review, 15*, 357–366.

Cappella, J. N. (1981). Mutual influence in expressive behavior: Adult-adult and infant-adult dyadic interaction. *Psychological Bulletin, 89*, 101–132.

Carlsmith, J. M., & Anderson, C. A. (1979). Ambient temperature and the occurrence of collective violence: A new analysis. *Journal of Personality and Social Psychology, 37*, 337–344.

Carlsmith, J. M., Collins, B. E., & Helmreich, R. L. (1966). Studies in forced compliance: I. The effect of pressure for compliance on attitude change produced by face-to-face role-playing and anonymous essay writing. *Journal of Personality and Social Psychology, 4*, 1–13.

Carlsmith, J. M., Ellsworth, P. C., & Aronson, E. (1976). *Methods of research in social psychology.* Reading, MA: Addison-Wesley.

Carpenter, C. R. (1958). Territoriality: A review of concepts and problems. In A. Roe & G. G. Simpson (Eds.), *Behavior and evolution* (pp. 224–250). New Haven, CT: Yale University Press.

Carron, A. V. (1980). *Social psychology of sport.* Ithaca, NY: Mouvement Publications.

Cartwright, D. (1979). Contemporary social psychology in historical perspective. *Social Psychology Quarterly, 42*, 82–93.

Carver, C. S. (1979). A cybernetic model of self-attention processes. *Journal of Personality and Social Psychology, 37*, 1251–1281.

Carver, C. S., & Scheier, M. F. (1978). Self-focusing effects of dispositional self-consciousness, mirror presence, and audience presence. *Journal of Personality and Social Psychology, 36*, 324–332.

Cavior, N., & Boblett, P. J. (1972). Physical attractiveness of dating versus married couples. *Proceedings of the Annual Convention of the American Psychological Association, 7*, 175–176.

Chaiken, S., & Eagly, A. H. (1976). Communication modality as a determinant of message persuasiveness and message comprehensibility. *Journal of Personality and Social Psychology, 34*, 605–614.

Chaikin, A. L., & Derlega, V. (1978). Nonverbal mediators of expectancy effects in black and white children. *Journal of Applied Social Psychology, 8*, 117–125.

Chaikin, A. L., Derlega, V. J., & Miller, S. J. (1976). Effects of room environment on self-disclosure in a counseling analogue. *Journal of Consulting Psychology, 23*, 479–481.

Chapman, L. J. (1967). Illusory correlation in observational report. *Journal of Verbal Learning and Verbal Behavior, 6*, 151–155.

Cheek, J. M., & Buss, A. H. (1981). Shyness and sociability. *Journal of Personality and Social Psychology, 41*, 330–339.

Chelune, G. J. (1975). Self-disclosure: An elaboration of its basic dimensions. *Psychological Reports, 36*, 79–85.

Chelune, G. J. (1976). Reactions to male and female disclosure at two levels. *Journal of Personality and Social Psychology, 34*, 1000–1003.

Chemers, M. M., & Skrzypek, G. J. (1972). An experimental test of the Contingency Model of Leadership effectiveness. *Journal of Personality and Social Psychology, 24*, 172–177.

Cherulnik, P. D., & Wilderman, S. K. (1986). Symbols of status in urban neighborhoods: Contemporary perceptions of nineteenth century Boston. *Environment and Behavior, 18*, 604–622.

Childers, T. L., Heckler, S. E., & Houston, M. J. (1986). Memory for the visual and verbal components of print advertisements. *Psychology and Marketing, 3*, 137–149.

Christensen, A. (1979). Naturalistic observation of families: A system for random audio recordings. *Behavior Therapy, 10*, 418–427.

Cialdini, R. B. (1985). *Influence: Science and practice.* Glenview, IL: Scott, Foresman.

Cialdini, R. B., & Ascani, K. (1976). Test of a concession procedure for inducing verbal, behavioral, and further compliance with a request to donate blood. *Journal of Applied Psychology, 61*, 295–300.

Cialdini, R. B., Bickman, L., & Caccioppo, J. T. (1979). An example of consumeristic social psychology: Bargaining tough in the new car showroom. *Journal of Applied Social Psychology, 9*, 115–126.

Cialdini, R. B., Borden, R., Thorne, A., Walker, M., Freeman, S., & Sloane, L. T. (1976). Basking in reflected glory: Three (football) field studies. *Journal of Personality and Social Psychology, 34*, 366–375.

Cialdini, R. B., Braver, S. L., & Lewis, S. K. (1974). Attributional bias and the easily persuaded other. *Journal of Personality and Social Psychology, 30*, 631–637.

Cialdini, R. B., Caccioppo, J. T., Bassett, R., & Miller, J. A. (1978). Low-ball procedure for producing compliance: Commitment then cost. *Journal of Personality and Social Psychology, 36*, 463–476.

Cialdini, R. B., Darley, B. L., & Vincent, J. E. (1973). Transgression and altruism: A case for hedonism. *Journal of Experimental Social Psychology, 9*, 502–516.

Cialdini, R. B., & Kenrick, D. T. (1976). Altruism as hedonism: A social developmental perspective on the relationship of negative mood state and helping. *Journal of Personality and Social Psychology, 34*, 907–914.

Cialdini, R. B., Kenrick, D. T., & Hoerig, J. H. (1976). Victim derogation in the Lerner paradigm: Just world or just justification? *Journal of Personality and Social Psychology, 33*, 719–724.

Cialdini, R. B., Petty, R. E., & Caccioppo, J. T. (1981). Attitude and attitude change. In M. R. Rosenzweig & L. W. Porter (Eds.), *Annual review of psychology* (Vol. 32, pp. 357–404). Palo Alto, CA: Annual Reviews.

Cialdini, R. B., Schaller, M., Houlihan, D., Arps, K., Fultz, J., & Beaman, A. L. (1987). Empathy-based helping: Is it selflessly or selfishly motivated? *Journal of Personality and Social Psychology, 52*, 749–758.

Cialdini, R. B., & Schroeder, D. A. (1976). Increasing compliance by legitimizing paltry contributions: When even a penny helps. *Journal of Personality and Social Psychology, 34*, 559–604.

Cialdini, R. B., Vincent, J. E., Lewis, S. K., Catalan, J., Wheeler, D., & Darby, B. L. (1975). Reciprocal concessions procedure for inducing compliance: The door-in-the-face technique. *Journal of Personality and Social Psychology, 31*, 206–215.

Clancey, M., & Robinson, M. J. (1985). General election coverage: Part I. *Public Opinion, 7*, 49–54, 59.

Clark, K. B. (1963). *Prejudice and your child* (2nd ed.). Boston, MA: Beacon Press.

Clark, K., & Clark, M. (1947). Racial identification and preference in Negro children. In T. M. Newcomb & E. L. Hartley (Eds.), *Readings in social psychology.* New York: Holt.

Clark, M. S. (1984). Record keeping in two types of relationships. *Journal of Personality and Social Psychology, 47*, 549–557.

Clark, M. S. (1985). Implications of relationship type for understanding compatibility. In W. Ickes (Ed.), *Compatible and incompatible relationships* (pp. 119–142). New York: Springer-Verlag.

Clark, M. S., & Mills, J. (1979). Interpersonal attraction in exchange and communal relationships. *Journal of Personality and Social Psychology, 37,* 12–24.

Clark, R., Crockett, W. H., & Archer, R. L. (1971). Risk as value hypothesis: The relationship between perception of self, others, and the risky shift. *Journal of Personality and Social Psychology, 20,* 425–429.

Clark, R. D., & Word, L. E. (1972). Why don't bystanders help? Because of ambiguity? *Journal of Personality and Social Psychology, 24,* 392–400.

Clark, R. D., & Word, L. E. (1974). Where is the apathetic bystander? Situational characteristics of the emergency. *Journal of Personality and Social Psychology, 29,* 279–287.

Clark, R. N., Burgess, R. L., & Hendee, J. C. (1972). The development of anti-litter behavior in a forest campground. *Journal of Applied Behavior Analysis, 5,* 1–5.

Clarke, A. C. (1952). An examination of the operation of residential propinquity as a factor in mate selection. *American Sociological Review, 17,* 17–22.

Clayton, P. J., Halikas, J. A., & Maurice, W. L. (1972). The depression of widowhood. *British Journal of Psychiatry, 120,* 71–78.

Cline, V. B., Croft, R. G., & Courrier, S. (1973). Desensitization of children to television violence. *Journal of Personality and Social Psychology, 27,* 360–365.

Clore, G. L., Bray, R. M., Itkin, S. M., & Murphy, P. (1978). Interracial attitudes and behavior at a summer camp. *Journal of Personality and Social Psychology, 36,* 107–116.

Clore, G. L., & Byrne, D. (1974). A reinforcement-affect model of attraction. In T. L. Huston (Ed.), *Foundations of interpersonal attraction.* New York: Academic Press.

Coates, T. J., Stall, R. D., Kegeles, S. M., Lo, B., Morin, S. F., & McKusick, L. (1988). AIDS antibody testing: Will it stop the AIDS epidemic? Will it help people infected with HIV? *American Psychologist (Special Issue: Psychology and AIDS), 43,* 859–864.

Cobb, S., & Rose, R. M. (1973). Hypertension, peptic ulcer, and diabetes in air traffic controllers. *Journal of the American Medical Association, 224,* 489–492.

Cochran, C. D., Hale, D., & Hissam, C. P. (1984). Personal space requirements in indoor versus outdoor locations. *Journal of Psychology, 117,* 121–125.

Cochran, C. D., & Urbanczych, S. (1982). The effect of availability of vertical space on personal space. *Journal of Psychology, 111,* 137–140.

Cohen, A. (1977). Extra-auditory effects of acoustic stimulation. In D. K. Lee, L. Falk, S. D. Murphy, & S. R. Geiger (Eds.), *Handbook of physiology: Reactions to environmental agents.* Baltimore, MD: Williams & Wilkins.

Cohen, A. R. (1962). An experiment on small rewards for discrepant compliance and attitude change. In J. W. Brehm & A. R. Cohen (Eds.), *Explorations in cognitive dissonance.* New York: Wiley.

Cohen, C. E. (1981). Person categories and social perception: Testing some boundaries of the processing effects of prior knowledge. *Journal of Personality and Social Psychology, 40,* 441–452.

Cohen, J. L., Sladen, B., & Bennett, B. (1975). The effects of situational variables on judgments of crowding. *Sociometry, 38,* 273–281.

Cohen, S. (1981, October). Sound effects on behavior. *Psychology Today,* pp. 38, 41–42, 44, 48–49.

Cohen, S. (1986). Contrasting the hassles scale and the perceived stress scale: Who's really measuring appraised stress? *American Psychologist, 41,* 716–718.

Cohen, S., Evans, G. W., Krantz, D. S., & Stokols, D. (1980). Physiological, motivational, and cognitive effects of aircraft noise on children: Moving from the laboratory to the field. *American Psychologist, 35,* 231–243.

Cohen, S., Evans, G. W., Stokols, D., & Krantz, D. S. (1986). *Behavior, health, and environmental stress.* New York: Plenum.

Cohen, S., Glass, D. C., & Phillips, S. (1979). Environment and health. In H. E. Freeman, S. Levine, & L. G. Reeder (Eds.), *Handbook of medical sociology.* Englewood Cliffs, NJ: Prentice-Hall.

Cohen, S., & Hoberman, H. M. (1983). Positive events and social supports as buffers of life change scores. *Journal of Applied Social Psychology, 13,* 99–125.

Cohen, S., Kamarck, T., & Mermelstein, R. (1983). A global measure of perceived stress. *Journal of Health and Social Behavior, 24,* 385–396.

Cohen, S., & Spacapan, S. (1978). The aftereffects of stress: An attentional interpretation. *Environmental Psychology and Nonverbal Behavior, 3,* 43–57.

Cohen, S., & Spacapan, S. (1984). The social psychology of noise. In D. M. Jones & A. J. Chapman (Eds.), *Noise and society* (pp. 221–245). New York: Wiley.

Cohen, S., & Syme, S. L. (Eds.) (1985). *Social support and health.* New York: Academic Press.

Cohen, S., & Wills, T. A. (1985). Stress, social support, and the buffering hypothesis. *Psychological Bulletin, 98,* 310–357.

Coke, J. S., Batson, C. D., & McDavis, K. (1978). Empathic mediation of helping: A two-stage model. *Journal of Personality and Social Psychology, 36,* 464–468.

Coleman, M., & Ganong, L. H. (1985). Love and sex role stereotypes: Do macho men and feminine women make better lovers? *Journal of Personality and Social Psychology, 49,* 170–176.

Collard, R. R. (1968). Social and play responses of first-born and later-born infants in an unfamiliar situation. *Child Development, 39,* 325–334.

Collins, D. L., Baum, A., & Singer, J. E. (1982). Coping with chronic stress at Three Mile Island: Psychological and biochemical evidence. *Health Psychology, 2,* 149–166.

Collins, W. A., & Getz, S. K. (1976). Children's social responses following modeled reactions to provocation: Prosocial effects of a television drama. *Journal of Personality, 44,* 488–500.

Colombotes, J. (1969). Physicians and medicare: A before-after study of the effects of legislation on attitudes. *American Sociological Review, 34,* 318–334.

Committee on Model Jury Instructions of the 9th Circuit Court. (1985). *Manual of model jury instructions for the 9th circuit.* St. Paul, MN: West Publishing.

Condon, J. W., & Crano, W. D. (1988). Inferred evaluation and the relation between attitude similarity and interpersonal attraction. *Journal of Personality and Social Psychology, 54,* 789–797.

Condry, J., & Dyer, S. (1976). Fear of success: Attribution of cause to the victim. *Journal of Social Issues, 32,* 63–83.

Cone, J. D., & Hayes, S. C. (1980). *Environmental problems/behavioral solutions.* Monterey, CA: Brooks/Cole.

Connor, R. L., & Levine, S. (1969). Hormonal influences on aggressive behaviour. In S. Garattini & E. B. Sigg (Eds.), *Aggressive behaviour.* New York: Wiley.

Constantinople, A. (1973). Masculinity-femininity: An exception to a famous dictum. *Psychological Bulletin, 80,* 389–407.

Conway, M., & Ross, M. (1984). Getting what you want by revising what you had. *Journal of Personality and Social Psychology, 47,* 738–748.

Cook, J. M. (1975). *In defense of homo sapiens.* New York: Dell.

Cook, M. (1969). Anxiety, speech disturbance, and speech rate. *British Journal of Social and Clinical Psychology, 8,* 13–21.

Cook, M. (1977). Gaze and mutual gaze in social encounters. *American Scientist, 65,* 328–333.

Cook, S. W. (1970). Motives in a conceptual analysis of attitude-related behavior. In W. J. Arnold & D. Levine (Eds.), *Nebraska symposium on motivation* (Vol. 17, pp. 179–235). Lincoln, NE: University of Nebraska Press.

Cook, S. W. (1978). Interpersonal and attitudinal outcomes in cooperating interracial groups. *Journal of Research and Development in Education, 12*, 97–113.

Cook, S. W. (1984). Cooperative interaction in multiethnic contexts. In N. Miller & M. B. Brewer (Eds.), *Groups in contact*. New York: Academic Press.

Cook, S. W. (1985a). Experimenting on social issues: The case of school desegregation. *American Psychologist, 40*, 452–460.

Cook, S. W. (1985b). *Helping and being helped in cooperating interracial groups: Effects on respect and liking for group members*. Paper presented at the Society of Experimental Social Psychology meeting, Evanston, IL.

Cook, T. D., & Campbell, D. T. (1979). *Quasi-experimentation: Design and analysis issues for field settings*. Chicago, IL: Rand McNally.

Cooley, C. (1902). *Human nature and the social order*. New York: Scribner.

Cooper, H. M. (1979). Statistically combining independent studies: A meta-analysis of sex differences in conformity research. *Journal of Personality and Social Psychology, 37*, 131–146.

Cooper, J. (1971). Personal responsibility and dissonance: The role of foreseen consequences. *Journal of Personality and Social Psychology, 18*, 354–363.

Cooper, J., & Duncan, B. L. (1971). Cognitive dissonance as a function of self-esteem and logical inconsistency. *Journal of Personality, 39*, 289–302.

Cooper, J., & Fazio, R. H. (1984). A new look at dissonance theory. In L. Berkowitz (Ed.), *Advances in experimental social psychology* (Vol. 17). New York: Academic Press.

Cooper, J., & Worchel, S. (1970). Role of undesired consequences in arousing dissonance. *Journal of Personality and Social Psychology, 16*, 199–206.

Cooper, J., Zanna, M. P., & Goethals, G. R. (1974). Mistreatment of an esteemed other as a consequence affecting dissonance reduction. *Journal of Experimental Social Psychology, 10*, 224–233.

Cooper, J., Zanna, M. P., & Taves, P. A. (1978). Arousal as a necessary for attitude change following induced compliance. *Journal of Personality and Social Psychology, 36*, 1101–1106.

Cooper, K. C. (1968). *Aerobics*. New York: Bantam Books.

Coopersmith, S. (1967). *The antecedents of self-esteem*. San Francisco: W. H. Freeman.

Cope, J. G., & Geller, E. S. (1984). Community-based interventions to increase the use of automobile litterbags. *Journal of Resource Management and Technology, 13*, 127–132.

Corliss, R. (1986, June 16). If heaven ain't a lot like Disney. *Time*, pp. 80–84.

Costanzo, F. S., Markel, N. N., & Costanzo, P. R. (1969). Voice quality profile and perceived emotion. *Journal of Counseling Psychology, 16*, 267–270.

Costanza, R. S., Derlega, V. J., & Winstead, B. A. (1988). Positive and negative forms of social support: Effects of conversational topics on coping and stress among same-sex friends. *Journal of Experimental Social Psychology, 24*, 182–193.

Cottrell, N. B. (1972). Social facilitation. In C. G. McClintock (Ed.), *Experimental social psychology*. New York: Holt, Rinehart & Winston.

Cousins, N. (1979). *Anatomy of an illness*. New York: Norton.

Coyne, J. C., & Lazarus, R. S. (1981). Cognitive style, stress perception, and coping. In I. L. Kutash & L. B. Schlesinger (Eds.), *Handbook of stress and anxiety* (pp. 144–158). Washington, DC: Jossey-Bass.

Cozby, P. C. (1972). Self-disclosure, reciprocity and liking. *Sociometry, 35*, 151–160.

Craik, K. H., & Feimer, N. R. (1987). Environmental assessment. In D. Stokols & I. Altman (Eds.), *Handbook of environmental psychology* (Vol. 2, pp. 891–918). New York: Wiley.

Craik, K. H., & Zube, E. H. (Eds.) (1976). *Perceiving environmental quality*. New York: Plenum.

Crano, W. D., & Cooper, R. E. (1973). Examination of Newcomb's extension of structural balance theory. *Journal of Personality and Social Psychology, 27*, 344–353.

Crano, W. D., & Messe, L. A. (1982). *Social psychology: Principles and themes of interpersonal behavior*. Homewood, IL: Dorsey Press.

Crocker, J., Thompson, L. L., McGraw, K. M., & Ingerman, C. (1987). Downward comparison, prejudice, and evaluations of others: Effects of self-esteem and threat. *Journal of Personality and Social Psychology, 52*, 907–916.

Crook, J. H. (1973). The nature and function of territorial aggression. In M. F. A. Montagu (Ed.), *Man and aggression* (2nd ed., pp. 183–220). New York: Oxford University Press.

Croyle, R., & Cooper, J. (1983). Dissonance arousal: Physiological evidence. *Journal of Personality and Social Psychology, 45*, 782–791.

Crusco, A. H., & Wetzel, C. G. (1984). The Midas touch: The effects of interpersonal touch on restaurant tipping. *Personality and Social Psychology Bulletin, 10*, 512–517.

Crutchfield, (1955). Conformity and character. *American Psychologist, 10*, 191–198.

Cunningham, M. R. (1979). Weather, mood, and helping behavior: Quasi-experiments with the sunshine Samaritan. *Journal of Personality and Social Psychology, 37*, 1947–1956.

D'Atri, D. A. (1975). Psychophysical responses to crowding. *Environment and Behavior, 7*, 237–252.

Dabbs, J. M., Jr. (1977). Does reaction to crowding depend upon sex of subject or sex of subject's partner? *Journal of Personality and Social Psychology, 35*, 343–344.

Dabbs, J. M., Jr., & Ruback, R. B. (1984). Vocal patterns in male and female groups. *Personality and Social Psychology Bulletin, 10*, 518–525.

Daly, J. A., Hogg, E., Sacks, D., Smith, M., & Zimring, L. (1983). Sex and relationship affect social self-grooming. *Journal of Nonverbal Behavior, 7*, 183–189.

Danford, S., Starr, N., & Willems, E. P. (1979). The case against subjective, cognitive reports in environmental design research: A critical test. In A. D. Seidel & S. Danford (Eds.), *Environmental design: Research, theory, and application* (pp. 181–189). Washington, DC: Environmental Design Research Association.

Darley, J. M., & Batson, C. D. (1973). From Jerusalem to Jericho: A study of situational and dispositional variables in helping behavior. *Journal of Personality and Social Psychology, 27*, 100–108.

Darley, J. M., & Fazio, R. H. (1980). Expectancy confirmation processes arising in the social interaction sequence. *American Psychologist, 35*, 867–881.

Darley, J. M., & Latane, B. (1968). Bystander intervention in emergencies: Diffusion of responsibility. *Journal of Personality and Social Psychology, 8*, 377–383.

Darley, J. M., Teger, A., & Lewis, L. (1973). Do groups always inhibit individuals' responses to potential emergencies? *Journal of Personality and Social Psychology, 26*, 395–399.

Darley, S. A., & Cooper, J. (1972). Cognitive consequences of forced non-compliance. *Journal of Personality and Social Psychology, 24*, 321–326.

Daves, W. F., & Swaffer, P. W. (1971). Effect of room size on critical interpersonal distance. *Perceptual and Motor Skills, 33*, 926.

Davidson, A. R., & Jaccard, J. J. (1979). Variables that moderate the attitude-behavior relation: Results of a longitudinal survey. *Journal of Personality and Social Psychology, 37,* 1364–1376.

Davies, J. C. (1962). Toward a theory of revolution. *American Sociological Review, 27,* 5–19.

Davies, J. C. (1969). The J-curve of rising and declining satisfactions as a cause of some revolutions and a contained rebellion. In H. D. Graham & T. R. Gurr (Eds.), *Violence in America* (Vol. 2). Washington, DC: U.S. Government Printing Office.

Davis, D. (1981). Implications for interaction versus effectance as mediators of the similarity-attraction relationship. *Journal of Experimental Social Psychology, 17,* 96–116.

Davis, D. (1982). Determinants of responsiveness in dyadic interaction. In W. Ickes & E. Knowles (Eds.), *Personality, roles and social behavior.* New York: Springer-Verlag.

Davis, D., & Perkowitz, W. T. (1979). Consequences of responsiveness in dyadic interaction: Effects of probability of response and proportion of content-related responses on interpersonal attraction. *Journal of Personality and Social Psychology, 37,* 534–550.

Davis, J. H. (1980). Group decision and social interaction. A theory of social decision schemes. *Psychological Review, 80,* 97–125.

Davis, K. E. (1985, February). Near and dear: Friendship and love compared. *Psychology Today,* pp. 22–30.

Davis, M. (1987, March 7). Violence rips life of quiet, gentle clerk. *Dayton Daily News, 110* (179), 3.

Dawkins, R. (1976). *The selfish gene.* New York: Oxford University Press.

DeBeer-Keston, K., Mellon, L., & Solomon, L. Z. (1986). Helping behavior as a function of personal space invasion. *Journal of Social Psychology, 126,* 407–409.

DeGree, C., & Snyder, C. (1985). Adler's psychology (of use) today: Personal history of traumatic life events as a self-handicapping strategy. *Journal of Personality and Social Psychology, 48,* 1512–1519.

DeLongis, A., Coyne, J. C., Dakof, G., Folkman, S., & Lazarus, R. S. (1982). Relationship of daily hassles, uplifts, and major life events to health status. *Health Psychology, 1,* 119–136.

DePaulo, B. M., Stone, J. I., & Lassiter, D. G. (1985). Telling ingratiating lies: Effects of target sex and target attractiveness on verbal and nonverbal deceptive success. *Journal of Personality and Social Psychology, 48,* 1191–1203.

DePaulo, B. M., Zuckerman, M., & Rosenthal, R. (1980). Detecting deception: Modality effects. In L. Wheeler (Ed.), *Review of personality and social psychology* (Vol. 1, pp. 125–162). Beverly Hills, CA: Sage.

DeVries, D. L., Edwards, K. J., & Slavin, R. E. (1978). Biracial learning teams and race relations in the classroom: Four field experiments using teams-games-tournaments. *Journal of Educational Psychology, 70,* 356–362.

Dean, J. (1976). *Blind ambition.* New York: Doubleday.

Deaux, K. (1972). Anticipatory attitude change: A direct test of the self-esteem hypothesis. *Journal of Experimental Social Psychology, 8,* 143–155.

Deaux, K., & Emswiller, T. (1974). Explanations of successful performance on sex-linked tasks: What is skill for the male is luck for the female. *Journal of Personality and Social Psychology, 29,* 80–85.

Deci, E. (1975). *Intrinsic motivation.* New York: Plenum.

Deci, E. L. (1980). *The psychology of self-determination.* Lexington, MA: Lexington Books.

Delgado, J. M. R. (1969). *Physical control of the mind.* New York: Harper & Row.

Delgado, J. M., Roberts, W. W., & Miller, N. E. (1954). Learning motivated by electrical stimulation of the brain. *American Journal of Physiology, 179,* 587–593.

Dembroski, T. M., & Costa, P. T., Jr. (1987). Coronary prone behavior: Components of the Type A pattern and hostility. *Journal of Personality, 55,* 211–235.

Demo, D. H. (1985). The measurement of self-esteem: Refining our methods. *Journal of Personality and Social Psychology, 48,* 1490–1502.

Derlega, V. J., & Chaikin, A. L. (1975). *Sharing intimacy: What we reveal to others and why.* Englewood Cliffs, NJ: Prentice-Hall.

Derlega, V. J., Wilson, M., & Chaikin, A. L. (1976). Friendship and disclosure reciprocity. *Journal of Personality and Social Psychology, 34,* 578–582.

Des Jarlais, D. C., & Friedman, S. R. (1988). The psychology of preventing AIDS among intravenous drug users: A social learning conceptualization. *American Psychologist (Special Issue: Psychology and AIDS), 43,* 865–870.

Desor, J. A. (1972). Toward a psychological theory of crowding. *Journal of Personality and Social Psychology, 21,* 79–83.

Deutsch, M. (1949). A theory of cooperation and competition. *Human Relations, 2,* 129–152

Deutsch, M., & Collins, M. (1951). *Interracial housing: A psychological evaluation of a social experiment.* Minneapolis, MN: University of Minnesota Press.

Deutsch, M., & Gerard, H. B. (1955). A study of normative and informational social influence upon individual judgement. *Journal of Abnormal and Social Psychology, 51,* 629–636.

Devine, P. G. (1989). Stereotypes and prejudice: Their automatic and controlled components. *Journal of Personality and Social Psychology, 56,* 5–18.

Dew, M. A., Bromet, E. J., & Schulberg, H. C. (1987). A comparative analysis of two community stressors' long-term mental health effects. *American Journal of Community Psychology, 15,* 167–184.

Dey, F. L. (1970). Auditory fatigue and predicted permanent hearing defects from rock-and-roll music. *New England Journal of Medicine, 282,* 467–469.

Dichter, E. (1960). *The strategy of desire.* Garden City, NY: Doubleday.

Dickoff, H. (1961). *Reactions to evaluations by another person as a function of self-evaluation and the interaction context.* Unpublished Ph.D. Dissertation, Duke University.

Dickson, H. (1988, July 2). Body-language reports: Glenn's not Duke's pick. *Boston Herald,* pp. 1, 9.

Diener, C. I., & Dweck, C. S. (1978). An analysis of learned helplessness: Continuous changes in performance, strategy, and achievement cognitions following failure. *Journal of Personality and Social Psychology, 36,* 451–462.

Diener, E. (1979). Deindividuation, self-awareness, and disinhibition. *Journal of Personality and Social Psychology, 37,* 1160–1171.

Diener, E. (1980). Deindividuation: The absence of self-awareness and self-regulation in group members. In P. B. Paulus (Ed.), *Psychology of group influence* (pp. 209–244). Hillsdale, NJ: Erlbaum.

Diener, E., Fraser, S. C., Beaman, A. L., & Kelem, R. T. (1976). Effects of deindividuating variables on stealing by Halloween trick-or-treaters. *Journal of Personality and Social Psychology, 33,* 178–183.

Diener, E., Lusk, R., DeFour, D., & Flax, R. (1980). Deindividuation: Effects of group size, density, number of observers, and group member similarity on self-consciousness and disinhibited behavior. *Journal of Personality and Social Psychology, 39,* 449–459.

Dion, K. (1972). Physical attractiveness and evaluations of children's transgressions. *Journal of Personality and Social Psychology, 24,* 207–213.

Dion, K. K., Berscheid, E., & Walster, E. (1972). What is beautiful is good. *Journal of Personality and Social Psychology, 24,* 285–290.

Dion, K. K., & Stein, S. (1978). Physical attractiveness and interpersonal influence. *Journal of Experimental Social Psychology, 14,* 97–108.

Dion, K. L., Baron, R. S., & Miller, N. (1970). Why do groups make riskier decisions than individuals? In L. Berkowitz (Ed.), *Advances in experimental social psychology* (Vol. 5). New York: Academic Press.

Dittmann, A. T. (1972). *Interpersonal messages of emotion.* New York: Springer.

Dohrenwend, B. P., & Shrout, P. E. (1985). "Hassles" in the conceptualization and measurement of life stress variables. *American Psychologist, 40,* 780–785.

Dohrenwend, B. S., & Dohrenwend, B. P. (Eds.) (1974). *Stressful life events: Their nature and effects.* New York: Wiley.

Dohrenwend, B. S., & Dohrenwend, B. P. (Eds.) (1981). *Stressful life events and their contexts.* New York: Prodist.

Dollard, J., Doob, L., Miller, N., Mowrer, O., & Sears, R. (1939). *Frustration and aggression.* New Haven, CT: Yale University Press.

Donaldson, K. (1976). *Insanity inside out.* New York: Crown.

Donnerstein, E. (1980). Aggressive erotica and violence against women. *Journal of Personality and Social Psychology, 39,* 269–277.

Donnerstein, E. (1983). Erotica and human aggression. In R. G. Geen & E. I. Donnerstein (Eds.), *Aggression: Theoretical and empirical reviews* (Vol. 2, pp. 127–154). New York: Academic Press.

Donnerstein, E., & Hallum, J. (1978). Facilitating effects of erotica on aggression against women. *Journal of Personality and Social Psychology, 36,* 1270–1277.

Donnerstein, E., & Wilson, D. W. (1976). Effects of noise and perceived control on ongoing and subsequent aggressive behavior. *Journal of Personality and Social Psychology, 34,* 774–781.

Dooley, D., Rook, K., & Catalano, R. (1987). Job and non-job stressors and their moderators. *Journal of Occupational Psychology, 60,* 115–132.

Dooley, D., & Catalano, R. (1984). Why the economy predicts help-seeking: A test of competing explanations. *Journal of Health and Social Behavior, 25,* 160–176.

Dosey, M. A., & Meisels, M. (1969). Personal space and self-protection. *Journal of Personality and Social Psychology, 11,* 93–97.

Drabman, R. S., & Thomas, M. H. (1974). Does media violence increase children's toleration of real life aggression? *Developmental Psychology, 10,* 418–421.

Duffy, M., Bailey, S., Beck, B., & Barker, D. G. (1986). Preferences in nursing home design: A comparison of residents, administrators, and designers. *Environment and Behavior, 18,* 246–257.

Duke, M. P., & Nowicki, S. (1972). A new measure and social-learning model for interpersonal distance. *Journal of Experimental Research in Personality, 6,* 119–132.

Duncan, S. D., Jr. (1972). Some signals and rules for taking speaking turns in conversations. *Journal of Personality and Social Psychology, 23,* 283–292.

Duncan, S. D., Jr., & Fiske, D. W. (1977). *Face-to-face interaction: Research, method, and theory.* Hillsdale, NJ: Erlbaum.

Dunkel-Schetter, C., Folkman, S., & Lazarus, R. S. (1987). Correlates of social support receipt. *Journal of Personality and Social Psychology, 53,* 71–80.

Dunnette, M. D., Campbell, J., & Jaastad, K. (1963). The effect of group participation on brainstorming effectiveness for two industrial samples. *Journal of Applied Psychology, 47,* 30–37.

Durdan, C. A., Reeder, G. D., & Hecht, P. R. (1985). Litter in a university cafeteria: Demographic data and the use of prompts as an intervention strategy. *Environment and Behavior, 17,* 387–404.

Dutton, D. G., & Aron, A. P. (1974). Some evidence for heightened sexual attraction under conditions of high anxiety. *Journal of Personality and Social Psychology, 30,* 510–517.

Dutton, D. G., & Lennox, V. L. (1974). Effect of prior "token" compliance on subsequent interracial behavior. *Journal of Personality and Social Psychology, 29,* 65–71.

Duval, S., & Wicklund, R. A. (1972). *A theory of objective self-awareness.* New York: Academic Press.

Eagly, A. H. (1974). Comprehensibility of persuasive arguments as a determinant of opinion change. *Journal of Personality and Social Psychology, 29,* 758–773.

Eagly, A. H. (1978). Sex differences in influenceability. *Psychological Bulletin, 85,* 86–116.

Eagly, A. H. (1987). *Sex differences in social behavior: A social role interpretation.* Hillsdale, NJ: Lawrence Erlbaum.

Eagly, A. H., & Chaiken, S. (1984). Cognitive theories of persuasion. In L. Berkowitz (Ed.), *Advances in experimental social psychology* (Vol. 17). New York: Academic Press.

Eagly, A. H., & Crowley, M. (1986). Gender and helping behavior: A meta-analytic review of the social psychological literature. *Psychological Bulletin, 100,* 283–308.

Eagly, A. H., & Steffen, V. J. (1986). Gender and aggressive behavior: A meta-analytic review of the social psychological literature. *Psychological Bulletin, 100,* 309–330.

Eagly, A. H., Wood, W., & Chaiken, S. (1978). Causal inferences about communicators and their effect on opinion change. *Journal of Personality and Social Psychology, 36,* 424–435.

Eagly, A. H., Wood, W., & Fishbaugh, L. (1981). Sex differences in conformity: Surveillance by the group as a determinant of male nonconformity. *Journal of Personal and Social Psychology, 40,* 384–394.

Eastman, C. M., & Harper, J. (1971). A study of proxemic behavior. *Environment and Behavior, 3,* 418–437.

Ebbesen, E. B., Kjos, G. L., & Konečni, V. J. (1976). Spatial ecology: Its effects on the choice of friends and enemies. *Journal of Experimental Social Psychology, 12,* 505–518.

Eckenrode, J. (1984). Impact of chronic and acute stressors on daily reports of mood. *Journal of Personality and Social Psychology, 46,* 907–918.

Eden, D. (1984). Self-fulfilling prophecy as a management tool: Harnessing Pygmalion. *Academy of Management Review, 9,* 64–73.

Eden, D., & Ravid, G. (1982). Pygmalion vs. self-expectancy: Effects of instructor- and self-expectancy on trainee performance. *Organizational Behavior and Human Performance, 30,* 351–364.

Edney, J. J. (1972a). Place and space: The effects of experience with a physical locale. *Journal of Experimental Social Psychology, 8,* 124–135.

Edney, J. J. (1972b). Property, possession, and permanence: A field study in human territoriality. *Journal of Applied Social Psychology, 2,* 275–282.

Edney, J. J. (1974). Human territoriality. *Psychological Bulletin, 81,* 959–975.

Edney, J. J. (1975). Territoriality and control: A field experiment. *Journal of Personality and Social Psychology, 31,* 1108–1115.

Edney, J. J. (1976). The psychological role of property rights in human behavior. *Environment and Planning A, 8,* 811–822.

Edney, J. J., & Uhlig, S. R. (1977). Individual and small group territories. *Small Group Behavior, 8,* 457–468.

Edwards, D. A. (1968).   Mice: Fighting by neonatally androgenized females. *Science, 161,* 1027–1028.

Egger, M. D., & Flynn, J. P. (1962). Amygdaloid suppression of hypothalamically elicited attack behavior. *Science, 136,* 43–44.

Ehrlich, H. J., & Graeven, D. B. (1971). Reciprocal self-disclosure in a dyad. *Journal of Experimental Social Psychology, 7,* 389–400.

Eibl-Eibesfeldt, I. (1972).   Similarities and differences between cultures in expressive movements. In R. A. Hinde (Ed.), *Nonverbal communication and movement.* New York: Academic Press.

Einhorn, H. J., & Hogarth, R. M. (1978). Confidence in judgment: Persistence in the illusion of validity. *Psychological Review, 85,* 395–416.

Eisenberg-Berg, N. (1979).   Development of childrens' prosocial moral judgment. *Developmental Psychology, 15,* 128–137.

Ekman, P., & Friesen, W. V. (1969). Nonverbal leakage and cues to deception. *Psychiatry, 32,* 88–108.

Ekman, P., & Friesen, W. V. (1975). *Unmasking the face.* Englewood Cliffs, NJ: Prentice-Hall.

Ekman, P., Friesen, W. V., & Ellsworth, P. (1972).   *Emotion in the human face.* New York: Pergamon.

Ekman, P., Friesen, W. V., O'Sullivan, M., & Scherer, K. (1980).   Relative importance of face, body, and speech in judgements of personality and affect. *Journal of Personality and Social Psychology, 38,* 270–277.

Eldersveld, S. J., & Dodge, R. W. (1954). Personal contact or mail propaganda? An experiment in voting turnout and attitude change. In D. Katz et al. (Eds.), *Public opinion and propaganda.* New York: Dryden Press.

Ellis, G. T., & Sekra, F., III. (1972).   The effect of aggressive cartoons on the behavior of first grade children. *Journal of Psychology, 81,* 37–43.

Ellsworth, P. C. (1975).   Direct gaze as a social stimulus: The example of aggression. In P. Pliner, L. Krames, & T. Allaway (Eds.), *Nonverbal communication of aggression.* New York: Plenum Press.

Ellsworth, P. C., & Carlsmith, J. M. (1968). Effects of eye contact and verbal content on affective responses to a dyadic interaction. *Journal of Personality and Social Psychology, 10,* 15–20.

Ellsworth, P. C., Carlsmith, J. M., & Henson, A. (1972).   The stare as a stimulus to flight in human subjects: A series of field experiments. *Journal of Personality and Social Psychology, 21,* 302–311.

Ellyson, S. L., Dovidio, J. F., Corson, R. L., & Vinicur, D. L. (1980).   Visual dominance behaviors in female dyads: Situational and personality factors. *Social Psychology Quarterly, 43,* 328–336.

Elman, D., Schulte, D. C., & Bukoff, A. (1977).   Effects of facial expression and stare duration on walking speed: Two field experiments. *Environmental Psychology and Nonverbal Behavior, 2,* 93–99.

Environmental Protection Agency. (1972). Report to the President and Congress on noise. Washington, DC: U.S. Government Printing Office.

Epstein, S. M. (1967).   Toward a unified theory of anxiety. In B. Maher (Ed.), *Progress in experimental personality research* (Vol. 4). New York: Academic Press.

Epstein, S., & Taylor, S. (1967). Instigation to aggression as a function of degree of defeat and perceived aggressive intent of the opponent. *Journal of Personality, 35,* 265–289.

Epstein, Y. M. (1982).   Crowding stress and human behavior. In G. W. Evans (Ed.), *Environmental stress.* New York: Cambridge University Press.

Epstein, Y. M., & Karlin, R. A. (1975). Effects of acute experimental crowding. *Journal of Applied Social Psychology, 5,* 34–53.

Erickson, B., Lind, E. A., Johnson, B. C., & O'Barr, W. M. (1978).   Speech style and impression formation in a court setting: The effects of "powerful" and "powerless" speech. *Journal of Experimental Social Psychology, 14,* 266–279.

Ernst, C., & Angst, J. (1983).   *Birth order: Its influence on personality.* New York: Springer-Verlag.

Eron, L. D., Huesmann, L. R., Lefkowitz, M. M., & Walder, L. O. (1972).   Does television violence cause aggression? *American Psychologist, 27,* 253–263.

Eron, L. D., Walder, L. O., & Lefkowitz, M. M. (1971).   *Learning of aggression in children.* Boston, MA: Little, Brown.

Etzioni, A. (1967).   The Kennedy experiment. *The Western Political Quarterly, 20,* 361–380.

Evans, G. W. (1979).   Behavioral and physiological consequences of crowding in humans. *Journal of Applied Social Psychology, 9,* 27–46.

Evans, G. W., & Cohen, S. (1987). Environmental stress. In D. Stokols & I. Altman (Eds.), *Handbook of environmental psychology.* New York: Wiley.

Evans, G. W., Colome, S. D., & Shearer, D. F. (1988).   Psychological reactions to air pollution. *Environmental Research, 45,* 1–15.

Evans, G. W., Jacobs, S. V., Dooley, D., & Catalano, R. (1987).   The interaction of stressful life events and chronic strains on community mental health. *American Journal of Community Psychology, 15,* 23–34.

Evans, G. W., & Tafalla, R. (1987). Measurement of environmental annoyance. In H. S. Koelega (Ed.), *Environmental annoyance: Characterization, measurement, and control* (pp. 11–25). New York: Amsterdam.

Evans, G. W., & Wood, K. W. (1980). Assessment of environmental aesthetics in scenic highway corridors. *Environment and Behavior, 12,* 255–273.

Evans, R. I. (1980).   Behavioral medicine: A new applied challenge to social psychologists. In L. Bickman (Ed.), *Applied social psychology annual* (Vol. 1, pp. 279–305). Beverly Hills, CA: Sage.

Exline, R. V. (1963).   Explorations in the process of person perception: Visual interaction in relation to competition, sex, and the need for affiliation. *Journal of Personality, 31,* 1–20.

Exline, R. V., Ellyson, S. L., & Long, B. D. (1975).   Visual behavior as an aspect of power role relationships. In P. Pliner, L. Krames, & T. Alloway (Eds.), *Advances in the study of communication and affect* (Vol. 2, pp. 21–25). New York: Plenum.

Exline, R. V., Gray, D., & Schuette, D. (1965).   Visual behavior in a dyad as affected by interview content and sex of respondent. *Journal of Personality and Social Psychology, 1,* 201–209.

Exline, R. V., & Winters, L. C.   Affective relations and mutual glances in dyads. In S. Tomkins & C. E. Izard (Eds.), *Affect, cognition, and personality.* New York: Springer.

Faranda, J. A., Kaminski, J. A., & Giza, B. K. (1979).   *An assessment of attitudes toward women with the bogus pipeline.* Paper presented at the American Psychological Association convention, New York, NY.

Farley, R., Schuman, H., Bianchi, S., Colasnto, D., & Hatchett, S. (1978). Chocolate city, vanilla suburbs: Will the trend toward racially separate communities continue? *Social Science Research, 7,* 319–344.

Fazio, R. H. (1986).   How do attitudes guide behavior? In R. Sorrentino & E. T. Higgins (Eds.), *The handbook of motivation and cognition: Foundations of social behavior.* New York: Guildford Press.

Fazio, R. H., Powell, M. C., & Herr, P. M. (1983).   Toward a process model of the attitude-behavior relation: Accessing one's attitude upon mere observation of the attitude object. *Journal of Personality and Social Psychology, 44,* 723–735.

Fazio, R. H., Sanbonmatsu, D. M., Powell, M. C., & Kardes, F. R. (1986).   On the automatic activation of attitudes. *Journal of Personality and Social Psychology, 50,* 229–238.

Fazio, R. H., & Zanna, M. P. (1981). Direct experience and attitude-behavior consistency. In L. Berkowitz (Ed.), *Advances in experimental social psychology* (Vol. 14). New York: Academic Press.

Fazio, R. H., Zanna, M. P., & Cooper, J. (1977).   Dissonance and self-perception: An integrative view of each theory's proper domain of application. *Journal of Experimental Social Psychology, 13,* 464–479.

Federal Bureau of Investigation. (1986). *Uniform crime reports—1985.* Washington, DC: U.S. Government Publications Office.

Feist, J., & Brannon, L. (1988).   *Health psychology: An introduction to behavior and health.* Belmont, CA: Wadsworth.

Feldman, R. S., & Prohaska, T. (1979). The student as Pygmalion: Effect of students' expectancy on the teacher. *Journal of Educational Psychology, 71,* 485–493.

Feldman, R. S., & Theiss, A. J. (1982). The teacher and student as Pygmalions: The joint effects of teacher and student expectation. *Journal of Educational Psychology, 74,* 217–223.

Felipe, N. J., & Sommer, R. (1966). Invasions of personal space. *Social Problems, 14,* 206–214.

Fenigstein, A. (1979).   Self-consciousness, self-attention, and social interaction. *Journal of Personality and Social Psychology, 37,* 75–86.

Fenigstein, A., Scheier, M. F., & Buss, A. H. (1975).   Public and private self-consciousness: Assessment and theory. *Journal of Consulting and Clinical Psychology, 43,* 522–527.

Feshbach, N. D. (1980).   *The child as "psychologist" and "economist": Two curricula.* Paper presented at the American Psychological Association convention.

Feshbach, S., & Singer, R. (1971). *Television and aggression.* San Francisco: Jossey-Bass.

Festinger, L. (1954).   A theory of social comparison processes. *Human Relations, 7,* 117–140.

Festinger, L. (1957).   *A theory of cognitive dissonance.* Stanford, CA: Stanford University Press.

Festinger, L. (1964).   *Conflict, decision and dissonance.* Stanford, CA: Stanford University Press.

Festinger, L. (1980).   Looking backward. In L. Festinger (Ed.), *Retrospections on social psychology* (pp. 236–254). New York: Oxford University Press.

Festinger, L., & Carlsmith, J. M. (1959). Cognitive consequences of forced compliance. *Journal of Abnormal and Social Psychology, 58,* 203–210.

Festinger, L., Riecken, H. W., & Schachter, S. (1956).   *When prophecy fails.* Minneapolis, MN: University of Minnesota Press.

Festinger, L., Schachter, S., & Back, K. (1950).   *Social pressures in informal groups.* New York: Harper.

Fiedler, F. E. (1954).   Assumed similarity measures as predictors of team effectiveness. *Journal of Abnormal and Social Psychology, 49,* 381–388.

Fiedler, F. E. (1964).   A contingency model of leadership effectiveness. In L. Berkowitz (Ed.), *Advances in experimental social psychology.* New York: Academic Press.

Fiedler, F. E. (1967).   *A theory of leadership effectiveness.* New York: McGraw-Hill.

Fiedler, F. E. (1971).   *Leadership.* New York: General Learning Press.

Fiedler, F. E. (1978).   Recent developments in research on the contingency model. In L. Berkowitz (Ed.), *Group processes.* New York: Academic Press.

Fiedler, F. E. (1981).   Leadership effectiveness. *American Behavioral Scientist, 24,* 619–632.

Fiedler, F. E., Chemers, M. M., & Mahar, L. (1977).   *Improving leadership effectiveness: The leader match approach* (Rev. ed.). New York: Wiley.

Fiedler, F. E., & Mahar, L. (1979).   The effectiveness of contingency model training: A review of the validation of leader match. *Personnel Psychology, 32,* 45–62.

Field, T. (1978).   Interaction behaviors of primary versus secondary caretaker fathers. *Developmental Psychology, 14,* 183–184.

Fincham, F., & O'Leary, K. D. (1983). Causal inferences for spouse behavior in maritally distressed and nondistressed couples. *Journal of Clinical and Social Psychology, 1,* 42–57.

Fine, B. J. (1955).   Conclusion-drawing, communicator credibility, and anxiety as factors in opinion change. *Journal of Abnormal and Social Psychology, 54,* 369–374.

Finnie, W. C. (1973).   Field experiments in litter control. *Environment and Behavior, 5,* 123–144.

Firestone, I. J., Lichtman, C. M., & Colamosca, J. V. (1975).   Leader effectiveness and leadership conferral as determinants of helping in a medical emergency. *Journal of Personality and Social Psychology, 31,* 343–348.

Fischer, C. S. (1984).   *The urban experience.* New York: Harcourt Brace Jovanovich.

Fischhoff, B., & Beyth, R. (1975).   "I knew it would happen"—Remembered probabilities of once-future things. *Organizational Behavior and Human Performance, 13,* 1–16.

Fishbein, M., & Ajzen, I. (1975).   *Belief, attitude, intention and behavior: An introduction to theory and research.* Reading, MA: Addison-Wesley.

Fisher, J. D., Bell, P. A., Baum, A., & Greene, T. C. (in press). *Environmental psychology* (3rd ed.). New York: Holt, Rinehart & Winston.

Fisher, J. D., & Byrne, D. (1975).   Too close for comfort: Sex differences in response to invasions of personal space. *Journal of Personality and Social Psychology, 32,* 15–21.

Fisher, J. D., Nadler, A., & Whitcher-Alagna, S. W. (1982).   Recipient reactions to aid. *Psychological Bulletin, 91,* 27–54.

Fisher, J. D., Rytting, M., & Heslin, R. (1976).   Hands touching. *Sociometry, 39,* 416–421.

Fisher, M. J., & Apostal, R. A. (1975). Selected vocal cues and counselors' perceptions of genuineness, self-disclosure, and anxiety. *Journal of Counseling Psychology, 22,* 92–96.

Fiske, S. T., & Taylor, S. E. (1984). *Social cognition.* Reading, MA.: Addison-Wesley.

Fleming, R., Baum, A., Gisriel, M. M., & Gatchel, R. J. (1982).   Mediating influences of social support on stress at Three Mile Island. *Journal of Human Stress, 8,* 14–22.

Fleming, R., Baum, A., & Singer, J. E. (1984).   Toward an integrative approach to the study of stress. *Journal of Personality and Social Psychology, 46,* 939–949.

Fleming, I., Baum, A., & Weiss, L. (1987). Social density and perceived control as mediators of crowding stress in high-density residential neighborhoods. *Journal of Personality and Social Psychology, 52,* 899–906.

Flowers, M. L. (1977).   A laboratory test of some implications of Janis's groupthink hypothesis. *Journal of Personality and Social Psychology, 35,* 888–896.

Flynn, J. P. (1967).   The neural basis of aggression in cats. In D. C. Glass (Ed.), *Neurophysiology and emotion* (pp. 40–60). New York: Rockefeller University Press.

Foa, E. B., & Foa, U. G. (1976). Resource theory of social exchange. In J. W. Thibaut, J. T. Spence, & R. C. Carson (Eds.), *Contemporary topics in social psychology* (pp. 99–131). Morristown, NJ: General Learning Press.

Foa, U. G., & Foa, E. B. (1974). *Societal structures of the mind.* Springfield, IL.: Charles C. Thomas.

Folkes, V. S., & Sears, D. O. (1977). Does everybody like a liker? *Journal of Experimental Social Psychology, 13,* 505–519.

Folkman, S., & Lazarus, R. S. (1980). An analysis of coping in a middle-age community sample. *Journal of Health and Social Behavior, 21,* 219–239.

Folkman, S., & Lazarus, R. S. (1985). If it changes it must be a process: Study of emotional responses and coping during three stages of a college examination. *Journal of Personality and Social Psychology, 48,* 150–170.

Folkman, S., Lazarus, R. S., Dunkel-Schetter, C., DeLongis, A., & Gruen, R. J. (1986a). Dynamics of a stressful encounter: Cognitive appraisal, coping, and encounter outcomes. *Journal of Personality and Social Psychology, 50,* 992–1003.

Folkman, S., Lazarus, R. S., Gruen, R. J., & DeLongis, A. (1986b). Appraisal, coping, health status, and psychological symptoms. *Journal of Personality and Social Psychology, 50,* 571–579.

Forgays, D. G., & Belinson, M. J. (1986). Is flotation isolation a relaxing environment? *Journal of Environmental Psychology, 6,* 19–34.

Foss, R. D., & Dempsey, C. B. (1979). Blood donation and the foot-in-the-door technique: A limiting case. *Journal of Personality and Social Psychology, 37,* 580–590.

Foushee, H. C. (1984). Dyads and triads at 35,000 feet: Factors affecting group process and aircrew performance. *American Psychologist, 39,* 885–893.

Fowler, F. J., McCall, M. E., & Magione, T. W. (1979). *Reducing residential crime and fear: The Hartford neighborhood crime prevention program.* Washington, DC: Government Printing Office.

Foy, D. W., & Card, J. J. (1987). Combat-related posttraumatic stress disorder etiology: Replicated findings in a national sample of Vietnam-era men. *Journal of Clinical Psychology, 43,* 28–31.

Foy, D. W., Carroll, E. M., & Donahoe, C. P., Jr. (1987). Etiological factors in the development of PTSD in clinical samples of Vietnam veterans. *Journal of Clinical Psychology, 43,* 17–27.

Francis, P. (1979). *How to serve on a jury* (2nd ed.). Dobbs Ferry, NY: Oceana Publications.

Freedman, D. G. (1979). *Human sociobiology: A holistic approach.* New York: Free Press.

Freedman, J. L. (1965). Long-term behavioral effects of cognitive dissonance. *Journal of Experimental Social Psychology, 1,* 145–155.

Freedman, J. L. (1975). *Crowding and behavior.* San Francisco: Freeman.

Freedman, J. L. (1984). Effect of television violence on aggressiveness. *Psychological Bulletin, 96,* 227–246.

Freedman, J. L. (1986). Television violence and aggression: A rejoinder. *Psychological Bulletin, 100,* 372–378.

Freedman, J. L., Birksy, J., & Cavouskian, A. (1980). Environmental determinants of behavioral contagion: Density and number. *Basic and Applied Social Psychology, 1,* 155–161.

Freedman, J. L., & Fraser, S. C. (1966). Compliance without pressure: The foot-in-the-door technique. *Journal of Personality and Social Psychology, 4,* 195–202.

Freedman, J. L., Levy, A. S., Buchanan, R. W., & Price, J. (1972). Crowding and human aggressiveness. *Journal of Experimental Social Psychology, 8,* 528–548.

Freeman, S., Walker, M., Borden, R., & Latane, B. (1975). Diffusion of responsibility and restaurant tipping: Cheaper by the bunch. *Personality and Social Psychology Bulletin, 1,* 584–587.

French, J. R. P., & Raven, B. H. (1959). The bases of social power. In D. Cartwright (Ed.), *Studies in social power* (pp. 150–167). Ann Arbor: University of Michigan Press.

Freud, S. (1920/1965). *A general introduction to psychoanalysis.* New York: Washington Square Press.

Freud, S. (1933). *New introductory notes on psychoanalysis.* New York: Norton.

Frey, D. L., & Gaertner, S. L. (1986). Helping and the avoidance of inappropriate interracial behavior: A strategy that perpetuates a nonprejudiced self-image. *Journal of Personality and Social Psychology, 50,* 1083–1090.

Fried, M. (1963). Grieving for a lost home. In L. J. Duhl (Ed.), *The urban condition* (pp. 151–171). New York: Simon & Schuster.

Friedenthal, J. H., Kane, M. K., & Miller, A. R. (1985). *Civil procedure.* St. Paul, MN: West Publishing.

Friedman, H. S. (1978). The relative strength of verbal versus nonverbal cues. *Personality and Social Psychology Bulletin, 4,* 147–150.

Friedrich, L. K., & Stein, A. H. (1975). Prosocial television and young children: The effects of verbal labeling and role playing on learning and behavior. *Child Development, 46,* 27–38.

Friedrich-Cofer, L., & Huston, A. C. (1986). Television violence and aggression: The debate continues. *Psychological Bulletin, 100,* 364–371.

Frieze, I. H., Parsons, J. E., Johnson, P. B., Ruble, D. N., & Zellman, G. L. (1978). *Women and sex roles: A social psychological perspective.* New York: Norton.

Frieze, I. H., & Weiner, B. (1971). Cue utilization and attributional judgments for success and failure. *Journal of Personality, 39,* 591–606.

Fromm, E. (1963). *War within man: A psychological inquiry into the roots of destructiveness.* Philadelphia. PA: American Friends Service Committee.

Fugita, B. N., Harper, R. G., & Weins, A. N. (1980). Encoding-decoding of nonverbal emotional messages: Sex differences in spontaneous and enacted expressions. *Journal of Nonverbal Behavior, 4,* 131–145.

Fugita, S. S. (1974). Effects of anxiety and approval on visual interaction. *Journal of Personality and Social Psychology, 29,* 586–592.

Gaertner, S. L. (1973). Helping behavior and racial discrimination among liberals and conservatives. *Journal of Personality and Social Psychology, 25,* 335–341.

Gaertner, S. L., & Dovidio, J. F. (1977). The sublety of white racism, arousal and helping behavior. *Journal of Personality and Social Psychology, 35,* 691–707.

Gal, C. A., Benedict, J. O., & Supinski, D. M. (1986). Territoriality and the use of library study tables. *Perceptual and Motor Skills, 63,* 567–574.

Galle, O. R., Gove, W. R., & McPherson, J. M. (1972). Population density and pathology: What are the relationships for man? *Science, 176,* 23–30.

Gallwey, W. T. (1974). *The inner game of tennis.* New York: Random House.

Gans, H. (1962). *The urban villagers.* New York: Free Press.

Ganster, D. C., Fusilier, M. R., & Mayes, B. T. (1986). Role of social support in the experience of stress at work. *Journal of Applied Psychology, 71,* 102–110.

Ganster, D., McCuddy, M., & Fromkin, H. L. (1977). *Similarity and undistinctiveness as determinants of favorable and unfavorable changes in self-esteem.* Paper presented at Midwestern Psychological Association convention, Chicago.

Gantner, A. B., & Taylor, S. P. (1988). Human physical aggression as a function of diazepam. *Personality and Social Psychology Bulletin, 14,* 479–484.

Garling, T., Book, A., & Lindberg, E. (1986). Spatial orientation and wayfinding in the designed environment: A conceptual analysis and some suggestions for postoccupancy evaluation. *Journal of Architectural Planning and Research, 3,* 55–64.

Geen, R. G. (1968). Effects of frustration, attack, and prior training in aggressiveness upon aggressive behavior. *Journal of Personality and Social Psychology, 9,* 316–321.

Geen, R. G. (1978). Effects of attack and uncontrollable noise on aggression. *Journal of Research in Personality, 12,* 15–29.

Geen, R. G. (1980). The effects of being observed on performance. In P. B. Paulus (Ed.), *Psychology of group influence* (pp. 61–98). Hillsdale, NJ: Erlbaum.

Geen, R. G., & Berkowitz, L. (1966). Name-mediated aggressive cue properties. *Journal of Personality, 34,* 456–465.

Geen, R. G., & McCown, E. J. (1984). Effects of noise and attack on aggression and physiological arousal. *Motivation and Emotion, 8,* 231–241.

Geen, R. G., & Quanty, M. B. (1977). The catharsis of aggression: An evaluation of a hypothesis. In L. Berkowitz (Ed.), *Advances in experimental social psychology* (Vol. 10, pp. 1–37). New York: Academic Press.

Gelbort, K. R., & Winer, J. L. (1985). Fear of success and fear of failure: A multitrait-multimethod validation study. *Journal of Personality and Social Psychology, 48,* 1009–1014.

Gelfand, D. M., Hartmann, D. P., Walder, P., & Page, B. (1973). Who reports shoplifters? A field-experimental study. *Journal of Personality and Social Psychology, 25,* 276–285.

Geller, E. S. (1986). The behavior change approach to litter management. *Journal of Resource Management and Technology, 14,* 117–122.

Geller, E. S. (1987). Environmental psychology and applied behavior analysis: From strange bedfellows to a productive marriage. In D. Stokols & I. Altman (Eds.), *Handbook of environmental psychology* (Vol. 2, pp. 361–388). New York: Wiley.

Geller, E. S., Erickson, J. B., & Buttram, B. A. (1983). Attempts to promote residential water conservation with educational, behavioral, and engineering strategies. *Population and Behavior, 6,* 96–112.

Geller, E. S., Winett, R. A., & Everett, P. B. (1982). *Preserving the environment: New strategies for behavior change.* New York: Pergamon.

Geller, E. S., Witmer, J. F., & Orebaugh, A. L. (1976). Instructions as a determinant of paper-disposal behaviors. *Environment and Behavior, 8,* 417–438.

Genthner, R. W., & Taylor, S. P. (1973). Physical aggression as a function of racial prejudice and the race of the target. *Journal of Personality and Social Psychology, 27,* 207–210.

Gerard, H. B., & Mathewson, G. (1966). The effects of severity of initiation on liking for a group: A replication. *Journal of Experimental Social Psychology, 2,* 278–287.

Gerard, H. B., & Miller, N. (1975). *School desegregation: A long-term study.* New York: Plenum.

Gerbner, G., Gross, L., Eleey, M. F., Jackson-Beeck, M., Jeffries-Fox, S., & Signorielli, N. (1977). TV profile no. 8: The highlights. *Journal of Communication, 27* (2), 171–180.

Gerbner, G., Gross, L., Morgan, M., & Signorelli, N. (1980). The mainstreaming of America: Violence profile no. 11. *Journal of Communication, 30,* 10–29.

Gerbner, G., Gross, L., Morgan, M., & Signorelli, N. (1981a). A curious journey into the scary world of Paul Hirsch. *Communication Research, 8,* 39–72.

Gerbner, G., Gross, L., Morgan, M., & Signorelli, N. (1981b). Final reply to Hirsch. *Communication Research, 8,* 259–280.

Gergen, K. J., Gergen, M. M., & Barton, W. H. (1973). Deviance in the dark. *Psychology Today, 10,* 129–130.

Gergen, K. J., Gergen, M. M., & Meter, K. (1972). Individual orientations to prosocial behavior. *Journal of Social Issues, 28,* 105–130.

Gibbons, F., & Wicklund, R. (1982). Self-focused attention and helping behavior. *Journal of Personality and Social Psychology, 43,* 462–474.

Gifford, R. (1987). *Environmental psychology: Principles and practices.* Boston: Allyn & Bacon.

Gilbert, D. T., Krull, D. S., & Pelham, B. W. (1988). Of thoughts unspoken: Social inference and the self-regulation of behavior. *Journal of Personality and Social Psychology, 55,* 685–694.

Gilbert, S. J. (1981). Another look at the Milgram obedience studies: The role of the graduated series of shocks. *Personality and Social Psychology Bulletin, 7,* 690–695.

Gillig, P. M., & Greenwald, A. G. (1974). Is it time to lay the sleeper effect to rest? *Journal of Personality and Social Psychology, 29,* 132–139.

Ginsburg, H. (1977). *Kinship altruism of grandparents.* Paper presented at Psychonomic Society convention, Washington, DC.

Ginzburg, R. (1962). *100 years of lynching.* New York: Lancer.

Givens, D. B. (1983). *Love signals: How to attract a mate.* New York: Crown.

Glass, D. C., & Singer, J. E. (1972). *Urban stress: Experiments on noise and social stressors.* New York: Academic Press.

Glenn, N. D. (1975). Psychological well-being in the post-parental stage: Some evidence from national surveys. *Journal of Marriage and the Family, 37,* 105–110.

Glenn, N. D., & McLanahan, S. (1982). Children and marital happiness: A further specification of the relationship. *Journal of Marriage and the Family, 44,* 63–72.

Gleser, G., Green, B., & Winget, C. (1981). *Prolonged psychosocial effects of disaster: A study of Buffalo Creek.* New York: Academic Press.

Glick, P., DeMorest, J. A., & Hotze, C. A. (1988). Keeping your distance: Group membership, personal space, and requests for small favors. *Journal of Applied Social Psychology, 18,* 315–330.

Glick, P., Zion, C., & Nelson, C. (1988). What mediates sex discrimination in hiring decisions? *Journal of Personality and Social Psychology, 55,* 239–247.

Goethals, G. R., & Darley, J. (1977). Social comparison theory: An attributional approach. In J. Suls & R. Miller (Eds.), *Social comparison processes: Theoretical and empirical perspectives.* Washington, DC: Halsted-Wiley.

Goethals, G. R., & Nelson, R. E. (1973). Similarity in the influence process: The belief-value distinction. *Journal of Personality and Social Psychology, 25,* 117–122.

Goethals, G. R., & Reckman, R. F. (1973). The perception of consistency in attitudes. *Journal of Experimental Social Psychology, 9,* 491–501.

Goffman, E. (1952). On cooling the mark out: Some aspects of adaptation to failure. *Psychiatry, 15,* 451–463.

Goffman, E. (1959). *The presentation of self in everyday life.* Garden City, NY: Doubleday.

Goffman, E. (1971). *Relations in public.* New York: Basic Books.

Goldman, M., Stockbauer, J. W., & McAuliffe, T. G. (1977). Intergroup and intragroup competition and cooperation. *Journal of Experimental Social Psychology, 13,* 81–88.

Gonzales, A. E. J., & Cooper, J. (1976). What to do with leftover dissonance: Blame it on the lights. (Reported in Zanna & Cooper, 1976).

Gonzales, M. H., Davis, J. M., Loney, G. L., Lukens, C. K., & Junghaus, C. H. (1983). Interactional approach to interpersonal attraction. *Journal of Personality and Social Psychology, 44,* 1192–1197.

Goodman, M. (1952). *Race awareness in young children.* Cambridge, MA: Addison-Wesley.

Goodrich, R. (1982). Seven office evaluations: A review. *Environment and Behavior, 8,* 175–180.

Gordon, C. (1968). Self-conceptions: Configurations of content. In C. Gordon & K. Gergen (Eds.), *The self in social interaction* (pp. 115–136). New York: Wiley.

Gould, R., & Sigall, H. (1977). The effects of empathy and outcome on attribution: An examination of the divergent-perspectives hypothesis. *Journal of Experimental Social Psychology, 13,* 480–491.

Gouldner, A. W. (1960). The norm of reciprocity: A preliminary statement. *American Sociological Review, 25,* 161–178.

Grass, R. C., & Wallace, W. H. (1969). Satiation effects of TV commercials. *Journal of Advertising Research, 9,* 3–9.

Green, R. G. (1980). The effects of being observed on performance. In P. B. Paulus (Ed.), *Psychology of group influence* (pp. 61–98). Hillsdale, NJ: Erlbaum.

Greenbaum, P., & Rosenfeld, H. M. (1978). Patterns of avoidance in response to interpersonal staring and proximity: Effects of bystanders on drivers at a traffic intersection. *Journal of Personality and Social Psychology, 36,* 575–587.

Greenbaum, P. E., & Greenbaum, S. D. (1981). Territorial personalization: Group identity and social interaction in a Slavic-American neighborhood. *Environment and Behavior, 13,* 574–589.

Greenberg, M. S., & Frisch, D. M. (1972). Effects of intentionality on willingness to reciprocate a favor. *Journal of Experimental Social Psychology, 8,* 99–111.

Greenwald, A., Baumgardner, M. H., & Leippe, M. R. (1979). *In search of reliable persuasion effects: III. The sleeper effect is dead. Long live the sleeper effect!* Unpublished manuscript, Ohio State University.

Greenwald, A. G., & Breckler, S. J. (1985). To whom is the self presented? In B. R. Schlenker (Ed.), *The self and social life.* New York: McGraw-Hill.

Greer, D. L. (1983). Spectator booing and the home advantage: A study of social influence in the basketball arena. *Social Psychology Quarterly, 46,* 252–261.

Griffiths, I. D., & Raw, G. J. (1987). Community and individual responses to changes in traffic noise exposure. In H. S. Koelega (Ed.), *Environmental annoyance: Characterization, measurement, and control* (pp. 333–341). New York: Elsevier.

Griffitt, W., & Veitch, R. (1971). Hot and crowded: Influence of population density and temperature on interpersonal affective behavior. *Journal of Personality and Social Psychology, 17,* 92–98.

Gruder, C. L., Cook, T. D., Hennigan, K. M., Flay, B. R., Alessis, C., & Halamaj, J. (1978). Empirical tests of the absolute sleeper effect predicted from the discounting cue hypothesis. *Journal of Personality and Social Psychology, 36,* 1061–1074.

Grusec, J. E., Kuczynski, L., Rushton, J. P., & Simutis, Z. (1978). Modeling, direct instruction, and attributions: Effects on altruism. *Developmental Psychology, 14,* 51–57.

Grusec, J. E., Saas-Korlsaak, P., & Simutis, Z. M. (1978). The role of example and moral exhortation in the training of altruism. *Child Development, 49,* 920–923.

Gump, P. V., & Friesen, W. V. (1964). Satisfactions derived from nonclass settings. In R. G. Barker & P. V. Gump (Eds.), *Big school, small school: High school size and student behavior.* Stanford, CA: Stanford University Press.

Haaga, D. A. (1987). Treatment of the Type A behavior pattern. *Clinical Psychology Review, 7,* 557–574.

Haan, N., Smith, M., & Block, J. (1968). Moral reasoning of young adults: Political-social behavior, family background and personality correlates. *Journal of Personality and Social Psychology, 10,* 183–201.

Haber, G. M. (1980). Territorial invasion in the classroom: Invadee responses. *Environment and Behavior, 12,* 17–31.

Hall, E. T. (1959). *The silent language.* Garden City, NY: Doubleday.

Hall, E. T. (1966). *The hidden dimension.* New York: Doubleday.

Hall, J. A. (1978). Gender effects in decoding nonverbal cues. *Psychological Bulletin, 85,* 845–857.

Hall, J. A. (1984). *Nonverbal sex differences: Communication accuracy and expressive style.* Baltimore, MD: Johns Hopkins University Press.

Hallinan, M. T., & Smith, S. S. (1985). The effects of classroom racial composition on students' interracial friendliness. *Social Psychology Quarterly, 48,* 3–16.

Hamilton, D. L. (1981). Cognitive representations of persons. In E. T. Higgins, C. P. Herman, & M. P. Zanna (Eds.), *Social cognition: The Ontarion symposium* (Vol. 1). Hillsdale, NJ: Erlbaum.

Hamilton, D. L., & Gifford, R. K. (1976). Illusory correlation in interpersonal perception: A cognitive basis of stereotypic judgments. *Journal of Experimental Social Psychology, 12,* 392–407.

Hamilton, D. L., Katz, L. B., & Leirer, V. O. (1980). Cognitive representation of personality impressions: Organizational processes in first impression formation. *Journal of Personality and Social Psychology, 39,* 1050–1063.

Hamilton, D. L., & Rose, T. L. (1980). Illusory correlation and the maintenance of stereotypic beliefs. *Journal of Personality and Social Psychology, 39,* 832–845.

Hamilton, W. D. (1964). The genetical evolution of social behaviour: I and II. *Journal of Theoretical Biology, 7,* 1–52.

Haney, C., Banks, C., & Zimbardo, P. (1973). Interpersonal dynamics in a simulated prison. *International Journal of Criminology and Penology, 1,* 69–97.

Hansen, R. D. (1980). Commonsense attribution. *Journal of Personality and Social Psychology, 39,* 996–1009.

Hanson, W. B., & Altman, I. (1976). Decorating personal spaces: A descriptive analysis. *Environment and Behavior, 8,* 491–504.

Hansson, R. O., Noulles, D., & Bellovich, S. J. (1982). Knowledge, warning, and stress: A study of comparative roles in an urban floodplain. *Environment and Behavior, 14,* 171–185.

Hapkiewicz, W. G. (1979). Children's reactions to cartoon violence. *Journal of Clinical Child Psychology, 8,* 30–34.

Harkins, S. G., & Petty, R. E. (1981a). Effects of source magnification of cognitive effort on attitudes: An information-processing view. *Journal of Personality and Social Psychology, 40,* 401–413.

Harkins, S. G., & Petty, R. E. (1981b). The multiple source effect in persuasion: The effects of distraction. *Personality and Social Psychology Bulletin, 7,* 627–633.

Harkins, S. G., & Petty, R. E. (1982). Effects of task difficulty and task uniqueness on social loafing. *Journal of Personality and Social Psychology, 43,* 1214–1229.

Harlow, H. (1958). The nature of love. *American Psychologist, 13,* 673–685.

Harries, K. D., & Stadler, S. J. (1988). Heat and violence: New findings from Dallas field data, 1980–1981. *Journal of Applied Social Psychology, 18,* 129–138.

Harrigan, J. A., Oxman, T. E., & Rosenthal, R. (1985). Rapport expressed through nonverbal behavior. *Journal of Nonverbal Behavior, 9*, 95–110.

Harris, M. B. (1972). The effects of performing one altruistic act on the likelihood of performing another. *Journal of Social Psychology, 88*, 665–673.

Harris, M. B. (1974). Mediators between frustration and aggression in a field experiment. *Journal of Experimental Social Psychology, 10*, 561–571.

Harris, M. B. (1977). Effects of altruism on mood. *Journal of Social Psychology, 102*, 197–208.

Harris, M. B., & Baudin, H. (1973). The language of altruism: The effects of language, dress and ethnic group. *Journal of Social Psychology, 91*, 37–41.

Harris, M. B., & Bays, G. (1973). Altruism and sex roles. *Psychological Reports, 32*, 1002.

Harris, M. B., Benson, S. M., & Hall C. L. (1975). The effects of confession on altruism. *Journal of Social Psychology, 96*, 187–192.

Harris, M. B., & Ho, J. (1984). Effects of degree, locus and controllability of dependency and sex of subject on anticipated and actual helping. *Journal of Social Psychology, 122*, 245–255.

Harris, M. B., & Huang, L. C. (1973a). Competence and helping. *Journal of Social Psychology, 89*, 203–210.

Harris, M. B., & Huang, L. C. (1973b). Helping and the attribution process. *Journal of Social Psychology, 90*, 291–297.

Harris, M. B., James, J., Chavez, J., Fuller, M. L., Kent, S., Massanari, C., & Walsh, F. (1983). Clothing: Communication, compliance and choice. *Journal of Applied Social Psychology, 13*, 88–97.

Harris, M. B., & Klingbeil, D. R. (1976). The effects of ethnicity of subject and accent and dependency of confederate on aggressiveness and altruism. *Journal of Social Psychology, 98*, 47–53.

Harris, M. B., Liguori, R., & Joniak, A. (1973). Aggression, altruism, and models. *Journal of Social Psychology, 91*, 343–344.

Harris, M. B., Liguori, R. A., & Stack, C. (1973). Favors, bribes, and altruism. *Journal of Social Psychology, 89*, 47–54.

Harris, M. B., & Samerotte, G. (1975). The effects of aggressive and altruistic modeling on subsequent behavior. *Journal of Social Psychology, 95*, 173–182.

Harris, M. B., & Samerotte, G. C. (1976). The effects of actual and attempted theft, need and a previous favor on altruism. *Journal of Social Psychology, 99*, 193–202.

Harris, M. B., & Siebel, C. E. (1975). Affect, aggression, and altruism. *Developmental Psychology, 11*, 623–627.

Harris, M. B., & Smith, R. J. (1975). Mood and helping. *Journal of Psychology, 91*, 215–221.

Harris, R. N., & Snyder, C. R. (1986). The role of uncertain self-esteem in self-handicapping. *Journal of Personality and Social Psychology, 51*, 451–458.

Harrison, A. A. (1977). Mere exposure. In L. Berkowitz (Ed.), *Advances in experimental social psychology* (Vol. 10, pp. 39–83). New York: Academic Press.

Harrison, A. A., & Saeed, L. (1977). Let's make a deal: An analysis of revelations and stipulations in lonely hearts advertisements. *Journal of Personality and Social Psychology, 35*, 257–264.

Harvey, J. H., Harris, B., & Barnes, R. D. (1975). Actor-observer differences in the perceptions of responsibility and freedom. *Journal of Personality and Social Psychology, 32*, 22–28.

Harvey, J. H., & Smith, W. P. (1977). *Social psychology: An attributional approach*. St. Louis, MO: C. V. Mosby.

Harvey, J. H., Wells, G. L., & Alvarez, M. D. (1978). Attribution in the context of conflict and separation in close relationships. In J. H. Harvey, W. J. Ickes, & R. F. Kidd (Eds.), *New directions in attribution research* (Vol. 2). Hillsdale, NJ: Erlbaum.

Hass, R. G., & Grady, K. (1975). Temporal delay, type of forewarning, and resistance to influence. *Journal of Experimental Social Psychology, 11*, 459–469.

Hastie, R. (1981). Schematic principles in human memory. In E. T. Higgins, C. P. Herman, & M. P. Zanna (Eds.), *Social cognition: The Ontario symposium* (Vol. 1). Hillsdale, NJ: Erlbaum.

Hastie, R. (1984). Causes and effects of causal attribution. *Journal of Personality and Social Psychology, 46*, 44–56.

Hastie, R., & Kumar, P. A. (1979). Person memory: Personality traits as organizing principles in memory for behavior. *Journal of Personality and Social Psychology, 37*, 25–38.

Hastie, R., Penrod, S. D., & Pennington, N. (1983). *Inside the jury*. Cambridge, MA: Harvard University Press.

Hastorf, A. H., & Cantril, H. (1954). They saw a game: A case study. *Journal of Abnormal and Social Psychology, 47*, 574–576.

Hatfield, E., Traupmann, J., Sprecher, S., Utne, M., & Hay, J. (1985). Equity and intimate relations: Recent research. In W. Ickes (Ed.), *Compatible and incompatible relationships* (pp. 91–118). New York: Springer-Verlag.

Hawkins, C. H. (1960). *Interaction and coalition realignments in consensus groups: A study of experimental jury deliberations*. Doctoral Dissertation, University of Chicago.

Hayduk, L. A. (1983). Personal space: Where we now stand. *Psychological Bulletin, 94*, 293–335.

Hayduk, L. A. (1985). Personal space: The conceptual and measurement implications of structural equation models. *Canadian Journal of Behavioral Science, 13*, 717–734.

Hazan, C., & Shaver, P. (1987). Romantic love conceptionalized as an attachment process. *Journal of Personality and Social Psychology, 52*, 511–524.

Hearn, G. (1957). Leadership and the spatial factor in small groups. *Journal of Abnormal and Social Psychology, 35*, 183–190.

Hearst, P. C. (1982). *Every secret thing*. Garden City, NY: Doubleday.

Hedge, A. (1982). The open-plan office: A systematic investigation of employee reactions to their work environments. *Environment and Behavior, 14*, 519–542.

Heider, F. (1958). *The psychology of interpersonal relationships*. New York: Wiley.

Heller, J., Groff, B., & Solomon, S. (1977). Toward an understanding of crowding: The role of physical interaction. *Journal of Personality and Social Psychology, 35*, 183–190.

Hemsley, G. D., & Doob, A. N. (1978). The effect of looking behavior on perceptions of a communicator's credibility. *Journal of Applied Social Psychology, 8*, 136–144.

Hendrick, C., Bixenstein, V., & Hawkins, G. (1971). Race versus belief similarity as determinants of attraction: A search for a fair test. *Journal of Personality and Social Psychology, 17*, 250–258.

Hendrick, C., Giesen, M., & Coy, S. (1974). The social ecology of free seating arrangements in a small group interaction context. *Sociometry, 37*, 262–274.

Hendrick, C., & Hendrick, S. (1983). *Liking, loving and relating*. Monterey, CA: Brooks/Cole.

Hendrick, C., & Page, H. (1970). Self-esteem, attitude similarity, and attraction. *Journal of Personality, 38*, 588–601.

Henley, N. M. (1973). Status and sex: Some touching observations. *Bulletin of the Psychonomic Society, 2*, 91–93.

Henley, N. M. (1977). *Body politics: Power, sex and nonverbal communication*. Englewood Cliffs, NJ: Prentice-Hall.

Hepworth, J. T., & West, S. G. (1988). Lynchings and the economy: A time-series reanalysis of Hovland and Sears (1940). *Journal of Personality and Social Psychology, 55,* 239–247.

Herek, G. M. (1986). The instrumentality of ideologies: Toward a neofunctional theory of attitudes and behavior. *Journal of Social Issues, 42,* 99–114.

Herr, P. M. (1986). Consequences of priming: Judgment and behavior. *Journal of Personality and Social Psychology, 51,* 1106–1115.

Herzog, T. R., Kaplan, S., & Kaplan, R. (1982). The prediction of preference for unfamiliar urban places. *Population and Environment, 5,* 43–59.

Herzog, T. R., & Smith, G. A. (1988). Danger, mystery, and environmental preference. *Environment and Behavior, 20,* 320–344.

Heshka, S., & Nelson, Y. (1972). Interpersonal speaking distance as a function of age, sex, and relationship. *Sociometry, 35,* 491–498.

Heslin, R., & Boss, D. (1980). Nonverbal intimacy in airport arrival and departure. *Personality and Social Psychology Bulletin, 6,* 248–252.

Heslin, R., & Patterson, M. L. (1982). *Nonverbal behavior and social psychology.* New York: Plenum.

Hewstone, M., & Brown, R. (1986). Contact is not enough: An intergroup perspective on the "contact hypothesis." In M. Hewstone and R. Brown (Eds.), *Contact and conflict in intergroup encounters* (pp. 1–44). New York: Basil Blackwell.

Hewstone, M., & Brown, R. (Eds.) (1986). *Contact and conflict in intergroup encounters.* New York: Basil Blackwell.

Hewstone, M., & Jaspars, J. (1987). Covariation and causal attribution: A logical model of the intuitive analysis of variance. *Journal of Personality and Social Psychology, 53,* 663–672.

Higgins, E. T. (1987). Self-discrepancy: A theory relating self and affect. *Psychological Review, 94,* 319–340.

Higgins, E. T. (1989). Self-discrepancy theory: What patterns of self-beliefs cause people to suffer? In L. Berkowitz (Ed.), *Advances in experimental social psychology* (Vol. 22, pp. 93–136). San Diego, CA: Academic Press.

Higgins, E. T., Bond, R. N., Klein, R., & Strauman, T. (1986). Self-discrepancies and emotional vulnerability: How magnitude, accessibility, and type of discrepancy influence affect. *Journal of Personality and Social Psychology, 51,* 5–15.

Higgins, E. T., King, G. A., & Mavin, G. H. (1982). Individual construct accessibility and subjective impressions and recall. *Journal of Personality and Social Psychology, 43,* 35–47.

Higgins, E. T., Klein, R., & Strauman, T. (1985). Self-concept discrepancy theory: A psychological model for distinguishing among different aspects of depression and anxiety. *Social Cognition, 3,* 51–76.

Higgins, E. T., Rhodewalt, F., & Zanna, M. P. (1979). Dissonance motivation: Its nature, persistence, and reinstatement. *Journal of Experimental Social Psychology, 15,* 16–34.

Higgins, E. T., Rholes, W. S., & Jones, C. R. (1977). Category accessibility and impression formation. *Journal of Experimental Social Psychology, 13,* 141–154.

High, T., & Sundstrom, E. (1977). Room flexibility and space use in a dormitory. *Environment and Behavior, 9,* 81–90.

Hill, G. W. (1982). Group versus individual performance: Are N + 1 heads better than one? *Psychological Bulletin, 91,* 517–539.

Hillier, B. (1973, November). In defense of space. *Royal Institute of British Architects Journal,* 539–544.

Hilton, I. (1967). Differences in the behavior of mothers toward first and later born children. *Journal of Personality and Social Psychology, 7,* 282–290.

Hirsch, P. M. (1980). The "scary world" of the nonviewer and other anomalies. *Communication Research, 7,* 403–456.

Hirsch, P. M. (1981a). Distinguishing good speculation from bad theory. *Communication Research, 8,* 73–95.

Hirsch, P. M. (1981b). On not learning from one's own mistakes. *Communication Research, 8,* 3–37.

Hirt, E. R. (1987). *Techniques of reconstructing the past: Implications for the accuracy of memories.* Unpublished doctoral dissertation, Indiana University.

Hirt, E., & Kimble, C. E. (1981). *The home-field advantage in sports: Differences and correlates.* Paper presented at the Midwestern Psychological Association Convention, Detroit.

Hobfoll, S. E., & Lieberman, J. R. (1987). Personality and social resources in immediate and continued stress resistance among women. *Journal of Personality and Social Psychology, 52,* 18–26.

Hobfoll, S. E., Nadler, A., & Lieberman, J. (1986). Satisfaction with social support during crisis: Intimacy and self-esteem as critical determinants. *Journal of Personality and Social Psychology, 51,* 296–304.

Hobfoll, S. E., & Penner, L. A. (1978). The effect of physical attraction on therapists' initial judgement of a person's self-concept. *Journal of Clinical and Consulting Psychology, 46,* 200–201.

Hochschild, A. R. (1983). *The managed heart: Commercialization of human feeling.* Berkeley, CA: University of California Press.

Hoffman, H. S., & Solomon, R. L. (1974). An opponent-process theory of motivation: III. Some affective dynamics in imprinting. *Learning and Motivation, 5,* 149–164.

Hoffman, M. L. (1977). Sex differences in empathy and related behaviors. *Psychological Bulletin, 84,* 712–722.

Hoffman, M. L. (1981). Is altruism part of human nature? *Journal of Personality and Social Pschyology, 40,* 121–137.

Hofling, C. K., Brotzman, E., Dalrymple, S., Graves, N., & Pierce, C. M. (1966). An experimental study in nurse-physician relationships. *Journal of Nervous and Mental Disease, 143,* 171–180.

Hogan, R., Jones, W., & Cheek, J. M. (1985). Socioanalytic theory: An alternative to armadillo psychology. In B. R. Schlenker (Ed.), *The self and social life* (pp. 175–198). New York: McGraw-Hill.

Hokanson, J. E. (1970). Psychophysiological evaluation of the catharsis hypothesis. In E. I. Megargee & J. E. Hokanson (Eds.), *The dynamics of aggression.* New York: Harper & Row.

Hokanson, J. E., & Burgess, M. (1962). The effects of status, type of frustration, and aggression on vascular processes. *Journal of Abnormal and Social Psychology, 65,* 232–237.

Holahan, C. J. (1976). Environmental change in a psychiatric setting: A social systems analysis. *Human Relations, 29,* 153–166.

Holahan, C. J., & Moos, R. H. (1986). Personality, coping, and family resources in stress resistance: A longitudinal analysis. *Journal of Personality and Social Psychology, 51,* 389–395.

Holahan, C. J., & Moos, R. H. (1987). Personal and contextual determinants of coping strategies. *Journal of Personality and Social Psychology, 52,* 946–955.

Holahan, C. J., & Saegert, S. (1973). Behavioral and attitudinal effects of large-scale variation in the physical environment of psychiatric wards. *Journal of Abnormal Psychology, 83,* 454–462.

Holland, J. L., Magoon, T. M., & Spokane, A. R. (1981). Counseling psychology: Career interventions, research, and theory. *Annual Review of Psychology, 32,* 279–305.

Hollander, E. P. (1964). *Leaders, groups, and influence.* New York: Oxford University Press.

Hollander, E. P. (1978). *Leadership dynamics: A Practical guide to effective relationships.* New York: Free Press.

Hollander, E. P. (1985). Leadership and power. In G. Lindzey & E. Aronson (Eds.), *Handbook of social psychology* (3rd ed., Vol. 2, pp. 485–537). New York: Random House.

Hollander, E. P., Julian, J. W., & Haaland, G. A. (1965). *Conformity process and prior group support*. Paper presented at American Psychological Association, Atlantic City, NJ.

Holmes, D. S. (1984). Meditation and somatic arousal reduction. *American Psychologist, 39*, 1–10.

Holmes, D. S., Solomon, S., Cappo, B. M., & Greenberg, J. L. (1983). Effects of transcendental meditation versus resting on physiological and subjective arousal. *Journal of Personality and Social Psychology, 44*, 1245–1252.

Holmes, T. H., & Masuda, M. (1974). Life change and illness susceptibility. In B. S. Dohrenwend & B. P. Dohrenwend (Eds.), *Stressful life events: Their nature and effects* (pp. 45–72). New York: Wiley.

Holmes, T. H., & Rahe, R. (1967). The social readjustment rating scale. *Journal of Psychosomatic Research, 11*, 213–218.

Holmes, T. S., & Holmes, T. H. (1970). Short-term intrusions into the life style routine. *Journal of Psychosomatic Research, 14*, 121–132.

Holtgraves, T. (1986). Language structure in social interaction: Perceptions of direct and indirect speech acts and interactants who use them. *Journal of Personality and Social Psychology, 51*, 305–314.

Holtzworth-Monroe, A., & Jacobson, N. S. (1985). Causal attributions of married couples: When do they search for causes? What do they conclude when they do? *Journal of Personality and Social Psychology, 48*, 1398–1412.

Homans, G. C. (1961). *Social behavior: Its elementary forms*. New York: Harcourt, Brace and World.

Homans, G. C. (1974). *Social behavior: Its elementary forms* (Rev. Ed.). New York: Harcourt Brace Jovanovich.

Horai, J., Naccari, N., & Fatoullah, E. (1974). The effects of expertise and physical attractiveness upon opinion agreement and liking. *Sociometry, 37*, 601–606.

Horner, M. S. (1970). Femininity and successful achievement: A basic inconsistency. In J. M. Bardwick, E. Douvan, M. S. Horner, & D. Guttman (Eds.), *Feminine personality and conflict*. Belmont, CA: Brooks/Cole.

Horner, M. S. (1972). Toward an understanding of achievement-related conflicts in women. *Journal of Social Issues, 28*, 157–175.

House, J. S. (1984). Barriers to work stress: I. Social support. In W. D. Gentry, H. Benson, & C. deWolff (Eds.), *Behavioral medicine: Work, stress, and health*. The Hague: Nijhoff.

Hovland, C. I., Harvey, O. J., & Sherif, M. (1957). Assimilation and contrast effects in reactions to communication and attitude change. *Journal of Abnormal and Social Psychology, 55*, 244–252.

Hovland, C. I., Janis, I. L., & Kelley, H. H. (1953). *Communication and persuasion*. New Haven, CT: Yale University Press.

Hovland, C. I., Lumsdaine, A. A., & Sheffield, F. D. (1949). *Experiments on mass communication*. Princeton, NJ: Princeton University Press.

Hovland, C. I., & Mandell, W. (1952). An experimental comparison of conclusion-drawing by the communicator and by the audience. *Journal of Abnormal and Social Psychology, 47*, 581–588.

Hovland, C. I., & Sears, R. R. (1940). Minor studies in aggression: VI. Correlations of lynchings with economic indices. *Journal of Personality, 9*, 301–310.

Hovland, C. I., & Weiss, W. (1951). The influence of source credibility on communication effectiveness. *Public Opinion Quarterly, 15*, 635–650.

Howard, H. E. (1948). *Territory in bird life*. London: Collins.

Howard, J. H., Cunningham, D. A., & Rechnitzer, P. A. (1986). Role ambiguity, Type A behavior, and job satisfaction: Moderating effects on cardiovascular and biochemical responses associated with coronary risk. *Journal of Applied Psychology, 71*, 95–101.

Howard, J. W., & Dawes, R. M. (1976). Linear prediction of marital happiness. *Personality and Social Psychology Bulletin, 2*, 478–480.

Howarth, E. (1980). Birth order, family structure and personality variables. *Journal of Personality Assessment, 44*, 299–301.

Howells, L. T., & Becker, S. W. (1962). Seating arrangement and leadership emergence. *Journal of Abnormal and Social Psychology, 64*, 148–150.

Hoyt, M. F., & Raven, B. H. (1973). Birth order and the 1971 Los Angeles earthquake. *Journal of Personality and Social Psychology, 28*, 123–128.

Huesmann, L. R. (1987). *Comments in alternative theories of aggression*. Symposium presentation at Midwestern Psychological Association convention, Chicago, IL.

Hull, J. G., Levenson, R. W., Young, R. D., & Sher, K. J. (1983). Self-awareness-reducing effects of alcohol consumption. *Journal of Personality and Social Psychology, 44*, 461–473.

Hull, J. G., Van Treuren, R. R., & Virnelli, S. (1987). Hardiness and health: A critique and alternative approach. *Journal of Personality and Social Psychology, 53*, 518–530.

Hull, J. G., & Young, R. D. (1983). Self-consciousness, self-esteem, and success-failure as determinants of alcohol consumption in male social drinkers. *Journal of Personality and Social 1097–1109.*

Hull, J. G., Young, R. D., & Jouriles, E. (1986). Applications of the self-awareness model of alcohol consumption: Predicting patterns of use and abuse. *Journal of Personality and Social Psychology, 51*, 790–796.

Hunter, A. (1978). Persistence of local sentiments in mass society. In D. Street (Ed.), *Handbook of contemporary urban life*. San Francisco: Jossey-Bass.

Hunter, M., Grinnell, R. M., Jr., & Blanchard, R. (1978). A test of a shorter privacy preference scale. *Journal of Psychology, 98*, 207–210.

Huston, T. L. (1973). Ambiguity of acceptance, social desirability, and dating choice. *Journal of Experimental Social Psychology, 9*, 32–42.

Ickes, W. (1982). A basic paradigm for the study of personality, roles, and social behavior. In W. Ickes & E. S. Knowles (Eds.), *Personality, roles and social behavior*. New York: Springer-Verlag.

Ickes, W. (Ed.) (1985). *Compatible and incompatible relationships*. New York: Springer-Verlag.

Ickes, W., & Barnes, R. D. (1977). The role of sex and self-monitoring in unstructured dyadic interactions. *Journal of Personality and Social Psychology, 35*, 315–330.

Ickes, W., & Barnes, R. D. (1978). Boys and girls together—and alienated: On enacting stereotyped sex roles in mixed-sex dyads. *Journal of Personality and Social Psychology, 36*, 669–683.

Ickes, W., & Turner, M. (1983). On the social advantages of having an older, opposite-sex sibling: Birth order influences in mixed-sex dyads. *Journal of Personality and Social Psychology, 45*, 210–222.

Im, S. (1984). Visual preferences in enclosed urban spaces: An exploration of a scientific approach to environmental design. *Environment and Behavior, 16*, 235–262.

Ingham, A. G., Levinger, G., Graves, J., & Peckham, V. (1974). The Ringelmann effect: Studies of group size and group performance. *Journal of Experimental Social Psychology, 10*, 371–384.

Irwin, M., Daniels, M., Bloom, E. T., Smith, T. L., & Weiner, H. (1987). Life events, depressive symptoms, and immune function. *American Journal of Psychiatry, 144,* 437–441.

Isen, A. M. (1970). Success, failure, attention and reactions to others: The warm glow of success. *Journal of Personality and Social Psychology, 15,* 294–301.

Isen, A. M., Clark, M., & Schwartz, M. F. (1976). Duration of the effect of good mood on helping: "Footprints on the sands of time." *Journal of Personality and Social Psychology, 34,* 385–393.

Isen, A. M., & Levin, P. G. (1972). The effects of feeling good on helping: Cookies and kindness. *Journal of Personality and Social Psychology, 21,* 384–388.

Ittelson, W. H. (1976). Environmental perception and contemporary perceptual theory. In H. M. Proshansky, W. H. Ittelson, & L. G. Rivlin (Eds.), *Environmental psychology: People and their physical settings.* New York: Holt, Rinehart & Winston.

Ittelson, W. H., Proshansky, H. M., & Rivlin, L. G. (1970). The environmental psychology of the psychiatric ward. In H. M. Proshansky, W. H. Ittelson, & L. G. Ittelson (Eds.), *Environmental psychology* (pp. 419–439). New York: Holt, Rinehart & Winston.

Ittelson, W. H., Proshansky, H. M., & Rivlin, L. G. (1972). Bedroom size and social interaction of the psychiatric ward. In J. Wohlwill & D. Carson (Eds.), *Environment and the social sciences* (pp. 95–113). Washington, DC: American Psychological Association.

Ittelson, W. H., Proshansky, H. M., Rivlin, L. G., & Winkel, G. H. (1974). *An introduction to environmental psychology.* New York: Holt, Rinehart & Winston.

Izard, C. E. (1960). Personality similarity and friendship. *Journal of Abnormal and Social Psychology, 61,* 47–51.

Izard, C. E. (1963). Personality similarity and friendship: A follow-up study. *Journal of Abnormal and Social Psychology, 66,* 598–600.

Jackson, J. M., & Harkins, S. G. (1985). Equity in effort: An explanation of the social loafing effect. *Journal of Personality and Social Psychology, 49,* 1199–1206.

Jackson, J. M., & Latané, B. (1981a). All alone in front of all those people: Stage fright as a function of number and type of co-performers and audience. *Journal of Personality and Social Psychology, 40,* 73–85.

Jackson, J. M., & Latané, B. (1981b). Strength and number of solicitors and the urge toward altruism. *Personality and Social Psychology Bulletin, 7,* 415–422.

Jacobs, B. S., & Moss, H. A. (1976). Birth order and sex of sibling as determinants of mother-infant interaction. *Child Development, 47,* 315–322.

Jacobs, J. (1961). *The death and life of great American cities.* New York: Vintage.

Jacobs, S. V., Evans, G. W., Catalano, R., & Dooley, D. (1984). Air pollution and depressive symptomology: Exploratory analysis of intervening psychosocial factors. *Population and Environment, 7,* 260–272.

Jacobson, N. S., McDonald, D. W., Follette, W. C., & Berley, R. A. (1985). Attributional processes in distressed and nondistressed married couples. *Cognitive Therapy and Research, 9,* 35–50.

Jaffe, Y., Malamuth, N., Feingold, J., & Feshbach, S. (1974). Sexual arousal and behavioral aggression. *Journal of Personality and Social Psychology, 30,* 759–764.

James, W. (1890). *The principles of psychology.* New York: Henry Holt.

Janis, I. L. (1972). *Victims of groupthink.* Boston: Houghton Mifflin.

Janis, I. L. (1975). Effectiveness of social support for stressful decisions. In M. Deutsch & H. A. Hornstein (Eds.), *Applying social psychology: Implications for research, practice, and training* (pp. 87–114). Hillsdale, NJ: Erlbaum.

Janis, I. L. (1983). The role of social support in adherence to stressful decisions. *American Psychologist, 38,* 143–160.

Janis, I. L., & Feshbach, S. (1953). Effects of fear-arousing communications. *Journal of Abnormal and Social Psychology, 48,* 78–92.

Janisse, M. P., & Peavler, W. S. (1974, February). Pupillary research today: Emotion in the eye. *Psychology Today,* pp. 60–63.

Jason, L. A., Zolik, E. S., & Matese, F. (1979). Prompting dog owners to pick up dog droppings. *American Journal of Community Psychology, 7,* 339–351.

Jecker, J., & Landy, D. (1969). Liking a person as a function of doing him a favor. *Human Relations, 22,* 371–378.

Jellison, J. M., & Arkin, R. M. (1977). Social comparison of abilities: A self presentational interpretation of decision making in groups. In J. Suls & R. L. Miller (Eds.), *Social comparison processes* (pp. 235–257). New York: Wiley.

Jennings, D. L., Amabile, T. M., & Ross, L. (1982). Informal covariation assessment: Data-based versus theory-based judgments. In D. Kahneman, P. Slovic, & A. Tversky (Eds.), *Judgment under uncertainty: Heuristics and biases* (pp. 211–230). New York: Cambridge University Press.

Jennings, D. L., Lepper, M. R., & Ross, L. (1980). *Persistence of impressions of personal persuasiveness: Perseverance of erroneous self-assessments outside the debriefing paradigm.* Unpublished manuscript, Stanford University.

Johnson, R. D., & Downing, L. L. (1979). Deindividuation and valence of cues: Effects on prosocial and antisocial behavior. *Journal of Personality and Social Psychology, 37,* 1532–1538.

Jones, E. E. (1964). *Ingratiation: A social-psychological analysis.* New York: Appleton-Century-Crofts.

Jones, E. E. (1986). Interpreting interpersonal behavior: The effects of expectancies. *Science, 234,* 41–46.

Jones, E. E., & Berglas, S. (1978). Control of attributions about the self through self-handicapping strategies: The appeal of alcohol and the role of underachievement. *Personality and Social Psychology Bulletin, 4,* 200–206.

Jones, E. E., & Davis, K. E. (1965). A theory of correspondent inferences: From acts to dispositions. In L. Berkowitz (Ed.), *Advances in experimental social psychology* (Vol. 2, pp. 219–266). New York: Academic Press.

Jones, E. E., Davis, K. E., & Gergen, K. J. (1961). Role playing variations and their informational value for person perception. *Journal of Abnormal and Social Psychology, 63,* 302–310.

Jones, E. E., & Gerard, H. B. (1967). *Foundations of social psychology.* New York: Wiley.

Jones, E. E., Gergen, K. J., Gumpert, P., & Thibaut, J. W. (1965). Some conditions affecting the use of ingratiation to influence performance evaluation. *Journal of Personality and Social Psychology, 1,* 613–625.

Jones, E. E., Gergen, K. J., & Jones, R. G. (1963). Some conditions affecting the evaluation of a conformist. *Journal of Personality, 31,* 270–288.

Jones, E. E., & Harris, V. A. (1967). The attribution of attitudes. *Journal of Experimental Social Psychology, 3,* 1–24.

Jones, E. E., & Nisbett, R. (1972). The actor and the observer: Divergent perceptions of the causes of behavior. In E. E. Jones et al. (Eds.), *Attribution: Perceiving the causes of behavior.* Morristown, NJ: General Learning Press.

Jones, E. E., & Pittman, T. S. (1982).
Toward a general theory of strategic
self-presentation. In J. Suls (Ed.),
Psychological perspectives on the self
(Vol. 1). Hillsdale, NJ: Erlbaum.

Jones, E. E., & Sigall, H. (1971). The
bogus pipeline: A new paradigm for
measuring affect and attitude.
Psychological Bulletin, 76, 349–364.

Jones, E. E., & Wortman, C. (1973).
*Ingratiation: An attributional
approach.* Morristown, NJ: General
Learning Press.

Jones, J. M. (1972). *Prejudice and racism.*
Reading, MA: Addison-Wesley.

Jones, J. M., & Hochner, A. R. (1973).
Racial differences in sports activities: A
look at the self-paced versus reactive
hypothesis. *Journal of Personality and
Social Psychology, 27,* 86–95.

Jones, R. A. (1977). *Self-fulfilling
prophecies: Social, psychological, and
physiological effects of expectancies.*
Hillsdale, NJ: Erlbaum.

**Jones, W. H., Cheek, J. M., & Briggs, S. R.
(Eds.) (1986).** *Shyness: Perspectives on
research and treatment.* New York:
Plenum.

**Jones, W. H., Chernovetz, M. O. C., &
Hansson, R. O. (1978).** The enigma of
androgyny: Differential implications for
males and females? *Journal of
Consulting and Clinical Psychology,
46,* 298–313.

Jorgenson, D. O., & Dukes, F. O. (1976).
Deindividuation as a function of density
and group membership. *Journal of
Personality and Social Psychology, 34,*
24–39.

Jourard, S. M. (1966). An exploratory
study of body-accessibility. *British
Journal of Social and Clinical
Psychology, 5,* 221–231.

Jourard, S. M. (1971). *Self-disclosure: An
experimental analysis of the
transparent self.* New York: Wiley.

Jourard, S. M., & Friedman, R. (1970).
Experimenter-subject "distance" and
self-disclosure. *Journal of Personality
and Social Psychology, 25,* 278–282.

Jourard, S. M., & Jaffee, P. E. (1970).
Influence of an interviewer's disclosure
on the self-disclosing behavior of
interviewees. *Journal of Consulting
Psychology, 17,* 252–257.

**Jue, G. M., Shumacher, S. A., & Evans,
G. W. (1984).** Community opinion
concerning airport noise-abatement
alternatives. *Journal of Environmental
Psychology, 4,* 337–345.

Jung, J. (1984). Social support and its
relation to health: A critical evaluation.
*Journal of Applied Social Psychology,
5,* 143–169.

Jussim, L. (1986). Self-fulfilling
prophecies: A theoretical and
integrative review. *Psychological
Review, 93,* 429–445.

Kagan, J. (1984). *The nature of the child.*
New York: Basic Books.

Kahneman, D., & Tversky, A. (1972).
Subjective probability: A judgment of
representativeness. *Cognitive
Psychology, 3,* 430–454.

Kahneman, D., & Tversky, A. (1973). On
the psychology of prediction.
Psychological Review, 80, 237–251.

Kahneman, D., & Tversky, A. (1982). The
simulation heuristic. In D. Kahneman,
P. Slovic, & A. Tversky (Eds.),
*Judgment under uncertainty: Heuristics
and biases.* New York: Cambridge
University Press.

**Kairys, D., Schulman, J., & Harring, S.
(Eds.) (1975).** *The Jury system: New
methods for reducing prejudice.*
Prepared by the National Jury Project
and the National Lawyers Guild.
Philadelphia, PA: Philadelphia
Resistance Print Shop.

Kalven, H., Jr., & Zeisel, H. (1966). *The
American jury.* Boston, MA: Little,
Brown.

**Kane, T. R., Joseph, J. M., & Tedeschi, J. T.
(1976).** Person perception and an
evaluation of the Berkowitz paradigm
for the study of aggression. *Journal of
Personality and Social Psychology, 33,*
663–673.

**Kanner, A. D., Coyne, J. C., Schaefer, C., &
Lazarus, R. S. (1981).** Comparison of
two modes of stress management: Daily
hassles and uplifts versus major life
events. *Journal of Behavioral Medicine,
4,* 1–39.

Kaplan, M. F. (1987). The influencing
process in group decision making. In C.
Hendrick (Ed.), *Review of personality
and social psychology: Vol. 8. Group
processes* (pp. 189–212). Beverly Hills:
Sage.

Kaplan, M. F., & Anderson, N. H. (1973).
Information integration theory and
reinforcement theory as approaches to
interpersonal attraction. *Journal of
Personality and Social Psychology, 28,*
301–312.

Kaplan, R. (1977). Preference and
everyday nature: Method and
application. In D. Stokols (Ed.),
*Perspectives on environment and
behavior: Theory, research, and
applications* (pp. 235–250). New York:
Plenum.

Kaplan, R. (1983). The role of nature in
the urban context. In I. Altman & J. F.
Wohlwill (Eds.), *Behavior and the
natural environment* (pp. 127–161).
New York: Plenum.

Kaplan, R. (1985). Nature at the footstep:
Residential satisfaction and the nearby
environment. *Journal of Architectural
and Planning Research, 2,* 115–127.

Kardes, F. R. (1988). Spontaneous
inference processes in advertising: The
effects of conclusion omission and
involvement on persuasion. *Journal of
Consumer Research, 15,* 225–233.

**Karlin, R. A., McFarland, D., Aiello, J. R.,
& Epstein, Y. M. (1976).** Normative
mediation of reactions to crowding.
*Environmental Psychology and
Nonverbal Behavior, 1,* 30–40.

**Kasl, S. V., Evans, A. S., & Neiderman,
J. C. (1979).** Psychosocial risk factors
in the development of infectious
mononucleosis. *Psychosomatic
Medicine, 41,* 445–467.

Kasl, S. V., & Mahl, G. F. (1965). The
relationship of disturbances and
hesitations in spontaneous speech to
anxiety. *Journal of Personality and
Social Psychology, 1,* 425–433.

Kasmer, J. V. (1970). The development of
a usable lexicon of environmental
descriptors. *Environment and Behavior,
2,* 153–169.

Katz, D. (1960). The functional approach
to the study of attitudes. *Public Opinion
Quarterly, 24,* 163–204.

Katz, D. (1968). Consistency for what?
The functional approach. In R. P.
Abelson, E. Aronson, W. J. McGuire,
T. M. Newcomb, M. J. Rosenberg, &
P. H. Tannenbaum (Eds.), *Theories of
cognitive consistency: A sourcebook*
(pp. 179–191). Chicago, IL: Rand
McNally.

Katz, E. (1957). The two-step flow of
communication: An up-to-date report on
a hypothesis. *Public Opinion Quarterly,
21,* 61–78.

Katz, E., & Lazarfeld, P. F. (1955).
Personal influence. Glencoe, IL: Free
Press.

Katz, I., Cohen, S., & Glass, D. C. (1975).
Some determinants of cross-racial
helping. *Journal of Personality and
Social Psychology, 32,* 964–970.

**Katz, I., Wackenhut, J., & Glass, D. C.
(1986).** An ambivalence-amplification
theory of behavior toward the
stigmatized. In S. Worchel & W. G.
Austin (Eds.), *Psychology of intergroup
relations* (pp. 103–117). Chicago, IL:
Nelson-Hall.

Katz, P. A. (1976). The acquisition of
racial attitudes in children. In P. A.
Katz (Ed.), *Towards the elimination of
racism* (pp. 125–154). New York:
Pergamon Press.

**Kaylor, J. A., King, D. W., & King, L. A.
(1987).** Psychological effects of
military service in Vietnam: A meta-
analysis. *Psychological Bulletin, 102,*
257–271.

Kelley, H. H. (1950). The warm-cold
variable in first impressions of persons.
Journal of Personality, 18, 431–439.

Kelley, H. H. (1967). Attribution theory in
social psychology. In D. Levine (Ed.),
Nebraska symposium on motivation
(Vol. 15, pp. 192–238). Lincoln:
University of Nebraska Press.

Kelley, H. H. (1971). *Attribution in social
interaction.* Morristown, NJ: General
Learning Press.

Kelley, H. H. (1983). Love and commitment. In H. H. Kelley, E. Bersheid, A. Christensen, J. H. Harvey, T. L. Huston, G. Levington, E. McClintock, L. A. Peplau, & D. R. Peterson. *Close relationships* (pp. 265–314). New York: W. H. Freeman.

Kelman, H. C. (1958). Compliance, identification and internalization: Three processes of attitude change. *Journal of Conflict Resolution, 2,* 51–60.

Kelman, H. C. (1974). Attitudes are alive and well and gainfully employed in the sphere of action. *American Psychologist, 29,* 310–324.

Kelman, H. C., & Hovland, C. I. (1953). "Reinstatement" of the communicator in delayed measurement of opinion change. *Journal of Abnormal and Social Psychology, 48,* 327–335.

Kemery, E. R., Mossholder, K. W., & Bedeian, A. G. (1987). Role stress, physical symptomology, and turnover intentions: A causal analysis of three alternative specifications. *Journal of Occupational Behaviour, 8,* 11–23.

Kendon, A. (1967). Some functions of gaze-direction in social interaction. *Acta Psychologica, 26,* 22–63.

Keniston, K. (1968). *Young radicals: Notes on committed youth.* New York: Harcourt, Brace and World.

Keniston, K. (1971). *Youth and dissent: The rise of a new opposition.* New York: Harcourt Brace Jovanovich.

Kennedy, J. F. (1955). *Profiles in courage.* New York: Harper.

Kenner, A. N. (1984). The effect of task differences, attention and personality on the frequency of body-focused hand movements. *Journal of Nonverbal Behavior, 8,* 159–171.

Kenrick, D. T., & Cialdini, R. B. (1977). Romantic attraction: Misattribution versus reinforcement explanations. *Journal of Personality and Social Psychology, 35,* 381–391.

Kenrick, D. T., & Johnson, G. A. (1979). Interpersonal attraction in aversive environments: A problem for the classical conditioning paradigm? *Journal of Personality and Social Psychology, 37,* 572–579.

Kerckhoff, A. C., & Davis, K. E. (1962). Value consensus and need complementarity in mate selection. *American Sociological Review, 27,* 295–303.

Kernan, J. B., & Reingen, P. H. (1985). Behavior influence: A new look in persuasion research. In J. N. Streth (Ed.), *Research in consumer behavior* (Vol. 1, pp. 159–199). Greenwich, CT: JAI Press.

Kerr, N. L. (1983). Motivation losses in small groups: A social dilemma analysis. *Journal of Personality and Social Psychology, 45,* 819–828.

Kerr, N. L., & Bruun, S. E. (1983). The dispensability of member effort and group motivation losses: Free-rider effects. *Journal of Personality and Social Psychology, 44,* 78–94.

Kerr, S., & Jermier, J. M. (1978). Substitutes for leadership: Their meaning and measurement. *Organizational Behavior and Human Performance, 22,* 375–403.

Kertzer, D. I. (1983). Generation as a sociological problem. *Annual Review of Sociology, 9,* 125–149.

Kessler, R. C., House, J. S., & Turner, J. B. (1987). Unemployment and health in a community sample. *Journal of Health and Social Behavior, 28,* 51–59.

Kessler, R. C., Price, R. H., & Wortman, C. B. (1985). Social factors in psychopathology: Stress, social support, and coping processes. *Annual Review of Psychology, 36,* 531–572.

Key, W. B. (1973). *Subliminal seduction.* Englewood Cliffs, NJ: Prentice-Hall.

Kiesler, C. A. (1971). *The psychology of commitment: Experiments linking behavior to belief.* New York: Academic Press.

Kiesler, C. A., & Kiesler, S. B. (1964). Role of forewarning in persuasive communications. *Journal of Abnormal and Social Psychology, 68,* 547–549.

Kimble, C. E. (1972). *The effects of acquaintanceship, disclosure level, and attributional variables on attraction and self-disclosure.* Ph.D. Dissertation, University of Texas at Austin.

Kimble, C. E. (1974). *A test of acquaintanceship theory.* Unpublished manuscript. University of Dayton.

Kimble, C. E. (1980). Factors affecting adults' attitudes toward school desegregation. *Journal of Social Psychology, 110,* 211–218.

Kimble, C. E. (1985). Commonsense attribution versus the covariation principle. *Social Behavior and Personality, 13,* 127–135.

Kimble, C. E., Arnold, E. M., & Hirt, E. R. (1985). An attributional perspective on interpersonal attraction using Kelley's cube. *Basic and Applied Social Psychology, 6,* 131–144.

Kimble, C. E., Fitz, D., & Onorad, J. (1977). Effectiveness of counteraggression strategies in reducing interactive aggression by males. *Journal of Personality and Social Psychology, 35,* 272–278.

Kimble, C. E., Forte, R. A., & Yoshikawa, J. C. (1981). Nonverbal concomitants of enacted emotional intensity and positivity: Visual and vocal behavior. *Journal of Personality, 49,* 271–283.

Kimble, C. E., Funk, S. C., & DaPolito, K. L. (1989). *Self-esteem certainty and behavioral self-handicapping.* Paper presented at Midwestern Psychological Association convention, Chicago.

Kimble, C. E., & Helmreich, R. (1972). Self-esteem and the need for social approval. *Psychonomic Science, 26,* 339–342.

Kimble, C. E., Hirt, E. R., & Arnold, E. M. (1985). Self-consciousness, public and private self-awareness and memory in a social setting. *Journal of Psychology, 119,* 59–69.

Kimble, C. E., & Kardes, F. R. (1987). Information patterns, attribution and attraction. *Social Psychology Quarterly, 50,* 338–345.

Kimble, C. E., Marsh, N. B., & Kiska, A. C. (1984). Sex, age, and cultural differences in self-reported assertiveness. *Psychological Reports, 55,* 419–422.

Kimble, C. E., & Moriarty, B. F. (1979). An attributional view of attraction: Evaluative gains versus favorable comparisons. *Psychological Reports, 45,* 199–207.

Kimble, C. E., & Musgrove, J. I. (1988). Dominance in arguing mixed-sex dyads: Visual dominance patterns, talking time, and speech loudness. *Journal of Research in Personality, 22,* 1–16.

Kimble, C. E., & Olszewski, D. A. (1980). Gaze and emotional expression: The effects of message positivity-negativity and emotional intensity. *Journal of Research in Personality, 14,* 60–69.

Kimble, C. E., Yoshikawa, J. C., & Zehr, H. D. (1981). Vocal and verbal assertiveness in same-sex and mixed-sex groups. *Journal of Personality and Social Psychology, 40,* 1047–1054.

Kimble, C. E., & Zehr, H. D. (1982). Self-consciousness, information load, self-presentation and memory in a social situation. *Journal of Social Psychology, 118,* 39–46.

Kinchlow, B. (1985). *Plain bread.* Waco, TX: Word Books.

Kinder, D. R., & Sears, D. O. (1981). Prejudice and politics: Symbolic racism versus racial threats to the good life. *Journal of Personality and Social Psychology, 40,* 414–431.

King, A. S. (1971). Self-fulfilling prophecies in training the hard-core: Supervisors' expectations and the underpriviledged workers' performance. *Social Science Quarterly, 52,* 369–378.

Kinzel, A. F. (1970). Body buffer zone in violent prisoners. *American Journal of Psychiatry, 127,* 99–104.

Kira, A. (1976). *The bathroom.* New York: Viking.

Kirk, R. E. (1968). *Experimental design: Procedures for the behavioral sciences.* Belmont, CA: Brooks/Cole.

Kleinke, C. L. (1986). Gaze and eye contact: A research review. *Psychological Bulletin, 100,* 78–100.

Kleinke, C. L., Meeker, F. B., & LaFong, C. L. (1974). Effects of gaze, touch and use of name on evaluation of "engaged" couples. *Journal of Research in Personality, 7,* 368–373.

Kleinke, C. L., Staneski, R. A., & Weaver, P. (1972). Evaluation of a person who uses another's name in ingratiating and noningratiating situations. *Journal of Experimental Social Psychology, 8,* 457–466.

Knipschild, P. (1977). Medical effects of aircraft noise. *International Archives of Occupational and Environmental Health, 40,* 185–204.

Knowles, E. S. (1980). An affiliative conflict theory of personal and group spatial behavior. In P. B. Paulus (Ed.), *Psychology of group influences* (pp. 133–188). Hillsdale, NJ: Erlbaum.

Knowles, E. S. (1983). Social physics and the effects of others: Tests of the effects of audience size and distance of social judgements and behavior. *Journal of Personality and Social Psychology, 45,* 1263–1279.

Knox, R. E., & Inkster, J. A. (1968). Postdecision dissonance at post time. *Journal of Personality and Social Psychology, 8,* 319–323.

Kobasa, S. C. (1979). Stressful life events, personality, and health: An inquiry into hardiness. *Journal of Personality and Social Psychology, 37,* 1–11.

Kobasa, S. C. (1982a). Commitment and coping in stress resistance among lawyers. *Journal of Personality and Social Psychology, 42,* 707–717.

Kobasa, S. C. (1982b). The hardy personality: Toward a social psychology of stress and health. In G. S. Sanders & J. Suls (Eds.), *Social psychology of health and illness* (pp. 3–32). Hillsdale, NJ: Erlbaum.

Kobasa, S. C., Maddi, R., & Puccetti, M. C. (1982). Personality and exercise as buffers in the stress-illness relationship. *Journal of Behavioral Medicine, 5,* 391–404.

Koch, H. L. (1960). The relation of certain formal attributes of siblings to attitudes held toward each other and toward their parents. *Monograph: Society for Research in Child Development, 25*(4), No. 78.

Koelega, H. S. (1987). Introduction: Environmental annoyance. In H. S. Koelega (Ed.), *Environmental annoyance: Characterization, measurement, and control* (pp. 1–7). New York: Elsevier.

Kogan, N., & Wallach, M. A. (1964). *Risk Taking: A study of cognition and personality.* New York: Holt, Rinehart & Winston.

Kohlberg, L. (1966). A cognitive-developmental analysis of children's sex-role concepts and attitudes. In E. E. Maccoby (Ed.), *The development of sex differences.* Stanford, CA: Stanford University Press.

Kohlberg, L. (1969). Stage and sequence: The cognitive-developmental approach to socialization. In D. A. Goslin (Ed.), *Handbook of socialization: Theory and research.* Chicago: Rand McNally.

Kohlenberg, R. J., & Phillips, T. (1973). Reinforcement and rate of litter deposit. *Journal of Applied Behavior Analysis, 9,* 13–18.

Kolditz, T. A., & Arkin, R. M. (1982). An impression management interpretation of the self-handicapping strategy. *Journal of Personality and Social Psychology, 43,* 492–502.

Komarovsky, M. (1971). *The unemployed man and his family.* New York: Arno Press.

Konar, E., Sundstrom, E., Brady, C., Mandel, D., & Rice, R. W. (1982). Status demarcation in the office. *Environment and Behavior, 14,* 561–580.

Konečni, V. J., Libuser, L., Morton, H., & Ebbesen, E. B. (1975). Effects of a violation of personal space on escape and helping responses. *Journal of Experimental Social Psychology, 11,* 288–299.

Koneya, M. (1976). Location and interaction in row-and-column seating arrangements. *Environment and Behavior, 8,* 265–283.

Koocher, G. P. (1977). Bathroom behavior and human dignity. *Journal of Personality and Social Psychology, 35,* 120–121.

Korte, C. (1981). Constraints on helping behavior in an urban environment. In J. P. Rushton & R. M. Sorrentino (Eds.), *Altruism and helping behavior: Social, personality, and developmental perspectives.* Hillsdale, NJ: Erlbaum.

Korte, C., & Kerr, N. (1975). Response to altruistic opportunities under urban and rural conditions. *Journal of Social Psychology, 95,* 183–184.

Korte, C., Ypma, I., & Toppen, A. (1975). Helpfulness in Dutch society as a function of urbanization and environmental input level. *Journal of Personality and Social Psychology, 32,* 996–1003.

Kovel, J. (1970). *White racism: A psychohistory.* New York: Pantheon.

Krauss, R. M., Apple, W., Morency, N., Wenzel, C., & Winton, W. (1981). Verbal, vocal, and visible factors in judgments of another's affect. *Journal of Personality and Social Psychology, 40,* 312–320.

Krauss, R. M., Freedman, J. L., & Whitcup, M. (1978). Field and laboratory studies of littering. *Journal of Experimental Social Psychology, 14,* 109–122.

Kraut, R. E., & Johnston, R. E. (1979). Social and emotional messages of smiling: An ethological approach. *Journal of Personality and Social Psychology, 37,* 1539–1553.

Kravitz, D. A., & Martin, B. (1986). Ringelmann rediscovered: The original article. *Journal of Personality and Social Psychology, 50,* 936–941.

Krebs, D. (1970). Altruism—An examination of the concept and review of the literature. *Psychological Bulletin, 73,* 258–302.

Krebs, D. (1975). Empathy and altruism. *Journal of Personality and Social Psychology, 32,* 1134–1146.

Krebs, D. L., & Rosenwald, A. (1977). Moral reasoning and moral behavior in conventional adults. *Merrill-Palmer Quarterly of Behavior and Development, 23,* 77–87.

Krebs, D. L., & Russell, C. (1981). Role-taking and altruism: When you put yourself in the shoes of another, will they take you to their owner's aid? In J. P. Rushton & R. M. Sorrentino (Eds.), *Altruism and helping behavior* (pp. 137–165). Hillsdale, NJ: Erlbaum.

Krieger, W. G. (1972). *The effects of visual aesthetics upon mood and problem-solving efficiency.* Unpublished master's thesis, Purdue University, West Lafayette, IN.

Kriss, M., Kinchla, R. A., & Darley, J. M. (1977). A mathematical model for social influences on perceptual judgments. *Journal of Experimental Social Psychology, 13,* 403–420.

Kryter, K. D. (1972). Non-auditory effects of environmental noise. *American Journal of Public Health, 62,* 389–398.

Kubler-Ross, E. (1969). *On death and dying.* New York: Macmillan.

Kuhn, D. Z., Madsen, C. H., & Becker, W. C. (1967). Effects of exposure to an aggressive model and "frustration" on children's aggressive behavior. *Child Development, 38,* 739–745.

Kuper, L. (1970). Neighbor on the hearth. In M. H. Proshansky, W. H. Ittelson, and L. G. Rivlin (Eds.), *Environmental psychology: Man and his physical setting* (pp. 246–255). New York: Holt, Rinehart & Winston.

Lacayo, R. (1985, June 10). Blood in the stands. *Time, 125*(23), 38–41.

LaFrance, M., & Carmen, B. (1980). The nonverbal display of psychological androgyny. *Journal of Personality and Social Psychology, 38,* 36–49.

LaFrance, M., & Mayo, C. (1976). Racial differences in gaze behavior during conversations: Two systematic observational studies. *Journal of Personality and Social Psychology, 33,* 547–552.

LaFrance, M., & Mayo, C. (1978). *Moving bodies: Nonverbal communication in social relationships.* Monterey, CA: Brooks/Cole.

Lamb, M. E. (1977). Father-infant and mother-infant interaction in the first year of life. *Child Development, 48,* 167–181.

Lamm, H., & Myers, D. G. (1978). Group-induced polarization of attitudes and behavior. In L. Berkowitz (Ed.), *Advances in experimental social psychology.* New York: Academic Press.

Lamm, H., & Trommsdorf, G. (1973). Group versus individual performance on tasks requiring ideational proficiency (brainstorming): A review. *European Journal of Social Psychology, 3,* 361–388.

Langer, E. J. (1978). Rethinking the role of thought in social interaction. In J. H. Harvey, W. Ickes, & R. F. Kidd (Eds.), *New directions in attribution research* (Vol. 2, pp. 35–58). Hillsdale, NJ: Erlbaum.

Langer, E. J. (1989). Minding matters: The consequences of mindlessness-mindfulness. In L. Berkowitz (Ed.), *Advances in experimental social psychology* (Vol. 22, pp. 137–173). New York: Academic Press.

Langer, E. J., Blank, A., & Chanowitz, B. (1978). The mindlessness of ostensibly thoughtful action: The role of "placebic" information in interpersonal interaction. *Journal of Personality and Social Psychology, 36,* 635–642.

Langer, E., & Saegert, S. (1977). Crowding and cognitive control. *Journal of Personality and Social Psychology, 34,* 191–198.

LaPiere, R. T. (1934). Attitudes versus action. *Social Forces, 13,* 230–237.

Latané, B. (1981). The psychology of social impact. *American Psychologist, 36,* 343–356.

Latané, B., & Dabbs, J. (1975). Sex, group size and helping in Columbus, Seattle and Atlanta. *Sociometry, 38,* 180–194.

Latané, B., & Darley, J. M. (1968). Group inhibition of bystander intervention in emergencies. *Journal of Personality and Social Psychology, 10,* 215–221.

Latané, B., & Darley, J. M. (1970). *The unresponsive bystander: Why doesn't he help?* New York: Appleton-Century-Crofts.

Latané, B., & Darley, J. M. (1976). Help in a crisis: Bystander response to an emergency. In J. W. Thibaut, J. T. Spence, & R. C. Carson (Eds.), *Contemporary topics in social psychology* (pp. 309–332). Morristown, NJ: General Learning Press.

Latané, B., Gabrenya, W., & Wang, Y. (1983). Social loafing in cross-cultural perspective: Chinese on Taiwan. *Journal of Cross-Cultural Psychology, 14,* 368–384.

Latané, B., & Harkins, S. (1976). Cross modality matches suggest anticipated stage fright a multiplicative power function of audience size and status. *Perception and Psychophysics, 20,* 482–488.

Latané, B., & Nida, S. (1981). Ten years of research on group size and helping. *Psychological Bulletin, 89,* 308–324.

Latané, B., Nida, S. A., & Wilson, D. W. (1981). The effects of group size and helping behavior. In J. P. Rushton & R. M. Sorrentino (Eds.), *Altruism and helping behavior: Social, personality and developmental perspectives.* Hillsdale, NJ: Erlbaum.

Latané, B., & Rodin, J. A. (1969). A lady in distress: Inhibiting effects of friends and strangers on bystander intervention. *Journal of Experimental Social Psychology, 5,* 189–202.

Latané, B., Williams, K., & Harkins, S. (1979). Many hands make light the work: The causes and consequences of social loafing. *Journal of Personality and Social Psychology, 37,* 823–832.

Latané, B., & Wolf, S. (1981). The social impact of majorities and minorities. *Psychological Review, 88,* 438–453.

Lau, R. R., & Russell, D. (1980). Attributions in the sports pages. *Journal of Personality and Social Psychology, 39,* 29–38.

Laudenslager, M. L., & Reite, M. L. (1984). Losses and separations: Immunological consequences and health implications. *Review of Personality and Social Psychology* (Vol. 5, pp. 285–312). Hillsdale, NJ: Erlbaum.

Laughlin, P. R., & Johnson, H. H. (1966). Group and individual performance on a complementary task as a function of initial ability level. *Journal of Experimental Social Psychology, 2,* 407–414.

Lavrakas, P. J. (1982). Fear of crime and behavioral restrictions in urban and suburban neighborhoods. *Population and Environment, 5,* 242–264.

Lazarus, R. S. (1966). *Psychological stress and the coping process.* New York: McGraw-Hill.

Lazarus, R. S. (1984). Puzzles in the study of daily hassles. *Journal of Behavioral Medicine, 7,* 375–389.

Lazarus, R. S., & Cohen, J. B. (1977). Environmental stress. In I. Altman & J. F. Wohlwill (Eds.), *Human behavior and environment: Advances in theory and research* (Vol. 2, pp. 89–127). New York: Plenum.

Lazarus, R. S., DeLongis, A., Folkman, S., & Gruen, R. (1985). Stress and adaptational outcomes: The problem of confounded measures. *American Psychologist, 40,* 770–779.

Lazarus, R. S., & Folkman, S. (1984). *Stress, appraisal, and coping.* New York: Springer.

Lazarus, R. S., & Launeir, R. (1978). Stress-related transactions between person and environment. In L. A. Pervin & M. Lewis (Eds.), *Perspectives in interactional psychology* (pp. 287–327). New York: Plenum.

LeCompte, W. A. (1981). The ecology of anxiety: Situational stress and rate of self-stimulation in Turkey. *Journal of Personality and Social Psychology, 40,* 712–721.

Leary, M. R., & Shepperd, J. A. (1986). Behavioral self-handicaps versus self-reported handicaps: A conceptual note. *Journal of Personality and Social Psychology, 51,* 1265–1268.

Lebo, C. P., & Oliphant, K. P. (1968). Music as a source of acoustical trauma. *Laryngoscope, 78,* 1211–1218.

Lee, J. A. (1973). *The colors of love.* New York: Bantam Books.

Lefcourt, H. M., & Martin, R. A. (1986). *Humor and life stress: Antidote to adversity.* New York: Springer-Verlag.

Lefkowitz, M., Blake, R. R., & Mouton, J. S. (1955). Status factors in pedestrian violation of traffic signals. *Journal of Abnormal and Social Psychology, 61,* 704–706.

Lehman, D. R., Wortman, C. B., & Williams, A. F. (1987). Long-term effects of losing a spouse or child in a motor vehicle crash. *Journal of Personality and Social Psychology, 52,* 218–231.

Lepper, M. R., Greene, D., & Nisbett, R. E. (1973). Undermining children's intrinsic interest with extrinsic reward: A test of the overjustification hypothesis. *Journal of Personality and Social Psychology, 28,* 129–137.

Lepper, M. R., Ross, L., & Lau, R. (1979). Persistence of inaccurate and discredited personal impressions: A field demonstration of attributional perseverance. Unpublished manuscript, Stanford University.

LeResche, L. (1982). Facial expression in pain: A study of candid photographs. *Journal of Nonverbal Behavior, 7,* 46–56.

Lerner, M. J. (1980). *The belief in a just world: A fundamental delusion.* New York: Plenum.

Lerner, M. J., & Simmons, C. H. (1966). Observer's reaction to the innocent victim: Compassion or rejection? *Journal of Personality and Social Psychology, 4,* 203–210.

Leventhal, G., & Levitt, L. (1979). Physical, social, and personal factors in the perception of crowding. *Journal of Nonverbal Behavior, 4,* 40–55.

Leventhal, H. (1970). Findings and theory in the study of fear communications. In L. Berkowitz (Ed.), *Advances in experimental social psychology* (Vol. 5). New York: Academic Press.

Levin, F. M., & Gergen, K. J. (1969). *Revealingness, ingratiation, and the disclosure of the self.* Paper presented at the American Psychological Association convention.

Levine, D. W., McDonald, P. J., O'Neal, E. C., & Garwood, S. G. (1980). Classroom ecology: The effects of seating position on grades and participation. *Personality and Social Psychology Bulletin, 6,* 409–412.

Levine, D. W., McDonald, P. J., O'Neal, E. C., & Garwood, S. G. (1982). Classroom seating effects: Environment or self-selection—Neither, either, or both. *Personality and Social Psychology Bulletin, 8,* 365–369.

Levine, R. A., & Campbell, D. T. (1972). *Ethnocentrism: Theories of conflict, ethnic attitudes and group behavior.* New York: Wiley.

Levine, R. V. (with E. Wolff) (1985, March). Social time: The heartbeat of culture. *Psychology Today,* pp. 28–30, 32, 34–35.

Levine, R. V., West, L. J., & Reis, H. T. (1980). Perceptions of time and punctuality in the United States and Brazil. *Journal of Personality and Social Psychology, 38,* 541–550.

Levinger, G. (1979). A social psychological perspective on marital dissolution. In G. Levinger & O. C. Moles (Eds.), *Divorce and separation: Context, causes, and consequences.* New York: Basic Books.

Levinger, G. (1983). Development and change. In Kelley, E. Bersheid, A., Christensen, J. H., Harvey, T. L. Huston, G. Levinger, E. McClintock, L. A. Peplau, & D. R. Peterson (Eds.), *Close relationships.* New York: Freeman.

Levinger, G., & Schneider, D. J. (1969). Test of the "risk is a value" hypothesis. *Journal of Personality and Social Psychology, 11,* 165–169.

Levinger, G., & Senn, D. J. (1967). Disclosure of feelings in marriage. *Merrill-Palmer Quarterly of Behavior and Development, 13,* 237–249.

Levinger, G., & Snoek, J. G. (1972). *Attraction in relationship: A new look at interpersonal attraction.* Morristown, NJ: General Learning Press.

Levitt, L., & Leventhal, G. (1986). Litter reduction: How effective is the New York state bottle law? *Environment and Behavior, 18,* 467–479.

Levitt, M. J. (in press). Attachment and close relationships: A life span perspective. In J. L. Gewirtz & W. F. Kurtines (Eds.), *Interactions with attachment.* Hillsdale, NJ: Erlbaum.

Levitt, M. J. (1989). Social involvement with peers in 2½-year-old toddlers: Environmental influences. *Environment and Behavior, 21,* 82–98.

Levitt, M. J., Clark, M. C., Rotton, J., & Finley, G. E. (1987). Social support, perceived control, and well-being: A study of an environmentally stressed population. *International Journal of Aging and Human Development, 25,* 249–260.

Levitt, M. J., & Weber, R. A. (1989). Social involvement with peers in 2½ toddlers: Environmental influences. *Environment and Behavior, 21,* 82–98.

Lewicki, P. (1985). Nonconscious biasing effects of single instances on subsequent judgments. *Journal of Personality and Social Psychology, 48,* 563–574.

Lewinsohn, P. M., Mischel, W., Chaplin, W., & Barton, R. (1980). Social competence and depression: The role of illusory self-perceptions. *Journal of Abnormal Psychology, 89,* 203–212.

Lewis, O. (1966). *La Vida.* New York: Random House.

Leyens, J. P., Camino, L., Parke, R. D., & Berkowitz, L. (1975). Effects of movie violence on aggression in a field setting as a function of group dominance and cohesion. *Journal of Personality and Social Psychology, 32,* 346–360.

Lichtenstein, S., Slovic, P., Fischhoff, B., Layman, M., & Combs, B. (1978). Judged frequency of lethal events. *Journal of Experimental Psychology: Human Learning and Memory, 4,* 551–578.

Liem, R., & Rayman, P. (1982). Health and the social costs of unemployment. *American Psychologist, 37,* 1116–1123.

Linden, W. (1987). On the impending death of the Type A construct: Or is there a phoenix rising from the ashes? *Canadian Journal of Behavioral Sciences, 19,* 179–190.

Linder, D. E., Cooper, J., & Jones, E. E. (1967). Decision freedom as a determinant of the role of incentive magnitude in attitude change. *Journal of Personality and Social Psychology, 6,* 245–254.

Linder, D. E., & Worchel, S. (1970). Opinion change as a result of effortfully drawing a counterattitudinal conclusion. *Journal of Experimental Social Psychology, 6,* 432–448.

Lindskold, S. (1981). Trust development, the GRIT proposal, and the effects of conciliatory acts on conflict and cooperation. *Psychological Bulletin, 85,* 772–793.

Linville, P. W. (1982). The complexity-extremity effect and age-based stereotyping. *Journal of Personality and Social Psychology, 42,* 193–211.

Linville, P. W. (1985). Self-complexity and affective extremity: Don't put all of your cognitive eggs in one basket. *Social Cognition, 3,* 94–120.

Linville, P. W. (1987). Self-complexity as a cognitive buffer against stress-related illness and depression. *Journal of Personality and Social Psychology, 52,* 663–676.

Linz, D. G., & Penrod, S. (1984). Increasing attorney persuasiveness in the courtroom. *Law and Psychology Review, 8,* 1–47.

Lippa, R. (1976). Expressive control and the leakage of dispositional introversion-extroversion during role teaching. *Journal of Personality, 44,* 541–559.

Lippa, R. (1978). The effect of expressive control on expressive consistency and on the relation between expressive behavior and personality. *Journal of Personality, 46,* 438–461.

Lippa, R., & Beauvais, C. (1983). Gender jeopardy: The effects of gender, assessed femininity and masculinity, and false success/failure feedback on performance in an experimental quiz game. *Journal of Personality and Social Psychology, 44,* 344–353.

Livingston, J. S. (1969). Pygmalion in management. *Harvard Business Review, 47*(4), 81–89.

Lord, C. G., Lepper, M. R., & Mackie, D. (1984). Attitude prototypes as determinants of attitude-behavior consistency. *Journal of Personality and Social Psychology, 37,* 2098–2109.

Lord, C. G., Ross, L., & Lepper, M. R. (1979). Biased assimilation and attitude polarization: The effects of prior theories on subsequently considered evidence. *Journal of Personality and Social Psychology, 37,* 2098–2109.

Lorenz, K. (1966). *On aggression.* New York: Harcourt Brace and World.

Lott, B. E., & Lott, A. J. (1960). The formation of positive attitudes toward group members. *Journal of Abnormal and Social Psychology, 61,* 297–300.

Lott, D. F., & Sommer, R. (1967). Seating arrangements and status. *Journal of Personality and Social Psychology, 7,* 90–95.

Lubinski, D., Tellegen, A., & Butcher, J. N. (1981). The relationship between androgyny and subjective indicators of emotional well-being. *Journal of Personality and Social Psychology, 40,* 722–730.

Lubinski, D., Tellegen, A., & Butcher, J. N. (1983). Masculinity, femininity, and androgyny viewed and assessed as distinct concepts. *Journal of Personality and Social Psychology, 44*, 428–439.

Lyman, S. M., & Scott, M. B. (1967). Territoriality: A neglected sociological dimension. *Social Problems, 15*, 236–249.

Lynn, S. J. (1978). Three theories of self-disclosure and exchange. *Journal of Experimental Social Psychology, 5*, 466–479.

Maas, A., & Clark, R. D. III. (1984). Hidden impact of minorities: Fifteen years of minority influence research. *Psychological Bulletin, 95*, 428–450.

Maccoby, E. E., & Jacklin, C. N. (1974). *The psychology of sex differences.* Stanford, California: Stanford University Press.

Maccoby, N., & Alexander, J. (1980). Use of media in lifestyle programs. In P. O. Davidson & S. M. Davidson (Eds.), *Behavioral medicine: Changing health lifestyles.* New York: Brunner/Mazel.

Mackie, D. M. (1986). Social identification effects in group polarization. *Journal of Personality and Social Psychology, 50*, 720–728.

MacLachlan, J. (1983–84). Making a message memorable and persuasive. *Journal of Advertising Research, 23*, 51–59.

Maddi, S. R., Bartone, P. T., & Puccetti, M. C. (1987). Stressful life events are indeed a factor in physical illness: Reply to Schroeder and Costa (1984). *Journal of Personality and Social Psychology, 52*, 833–843.

Madsen, D. B., & Finger, J. R., Jr. (1978). Comparison of a written feedback procedure, group brainstorming, and individual brainstorming. *Journal of Applied Psychology, 63*, 120–123.

Mahl, G. F. (1956). Disturbances and silences in the patients' speech in psychotherapy. *Journal of Abnormal Social Psychology, 53*, 1–15.

Mallick, S. K., & McCandless, B. R. (1966). A study of catharsis of aggression. *Journal of Personality and Social Psychology, 4*, 591–596.

Manucia, G. K., Baumann, D. J., & Cialdini, R. B. (1984). Mood influences on helping: Direct effects or side effects? *Journal of Personality and Social Psychology, 46*, 357–364.

Marans, R. W., & Sprekelmeyer, K. F. (1982). Evaluating open and conventional office design. *Environment and Behavior, 14*, 333–351.

Marjoribanks, K., & Walberg, H. J. (1975). Birth order, family size, social class, and intelligence. *Social Biology, 22*, 261–268.

Markiewicz, D. (1974). Effects of humor on persuasion. *Sociometry, 37*, 407–422.

Markus, E. M., Blenkner, M., Bloom, M., & Downs, T. (1972). Some factors and their association with post-relocation mortality among institutionalized aged persons. *Journal of Gerontology, 27*, 376–382.

Markus, H. (1981, June). Sibling personalities: The luck of the draw. *Psychology Today*, pp. 35–37.

Marshall, J. E., & Heslin, R. (1975). Boys and girls together: Sexual composition and the effects of density and group size on cohesiveness. *Journal of Personality and Social Psychology, 31*, 952–961.

Marshall, N. J. (1974). Dimensions of privacy preferences. *Multivariate Behavioral Research, 9*, 255–272.

Martens, R., & Landers, D. M. (1972). Evaluation potential as a determinant of coaction effects. *Journal of Experimental Social Psychology, 8*, 347–359.

Martin, R. A., Kuiper, N. A., Olinger, L. J., & Dobbin, J. (1987). Is stress always bad? Telic versus paratelic dominance as a stress-moderating variable. *Journal of Personality and Social Psychology, 53*, 970–982.

Martinsen, E. W. (1987). The role of aerobic exercise in the treatment of depression. *Stress Medicine, 3*, 93–100.

Maslach, C. (1982). *Burnout: The cost of caring.* Englewood Cliffs, NJ: Prentice-Hall.

Maslach, C., & Jackson, S. E. (1984). Burnout in organizational settings. In S. Oskamp (Ed.), *Applied social psychology annual* (Vol. 5, pp. 133–153). Beverly Hills, CA: Sage.

Maslow, A. H., & Mintz, N. C. (1956). Effects of esthetic surroundings: I. Initial effects of three esthetic conditions upon perceiving "energy" and "well-being" in faces. *Journal of Psychology, 41*, 247–254.

Mathews, K. E., Canon, L. K., & Alexander, K. (1974). The influence of level of empathy and ambient noise on the body buffer zone. *Personality and Social Psychology Bulletin, 1*, 367–369.

Mathews, K. E., Jr., & Canon, L. K. (1975). Environmental noise level as a determinant of helping behavior. *Journal of Personality and Social Psychology, 32*, 571–577.

Mazur, A. (1977). Interpersonal spacing on public benches in contact vs. noncontact cultures. *Journal of Social Psychology, 101*, 53–58.

McArthur, L. A. (1972). The how and what of why: Some determinants and consequences of causal attribution. *Journal of Personality and Social Psychology, 22*, 171–193.

McArthur, L. Z., & Post, D. L. (1977). Figural emphasis and person perception. *Journal of Experimental Social Psychology, 13*, 520–535.

McCann, I. L., & Holmes, D. S. (1984). Influence of aerobic exercise on depression. *Journal of Personality and Social Psychology, 46*, 1142–1147.

McClelland, L. (1976). Interaction level and acquaintance as mediators of density effects. *Personality and Social Psychology Bulletin, 2*, 175–178.

McConahay, J. B. (1982). Self-interest versus racial attitudes as correlates of anti-busing attitudes in Louisville: Is it the buses or the blacks? *Journal of Politics, 44*, 692–720.

McConahay, J., Mullin, C., & Frederick, J. (1977). The uses of social science in trials with political and racial overtones: The trial of Joan Little. *Law and Contemporary Problems, 41*, 205–229.

McConnell, J. V., Cutler, R. L., & McNeil, E. B. (1958). Subliminal stimulation: An overview. *American Psychologist, 13*, 229–239.

McElroy, J. C., Morrow, P. C., & Wall, L. C. (1983). Generalizing impact of object language to other audiences: Peer response to office design. *Psychological Reports, 53*, 315–322.

McGill, W., & Korn, J. H. (1982). Awareness of an urban environment. *Environment and Behavior, 14*, 186–201.

McGinnies, E., & Ward, C. D. (1980). Better liked than right: Trustworthiness and expertise as factors in credibility. *Personality and Social Psychology Bulletin, 6*, 467–472.

McGuire, W. J. (1964). Inducing resistance to persuasion. In L. Berkowitz (Ed.), *Advances in experimental social psychology* (Vol. 1, pp. 191–229). New York: Academic Press.

McGuire, W. J. (1968a). Personality and susceptibility to social influence. In E. F. Borgatta & W. W. Lambert (Eds.), *Handbook of personality theory and research* (pp. 1130–1187). Chicago: Rand McNally.

McGuire, W. J. (1968b). Theory of the structure of human thought. In R. P. Abelson et al. (Eds.), *Theories of cognitive consistency: A sourcebook.* Chicago, IL: Rand McNally (pp. 140–162).

McGuire, W. J. (1985). Attitudes and attitude change. In G. Lindzey & E. Aronson (Eds.), *The handbook of social psychology* (3rd ed., Vol. 2, pp. 233–346). New York: Random House.

McGuire, W. J., McGuire, C. V., Child, P., & Fujioka, T. (1978). Salience of ethnicity in the spontaneous self-concept as a function of one's ethnic distinctiveness in the social environment. *Journal of Personality and Social Psychology, 36*, 511–520.

McGuire, W. J., & Papageorgis, D. (1961). The relative efficacy of various types of prior belief-defense in producing immunity against persuasion. *Journal of Abnormal and Social Psychology, 62,* 327–337.

McNees, M. P., Schnelle, J. F., Gendrich, J., Thomas, M. M., & Beegle, G. P. (1979). McDonald's litter hunt: A community litter control system for youth. *Environment and Behavior, 11,* 131–138.

Megargee, E. I. (1966). Undercontrolled and overcontrolled personality types in extreme antisocial aggression. *Psychological Monographs, 80* (Whole No. 611).

Mehrabian, A. (1969). Significance of posture and position in the communication of attitude and status relationships. *Psychological Bulletin, 71,* 359–372.

Mehrabian, A. (1970). The development and validation of measures of affiliative tendency and sensitivity to rejection. *Educational and Psychological Measurement, 30,* 417–428.

Mehrabian, A. (1972). *Nonverbal communication.* Chicago: Aldine.

Mehrabian, A. (1976). *Public places and private spaces: The psychology of work, play, and living environments.* New York: Basic Books.

Mehrabian, A., & Diamond, S. G. (1971a). Effects of furniture arrangement, props, and personality on social interaction. *Journal of Personality and Social Psychology, 20,* 18–30.

Mehrabian, A., & Diamond, S. G. (1971b). Seating arrangement and conversation. *Sociometry, 34,* 281–289.

Mehrabian, A., & Ferris, S. R. (1967). Inference of attitudes from nonverbal communication in two channels. *Journal of Consulting Psychology, 31,* 248–252.

Mehrabian, A., & Russell, J. A. (1974). *An approach to environmental psychology.* Cambridge, MA: M. I. T. Press.

Mehrabian, A., & Weiner, M. (1967). Decoding of inconsistent communications. *Journal of Personality and Social Psychology, 6,* 109–114.

Meindl, J. R., & Lerner, M. J. (1983). The heroic motive: Some experimental demonstrations. *Journal of Experimental Social Psychology, 19,* 1–20.

Meindl, J. R., & Lerner, M. J. (1985). Exacerbation of extreme responses to an out-group. *Journal of Personality and Social Psychology, 47,* 71–84.

Mendelson, R., & Orcutt, G. (1979). An empirical analysis of air pollution dose-response curves. *Journal of Environmental Economics and Management, 6,* 85–106.

Menzel, H., & Katz, E. (1956). Social relations and innovations in the medical profession: The epidemiology of a new drug. *Public Opinion Quarterly, 19,* 337–352.

Mercer, G. W., & Benjamin, M. L. (1980). Spatial behavior of university undergraduates in double occupancy residence rooms: An inventory of effects. *Journal of Applied Social Psychology, 10,* 32–44.

Merkl, P. H. (1980). *The making of a storm trooper.* Princeton, NJ: Princeton University Press.

Merton, R. K. (1948). The self-fulfilling prophecy. *Antioch Review, 8,* 193–210.

Meyer, J. P., & Pepper, S. (1977). Need compatibility and marital adjustment in young married couples. *Journal of Personality and Social Psychology, 35,* 331–342.

Mezei, L. (1971). Perceived social pressure as an explanation of shifts in the relative influence of race and belief on prejudice across social interactions. *Journal of Personality and Social Psychology, 19,* 69–81.

Michaels, J. W., Blommel, J. M., Brocato, R. M., Linkous, R. A., & Rowe, J. S. (1982). Social facilitation and inhibition in a natural setting. *Replications in Social Psychology, 2,* 21–24.

Middlebrook, P. N. (1980). *Social psychology and modern life* (2nd ed.). New York: Alfred A. Knopf.

Middlemist, R. D., Knowles, E. S., & Matter, C. F. (1976). Personal space invasions in the lavatory: Suggestive evidence for arousal. *Journal of Personality and Social Psychology, 33,* 541–546.

Middlemist, R. D., Knowles, E. S., & Matter, C. F. (1977). What to do and what to report: A reply to Koocher. *Journal of Personality and Social Psychology, 35,* 122–124.

Midlarsky, M., & Midlarsky, E. (1976). Status inconsistency, aggressive attitude, and helping behavior. *Journal of Personality, 44,* 371–391.

Milgram, S. (1970). The experience of living in cities. *Science, 167,* 1461–1468.

Milgram, S. (1974). *Obedience to authority.* New York: Harper & Row.

Miller, C. T. (1982). The role of performance-related similarity in social comparison of abilities: A test of the related attributes hypothesis. *Journal of Experimental Social Psychology, 18,* 513–523.

Miller, D. T., & Ross, M. (1975). Self-serving biases in attributions of causality: Fact or fiction? *Psychological Bulletin, 82,* 213–225.

Miller, L. K., & Hamblin, R. L. (1963). Interdependence, differential rewarding, and productivity. *American Sociological Review, 28,* 768–777.

Miller, N. E. (1941). The frustration-aggression hypothesis. *Psychological Review, 48,* 337–342.

Miller, N., & Campbell, D. T. (1959). Recency and primacy in persuasion as a function of the timing of speeches and measurement. *Journal of Abnormal and Social Psychology, 59,* 1–9.

Miller, N., & Maruyama, G. (1976). Ordinal position and peer popularity. *Journal of Personality and Social Psychology, 33,* 123–131.

Miller, N., Maruyama, G., Beaber, R. J., & Valone, K. (1976). Speed of speech and persuasion. *Journal of Personality and Social Psychology, 34,* 615–624.

Mills, J., & Clark, M. S. (1982). Communal and exchange relationships. In L. Wheeler (Ed.), *Review of personality and social psychology* (Vol. 3, pp. 121–144). Beverly Hills, CA: Sage.

Mills, J., & Jellison, J. M. (1967). Effect on opinion change of how desirable the communication is to the audience the communicator addressed. *Journal of Personality and Social Psychology, 6,* 98–101.

Mills, J., & Harvey, J. H. (1972). Opinion change as a function of when information about the communicator is received and whether he is attractive or expert. *Journal of Personality and Social Psychology, 21,* 52–55.

Mills, J., & Kimble, C. E. (1973). Opinion change as a function of similarity to the communicator and subjectivity of the topic. *Bulletin of the Psychonomic Society, 2,* 35–36.

Mineka, S., & Hendersen, R. W. (1985). Controllability and predictability in acquired motivation. *Annual Review of Psychology, 36,* 495–529.

Mintz, N. L. (1956). Effects of esthetic surroundings: II. Prolonged and repeated experience in a "beautiful" and an "ugly" room. *Journal of Psychology, 41,* 459–466.

Mischel, W. (1981). *Introduction to personality.* New York, Holt, Rinehart & Winston.

Molloy, J. T. (1975). *Dress for success.* New York: P. H. Wyden.

Molloy, J. T. (1977). *Woman's dress for success book.* Chicago: Follett.

Monahan, J., & Walker, L. (1988). Social science research and law: A new paradigm. *American Psychologist, 43,* 465–472.

Monroe, S. M. (1983). Major and minor life events as predictors of psychological distress: Further issues and findings. *Journal of Behavioral Medicine, 6,* 189–205.

Morasch, B., Groner, N., & Keating, J. P. (1979). Type of activity and failure as mediators of perceived crowding. *Personality and Social Psychology Bulletin, 5,* 223–226.

Moreland, R. L., & Zajonc, R. B. (1979). Exposure effects may not depend on stimulus recognition. *Journal of Personality and Social Psychology, 37,* 1085–1089.

Morgan, B. S. (1976). Intimacy of disclosure topics and sex differences in self-disclosure. *Sex Roles, 2,* 161–166.

Morgan, S. W., & Mausner, B. (1973). Behavioral and fantasied indicators of avoidance of success in men and women. *Journal of Personality, 41,* 457–470.

Moriarty, T. (1974). Criminal justice and psychology. Symposium presentation at the American Psychological Association convention, New Orleans, LA.

Moriarty, T. (1975). Crime, commitment and the responsive bystander: Two field experiments. *Journal of Personality and Social Psychology, 31,* 370–376.

Morrow, P. C., & McElroy, J. C. (1981). Interior office design and visitor response: A constructive replication. *Journal of Applied Psychology, 66,* 646–650.

Morton, T. U. (1978). Intimacy and reciprocity of exchange: A comparison of spouses and strangers. *Journal of Personality and Social Psychology, 36,* 72–81.

Moscovici, S. (1976). *Social influence and social change.* New York: Academic Press.

Moscovici, S. (1980). Toward a theory of conversion behavior. In L. Berkowitz (Ed.), *Advances in experimental social psychology* (Vol. 13, pp. 209–239). New York: Academic Press.

Moscovici, S. (1985). Social influence and conformity. In G. Lindzey & E. Aronson (Eds.), *Handbook of social psychology* (3rd ed., Vol. 2, pp. 347–412). New York: Random House.

Moscovici, S., & Faucheux, C. (1972). Social influence, conforming bias, and the study of active minorities. In L. Berkowitz (Ed.), *Advances in experimental social psychology* (Vol. 6, pp. 149–202). New York: Academic Press.

Moscovici, S., Lage, S., & Naffrechoux, M. (1969). Influence on a consistent minority on the responses of a majority in a color perception task. *Sociometry, 32,* 365–380.

Moscovici, S., & Zavalloni, M. (1969). The group as a polarizer of attitudes. *Journal of Personality and Social Psychology, 12,* 125–135.

Moss, M. K., & Page, R. A. (1972). Reinforcement and helping behavior. *Journal of Applied Social Psychology, 2,* 360–371.

Mowen, J. C., & Cialdini, R. B. (1980). On implementing the door-in-the-face compliance strategy in a marketing context. *Journal of Marketing Research, 17,* 253–262.

Mowrer, O. H. (1968). Loss and recovery of community: A guide to the theory and practice of integrity therapy. In G. Gazda (Ed.), *Innovation to group psychotherapy* (pp. 130–189). Springfield, IL: Charles C. Thomas.

Moyer, K. E. (1971). *The physiology of hostility.* Chicago: Markham.

Moyer, K. E. (1982). Aggression theories. *Academic Psychology Bulletin, 4,* 415–423.

Muehlenhard, C. L., & Hollabaugh, L. C. (1988). Do women sometimes say no when they mean yes? The prevalence and correlates of women's token resistance to sex. *Journal of Personality and Social Psychology, 54,* 872–879.

Mullen, B. (1983). Operationalizing the effect of the group on individual: A self-attention perspective. *Journal of Experimental Social Psychology, 14,* 295–322.

Mullen, B. (1984). Participation in religious groups as a function of group composition: A self-attention perspective. *Journal of Applied Social Psychology, 14,* 509–518.

Mullen, B. (1985a). *Participation in classroom discussion as a function of class composition: A self-attention perspective.* Paper presented at American Educational Research Association convention, Chicago.

Mullen, B. (1985b). Strength and immediacy of sources: A meta-analytic evaluation of the forgotten elements of social impact theory. *Journal of Personality and Social Psychology, 48,* 1458–1466.

Mullen, B. (1985c). *The effect of multiple subgroups on the individual: A self-attention perspective.* Paper presented at Eastern Psychological Association convention, Boston.

Mullen, B. (1986a). Atrocity as a function of lynch mob composition: A self-attention perspective. *Personality and Social Psychology Bulletin, 12,* 187–197.

Mullen, B. (1986b). Stuttering, audience size and the Other-Total ratio: A self-attention perspective. *Journal of Applied Social Psychology, 16,* 139–149.

Mullen, B. (1986c). *The effect of seating position on participation and leadership: A self-attention perspective.* Paper presented at Eastern Psychological Association convention, New York, NY.

Mullen, B., Futrell, D., Stairs, D., Tice, D., Baumeister, R., Dawson, K., Riordan, C., Radloff, C. Goethals, G., Kennedy, J., & Rosenfeld, P. (1986). Newcasters' facial expressions and voting behavior of viewers: Can a smile elect a president? *Journal of Personality and Social Psychology, 51,* 291–295.

Murstein, B. I. (1976). *Who will marry whom: Theories and research in marital choice.* New York: Springer.

Murstein, B. I., & Christy, P. (1976). Physical attractiveness and marriage adjustment in middle-aged couples. *Journal of Personality and Social Psychology, 34,* 537–542.

Myers, D. G. (1978). Polarizing effects of social comparison. *Journal of Experimental Social Psychology, 14,* 554–563.

Myers, D. G. (1982). Polarizing effects of social interaction. In M. Brandstatter, J. H. Davis, & G. Stocker-Kreichgauer (Eds.), *Group decision making* (pp. 125–161). London: Academic Press.

Myers, D. G., Bach, P. J., & Schreiber, F. B. (1974). Normative and informational effects of group interaction. *Sociometry, 37,* 275–286.

Myers, D. G., & Bishop, G. D. (1971). The enhancement of dominant attitudes in group discussion. *Journal of Personality and Social Psychology, 20,* 386–391.

Myers, D. G., & Kaplan, M. F. (1976). Group-induced polarization in simulated juries. *Personality and Social Psychology Bulletin, 2,* 63–66.

Myerscough, R., & Taylor, S. (1985). The effects of marijuana on human physical aggression. *Journal of Personality and Social Psychology, 49,* 1541–1546.

Mynatt, C. R., Doherty, M. E., & Tweney, R. D. (1978). Consequences of confirmation and disconfirmation in a simulated research environment. *Quarterly Journal of Experimental Psychology, 30,* 395–406.

Nahemow, L. (1971). Research in a novel environment. *Environment and Behavior, 3,* 81–102.

Nahemow, L., & Lawton, M. P. (1975). Similarity and propinquity in friendship formation. *Journal of Personality and Social Psychology, 32,* 204–213.

Nasar, J. L. (1981–82). Environmental factors and commercial burglary. *Journal of Environmental Systems, 11,* 49–56.

Nasar, J. L. (1983). Adult viewers' preferences in residential scenes: A study of the relationship of environmental attributes to preference. *Environment and Behavior, 15,* 589–614.

National Academy of Sciences. (1981). *The effect on human health from long-term exposure to noise* (Report of Working Group 81). Washington, DC: National Academy Press.

Nel, E., Helmreich, R., & Aronson, E. (1969). Opinion change in the advocate as a function of the persuasibility of his audience: A clarification of the meaning of dissonance. *Journal of Personality and Social Psychology, 12,* 117–124.

Nemecek, J., & Grandjean, E. (1973). Results of an ergonometric investigation of large space offices. *Human Factors, 15,* 111–124.

Nemeth, C., Swedlund, M., & Kanki, B. (1974). Patterning of the minority's responses and their influence on the majority. *European Journal of Social Psychology, 4,* 53–64.

Nemeth, C., & Wachtler, J. (1973a). Consistency and modification of judgment. *Journal of Experimental Social Psychology, 9,* 65–79.

Nemeth, C., & Wachtler, J. (1973b). Creative problem solving as a result of majority vs. minority influence. *European Journal of Social Psychology, 3,* 45–55.

Nemeth, C., & Wachtler, J. (1974). Creating the perceptions of consistency and confidence: A necessary condition for minority influence. *Sociometry, 37,* 529–540.

Nemeth, C., Wachtler, J., & Endicott, J. (1977). Increasing the size of the minority: Some gains and some losses. *European Journal of Social Psychology, 7*(1), 15–27.

Nemeth, C. J. (1986a). Differential contributions of majority and minority influence. *Psychological Review, 93,* 23–32.

Nemeth, C. J. (1986b). Intergroup relations between majority and minority. In S. Worchel & W. G. Austin (Eds.), *Psychology of intergroup relations* (pp. 229–243). Chicago: Nelson-Hall.

Nesbitt, P. D., & Steven, G. (1974). Personal space and stimulus intensity at a Southern California amusement park. *Sociometry, 37,* 105–115.

Newcomb, T. M. (1943). *Personality and social change.* New York: Dryden Press.

Newcomb, T. M. (1961). *The acquaintance process.* New York: Holt, Rinehart & Winston.

Newcomb, T. M. (1968). Interpersonal balance. In R. P. Abelson et al. (Eds.), *Theories of cognitive consistency: A sourcebook.* Skokie, IL: Rand McNally.

Newcomb, T., Koenig, K., Flacks, R., & Warwick, D. (1967). *Persistence and change: Bennington College and its students after 25 years.* New York: Wiley.

Newman, J., & McCauley, C. (1977). Eye contact with strangers in city, suburb, and small town. *Environment and Behavior, 9,* 547–558.

Newman, O. (1972). *Defensible space.* New York: Macmillan.

Newman, O. (1980). *Community of interest.* New York: Anchor Press/ Doubleday.

Nezu, A. M., Nezu, C. M., & Blissett, S. E. (1986). Sense of humor as a moderator of the relation between stressful events and psychological distress: A prospective analysis. *Journal of Personality and Social Psychology, 54,* 520–525.

Nguyen, T., Heslin, R., & Nguyen, M. L. (1975). The meaning of touch: Sex differences. *Journal of Communication, 25,* 92–103.

Nicosia, G. J., Hyman, D., Karlin, R. A., Epstein, Y. M., & Aiello, J. R. (1979). Effects of bodily contact on reactions to crowding. *Journal of Applied Social Psychology, 9,* 508–523.

Nisbett, R. E., & Ross, L. (1980). *Human inference: Strategies and shortcomings of social judgment.* Englewood Cliffs, NJ: Prentice-Hall.

Nishida, T., & Kawanaka, K. (1972). Inter-unit group relations among wild chimpanzees of the Mahali Mountains. *Kyoto University African Studies, 7,* 131–169.

Noller, P. (1980). Marital misunderstanding: A study of couples' nonverbal communication. *Journal of Personality and Social Psychology, 39,* 1135–1148.

Noller, P. (1981). Gender and marital adjustment level differences in decoding messages from spouses and strangers. *Journal of Personality and Social Psychology, 41,* 272–278.

Noller, P. (1982). Channel consistency and inconsistency in the communications of married couples. *Journal of Personality and Social Psychology, 43,* 732–741.

Noller, P. (1985). Video primacy: A further look. *Journal of Nonverbal Behavior, 9,* 28–47.

Nowack, K. M. (1986). Type A, hardiness, and psychological distress. *Journal of Behavioral Medicine, 9,* 537–548.

O'Quin, K., & Aronoff, J. (1981). Humor as a technique of social influence. *Social Psychology Quarterly, 44,* 349–357.

Olds, J., & Milner, P. (1954). Positive reinforcement produced by electrical stimulation of septal area and other regions of the rat brain. *Journal of Comparative and Physiological Psychology, 47,* 419–427.

Opeil, D. (1976). *Similarity of disclosure and the acquaintanceship process.* Unpublished master's thesis, University of Dayton.

Orne, M. (1962). On the social psychology of the psychological experiment. *American Psychologist, 17,* 776–783.

Ortega y Gasset, J. (1933). *The modern theme.* New York: W. W. Norton.

Orvis, B. R., Cunningham, J. D., & Kelley, H. H. (1975). A closer examination of causal inference: The roles of consensus, distinctiveness, and consistency information. *Journal of Personality and Social Psychology, 32,* 605–616.

Orvis, B. R., Kelley, H. H., & Butler, D. (1976). Attributional conflict in young couples. In J. H. Harvey, W. Ickes, & R. F. Kidd (Eds.), *New directions in attribution research* (Vol. 1, pp. 353–386). Hillsdale, NJ: Erlbaum.

Osborn, A. F. (1957). *Applied imagination.* New York: Scribner.

Osgood, C. E. (1962). *An alternative to war and surrender.* Urbana, IL: University of Illinois Press.

Osgood, C. E., & Tannenbaum, P. H. (1955). The principle of congruity in the prediction of attitude change. *Psychological Review, 62,* 42–55.

Osherow, N. (1984). Making sense of the nonsensical: An analysis of Jonestown. In E. Aronson (Ed.), *Readings about the social animal* (4th ed., pp. 68–86). New York: W. H. Freeman.

Oskamp, S. (1984). *Applied social psychology.* Englewood Cliffs, NJ: Prentice-Hall.

Osmond, H. (1957). Function as the basis of psychiatric ward design. *Mental Hospital, 8,* 23–30.

Oxley, D., Haggard, L. M., Werner, C. M., & Altman, I. (1986). Transactional qualities of neighborhood social networks: A case study of "Christmas Street." *Environment and Behavior, 18,* 640–677.

Pablant, P., & Baxter, J. C. (1975, July). Environmental correlates of school vandalism. *Journal of the American Institute of Planners,* pp. 270–279.

Paffenbarger, R. S., Jr., Hyde, R. T., Wing, A. L., & Hsieh, C. (1986). Physical activity, all cause mortality, and longevity of college alumni. *New England Journal of Medicine, 314,* 605–613.

Page, M. P., & Scheidt, R. J. (1971). The elusive weapons effect: Demand awareness, evaluation apprehension, and slightly sophisticated subjects. *Journal of Personality and Social Psychology, 20,* 304–318.

Page, R. A. (1977). Noise and helping behavior. *Environment and Behavior, 9,* 311–334.

Pagel, M. D., Erdly, W. W., & Becker, J. (1987). Social networks: We get by with (and in spite of) a little help from our friends. *Journal of Personality and Social Psychology, 53,* 793–804.

Palamarek, D. L., & Rule, B. G. (1979). The effects of temperature and insult on the motivation to retaliate or escape. *Motivation and Emotion, 3,* 83–92.

Park, B., & Rothbart, M. (1982). Perception of out-group homogeneity and levels of social categorization: Memory for the subordinate attributes of in-group and out-group members. *Journal of Personality and Social Psychology, 42,* 1051–1068.

Parke, R. D., Berkowitz, L., Leyens, J. P., West, S. G., & Sebastian, J. (1977). Some effects of violent and nonviolent movies on the behavior of juvenile delinquents. In L. Berkowitz (Ed.), *Advances in experimental social psychology* (Vol. 10). New York: Academic Press.

Paterson, R. J., & Neufeld, R. W. J. (1987). Clear danger: Situational determinants of the appraisal of threat. *Psychological Bulletin, 101,* 404–416.

Patterson, G. R., Littman, R. A., & Bricker, W. (1967). Assertive behavior in children: A step toward a theory of aggression. *Monographs of the Society for Research in Child Development, 32*(5), (No. 113).

Patterson, M. L. (1973). Compensation in nonverbal immediacy behaviors: A review. *Sociometry, 36,* 237–252.

Patterson, M. L. (1975). Personal space—time to burst the bubble? *Man-Environment System, 5,* 67.

Patterson, M. L. (1976). An arousal model of interpersonal intimacy. *Psychological Review, 83,* 235–245.

Patterson, M. L. (1982). A sequential model of nonverbal exchange. *Psychological Review, 89,* 231–249.

Patterson, M. L., & Holmes, D. S. (1966). Social interaction correlates of the MMPI extraversion-introversion scale. *American Psychologist, 21,* 724–725.

Patterson, M. L., Jordan, A., Hogan, M. B., & Frerker, D. (1981). Effects of nonverbal intimacy on arousal and behavioral adjustment. *Journal of Nonverbal Behavior, 5,* 184–198.

Patterson, M. L., Kelly, C. E., & Romano, J. (1971). Compensatory reactions to spatial intrusion. *Sociometry, 34,* 114–121.

Patterson, T. E. (1980). *The mass media: How Americans choose their president.* New York: Praeger.

Pattison, J. E. (1973). Effects of touch on self-exploration and the therapeutic relationship. *Journal of Consulting and Clinical Psychology, 40,* 170–175.

Paulus, P. B., Annis, A. B., Seta, J. J., Schkode, J. K., & Matthews, R. W. (1976). Crowding does affect task performance. *Journal of Personality and Social Psychology, 34,* 248–253.

Paulus, P. B., Cox, V. C., & McCain, G. (1988). *Prison crowding: A psychological perspective.* New York: Springer-Verlag.

Paulus, P. B., & Matthews, R. W. (1980). When density affects task performance. *Personality and Social Psychology Bulletin, 6,* 119–124.

Pearlin, L. I., Lieberman, M. A., Meneghan, E. G., & Mullen, J. T. (1981). The stress process. *Journal of Health and Social Behavior, 22,* 337–356.

Pedersen, D. M. (1982). Personality correlates of privacy. *Journal of Psychology, 112,* 11–14.

Peele, S., & Brodsky, A. (1974, August). Interpersonal heroin: Love can be an addiction. *Psychology Today,* pp. 22–26.

Pellegrini, R. J., & Empey, J. (1970). Interpersonal spatial orientation in dyads. *Journal of Psychology, 76,* 67–70.

Pempus, E., Sawaya, C., & Cooper, R. E. (1975). *"Don't fence me in": Personal space depends on architectural enclosure.* Paper presented at the Annual Meeting of the American Psychological Association, Chicago.

Pennebaker, J. W. (1989). Confession, inhibition, and disease. In L. Berkowitz (Ed.), *Advances in experimental social psychology* (Vol. 22, pp. 211–244). New York: Academic Press.

Pennebaker, J. W., & O'Heeron, R. C. (1984). Confiding in others and illness rate among spouses of suicide and accidental death victims. *Journal of Abnormal Psychology, 93,* 473–476.

Pennebaker, J. W., Dyer, M. A., Caulkins, R. S., Litowitz, D. L., Ackreman, P. L., Anderson, D. B., & McGraw, K. M. (1979). Don't the girls get prettier at closing time: A country and western application to psychology. *Personality and Social Psychology Bulletin, 5,* 122–125.

Pennebaker, J. W., Hughes, C. F., & O'Heeron, R. C. (1987). The psychophysiology of confession: Linking inhibitory and psychosomatic processes. *Journal of Personality and Social Psychology, 52,* 781–793.

Pennington, N., & Hastie, R. (1981). Juror decision-making models: The generalization gap. *Psychological Bulletin, 89,* 246–287.

Peplau, L. A. (1983). Roles and gender. In H. H. Kelley et al. (Eds.), *Close relationships* (pp. 220–264). New York: W. H. Freeman.

Peplau, L. A., & Perlman, D. (1979). Blueprint for a social psychological theory of loneliness. In M. Cook & G. Wilson (Eds.), *Love and attraction.* Oxford, England: Pergamon.

Peplau, L. A., & Perlman, D. (Eds.) (1982). *Loneliness: A sourcebook of current theory, research, and therapy.* New York: Wiley.

Perry, R. W., & Lindell, M. K. (1978). The psychological consequences of natural disaster: A review of research on American communities. *Mass Emergencies, 3,* 105–115.

Peterson, C., & Seligman, M. E. P. (1984). Causal explanations as a risk factor in depression: Theory and evidence. *Psychological Review, 91,* 347–374.

Peterson, C., Seligman, M. E. P., & Vaillant, G. E. (1988). Pessimistic explanatory style is a risk factor for physical illness: A thirty-five-year longitudinal study. *Journal of Personality and Social Psychology, 55,* 23–27.

Peterson, D. R. (1979). Assessing interpersonal relationships by means of interaction records. *Behavioral Assessment, 1,* 221–236.

Pettigrew, T. F. (1961). Social psychology and desegregation research. *American Psychologist, 16,* 105–112.

Pettigrew, T. F. (1971). *Racially separate or together?* New York: McGraw-Hill.

Pettigrew, T. F. (1986). The intergroup contact hypothesis reconsidered. In M. Hewstone & R. Brown (Eds.), *Contact and conflict in intergroup encounters* (pp. 169–195). New York: Basil Blackwell.

Petty, R. E., & Cacioppo, J. T. (1979a). Effects of forewarning of persuasive intent and involvement on cognitive responses in persuasion. *Personality and Social Psychology Bulletin, 5,* 173–176.

Petty, R. E., & Cacioppo, J. T. (1979b). Issue involvement can increase or decrease persuasion by enhancing message-relevant cognitive responses. *Journal of Personality and Social Psychology, 37,* 1915–1926.

Petty, R. E., & Cacioppo, J. T. (1981). *Attitudes and persuasion: Classic and contemporary approaches.* Dubuque, IA: William C. Brown.

Petty, R. E., & Cacioppo, J. T. (1986). The elaboration likelihood model of persuasion. In L. Berkowitz (Ed.), *Advances in experimental social psychology* (Vol. 19, pp. 123–205). New York: Academic Press.

Petty, R. E., Cacioppo, J. T., & Goldman, R. (1981). Personal involvement as a determinant of argument-based persuasion. *Journal of Personality and Social Psychology, 41,* 847–855.

Petty, R. E., Harkins, S. G., & Williams, K. D. (1980). The effects of group diffusion of cognitive effort on attitudes: An information processing view. *Journal of Personality and Social Psychology, 38,* 81–92.

Phillips, D. P. (1982). The impact of fictional television stories on U.S. adult fatalities: New evidence on the effect of mass media on violence. *American Journal of Sociology, 87,* 1340–1359.

Phillips, D. P. (1983). The impact of mass media violence on U.S. homicides. *American Sociological Review, 48,* 560–568.

Piaget, J. (1952). *The origins of intelligence in children.* New York: International Universities Press.

Piliavin, I. M., Rodin, J., & Piliavin, J. A. (1969). Good Samaritanism: An underground phenomenon? *Journal of Personality and Social Psychology, 13,* 289–299.

Piliavin, J. A., Callero, P. L., & Evans, D. E. (1982). Addiction to altruism? Opponent-process theory and habitual blood donation. *Journal of Personality and Social Psychology, 43,* 1200–1213.

Piliavin, J. A., Dovidio, J. F., Gaertner, S. L., & Clark, R. D., III. (1981). *Emergency intervention.* New York: Academic Press.

Piliavin, J. A., & Piliavin, I. M. (1972). Effect of blood on reactions to a victim. *Journal of Personality and Social Psychology, 23,* 353–362.

Piliavin, J. A., Piliavin, I. M., & Broll, L. (1976). Time of arrival at an emergency and likelihood of helping. *Personality and Social Psychology Bulletin, 2,* 273–276.

Pines, A., & Aronson, E. (1982). *Burnout: From tedium to personal growth.* New York: Free Press.

Pisano, R., & Taylor, S. P. (1971). Reduction of physical aggression: The effects of four strategies. *Journal of Personality and Social Psychology, 19,* 237–242.

Platt, J. (1973). Social traps. *American Psychologist, 28,* 641–651.

Polit, D., & LaFrance, M. (1977). Sex differences in reaction to spatial invasions. *Journal of Social Psychology, 100,* 59–60.

Pope, B., Siegman, A. W., & Blass, T. (1970). Anxiety and speech in the initial interview. *Journal of Consulting and Clinical Psychology, 35,* 233–238.

Porteous, J. D. (1985). Smellscape. *Progress in Human Geography, 9,* 358–378.

Powell, M. C., & Fazio, R. H. (1984). Attitude accessibility as a function of repeated attitudinal expression. *Personality and Social Psychology Bulletin, 10,* 139–148.

Prentice-Dunn, S., & Rogers, R. W. (1983). Deindividuation in aggression. In R. G. Geen & E. I. Donnerstein (Eds.), *Aggression: Theoretical and empirical reviews* (Vol. 2, pp. 155–172). New York: Academic Press.

Proshansky, H. M. (1978). The city and self-identity. *Environment and Behavior, 10,* 147–169.

Proshansky, H. M., & Altman, I. (1979). Overview of the field. In W. P. White (Ed.), *Resources in environment and behavior* (pp. 3–36). Washington, DC: American Psychological Association.

Proshansky, H. M., Fabian, A. K., & Kaminoff, R. (1983). Place-identity: Physical world socialization of the self. *Journal of Environmental Psychology, 3,* 57–83.

Pyszczynski, T., Holt, K., & Greenberg, J. (1987). Depression, self-focused attention, and expectancies for positive and negative future life events for self and others. *Journal of Personality and Social Psychology, 52,* 994–1001.

Quattrone, G. A., & Jones, E. E. (1980). The perception of variability within in-groups and out-groups: Implications for the law of small numbers. *Journal of Personality and Social Psychology, 38,* 141–150.

Rabbie, J. M., Brehm, J. W., & Cohen, A. R. (1959). Verbalization and reactions to cognitive dissonance. *Journal of Personality, 27,* 407–417.

Radloff, R., & Helmreich, R. L. (1968). *Groups under stress: Psychological research in sealab II.* New York: Appleton-Century-Crofts.

Rands, M., Levinger, G., & Mellinger, G. (1981). Patterns of conflict resolution and marital satisfaction. *Journal of Family Issues, 2,* 297–321.

Raush, H. L., Barry, W. A., Hertel, R. K., & Swain, M. A. (1974). *Communication, conflict and marriage.* San Francisco: Jossey-Bass.

Read, P. B. (1974). Source of authority and the legitimation of leadership in small groups. *Sociometry, 37,* 189–204.

Reedy, G. E. (1970). *The twilight of the presidency.* New York: World.

Regan, D. T. (1971). Effects of a favor and liking on compliance. *Journal of Experimental Social Psychology, 1,* 627–639.

Regan, D. T., & Fazio, R. H. (1977). On the consistency between attitudes and behavior: Look to the method of attitude formation. *Journal of Experimental Social Psychology, 13,* 28–45.

Reich, J. W., & Robertson, J. L. (1979). Reactance and normal appeal in antilittering messages. *Journal of Applied Social Psychology, 9,* 91–101.

Reingen, P. H. (1978). On inducing compliance with requests. *Journal of Consumer Research, 5,* 96–102.

Reiss, M., Rosenfeld, P., Melburg, V., & Tedeschi, J. T. (1981). Self-serving attributions: Biased private perceptions and distorted public descriptions. *Journal of Personality and Social Psychology, 41,* 224–231.

Report of the Presidential Commission on the space shuttle Challenger accident (1986, June 6). (W. Rogers, Chair). Washington, DC: U.S. Government Printing Office.

Reynolds, V., & Reynolds, F. (1965). Chimpanzees of the Budongo Forests. In I. Devore (Ed.), *Primate behavior.* New York: Holt, Rinehart & Winston.

Rice, M. E., & Grusec, J. E. (1975). Saying and doing: Effects on observer performance. *Journal of Personality and Social Psychology, 32,* 584–593.

Riley, D., & Eckenrode, J. (1986). Social ties: Subgroup differences in costs and benefits. *Journal of Personality and Social Psychology, 51,* 770–778.

Riley, R. T., & Pettigrew, T. F. (1976). Dramatic events and attitude change. *Journal of Personality and Social Psychology, 34,* 1004–1015.

Rimland, B. (1964). *Infantile autism: The syndrome and its implications for a neural theory of behavior.* New York: Appleton-Century-Crofts.

Rizzo, J., House, R., & Lirtzman, S. (1970). Role conflict and ambiguity in complex organizations. *Administrative Science Quarterly, 15,* 150–163.

Roberts, W. R., Penk, W. E., Gearing, M. L., Rabinowitz, R., Dolan, M. P., & Patterson, E. T. (1982). Interpersonal problems of Vietnam combat veterans with symptoms of posttraumatic stress disorder. *Journal of Abnormal Psychology, 91,* 444–450.

Robinson, S. N., & Frisch, M. H. (1975, April). *Social and Environmental Influences on Littering Behavior.* Paper presented at annual meeting of the Eastern Psychological Association, New York.

Robles, R., Smith, R., Carver, C. S., & Wellens, A. R. (1987). Influence of subliminal visual images on the experience of anxiety. *Personality and Social Psychology Bulletin, 13,* 399–410.

Rodin, J., Solomon, S. K., & Metcalf, J. (1978). Role of control in mediating perceptions of density. *Journal of Personality and Social Psychology, 36,* 988–999.

Rogers, C. (1959). Therapy, personality, and interpersonal relationships. In S. Koch (Ed.), *Psychology: A study of a science* (Vol. 3). New York: McGraw-Hill.

Rogers, R. W. (1975). A protection motivation theory of fear appeals and attitude change. *Journal of Psychology, 91,* 93–114.

Rogers, R. W., & Mewborn, R. (1976). Fear appeals and attitude change: Effects of a threat's noxiousness, probability of occurrence, and the efficacy of coping responses. *Journal of Personality and Social Psychology, 34,* 54–61.

Rokeach, M. (Ed.) (1960). *The open and closed mind.* New York: Basic Books.

Rokeach, M. (1968). *Beliefs, attitudes and values.* San Francisco Jossey-Bass.

Rokeach, M., & Mezei, L. (1966). Race and shared belief as factors in social choice. *Science, 151,* 167–172.

Rollins, B. C., & Cannon, K. (1974). Marital satisfaction over the family life cycle: A reevaluation. *Journal of Marriage and the Family, 36,* 271–282.

Rollins, B. C., & Galligan, R. (1978). The developing child and marital satisfaction of parents. In R. M. Lerner & G. B. Spanier (Eds.), *Child influences on marital and family interaction.* New York: Academic Press.

Rook, K. S. (1987). Social support versus companionship: Effects on life stress, loneliness, and evaluations by others. *Journal of Personality and Social Psychology, 52,* 1132–1147.

Roper, R. T. (1980). Jury size and verdict consistency: A line has to be drawn somewhere. *Law and Society Review, 14,* 977–995.

Roper, R. T., & Flango, V. E. (1983). Trials before judges and juries. *The Justice System Journal, 8,* 186–198.

Rose, R. M., Holaday, J. W., & Bernstein, I. S. (1971). Plasma testosterone, dominance rank and aggressive behaviour in male rhesus monkeys. *Nature, 231,* 366–368.

Rosen, S., Bergman, M., Plestor, D., El-Mofty, A., & Satti, M. (1962). Presbycosis study of a relatively noise-free population in the Sudan. *Annals of Otology, Rhinology, and Laryngology, 71,* 727–743.

Rosenberg, M. (1965). *Society and the adolescent self-image.* Princeton, NJ: Princeton University Press.

Rosenberg, S., Nelson, C., & Vivekananthan, P. S. (1968). A multidimensional approach to the structure of personality impressions. *Journal of Personality and Social Psychology, 9,* 283–294.

Rosenfeld, H. M. (1966). Approval-seeking and approval-inducing functions of verbal and nonverbal responses in the dyad. *Journal of Personality and Social Psychology, 4,* 597–605.

Rosenfeld, H. M. (1967). Nonverbal reciprocation of approval: An experimental analysis. *Journal of Experimental Social Psychology, 3,* 102–111.

Rosenfeld, H. M. (1978). Conversational control functions of nonverbal behavior. In A. W. Siegman & S. Feldstein (Eds.), *Nonverbal behavior and communication* (pp. 291–328). Hillsdale, NJ: Erlbaum.

Rosenfeld, H. M., Breck, B. E., Smith, S. M. H., & Kehoe, S. (1984). Intimacy-mediators of the proximity-gaze compensation effect: Movement, conversational role, acquaintance, and gender. *Journal of Nonverbal Behavior, 8,* 235–249.

Rosenfeld, H. M., & Hancks, M. (1980). The nonverbal context of verbal listener responses. In M. R. Key (Ed.), *The relationship of verbal and nonverbal communication.* The Hague: Mouton.

Rosenhan, D. L. (1973). On being sane in insane places. *Science, 179,* 250–258.

Rosenthal, R. (1973). The mediation of Pygmalion effects: A four-factor "theory." *Papua New Guinea Journal of Education, 9,* 1–12.

Rosenthal, R. (1974). *On the social psychology of the self-fulfilling prophecy: Further evidence for Pygmalion effects and mediating mechanisms* (Module 53, pp. 1–28). New York: MSS Modular Publications.

Rosenthal, R., & DePaulo, B. M. (1979). Sex differences in eavesdropping on nonverbal cues. *Journal of Personality and Social Psychology, 37,* 273–285.

Rosenthal, R., & Jacobson, L. (1968). *Pygmalion in the classroom.* New York: Holt, Rinehart & Winston.

Rosenthal, R., & Rubin, D. B. (1978). Interpersonal expectancy effects: The first 345 studies. *Behavioral and Brain Sciences, 2,* 377–415.

Ross, L. (1977). The intuitive psychologist and his shortcomings: Distortions in the attribution process. In L. Berkowitz (Ed.), *Advances in experimental social psychology* (Vol. 10, pp. 172–220). New York: Academic Press.

Ross, L., Amabile, T. M., & Steinmetz, J. L. (1977). Social roles, social control, and biases in social-perception processes. *Journal of Personality and Social Psychology, 35,* 485–494.

Ross, L., Greene, D., & House, P. (1977). The "false consensus effect": An egocentric bias in social perception and attributional processes. *Journal of Experimental Social Psychology, 13,* 279–301.

Ross, L., Lepper, M. R., & Hubbard, M. (1975). Perseverance in self-perception and social perception: Biased attribution processes in the debriefing paradigm. *Journal of Personality and Social Psychology, 32,* 880–892.

Ross, L., Lepper, M. R., Strack, F., & Steinmetz, J. (1977). Social explanation and social expectation: Effects of real and hypothetical explanations on subjective likelihood. *Journal of Personality and Social Psychology, 35,* 817–829.

Ross, M., & Conway, M. (1986). Remembering one's own past: The construction of personal histories. In R. M. Sorrentino & E. T. Higgins (Eds.), *Handbook of motivation and cognition* (pp. 122–144). New York: Guilford Press.

Ross, M., McFarland, C., & Fletcher, G. J. O. (1981). The effect of attitude on the recall of personal histories. *Journal of Personality and Social Psychology, 40,* 627–634.

Ross, M., & Sicoly, F. (1979). Egocentric biases in availability and attribution. *Journal of Personality and Social Psychology, 37,* 322–337.

Rothbart, M., Evans, M., & Fulero, S. (1979). Recall for confirming events: Memory processes and the maintenance of social stereotyping. *Journal of Experimental Social Psychology, 15,* 343–355.

Rothbart, M. K. (1971). Birth order and mother-child interaction in an achievement situation. *Journal of Personality and Social Psychology, 17,* 113–120.

Rotton, J. (1983). Affective and cognitive consequences of malodorous pollution. *Basic and Applied Social Psychology, 4,* 171–191.

Rotton, J. (1985, August). *Pedestrian movement in warm and cool settings: Three quasi-experiments.* Paper presented at the Annual Convention of the American Psychological Association, Los Angeles, CA.

Rotton, J. (1987a). Hemmed in and hating it: Effects of shape of room on tolerance for crowding. *Perceptual and Motor Skills, 64,* 285–286.

Rotton, J. (1987b). Indirect measures of annoyance: What price pollution? In H. S. Koelega (Ed.), *Environmental annoyance: Characterization, measurement, and control* (pp. 153–162). New York: Elsevier.

Rotton, J., Barry, T., Frey, J., & Soler, E. (1978). Air pollution and interpersonal attraction. *Journal of Applied Social Psychology, 8,* 57–71.

Rotton, J., Barry, T., & Kimble, C. E. (1985, August). *Climate and crime: Coping with multicollinearity.* Paper presented at the Annual Convention of the American Psychological Association, Los Angeles, CA.

Rotton, J., Blake, B. F., & Heslin, R. (1983). Good news is no news: Some determinants of pre-attributional information search. *Representative Research in Social Psychology, 13,* 171–191.

Rotton, J., & Frey, J. (1984). Psychological costs of air pollution: Atmospheric conditions, seasonal trends, and psychiatric emergencies. *Population and Environment, 7,* 3–16.

Rotton, J., & Frey, J. (1985). Air pollution, weather, and violent crimes: Concomitant time-series analysis of archival data. *Journal of Personality and Social Psychology, 49,* 1207–1220.

Rotton, J., Frey, J., Barry, T., Milligan, M., & Fitzpatrick, M. (1979). The air pollution experience and interpersonal aggression. *Journal of Applied Social Psychology, 9,* 397–412.

Rotton, J., & Kimble, C. E. (1989). Climate, culture, and criminal behavior: Toward a causal model. *Proceedings of the 9th Annual Conference on Biometerology and Aerobiology, 9,* 316–319.

Rotton, J., Olszewski, D. A., Charleton, M. E., & Soler, E. (1978). Loud speech, conglomerate noise, and behavioral aftereffects. *Journal of Applied Psychology, 63,* 360–365.

Rotton, J., Tikofsky, R. S., & Feldman, H. M. (1982). Behavioral effects of chemicals in drinking water. *Journal of Applied Psychology, 69,* 397–412.

Ruback, R. B., Dabbs, J. M., & Hopper, C. H. (1984). The process of brainstorming: An analysis with individual and group vocal parameters. *Journal of Personality and Social Psychology, 47,* 558–567.

Rubin, Z. (1970). Measurement of romantic love. *Journal of Personality and Social Psychology, 16,* 265–273.

Rubin, Z. (1973). *Liking and loving: An invitation to social psychology.* New York: Holt, Rinehart & Winston.

Rubin, Z. (1975). Disclosing oneself to a stranger: Reciprocity and its limits. *Journal of Experimental Social Psychology, 11,* 233–260.

Rubin, Z., & Mitchell, C. (1976). Couples research as couples counseling: Some unintended effects of studying close relationships. *American Psychologist, 31,* 17–25.

Rubin, Z., & Schenker, S. (1977). Friendship, proximity, and self-disclosure. *Journal of Personality, 46,* 1–22.

Rubovits, P., & Maehr, M. (1973). Pygmalion black and white. *Journal of Personality and Social Psychology, 25,* 210–218.

Rusbult, C. E. (1983). A longitudinal test of the investment model: The development (and deterioration) of satisfaction and commitment in heterosexual involvements. *Journal of Personality and Social Psychology, 45,* 101–117.

Rusbult, C. E., Zembrodt, I. M., & Gunn, L. K. (1982). Exit, voice, loyalty, and neglect: Responses to dissatisfaction in romantic involvements. *Journal of Personality and Social Psychology, 43,* 1230–1242.

Rushton, J. P. (1975). Generosity in children: Immediate and long-term effects of modeling, preaching and moral judgment. *Journal of Personality and Social Psychology, 31,* 459–466.

Rushton, J. P. (1979). Effects of prosocial television and film material on behavior of viewers. In L. Berkowitz (Ed.), *Advances in experimental social psychology* (Vol. 12). New York: Academic Press.

Rushton, J. P. (1980). *Altruism, socialization, and society.* Englewood Cliffs, NJ: Prentice-Hall.

Rushton, J. P. (in press). Genetic similarity, human altruism, and group selection. *Behavioral and Brain Sciences.*

Rushton, J. P., & Teachman, G. (1978). The effects of positive reinforcement, attributions, and punishment on model-induced altruism in children. *Personality and Social Psychology Bulletin, 4,* 322–325.

Russell, D. W., Altmaier, E., & Van Velzen, D. (1987). Job-related stress, social support, and burnout among college classroom teachers. *Journal of Applied Psychology, 72,* 269–274.

Russell, D., & Kimble, C. E. (1979). *Male aggression as a function of sexual arousal, shared experience, and sex of target.* Paper presented at the Midwestern Psychological Association convention, Chicago, IL.

Russell, D., Peplau, L. A., & Cutrona, C. E. (1980). The revised UCLA Loneliness Scale: Concurrent and discriminant validity evidence. *Journal of Personality and Social Psychology, 39,* 472–480.

Russell, J. A. (1979). Affective space is bipolar. *Journal of Personality and Social Psychology, 37,* 345–356.

Russell, J. A., & Mehrabian, A. (1978). Approach-avoidance and affiliation as functions of the emotion-eliciting qualities of an environment. *Environment and Behavior, 10,* 355–387.

Russell, J. A., & Snodgrass, J. (1987). Emotion and the environment. In D. Stokols & I. Altman (Eds.), *Handbook of environmental psychology* (Vol. 1, pp. 245–280). New York: Wiley.

Russell, J. A., Ward, L. M., & Pratt, G. (1981). Affective quality attributed to environments: A factor analytic study. *Environment and Behavior, 13,* 259–288.

Russo, N. F. (1975). Eye contact, interpersonal distance, and the equilibrium theory. *Journal of Personality and Social Psychology, 31,* 497–502.

Ryan, E. D. (1970). The cathartic effect of vigorous motor activity on aggressive behavior. *Research Quarterly, 41,* 542–551.

St John, N. H. (1975). *School desegregation: Outcomes for children.* New York: Wiley.

Samerotte, G. C., & Harris, M. B. (1976). Some factors influencing helping: The effects of a handicap, responsibility, and requesting help. *Journal of Social Psychology, 98,* 39–45.

Samuelson, D. J., & Lindauer, M. S. (1976). Perception, evaluation, and performance in a neat and messy room by high and low sensation seekers. *Environment and Behavior, 8,* 291–306.

Sanders, G. S., & Baron, R. S. (1975). The motivating effects of distraction on task performance. *Journal of Personality and Social Psychology, 32,* 956–963.

Sanders, G. S., & Baron, R. S. (1977). Is social comparison irrelevant for producing choice shifts? *Journal of Experimental Social Psychology, 13,* 303–314.

Santee, R., & Maslach, C. (1982). To agree and not to agree: Personal dissent amid pressure to conform. *Journal of Personality and Social Psychology, 42,* 690–700.

Santee, R. T. (1976). The effect on attraction of attitude similarity as information about interpersonal reinforcement contingencies. *Sociometry, 39,* 153–156.

Sarason, B. R., Shearin, E. N., Pierce, G. R., & Sarason, I. G. (1987). Interrelations of social support measures: Theoretical and practical implications. *Journal of Personality and Social Psychology, 52,* 813–832.

Sarason, I. G. (1984). Stress, anxiety, and cognitive interference: Reactions to tests. *Journal of Personality and Social Psychology, 46,* 929–938.

Sarason, I. G., Johnson, J. H., & Siegel, J. M. (1978). Assessing the impact of life changes: Development of the life experiences survey. *Journal of Clinical and Consulting Psychology, 46,* 932–946.

Sauser, W. I., Jr., Arauz, C. G., & Chambers, R. M. (1978). Exploring the relationship between level of office noise and salary recommendations: A preliminary research note. *Journal of Management, 4,* 57–63.

Savinar, J. (1975). The effect of ceiling height on personal space. *Man-Environment System, 5,* 321–324.

Schachter, S. (1951). Deviation, rejection, and communication. *Journal of Abnormal and Social Psychology, 46,* 190–207.

Schachter, S. (1959). *The psychology of affiliation.* Stanford, CA: Stanford University Press.

Schachter, S., & Singer, J. (1962). Cognitive, social, and physiological determinants of the emotional state. *Psychological Review, 69,* 379–399.

Schaeffer, M. H., Baum, A., Paulus, P. B., & Gaes, G. G. (1988). Architecturally mediated effects of social density in prisons. *Environment and Behavior, 20,* 3–19.

Schaeffer, M. H., Street, S. W., Singer, J. E., & Baum, A. (1988). Effects of control on the stress reactions of commuters. *Journal of Applied Social Psychology, 11,* 944–957.

Schaffner, P. E. (1985). Specious learning about reward and punishment. *Journal of Personality and Social Psychology, 48,* 1377–1386.

Schank, R. C., & Abelson, R. P. (1977). *Scripts, plans, goals, and understanding.* Hillsdale, NJ: Erlbaum.

Scheflen, A. E. (1965). Quasi-courtship behavior in psychotherapy. *Psychiatry, 28,* 245–257.

Scheier, M. (1976). Self-awareness, self-consciousness, and angry aggression. *Journal of Personality, 44,* 627–644.

Scheier, M. F., & Carver, C. S. (1977). Self-focused attention and the experience of emotion: Attraction, repulsion, elation, and depression. *Journal of Personality and Social Psychology, 35,* 625–636.

Scheier, M. F., & Carver, C. S. (1985). Optimism, coping, and health: Assessment and implications of generalized outcome expectancies. *Health Psychology, 4,* 219–247.

Scheier, M. F., Weintraub, J. K., & Carver, C. S. (1986). Coping with stress: Divergent strategies of optimists and pessimists. *Journal of Personality and Social Psychology, 51,* 1257–1264.

Schein, E. H. (1956). The Chinese indoctrination program for prisoners of war: A study of attempted brainwashing. *Psychiatry, 19,* 149–172.

Scherer, K. R. (1972). Judging personality from voice: A cross-cultural approach to an old issue in interpersonal perception. *Journal of Personality, 40,* 191–210.

Schiffenbauer, A., & Schiavo, R. S. (1976). Physical distance and attraction: An intensification effect. *Journal of Experimental Social Psychology, 12,* 274–282.

Schlenker, B. R. (1980). *Impression management: The self-concept, social identity, and interpersonal relations.* Monterey, CA: Brooks/Cole.

Schlenker, B. R. (1982). Translating actions into attitudes: An identity-analytic approach to the explanation of social conduct. In L. Berkowitz (Ed.), *Advances in experimental social psychology.* New York: Academic Press.

Schlenker, B. R. (Ed.) (1985). *The self and social life.* New York: McGraw-Hill.

Schlenker, B., Forsyth, D., Leary, M., & Miller, R. (1980). A self-presentational analysis of the effects of incentives and attitude change following counterattitudinal behavior. *Journal of Personality and Social Psychology, 39,* 553–577.

Schneider, D. J. (1973). Implicit personality theory: A review. *Psychological Bulletin, 79,* 294–319.

Schofield, J. W. (1979). The impact of positively structured contact on intergroup behavior: Does it last under adverse conditions? *Social Psychology Quarterly, 42,* 280–284.

Schofield, J. W. (1986). Black-white contact in desegregated schools. In M. Hewstone & R. Brown (Eds.), *Contact and conflict in intergroup encounters* (pp. 79–92). New York: Basil Blackwell.

Schofield, J. W., & Sagar, H. A. (1977). Peer interaction patterns in an integrated middle school. *Sociometry, 40,* 130–138.

Schopler, J. (1967). An investigation of sex differences on the influence of dependence. *Sociometry, 30,* 50–63.

Schopler, J., & Thompson, V. D. (1968). Role of attribution processes in mediating amount of reciprocity for a favor. *Journal of Personality and Social Psychology, 10,* 243–250.

Schopler, J., & Walton, M. (1974). *The effects of expected structure, expected enjoyment and participants' internality-externality upon feelings of being crowded.* Unpublished manuscript, University of North Carolina, Chapel Hill, NC.

Schroeder, D. H., & Costa, P. T., Jr. (1984). Influence of life event stress on physical illness: Substantive effect or methodological flaws? *Journal of Personality and Social Psychology, 46,* 853–863.

Schroeder, H. W., & Daniel, T. C. (1980). Predicting the scenic quality of forest road corridors. *Environment and Behavior, 12,* 349–366.

Schulman, J., Shaver, P., Colman, R., Emrick, B., & Christie, R. (1973, June). Recipe for a jury. *Psychology Today,* pp. 37–44, 77–84.

Schuman, H., & Johnson, M. P. (1976). Attitudes and behavior. *Annual Review of Sociology, 2,* 161–207.

Schwab, M. R., & Lundgren, D. C. (1978). Birth order, perceived appraisals by significant others, and self-esteem. *Psychological Reports, 43,* 443–454.

Schwartz, B., & Barsky, S. (1977). The home advantage. *Social Forces, 55,* 641–661.

Schwartz, S. H., & Ben David, T. (1976). Responsibility and helping in an emergency. *Sociometry, 39,* 406–415.

Schwartz, S. H., & Clausen, G. T. (1970). Responsibility, norms, and helping in an emergency. *Journal of Personality and Social Psychology, 16,* 299–310.

Schwartz, S. H., & Gottlieb, A. (1976). Bystander reactions to a violent theft: Crime in Jerusalem. *Journal of Personality and Social Psychology, 34,* 1188–1199.

Schwartz, S. H., & Howard, J. A. (1981). A normative decision-making model of altruism. In J. P. Rushton & R. M. Sorrentino (Eds.), *Altruism and helping behavior: Social, personality and developmental perspectives.* Hillsdale, NJ: Erlbaum.

Scott, J. A. (1984). Comfort and seating distance in living rooms: The relationship of interactants and topic of conversation. *Environment and Behavior, 16,* 33–54.

Searle, J. R. (1975). Indirect speech acts. In P. Cole & J. L. Morgan (Eds.), *Syntax and semantics 3: Speech acts* (pp. 59–82). New York: Academic Press.

Sears, R. R., Maccoby, E. E., & Levin, H. (1957). *Patterns of child rearing.* New York: Harper & Row.

Seavey, C. A., Katz, P. A., & Zalk, S. R. (1975). Baby X: The effect of gender labels on adult responses to infants. *Sex Roles, 1,* 61–73.

Sebba, R., & Churchman, A. (1983). Territories and territoriality in the home. *Environment and Behavior, 15,* 191–210.

Secord, P. F., & Backman, C. W. (1964). *Social psychology.* New York: McGraw-Hill.

Seidel, S., & Kimble, C. E. (1989). *Manifestations of confidence in paralanguage.* Unpublished manuscript, University of Dayton.

Seligman, C. (1986). Energy consumption, attitudes, and behavior. In M. J. Saks & L. Saxe (Eds.), *Advances in applied social psychology* (Vol. 3, pp. 153–180). Hillsdale, NJ: Erlbaum.

Seligman, M. E. P. (1975). *Helplessness: On depression, development, and death.* San Francisco: Freeman, Cooper.

Selye, H. (1956). *The stress of life.* New York: McGraw-Hill.

Selye, H. (1973). The evolution of the stress concept. *American Scientist, 61,* 692–699.

Selye, H. (1981). The stress concept today. In L. M. Kutash & L. B. Schlesinger (Eds.), *Handbook of stress and anxiety* (pp. 127–143). Washington, DC: Jossey-Bass.

Seta, J. J., & Hassan, R. K. (1980). Awareness of prior success of failure: A critical factor in task performance. *Journal of Personality and Social Psychology, 39,* 70–76.

Shaffer, D. R., & Sadowsky, C. (1975). This table is mine: Respect for marked barroom tables as a function of gender and the desirability of locale. *Sociometry, 38,* 408–419.

Shaklee, H., & Fischhoff, B. (1982). Strategies of information search in causal analysis. *Memory and Cognition, 10,* 520–530.

Shanteau, J., & Nagy, G. F. (1979). Probability of acceptance in dating choice. *Journal of Personality and Social Psychology, 37,* 522–533.

Shavitt, S., & Brock, T. C. (1986). *Attitude functions affect persuasiveness of appeals.* Paper presented at the Midwestern Psychological Association convention, Chicago.

Shaw, G. (1972). *Meat on the hoof.* New York: Dell.

Shaw, M. E. (1981). *Group dynamics: The psychology of small group behavior* (3rd ed.). New York: McGraw-Hill.

Sherif, M. (1935). *A study of some social factors in perception.* Archives of Psychology, No. 187.

Sherif, M., Harvey, O. J., White, B. J., Hood, W. E., & Sherif, C. W. (1961). *Intergroup conflict and cooperation: The Robber's Cave experiment.* Norman, OK: Institute of Group Relations.

Sherif, M., & Hovland, C. I. (1961). *Social judgment.* New Haven, CT: Yale University Press.

Sherif, M., & Sherif, C. W. (1967). Attitude as the individual's own categories: The social judgement-involvement approach to attitude change. In C. W. Sherif & M. Sherif (Eds.), *Attitude, ego-involvement and change.* New York: Wiley.

Sherman, L. W., & Berk, R. A. (1984). Deterrent effects of arrest for domestic violence. *American Sociological Review, 49,* 261–272.

Sherman, S. J. (1980). On the self-erasing nature of errors of prediction. *Journal of Personality and Social Psychology, 39,* 211–221.

Sherman, S. J., Chassin, L, Presson, C. C., & Agostinelli, G. (1984). The role of the evaluation and similarity principles in the false consensus effect. *Journal of Personality and Social Psychology, 47,* 1244–1262.

Sherman, S. J., & Corty, E. (1984). Cognitive heuristics. In R. S. Wyer & T. K. Srull (Eds.), *Handbook of social cognition* (Vol. 1, pp. 189–286). Hillsdale, NJ: Erlbaum.

Sherman, S. J., Presson, C. C., Chassin, L., Corty, E., & Olshavsky, R. (1983). The false consensus effect in estimates of smoking prevalence: Underlying mechanisms. *Personality and Social Psychology Bulletin, 9,* 197–207.

Sherman, S. J., Skov, R. B., Hervitz, E. F., & Stock, C. B. (1981). The effects of explaining hypothetical future events: From possibility to probability to actuality and beyond. *Journal of Experimental Social Psychology, 17,* 142–158.

Sherman, S. J., Zehner, K. S., Johnson, J., & Hirt, E. R. (1983). Social explanation: The role of timing, set, and recall on subjective likelihood estimates. *Journal of Personality and Social Psychology, 44,* 1127–1143.

Sherrod, D. (1985). Trial delay as a source of bias in jury decision making. *Law and Human Behavior, 9,* 101–108.

Sherrod, D. R., Armstrong, D., Hewitt, J., Madonia, B., Speno, S., & Fenyd, D. (1977). Environmental attention, affect, and altruism. *Journal of Applied Social Psychology, 7,* 359–371.

Shinn, M., Rosario, M., Moch, H., & Chestnut, D. E. (1984). Coping with job stress and burnout in the human services. *Journal of Personality and Social Psychology, 46,* 864–878.

Shneidman, E. S. (1973). *Deaths of man.* New York: The New York Times Book Company, Quadrangle.

Shotland, R. L., & Heinold, W. D. (1985). Bystander response to arterial bleeding: Helping skills, the decision-making process, and differentiating the helping response. *Journal of Personality and Social Psychology, 49,* 347–356.

Shotland, R. L., & Huston, T. L. (1979). Emergencies: What are they and do they influence bystanders to intervene? *Journal of Personality and Social Psychology, 37,* 1822–1834.

Shumaker, S. A., & Taylor, R. B. (1983). Toward a clarification of people-place relationships: A model of attachment to place. In N. R. Feimer & E. S. Geller (Eds.), *Environmental psychology: Directions and perspectives* (pp. 219–251). New York: Praeger.

Shuntich, R. J., & Taylor, S. P. (1972). The effects of alcohol on human physical aggression. *Journal of Experimental Research in Personality, 6,* 34–38.

Shuter, R. (1976). Proxemics and tactility in Latin America. *Journal of Communication, 26,* 46–52.

Siegel, J. M., & Steele, C. M. (1980). Environmental distraction and interpersonal judgments. *British Journal of Social and Clinical Psychology, 19,* 23–32.

Siegman, A. W. (1978). The telltale voice: Nonverbal messages of verbal communication. In A. W. Siegman & S. Feldstein (Eds.), *Nonverbal behavior and communication.* Hillsdale, NJ: Erlbaum.

Sigall, H., & Aronson, E. (1969). Liking for an evaluator as a function of her physical attractiveness and nature of the evaluations. *Journal of Experimental Social Psychology, 5,* 93–100.

Sigall, H., & Landy, D. (1973). Radiating beauty: The effect of having a physically attractive partner on person perception. *Journal of Personality and Social Psychology, 28,* 218–224.

Sigall, H., & Ostrove, N. (1975). Beautiful but dangerous: Effects of offender attractiveness and nature of the crime on juridic judgment. *Journal of Personality and Social Psychology, 31,* 410–414.

Sigall, H., & Page, R. (1971). Current stereotypes: A little fading, a little faking. *Journal of Personality and Social Psychology, 18,* 247–255.

Silverstein, C. H., & Stang, D. J. (1976). Seating position and interaction in triads: A field study. *Sociometry, 39,* 166–170.

Simons, H. W., Berkowitz, N. N., & Moyer, R. J. (1970). Similarity, credibility and attitude change: A review and a theory. *Psychological Bulletin, 73,* 1–16.

Singer, J. L., Singer, D. G., & Rapaczynski, W. (1984). Children's imagination as predicted by family patterns and television viewing: A longitudinal study. *Genetic Psychology Monographs, 110,* 43–69.

Sistrunk, F., & McDavid, J. W. (1971). Sex variable in conforming behavior. *Journal of Personality and Social Psychology, 17,* 200–207.

Sivacek, J., & Crano, W. D. (1982). Vested interest as a moderator of attitude-behavior consistency. *Journal of Personality and Social Psychology, 43,* 210–221.

Skinner, B. F. (1938). *The behavior of organisms.* New York: Appleton-Century-Crofts.

Skinner, B. F. (1971). *Beyond freedom and dignity.* New York, NY: Alfred A. Knopf.

Skolnick, A. (1981). Married lives: Longitudinal perspectives on marriage. In D. Eichorn, J. Clausen, N. Haan, M. Honzik & P. Mussen (Eds.), *Present and past in middle life.* New York: Academic Press.

Slater, D., & Elliot, W. R. (1982). Television's influence on social reality. *Quarterly Journal of Speech, 68,* 69–79.

Slovic, P., Fischhoff, B. & Lichtenstein, S. (1979). Rating the risks. *Environment, 21,* 14–20, 36–39.

Smedley, J. W., & Bayton, J. A. (1978). Evaluative race-class stereotypes by race and perceived class of subjects. *Journal of Personality and Social Psychology, 36,* 530–535.

Smith, C. A., & Ellsworth, P. C. (1987). Patterns of appraisal and emotion related to taking an exam. *Journal of Personality and Social Psychology, 52,* 475–488.

Smith, H. W. (1981). Territorial spacing on a beach revisited: A cross-national exploration. *Social Psychology Quarterly, 44,* 132–137.

Smith, M. L., Glass, G. V., & Miller, T. L. (1980). *The benefits of psychotherapy.* Baltimore: Johns Hopkins University Press.

Smith, P., & Connolly, K. (1977). Social and aggressive behavior in preschool children as a function of crowding. *Social Science Information, 16,* 601–620.

Smith, R. J., & Knowles, E. S. (1978). Attributional consequences of personal space invasions. *Personality and Social Psychology Bulletin, 4,* 429–433.

Smith, T. W., Snyder, C. R., & Handelsman, M. M. (1982). On the self-serving function of an academic wooden leg: Test anxiety as a self-handicapping strategy. *Journal of Personality and Social Psychology, 42,* 314–321.

Smith, T. W., Snyder, C. R., & Perkins, S. C. (1983). The self-serving function of hypochondriacal complaints: Physical symptoms as self-handicapping strategies. *Journal of Personality and Social Psychology, 44*, 787–797.

Snyder, C., & Fromkin, H. (1980). *Uniqueness: The human pursuit of difference.* New York: Plenum.

Snyder, C. R., Lassegard, M. A., & Ford, C. (1986). Distancing after group success and failure: Basking in reflected glory and cutting off reflected failure. *Journal of Personality and Social Psychology, 51*, 382–388.

Snyder, C., Smith, T., Augelli, R., & Ingram, R. (1985). On the self-serving function of social anxiety: Shyness as a self-handicapping strategy. *Journal of Personality and Social Psychology, 48*, 970–980.

Snyder, M. (1974). Self-monitoring of expressive behavior. *Journal of Personality and Social Psychology, 30*, 526–537.

Snyder, M., & Monson, T. (1975). Persons, situations, and the control of social behavior. *Journal of Personality and Social Psychology, 32*, 637–644.

Snyder, M., & Simpson, J. A. (1984). Self-monitoring and dating relationships. *Journal of Personality and Social Psychology, 47*, 1281–1291.

Snyder, M., & Swann, W. B., Jr. (1976). When actions reflect attitudes: The politics of impression management. *Journal of Personality and Social Psychology, 34*, 1034–1042.

Snyder, M., & Swann, W. B., Jr. (1978). Hypothesis testing processes in social interaction. *Journal of Personality and Social Psychology, 36*, 1202–1212.

Snyder, M., Tanke, E., & Berscheid, E. (1977). Social perception and interpersonal behavior: On the self-fulfilling nature of social stereotypes. *Journal of Personality and Social Psychology, 35*, 656–666.

Snyder, M., & Uranowitz, S. W. (1978). Reconstructing the past: Some cognitive consequences of person perception. *Journal of Personality and Social Psychology, 36*, 941–950.

Solano, C. H., Batten, P. G., & Parish, E. A. (1982). Loneliness and patterns of self-disclosure. *Journal of Personality and Social Psychology, 43*, 524–531.

Solomon, R. L. (1980). The opponent-process theory of acquired motivation: The costs of pleasure and the benefits of pain. *American Psychologist, 35*, 691–712.

Solomon, R. L., & Corbit, J. D. (1974). An opponent-process theory of motivation: I. Temporal dynamics of affect. *Psychological Review, 81*, 119–145.

Solomon, Z., Mukulincer, M., & Avitzur, E. (1988). Coping, locus of control, social support, and combat-related posttraumatic stress disorder: A prospective study. *Journal of Personality and Social Psychology, 55*, 279–285.

Solomon, Z., Mukulincer, M., & Hobfoll, S. E. (1986). Effects of social support and battle intensity on loneliness and breakdown during combat. *Journal of Personality and Social Psychology, 51*, 1269–1276.

Solomon, Z., Weisenberg, M., Schwarzwald, J., & Mikulincer, M. (1987). Posttraumatic stress disorder among frontline soldiers with combat stress reaction: The 1982 Israeli experience. *American Journal of Psychiatry, 144*, 448–454.

Sommer, R. (1966). The ecology of privacy. *The Library Quarterly, 36*, 234–248.

Sommer, R. (1969). *Personal space: The behavioral basis of design.* New York: Holt, Rinehart & Winston.

Sommer, R. (1974). *Tight spaces: Hard architecture and how to humanize it.* Englewood Cliffs, NJ: Prentice-Hall.

Sommer, R. (1987). Crime and vandalism in university residence halls: A confirmation of defensible space theory. *Journal of Environmental Psychology, 7*, 1–12.

Sommer, R., & Becker, F. D. (1969). Territorial defense and the good neighbor. *Journal of Personality and Social Psychology, 11*, 85–92.

Sommer, R., & Ross, H. (1958). Social interaction on a geriatric ward. *International Journal of Social Psychiatry, 4*, 128–133.

Sonnenfeld, J. (1966). Variable values in space and landscape: An inquiry into the nature of the environment. *Journal of Social Issues, 22*(4), 71–82.

Sorrentino, R. M., & Boutillier, R. G. (1975). The effect of quantity and quality of verbal interaction on ratings of leadership ability. *Journal of Experimental Research in Personality, 11*, 403–411.

Sorrentino, R. M., & Field, N. (1986). Emergent leadership over time: The functional value of positive motivation. *Journal of Personality and Social Psychology, 50*, 1091–1099.

Spacapan, S., & Cohen, S. (1983). Effects and aftereffects of stressor expectations. *Journal of Personality and Social Psychology, 45*, 1243–1254.

Spanier, G. B., Lewis, R. A., & Cole, C. L. (1975). Marital adjustment over the family life cycle: The issue of curvilinearity. *Journal of Marriage and the Family, 37*, 263–275.

Spence, J. (1983). Comment on Lubinski, Tellegen, and Butcher's "Masculinity, femininity, and androgyny viewed and assessed as distinct concepts." *Journal of Personality and Social Psychology, 44*, 440–446.

Spence, J. T., & Helmreich, R. L. (1978). *Masculinity and femininity: Their psychological dimensions, correlates and antecedents.* Austin, TX: University of Texas Press.

Spence, J. T., Helmreich, R. L., & Stapp, J. (1975). Ratings of self and peers on sex role attributes and their relation to self-esteem and conceptions of masculinity and femininity. *Journal of Personality and Social Psychology, 32*, 29–39.

Spitz, R. A. (1945). Hospitalism: An inquiry into the genesis of psychiatric conditions in early childhood. *The Psychoanalytic Study of the Child, 1*, 53–74.

Sprafkin, J. N., Liebert, R. M., & Poulos, R. W. (1975). Effects of a televised prosocial example on children's helping. *Journal of Experimental Child Psychology, 20*, 119–126.

Srull, T. K., Lichtenstein, M., & Rothbart, M. (1985). Associative storage and retrieval processes in person memory. *Journal of Experimental Psychology: Learning, Memory, and Cognition, 11*, 316–345.

Srull, T. K., & Wyer, R. S. (1979). The role of category accessibility in the interpretation of information about persons: Some determinants and implications. *Journal of Personality and Social Psychology, 37*, 1660–1672.

Srull, T. K., & Wyer, R. S. (1980). Category accessibility and social perception: Some implications for the study of person memory and interpersonal judgments. *Journal of Personality and Social Psychology, 38*, 841–856.

Stack, S., & Haas, A. (1984). The effect of unemployment duration on national suicide rates: A time series analysis, 1948–1982. *Sociological Focus, 17*, 17–29.

Stall, R. D., Coates, T. J., & Hoff, C. (1988). Behavioral risk reduction for HIV infection among gay and bisexual men. (Special Issue: Psychology and AIDS), *American Psychologist, 43*, 878–885.

Stasser, G., & Titus, W. (1985). Pooling of unshared information in group decision making: Biased information sampling during discussion. *Journal of Personality and Social Psychology, 48*, 1467–1478.

Stasser, G., & Titus, W. (1987). Effects of information load and percentage of shared information on the dissemination of unshared information during group discussion. *Journal of Personality and Social Psychology, 53*, 81–93.

Staub, E. (1970). A child in distress: The influence of age and number of witnesses on children's attempts to help. *Journal of Personality and Social Psychology, 14,* 130–140.

Staub, E. (1971). Helping a person in distress: The influence of implicit and explicit "rules" of conduct on children and adults. *Journal of Personality and Social Psychology, 17,* 137–145.

Staub, E. (1974). Helping a distressed person: Social, personality, and stimulus determinants. In L. Berkowitz (Ed.), *Advances in experimental social psychology* (Vol. 7). New York: Academic Press.

Staub, E., & Baer, R. S., Jr. (1974). Stimulus characteristics of a sufferer and difficulty of escape as determinants of helping. *Journal of Personality and Social Psychology, 30,* 279–285.

Steele, C. M., & Liu, T. J. (1981). Making the dissonance act unreflective of self: Dissonance avoidance and the expectancy of a value-affirming response. *Personality and Social Psychology Bulletin, 7,* 393–397.

Steele, C. M., & Liu, T. J. (1983). Dissonance processes as self-affirmation. *Journal of Personality and Social Psychology, 45,* 5–19.

Steele, C. M., Southwick, L. L., & Critchlow, B. (1981). Dissonance and alcohol: Drinking your troubles away. *Journal of Personality and Social Psychology, 41,* 831–846.

Stein, R. T., & Heller, T. (1979). An empirical analysis of the correlations between leadership status and participation rates reported in the literature. *Journal of Personality and Social Psychology, 37,* 1993–2002.

Steiner, I. D. (1966). Models for inferring relationships between group size and potential group productivity. *Behavioral Science, 11,* 273–283.

Steiner, I. D. (1972). *Group process and productivity.* New York: Academic Press.

Steinzor, B. (1950). The spatial factor in face-to-face groups. *Journal of Abnormal and Social Psychology, 45,* 552–555.

Stephan, W. G. (1978). School desegregation: An examination of predictions made in Brown v. Board of Education. *Psychological Bulletin, 85,* 217–238.

Stephan, W. G. (1985). Intergroup relations. In G. Lindzey & E. Aronson (Eds.), *Handbook of social psychology* (3rd ed., Vol. 2, pp. 599–658). New York: Random House.

Stephan, W. G., & Rosenfield, D. (1978). Effects of desegregation on racial attitudes. *Journal of Personality and Social Psychology, 36,* 795–804.

Stephan, W. G., & Stephan, C. W. (1984). The role of ignorance in intergroup relations. In N. Miller & M. B. Brewer (Eds.), *Groups in contact.* New York: Academic Press.

Stern, P. C., & Oskamp, S. (1987). Managing scarce environmental resources. In D. Stokols & I. Altman (Eds.), *Handbook of environmental psychology* (Vol. 2, pp. 1043–1088). New York: Wiley.

Sternberg, R. J. (1986). A triangular theory of love. *Psychological Review, 93,* 119–135.

Stewart, T. R. (1987). Developing an observer-based measure of environmental annoyance. In H. S. Koelega (Ed.), *Environmental annoyance: Characterization, measurement, and control* (pp. 213–222). New York: Elsevier.

Stier, D. S., & Hall, J. A. (1984). Gender differences in touch: An empirical and theoretical review. *Journal of Personality and Social Psychology, 47,* 440–459.

Stires, L. K. (1980). Classroom seating location, student grades, and attitudes: Environment or self-selection? *Environment and Behavior, 12,* 241–254.

Stires, L. K. (1982). Classroom seating location, order effects, and reactivity. *Personality and Social Psychology Bulletin, 8,* 362–364.

Stogdill, R. M. (1974). *Handbook of leadership: A survey of theory and research.* New York: Free Press.

Stokols, D. (1972). On the distinction between density and crowding: Some implications for future research. *Psychological Review, 79,* 275–278.

Stokols, D. (1976). The experience of crowding in primary and secondary environments. *Environment and Behavior, 8,* 49–86.

Stokols, D., Ohlig, W., & Resnick, S. M. (1978). Perception of residential crowding, classroom experiences, and student health. *Human Ecology, 6,* 233–252.

Stokols, D., Rall, M., Pinner, B., & Schopler, J. (1973). Physical, social and personal determinants of the perception of crowding. *Environment and Behavior, 5,* 87–115.

Stoneman, Z., & Brody, G. H. (1981). Peers as mediators of television food advertisements aimed at children. *Developmental Psychology, 17,* 853–858.

Stoner, J. A. F. (1961). *A comparison of individual and group decisions involving risk.* Unpublished master's thesis. MA Institute of Technology, School of Industrial Management. Cambridge, MA.

Stoner, J. A. F. (1968). Risky and cautious shifts in group decisions: The influence of widely held values. *Journal of Experimental Social Psychology, 4,* 442–459.

Storms, M. D. (1973). Videotape and the attribution process: Reversing actors' and observers' points of view. *Journal of Personality and Social Psychology, 27,* 165–175.

Storms, M. D., & Nisbett, R. E. (1970). Insomnia and the attribution process. *Journal of Personality and Social Psychology, 16,* 319–328.

Storms, M. D., & Thomas, G. C. (1977). Reactions to physical closeness. *Journal of Personality and Social Psychology, 35,* 412–418.

Stotland, E. (1969). Exploratory studies in empathy. In L. Berkowitz (Ed.), *Advances in experimental social psychology* (Vol. 4, pp. 271–313). New York: Academic Press.

Strack, S., Carver, C. S., & Blaney, P. H. (1987). Predicting successful completion of an aftercare program following treatment for alcoholism: The role of dispositional optimism. *Journal of Personality and Social Psychology, 53,* 579–584.

Strauman, T. J., & Higgins, E. T. (in press). Self-discrepancies as predictors of distinct syndromes of chronic emotional distress. *Journal of Personality.*

Straus, M. A. (1974). Leveling, civility, and violence in the family. *Journal of Marriage and the Family, 36,* 13–29.

Straus, M. A., Gelles, R. J., & Steinmetz, S. K. (1979). *Behind closed doors: Violence in the American family.* New York: Doubleday.

Streeter, L. A., Krauss, R. M., Geller, V., Olson, C., & Apple, W. (1977). Pitch changes during attempted deception. *Journal of Personality and Social Psychology, 35,* 345–350.

Strodtbeck, F., & Hook, H. (1961). The social dimensions of a 12-man jury table. *Sociometry, 24,* 397–415.

Strodtbeck, F., & Mann, R. (1956). Sex role differentiation in jury deliberations. *Sociometry, 19,* 3–11.

Suedfeld, P. (1982). Aloneness as a healing experience. In L. A. Peplau & D. Perlman (Eds.), *Loneliness: A sourcebook of current theory, research, and therapy* (pp. 54–67). New York: Wiley.

Suedfeld, P. (1984). Restricted environmental stimulation therapy (REST). In J. D. Matarazzo, S. M. Weiss, J. A. Herd, N. E. Miller, & S. Weiss (Eds.), *Behavioral health: A handbook of health enhancement and disease prevention* (pp. 755–764). New York: Wiley.

Suedfeld, P., & Baker-Brown, G. (1986). Restricted environmental stimulation therapy and aversive conditioning in smoking cessation: Active and placebo effects. *Behavioral Research and Therapy, 24,* 421–428.

Suedfeld, P., & Clark, J. C. (1981). Specific food aversion acquired during restricted environmental stimulation. *Journal of Applied Social Psychology, 11,* 538–547.

Suedfeld, P., & Ikard, F. F. (1973). Attitude manipulation in restricted environments: Psychologically addicted smokers treated in sensory deprivation. *British Journal of Addiction, 68,* 170–176.

Suinn, R. M. (1982). Intervention with Type A behaviors. *Journal of Consulting and Clinical Psychology, 50,* 933–949.

Suls, J., & Mullen, B. (1981). Life change and psychological distress: The role of perceived control and desirability. *Journal of Applied Social Psychology, 11,* 379–389.

Sundstrom, E. (1975). An experimental study of crowding: Effects of room size, intrusion, and goal-blocking on nonverbal behavior, self-disclosure, and self-reported stress. *Journal of Personality and Social Psychology, 32,* 645–654.

Sundstrom, E., & Altman, I. (1974). Field study of territorial behavior and dominance. *Journal of Personality and Social Psychology, 30,* 115–124.

Sundstrom, E., Herbert, R. K., & Brown, D. W. (1982). Privacy and communication in an open-plan office: A case study. *Environment and Behavior, 14,* 543–559.

Sundstrom, E., & Sundstrom, M. G. (1986). *Workplaces: Psychology of the physical environment in offices and factories.* New York: Cambridge University Press.

Sundstrom, E., Town, J. P., Brown, D. W., Forman, A., & McGee, C. (1982). Physical enclosure, type of job, and privacy in the office. *Environment and Behavior, 14,* 543–559.

Sussman, N. M., & Rosenfeld, H. M. (1982). Influence of culture, language, and sex on conversational distance. *Journal of Personality and Social Psychology, 42,* 66–74.

Switzer, R., & Taylor, R. B. (1983). Sociability versus privacy of residential choice: Impacts of personality and local social ties. *Basic and Applied Social Psychology, 4,* 123–136.

Tajfel, H. (1981). *Human groups and social categories: Studies in social psychology.* London: Cambridge University Press.

Tajfel, H. (1982). Social psychology of intergroup relations. *Annual Review of Psychology, 33,* 1–39.

Tajfel, H., & Billig, M. (1974). Familiarity and categorization in intergroup behavior. *Journal of Experimental Social Psychology, 10,* 159–170.

Tajfel, H., Billig, M. G., Bundy, R. P., & Flament, C. (1971). Social categorization and intergroup behavior. *European Journal of Social Psychology, 1,* 149–178.

Tajfel, H., & Turner, J. C. (1986). The social identity theory of intergroup behavior. In S. Worchel & W. G. Austin (Eds.), *Psychology of intergroup relations* (pp. 7–24). Chicago: Nelson-Hall.

Tanaka, J. S., & Huba, G. J. (1984). Confirmatory hierarchical factor analysis of psychological distress measures. *Journal of Personality and Social Psychology, 46,* 621–635.

Tannenbaum, P. H. (1967). The congruity principle revisited: Studies in the reduction, induction and generalization of persuasion. In L. Berkowitz (Ed.), *Advances in experimental social psychology* (Vol. 3, pp. 271–320). New York: Academic Press.

Tashakkori, A., & Insko, C. A. (1981). Interpersonal attraction and person perception: Two tests of three balance models. *Journal of Experimental Social Psychology, 17,* 266–285.

Tavris, C. (1974, June). The frozen world of the familiar stranger. *Psychology Today, 8*(1), 71–80.

Taylor, D. A. (1968). Some aspects of the development of interpersonal relationships: Social penetration processes. *Journal of Social Psychology, 75,* 79–90.

Taylor, D. A. (1973). Should we integrate organizations? In H. L. Fromkin & J. J. Sherwood (Eds.), *Integrating the organization: A social psychological analysis.* Glencoe, IL: Free Press.

Taylor, D. A. (1984). Race prejudice, discrimination, and racism. In A. S. Kahn (Ed.), *Social psychology* (pp. 324–351). Dubuque, IA: Wm. C. Brown.

Taylor, D. A., & Altman, I. (1966). Intimacy-scaled stimuli for use in studies of interpersonal relations. *Psychological Reports, 19,* 729–730.

Taylor, D. M., Dube, L., & Bellerose, J. (1986). Intergroup contact in Quebec. In M. Hewstone & R. Brown (Eds.), *Contact and conflict in intergroup encounters* (pp. 107–118). New York: Basil Blackwell.

Taylor, D. W., Berry, P. C., & Block, C. H. (1958). Does group participation when using brainstorming facilitate or inhibit creative thinking? *Administrative Science Quarterly, 3,* 23–47.

Taylor, R. B. (1987). Toward an environmental psychology of disorder: Delinquency, crime, and fear of crime. In D. Stokols & I. Altman (Eds.), *Handbook of environmental psychology* (Vol. 2, pp. 951–986). New York: Wiley.

Taylor, R. B., & Brooks, D. K. (1980). Temporary territories: Responses to intrusions in a public setting. *Population and Environment, 3,* 135–145.

Taylor, R. B., & Ferguson, G. (1980). Solitude and intimacy: Linking territoriality and privacy experiences. *Journal of Nonverbal Behavior, 4,* 227–239.

Taylor, R. B., & Strough, R. R. (1978). Territorial cognition: Assessing Altman's typology. *Journal of Personality and Social Psychology, 36,* 418–423.

Taylor, S. E. (1975). On inferring one's own attitudes from one's behavior: Some delimiting conditions. *Journal of Personality and Social Psychology, 31,* 126–131.

Taylor, S. E. (1981). The interface of cognitive and social psychology. In J. Harvey (Ed.), *Cognition, social behavior, and the environment.* Hillsdale, NJ: Erlbaum.

Taylor, S. E., & Fiske, S. T. (1975). Points-of-view and perceptions of causality. *Journal of Personality and Social Psychology, 32,* 439–445.

Taylor, S. E., & Fiske, S. T. (1978). Salience, attention, and attribution: Top of the head phenomena. In L. Berkowitz (Ed.), *Advances in experimental social psychology* (Vol. 11, pp. 249–288). New York: Academic Press.

Taylor, S. P. (1967). Aggressive behavior and physiological arousal as a function of provocation and the tendency to inhibit aggression. *Journal of Personality, 35,* 297–310.

Taylor, S. P., & Gammon, C. B. (1975). Effects of type and dose of alcohol on human physical aggression. *Journal of Personality and Social Psychology, 32,* 169–175.

Taylor, S. P., & Gammon, C. B. (1976). Aggressive behavior of intoxicated subjects: The effect of third-party intervention. *Journal of Studies on Alcohol, 37,* 917–930.

Taylor, S. P., Gammon, C. B., & Capasso, D. R. (1976). Aggression as a function of alcohol and threat. *Journal of Personality and Social Psychology, 34,* 938–941.

Taylor, S. P., & Leonard, K. E. (1983). Alcohol and human physical aggression. In R. G. Geen & E. I. Donnerstein (Eds.), *Aggression: Theoretical and empirical reviews* (Vol. 2, pp. 77–102). New York: Academic Press.

Taylor, S. P., & Pisano, R. (1971). Physical aggression as a function of frustration and physical attack. *Journal of Social Psychology, 84,* 261–267.

Taylor, S. P., Schmutte, G. T., Leonard, K. E., & Cranston, J. W. (1979). The effects of alcohol and extreme provocation on the use of a highly noxious shock. *Motivation and Emotion, 3,* 73–81.

Taylor, S., Vardaris, R., Rawitch, A., Gammon, C., Cranston, J., & Lubetkin, A. (1976). The effects of alcohol and delta-9-tetrahydrocannabinol on human physical aggression. *Aggressive Behavior, 2,* 153–161.

Taylor, V. (1977, October). Good news about disaster. *Psychology Today, 11*(10), 93–94, 124–125.

Tedeschi, J. T., (Ed.) (1981). *Impression management theory and social psychological research.* New York: Academic Press.

Tedeschi, J. T. (1983). Social influence theory and aggression. In R. G. Geen & E. I. Donnerstein (Eds.), *Aggression: Theoretical and empirical reviews* (Vol. 1, pp. 135–162). New York: Academic Press.

Tedeschi, J. T., & Rosenfeld, P. (1981). Impression management and the forced compliance situation. In J. T. Tedeschi (Ed.), *Impression management theory and social psychological research.* New York: Academic Press.

Tedeschi, J. T., Schlenker, B. R., & Bonoma, T. V. (1971). Cognitive dissonance: Private ratiocination or public spectacle? *American Psychologist, 26,* 685–695.

Tennov, D. (1979). *Love and limerance: The experience of being in love.* New York: Stein and Day.

Tesser, A. (1980). Self-esteem maintenance in family dynamics. *Journal of Personality and Social Psychology, 39,* 77–91.

Tesser, A. (1985). Some effects of self-evaluation maintenance on cognition and action. In R. M. Sorrentino & E. T. Higgins (Eds.), *The handbook of motivation and cognition: Foundations of social behavior.* New York: Guilford.

Tetlock, P. E. (1979). Identifying victims of groupthink from public statements of decision makers. *Journal of Personality and Social Psychology, 37,* 1314–1324.

Thalhofer, N. N. (1980). Violation of a spacing norm in high social density. *Journal of Applied Social Psychology, 10,* 175–183.

Thibaut, J. W., & Kelley, H. H. (1959). *The social psychology of groups.* New York: Wiley.

Thistlethwaite, D. L., de Haan, H., & Kamenetsky, J. (1955). The effects of "directive" and "nondirective" communication procedures on attitudes. *Journal of Abnormal and Social Psychology, 51,* 107–113.

Thoits, P. A. (1983). Dimensions of life events that influence psychological distress: An evaluation of the literature. In H. B. Kaplan (Ed.), *Psychological stress: Trends in theory and research* (pp. 33–103). New York: Academic Press.

Thomas, W. A. (1972). *Indicators of environmental quality.* New York: Plenum.

Thompson, D. E., Aiello, J. R., & Epstein, Y. (1979). Interpersonal distance preferences. *Journal of Nonverbal Behavior, 4,* 113–118.

Thompson, H. L., & Richardson, D. R. (1983). The rooster effect: Same-sex rivalry and inequity as factors in retaliative aggression. *Personality and Social Psychology Bulletin, 9,* 415–425.

Thompson, S. C. (1981). Will it hurt less if I can control it? A complex answer to a simple question. *Psychological Bulletin, 90,* 89–101.

Thompson, W. C., Fong, G. T., & Rosenhan, D. L. (1981). Inadmissible evidence and juror verdicts. *Journal of Personality and Social Psychology, 40,* 453–463.

Thorndike, E. L. (1933). A proof of the law of effect. *Science, 77,* 173–175.

Thorne, S. B. (1984). *The role of suggestion in the perception of satanic messages in rock-and-roll recordings.* Paper presented at the Southwestern Psychological Association convention, New Orleans, LA.

Tice, D. M., & Baumeister, R. F. (1985). Masculinity inhibits helping in emergencies: Personality does predict the bystander effect. *Journal of Personality and Social Psychology, 49,* 420–428.

Tice, D. M., Buder, J., & Baumeister, R. F. (1985). Development of self-consciousness: At what age does audience pressure disrupt performance? *Adolescence, 20,* 301–305.

Tilker, H. A. (1970). Socially responsible behavior as a function of observer responsibility and victim feedback. *Journal of Personality and Social Psychology, 14,* 95–100.

Tinbergen, N. (1952). The curious behavior of stickleback. *Scientific American, 187,* 22–26.

Toch, H. H. (1969). *Violent men: An inquiry into the psychology of violence.* Chicago: Aldine.

Toepler, J., Diago, G., & Kimble, C. E. (1989). *Making eye contact with a stranger in post offices: A replication.* Unpublished manuscript, University of Dayton.

Tognoli, J., & Keisner, R. (1972). Gain and loss as determinants of interpersonal attraction: A replication and extension. *Journal of Personality and Social Psychology, 23,* 201–204.

Toi, M., & Batson, C. D. (1982). More evidence that empathy is a source of altruistic motivation. *Journal of Personality and Social Psychology, 43,* 281–292.

Tolstedt, B. E., & Stokes, J. P. (1984). Self-disclosure, intimacy, and the depenetration process. *Journal of Personality and Social Psychology, 46,* 84–90.

Tresemer, D. (1976). The cumulative record of research on "Fear of Success." *Sex Roles, 2,* 217–236.

Triandis, H. C., Marin, G., Lisansky, J., & Betancourt, H. (1984). Simpatia as a cultural script of hispanics. *Journal of Personality and Social Psychology, 47,* 1363–1375.

Triandis, H. C., & Triandis, L. M. (1962). A cross-cultural study of social distance. *Psychological Monographs, 76,* 1–21.

Triplett, N. (1897). The dynamogenic factors in pacemaking competition. *American Journal of Psychology, 9,* 507–533.

Trivers, R. L. (1971). The evolution of reciprocal altruism. *Quarterley Review of Biology, 46,* 35–37.

Trolier, T. K., & Hamilton, D. L. (1986). Variables influencing judgments of correlational relations. *Journal of Personality and Social Psychology, 50,* 879–888.

Trout, D. L., & Rosenfeld, H. M. (1980). The effect of postural lean and body congruence on the judgment of psychotherapeutic rapport. *Journal of Nonverbal Behavior, 4,* 176–190.

Tuan, Y. (1974). *Topophilia: A study of environmental perception, attitudes, and values.* Englewood Cliffs, NJ: Prentice-Hall.

Tunnell, G. B. (1977). Three dimensions of naturalness: An expanded definition of field research. *Psychological Bulletin, 84,* 426–437.

Turner, C. W., Layton, J. F., & Simons, L. S. (1975). Naturalistic studies of aggressive behavior: Aggressive stimuli, victim visibility, and horn honking. *Journal of Personality and Social Psychology, 31,* 1098–1107.

Turner, C. W., Simons, L. S., Berkowitz, L., & Frodi, A. (1977). The stimulating and inhibiting effects of weapons on aggressive behavior. *Aggressive Behavior, 3,* 355–378.

Tversky, A., & Kahneman, D. (1971). Belief in the law of small numbers. *Psychological Bulletin, 76,* 105–110.

Tversky, A., & Kahneman, D. (1973). Availability: A heuristic for judging frequency and probability. *Cognitive Psychology, 5,* 207–232.

Tybout, A. M., Sternthal, B., & Calder, B. J. (1983). Information availability as a determinant of multiple request effectiveness. *Journal of Marketing Research, 20,* 280–290.

Tyler, V. O., Jr., & Brown, G. D. (1967). The use of swift, brief isolation as a group control device for institutionalized delinquents. *Behavior Research and Therapy, 5,* 1–9.

Ulrich, R. E. (1966). Pain as a cause of aggression. *American Zoologist, 6,* 643–662.

Ulrich, R. E., & Azrin, N. H. (1962). Reflexive fighting in response to aversive stimulation. *Journal of the Experimental Analysis of Behavior, 5,* 511–520.

Ulrich, R. S. (1981). Natural versus urban scenes: Some psychophysiological effects. *Environment and Behavior, 13,* 523–556.

Ulrich, R. S. (1983). Aesthetic and affective responses to natural environment. In I. Altman & J. F. Wohlwill (Eds.), *Behavior and the natural environment* (pp. 85–125). New York: Plenum.

Ulrich, R. S. (1984). View through window may influence recovery from surgery. *Science, 224,* 420–421.

Ulrich, R. S. (1986). Human responses to vegetation and landscapes. *Journal of Urban Planning, 13,* 29–44.

U.S. Bureau of the Census. (1989). *Statistical abstract of the United States* (109th ed.). Washington, DC: U.S. Printing Office.

Valins, S., & Nisbett, R. E. (1972). Attributional processes in the development and treatment of emotional disorders. In E. E. Jones et al. (Eds.), *Attribution: Perceiving the causes of behavior* (pp. 137–149). Morristown, NJ: General Learning.

Van den Berghe, P. L. (1981). *The ethnic phenomenon.* New York: Elsevier.

Van de Ven, A. H., & Delbecq, A. L. (1974). The effectiveness of nominal, delphi, and interacting group decision-making processes. *Journal of the Academy of Management, 17,* 605–621.

Vine, I. (1974). Social spacing in animals and man. *Social Science Information, 12,* 7–50.

Vinokur, A., & Selzer, M. L. (1975). Desirable versus undesirable life events: Their relationship to stress and mental distress. *Journal of Personality and Social Psychology, 32,* 329–337.

Vinsel, A., Brown, B. B., Altman, I., & Foss, C. (1980). Privacy regulation, territorial displays, and effectiveness of individual functioning. *Journal of Personality and Social Psychology, 39,* 1104–1115.

Vitaliano, P. P., Maiuro, R. D., Bolton, P. A., & Armsden, G. C. (1987). A psychoepidemiologic approach to the study of disaster. *Journal of Community Psychology, 15,* 99–122.

Von Gierke, H. E., & Harris, C. S. (1987). Annoyance response to military flight operations and the development of standard criteria for community annoyance. In H. S. Koelega (Ed.), *Environmental annoyance: Characterization, measurement, and control* (pp. 257–268). New York: Elsevier.

Wagstaff, A. (1985). Time series analysis of the relationship between unemployment and mortality: A survey of econometric critiques and replications of Brenner's studies. *Social Science and Medicine, 21,* 985–996.

Walden, T. A., & Forsyth, D. (1981). Close encounters of the stressful kind: Affective, physiological, and behavioral reactions to the experience of crowding. *Journal of Nonverbal Behavior, 6,* 46–64.

Walker, M. B., & Trimboli, C. (1983). The expressive function of the eye flash. *Journal of Nonverbal Behavior, 8,* 3–13.

Waller, W. W., & Hill, R. (1951). *The family: A dynamic interpretation.* New York: Dryden.

Walster (Hatfield), E. (1964). The temporal sequence of post-decision processes. In L. Festinger (pp. 112–128). *Conflict, decision, and dissonance* (pp. 112–128). Stanford, CA: Stanford University Press.

Walster (Hatfield), E., Aronson, E., & Abrahams, D. (1966). On increasing the persuasiveness of a low-prestige communicator. *Journal of Experimental Social Psychology, 2,* 325–342.

Walster (Hatfield), E., Aronson, V., Abrahams, D., & Rottman, L. (1966). Importance of physical attractiveness in dating behavior. *Journal of Personality and Social Psychology, 4,* 508–516.

Walster (Hatfield), E., Berscheid, E., & Walster, G. W. (1973). New directions in equity research. *Journal of Personality and Social Psychology, 25,* 151–176.

Walster (Hatfield), E., & Festinger, L. (1962). The effectiveness of "overheard" persuasive communications. *Journal of Abnormal and Social Psychology, 65,* 395–402.

Walster, (Hatfield) E., & Piliavin, J. A. (1972). Equity and the innocent bystander. *Journal of Social Issues, 28,* 165–189.

Walster (Hatfield), E., & Walster, G. W. (1978). *A new look at love.* Reading, MA: Addison-Wesley.

Walster (Hatfield), E., Walster, G. W., & Berscheid, E. (1978). *Equity: Theory and research.* Boston: Allyn & Bacon.

Walster (Hatfield), E., Walster, G. W., Piliavin, J., & Schmidt, L. (1973). Playing hard to get: Understanding an elusive phenomenon. *Journal of Personality and Social Psychology, 26,* 113–121.

Walster (Hatfield), E., Walster, G. W., & Traupmann, J. (1978). Equity and premarital sex. *Journal of Personality and Social Psychology, 36,* 82–92.

Walters, G. C., & Grusec, J. E. (1977). *Punishment.* San Francisco, CA: W. H. Freeman.

Wankel, L. M. (1972). Competition in motor performance: An experimental analysis of motivational components. *Journal of Experimental Social Psychology, 8,* 427–437.

Watson, J. B. (1913). Psychology as the behaviorist views it. *Psychological Review, 20,* 158–177.

Weary, G., Harvey, J. H., Schwieger, P., Olson, C. T., Perloff, R., & Pritchard, S. (1982). Self-presentation and the moderation of self-serving attributional biases. *Social Cognition, 1,* 140–159.

Weatherley, D. (1963). Maternal response to childhood aggression and subsequent anti-Semitism. *Journal of Abnormal and Social Psychology, 66,* 183–185.

Wegner, D. M., & Schaefer, D. (1978). The concentration of responsibility: An objective self-awareness analysis of group size effects in helping situations. *Journal of Personality and Social Psychology, 36,* 147–155.

Wegner, D. M., & Vallacher, R. R. (1977). *Implicit psychology: An introduction to social cognition.* New York: Oxford University Press.

Weigel, R. H., Wiser, P. L., & Cook, S. W. (1975). The impact of cooperative learning experience on cross-ethnic relations and attitudes. *Journal of Social Issues, 31,* 219–244.

Weinberger, M., Hiner, S. L., & Tierney, W. M. (1987). In support of hassles as a measure of stress in predicting health outcomes. *Journal of Behavioral Medicine, 10,* 19–31.

Weiner, B., & Kukla, A. (1970). An attributional analysis of achievement motivation. *Journal of Personality and Social Psychology, 15,* 1–20.

Weiner, B. et al. (1972). Perceiving the causes of success and failure. In E. E. Jones et al. (Eds.), *Attribution: Perceiving the causes of behavior.* Morristown, NJ: General Learning Press.

Weiner, F. H. (1976). Altruism, ambiance, and action: The effects of rural and urban rearing on helping behavior. *Journal of Personality and Social Psychology, 34,* 112–124.

Weiss, B. (1983). Behavioral toxicology and environmental health science. *American Psychologist, 38,* 1174–1187.

Weiss, R. F., Lombardo, J. P., Warren, D. R., & Kelley, K. A. (1971). The reinforcing effects of speaking in reply. *Journal of Personality and Social Psychology, 20,* 186–199.

Weiss, R. S. (1975). *Marital separation.* New York: Basic Books.

Wener, R. E., & Keys, C. (1988). The effects of changes in jail population densities on crowding, sick call, and spatial behavior. *Journal of Applied Social Psychology, 10,* 852–866.

Wener, R., & Szigeti, F. (Eds.) (1987). *Cumulative index to the EDRA proceedings: Volumes 1–18.* Washington, DC: Environmental Design Research Association.

Werner, A., & Reis, H. T. (1974). *Do the eyes have it? Some interpersonal consequences of the stare.* Paper presented at the meeting of the Eastern Psychological Association, Philadelphia.

Werner, C., Brown, B., & Damron, G. (1981). Territorial marking in a game arcade. *Journal of Personality and Social Psychology, 41,* 1094–1104.

Werner, C., & Parmelee, P. (1979). Similarity of activity preference among friends: Those who play together stay together. *Social Psychology Quarterly, 42,* 62–65.

West, S, G., Whitney, G., & Schnedler, R. (1975). Helping a motorist in distress: The effects of sex, race, and neighborhood. *Journal of Personality and Social Psychology, 31,* 691–698.

Westin, A. (1970). *Privacy and freedom.* New York: Atheneum.

Weyant, J. M. (1978). Effects of mood states, costs and benefits on helping. *Journal of Personality and Social Psychology, 36,* 1169–1176.

Weyant, J. M. (1984). Applying social psychology to induce charitable donations. *Journal of Applied Social Psychology, 14,* 441–447.

Weyant, J. M. (1986). *Applied social psychology.* New York: Oxford University Press.

Weyant, J. M., & Smith, S. L. (1987). Getting more by asking for less: The effects of request size on donations to charity. *Journal of Applied Social Psychology, 17,* 392–400.

Whitcher, S. J., & Fisher, J. D. (1979). Multidimensional reaction to therapeutic touch in a hospital setting. *Journal of Personality and Social Psychology, 37,* 87–96.

White, G. L. (1980). Physical attractiveness and courtship progress. *Journal of Personality and Social Psychology, 39,* 660–668.

White, G. L., Fishbein, S., & Rutstein, J. (1981). Passionate love and the misattribution of arousal. *Journal of Personality and Social Psychology, 41,* 56–62.

White, M. (1975). Interpersonal distance as affected by room size, status, and sex. *Journal of Social Psychology, 95,* 241–249.

Wicker, A. W. (1968). Undermanning, performances, and students' subjective experiences in behavior settings of large and small high schools. *Journal of Personality and Social Psychology, 10,* 255–261.

Wicker, A. W. (1969). Attitudes versus actions: The relationship of verbal and overt behavioral responses to attitude objects. *Journal of Social Issues, 25,* 41–78.

Wicker, A. W. (1979). *An introduction to ecological psychology.* Monterey, CA: Brooks/Cole.

Wicklund, R. A. (1974). *Freedom and reactance.* Hillsdale, NJ: Erlbaum.

Wicklund, R. A., & Brehm, J. W. (1976). *Perspectives on cognitive dissonance.* Hillsdale, NJ: Erlbaum.

Wiggins, J. S., Wiggins, N., & Conger, J. C. (1968). Correlates of heterosexual somatic preference. *Journal of Personality and Social Psychology, 10,* 82–90.

Wilder, D. A. (1977). Perception of groups, size of opposition, and social influence. *Journal of Experimental Social Psychology, 13,* 253–268.

Wilder, D. A. (1978). Perceiving persons as a group: Effects on attributions of causality and beliefs. *Social Psychology, 41,* 13–23.

Wilder, D. A. (1984). Intergroup contact: The typical member and the exception to the rule. *Journal of Experimental Social Psychology, 20,* 177–194.

Wildman, R. C. (1978). Life change and college grades as a role-performance variable. *Social Psychology, 41,* 34–46.

Williams, K. (1981). *Social loafing and group cohesion.* Paper presented at Midwestern Psychological Association, Detroit, MI.

Williams, K., Harkins, S., & Latané, B. (1981). Identifiability as a deterrent to social loafing: Two cheering experiments. *Journal of Personality and Social Psychology, 40,* 303–311.

Wills, T. A. (1981). Downward comparison principles in social psychology. *Psychological Bulletin, 90,* 245–271.

Wills, T. A., Weiss, R. L., & Patterson, G. R. (1974). A behavioral analysis of the determinants of marital satisfaction. *Journal of Consulting and Clinical Psychology, 42,* 802–811.

Wilson, E. O. (1975). *Sociobiology: The new synthesis.* Cambridge, MA: Harvard University Press.

Wilson, E. O. (1978). *On human nature.* Cambridge, MA: Harvard University Press.

Wilson, J. P. (1976). Motivation, modeling and altruism: A person X situation analysis. *Journal of Personality and Social Psychology, 34,* 1078–1086.

Wilson, J. Q., & Herrnstein, R. J. (1985). *Crime and human nature.* New York: Simon & Schuster.

Wilson, T., & Linville, P. (1982). Improving academic performance of college freshmen: Attribution therapy revisited. *Journal of Personality and Social Psychology, 42,* 367–376.

Winch, R. F. (1958). *Mate selection: A study of complementary needs.* New York: Harper & Row.

Wineman, J. D. (1982). Office design and evaluation: An overview. *Environment and Behavior, 14,* 271–298.

Winsberg, M. D. (1986). Racial polarization gauged in top metropolitan areas. *USA Today,* p. 13A, date unknown.

Wispé, L., & Freshley, H. (1971). Race, sex and sympathetic helping behavior: The broken bag caper. *Journal of Personality and Social Psychology, 17,* 59–65.

Wober, J. M., & Gunter, B. (1986). Television audience research at Britain's independent broadcasting authority, 1974–1984. *Journal of Broadcasting and Electronic Media, 30,* 15–31.

Wohlwill, J. F. (1983). The concept of nature: A psychologist's view. In I. Altman & J. F. Wohlwill (Eds.), *Behavior and the natural environment* (pp. 5–37). New York: Plenum.

Wolf, S. (1985). Manifest and latent influence on majorities and minorities. *Journal of Personality and Social Psychology, 48,* 899–908.

Wolf, S., & Latané, B. (1983). Majority and minority influence on restaurant preferences. *Journal of Personality and Social Psychology, 45,* 282–292.

Wolfgang, M. E., & Strohm, R. B. (1956). The relationship between alcohol and criminal homicide. *Quarterly Journal of Studies on Alcohol, 17,* 411–425.

Wolman, C., & Frank, H. (1975). The solo woman in a professional peer group. *American Journal of Orthopsychiatry, 45,* 164–171.

Wong, P., & Weiner, B. (1981). When people ask "why" questions, and the heuristics of attributional search. *Journal of Personality and Social Psychology, 40,* 650–663.

Worchel, S. (1974). The effect of three types of arbitrary thwarting on the instigation to aggression. *Journal of Personality, 42,* 301–318.

Worchel, S. (1986a). The influence of contextual variables on interpersonal spacing. *Journal of Nonverbal Behavior, 10,* 230–254.

Worchel, S. (1986b). The role of cooperation in reducing intergroup conflict. In S. Worchel & W. G. Austin (Eds.), *Psychology of intergroup relations* (pp. 288–304). Chicago: Nelson-Hall.

Worchel, S., & Andreoli, V. A., & Folger, R. (1977). Intergroup cooperation and intergroup attraction: The effect of previous interaction and outcome of combined effort. *Journal of Experimental Social Psychology, 13,* 131–140.

Worchel, S., & Brown, E. H. (1984). The role of plausibility in influencing environmental attributions. *Journal of Experimental Social Psychology, 20,* 86–96.

Worchel, S., & Lollis, M. (1982). Reactions to territorial contamination as a function of culture. *Personality and Social Psychology Bulletin, 6,* 370–375.

Worchel, S., & Teddlie, C. (1976). The experience of crowding: A two-factor theory. *Journal of Personality and Social Psychology, 34,* 30–40.

Worchel, S., & Yohai, S. M. L. (1979). The role of attribution in the experience of crowding. *Journal of Experimental Social Psychology, 15,* 91–104.

Word, C. O., Zanna, M. P., & Cooper, J. (1974). The nonverbal mediation of self-fulfilling prophecies in interracial interaction. *Journal of Experimental Social Psychology, 10,* 109–120.

Worringham, C. J., & Messick, D. M. (1983). Social facilitation of running: An unobtrusive study. *Journal of Social Psychology, 121,* 23–29.

Worthy, M., Gary, A. L., & Kahn, G. (1969). Self-disclosure as an exchange process. *Journal of Personality and Social Psychology, 3,* 59–63.

Wortman, S., & Brehm, J. W. (1975). Responses to uncontrollable outcomes: An integration of reactance theory and the learned helplessness model. In L. Berkowitz (Ed.), *Advances in experimental social psychology* (Vol. 8, pp. 277–336). New York: Academic Press.

Wright, P. H. (1971). Bryne's paradigmatic approach to the study of attraction: Misgivings and alternatives. *Representative Research in Social Psychology, 2,* 66–70.

Wrightsman, L. S. (1978). The American trial jury on trial: Empirical evidence and procedural modifications. *Journal of Social Issues, 34*(4), 137–164.

Wyer, R. S., & Carlston, D. E. (1979). *Social cognition, inference, and attribution.* Hillsdale, NJ: Erlbaum.

Wyer, R. S., & Gordon, S. E. (1982). The recall of information about persons and groups. *Journal of Experimental Social Psychology, 18,* 128–164.

Yancey, W. L. (1972). Architecture, interaction, and social control: The case of a large scale housing project. In J. F. Wohlwill & D. H. Carson (Eds.), *Environment and the social sciences: Perspectives and applications* (pp. 126–136). Washington: American Psychological Association.

Yinon, Y., & Bizman, A. (1980). Noise, success and failure as determinants of helping behavior. *Personality and Social Psychology Bulletin, 6,* 125–130.

Yngve, V. H. (1970). *On getting a word in edgewise.* Papers presented at the sixth regional meeting Chicago Linguistic Society, 567–577.

Younger, J. C., Walker, L., & Arrowood, A. J. (1977). Post-decision dissonance at the fair. *Personality and Social Psychology Bulletin, 3,* 247–287.

Zajonc, R. B. (1960). The process of cognitive tuning in communication. *Journal of Abnormal and Social Psychology, 61,* 159–167.

Zajonc, R. B. (1965). Social facilitation. *Science, 149,* 269–274.

Zajonc, R. B. (1980). Compresence. In P. B. Paulus (Ed.), *Psychology of group influence* (pp. 35–60). Hillsdale, NJ: Erlbaum.

Zajonc, R. B., & Bargh, J. (1980). Birth order, family size, and decline of SAT scores. *American Psychologist, 35,* 662–668.

Zajonc, R. B., & Markus, G. B. (1975). Birth order and intellectual development. *Psychological Review, 82,* 74–88.

Zajonc, R. B., Markus, H., & Markus, G. B. (1979). The birth order puzzle. *Journal of Personality and Social Psychology, 37,* 1325–1341.

Zander, A. (1976). The psychology of removing group members and recruiting new ones. *Human Relations, 29,* 969–987.

Zanna, M. P., & Cooper, J. (1974). Dissonance and the pill: An attributional approach to studying the arousal properties of dissonance. *Journal of Personality and Social Psychology, 29,* 703–709.

Zeidner, M., & Schechter, M. (1988). Psychological responses to air pollution: Some personality and demographic correlates. *Journal of Environmental Psychology, 8,* 191–208.

Zeldow, P. B., Clark, D., & Daugherty, S. R. (1985). Masculinity, femininity, Type A behavior, and psychosocial adjustment in medical students. *Journal of Personality and Social Psychology, 48,* 481–492.

Zika, S., & Chamberlain, K. (1987). Relation of hassles and personality to subjective well-being. *Journal of Personality and Social Psychology, 53,* 155–162.

Zillman, D. (1971). Excitation transfer in communication-mediated aggressive behavior. *Journal of Experimental Social Psychology, 7,* 419–434.

Zillman, D. (1979). *Hostility and aggression.* Hillsdale, NJ: Erlbaum.

Zillman, D. (1983). Arousal and aggression. In R. G. Geen and E. I. Donnerstein (Eds.), *Aggression: Theoretical and empirical reviews* (Vol. 1, pp. 75–102). New York: Academic Press.

Zillman, D. (1988). Cognitive-excitation interdependencies in aggressive behavior. *Aggressive Behavior, 19,* 51–64.

Zillman, D., Hoyt, J. L., & Day, K. D. (1974). Strength and duration of the effect of aggressive, violent, and erotic communications on subsequent aggressive behavior. *Communication Research, 1,* 286–306.

Zimbardo, P. (1965). The effect of effort and improvisation on self-persuasion produced by role playing. *Journal of Experimental Social Psychology, 1,* 103–120.

Zimbardo, P. G. (1970). The human choice: Individuation, reason, and order versus deindividuation, impulse, and chaos. In W. J. Arnold & D. Levine (Eds.), *Nebraska symposium on motivation, 1969.* Lincoln: University of Nebraska Press.

Zimbardo, P. G. (1974). *Psychology and criminal justice.* Symposium presented at the American Psychological Association convention, New Orleans, LA.

Zimbardo, P. G. (1977). *Shyness: What it is; What to do about it.* Reading, MA: Addison-Wesley.

Zimbardo, P. G., Ebbesen, E. B., & Maslach, C. (1977). *Influencing attitudes and changing behavior.* Reading, MA: Addison-Wesley.

Zimbardo, P., Weisenberg, M., Firestone, I., & Levy, B. (1965). Communicator effectiveness in producing public conformity and private attitude change. *Journal of Personality, 33,* 233–255.

Zimmerman, D. H., & West, C. (1975). Sex roles: Interuptions and silences in conversation. In B. Thorne & N. M. Henley (Eds.), *Language and sex: Differences and domination.* Rowly, MA: Newbury House Publishers.

Zube, E. H. (1980). *Environmental evaluation: Perception and public policy.* Monterey, CA: Brooks/Cole.

Zuckerman, M. (1978). Sensation seeking. In H. London & J. Exner (Eds.), *Dimensions of personality.* New York: Wiley.

Zuckerman, M. (1979). Attribution of success and failure revisited, or: The motivational bias is alive and well in attribution theory. *Journal of Personality, 47,* 245–287.

Zuckerman, M., DePaulo, B. M., & Rosenthal, R. (1981). Verbal and nonverbal communication of deception. In L. Berkowitz (Ed.), *Advances in experimental social psychology* (Vol. 14, pp. 1–59). New York: Academic Press.

Zuckerman, M., Schimitz, M., & Yosha, A. (1977). Effects of crowding in a student environment. *Journal of Applied Social Psychology, 7,* 67–72.

Zurcher, L. A. (1977). *The mutable self.* Beverly Hills, CA: Sage.

CREDITS

Illustrations

Hans and Cassady, Inc. Fig. 1.1, 2.1, pg. 38, Fig. 2.2, 2.3, 2.4, 3.1, 3.2, 3.3, 3.4, 4.1, 4.2, 4.3, 4.4, 5.1, 5.2, 5.3, 6.1, 6.2, 6.3, 6.4, 6.5, 6.6–6.10, 6.11, 6.12, 6.13, Bx6.A, 6.14, pg. 173, Fig. 7.1–7.3, 7.4, 7.5, 7.6–7.9, 8.1, 8.2, 8.3, 8.4, 8.5, 8.6, 8.7, Bx8.A, Bx 8.B, 9.1–9.3, 9.4, 9.5, 9.6, 9.7, 9.8, 9.9, 10.1, 10.2, 10.3, 10.4, 10.5, 10.6, 10.7, 10.8, 11.1–11.3, 11.4–11.9, 11.10, 11.11, 11.12, 11.13, pg. 350, Fig. 12.1, pg 361, Fig. 12.2–12.5, 12.6–12.9, 12.10, 12.11, 13.1, Bx13.A, 13.2–13.6, 13.7, 13.8, 14.1, 14.2, 14.3, 14.4, 14.5, 14.6–14.8, 15.1–15.4, 15.6–15.10, 15.12, 15.13B, 15.14–15.16, pg. 506, Fig. 16.3, 16.4, 16.8, 16.10–16.13

Photographs

Table of Contents and Part Openers

1: © Bill Aron/Photo Researchers, Inc.; **2:** © Larry Mangino/The Image Works; **3:** © Nita Winter/The Image Works; **4:** © Frank Siteman/The Picture Cube; **5:** © Will McIntyre/Photo Researchers, Inc.

Chapter 1

Page 3 top left: © Robert E. Murowhick/Photo Researchers, Inc., **top right:** © Robert A. Isaacs/Photo Researchers, Inc.; **both middle:** © C&W Shields, Inc., **bottom left:** © 1980, Melissa Hayes English/Photo Researchers, Inc., **bottom right:** © Michael Yada/Zephyr Pictures; **page 7:** © James L. Shaffer; **page 9:** AP/Wide World Photos; **page 11:** © H. Armstrong Roberts, Inc.; **page 15:** courtesy of Donald Dutton, Department of Psychology, University of British Columbia, Vancouver; **page 17:** © Harriet Gans/The Image Works; **page 19 both:** © Alexandra Milgram.

Chapter 2

Page 28: © Paul Buddle; **page 33:** courtesy of Charles E. Kimble; **page 35:** © Royce Bair/The Stock Solution; **page 45:** © Alan Carey/The Image Works; **page 49 both:** courtesy of Philip G. Zimbardo, Stanford University.

Chapter 3

Page 55: © Robert Kalman/The Image Works; **page 58:** © Spencer Grant/Photo Researchers, Inc.; **page 65:** AP/Wide World Photos; **page 68:** © Bob Daemmrich/The Image Works.

Chapter 4

Page 79: © Mark Antman/The Image Works; **page 88:** R. P. McMurphy (Jack Nicholson) and Nurse Ratched (Louise Fletcher) in a scene from *"ONE FLEW OVER THE CUCKOO'S NEST."* Directed by Milos Forman, produced by Saul Zaentz and Michael Douglas. © 1975. Fantasy Films. All Rights Reserved; **page 91:** © Charles Gatewood/The Image Works; **page 94:** © James L. Shaffer.

Chapter 5

Page 102 left: AP/Wide World Photos, **right:** © M. Childers/Sygma; **page 106:** AP/Wide World Photos; **page 110:** © The Stock Solution/Zephyr Picture Agency; **page 114:** © Spencer Grant/Photo Researchers, Inc.; **page 118:** © Steve Whalen/Zephyr Picture Agency; **page 119:** © Topham/The Image Works; **page 120:** © Spencer Grant/Photo Researchers, Inc.; **page 124:** © Cleo Freelance Photo; **page 127 top:** © Spencer Grant/Photo Researchers, Inc., **bottom:** AP/Wide World Photos; **page 131 top:** © Paul Buddle, **bottom:** © Sygma; **page 135:** © Shelley Gazin/The Image Works.

Chapter 6

Page 140: © Spencer Grant/Photo Researchers, Inc.; **page 145:** © Alan Carey/The Image Works; **page 153:** © Jack Spratt/The Image Works; **page 154:** © Teri Leigh Stratford/Photo Researchers, Inc.; **page 163:** © Spencer Grant/Photo Researchers, Inc.; **page 165:** © Alan Carey/The Image Works.

Chapter 7

Page 183 left: © Spencer Grant/Photo Researchers, Inc., **right:** © Barbara Rios/Photo Researchers, Inc; **page 191:** © David M. Grossman; **page 192:** © Rhoda Galyn/Photo Researchers, Inc.; **page 193:** © Dion Ogust/The Image Works; **page 194:** © Dan Chidester/The Image Works; **page 201:** © Bettye Lane/Photo Researchers, Inc.; **page 203:** AP/Wide World Photos; **page 206:** © Charles Schabes/Viewfinders; **page 207:** © Barbara Rios/Photo Researchers, Inc.

Chapter 8

Page 213: © David Wells/The Image Works; **page 217:** © William Vandivert and *Scientific American* **page 222:** © Michael Siluk; **page 229:** © 1989 David H. Wells/The Image Works; **page 230:** © Janet & Ben Mathes; **page 238:** © Alan Carey/The Image Works.

Chapter 9

Page 242 left: © Michael Siluk, **right:** © Jim Whitmer/Vantage Photo Dynamics; **page 252:** © Alan Carey/The Image Works; **page 255:** AP/Wide World Photos; **page 256:** © Michael Siluk; **page 262:** © Howard Diatch/The Image Works; **page 268:** © Bill McCarthy/Viewfinders; **page 276:** NASA/The Image Works.

Chapter 10

Page 281: © Michael Siluk; **page 285:** © Alan Carey/The Image Works; **page 291:** © David Wells/The Image Works; **page 295:** © Alan Carey/The Image Works; **page 297:** © Michael Siluk; **pages 300, 305:** AP/Wide World Photos.

Chapter 11

Page 313 left: © Jim Whitmer/Vantage Photo Dynamics, **right:** © Wendell Dickinson/Vantage Photo Dynamics; **page 325:** © Alan Carey/The Image Works; **page 341:** © Jim Whitmer/Vantage Photo Dynamics; **page 345:** © Charles E. Kimble.

Chapter 12

Page 358: © Jim Mahoney/The Image Works; **page 363:** © Robert Kalman/The Image Works; **page 368:** © James L. Shaffer; **page 372:** © Michael Siluk; **page 375:** © Jean-Claude Lejeune; **page 379:** © Michael Siluk; **page 381:** © Chris Grayczyk/Viewfinders; **page 385 left:** © Jean-Claude Lejeune, **right:** © Arnold Kapp/Van Cleve Photography; **page 392:** © Berenger/Dratch/The Image Works.

Chapter 13

Page 398: © Paul Sequeira/Photo Researchers, Inc.; **page 402:** © Spencer Grant/Photo Researchers, Inc.; **page 406:** © Topham/The Image Works; **page 409:** © Michael Siluk; **pages 416, 417:** AP/Wide World Photos; **page 426:** © Mark Antman/The Image Works; **page 432:** © 1984 Ed Lettau/Photo Researchers, Inc.

Chapter 14

Page 441: © Charles Gatewood/The Image Works; **page 442:** © Tannenbaum/Sygma; **page 444:** © Joan Albert/The Image Works; **page 448:** © Bill Bachman/Photo Researchers, Inc; **page 449:** © Rona Beame/Photo Researchers, Inc.; **page 460:** AP/Wide World Photos; **page 464:** © Elizabeth Crews/Stock, Boston.

Chapter 15

Page 472: AP/Wide World Photos; **page 485 left:** © Mark Antman/The Image Works, **right:** © Barbara Rios/Photo Researchers, Inc.; **page 494 left:** © Spencer Grant/Photo Researchers, Inc., **right:** © Ray Ellis/Photo Researchers, Inc.; **page 498:** Reprinted with permission of Macmillan Publishing Company from *DEFENSIBLE SPACE* by Oscar Newman. Copyright © 1972, 1973 by Oscar Newman.

Chapter 16

Page 507 top left: © Michael Siluk, **bottom left:** © Mark Antman/The Image Works, **right:** © Sam C. Pierson, Jr./Photo Reserchers, Inc.; **page 508:** © Hans Selye *AMERICAN SCIENTIST 61 (1973)* 692; **page 519:** © Lionel J-M Delevingne/Stock, Boston; **page 520:** AP/Wide World Photos; **page 524:** © Billy Gallery/Stock, Boston; **page 530:** © James L. Shaffer.

Text

Chapter 4

Figure 4.1: From Bonnie Erickson, et al., "Speech Style and Impression Formation in a Court Setting: The Affects of 'Powerful' and 'Powerless' Speech" in *Journal of Experimental Social Psychology,* *14*(3):266–279, 1978. Copyright © 1978 Academic Press, Inc., San Diego, CA.
Figure 4.2: From Valerie S. Folkes & David O. Sears, "Does Everybody Like a Liker?" in *Journal of Experimental Social Psychology, 13*(6):505–519, 1977. Copyright © 1977 Academic Press, Inc., San Diego, CA.
Figure 4.3: Figure 7–1 from *Pygmalion in the Classroom: Teacher Expectation and Pupil's Intellectual Development* by Robert Rosenthal and Lenore Jacobson, copyright © 1968 by Holt, Rinehart and Winston, Inc., reprinted by permission of the publisher.
Figure 4.4: From Timothy D. Wilson & Patricia W. Linville, *Journal of Personality and Social Psychology, 42*:372, 1982. Copyright 1982 by the American Psychological Association.

Chapter 10

Figure 10.8: From R. E. Kraut & R. E. Johnston, "Social and Emotional Messages of Smiling: An Ethological Approach" in *Journal of Personality and Social Psychology, 37*:1539–1553, 1979. Copyright 1979 by the American Psychological Association.

Chapter 13

Figure 13.7: From A. Bandura, "Influence of Models' Reinforcement Contingencies on the Acquisition of Imitative Responses" in *Journal of Personality and Social Psychology, 1*:589–595, 1965. Copyright 1965 by the American Psychological Association.
Figure 13.8: From C. E. Kimble, et al., "Effectiveness of Counteraggression Strategies in Reducing Interactive Aggression by Males" in *Journal of Personality and Social Psychology, 35*:272–278, 1977. Copyright 1977 by the American Psychological Association.

Chapter 15

Figure 15.13b: From O. Newman, *Defensible Space.* Copyright © 1972 Macmillan Publishing Company, New York, NY.
Figure 15.14: From R. Sommer, "Crime & Vandalism in University Residence Halls: A Confirmation of Defensible Space Theory" in *Journal of Environmental Psychology, 7*:1–12, 1987. Copyright © 1987 Academic Press, London, England.
Figure 15.15: This article first appeared in the *Journal of Architectural and Planning Research,* Volume 5, Issue 2, 1985, pp. 231–243. Reprinted with permission of the publisher.
Figure 15.16: From Levitt & Leventhal, *Environment and Behavior, 18* pp 467–479, copyright 1986 by Sage Publications, Inc. Reprinted by permission of Sage Publications, Inc.

Chapter 16

Figure 16.11: From A. Baum and S. Valins, *Architecture and Social Behavior: Psychological Studies of Social Density.* Copyright © 1977 Lawrence Erlbaum Associates, Inc., Hillsdale, NJ. Reprinted by permission.
Figure 16.12: From D. T. Kenrick and G. A. Johnson, "Interpersonal Attraction in Aversive Environments: A Problem for the Classical Conditioning Paradigm?" in *Journal of Personality and Social Psychology, 37*:572–579, 1979. Copyright 1979 by the American Psychological Association.
Figure 16.13: Courtesy of Professor K. D. Harries. Used with permission.